Handbook of Research on Creating Meaningful Experiences in Online Courses

Lydia Kyei-Blankson
Illinois State University, USA

Esther Ntuli
Idaho State University, USA

Joseph Blankson
Ohio Northern University, USA

A volume in the Advances in Educational Technologies and Instructional Design (AETID) Book Series

Published in the United States of America by
IGI Global
Information Science Reference (an imprint of IGI Global)
701 E. Chocolate Avenue
Hershey PA, USA 17033
Tel: 717-533-8845
Fax: 717-533-8661
E-mail: cust@igi-global.com
Web site: http://www.igi-global.com

Copyright © 2020 by IGI Global. All rights reserved. No part of this publication may be reproduced, stored or distributed in any form or by any means, electronic or mechanical, including photocopying, without written permission from the publisher. Product or company names used in this set are for identification purposes only. Inclusion of the names of the products or companies does not indicate a claim of ownership by IGI Global of the trademark or registered trademark.
Library of Congress Cataloging-in-Publication Data

Names: Kyei-Blankson, Lydia, editor. | Ntuli, Esther, 1976- editor. |
   Blankson, Joseph, 1960- editor.
Title: Handbook of research on creating meaningful experiences in online
   courses / Lydia Kyei-Blankson, Esther Ntuli, and Joseph Blankson,
   editors.
Description: Hershey, PA : Information Science Reference, [2020] | Includes
   bibliographical references. | Summary: "This book examines strategies
   and practices used by online instructors to create meaningful teaching
   and learning experiences in online courses. It also demonstrates the
   kinds of learning outcomes that can be realized through online
   education"-- Provided by publisher.
Identifiers: LCCN 2019016733 | ISBN 9781799801153 (h/c) | ISBN
   9781799801160 (eISBN)
Subjects: LCSH: Internet in higher education. | Web-based instruction. |
   Education, Higher--Computer-assisted instruction. | Distance education.
   | Open learning.
Classification: LCC LB2395.7 .H2345 2020 | DDC 378.1/7344678--dc23
LC record available at https://lccn.loc.gov/2019016733

This book is published in the IGI Global book series Advances in Educational Technologies and Instructional Design (AETID) (ISSN: 2326-8905; eISSN: 2326-8913)

British Cataloguing in Publication Data
A Cataloguing in Publication record for this book is available from the British Library.

All work contributed to this book is new, previously-unpublished material. The views expressed in this book are those of the authors, but not necessarily of the publisher.

For electronic access to this publication, please contact: eresources@igi-global.com.

Advances in Educational Technologies and Instructional Design (AETID) Book Series

Lawrence A. Tomei
Robert Morris University, USA

ISSN:2326-8905
EISSN:2326-8913

Mission

Education has undergone, and continues to undergo, immense changes in the way it is enacted and distributed to both child and adult learners. In modern education, the traditional classroom learning experience has evolved to include technological resources and to provide online classroom opportunities to students of all ages regardless of their geographical locations. From distance education, Massive-Open-Online-Courses (MOOCs), and electronic tablets in the classroom, technology is now an integral part of learning and is also affecting the way educators communicate information to students.

The **Advances in Educational Technologies & Instructional Design (AETID) Book Series** explores new research and theories for facilitating learning and improving educational performance utilizing technological processes and resources. The series examines technologies that can be integrated into K-12 classrooms to improve skills and learning abilities in all subjects including STEM education and language learning. Additionally, it studies the emergence of fully online classrooms for young and adult learners alike, and the communication and accountability challenges that can arise. Trending topics that are covered include adaptive learning, game-based learning, virtual school environments, and social media effects. School administrators, educators, academicians, researchers, and students will find this series to be an excellent resource for the effective design and implementation of learning technologies in their classes.

Coverage

- E-Learning
- Game-Based Learning
- Instructional Design
- Classroom Response Systems
- Instructional Design Models
- Higher Education Technologies
- Educational Telecommunications
- Virtual School Environments
- Bring-Your-Own-Device
- Collaboration Tools

IGI Global is currently accepting manuscripts for publication within this series. To submit a proposal for a volume in this series, please contact our Acquisition Editors at Acquisitions@igi-global.com or visit: http://www.igi-global.com/publish/.

The Advances in Educational Technologies and Instructional Design (AETID) Book Series (ISSN 2326-8905) is published by IGI Global, 701 E. Chocolate Avenue, Hershey, PA 17033-1240, USA, www.igi-global.com. This series is composed of titles available for purchase individually; each title is edited to be contextually exclusive from any other title within the series. For pricing and ordering information please visit http://www.igi-global.com/book-series/advances-educational-technologies-instructional-design/73678. Postmaster: Send all address changes to above address. Copyright © 2020 IGI Global. All rights, including translation in other languages reserved by the publisher. No part of this series may be reproduced or used in any form or by any means – graphics, electronic, or mechanical, including photocopying, recording, taping, or information and retrieval systems – without written permission from the publisher, except for non commercial, educational use, including classroom teaching purposes. The views expressed in this series are those of the authors, but not necessarily of IGI Global.

Titles in this Series

For a list of additional titles in this series, please visit:
https://www.igi-global.com/book-series/advances-educational-technologies-instructional-design/73678

Form, Function, and Style in Instructional Design Emerging Research and Opportunities
Shalin Hai-Jew (Kansas State University, USA)
Information Science Reference • copyright 2020 • 203pp • H/C (ISBN: 9781522598336) • US $155.00 (our price)

The Roles of Technology and Globalization in Educational Transformation
Blessing F. Adeoye (Walden University, USA) and Gladys Arome (Marian University, USA)
Information Science Reference • copyright 2020 • 259pp • H/C (ISBN: 9781522597469) • US $195.00 (our price)

Utilizing Educational Data Mining Techniques for Improved Learning Emerging Research and Opportunities
Chintan Bhatt (Charotar University of Science and Technology, India) Priti Srinivas Sajja (Sardar Patel University, India) and Sidath Liyanage (University of Kelaniya, Sri Lanka)
Information Science Reference • copyright 2020 • 166pp • H/C (ISBN: 9781799800101) • US $165.00 (our price)

Claiming Identity Through Redefined Teaching in Construction Programs
Sherif Mostafa (Griffith University, Australia) and Payam Rahnamayiezekavat (Western Sydney University, Australia)
Information Science Reference • copyright 2020 • 259pp • H/C (ISBN: 9781522584520) • US $185.00 (our price)

Global Perspectives on Teaching and Learning Paths in Islamic Education
Miftachul Huda (Universiti Pendidikan Sultan Idris Malaysia, Malaysia) Jimaain Safar (Universiti Teknologi Malaysia, Malaysia) Ahmad Kilani Mohamed (Universiti Teknologi Malaysia, Malaysia) Kamarul Azmi Jasmi (Universiti Teknologi Malaysia, Malaysia) and Bushrah Basiron (Universiti Teknologi Malaysia, Malaysia)
Information Science Reference • copyright 2020 • 341pp • H/C (ISBN: 9781522585282) • US $195.00 (our price)

Social Justice and Putting Theory Into Practice in Schools and Communities
Susan Trostle Brand (University of Rhode Island, USA) and Lori E. Ciccomascolo (University of Rhode Island, USA)
Information Science Reference • copyright 2020 • 359pp • H/C (ISBN: 9781522594345) • US $195.00 (our price)

Handbook of Research on Diverse Teaching Strategies for the Technology-Rich Classroom
Lawrence A. Tomei (Robert Morris University, USA) and David D. Carbonara (Duquesne University, USA)
Information Science Reference • copyright 2020 • 426pp • H/C (ISBN: 9781799802389) • US $265.00 (our price)

Emerging Technologies in Virtual Learning Environments
Kim Becnel (Appalachian State University, USA)
Information Science Reference • copyright 2019 • 348pp • H/C (ISBN: 9781522579878) • US $205.00 (our price)

701 East Chocolate Avenue, Hershey, PA 17033, USA
Tel: 717-533-8845 x100 • Fax: 717-533-8661
E-Mail: cust@igi-global.com • www.igi-global.com

Editorial Advisory Board

Jennifer Aucoin, *Gwynedd Mercy University, USA*
Tridib Bandyopadhyay, *Kennesaw State University, USA*
Danielle Budenz, *Gwynedd Mercy University, USA*
Desiree Caldwell, *Gwynedd Mercy University, USA*
Kristin Carlson, *Illinois State University, USA*
Lesley Farmer, *California State University, Long Beach, USA*
Yasemin Gulbahar, *Ankara University, Turkey*
Yowei Kang, *National Taiwan Ocean University, Taiwan*
Christina Liebrecht, *Ohio Northern University, USA*
Lauren Logan, *Ohio Northern University, USA*
Haruni Machumu, *Mzumbe University, Tanzania*
Liliana Cuesta Medina, *Universidad de La Sabana, Colombia*
Amy O'Brien, *Pennsylvania Cyber Charter School, USA*
Mohamed Nur-Awaleh, *Illinois State University, USA*
Anthony Owusu-Ansah, *Albany State University, USA*
Celal Perihan, *Idaho State University, USA*
Kathleen Pierce-Friedman, *Ashford University, USA*
Dorothy Sammons, *Idaho State University, USA*
Joanne Schieltz, *Ohio Northern University, USA*
Kwesi Tandoh, *Ball State University, USA*
Steven Tolman, *Georgia Southern University, USA*
Shaunna Waltemeyer, *Grand Canyon University, USA*
Jill Winnington, *Gwynedd Mercy University, USA*
Dazhi Yang, *Boise State University, USA*
Kenneth C. C. Yang, *The University of Texas at El Paso, USA*

Table of Contents

Preface xvi

Section 1
Preparing Faculty to Offer Meaningful Experiences

Chapter 1
Faculty Professional Development in Creating Significant Teaching and Learning Experiences
Online 1
    Kathleen Pierce-Friedman, Ashford University, USA
    Laurie Wellner, Northcentral University, USA

Chapter 2
Closing the Distance in Distance Learning 14
    Shaunna Waltemeyer, Grand Canyon University, USA
    Jeff Cranmore, Grand Canyon University, USA

Chapter 3
Comprehensive Faculty Development: An Innovative Approach in Online Education 25
    Desiree' Caldwell, Gwynedd Mercy University, USA
    Mary Sortino, Gwynedd Mercy University, USA
    Jill Winnington, Gwynedd Mercy University, USA
    Tiffany Cresswell-Yeager, Gwynedd Mercy University, USA

Chapter 4
Faculty Professional Development in Creating Significant Teaching and Learning Experiences
Online 37
    Yasemin Gülbahar, Ankara University, Turkey
    Müge Adnan, Mugla Sitki Kocman University, Turkey

Chapter 5
Flexible Higher Education Through Swayam 59
    Varun Gupta, Universidade da Beira Interior, Portugal
    Durg Singh Chauhan, GLA University, India
    Thomas Hanne, University of Applied Sciences and Arts Northwestern Switzerland,
      Switzerland

Section 2
Designing Online Courses for Meaningful Learning Experiences

Chapter 6
The Transition From Teaching F2F to Online 67
Steven Tolman, Georgia Southern University, USA
Matt Dunbar, Georgia Southern University, USA
K. Brooke Slone, Georgia Southern University, USA
Allie Grimes, Georgia Southern University, USA
Christopher A. Trautman, Fairleigh Dickinson University, USA

Chapter 7
Online Education Past, Current, and Future 85
Kieran Chidi Nduagbo, Independent Researcher, USA

Chapter 8
Quality Assurance: Breaking Through the Online Learning Plateau 101
Jermaine S. McDougald, Universidad de La Sabana, Colombia

Section 3
Fostering Faculty-Student and Student-Student Interactions

Chapter 9
The Effect of Membership in an Online Cohort Major on Baccalaureate Degree Completion 119
Mary Dobransky, Bellevue University, USA

Chapter 10
Relationships in Online Learning Experiences: Identifying and Creating Positive Relationships in
Online Learning 140
Robyn J. Emde, The University of the Cumberlands, USA
Erin Kathleen Doherty, The University of the Cumberlands, USA
Bradley 'Scott' Ellis, The University of the Cumberlands, USA
Dina Flynt, The University of the Cumberlands, USA

Chapter 11
A Framework for Student Engagement: Strategies for Faculty Teaching Online 153
Desiree' Caldwell, Gwynedd Mercy University, USA
Tiffany Cresswell-Yeager, Gwynedd Mercy University, USA
Jennifer Aucoin, Gwynedd Mercy University, USA
Danielle Budenz, Gwynedd Mercy University, USA

Section 4
Considering Power, Privilege, and Inclusion in Online Courses

Chapter 12
Intentionally Creating an Inclusive and Welcoming Climate in the Online Learning Classroom 173

Jon P. Humiston, Central Michigan University, USA
Sarah M. Marshall, Central Michigan University, USA
Nicole L. Hacker, Central Michigan University, USA
Luis M. Cantu, Central Michigan University, USA

Chapter 13
Strategies for Efficient, Meaningful, and Inclusive Online Learning Environments: It's About Time 187
Naomi Jeffery Petersen, Central Washington University, USA

Chapter 14
Universal Design for Learning Enables Significant Learning in Digital Courses 227
Kimberly Coy, California State University, Fresno, USA

Section 5
Student Outcomes and Experiences

Chapter 15
Expectations, Experiences, and Preferences of Students in a Dual Mode Program: A Thematic Analysis 248
Linh Cuong Nguyen, Charles Sturt University, Australia
Kate Davis, University of Southern Queensland, Australia
Elham Sayyad Abdi, University of Southern Queensland, Australia
Clare Thorpe, University of Southern Queensland, Australia
Katya Henry, Queensland University of Technology, Australia
Helen Partridge, University of Southern Queensland, Australia

Chapter 16
Supporting the Spiritual Experience in Online Faith-Based Education 270
Amanda Lanae Jones Ziemendorf, Grand Canyon University, USA
Sarah Schroyer, Grand Canyon University, USA

Chapter 17
The Effectiveness of Gamification on Student Engagement, Learning Outcomes, and Learning Experiences 286
Kenneth C. C. Yang, The University of Texas at El Paso, USA
Yowei Kang, National Taiwan Ocean University, Taiwan

Compilation of References 306

About the Contributors 345

Index 353

Detailed Table of Contents

Preface xvi

Section 1
Preparing Faculty to Offer Meaningful Experiences

Chapter 1
Faculty Professional Development in Creating Significant Teaching and Learning Experiences
Online 1

    Kathleen Pierce-Friedman, Ashford University, USA
    Laurie Wellner, Northcentral University, USA

Teaching in the online world means a new way of delivering content that may be abstract for some professors. When teaching online, you need to take into consideration the content of the course and the methods in which the students will assimilate knowledge. Understanding the history, arguments for and against online teaching, along with the basic theory of adult learning may help the professor understand the initial move to online teaching. After the initial understanding of online delivery, there is a continued need for professional development that is applicable for the online instructor.

Chapter 2
Closing the Distance in Distance Learning 14

    Shaunna Waltemeyer, Grand Canyon University, USA
    Jeff Cranmore, Grand Canyon University, USA

This chapter will outline various best practices to assist instructors in closing the distance for online students. Topics include the theory of transactional distance as well as creating an engaging learning environment and overall student satisfaction. Best practices include live conferencing, instant communication tools, effective feedback, group discussions, announcements and reminders, the ease of using an online learning platform, and establishing personal connections. This chapter also provides examples and practical applications for technology in the online learning environment.

Chapter 3
Comprehensive Faculty Development: An Innovative Approach in Online Education 25

    Desiree' Caldwell, Gwynedd Mercy University, USA
    Mary Sortino, Gwynedd Mercy University, USA
    Jill Winnington, Gwynedd Mercy University, USA
    Tiffany Cresswell-Yeager, Gwynedd Mercy University, USA

There is a significant need for faculty development and support as it relates to online teaching. Researchers assert that the success of online education may be a direct result of the training and support of the institution's faculty. Higher education institutions implement a variety of online faculty development practices; however, little is known about which practices are seen as the most effective and efficient. In this chapter, the authors propose a strategic approach to building a comprehensive faculty development program that supports and engages online faculty from initial hire and beyond. The purpose of this chapter is to provide new insights to support faculty. The authors identify evidence-based strategies to incorporate adjunct and full-time online faculty into the university community. In addition, the authors share their experiences developing a comprehensive faculty development plan.

Chapter 4
Faculty Professional Development in Creating Significant Teaching and Learning Experiences Online.. 37
Yasemin Gülbahar, Ankara University, Turkey
Müge Adnan, Mugla Sitki Kocman University, Turkey

With faculty members and instructors struggling with the massive transformational challenges stemming from technological innovation, the establishment of a digital teaching-learning culture to ensure that university graduates are ready to join the 21st-century workforce is of the utmost importance. At this juncture, the key players are those who lead the learning experience, namely faculty members and instructors. Being an experienced faculty member and possessing advanced skills of using technology does not necessarily lead to an instructor becoming an effective e-instructor. This chapter, therefore, discusses the changing nature of digital teaching and learning from the perspective of faculty members, within the framework of certain required competencies and skills that every faculty member should possess. The chapter also includes a brief overview of the literature regarding the professional development of faculty members, synchronized with reflections and experiences from an online e-Tutor course.

Chapter 5
Flexible Higher Education Through Swayam 59
Varun Gupta, Universidade da Beira Interior, Portugal
Durg Singh Chauhan, GLA University, India
Thomas Hanne, University of Applied Sciences and Arts Northwestern Switzerland, Switzerland

Challenges in MOOC education for both practical and theoretical courses are identified by the researchers, both experimentally and through a case study. The insights brought by empirical studies helped researchers to propose a framework to make higher education in engineering and management truly online and tuition free. The objective of this chapter is to propose a flexible online degree framework through SWAYAM or any other online platform being approved by education regulator. The process involving course enrollment, learning, evaluation, and outcome is contained in the proposed flexible system that leads to tuition free online degrees. The proposed system not only gives students a freedom to choose their courses in accordance with their flexibility but also use earned credit towards online degrees of any university of their choice.

Section 2
Designing Online Courses for Meaningful Learning Experiences

Chapter 6
The Transition From Teaching F2F to Online 67
   Steven Tolman, Georgia Southern University, USA
   Matt Dunbar, Georgia Southern University, USA
   K. Brooke Slone, Georgia Southern University, USA
   Allie Grimes, Georgia Southern University, USA
   Christopher A. Trautman, Fairleigh Dickinson University, USA

As online education continues to grow, more and more faculty find themselves transitioning from teaching face-to-face to online environments. Unsurprisingly, this can be challenging for many faculty as they go through this process. This book chapters examines the experience of a faculty member who transitioned from teaching exclusively face-to-face to online and lessons learned are shared. Additionally, four students share their experience learning online and provide recommendations to faculty members.

Chapter 7
Online Education Past, Current, and Future 85
   Kieran Chidi Nduagbo, Independent Researcher, USA

This chapter addresses the paradigmatic shift in traditional education. It presents a historical overview of online education as a content and framework for understanding its current state and highlights how online education has become entrenched in business and in higher education worldwide. Beginning with distance education's contributions to the paradigmatic shift, this chapter provides a framework for understanding online education. It focuses on the connections and contributions of distance education to present day online education, the current trends in online education, and the projections of the future of online education. This chapter concludes that the nature and practice of online education across the globe will change in the next few years.

Chapter 8
Quality Assurance: Breaking Through the Online Learning Plateau 101
   Jermaine S. McDougald, Universidad de La Sabana, Colombia

Online education has continued to increase at a rapid rate over the past decades, offering diverse learning programs at all levels of education. As a result, online programs continue to shift and change according to the demands of society. However, the demands for qualified online instructors (OI) are not increasing at the same rate and are not proportional to the number of instructors directly responsible for delivering quality online courses. Many OI do not know their learners; therefore, a gap is left in terms of their needs in an online environment. This chapter will provide insights into how the strategy "module hosts" for online discussion boards, and learner profiles are used in an online graduate program to promote effective communication, leadership, and collaboration. Moreover, the chapter discusses varied ways through which online instructors can incorporate a "bottom-up" approach in their instruction as part of being a change agent.

Section 3
Fostering Faculty-Student and Student-Student Interactions

Chapter 9
The Effect of Membership in an Online Cohort Major on Baccalaureate Degree Completion.......... 119

Mary Dobransky, Bellevue University, USA

Attaining an undergraduate college degree contributes to increased employment opportunities and greater compensation, yet many students who enroll fail to graduate within six years, including a growing number of online students. One promising model for increasing retention is cohort education, in which students take multiple courses together as a group. This chapter uses a quantitative data analysis to examine the relationship between membership in an online cohort major and degree completion of baccalaureate students. The study population includes students at a Midwestern university that offers online programs in cohort and non-cohort formats. Study results show a significant positive relationship between membership in an online cohort major and baccalaureate degree completion. The results suggest that higher education leaders seeking to improve baccalaureate degree completion rates may benefit from offering online courses in a cohort format.

Chapter 10
Relationships in Online Learning Experiences: Identifying and Creating Positive Relationships in Online Learning 140

    Robyn J. Emde, The University of the Cumberlands, USA
    Erin Kathleen Doherty, The University of the Cumberlands, USA
    Bradley 'Scott' Ellis, The University of the Cumberlands, USA
    Dina Flynt, The University of the Cumberlands, USA

A relationship is documented as a personal investment in another's life. Relationships add to learning environments as substantial to the growth of students. In an online learning environment, a relationship is defined by the mutual agreement between an educator and a learner in which expectations of increased knowledge gained through the education experience provided by the educator. It is evident that in an online environment it is vital to consistently evaluate in order to have the enrichment of relationships between student to professors and student to student. Research has shown that the creation of such environments results in a feeling of community and social presence for the students. Student satisfaction extends to the relationship students feel toward their professors. The strength of the student to professor relationship results in a key component in student retention. The method in which the relationships are established and built in an online environment are vital for student satisfaction and retention of students within a program of study.

Chapter 11
A Framework for Student Engagement: Strategies for Faculty Teaching Online 153

    Desiree' Caldwell, Gwynedd Mercy University, USA
    Tiffany Cresswell-Yeager, Gwynedd Mercy University, USA
    Jennifer Aucoin, Gwynedd Mercy University, USA
    Danielle Budenz, Gwynedd Mercy University, USA

When teaching online, many instructors are provided with a master course that contains the learning materials, discussion forums, assignments, and assessments. With more higher education institutions opting to offer master course shells, it can be difficult for instructors to know how to incorporate their personality, experiences, and insights into a pre-designed course. Faculty who teach online may be searching for ideas on how to personalize their master course and increase student engagement. Many faculty express concerns about students who are disconnected. Personalization of master courses increases student engagement while allowing students and instructors to feel more connected during the course.

The authors will explore best practices to increase student engagement and provide a framework to implement these strategies that assist online instructors in demonstrating their personalities and expertise in master courses.

Section 4
Considering Power, Privilege, and Inclusion in Online Courses

Chapter 12
Intentionally Creating an Inclusive and Welcoming Climate in the Online Learning Classroom...... 173
    Jon P. Humiston, Central Michigan University, USA
    Sarah M. Marshall, Central Michigan University, USA
    Nicole L. Hacker, Central Michigan University, USA
    Luis M. Cantu, Central Michigan University, USA

The online classroom environment may feel safer for students in marginalized groups because the sense of anonymity the environment can provide. While faculty purposely strive to ensure all students are treated equitably in traditional, in-person classrooms, faculty should not assume power and privilege are not impacting the online classroom environment for students, particularly students from underrepresented identities. Research indicates that marginalized students face different challenges in online classrooms than in traditional, in-person classrooms. Further, power and privilege manifests in the online classroom in different ways than in traditional classrooms. This chapter positions a critical lens on the ways that power and privilege impact the online environment, why marginalized students are drawn to the online classroom, the challenges they face, and how faculty contribute to the creation or resolution of these problems. Finally, the chapter concludes with strategies for intentionally promoting inclusion in online classrooms.

Chapter 13
Strategies for Efficient, Meaningful, and Inclusive Online Learning Environments: It's About Time 187
    Naomi Jeffery Petersen, Central Washington University, USA

Students and faculty rely on clear and unambiguous time targets to exchange information and pace their intersecting lives. Most students juggle work, family, and commuting demands, and increasing numbers also struggle with language needs and disabilities, requiring additional and flexible time to grasp the scope of assignments, read and gather information, process concepts into written products, and finally make sense of the experience. It all takes time. In this chapter, practical strategies for structuring time expectations are introduced in the context of a commitment to empower self-regulation and lifelong learning with particular attention to accessibility. The time dimension of each component of the syllabus, assignments, and gradebook are described with examples from a successful online course, with reference to theory and research on student engagement and satisfaction.

Chapter 14
Universal Design for Learning Enables Significant Learning in Digital Courses 227
    Kimberly Coy, California State University, Fresno, USA

Universities serve a more diverse group of students than ever before, including students who are first generation, students from poverty, and students with learning disabilities. These institutions are also increasing the amount and types of digital learning environments students use. Meeting the needs of such a diverse student group with changing resources is a dynamic problem. The universal design for learning (UDL) framework has the potential to support professors, lecturers, and course designers as they create academic events for this wide group of learners in every field of study. This chapter examines the core concepts of UDL and presents specific examples in digital university teaching constructs. Students with diverse learning needs can be served in the same environments as more traditional students when this design framework is employed. UDL can be leveraged as an instructional superpower to the benefit of all learners in universities and post-secondary courses.

Section 5
Student Outcomes and Experiences

Chapter 15
Expectations, Experiences, and Preferences of Students in a Dual Mode Program: A Thematic Analysis 248

    Linh Cuong Nguyen, Charles Sturt University, Australia
    Kate Davis, University of Southern Queensland, Australia
    Elham Sayyad Abdi, University of Southern Queensland, Australia
    Clare Thorpe, University of Southern Queensland, Australia
    Katya Henry, Queensland University of Technology, Australia
    Helen Partridge, University of Southern Queensland, Australia

While online-only programs are increasingly common, many universities today offer dual mode programs with both online and on campus cohorts undertaking the same program at the same time. This results in students having a range of experiences along a continuum from fully online study to a mix of online and face-to-face study. This research aimed to develop an understanding of preferences, expectations, and experiences of students enrolled in a dual mode postgraduate coursework program in Australia. Outcomes are presented in themes along with rich description and explanation that capture different facets of recurring singular ideas delineating the experiences of students in relation to their learning in a flexible dual mode. The research findings provide insight into the student experience of online study as well as the broader experience of study in a dual mode cohort.

Chapter 16
Supporting the Spiritual Experience in Online Faith-Based Education 270

    Amanda Lanae Jones Ziemendorf, Grand Canyon University, USA
    Sarah Schroyer, Grand Canyon University, USA

Faith-based institutions offer educators a unique set of challenges and opportunities as they are tasked with the integration of faith in the classroom experience while delivering content necessary to meet subject matter objectives. Evaluation of audience, context, and protection of the learning environment are key elements for consideration when incorporating faith within the online classroom. The purpose of this chapter is to support knowledge and competency in implementing faith-based content, integration techniques, and usable instructional solutions that promote authentic connections. When applied strategically and mindfully, faith components can support mutual trust between the learner and the educator, establish a foundation for deep personal growth, and actively fulfill the online instructional objectives. This chapter will cover the background and history of faith in adult education, evaluation of audience and context, protection of the learning environment, utility of faith-based instruction, mindfulness, and techniques for integration.

Chapter 17
The Effectiveness of Gamification on Student Engagement, Learning Outcomes, and Learning Experiences 286
    Kenneth C. C. Yang, The University of Texas at El Paso, USA
    Yowei Kang, National Taiwan Ocean University, Taiwan

Gamification has been widely used in the higher education to enhance users' learning experiences through the integration of game-like elements into the course materials. This study explores whether and how different levels of gamification in the instructional methods will influence student engagement with the course, overall learning experiences with the course, and learning outcomes with the course materials. The findings suggest that, among four indices to measure the success of gamification, three out of four show the positive gamification effects with a highly gamified class leads to higher level of student engagement than no or lowly gamified classes. The same positive gamification effects can be found in students' overall learning experience. Highly gamified classes result in better student learning outcomes as measured by their grades at different data collection points. Limitations of this study include small class sizes and no statistically significant results and only two gamified elements used. Implications and discussions were presented.

Compilation of References 306

About the Contributors 345

Index 353

Preface

The number of online courses and programs have grown rapidly over the years with the development of technology. Many reputable brick and mortar higher education institutions are now offering undergraduate and graduate programs in addition to massive open online courses (MOOC) to anyone willing to develop their knowledge and skills in an area of study or discipline. The number of higher education institutions that view online education as an important part of their long-term strategy for growth is on the rise (Allen & Seaman, 2016) and the proportion of students taking online courses continues to increase (Seaman, Allen & Seaman, 2018), yet concerns regarding quality and rigor remain among certain stakeholders. With the growth in online enrollment has come ongoing debate regarding the benefits and challenges of teaching and learning online as well as on issues related to credibility and acceptability of online learning. Given this, there is still reluctance among some educators to teach online. Not only is there hesitation to teach online, but there is also doubt as to how well-prepared students who have enrolled in online programs are for further study and for their career.

To help quell these concerns for online learning and demonstrate that online programs and courses are comparable to what is offered in traditional settings, it is essential that expert or master teachers and researchers in the field share the significant and meaningful teaching and learning experiences and outcomes that occur in online classrooms and highlight pedagogical practices used by online instructors to make their courses and programs comparable to those offered face-to-face.

This handbook of research details strategies and practices used by online instructors to create meaningful teaching and learning experiences in online courses and programs. The contents of the book demonstrate the kinds of learning outcomes that can be realized through online education. As more students opt for online courses and programs it is necessary to share how best teaching and learning can be done and valued in online settings.

Target audience for this handbook include instructors who teach online. The book may also be of importance to researchers interested in topics related to online teaching and learning.

The book comprises 17 chapters covering topics such as online education: past, current, and future; faculty professional development in creating significant teaching and learning experiences online; envisioning significant learning in online courses; designing and implementing significant experiences in online courses; technology tools for creating significant experiences; and assessing significant learning experiences online. The information in the book is organized into five sections: "Preparing Faculty to Offer Meaningful Experiences," "Designing Online Courses for Meaningful Learning Experiences," "Fostering Faculty-Student and Student-Student Interactions," "Considering Power, Privilege, and Inclusion in Online Courses," and "Student Outcomes and Experiences."

Preface

Lydia Kyei-Blankson
Illinois State University, USA

Esther Ntuli
Idaho State University, USA

Joseph Blankson
Ohio Northern University, USA

REFERENCES

Allen, I. E., & Seaman, J. (2016). *Online report card: Tracking online education in the United States*. Babson Park, MA: Babson Survey Research Group and Quahog Research Group. Retrieved from http://onlinelearningsurvey.com/reports/onlinereportcard.pdf

Seaman, J. E., Allen, I. E., & Seaman, J. (2018). *Grade increase: Tracking distance education in the United States*. The Babson Survey Research Group. Retrieved from http://www.onlinelearningsurvey.com/highered.html

Section 1
Preparing Faculty to Offer Meaningful Experiences

Chapter 1
Faculty Professional Development in Creating Significant Teaching and Learning Experiences Online

Kathleen Pierce-Friedman
Ashford University, USA

Laurie Wellner
Northcentral University, USA

ABSTRACT

Teaching in the online world means a new way of delivering content that may be abstract for some professors. When teaching online, you need to take into consideration the content of the course and the methods in which the students will assimilate knowledge. Understanding the history, arguments for and against online teaching, along with the basic theory of adult learning may help the professor understand the initial move to online teaching. After the initial understanding of online delivery, there is a continued need for professional development that is applicable for the online instructor.

INTRODUCTION

Teaching courses in the virtual environment is not only a new means of delivering course content to students but is an increasingly innovative way of facilitating information for the success of learning across age groups and geographic spaces. Incorporating new and changing pedagogical approaches, instructors must be continually supported in their quest to provide excellent teaching. For many instructors who are making the transition from the traditional classrooms in a face-to-face environment to that of the online environment, there can be misunderstandings, angst, and even confusion over what the most effective role an online instructor plays (Dolan, 2011). Similarly, determining what and how to implement those proven best practices for delivering instruction is essential for the success of the instructor and student

DOI: 10.4018/978-1-7998-0115-3.ch001

alike. Supporting these new or even veteran instructors may be challenging as the previously established methods of professional development support for the traditional classroom teachers may not be as effective.

More specifically, the move from classroom-based learning to that of online learning, which is typically multimedia based, has placed greater (and different) demands on instructors. Students in the online setting are seeking more of a learning partner in education and not simply facilitators of information. Instructors in the online setting are forced to move away from the daily face-to-face teaching model and into the online environment where a combination of asynchronous and synchronous learning environments are utilized. This change of emphasis in the instructional setting may prove difficult for some instructors who transition from the traditional teaching setting into the online environment (Ormrod, 2008). With the change from the daily face-to-face contact to the online environment, instructors are now working, for the most part, in settings where they are physically separated from their colleagues and could have an increased feeling of isolation. Professional development opportunities can support faculty to feel less isolated and disconnected from colleagues, build a community of learners, improve teaching, and increase organizational capacity (Alexiou-Ray, & Bentley, 2015).

However, professional development opportunities for online faculty often emphasizes on topics related to technological training with little to no guidance on effective online pedagogical practices and their application in the online environment (Moskal, Thompson, & Futch, 2015). Taking into consideration the distinct needs of adult learners, faculty must apply research-based methodologies, innovative instructional technologies, and comprehensive assessment practices to strengthen their own craft and improve student learning outcomes. Vaill & Testori (2012) note that support for professional development pertaining to online education is critical to allow faculty the opportunity for pedagogical problem solving and discovery.

This chapter will explore the professional development topics online instructors may require in order to equip them and others who are interested in applying their skills to the online teaching and learning platform. This chapter is also intended to bring together the wide array of strategies to prepare instructors for teaching online courses or to advancing the skills of veteran online instructors. Providing a rich initial presentation of valuable and proven themes to reinforce faculty professional development, this chapter will explore the trends in the literature that support faculty's growth and their success in practice within the online platform. With this type of instruction significantly increasing in popularity, more and more faculty are requiring initial and ongoing support for their own success and that of their students.

A BRIEF HISTORY OF ONLINE EDUCATION

In today's world of learning, online education has become more popular than ever and has a somewhat brief history of its development within the scope of education in its entirety. Important to note that with this brief history, the pedagogy has not yet had ample time to catch up with the fast expansion of popularity and growth (Zawacki-Richter & Latchem, 2017). Learning and teaching in the online platform, conducted in the convenience of one's home, has proven to be increasingly attractive to both students and instructors (Ching, Hsu, & Baldwin, 2018; Kincey, Farmer, Wilsher, McKenzie & Mbiza, 2019). The premise of quality teaching is at the heart of this profession no matter the environment, however this takes ongoing professional development for online instructors in the application of best practices, training, and support (Adnan, 2018; Barlett, 2018; Ching, Hsu, & Baldwin, 2018; Roberts, 2018).

Online education, while today is considered to be mainstream practice, was not the first form of distance learning. Distance learning can be traced back to correspondence courses used in the early 19th century when improved mail delivery made it possible for students to complete courses via print-based media. With the invention of radio and then television in the early 1950s and 1960s, broadcast educational programming was being used to deliver educational information to a greater number of students than just those attending a collegial setting (Bozkurt, 2019; Xiao, 2017; Weller, Jordan, DeVries & Rolfe, 2018). Distance education can be broken down into five main timelines:

1. **Correspondence Education:** Was based on print and postal delivery and offered the flexibility of time, as well as the pace at which a student completed his/her work.
2. **Multi-Media:** Combined print, audiotape, videotape and computer-disc technologies. It offered the flexibility of time, place and pace of the first method of distance education, but it also incorporated speech-to-text interaction.
3. **Television:** Was the first form of what we now know as synchronous communication learning. The use of broadcast TV and radio (audio) teleconferencing which was the first time that students could watch their instructor on TV (public access) at home and call into a phone line to ask questions as the lecture was being given.
4. **First Generation Internet Delivery:** Interactive media was delivered through the Internet for online delivery. Students and teachers could interact both asynchronous and synchronous for the first time.
5. **Second Generation Internet Delivery:** The main difference between this and the first generation is that it provides a customizable e-interface in which students, staff and other stakeholders can interact with the inclusion of a campus based portal (Bozkurt, 2019; Xiao, 2017; Weller, Jordan, DeVries & Rolfe, 2018).

Each generation of distance education as noted above was not eliminated by the next generation, but rather was built upon by the next generation. This history of online education is important to note as there are over 4,358 higher education institutions in the United States (US) and 1.8% of those offer some type of online degree or program (US Department of Education, National Center for Education Statistics, Integrated Postsecondary Education Data System, 2016). However, often the credibility of the online program is called into question with arguments for and against online instruction.

Arguments in Support of Online Instruction

Herman (2012) stated, "Online education is no longer a peripheral phenomenon in higher education," (p. 87). The online teaching and learning experience are becoming more and more common and sophisticated. Flexibility, cost, and diversity are three of the key items noted from those in favor of online instruction. As a result, online education has become more popular in today's fast-paced environment. Many online institutions offer flexibility in core course requirements for a degree and completely asynchronous learning. Cost is a huge factor in the argument in support of online learning. While it is true that there is no physical buildings, grounds or similar investment as a brick and mortar university, online universities must maintain their technology infrastructure to maintain current in the field and to provide up to date curricula. However, the overall costs to maintain an online program are far less than that of the traditional university (Money & Dean, 2019).

Online education can be a beneficial option for adults who work full-time and can use the flexibility to complete assignments when most convenient for their schedules. For students who serve in the military, online education has been the most popular access to higher education while on active duty or traveling to other countries. As Chickering and Ehrmann (1996) stated "any given instructional strategy can be supported by a number of contrasting technologies (old and new), just as any given technology might support different instructional strategies. But for any given instructional strategy, some technologies are better than others: Better to turn a screw with a screwdriver than a hammer - a dime may also do the trick, but a screwdriver is usually better" (para 2).

This common assumption that good teaching is just that, given any modality or platform, and similarity that poor instruction is also just that, no matter the method of delivery is partially true. Simply because instruction is provided in a virtual setting does not directly translate to it being bad teaching. It is in the craft of the instructor related to engagement of the student and delivery of the content, instructional design, curricula and the ongoing support provided to the instructors to continue to increase their capacity for the application of best practices. The concept of what is considered 'good teaching' can indeed be good teaching given the support, training, and the application of proper pedagogy is present in whatever platform is leveraged.

Arguments Against Online Instruction

Over the years, many have questioned the effectiveness of online instruction. Proving difficult to measure are the positive characteristics and outcomes of the effectiveness of online instruction as compared to that of traditional face-to-face instructional settings even though this delivery model continues to become more popular. While convenient in the eyes of the students, opponents in the field of education believe that the quality and rigor provided in online instruction are often sacrificed (VanPortfliet & Anderson, 2013) for easy access to higher education learning opportunities. Others propose that the lack of direct interaction with their instructor and peers within the classroom setting is credited for the lack of academic achievement and retention (Tinto, 1993).

One of the main arguments from instructors is that students often do not possess time management skills and organization skills necessary to stay on top of coursework. The balance between coursework and other priorities in life may mitigate persistence. Online courses typically require a greater amount of reading and assignments than traditional classes and students may not only need to possess management and organizational skills they need to be prepared for greater amount of research to ensure they understand the content being assessed for the course as there is often limited access to the instructor for clarification of content. Students have noted that little or no face-to-face interaction which hampers the ability to make connections with other students or instructor for help with coursework, or moral support is a limiting factor (Rios, 2019).

Being unable to adequately measure the academic achievement in student outcomes is mainly due to the lack of continuity in the literature, inconsistent terminology, and multiple views of the stakeholders in the application of data obtained by researchers. However, research shows there to be between 10% to 20% failure rate in students who are taking online courses (Bawa, 2016). Additionally, it has been stated that the primary cause of student failures in an online course of study is the inability for the student to maintain interest and direct involvement in the course (Simplico, 2019). Students may require more than minimal support from their instructors, structured content, and convenience of access to be successful in their online learning endeavors. With perceived minimal direct contact from the instructor, lack of motivation on the part of the student, and limited persistence to succeed, it is easy to see how the lesser motivated student can experience challenges in their achievements in this teaching and learning environment.

Factors Leading to Successful Online Instruction

Online teaching just didn't happen overnight, there were several iterations of distance learning before the onslaught of online learning from many for and not for profit universities, private and public. There will always be a debate for or against online learning. Scholars and others will argue the merits of learning and teaching in this online world. From the quality of instruction to the knowledge acquired towards a degree requirement. However, one thing we can agree on is that in this postmodern world anyone can consider themselves experts (you can thank the internet for this) and there is a fine line between the actual expert and simply having general knowledge of a subject (Reed, 2015).

Adult Learning Theory

The premise of adult learning theory is that adults' lived experiences and needs are unique and require a different approach than elementary and high school children. Adult learning theory is guided by a set of principles that indicate the ways in which adults learn, experience their education, and make sacrifices to achieve a degree. Adult learners experience different types of barriers and apprehension regarding higher education and have varied experiences and perceptions of learning modalities (Nicolaides & Marsick, 2016). Anxiety about the ability to effectively learn, perform well on exams, and write competently are the most common concerns among adult learners in higher education with the primary barriers and challenges faced by adult learners include childcare, conflict with schedules, apprehension about the viability and usefulness of a college degree in today's job market and economy, and concerns with navigating new technologies often used in pedagogy (Cox, 2015; Nicolaides & Marsick, 2016). Online students returning to school after over a decade, experience the highest levels of uncertainty with mediated communication and the use of learning management systems to facilitate learning (Jaafar & Schwartz, 2018; Kelly, 2017). While adult learning theory is important to understand as it relates to online learners, there are three main factors that contribute to effective online instruction; technology, delivery of content and instructor and student characteristics (Patterson, 2019).

Technology

In short, technology needs to be available, reliable and provide for quick synchronous and asynchronous exchanges between instructor and student. Adult learners that have likely been out of formal education for a while, may find it difficult to navigate the complex structures of the online university (Templeton & Linder, 2017). The problem with navigation (technology) is the one common issue reported by faculty teaching online (Templeton & Linder, 2017). Singh (2014) notes that the best way to reduce concerns and fears about teaching online is to implement training programs specifically designed to provide faculty with some successful teaching experiences online. Faculty should be able to access the appropriate tools needed to deliver online learning. In the traditional classroom, tools include the dry erase board, overhead projectors, and PowerPoint slides; online, these are replaced with discussion boards, chat rooms, interactive video lessons, and other technologies (Singh, 2014; Violino, 2014).

Delivery of the Content

As online resources and tools become diverse and complex, online pedagogy and course design should adapt to these changes in the learning environment. Course design should prioritize practical transfer of knowledge to theoretical understanding. Students are motivated by rapidly transferring course knowledge to workplace applications which promote career advancement (Ginda, Richey, Cousino & Börner 2019). As courses are designed in the online environment course developers should take into consideration not only student motivation to learn, but that adults learn best when their skills and experiences are leveraged and taken into consideration by their instructors. More specifically, adult learners tend to feel affirmed when their higher education coursework feels like it informs their career field and provides a sense of personal growth and understanding (Ginda, Richey, Cousino & Börner 2019). At a more micro level course content should include design elements that are low stress tasks both synchronously within the course meeting time and asynchronously for external student and group task working arrangements and after class homework, etc. (Boettcher, 2013).

Instructor Characteristics

From the instructors' perspective, providing positive and corrective types of feedback helps students persist and understand the scope of the course learning outcomes. Personalized, specific, and timely feedback is considered most helpful by students. Strategies for instructors to integrate different types of feedback into course design are paramount, text, speech and video (Uppal, Ali & Gulliver 2018).

Student motivation is a key factor in student retention. If students do not feel or maintain motivation, they may lack persistence in their education. Instructors need to not only provide motivation, support, and feedback for discussions. Summarize responses; bring the discussion back on track. Encourage student-to-student interaction. Tap learners' knowledge. Make students responsible for summarizing the week's discussion. Teach others a concept. Assign group projects. Arrange students' role-plays. Use peer-review for projects. Motivate them to display their work publicly. Instructor characteristics include interactive teaching styles which encourage interaction between the students and with the instructor. Along with some technical knowledge and most important knowledge of the subject matter. Student characteristics include having some prior computer knowledge, a support system and willingness to trust in the instructor and institution (Patterson, 2019).

Initiatives

The most difficult challenge faced by instructors is the onslaught of new initiatives by universities to customize instruction to different learning styles to be more accessible for more students in an effort to meet the population trends and shift in student demographics (Vedder, 207; Serrano, Dea-Avuela., Gonzalez-Burgos, Serrano-Gil, & Lalatsa 2019). The National Center for Education Statistics (2014) noted that enrollment in higher education will increase by 14% between 2011 and 2022 which is much slower than the increase from 2007 - 2011 of 45%. More specifically, the Center notes that student demographics will change the 18 - 24-year-old population will increase by only 9% while the 25 - 34-year old's and the 35+ student population will increase by 26% (Hassar & Bailey 2014). This shift in population notes that universities will need to adjust their program offerings to meet the demands of a changing student demographic of working professionals. Several top-rated MBA programs have already moved from traditional face to face instruction to that of blended or fully online for example; Babson College F.W. Olin Graduate School of Business has a fast track MBA which is a part-time program combining traditional classroom instruction with Web-based learning and UNC- Chapel Hill has an online MBA program at the Kenan-Flagler business school.

Professional Development: Supports Needed for Online Instructors

Professional development not only plays a crucial role in preparing faculty to teach online, it is becoming increasingly prevalent over the past ten years as the popularity of online instruction continues to grow. The current state of support for online instructors varies on the type, size, and emphasis on online instruction at the institutional level. While the literature in this area support a variety of professional development methods for online instructors, the Sloan Consortium data survey reports that training occurs in 81% of institutions that offer online instruction. Additionally, most of this training is provided through formal training courses paired with informal mentoring (Herman, 2012).

The practice of teaching and learning in the online setting must be examined by first having an appreciation for best practices in the face-to-face setting. As such, there are similarities between the characteristics and skills of theses opposing styles of instruction and often, those relevant skills are translatable between the two platforms. As an example, Chickering and Ehrmann (1996) researched the literature and identified seven principles of good instruction practice in the face-to-face environment which can be easily translated to the online setting. Often, these seven concepts are areas that are included, or are argued they should be included, in professional development activities for online instructors, both new and veteran. These seven areas are student-faculty contact, reciprocity and cooperation, active learning, promptness of feedback, time on task, high expectations, and diverse talents and student learning styles.

According to Schön (2017) reflection refers to teachers' thinking about their practice both outside of the learning environment ('reflection on action') and during the teaching process ('reflection in action'). Online tools for reflective actions of online teaching practices can contribute to teachers' learning and their acceptance of teaching with technology (van der Meij, Coenders, & McKenney, 2017). Moreover, successful instruction can be obtained through the continued support of professional development when it is authentic, integrated, subject-specific, and consistent (Gunter and Reeves, 2017). Unlike a traditional learning environment, the focus of the learner's interactions turns toward peers in discussion board formatting, more than the instructor. According to Gunter and Reeves (2017) these interactions are important to note as students may attribute difficulties or barriers towards the instructor as opposed to the learning platform or learning apart from others.

Professional development is vital to teachers' ongoing growth (Fisher et al., 2018). While evolving technologies have given way to new and different forms of professional development, the majority of educators (Campana, 2014; Trust, 2017) report spending several hours a week in online learning spaces like websites, forums, and social networks that are outside of formal professional development often offered by their institutions. Which is not surprising as research has indicated that teacher learning is social and best supported within a network, or community of other educators (Geldenhuys & Oosthuizen, 2015). Moreover, one-time workshops are unlikely to change teachers' practices and that learning should be sustained over time through professional development (Darling-Hammond, 2017; Kragler, Martin & Sylvester, 2014). How online professional development delivered online can look different based on the format utilized (Schlager, Farooq, Fusco, Schank, & Dwyer, 2009). Online professional development should include; the use of informal PD networks, provide for interaction between learners often using webinars and also be available as on-demand courses. Regardless of the format, to be effective, online PD must enable learners to have thoughtful, sustained engagements with their peers. Rienties, Brouwer, & Lygo-Baker, (2013) note that "optimal learning occurs when online professional development is job-embedded and flexible with teachers able to experience meaningful interactions" (p.125). With the flexibility of online professional development instructors are able to process content at their own pace and revisit as necessary, something that does not happen in traditional face-to-face professional development.

Application of Professional Development

Effective professional development must be responsive to the needs of the individual and the greater group as well as acknowledging that some are often in the beginning stages of transitioning to the online teaching environment. Knowing the strengths and areas of challenge for the team of instructors involved in faculty professional development can support the targeted instruction, and specific methods that are leveraged to provide professional development. A variety of methods to furnish instructors with technology and best practices should be offered to structure sessions with multiple opportunities for demonstration of skills and the application of new learning.

Establishing a positive culture for professional development is a key part of determining how it should best be delivered. Fink's model of Significant Learning Taxonomy (2003) is important for faculty to consider in light of selecting courses and determining the proper pedagogical approach. Having the knowledge and skills to design a nonlinear curriculum rather the scaffolded model previously prescribed

Figure 1. Fink's model of significant learning taxonomy

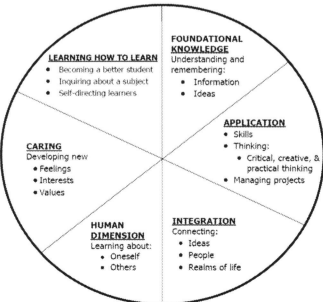

by Bloom, is believed to support instructors in their successful progress with students. Significant learning is believed to occur when these six critical components are simultaneously at work in an instructor's practice.

Ensuring that faculty are engaged in ongoing training in Fink's Taxonomy and other related concepts during the course of their tenure serving as an essential area of professional development.

SOLUTIONS AND RECOMMENDATIONS

With online instruction significantly increasing in popularity, more and more faculty are requiring initial and ongoing support for their own success and that of their students to demonstrate initial and long-term success. Faculty require training in both technology and online pedagogy before the initiate their work. Proactive training and support that not only advances their motivation and strengths but also is intended to support their increased skill development is essential. Trends in the literature that support faculty's growth and success in their practice within the online platform. With this type of instruction significantly increasing in popularity, more and more faculty are requiring initial and ongoing support for their own success and that of their students.

REFERENCES

Adnan, M. (2018). Professional development in the transition to online teaching: The voice of entrant online instructors. *ReCALL*, *30*(1), 88–111. doi:10.1017/S0958344017000106

Alexiou-Ray, J., & Bentley, C. C. (2015). Faculty professional development for quality online teaching. *Online Journal of Distance Learning Administration*, *18*(4), 1–7.

Bartlett, M. (2018). Online Professional Development for Part-time Instructors: FaculTEA. In E. Langran & J. Borup (Eds.), *Proceedings of Society for Information Technology & Teacher Education International Conference* (pp. 514-519). Washington, DC: Association for the Advancement of Computing in Education (AACE). Retrieved from https://www.learntechlib.org/primary/p/182573/

Bawa, P. (2016). *Retention in online courses: Exploring issues and solutions*. Purdue University. doi:10.1177/2158244015621777

Boettcher, J. V. (2013). *Ten best practices for teaching online: Quick guide for new online faculty*. Retrieved from http://www.designingforlearning.info/services/writing/ecoach/tenbest.html

Bozkurt, A. (2019). From Distance Education to Open and Distance Learning: A Holistic Evaluation of History, Definitions, and Theories. In S. Sisman-Ugur, & G. Kurubacak (Eds.), Handbook of Research on Learning in the Age of Transhumanism (pp. 252-273). Hershey, PA: IGI Global. doi:10.4018/978-1-5225-8431-5.ch016

Campana, J. (2014). *Learning for work and professional development: The significance of Informal learning networks of digital media industry professionals*. Academic Press.

Chickering, A. W., & Ehrmann, S. C. (1996). Implementing the seven principles: Technology as a lever. *AAHE Bulletin, 49*(2), 3–6. Retrieved from https://www.aahea.org/articles/sevenprinciples.htm

Ching, Y. H., Hsu, Y. C., & Baldwin, S. (2018). Becoming an Online Teacher: An Analysis of Prospective Online Instructors' Reflections. *Journal of Interactive Learning Research, 29*(2), 145-168. Retrieved from https://www.learntechlib.org/primary/p/181339/

Cox, E. (2015). Coaching and adult learning: Theory and practice. *New Directions for Adult and Continuing Education, 2015*(148), 27–38. doi:10.1002/ace.20149

Darling-Hammond, L., Hyler, M. E., & Gardner, M. (2017). *Effective teacher professional development.* Palo Alto, CA: Learning Policy Institute.

Dolan, V. (2011, Feb). The isolation of online adjunct faculty and its impact on their performance. *The International Review of Research in Open and Distributed Learning, 12*(2).

Fink, L. D. (2003). *Creating Significant Learning Experiences: An Integrated Approach to Designing College Courses.* Hoboken, NJ: John Wiley & Sons.

Fischer, C., Fishman, C., Dede, C., Eisenkraft, A., Frumin, K., Foster, B., & McCoy A. (2018). *Investigating relationships between school context, teacher professional development, teaching practices, and student achievement in response to a nationwide science reform.* Academic Press.

Geldenhuys, J. L., & Oosthuizen, L. C. (2015). Challenges influencing teachers' involvement in continuous professional development: A South African perspective. *Teaching and Teacher Education, 51,* 203–212. doi:10.1016/j.tate.2015.06.010

Ginda, M., Richey, M. C., Cousino, M., & Börner, K. (2019). Visualizing learner engagement, performance, and trajectories to evaluate and optimize online course design. *PLoS One, 14*(5). doi:10.1371/journal.pone.0215964 PMID:31059546

Hassar, W., & Bailey, T. (2014). *Projections of education statistics to 2022.* National Center for Education Statistics, US Dept. of Education.

Herman, J. H. (2012). Faculty development programs: The frequency and variety of professional development programs available to online instructors. *Journal of Asynchronous Learning Networks, 16*(5), 87–106. https://doi-org.proxy1.ncu.edu/10.24059/olj.v16i5.282

Jaafar, R., & Schwartz, J. (2018). Applying holistic adult learning theory to the study of calculus. *Journal of University Teaching & Learning Practice, 15*(3), 6–16.

Kelly, J. (2017). Professional learning and adult learning theory: A connection. *Northwest Journal of Teacher Education, 12*(2), 4–18. doi:10.15760/nwjte.2017.12.4

Kincey, S., Farmer, E., Errick, D., Wiltsher, C., McKenzie, D., & Mibiza, S. (2019, January). From chalkboard to digital media: The evolution of technology and its relationship to minority students' learning experiences. *Journal of Faculty Development, 33*(1), 65–76.

Kragler, S., Martin, L. E., & Sylvester, R. (2014). Lessons learned: What our history and research tell us about teachers' professional learning. In Handbook of professional development in education: Successful models and practices, preK-12. Guilford.

Money, W., & Dean, B. P. (2019). Incorporating student population differences for effective online education: A content-based review and integrative model. *Computers & Education, 138*, 57–82. doi:10.1016/j.compedu.2019.03.013

Moskal, P., Thompson, K., & Futch, L. (2015). Enrollment, engagement, and satisfaction in the BlendKit faculty development open, online course. *Online Learning, 19*(4), 1–12. doi:10.24059/olj.v19i4.555

Nicolaides, A., & Marsick, V. J. (2016). Understanding adult learning in the midst of complex social "Liquid Modernity.". *New Directions for Adult and Continuing Education, 2016*(149), 9–20. doi:10.1002/ace.20172

Ormrod, J. (2008). *Human learning*. Pearson Prentice-Hall.

Patterson, D. (2019). The Power of the Human Face in Online Education. *International Journal of Adult Vocational Education and Technology, 10*(1), 13–26. doi:10.4018/IJAVET.2019010102

Reed, P. (2015, July). Technology and the contemporary library. *Insights, 28*(2).

Rienties, B., Brouwer, N., & Lygo-Baker, S. (2013). The effects of online professional development on higher education teachers' beliefs and intentions towards learning facilitation and technology. *Teaching and Teacher Education, 29*, 122–131. doi:10.1016/j.tate.2012.09.002

Rios, T. (2019, January). The relationship between students' personalities and their perception of online course experiences. *Journal of Educators Online., 16*(1). doi:10.9743/jeo.2019.16.1.11

Roberts, J. (2018). Future and changing roles of staff in distance education: A study to identify training and professional development needs. *Distance Education, 39*(1), 37–53. doi:10.1080/01587919.2017.1419818

Schlager, M. S., Farooq, U., Fusco, J., Schank, P., & Dwyer, N. (2009). Analyzing online teacher networks: Cyber networks require cyber research tools. *Journal of Teacher Education, 60*(1), 86–100. doi:10.1177/0022487108328487

Serrano, D., Dea-Avuela, M., Gonzalez-Burgos, E., Serrano-Gil, A., & Lalatsa, A. (2019, April 5). Technology-enhanced learning in higher education: How to enhance student engagement through blended learning. *European Journal of Education: Research. Development and Policy, 54*(2), 273–286.

Simplico, J. (2019). Strategies to improve online student academic success and increase university persistence rates. *Education, 139*(3), 173–177.

Singh, E. (2014). Learning theory and online technologies. *Open Learning: The Journal of Open, Distance and e-Learning, 29*(1), 89-92.

Templeton, L., & Linder, K. E. (2017). *Establishing an e-Learning Division. In Leading and managing e-learning: What the e-learning leader needs to know*. Springer.

Tinto, V. (1993). *Leaving college: Rethinking the causes and cures of student attrition* (2nd ed.). Chicago: University of Chicago Press.

Trust, T. (2017). Motivation, empowerment, and innovation: Teachers' beliefs about how participating in the Edmodo Math Subject Community shapes teaching and learning. *Journal of Research on Technology in Education, 49*(1), 16–30. doi:10.1080/15391523.2017.1291317

Uppal, M. A., Ali, S., & Gulliver, S. R. (2018). Factors determining e-learning service quality. *British Journal of Educational Technology, 49*(3), 412–426. doi:10.1111/bjet.12552

U.S. Department of Education, National Center for Education Statistics, Integrated Postsecondary Education Data System (NCES). (2017). *Fall Enrollment component; IPEDS, Fall 2016, Completions component; and IPEDS, Winter 2016-17, Graduation Rates component*. Retrieved from https://nces.ed.gov/programs/digest/d17/tables/dt17_311.33.asp?current=yes

Vaill, A. L., & Testori, P. A. (2012). Orientation, mentoring and ongoing support: A three-tiered approach to online faculty development. *Journal of Asynchronous Learning Networks, 16*(2), 111–119. doi:10.24059/olj.v16i2.256

VanPortfliet, P., & Anderson, M. (2013). Moving from online to hybrid course delivery: Increasing positive student outcomes. *Journal of Research in Innovative Teaching, 6*(1), 80–87. Retrieved from https://search-ebscohost-com.proxy1.ncu.edu/login.aspx?direct=true&db=ehh&AN=88176006&site=eds-live

Vedder, R. (2017, Aug 29). *Seven challenges facing higher education*. Center for College Affordability and Productivity. Retrieved from https://www.forbes.com/sites/ccap/2017/08/29/seven-challenges-facing-higher-education/#4e96eac43180

Violino, B. (2014, Aug/Sep). The future is now. *Community College Journal, 85*(1), 18-23.

Weller, M., Jordan, K., DeVries, I., & Rolfe, V. (2018). Mapping the open education landscape: Citation network analysis of historical open and distance education research. *Open Praxis, 10*(2), 109–126. doi:10.5944/openpraxis.10.2.822

Xiao, J. (2018, January 28). On the margins or at the center? Distance education in higher education. *Journal of Distance Education, 29*(2), 22–36.

Zawacki-Richter, O., & Latchem, C. (2017, June 14). Exploring four decades of research in computer & education. *Computers & Education, 122*(36), 136–152.

ADDITIONAL READING

Kotluk, N., & Kocakaya, S. (2017). The effect of creating digital storytelling on secondary school students' academic achievement, self-efficacy perceptions and attitudes toward physics. *International Journal of Research in Education and Science.*, *3*(1), 218–227.

Mahnane, L. (2017). Recommending learning activities in social network using data mining algorithms. *Journal of Educational Technology & Society*, *20*(4), 11–23.

Mohamed, H., & Lamia, M. (2018). Implementing flipped classroom that used an intelligent tutoring system into learning process. *Computers & Education*, *124*, 62–76. doi:10.1016/j.compedu.2018.05.011

Tsai, C. W., & Chiang, Y. C. (2013). Research trends in problem-based learning (PBL) research in e-learning and online education environments: A review of publications in SSCI-indexed journals from 2004 to 2012. Colloquium. *British Journal of Educational Technology*, *44*(6), E185–E190. doi:10.1111/bjet.12038

Tsui, E. K., & Starecheski, A. (2018). Uses of oral history and digital storytelling in public health research and practice. *Public Health*, *154*, 24–30. doi:10.1016/j.puhe.2017.10.008 PMID:29153972

Chapter 2
Closing the Distance in Distance Learning

Shaunna Waltemeyer
Grand Canyon University, USA

Jeff Cranmore
Grand Canyon University, USA

ABSTRACT

This chapter will outline various best practices to assist instructors in closing the distance for online students. Topics include the theory of transactional distance as well as creating an engaging learning environment and overall student satisfaction. Best practices include live conferencing, instant communication tools, effective feedback, group discussions, announcements and reminders, the ease of using an online learning platform, and establishing personal connections. This chapter also provides examples and practical applications for technology in the online learning environment.

INTRODUCTION: CLOSING THE DISTANCE IN DISTANCE LEARNING

With the increase of online opportunities in higher education, there are more options for access to continuing education than ever before. While on-line course work can remove barriers related to access, time, and finances, many learners find themselves feeling isolated and missing face-to-face contact. Experienced faculty may also find themselves at a loss, when their traditional pedagogical methods do not translate to a digital setting. This chapter will focus on the concept of transactional distance, learner satisfaction, and strategies for online instructors to bring the "human element" into their classroom.

There are many benefits to the online learning modality. At the institutional level, online classes can reduce the cost of instruction through reductions in salaries and building upkeep. For students, online learning provides opportunities for students to take classes at times convenient to them, or even provide access to classes for students that have no other options. As in all courses, whether on campus or online, class instruction must be engaging, offer connections, and provide the best option for meeting all course objectives (Baker & Unni, 2018; Moore, 2016).

DOI: 10.4018/978-1-7998-0115-3.ch002

Instructors often have to change their behavior and shift their thinking regarding the move to online classes. Online courses cannot simply be the face-to-face version of the class recorded and placed online. Many times, this may make online learning more laborious than traditional face to face classes. Moore (2016) noted that "in the online environment, the instructor may spend additional time observing and commenting on activities in the discussion forum and creating videos or written tutorials and instructions for technological tools being used in the class" (p. 411). As such, online instructors face the ongoing challenges as it relates to their technological proficiencies that is required on top of existing academic responsibilities (Gillett-Swan, 2017). Therefore, the importance of increasing competencies related to technology and learning is essential for both instructors and students.

The increased enrollment numbers in online education over the last several years has greatly outpaced that of traditional onsite learning environments (Hewett & Bourelle, 2017). This increase, in part, is due to the convenience and flexibility of online learning (Hersman, 2014). Such benefits include the ability for students to work on their own time and in an environment conducive to their personal learning styles. Online students the opportunity to attend school during the times that best work with their personal and professional commitments. According to (Goodman, Melkers, and Pallais, 2019), online education offers opportunities for students to attend college who may otherwise not have access to higher education.

Transactional Distance

In 1972, the first attempt to articulate a theory associated with distance learning lead to the creation of the theory of transactional distance. According to Moore (1997), the theory stated,

Distance education is not simply a geographic separation of learners and teachers, but, more importantly, is a pedagogical concept. It is a concept describing the universe of teacher-learner relationships that exist when learners and instructors are separated by space and/or by time. This universe of relationships can be ordered into a typology that is shaped around the most elementary constructs of the field - namely, the structure of instructional programmes, the interaction between learners and teachers, and the nature and degree of self-directedness of the learner. (p. 22)

Since its introduction, the theory of transactional distance has grown and developed into its current form, but the primary tenets of transactional distance learning have remained constant.

Moore's original model indicated that transactional distance (TD) is the interplay between dialogue, course structure, and the autonomy of the learner. While instructors can control elements such as course structure and the amount of dialogue of students, learner autonomy remains an element that relies solely on the learner. Xiaoxia, Chandra, DePaolo, and Simmons (2016) found that perceived TD can be reduced. Elements related to structure, such as clearly defined objectives, instructions, and material, showed a strong correlation to reducing the perceived TD. Further, both the quantity and quality of dialogue also lowered perceived TD. Frequent and purposeful communication between learner-to-instructor and learner-to-learner are ways to build connections. Finally, Xiaoxia, et al (2016) found enhanced technology such as videos, live chats, and other synchronous communication tools lowered the perceived TD. Each of these strategies help in reducing the transactional distance, and creating an engaged learning environment. Larkin and Jamieson-Proctor (2015) found similar results to the advantage of increased dialogue. They do note that certain structural elements originally thought to decrease TD, had the opposite effect. In their study, lectures were audio recorded and made available; however, based on student feedback, they found students who could only listen had increased TD, over those that could both listen to and view the lesson.

Learner Satisfaction

In 2018, between 25-33% of all students enrolled in higher education are currently taking at least one online class (Babson Survey Research Group, 2018). This number has steadily increased since 2004. Students continue to cite a number of reasons for online enrollment; however, the most common reasons reported are flexibility of scheduling, cost, and the ability to work on their own time. A large number of students report taking on-line and ground based courses simultaneously, although fully online programs continue to grow. Social networking in classes may provide the opportunity for students to connect in new ways. In a study of social networking in Australian schools, Casey and Evans (2011) found that "Enabling students to work online allowed them to access the classroom anytime they wished" (p. 20). This flexibility is a large draw for online learning.

Flexibility and the ability for students to work at their own convenience are often listed as the major draws of online courses. Even with these benefits, high attrition rates remain a concern. The most mitigating factor in reducing students from dropping out of online course is student satisfaction. Higher satisfaction rates in courses positively correlates to student retention and completion of online courses. One possible connection to satisfaction may have to do with student motivation (Weidlich & Bastiaens, 2018).

Rios, Elliott, and Mandernach (2018) noted that "student satisfaction with what they learn and how they learn in an online classroom is an important variable to understand, as it can help instructors and course designers create an environment that fits students' needs" (p. 163). The authors provided several ideas for increased satisfaction. These included the instructor providing a brief biography and picture, as well as contact information. Additionally, they suggested that the instructor may want to model appropriate and acceptable behavior in class discussion boards (Ross, et al, 2018).. Finally, instructors should set clear expectations and send reminders of these expectations. Holbeck and Hartman (2018) identified increase communication as one way to increase perceived student satisfaction. Video and text communication allow instructors to have more direct contact with distance learners. These communications tools are especially helpful when used to remind learners of upcoming events. Costley and Lange (2016) found increased interaction also showed to increase student satisfaction and their perceived learning.

In addition to teacher created video/audio content, instructors may wish to include other media in their class. These might be short videos or audio recordings that can support the lesson's topic. One advantage of additional media is the ability to utilize multiple learning styles. A visual learner may appreciate seeing an example, while auditory learners may gain more insight from hearing a discussion or podcast. Examples may include demonstrations of labs in a science classroom, an explanation of conducting a statistical test on spss, examples of songs with lyrics that address school violence, or a podcast on the tools used in early civilizations. When including any media, make sure to abide by all copyright laws.

Strategies

Based on the desire to lower perceived TD, and increase student satisfaction and retention rates, the following are best practices that can be developed and applied in courses. Many of these strategies may already be aspects of the platform that allow these practices. Most if not all platforms will allow for instructors to make announcements and communicate directly with learners. Other practices may require additional software tools. Video conferencing, screen capture, and the ability to make short videos that can be posted or sent to students are more and more readily available, often at no cost. Each of these practices adds to the social presence, cognitive presence, or teaching presence of the instructor, all of which are factors to increase engagement (Moore, 2016; Rios, et al, 2018).

"Live" Conferencing

Students report the flexibility of time as a major reason for choosing online class options (Moore, 2016). In asynchronous courses, this truly means that they can work on their own at any time. One way to help keep the human connection, is to offer live/real time opportunities to communicate. This may be in the form of virtual office hours, optional conference calls, or virtual meetings. If these times and dates are posted well in advance, students are empowered to join in, if they wish. (Note- it is often critical to clearly post times and time zones for these)

These types of meetings may be in a video classroom, a phone call, or a live chat session. Any of these formats allow the student immediate access to ask their questions and receive feedback. While the chat or phone call provides that type of support, students often rate the live video conference as their preferred method. The ability to see the person on the other end gives a perceived feeling of more connection (Rios, et al, 2018).

A weekly meeting or office hour allows students to connect at their discretion. If they have a question or need clarification, they know they have an avenue to reach out to the instructor and have an immediate answer- without multiple emails to clarify the issue at hand. Much like a brick and mortar classroom, students can "pop" in with these types of questions. This access to the instructor can greatly increase the feeling of support of the learners.

Besides offering regularly scheduled office hours, some instructors may hold special topics sessions. This may be an additional tutorial when going over difficult concepts, a guide to a specific process (such as completing the next steps in the dissertation phase), or providing a forum for students interested in a certain field, just to name a few examples. These optional sessions can work to build a sense of community and increased perceived support from the instructor.

Instructional Presentations

Depending on the format of instruction- live versus asynchronous, learning will need some way to interact with the course material. If there are live lectures, learners can view the instructor as a live person. If there are live lectures, it may be worth considering converting them to a video format, that can be viewed multiple times. Loudon and Sharp (2006) found increased student outcomes in courses where lectures were converted into streaming media. The streaming media could be reviewed multiple times, and it allowed students that missed a live lecture to still participate. This approach could be applied to both face to face and synchronous on-line classes.

If the course is fully asynchronous and learners must read class notes and articles on their own, there may be an increased feeling of TD. If this is the case, various items might be incorporated to close perceptions of TD. Video clips of the instructor or of examples may be helpful here. Additionally, opportunity to interact with peers or the instructor, such as discussion boards over the instructional material can help provide a sense of connection.

Instant Communication Tools

If the class has a synchronous component, such as live class meetings, tools that provide instant feedback can greatly close perceived TD. These include live chat features, break out rooms, and polling tools. Most learning platforms have features that allow for some level of instant communication. If not, it may be possible to use supplemental programs to provide alternative forms of communication.

A live chat or video session allows students to instantly access you as the instructor and other students. Being able to put a face to a name, or get immediate responses can lower the perceived TD. These may be done as part of a class lecture, or as a special session to opt into. Students that crave this type of interaction will often make every effort to attend these types of sessions.

Breakout rooms may be used for group conversations or for collaborating on group projects. More recently, it has become popular to create digital "escape rooms." Holbeck and Hartman (2018) noted the increased popularity of these types of exercise, where students must complete a series of tasks to move to the next room or level. By providing an element of gamification, this may increase the engagement level and satisfaction of students. These types of activities can be synchronous or asynchronous.

A final example of instant feedback may come in the form of polling or questioning. If you as the instructor has the ability to write content into the platform, you may be able to create a no point test question that allows you to poll the class. If not, several free polling websites are available where students can poll in answers. In a similar approach, review games also allow instant feedback and add the gamiifaction element. Ideally, these games or polls are meant to be synchronous, but with some modification could be completed asynchronous

Feedback

Student feedback is essential for their learning. Quality constructive feedback directs the learner in areas to improve. In a virtual setting, there are not always ways to build rapport with students, and some students perceive feedback as harsh or overly critical. "Receiving personalized feedback on the assignments and completing quizzes can provide students with checkpoints on their academic achievement throughout the class" (Rios et al., 2018, p.161).

Best practices for feedback should include:

- Refer to the student by name
- Be precise
- Making real world connections
- Be timely in giving feedback
- Consider giving an example
- Give an upper level of review as well as specific comments
- Offer actionable items to improve on the next assignment

Each of these show a positive regard to each of the learners, as well as increase the teaching presence of the instructor.

One practice that may be helpful for instructors is keeping a list of saved feedback responses that can be used multiple times. An example of this may be a set of instructions on correctly citing a source in APA format. A detailed explanation along with resources can be saved and used each time the same citation issue appears. Comments such as these can be saved on a word document and copy and pasted, or other programs exist where comments (or macros) can be stored and pasted as needed

Another way to incorporate feedback is through screencasting technology that allows you to make short and personalized videos. For example, instructors can use screencasting technology to provide audio and visual feedback specific to each student. Not only does this help increase the personal connection between online instructors and students, it also allows the student to view the assignment feedback multiple times. This type of feedback is appropriate for instruction related to content, formatting, spelling, grammar, etc. West and Turner (2016) suggested students perceive video feedback as individualized, easy to understand, and more robust than traditional assignment feedback done in text form.

Group Discussions

Discussion boards offer students the ability to communicate their own thoughts and ideas with the instructor and with classmates. This is also the primary source of social interaction in an online class (Rios, et al, 2018). Discussion posts can greatly enhance feelings of connectedness to the class, if used in meaningful ways. Open two-way communication mirrors class discussions that take place in real time. As with all assignments, one key here is to make sure the discussion is relevant and has practical applications. If the discussion is centered on the topic or an application of the topic, students have a chance to share their voice and opinion. Discussion boards should be considered a safe place for students to have meaningful discourse. It is important to make sure conversations continue in a civil manner. As the instructor, you should model the expected behaviors in responding to posts, this may include the correct academic language, use of citation, and the expected civil tone. Disagreement is not discouraged, but personal attacks should not be tolerated.

As the instructor, this also provides a voice for you to be engaged in students' discussions, and increases your social, cognitive and teaching presence. Responding to a discussion thread allows you a chance to share your own experiences and expertise. Personal examples can also be helpful in building rapport and making the conversation more meaningful. It may be wise to respond later in the thread, so as not to discourage opinions or experiences that differ from your own. . Often your response will generate additional multi-way communication that builds a relationship with students. It is also a best practice to be "visible" on the class discussion at least once every 24-48 hours.

If the learning platform allows, the instructor might also have more detailed conversation in the private forum or through emails. Information about grades, academic concerns, or personal matters should not be discussed in front of the entire class, just as they should not be in a brick and mortar classroom. A private chat may allow you to give specific feedback to an issue that only involves that student.

Other Group Interactions

Group projects allow learners a chance for collaboration with peers. Many learning platforms allow the instructor to create a space for groups to "meet" to discuss the project or even to work on a draft. If the platform does not allow this, free sites meeting sites allow distance learners to virtual meet for group discussions. Additionally, applications such as Google Docs provide a platform for multiple users to contribute to a single document.

Breakout rooms can be used for discussions in both real time class meetings and asynchronous discussions. An example of this might include a classroom discussion. If students agree with one answer they may be directed to one breakout room, while other students disagreeing might be sent to a different room. These rooms can also be used for quick interactive conversations, such as a think-pair-share. Other activities involving breakout rooms might allow students to interact in a certain number of rooms. This can be set up as an "escape room" concept where students can work together to solve problems. Additionally, these rooms can be used for students to make quick posts or comments regarding a topic. For example, learners can be directed to visit four different break out rooms and comment on a topic. The learners can then visit all four rooms after all posts have been made to "gallery walk" the completed comments

Breakout rooms can also be utilized for providing differentiated instruction. After a pre-test, students may be assigned to different breakout rooms based on their score. Additional review materials can be aligned to cover material based on those scores. This can be used as a form of a review or as an extension of instructional practices.

A variety of interaction opportunities with peers can be helpful in reducing feelings of learning in isolation, and lowering the perceived TD. Virtual group activity mirrors that of face-to-face group interactions. For many students, this small additional of peer to peer exchange can make a big difference in their perception of the class.

Weekly Announcements/Reminders

Just as in a traditional classroom, there should be a venue for making announcements or giving reminders. This may include reminding students of upcoming assignments, providing technological assistance (such as addressing a problem with a link on the platform), or even giving a weekly word of encouragement. Each of these mirrors the practices of educators in a class setting, and can easily be applied to a virtual one. Most platforms will have options to make general announcements, as well as, announcements or messages to a specific student.

Rios et al (2018) suggested that weekly announcements can lower perceived TD, as well as increase engagement through the use of communication. Announcements should be posted weekly, and provide important information about the upcoming week. They further suggest the use of announcements to remind students of weekly expectations, such as reminders of upcoming assignments or assessments, as well as remind students of expectations for these activities. A pre-course announcement that outlines the expectations of the course can also remove student fears.

Weekly announcements also provide a venue to get out important information quickly. If the learning platform will be down for maintenance, you can announce that early so students can plan or if any piece of the class platform is not functioning correctly (such as a missing or broken link) you can also announce that. Announcements also allow you to notify the class if you will be unavailable. If you will be traveling or unable to respond in a 24 hour period, you would want to announce that early, along with instructions of what to do if there is an issue, and when you will return to normal availability.

Ease of Use of Platform

Many students become frustrated with online learning when aspects of the technology do not work, or are not intuitively manageable. If you notice a glitch in the platform, such as a missing link to an article or a particular function (such as submitting an assignment) is not working, it is important to make an immediate announcement of the problem, the anticipated length of the problem, and any instructions for working around the problem. If the submission link is not working and the assignment is due that day, many students will have increased anxiety about not being able to complete the assignment on time. A brief word from you, such as the submission deadline is being pushed back two days due to technical issues provides immediate relief to student fears of the unknown.

It is important for instructors to understand the form and functionality of the learning platform being used (Moore & Fodrey, 2018). This includes the format of the class (such as being synchronous or asynchronous) and the format of instruction (such as being a webinar or elearning). The understanding of the basic aspects of the classroom environment, allows instructors to answer any student questions. Additionally, if the functionality of a particular aspect of the learning platform is difficult to navigate, it is important to provide step by step directions. These should include screenshots or perhaps a short "how to" video.

Tutorials and "how to" videos are a valuable technology tool to help online students navigate the classroom or perform certain assignment activities. Screencasting allows instructors to video capture what is on their own computer screen, make it into a video, and ultimately share with students. This can be used for something as simple as how to upload and submit a completed assignment by offer both visual and audio directions. Screencasting can also be used for more complex scenarios by creating a video and providing step-by-step instructions on how to complete an algebra equation or accounting problem. Once completed, these videos can be used again. In a very short time, an instructor can compile a large video library that can be uploaded at the start of every class.

Finally, it is important students have instructions on what to do if technology does not work. This may include a link or number of the school's helpdesk, your email to contact you with questions, or even an office phone line to reach you. Even if the problem is one that you cannot address, being able to point students in the correct direction can go a long way in solving the heightened anxiety associated with technology failures.

Personal Contact

Interaction between students and instructors is via the online environment is oftentimes viewed as limited; however, there is still ample opportunity for personal contact. The use of technology tools, such as screencasting, allows instructors to record and share personal comments. Screencasting video recordings allow students to see and hear a personal message from that can be viewed multiple times; thus creating an individual connection with the instructor even in an online learning environment (Waltemeyer & Cranmore, 2019). This technology has many applications in the online classroom appropriate for establishing personal contact between instructors and students. Although the primary outcome is to teach students, personal contact with the instructor plays a vital role in student engagement and success in the online classroom (Glazier, 2016). This increased engagement is important to lower the perceived TD felt by online students.

Establishing and building rapport between online students and instructors is in many ways similar to a traditional learning environment. For example, instructors can share anecdotes and personal accounts as a means to form a personal connection. This can be related to shared struggles and challenges of attending school in online and can translate to instructors providing examples of specific struggles and how they were able to overcome these obstacles. Examples might include shared experiences related to time management, incorporating school into a busy schedule, technology challenges, and self-motivation. Not only does this provide a human element but also increases the important personal connection between the online instructor and students.

Additional ways in which instructors can increase their personal connection with online students is through the use of a welcome video posted at the beginning of class. A welcome video allows the instructor to personally introduce themselves, share their educational background and professional experiences, or even hobbies and favorite vacation places. This does not need to be an extensive or in-depth video but rather a short, energetic, informational welcome is more than sufficient.

Online learning is largely done in an asynchronous environment in which instructors and students communicate when it best fits their schedule as opposed to a set time of the day or week. Given this, it can be difficult to have a conversation in the classroom in "real time" as students often times live in various parts of the country or world. Therefore, it is important for instructors to connect with students in ways that are appropriate for all different types of learning and communication styles. Screencasting is a valuable tool to help bridge the gap in an asynchronous environment as students are able to view the videos multiple times and within their own schedules. Mahoney, Macfarlane, and Ajjawi (2019) suggested students value the use of screencasting technology and perceive this type of feedback as more personalized by simulating a face-to-face interaction with their instructor, and lowering their perception of the TD.

CONCLUSION

As in face to face classes, the instructor plays a major role in student satisfaction and retention. While there may be increased challenges in online settings, such as feelings of increased transactional distance, they can be overcome by the instructor having social, cognitive, and teaching presences. Teaching in an online setting can be as equally rewarding as teaching in face to face settings, but it does require a change in thought process and action. This chapter outlined several best practices that have research based evidence that supports their effectiveness in lowered perceived TD and increasing student satisfaction. These best practices can easily be incorporated into your classroom teaching and lesson design.

REFERENCES

Babson Survey Research Group. (2018). *Babson College, New Study: Distance Education up, Overall Enrollment Down*. Retrieved from http://www.babson.edu/about/news- events/babson-announcements/babson-survey-research-group-tracking-distance- education-report/

Baker, D. M., & Unni, R. (2018). USA and Asia hospitality & tourism students' perceptions and satisfaction with online learning versus traditional face-to-face instruction. *E-Journal of Business Education & Scholarship of Teaching, 12*(2), 40–54. Retrieved from https://lopes.idm.oclc.org/login?url=https://search.ebscohost.com/login.aspx?direct=true&db=ehh&AN=132335757&site=eds-live&scope=site

Casey, G., & Evans, T. (2011). Designing for learning: Online social networks as a classroom environment. *International Review of Research in Open and Distance Learning, 12*(7), 1–26. doi:10.19173/irrodl.v12i7.1011

Costley, J., & Lange, C. (2016). The effects of instructor control of online learning environments on satisfaction and perceived learning. *Electronic Journal of E-Learning, 14*(3), 169–180.

Gillett-Swan, J. (2017). The challenges of online learning: Supporting and engaging the isolated learner. *Journal of Learning Design, 10*(1), 20–30. doi:10.5204/jld.v9i3.293

Glazier, R. A. (2016). Building rapport to improve retention and success in online classes. *Journal of Political Science Education, 12*(4), 437–456. doi:10.1080/15512169.2016.1155994

Goodman, J., Melkers, J., & Pallais, A. (2019). Can online delivery increase access to education? *Journal of Labor Economics, 37*(1), 1–34. doi:10.1086/698895

Hersman, B. L. (2014). Increasing student engagement in online classes. *Chronicle of Kinesiology & Physical Education in Higher Education, 25*(2), 23–25.

Hewett, B. L., & Bourelle, T. (2017). Online teaching and learning in technical communication: Continuing the conversation. *Technical Communication Quarterly, 26*(3), 217–222. doi:10.1080/10572252.2017.1339531

Holbeck, R., & Hartman, J. (2018). Efficient strategies for maximizing online student satisfaction: Applying technologies to increase cognitive presence, social presence, and teaching presence. *Journal of Educators Online, 15*(3), 91–95. https://doi- org.lopes.idm.oclc.org/10.9743/jeo.2018.15.3.6

Larkin, K., & Jamieson-Proctor, R. (2015). Using transactional distance theory to redesign an online mathematics education course for pre-service primary teachers. *Mathematics Teacher Education and Development, 17*(1), 44–61.

Loudon, M., & Sharp, M. (2006). Online class review: Using streaming-media technology. *Journal of College Science Teaching, 36*(3), 39–43.

Mahoney, P., Macfarlane, S., & Ajjawi, A. (2019). A qualitative synthesis of video feedback in higher education. *Teaching in Higher Education, 24*(2), 157–179. doi:10.1080/13562517.2018.1471457

Moore, M. (1997). Theory of transactional distance. In Theoretical Principles of Distance Education. Routledge.

Moore, R. L. (2016). Interacting at a distance: creating engagement in online learning environments. In L. Kyei-Blankson, J. Blankson, E. Ntulli, & C. Agyeman (Eds.), *Handbook of Research on Strategic Management of Interaction, Presence, and Participation in Online Courses* (pp. 401–425). Hershey, PA: IGI Global. doi:10.4018/978-1-4666-9582-5.ch016

Moore, R. L., & Fodrey, B. (2018). Distance education and technology infrastructure: Strategies and opportunities. In A. Pina, V. Walker, & B. Harris (Eds.), *Leading and Managing elearning: What the e-learning learner needs to know* (pp. 87–100). Cham: Springer. doi:10.1007/978-3-319-61780-0_7

Rios, T., Elliott, M., & Jean Mandernach, B. (2018). Efficient instructional strategies for maximizing online student satisfaction. *Journal of Educators Online*, *15*(3), 158–166. doi:10.9743/jeo.2018.15.3.7

Waltemeyer, S. & Cranmore, J. (2018). Screencasting technology to increase student engagement in online higher education courses. *e-Learn, 2018*(12), 50-54.

Weidlich, J., & Bastiaens, T. J. (2018). Technology matters--The impact of transactional distance on satisfaction in online distance learning. *International Review of Research in Open and Distributed Learning*, *19*(3), 222–242. doi:10.19173/irrodl.v19i3.3417

West, J., & Turner, W. (2016). Enhancing the assessment experience: Improving student perceptions, engagement and understanding using online video feedback. *Innovations in Education and Teaching International*, *53*(4), 400–410. doi:10.1080/14703297.2014.1003954

Xiaoxia, H., Chandra, A., DePaolo, C. A., & Simmons, L. L. (2016). Understanding transactional distance in web-based learning environments: An empirical study. *British Journal of Educational Technology*, *47*(4), 734–747. https://doi- org.lopes.idm.oclc.org/10.1111/bjet.12263

Chapter 3
Comprehensive Faculty Development:
An Innovative Approach in Online Education

Desiree' Caldwell
Gwynedd Mercy University, USA

Mary Sortino
Gwynedd Mercy University, USA

Jill Winnington
Gwynedd Mercy University, USA

Tiffany Cresswell-Yeager
Gwynedd Mercy University, USA

ABSTRACT

There is a significant need for faculty development and support as it relates to online teaching. Researchers assert that the success of online education may be a direct result of the training and support of the institution's faculty. Higher education institutions implement a variety of online faculty development practices; however, little is known about which practices are seen as the most effective and efficient. In this chapter, the authors propose a strategic approach to building a comprehensive faculty development program that supports and engages online faculty from initial hire and beyond. The purpose of this chapter is to provide new insights to support faculty. The authors identify evidence-based strategies to incorporate adjunct and full-time online faculty into the university community. In addition, the authors share their experiences developing a comprehensive faculty development plan.

DOI: 10.4018/978-1-7998-0115-3.ch003

INTRODUCTION

Researchers assert that the success of online education may be a direct result of the training and support of the institution's faculty (Vaill & Testori, 2012). It has been asserted that supporting online instructors is paramount to developing high quality experiences for online teaching (Baran & Correia, 2014; Rhode, Richter, & Miller, 2017). This support empowers and challenges instructors to create transformative learning experiences (Mezirow, 1997). Professional development is a central factor leading to student success (O'Hara & Pritchard, 2012). Well-trained and supported faculty transfer their skills into the online classroom resulting in an improved student experience.

Professional development opportunities should include a variety of components including technology, pedagogy, mentoring/peer support, targeted modules for skill-set deficits, and disciple-based opportunities of scholarship (Baran & Correia, 2014; Scarpena et al., 2018; Schmit et al., 2016). The need for faculty members to engage in and complete training along their own time schedule, have access to archived live sessions, and be able to repeat trainings if necessary is of utmost importance (Scarpena, Riley, & Keathley, 2018). Because faculty have specific expectations and desires when it comes to professional development, it is important for institutions to assess the needs of faculty to develop an effective professional development plan (Mohr & Shelton, 2017). Administrators should seek to have faculty members self-identify weaknesses in skills important to online teaching and then provide the development opportunities needed to help faculty grow in those targeted areas (Rhode et al., 2017).

Chapter Objectives

- Examine current research related to strategies for online faculty development.
- Explore a strategic approach to building a comprehensive faculty development program which supports and engages online faculty from initial hire and beyond.

CURRENT RESEARCH

Comprehensive Professional Development

The authors of this chapter propose a comprehensive faculty development plan based on implementation of the most effective evidence-based strategies. This section explores some of those strategies. Development programs are critical in helping faculty engage in the process of pedagogical inquiry as they reflect on the interactions between content, online technologies, and pedagogical methods within their unique online classroom environment (Baran, Correia, & Thompson, 2013). Characteristics of successful professional development programs include information that is able to be used immediately (Baran & Correia, 2014), focuses on smaller and more focused opportunities (Schmidt, Tschida, & Hodge, 2016) and a shorter delivery format (Scarpena et al., 2018). Baran and Correia (2014) recommend departments offer many types of professional development opportunities with a comprehensive approach to teaching. Schmidt et al. (2016) explain that modules or sessions may focus on discipline-specific content, practical pedagogical techniques, theoretical approaches, and institutional expectations.

The most effective professional development programs include both formal approaches and informal opportunities. Elliot, Rhoades, Jackson, & Mandernach (2015) recommend that professional development programs include understanding of college teaching with an emphasis on practical teaching strategies. Baran and Correia (2014) suggest a three-tiered approach (organizational, community and teaching) for online faculty professional development. The first tier includes understanding the *organization*. This supports research by others that show professional development should include understanding of university policies and faculty expectations (Elliot et al., 2015; Schmidt et al., 2016). Baran and Correia (2014) assert the second tier is *teaching* in which professional development incorporates pedagogical understanding and practice with technological tools. The final tier in Baran and Correia's framework is *community* which encourages faculty members to engage in the campus community and create meaningful relationships with administrators and peers. By creating a community of practice, administrators help faculty become connected and active within an online environment. This community is crucial for online faculty support and development as it focuses on peer support, helps to extend conversations among faculty, and allows for an additional flow of knowledge and information, which can lead to transformative practice (Scarpena et al., 2018).

In both formal and informal opportunities, mentoring is an essential component of online faculty development. Mentoring can be part of a formal professional development program or evolve from an informal relationship between peers (Herman, 2012). Through formal mentoring, faculty can share opportunities, strengths, challenges and areas for improvement in their approach to teaching (Baran & Correia, 2014). Access to a mentor provides faculty with an experienced colleague who can share his/her experiences of what works and what does not work in an online classroom. Peer observation is another form of mentoring that has been integrated into professional development programs, such as at the authors' university. Through observation, faculty can provide colleagues with feedback and suggestions to improve teaching methods. Taking part in this observation and critiquing process can help faculty members visualize their own online teaching practices and develop their own strategies for improvement. This process can also help foster the learning community and sustain the conversation about effective online teaching practices (Baran & Correia, 2014). Researchers also espouse the importance of informal professional development including faculty to faculty conversations and discipline-specific networks (Schmidt et al., 2016). Baran and Correia (2014) assert the importance of this informal engagement in the community tier of their framework. Schmidt et al. (2016) argue that smaller more-focused informal opportunities are most effective and more helpful, especially when connecting experienced faculty with inexperienced faculty.

Despite the need for effective professional development and the evidence to support its effectiveness, institutional leaders and administrators face challenges to create and implement these programs. The next section of the chapter addresses some of these challenges.

Challenges in Implementation

Academic and institutional administrators are challenged with creating and implementing professional development opportunities for online faculty members that are of high quality, provide continued support, yield high impact results, produce faculty interaction, and respect faculty members' busy schedules (Baran & Correia, 2014; Scarpena et al., 2018; Schmit et al., 2016). A one size fits all development plan is not the solution (Elliot et al., 2015). Simply putting the development opportunities online does not make it easier for faculty to participate. Administration must take into account the amount of time development opportunities will take (Chen et al., 2017). Scheduling conflicts and a lack of interest prevent online faculty from participating in development opportunities.

To overcome these challenges and increase the effectiveness of online instruction, institutions must invest in faculty development through policies that provide for adequate resources for effective development (Herman, 2012). Because effective professional development involves multiple layers, activities, and learning, the authors of this chapter argue that a comprehensive plan is the most effective approach to faculty development.

IMPLEMENTING A COMPREHENSIVE FACULTY DEVELOPMENT PLAN

Quality professional development opportunities for both experienced and novice online educators are key to the success of any online program (Vaill & Testori, 2012). These opportunities must be derived from adult learning theories, such as the Transformative Learning Theory (Meyer, 2014). Development opportunities must reflect pedagogical considerations of the online classroom as well as the theoretical and practical needs of online faculty (Elliot et al., 2015). To help ensure a positive experience occurs for all involved, a faculty development approach must include initial training, mentorship, and ongoing support (Vaill & Testori, 2012). Mohr and Shelton (2017) add that a comprehensive approach requires all constituents to be involved. Faculty development for the online instructor must continually evolve its offerings including support for quality and training on new technological tools (Baran & Correia, 2014; Meyer & Murrell, 2014).

Online programs serving graduate and professional students often follow a Practitioner Faculty model. This model requires only a small core group of full time faculty with the majority of courses being taught by adjunct instructors who are practicing professionals in their respective field. The heavy reliance on adjunct faculty exacerbates the need for focused and dedicated faculty development.

In 2013, this university made the decision to move all graduate education, graduate business, and undergraduate adult degree completion programs to a fully online model. At the time of this transition, there were no established online faculty; either adjunct or full-time. Recognizing that online instruction is fundamentally different than face-to-face instruction, the university took the initial step of establishing an Online Faculty Certification course which provided basic training on the learning management system and the logistics of online instruction. However, there was little emphasis on pedagogy, student engagement, or best practices of online teaching and learning. As enrollment in online programs rapidly grew, the adjunct roles expanded, eventually including over 200 active adjunct faculty just within the School of Graduate and Professional Studies (GPS).

Culture of Engagement and Development

Following Baran and Correia's (2014) three-tiered approach, professional development must include establishing community. The first step in establishing this Comprehensive Faculty Development Program focused on creating a culture of engagement and development among the faculty—or community. While the faculty were teaching online, the majority of the students were local to the university. Therefore, onsite semi-annual Faculty Development Days were instituted. These days took the form of a mini conference with a general session, followed by a selection of concurrent breakout sessions and ending with program meetings. Adjunct faculty were invited, but not compensated for attending. These days were immediately well received with approximately 100 adjunct faculty members attending each time. The general session typically included university updates, policy reminders and a variety of guest speakers.

Guest speakers have included the new university president, the accessibility coordinator and external experts on collaborative learning communities. Breakout sessions vary from year to year and have included topics such as: grading, handling challenging student issues, the ethics of teaching, writing across the curriculum, academic integrity, integration of University mission, and facilitating discussion boards.

Online Faculty Expectations

The next step, therefore, centered upon creating a shared understanding of best practices in online instruction. This aligns with Baran and Correia's (2014) tier—*teaching*. After researching various models of online instruction and pedagogy, full time faculty within GPS developed the Online Faculty Expectations document. This set of guidelines addressed course preparation, frequency and level of faculty engagement in the online learning environment, expectations for grading and feedback, as well as procedural and policy related topics such as reporting attendance. This document would serve as the foundation for the Self-Assessment Tool and the Peer Observation Tool discussed below. The newly developed Online Faculty Expectations were socialized to the adjunct faculty over the course of a year. They were first presented and discussed at a Faculty Development Day, and then further discussed by the Program Directors in program meetings.

As mentioned above, the Online Faculty Expectations document formed the foundation for the development of a Self-Assessment Tool and a Peer Observation Tool. Once a shared understanding of expectations and best practices for online instruction was established, these tools were introduced. Adjunct faculty were asked to complete a Self-Assessment and reflect upon their own teaching. Program Directors offered to review these Self Assessments with faculty to provide coaching and mentoring. Additionally, feedback from the Self-Assessments helped to inform topics for future breakout sessions on Faculty Development Days. After faculty became comfortable with using the Self-Assessment Tool, Program Directors and full-time faculty began conducting Peer Observations. These observations were intended to be developmental and formative rather than summative evaluations. The use of the Peer Observation Tool in conjunction with the Self-Assessment Tool provided a framework for discussions about the implementation of established best practices. These Coaching and Mentoring meetings, which were originally perceived as stressful, formal, evaluations, have evolved to be mutually understood as opportunities for supportive, meaningful conversations around individual faculty strengths and challenges in meeting the established Faculty Expectations.

As the assessment and observation tools were being implemented, an Adjunct Faculty Manual was developed to provide a single source of information on policy and procedures. This manual provides guidance on issues such as attendance policy, accessibility services, academic support services, and the role of academic advising, along with summaries of relevant University policy. The presentation of this manual at a Faculty Development Day led to the realization that faculty who had been hired at different times had very different understanding of and comfort levels with various policies. It became evident that there needed to be an across the board recalibration of policies and procedures. This resulted in the creation of an online faculty orientation, called FAC100.

Online Faculty Orientation

To better understand the university policy and the school's expectations, this plan provides development that is consistent with Baran and Correia's (2014) tier of *organization*. FAC100 is a three-week online training course required of all faculty teaching within GPS. The course is facilitated by full time faculty and is designed to provide opportunities to model best practices in online pedagogy while providing adjunct faculty participants to experience a course from the student's perspective. FAC 100 includes discussion boards, written reflections, case studies and a policy quiz. The first week focuses on integration of the University mission into teaching, and how Practitioner Faculty can bring their own expertise to a pre-designed Master Course to enhance the curriculum and deepen student learning. It also included an overview of key policies and resources within the Adjunct Faculty Manual and the University website. Faculty facilitators are able to model engagement in the discussion boards to create a collaborative learning community. This allows participants to gain a deeper understanding of why their presence in the discussion boards is important to the learning that takes place. In week two, faculty review their administrative responsibilities and explore strategies for resolving student issues by completing a number of short case studies. In the final week, issues related to academic success are explored including academic integrity, access to academic support services and the importance of maintaining academic standards through establishing clear grading guidelines and late assignment policies.

With the establishment of the Adjunct Manual, Online Faculty Expectations, Self-Assessment Tool and Peer Observation Tool, it became necessary to develop a repository for these faculty development resources. A dedicated GPS Faculty Development Portal page was developed. This page houses all internal GPS faculty development resources as well as links to other important University portal and web pages that house needed policies and forms. This universal "one stop shop" allows adjunct faculty to have a single point of access to School and University policies, documents and forms.

Faculty Development Days

After four years of Faculty Development Days, the attendance and feedback continue to be strong. The general session and program meetings are now available for distance faculty to attend online. Assessment of data from Self Assessments, Peer Observations and feedback received during Coaching and Mentoring meetings have identified major themes that deserve more focused attention can be offered in a 45-minute break out session. Therefore, a new format has been developed for the Faculty Development Days. The meeting to be held in the Fall of 2019 will focus on a single theme and incorporate round table discussions sharing individual best practices and table exercises designed to strengthen particular pedagogical strategies. When this proposed change was presented to the faculty, it was very well received. While the spring meeting will maintain the original format, it will more closely resemble a conference in that a call for proposals will be issued and adjunct faculty will have the opportunity to develop and facilitate break-out sessions.

FEEDBACK DISCUSSION

Feedback from Faculty

Feedback from attendees at the Faculty Development Days was extremely positive with faculty indicating that they would like further opportunities for development. While this was a positive indicator of faculty commitment to developing their teaching, it became evident from student feedback that there was significant variation in the engagement and instructional practices of faculty across programs. Like many

Comprehensive Faculty Development

online programs utilizing the Practitioner Faculty model, the GPS programs utilized a Master Course within the learning management system. While this approach serves to ensure standardization in curriculum across courses taught by a variety of adjuncts, it can lead to a lack of faculty ownership for the teaching and learning that takes place within the pre-planned course. Rather than seeing themselves as content experts who are facilitating learning, adjunct faculty can fall into patterns of course monitoring and assignment grading. It became clear that, despite having a standardized curriculum, there were no shared expectations of the faculty role in facilitating learning in the online environment.

Break-Out Session Explanation and Feedback

At the university's spring 2019 Faculty Development Day, a break-out session on strategies for grading student work was conducted. The session was planned to put instructors in similar situations as when they are teaching a course; however, they were placed in a small group to be able to have a discussion while grading. First, instructors were presented with a discussion post worth 20 points. The presenter explained that the instructors would be split up into three groups: one group would have nothing (which is often the case when it comes to grading), one group would have a general discussion post rubric, and one group would have a specific rubric made specifically for that discussion post.

Once the small groups were in place, they were presented with an anonymous student's initial post as well as the required peer responses. The group that was given nothing had to come up with a grade for this discussion. The group that was given the general rubric had to use it to determine a grade for the discussion. The group that was given the specific discussion rubric had to use it determine a grade for the discussion. Each group's grades were recorded on a whiteboard and the presenter shared the grade she actually gave this particular discussion. The grades given ranged from 10 to 16 points.

Each group was then asked to explain why they gave the discussion post the grade they did. The discussions that occurred among the groups brought up issues that instructors face when grading students' assignments. Some instructors said they just make up the amount of points they want to take off for various things, so having the rubric helped with that. One instructor said the rubric did not really distinguish enough between the levels of competencies, so it was hard to choose a level for scoring. Some instructors said they allow the students to redo assignments if they are going to be low scoring depending on the week of the course. This workshop the importance of consistency in grading if instructors expect to see consistency in the students' work from course to course.

In the evaluation of break-out session data showed the faculty members appreciated the discussion and information. One faculty member wrote, "The grading session was a great interaction opportunity; the suggestions provided were very helpful." Another faculty member wrote, "The grading session was very helpful on grading discussions." When asked w*hat did you learn today that you will implement in your teaching?,* one faculty member wrote, "ways to improve my grading and feedback." Another faculty member wrote, "grading techniques" and another faculty member wrote, "other strategies for grading discussions." The data collected reiterates the need for online instructors to have opportunities to collaborate on basic components of online instruction such as grading.

Feedback on Online Faculty Peer Observation Form

Recently, a full-time faculty member used the Online Faculty Peer Observation Form (see Table 1) to peer review two adjunct instructors in the Master Teacher Program.

Table 1. Online faculty expectation document sample

Component	Explanation
Course Preparation	Faculty are instructed to check all components (course policies, welcome announcement, and faculty information) are available to students no less than three weeks before course start date.
Effective Communication	Level of communication is appropriate and consistent with course-level. Instructor indicates clear expectations and responds to student questions within 24 hours of receipt.
Active Engagement	Instructor creates an environment that welcomes collaboration, supports learning, and provides for open communication.
Assignment Feedback	Instructor provides timely, holistic feedback that supports and explains the numerical score provided.

In this example, the faculty member who was conducting the review, decided to go with a coaching approach rather than an evaluative approach. The reviewer was very nervous about conducting this peer observation as both of the instructors have many more years of experience both in the realm of education as well as being an online adjunct instructor. However, this also made her feel like she could learn a lot about herself as an online instructor. Prior to the course start date, the Online Faculty Peer Observation Form was sent out to each instructor for preparation ahead of time about the components of the review and observation. Each course was seven weeks in length. About three weeks in, the instructors' online presence was reviewed, and feedback was provided on what the instructors were doing a great job with as well as a couple of areas they could improve or try differently. The reviewer was not quite sure how the instructors were going to take the feedback; the fact that the only responses they provided were "thank you" did not make the reviewer feel any better. During Week Six, the reviewer reached out to the instructors again, merely as a check in, to review the Online Faculty Peer Observation Form to see if there was anything that could be changed as they moved into the final week of the course.

Once the course was over, the reviewer reached out to the instructors again to schedule a meeting to discuss the findings. The instructors were asked to complete the Online Faculty Peer Observation Form on their own prior to their meeting and were told the author would be doing the same. As the reviewer was completing the form, she started to get nervous when she had to check *disagree* or *strongly disagree* for any of the items. She made sure to have evidence from the online course to support her decisions in case the instructors challenged her decision. One meeting took place via phone and the other took place face to face. During the meetings, the reviewer went through the items on the Online Faculty Peer Observation Form one by one. She and the instructor shared their scores and the supporting evidence from the course. Each time they did this, it led to a deeper conversation about the item, sometimes even as far as questioning the item and needing further clarification. This was a very different outcome than what was expected. This was the reviewer's favorite part of the coaching process as she learned so much from both of the instructors. Each instructor has a very different educational background than the author and she found herself learning just as much from them as she did trying to coach them to improve in their online instruction. It really helped the reviewer and the instructor develop a different type of relationship than they previously had with each other just as colleagues.

Notes were made on the Online Faculty Peer Observation Form and the reviewer followed up with the Dean for further clarification on some of the items. She then reached back out to the instructors to explain and clarify some of the items discussed. The reviewer completed a copy of the Online Faculty

Peer Observation Form, attached a narrative from the follow up discussion, and sent everything to the adjunct instructors to review and sign. The signed copies were placed into the instructors' files held within the university. When asked to share thoughts about the process with other adjunct instructors who have not had a peer review session yet, one of the reviewed adjunct instructors said:

I have to say it was awkward at first, but after hearing from the reviewer the first time and reading her ideas and suggestions, I started to change how I felt. I could tell she was not there as an evaluator, but rather a colleague I could learn from. We had a great conversation when we discussed the items on the sheet; we talked for two hours! I felt like it was a joint effort and even when we didn't agree on something, we still had a good discussion about it. I feel like we have a different relationship now and I would like to work with her more. I think we need more opportunities for all of us to have the type of discussion she and I had.

This quote summarizes the process of observation, the importance of feedback and communication, as well as the coaching approach to peer evaluation for faculty development.

FUTURE DIRECTIONS

Future Initiatives

Over the last four years, GPS has evolved from a single technology based Online Faculty Certification course to a Comprehensive Faculty Development Program which includes Faculty Development Days, an Online Faculty Expectations document, a Self-Assessment Tool, a Peer Observation Tool, Coaching and Mentoring meetings, an Adjunct Faculty Manual, FAC100 Faculty Orientation, and a GPS faculty portal page. However, this Program is far from complete. Next steps include the establishment of a Comprehensive Professional Development Plan, a formal Mentoring program, and the development of online mini modules and badges.

Table 2. Online faculty peer observation form

Instructor Last Name:		Instructor First Name:	
Department:		Campus Email:	
Course # and Course name being reviewed:			
Faculty Status:	Full Adjunct	Teaching Environments (Select all that apply):	Online On campus Combination
Number of Semesters Teaching Online:		1 - 2 3 - 4 5 or more	
Number of courses taught each fall and/or spring semester, online and on campus combined:		1 2	
Number of online courses taught each fall and/or spring semester:		1 2	

A Comprehensive Faculty Development Plan will provide a format for adjunct Practitioner Faculty to reflect upon their own development as faculty and establish a plan for how they will continue to inform their teaching. This plan will incorporate their own reflection from the Self-Assessment Tool, the feedback they receive from the Peer Observation Tool, and subsequent Coaching and Mentoring meetings to identify areas of development. The plan will strive to turn this reflection into action. With the support of their Program Director, faculty will develop a plan for addressing these developmental needs through university sponsored events such as Faculty Development Days, and external resources such as conferences, workshops, and further research of best practices.

A formal mentoring program could identify exceptional adjunct faculty to serve as mentors to new faculty, as well as to those faculty in need of additional developmental support. Mentors could be faculty who successfully implement best practices and demonstrate a strong understanding of University policy and online instructional pedagogy. The mentoring program is expected to include mutual observation of instruction, along with regular meetings to discuss challenges and strategies. Ideally, all new faculty will be assigned a mentor for their first year. Subsequently, faculty who either self-identify, or are identified through peer observation or coaching and mentoring meetings, as needing additional support in the mastery and implementation of best practices, will be assigned a Mentor for a specified period of time.

Finally, the formal development offered through the Faculty Development Days will be expanded. These days are extremely well received and well attended. However, they are limited by time and location constraints. Creating mini-modules and the opportunity to earn badges will provide access to distance faculty and also allow faculty to select modules related specifically to their own developmental needs identified in their Comprehensive Faculty Development Plan.

FUTURE RESEARCH

The authors would like to explore the opportunity to assess the implementation and the effectiveness of these strategies through both qualitative and quantitative methods. Research could be conducted about the engagement of faculty through the use of strategies and the faculty satisfaction and self-reflection related to participation in development programs or training initiatives. In addition, focus groups or interviews could provide valuable data about faculty's perceptions and experiences related to teaching and learning.

CONCLUSION

Using Baran and Correia's (2014) three-tiered model as a framework, the authors of this chapter assert that the comprehensive faculty development plan includes understanding organization, building community, and applying outstanding pedagogy and teaching practices. It has taken significant time and energy to develop the foundations of the Comprehensive Faculty Development Program, and much work remains to be done. The investment of time and resources has resulted in a more engaged faculty who feel highly connected to the university and valued for their contributions. Faculty have responded positively to all aspects of the plan, demonstrating that even extremely busy adjunct Practitioner Faculty with demanding careers outside of the university are eager to inform and improve the practice of their teaching. They simply need the support to do so.

In conclusion, this chapter addressed the importance in faculty development in creating supportive, transformative online experiences for students. Well-trained, engaged faculty impact student success by developing courses with learning in mind. Understanding the importance of faculty development, institutions must develop a strategic approach to this process, training, and learning. As the current research shows, the approach must be multi-faceted and comprehensive (Baran & Correia, 2014; Schmidt et al., 2016). In addition, the most effective approaches include formal and informal organizational, community, and teaching components (Scarpena et al., 2018). This chapter offers administrators and faculty leaders with insight to develop a comprehensive faculty development plan at their institution using evidence-based strategies and examples of practical application.

REFERENCES

Alexiou-Ray, J., & Bentley, C. C. (2016). Faculty professional development for quality online teaching. *Journal of Distance Learning Administration*, *18*(4), 1–6.

Baran, E., & Correia, A. (2014). A professional development framework for online teaching. *TechTrends*, *58*(5), 96–102. doi:10.100711528-014-0791-0

Baran, E., Correia, A., & Thompson, A. D. (2013). Tracing successful online teaching in higher education: Voices of exemplary online teachers. *Teachers College Record*, *115*(3), 1–41.

Chen, K., Lowenthal, P. R., Bauer, C., Heaps, A., & Nielsen, C. (2017). Moving beyond smile sheets: A case study on the evaluation and iterative improvement of an online faculty development program. *Online Learning*, *21*(1), 85–111. doi:10.24059/olj.v21i1.810

Elliott, M., Rhoades, N., Jackson, C. M., & Mandernach, B. J. (2015). Professional development: Designing initiatives to meet the needs of online faculty. *Journal of Educators Online*, *12*(1), 160–188. doi:10.9743/JEO.2015.1.2

Gregory, J., & Salmon, G. (2013). Professional development for online university teaching. *Distance Education*, *34*(3), 256–270. doi:10.1080/01587919.2013.835771

Herman, J. H. (2012). Faculty development programs: The frequency and variety of professional development programs available to online instructors. *Journal of Asynchronous Learning Networks*, *16*(5), 87–106.

Meyer, K. A. (2014). An analysis of the research on faculty development for online teaching and identification of new directions. *Journal of Asynchronous Learning Networks*, *17*(4), 93–112.

Meyer, K. A., & Murrell, V. S. (2014). A national study of training content and activities for faculty development for online learning. *Journal of Asynchronous Learning Networks*, *18*(1), 3–18.

Mezirow, J. (1997). Transformative Learning: Theory to Practice. In P. Cranton (Ed.), *New Directions for Adult and Continuing Education 74*. San Francisco, CA: Jossey-Bass. doi:10.1002/ace.7401

Mohr, S., & Shelton, K. (2017). Best practices framework for online faculty professional development: A Delphi study. *Online Learning*, *21*(4), 123–143.

O'Hara, S., & Pritchard, R. (2012). "I'm teaching what?!": Preparing university faculty for online instruction. *Journal of Educational Research and Practice*, *2*(1), 42–53.

Ragan, L. C., Bigatel, P. M., Kennan, S. S., & Dillon, J. M. (2012). From research to practice: Towards the development of an integrated and comprehensive faculty development program. *Journal of Asynchronous Learning Networks*, *16*(5), 71–86.

Scarpena, K., Riley, M., & Keathley, M. (2018). Creating successful professional development activities for online faculty: A reorganized framework. *Journal of Distance Learning Administration*, *2*(1), 1–8.

Schmidt, S. W., Tschida, C. M., & Hodge, E. M. (2016). How faculty learn to teach online: What administrators need to know. *Online Journal of Distance Learning Administration*, *19*(1), 1–8.

Vaill, A. L., & Testori, P. A. (2012). Orientation, mentoring and ongoing support: A three-tiered approach to online faculty development. *Journal of Asynchronous Learning Networks*, *16*(2), 111–119.

ADDITIONAL READING

Darby, F., & Lang, J. (2019). *Small teaching online: Applying learning science in online classes*. San Franscisco, CA: Jossey-Bass Publishers.

Gillespie, K., & Robertson, D. (2010). *A guide to faculty development*. San Franscisco, CA: Wiley & Sons.

Stachowiak, B. (2019). *Teaching in Higher Ed*. [Blog]. Retrieved from https://teachinginhighered.com/blog/

KEY TERMS AND DEFINITIONS

Evidence-Based Strategies: Strategies proven through research and application to be effective.
Faculty Development: Training and support of faculty to improve teaching in an effort to improve student success and student learning.
Online Engagement: Interaction and connection of faculty and students within the online learning community.

Chapter 4
Faculty Professional Development in Creating Significant Teaching and Learning Experiences Online

Yasemin Gülbahar
Ankara University, Turkey

Müge Adnan
https://orcid.org/0000-0003-3256-7418
Mugla Sitki Kocman University, Turkey

ABSTRACT

With faculty members and instructors struggling with the massive transformational challenges stemming from technological innovation, the establishment of a digital teaching-learning culture to ensure that university graduates are ready to join the 21st-century workforce is of the utmost importance. At this juncture, the key players are those who lead the learning experience, namely faculty members and instructors. Being an experienced faculty member and possessing advanced skills of using technology does not necessarily lead to an instructor becoming an effective e-instructor. This chapter, therefore, discusses the changing nature of digital teaching and learning from the perspective of faculty members, within the framework of certain required competencies and skills that every faculty member should possess. The chapter also includes a brief overview of the literature regarding the professional development of faculty members, synchronized with reflections and experiences from an online e-Tutor course.

DOI: 10.4018/978-1-7998-0115-3.ch004

INTRODUCTION

Living in today's digital age, we are immersed in technology that is exponentially growing and transforming our lives to an extent never previously imaginable. The technological and knowledge revolution along with the dynamic social and economic structure of this age has also altered the skills and qualifications required from individuals to survive in this "agile and volatile" landscape, as Bates (2015) referred to it. We need to encompass communications and social media skills in addition to traditional communication skills such as reading or speaking; thinking skills including critical thinking, problem-solving, originality and creativity; teamwork including collaborative working and knowledge sharing at a distance; the ability to learn independently; working ethically and responsibly; digital skills assisting individuals' healthy inclusion in digital society; and knowledge management including how to find, evaluate, analyze, apply and disseminate information. It has also changed the profile of students, particularly within higher education. Higher education institutions now serve not only to full-time students that recently graduated from high school, but also to part-time mature learners often with their own family, job responsibilities and commitments.

This shift in the skills and qualifications of the digital age, as well as the changing profile of learners, requires significant repositioning of the teaching-learning processes and environments. Hence, as stated by Garrison and Anderson (2003), "expectations are changing, and there is little question that institutions of higher education are being transformed as a result of e-learning innovations" (p. 105). Today, such institutions are faced with rethinking their roles and responsibilities in order to respond to the premises of the digital era within a well-established digital teaching and learning culture. Building up a digital teaching-learning culture should encompass all aspects so as to train the kind of graduate workforce called for in today's digital era. Being at the core of any teaching-learning process, faculty members and instructors are challenged with overcoming this difficult task. Changing faculty roles during this shift have been contemplated by various researchers (e.g., Anderson, Rourke, Garrison, & Archer, 2001; Berge, 2001; Garrison & Anderson, 2003; Goodyear, Salmon, Spector, Steeples, & Tickner, 2001; Laurillard, 2002), where the online roles of instructors are typically categorized as pedagogical, managerial, social, technical and instructional, and include several aspects such as course management, instruction, instructional design, research, collaboration, coordination, guidance and interaction (Adnan, 2018). Ergo, a faculty member of the digital era is expected to have competencies that include:

- designing instruction for online and blended courses as well as face-to-face;
- delivering instruction effectively for online, blended and face-to-face courses;
- implementing innovative instructional methods and techniques based on emerging learning theories;
- orchestrating online systems and tools duly according to key characteristics; and,
- evaluating system components along with learners' progress.

Only through competent instructors can educational institutions fully utilize the potential of information and communication technologies within a responsible and accurate approach to teaching in a digital context. Today, many universities provide support and training to faculty members in various formats including informal learning environments, mentoring, in-service training or structured certificate programs (Adnan, Kalelioğlu, & Gülbahar, 2017; Rapp, Gülbahar, & Adnan, 2016) through different organizational structures such as centers for teaching and learning, distance learning centers, instructional technology support units or centers for excellence. Yet still, there are faculty members untended in this process who are either trying to fulfil this need through self-learning or attempting to learn from their peers in the absence of any organizational guidance or support.

This chapter discusses the changing nature of digital teaching and learning, putting faculty members at the core within a framework of the required knowledge, competencies and skills, and the significance of professional development in order to involve them fully in this transformational process. It also aims to highlight a structured online faculty development program for teaching online (*e-Tutor*) by means of educator students' reflections and experiences. The chapter commences with a look at the International Society for Technology in Education (ISTE) Standards for Educators that provides a roadmap for educators in assisting their students to be empowered learners in the digital age. Following a general outlook at the skills, qualifications and competencies of online instructors, the chapter continues with a brief explanation of professional development models, and reviews professional development's role in encouraging and equipping teachers, instructors and faculty members with knowledge and skills required for digital teaching and learning culture.

Attributes of an Educator in the Digital Age

Aiming to help educators and education leaders in reforming schools and classrooms for digital-age learning, the ISTE recently updated its Standards for Educators, listing seven attributes of an educator in the digital age (see Figure 1) seen as being required in order to embrace, adopt and integrate the ever-changing innovations of today into learning-teaching processes.

The first standard is that of being a ***learner***, where educators are supposed to be a learner themselves and thereby improve their teaching practice through perpetual learning, either by way of self-study or along with their students and peers, or within online or face-to-face professional communities so as to realize their overall goal: the improvement of student learning. Recent developments in digital learning have made vast amounts of information freely accessible through the Internet. Online video platforms have become a particularly popular media of choice and a primary source of information for individual learning by means of video sharing websites and applications and video streaming channels. Video-based courses in Massive Open Online Courses (MOOCs), open educational resources (OERs) and open courseware, self-recorded lecture captures and informative videos, along with live feeds and recordings from academic meetings and seminars, are available to individuals seeking information and skills for their own personal and career development. Thanks to artificial and semantic functions of the computer sciences, it is now even easier to locate the true source of knowledge and instruction of preference within a few seconds.

As ***leaders***, educators should pursue leadership opportunities for the empowerment of their students and to improve teaching and learning. This attribute envisions educators as influential professionals vigorously taking part in the creation and sharing of a common vision for teaching and learning with technology, advocating equal access to digital technologies in awareness of the digital divide, and acting as role models to their peers in the adoption and integration of digital resources into learning environments.

As ***citizens*** of a digital society, educators should serve as model digital citizens and inspire their students to participate in the digital world as responsible citizens through the establishment of a digital learning culture, mentoring and coaching students regarding legal and ethical considerations, digital privacy and digital identity, fostering digital literacy, and creating experiences for them to actively engage in digital communities. This attribute is particularly important in light of recent increases in social media

Figure 1. ISTE standards for educators (International Society for Technology in Education, 2018)

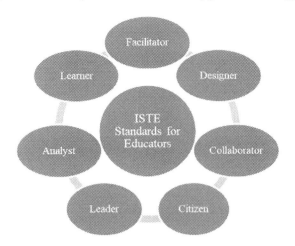

tools, applications, and networks where ethical concerns, data protection and data privacy have come to the fore. It is crucial for educators to fulfil this role and to provide guidance to students owing to the functionality of such environments, not only for learners' social presence but also for the instructional and collaborative opportunities they afford.

As *collaborators*, educators are expected to encourage and practice collaboration with their colleagues and students for better teaching and learning experiences that leverage technology. Using collaborative tools to expand students' learning experiences, engaging with experts and collaborating with parents and other stakeholders to enhance student learning. Today's networked lifestyle forces us to communicate, collaborate, and to work together more each day. This is particularly true for the digital learning environment that surrounds us, and furthermore provides various flexible channels for communication and collaboration through emerging and innovative technologies.

Educators are also *designers*, who create authentic learning environments enriched with learner-centered activities to address diverse learner needs for personalized learning experiences. Mobile applications have become popular, facilitating ubiquitous learning by making instructional content more accessible to a larger and more diverse student population. However, this brings about a challenge for educators regarding the design and delivery of course content, as well as concerns of a pedagogical and assessment-based nature. Although instructional design could by no means be considered a new topic, designing instruction for different media based on more diverse needs and in an adaptive or personalized way requires considerable new insight to the field.

As *facilitators*, educators are expected to be able to promote learning with technology so as to support student performance. This initiative includes fostering a learning culture and creating challenging learning opportunities for students. Over the past several years, the number of research studies conducted on the human brain and cognition have dramatically increased as researchers explore not only how the digital environment is impacting our brains, but also in exploring the relationship between technology, culture and cognitive processes. Wolf's (2018) "Reader, Come Home" and Carr's (2011) "The Shallows" are well worth a read in order to grasp the phenomenon from different perspectives. Once we see the bigger picture for this digital transformation of education, it becomes easier to foster a culture for individual and collective learning opportunities.

Educators are also ***analysts***, attempting to understand and use data in order to guide their teaching processes and to support students to achieve their learning goals. Recent evolution of various digital teaching and learning tools, pedagogical practices, adaptive and personalized learning approaches, as well as big data and learning analytics has become of significant importance; and perhaps is now more important than the learning environment itself. The vast amount of data now available about students, their engagement, courses and programs, and teaching and learning processes has enthralled us with the opportunity of being able to grasp useful insight and thereby provide more meaningful feedback than was previously feasible. By taking on the role of an analyst, educators are more likely to become capable of interpreting learning analytics to a level necessary for the instigation of improvements to their own teaching in the near future.

Changing Roles of Instructors in Online Learning Environments

Instructors have a presence to uphold in the classroom. Their appearance, how they communicate with their students, what classroom management practices they employ, and their use of pedagogical approaches for teaching are of significant importance. In the online environment, instructors also become a role model, not merely for their content delivery, but also in terms of creating an effective communication that carefully orchestrates online tools and processes for the purposes of student learning. In online learning environments, content, activities and assessment tools may have been designed and provided by professional teams external to the institution; but it is the responsibility of the instructor to arrange and integrate these components so as to create meaningful learning experiences for the students in their charge. Alternatively, in largely asynchronous programs, there may be situations where the instructor and students never even physically meet or see each other, especially if monthly meetings or video conferencing methods are not put into action. Hence, compared with face-to-face teaching, instructors' roles can vary according to different pedagogical approaches and learning tools before, during and after the delivery of a course or program.

Before the Course

In e-learning, it is crucial to undertake careful planning prior to the commencement of the process. A detailed syllabus is an important means to respond to the possible questions that may arise from students such as which subjects will be covered, what kind of activities and collaborative studies will be carried out, what kind of tasks and projects will be evaluated, what criteria will be used for evaluation, the rules to be followed throughout the process, how the content will be presented, and how the students should work. The syllabus and other means to provide detailed information about the course should be shared prior to the course commencing in order that students may arrange their own time and study plans (catering for work and family commitments etc.) and successfully complete the course within the allotted time. This type of information includes the timing of exams and quizzes, deadlines for projects, tasks, and assignments, available chat hours, as well as discussions, and face-to-face meetings.

The online instructor should clearly state how the content will be delivered and how it can be accessed. All teaching materials including readings, research assignments, presentations, interactive exercises, practice questions, projects, animations, videos and audio recordings should be made available to all students at the beginning of the semester. The materials presented should be as rich and diverse as possible, taking into account students' different learning preferences. It is important, wherever possible, to take student expectations into consideration beforehand, and as different teaching methods and techniques are decided jointly upon and materials made accessible through the system. Therefore, the course should be pre-structured and ready for implementation at short notice. Moreover, a proactive approach should be taken towards the occurrence of potential problems, and an alternative emergency management plan should be in place ready to address all such eventualities.

During the Course

An online instructor must be active near enough 24x7 throughout the course; constantly monitoring the process, addressing possible problems, reviewing students' progress, and providing feedback as and when necessary. It is important that instructors respond quickly to potential issues or misunderstandings in communication as they arise. Using instructional materials as support for transferring content within the virtual classroom environment and enriching these practices with other components such as chats and whiteboard activities will have the effect of increasing the teaching impact.

Managing real-time discussion environments such as chat sessions, voice or video conferencing is a matter of experience. During this process, it is important for instructors to act as moderator to ensure efficient discussions are held and that everyone's time is used effectively. Another important aspect is to incorporate different activities for individual projects and group work. Online instructors should monitor the process regularly and closely, and provide timely feedback in order to engage their students.

Online instructors must develop different pedagogical approaches whenever necessary in order to follow the interests of the students during the course, and thereby to motivate them. In addition, students should be provided with adequate technical, theoretical and practical support when needed by the instructor.

Interaction is crucial in an online course. There are basically six types of interaction among three main pillars of the learning process: student-content; student-student; student-instructor; content-content; instructor-content; and, instructor-instructor (Garrison & Anderson, 2003). It is expected that students will learn by interacting with the content as planned. This process might be guided by the instructor; yet, students may also create their own meaningful knowledge and perspective by adding new information to their existing knowledge as a result of the interaction process. The role of the instructor is therefore to monitor these individual processes, and to provide guidance and support when and where necessary. Within this process, it is very important for students to be able to access the desired information quickly and efficiently. It is of equal importance that instructors use visual teaching materials effectively, and to ensure student engagement and active participation.

Teacher-student interaction is mainly provided by means of technological tools. This type of interaction may be simultaneous or not, depending on the use of different tools which may range from e-mails to virtual classes, chats, forums, and voice or video conferencing. This may start with suggestions from the instructor, and continue with constant guidance, support, and encouragement. It is imperative that instructors maintain a positive attitude, and exhibit appropriate behaviors, as well as provide timely feedback and encouragement throughout the course. Communication and interaction among students may also be assured through different means such as in a forum discussion with participation by all students, or in a chat environment between a number of students within a group. Interpersonal interaction may be more motivating and engaging for the students. Students are said to express themselves more easily and freely when there is no instructor in the environment; yet, they will more likely maintain a certain level of communication if they know that the instructor can reach and see records of their interaction. It is known that collaborative activities can significantly contribute to the e-learning process; therefore, online instructors should provide sufficient time and space to accommodate such activities.

Content-content interaction is original, where various implications and suggestions are made on the basis of student records and data. Such software are known as educational agents, and they collect data based on students' preferences and demographic information. These are self-learning and developing programs making generalizations over a period of time. For instance, individual student's learning preferences may be determined by such systems at the onset of a course, and the content may then be presented in an adaptive way through instructional materials that are selected and presented appropriately according to students' preferences.

Instructor-content interaction is when an instructor uses the content to prepare, update, or utilize the course transfer process even if it is ready. This type of interaction also includes an important role for the online instructor: to provide written feedback for students' assignments and, where necessary, to suggest different resources that could be used. Interaction between instructors is the process whereby instructors share information and experience among themselves. This type of interaction will likely strengthen and increase the success of any e-learning venture as it is deemed essential to always consider and try out different perspectives for instructional delivery and teaching.

After the Course

E-learning process is a 24x7 process with no set "working hours." Students may therefore ask questions or submit assignments at any time of the night or day, which should be received and assessed by the instructor based on predetermined times. The instructor is then responsible for making formative and summative assessments whereby the whole process is evaluated, and the academic achievement level of students determined at the end of the course. This evaluation may be done manually by the instructor based on reports, or realized automatically by way of utilizing functionality within the system. Nevertheless, online instructors should also evaluate the different dimensions of the process in addition to just the measurable student performance such as the effectiveness of the course, the teaching materials used, the teaching methods and techniques employed, and the assessment tools that they used. Such assessments will help instructors to critically review the course, and to use the findings in order to apply any changes necessary or to update the course so as to make it run more efficiently.

Learning management systems (LMSs) are the most common method of facilitating these various roles, as well as for organizing all the different aspects of the teaching-learning process within online or blended learning environments. Most LMS configurations offer numerous opportunities. However, many of these are not utilized to their fullest extent due to lack of knowledge, skills or experience on behalf of the instructors and/or their students. Configured at a program and course level, the LMS can assist instructors and instructional designers in organizing a course on a time (e.g., weekly) or topic basis, and then to share all course materials including syllabi, documents, videos, podcasts, and weblinks to other relevant resources.

In parallel with today's technological developments, several learning management systems also provide instructors with the tools to create interactive activities as well as various forms of alternative assessment. It now takes but a few clicks to prepare a drag-and-drop activity, or a matching exercise or quiz which provides immediate and informative feedback to the course participants. Thanks to learning analytics, students can now learn about their progress from individualized reports and manage their learning accordingly, while instructors have access to different types of customized management reports that they can analyses and then make the necessary revisions to the course or course materials in order to provide an enhanced learning experience. Besides, communication tools in LMS and other online systems allow students and instructors to communicate, interact and support the teaching-learning process through discussion forums, blogs and wikis. Such developments have contributed to enhance learning environments, not only by providing enriched learning opportunities, but also by making predictions about student performance, providing reminders and warnings when necessary, and creating a more personalized learning experience.

Although they have been criticized from time to time regarding their limitations, LMSs provide notable opportunities for all stakeholders in the online and blended learning environment. Since it is difficult, if not impossible, to accomplish many of these facilities within traditional learning environments, such systems are heavily used for campus-based courses in several higher education institutions.

Acknowledging and making adjustments according to learners' needs, providing learners with personalized content, and automated feedback for assessments combined with meaningful and relevant learning activities for motivation can contribute to improved student performance and achievement in online and blended learning. Nonetheless, as with all novel approaches, using such a rich and promising environment effectively for addressing learners' needs requires instructors to possess specific competencies and skills.

Competencies and Skills of Online Instructors

Teaching online requires instructors to possess individual assets of moderation and communications skills suited to the online environment, in addition to being a content expert, having adequate prior teaching experience, and being competent with the required technologies. Furthermore, an online instructor needs to have reflection and adaptation skills balanced to changing learner profiles, the different needs of the various stakeholders, and the organizational goals and vision of the institution, notwithstanding the ever-present technological advances that face today's instructors (see Figure 2).

The epistemological stance and knowledge of theoretical approaches to learning have direct practical results on how teachers teach. Instructors will be better able to address the needs of their students through applying various approaches that are based on sound learning principles and informed selection, as well as the use of appropriate technologies to support the teaching-learning environment. Whether face-to-face, blended, or online, all learning environments require the application of learning theories that are combined with effective instructional strategies, techniques and methods. This magical combination of epistemology, theory, strategy, technique, method and technology or media will more likely lead to the expected level of learner motivation and achievement. This combination requires training, practice and experience gained over time. Bates (2015) spoke of theory and research as the "science of teaching,"

Figure 2. What makes an effective online instructor?

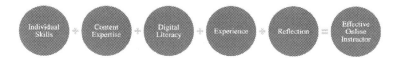

whereas instructors dealing with numerous changing variables in a learning environment with passion as the "art of teaching."

The ability to create this combination, to deliver content, to assess performance, to manage technology, and to communicate efficiently is of particular importance in the online learning environment, where instructors are challenged by time-related constraints as well as significant challenges in acclimation to new tools and operating environments (Roddy et al., 2017). Besides, instructors are under continual threat by the potential for student drop-out, with a higher likelihood seen in the online environment compared to the traditional classroom. Instructors are required to conduct task follow-ups in order to improve performance and overcome barriers that may impede student engagement. Hence, there has been a notable shift in online teaching from the mere management of content to the whole learning process.

Although taxonomies for learning such as Bloom's Revised Taxonomy (Krathwohl, 2002) provide teachers with a framework for learning design that promotes different types and levels of knowledge and cognitive processing, digital learning is an altogether different phenomenon, and designing instruction for the online learning environment is considerably challenging due to the complexity of structure and dimensions of learning in the digital environment. Thus, rather than considering merely cognitive levels and behaviors, the focus is aimed at the whole learning process of the individual, including their active engagement as well as the social aspects of learning.

In 2007, the International Board of Standards for Training, Performance and Instruction initiated a research project to survey learners enrolled in diverse education and training being delivered in an online format (Beaudoin, 2010). A total of 375 respondents from four different countries participated in the study. Analysis of the findings revealed that the strongest determinant for success in online learning was self-motivation of the learner, followed by time management, and their capacity to learn with limited support, which implies that dealing with the prevention of students dropping-out from a course is considerably more important than the content itself.

In 2011, Starkey designed a digital learning matrix which shifted the focus of learning from knowledge to that of critical thinking, knowledge creation, collaborative practices, and learning through connections. The researcher classified digital technology usage in terms of accessing, presenting and processing information, as well as the use of gaming and interactive programs, and criticized each class of use from the perspective of learning level as; doing, thinking about connections and concepts, critiquing and evaluating, and creating and sharing knowledge.

There have been numerous studies conducted in the past decade that have focused on the competencies and skills of online instructors (e.g., Dennis, Watland, Pirotte, & Verday, 2004; Goodyear et al., 2001; UNESCO, 2011). Roddy et al. (2017) examined some of these studies, and listed the following as the most important online teacher competencies:

- communication skills;
- technological competence;
- provision of informative feedback;
- administrative skills;
- responsiveness;
- monitoring learning;
- providing student support.

Quality Matters (2016) presented The Online Instructor Skills Set (OISS) as a validated set of instructor skills. Composed of six competency areas for online instruction, the list can also be used as a framework for assessing the presence of certain competencies necessary for effective online instruction:

1. Institutional Context;
2. Technologies;
3. Instructional Design;
4. Pedagogy;
5. Assessment;
6. Social Presence.

Although defined through different concepts and terminology, what is meant by "online instructor" is evident. An online instructor is expected to incorporate theory to design online instruction in an appropriate manner; to use technology effectively as a role model for teaching and for management; to create effective communication channels inspiring and motivating engagement through social means; to use pedagogical theories in support of learning processes; to provide immediate and relevant feedback and support in a responsive way; to monitor student learning and conduct reliable student assessment and evaluation by employing various methods to measure student performance; and finally to realize all these responsibilities from a leadership point of view within the institutional context.

What is expected from online instructors is not always innate. They need to learn how to deal with this challenge in a novel and unusual digital landscape. Several studies have indicated the need for professional development and continuous support for online instructors. Kebritchi, Lipschuetz, and Santiague (2017) conducted a literature review of such studies regarding major issues and strategies that may affect the quality of teaching online within higher education. The researchers concluded that

…higher education institutions need to provide professional development for instructors, trainings for learners, and technical support for the content development and delivery of online courses to address the challenges in online education and enhance the effectiveness of online teaching and learning. (p. 21)

No matter how experienced as an instructor or faculty member, the online instructor needs to accommodate certain knowledge and skills in the digital teaching and learning environment employing relevant and appropriate usage of media and technology. This needs an informed decision-making process on the basis of epistemological perspective, students' expected learning outcomes, teaching methods to achieve these outcomes, pedagogical affordances of the preferred media and technology, and the applicable institutional aspects (Bates, 2015). This may present considerable challenges for many instructors, since it is not easy to cope with the constant technological changes, innovations and implementations of today's educational world.

Pedagogical Approaches and Scope for Effective Professional Development

The principle questions that dominate are how educators can learn the appropriate online teaching skills, and what role professional development plays in improving instructors' delivery in the virtual classroom. Prior to exploring the pedagogical approaches and scope for professional development, it is important at this juncture to understand how traditional focus has changed for professional development in the 21st

Faculty Professional Development in Creating Significant Teaching and Learning Experiences Online

century. Boudreaux (2018) referred to Sornicelli, Austin, Eddy, and Beach (2006) for an era map for faculty development in order to illustrate its move towards a holistic and systemic view of professional development:

1. The Age of the Scholar (1950s-1960s), where the focus was on improving scholarly proficiency;
2. The Age of the Teacher (1960s-1970s), where the focus was on improving faculty teaching;
3. The Age of the Developer (1980s), where the focus was on the measurement of outcomes;
4. The Age of the Learner (1990s), where the focus was organizational structuring; and,
5. The Age of the Network (2000s), with increased clarity towards faculty development and networking between faculty members and management.

It is crystal clear that instructors need to adapt themselves and update their knowledge in line with emerging tools and technologies for teaching and learning; however, today it is more than about simply what an instructor needs. Consideration also needs to be paid to the needs of students, and how instructors manage those needs so as to help students to learn better and deeper. Hence, it is not just about instructors knowledge, but also about their skills and competencies. In other words, professional development is not only aimed at improving instructors, but also at enhancing student learning and improving student achievement. For this reason, a wider group of beneficiaries should be considered in the design, development and implementation of professional development programs, instead of just focusing on the individual (instructor) level. It should not be considered as the mere transfer of knowledge, but should also promote inquiry. It should be standalone, but at the same time embedded as an on-the-job training exercise. It should be designed as part of a continuous learning program that includes practice and follow-up, and not as a one-shot event. It should be perceived as professional "learning" rather than professional "development," which requires a change in the role of individuals who are responsible for professional development such as mentors as well as instructors.

This concept was significantly well-elaborated within a report by Learning Forward (2011), in which it defined professional development as "professional learning that increases educator effectiveness and results for all students." The report visualizes this conceptual relationship between professional learning and students as a cycle of four stages: (1) standards-based professional learning; (2) changes in educator knowledge, skills and dispositions; (3) changes in educator practices; and, (4) changes in students' results. The report also sets standards for professional learning to increase educator effectiveness and results for all students (see Table 1):

A comparative review by the Organization for Economic Co-operation and Development (OECD) on teachers defined effective professional development as,

...on-going, includes training, practice and feedback, and provides adequate time and follow-up support. Successful programmes involve teachers in learning activities that are similar to ones they will use with their students, and encourage the development of teachers' learning communities. There is growing interest in developing schools as learning organizations, and in ways for teachers to share their expertise and experience more systematically. (OECD, 2005, p. 49)

A recent review of the literature by Darling-Hammond, Hyler, and Gardner (2017) examined 35 studies regarding professional development, and reported that professional development was defined in 31 of the studies as a process "sustained over time through recurring workshops, coaching sessions, or

Table 1. Standards for professional learning (Learning Forward, 2011, p. 42)

LEARNING COMMUNITIES	LEADERSHIP	RESOURCES	DATA	LEARNING DESIGNS	IMPLEMENTATION	OUTCOMES
… since professional learning increases educator effectiveness and results for all students …							
occurs within learning communities committed to continuous improvement, collective responsibility, and goal alignment	requires skillful leaders who develop capacity, advocate, and create support systems for professional learning	requires prioritizing, monitoring, and coordinating resources for educator learning	uses a variety of sources and types of student, educator, and system data to plan, assess, and evaluate professional learning	integrates theories, research, and models of human learning to achieve its intended outcomes	applies research on change and sustains support for implementation of professional learning for long-term change	aligns its outcomes with educator performance and student curriculum standards

engagement with online platforms" (p. 15). The researchers stated seven common design elements for effective professional development approaches as:

1. They are content focused;
2. They incorporate active learning strategies;
3. They engage teachers in collaboration;
4. They use models and/or modeling;
5. They provide coaching and expert support;
6. They include time for feedback and reflection;
7. They are of sustained duration.

On the other hand, Nelson, Spence-Thomas, and Taylor (2015) listed nine important points for good and sound professional development consistently leading to significantly appropriate and successful pedagogy. The researchers stated that an effective professional development:

1. starts with the end in mind;
2. challenges thinking as part of changing practice;
3. is based on assessment of individual and school needs;
4. involves connecting work-based learning and external expertise;
5. opportunities are varied, rich and sustainable;
6. uses research and enquiry as essential tools;
7. is strongly enhanced through collaborative learning and joint practice development;
8. is enhanced by creating professional learning communities within and between schools; and,
9. requires leadership to create the necessary conditions.

From an online teaching perspective at the higher education level, a recent study by Mohr and Shelton (2017) focused on continuing growth in online enrolment, and indicated that higher educational institutions should prepare "faculty throughout their teaching career for learning theory, technical expertise, and pedagogical shifts for teaching in the online environment" (p. 123). Mohr and Shelton's (2017) study, using the Delphi method and reaching a consensus after four survey rounds, identified best practices of essential professional development strategies for supporting faculty teaching online, and listed 59 options as professional development opportunities under five headings: (1) pedagogy; (2) instructional design and materials; (3) technology integration; (4) facilitation and management; and, (5) assessment (see Table 2). Finally, the researchers suggested topics for online faculty professional development programs as faculty roles, classroom design, learning processes, and understanding legal issues in the online classroom.

Gregory and Salmon (2013) underlined that professional development for online teaching should be rapid and cost-effective, leading directly to practical outcomes. Accordingly, they suggested four guiding principles for efficient and sustainable professional development activities. The first principle marks the value of adoption of existing instructional course materials and processes, followed by a second principle about contextualization ensuring authentic learning. Recognizing the value of apprenticeship and mentoring in their third principle, the researchers suggested rapid scaling of the professional development activities. The last principle related to the encouragement of additional staff to take part in e-moderating courses.

Macdonald and Poniatowska (2011) presented a case study regarding the development of an online module at the Open University in the UK for helping faculty members understand how to use online tools in the support of their students. The initiative aimed at introducing innovations in learning and teaching practice by using social learning techniques and exploring business context reasons for undertaking professional development, their environment, and the need for contact with their colleagues. The study indicated that such context-aware approaches are favored by faculty members due to its effort to meet the diverse needs of the student and faculty population. Faculty members value the opportunity to experiment with digital tools in the context of their working environment, and appreciate the experience to learn from their peers.

Recent research by Brinkley-Etzkorn (2018) developed a model for training new online instructors, and measured its impact on the effectiveness of teaching and knowledge integration on the basis of the Technological Pedagogical Content Knowledge (TPACK) model as its conceptual framework. The study's findings showed no significant impact of the training on the effectiveness of teaching, which was interpreted and discussed by the researcher using multiple data sources for a deeper understanding of the phenomenon, participants' prior knowledge and skills, or a difficulty in fully integrating the pedagogy and technology as intended.

Table 2. Professional development opportunities for faculty members (Mohr & Shelton, 2017)

Pedagogy	Adaptation of teaching pedagogy for online, using active learning strategies, creating student-centered learning environments, incorporating learning theories, creating and maintaining teaching presence in online classroom.
Instructional design & materials	Planning, designing, structuring and organizing an online classroom by developing coherence between learning outcomes, course materials, assessment in an ethical way.
Technology integration	Using technology tools to enhance students learning, being flexible and adapting within an online classroom, creating innovative learning opportunities, integrating a rich variety of information and communication tools and resources, creating classroom policies.
Facilitation & management	Implementing strategies that enhance online communication and discussion in a friendly atmosphere, providing guidance to students throughout their learning journey, assisting students with special needs, facilitating individual and group work effectively.
Assessment	Adopting online assessment strategies, developing rubrics, grading online.

Similarly, Elliott, Rhoades, Jackson, and Mandernach's (2015) study examined online faculty preferences for participating in optional faculty development institutional initiatives, and indicated no significant interactions or major effects regarding the focus and format of the faculty development programs offered to online faculty members. Based on the findings, flexibility and diversity were suggested in faculty development initiatives in order to accommodate diverse needs for a heterogeneous faculty population based on a needs analysis. Yet, it should be acknowledged that measuring the educational effectiveness of a professional development program is not an easy task, and was defined as a major challenge by Dede (2004), due to the various components and dimensions of the whole process.

In a hands-on guide to teacher-centered professional development, Díaz-Maggioli (2004) questioned the constraints against professional development practices, and indicated that traditional professional development should be transformed into a visionary practice emphasizing collaborative decision-making with the collaborative construction of programs, rather than relying on a top-down decision-making process whereby instructors do not embrace the program, inquiry-based ideas or tailor-made techniques with adequate support systems, and context-specific programs delivered through adult-centered andragogical rather than pedagogical instruction.

Based on different insights and outcomes from studies conducted on professional development across various levels, it is safe to say that professional development initiatives should be tailored to address diversity in learners' needs, as well as their level of knowledge and experience framed through more than one pedagogical approach incorporated in a flexible manner.

Mainstream Models for Professional Development

Professional development programs are very diverse in their models. As an outcome of a collaboration between more than 45 participating countries, the Teaching and Learning International Survey (TALIS) of the OECD is a periodic international survey. Reporting its findings from its first cycle in 2008 in "Creating Effective Teaching and Learning Environments: First Results from TALIS," it was stated that TALIS broadly defines professional development as "activities that develop an individual's skills, knowledge, expertise and other characteristics as a teacher" (OECD, 2005, p. 49). This definition is said to acknowledge that professional development can be delivered in many ways such as courses, workshops or formal qualification programs, through collaboration between schools or teachers across or within schools through coaching, mentoring, collaborative teaching, and sharing good practices. In the survey, TALIS classified professional development activities under seven headings: (1) courses/workshops; (2) education conferences or seminars; (3) qualification programs; (4) observation visits to other schools; (5) participation in a network of instructors for the purposes of professional development; (6) individual or collaborative research; and, (7) mentoring, peer observation and coaching.

Díaz-Maggioli's book (2004), published by the Association for Supervision and Curriculum Development (ASCD) on teacher-centered professional development, explained professional development models as specific learning communities, mentoring, peer coaching, collaborative action research, critical development teams, conferences and seminars, and professional development through writing.

InfoDev's report on teacher professional development in developing countries (Gaible & Burns, 2005) placed professional development models into three broad categories:

1. Standardized programs focusing on rapid dissemination of specific skills and content (e.g., "train-the-trainer" approach);

Faculty Professional Development in Creating Significant Teaching and Learning Experiences Online

2. School-centered programs focusing on long-term change processes; and,
3. Individual or self-directed programs with little formal structure or support (p. 19).

Villegas-Reimers (2003), on the other hand, in her review of literature on teacher professional development, grouped professional development models under two main headings. The first heading includes macro- or meso-level models at the institutional or supra-institutional level, while the models under the second heading are implemented on a much smaller scale such as a school or classroom. Villegas-Reimers (2003) defined those in the second group as more like techniques which are used standalone or as part of the models included in the first group.

Emerging new models, or "techniques" as Villegas-Reimers (2003) put it, can be added to the second column of Table 3. In current terms, one example would be *joint practice development* (JPD), as defined by Fielding as "learning new ways of working through mutual engagement that opens up and shares practice with others" (British Council, 2017). Fielding et al. (2005) explained JPD as a practitioner-centered approach which "takes into account of the existing practice of teachers who are trying to learn new ways working and acknowledges the effort of those who are trying to support them. It also underscores the necessity of mutual engagement" (p. 72). JPD differs from other traditional models in that there is no expert in possession of valuable knowledge and skills to transfer or deliver to the audience. In JPD, the knowledge gained from research, combined with local experience and the individual insight of educators from real-life experience is crucial for the change (Gregson & Hillier, 2015).

Serious games for faculty development is another fresh technique, yet with a scarcity of research for the adoption of serious games for the purposes of training and professional development. Having come to the fore in the 1980s with the advent of the videogaming industry, serious games today are in consid-

Table 3. Models of teacher professional development (Villegas-Reimers, 2003, p. 70)

Organizational Partnership Models	Small group or Individual Models
Professional development schools	Supervision: traditional and clinical
Other university-school partnerships	Students' performance assessment
Other inter-institutional collaboration	Workshops, seminars, courses etc.
Schools' networks	Case-based study
Teachers' networks	Self-directed development
Distance education	Co-operative or collegial development
	Observation of excellent practice
	Teachers' participation in new roles
	Skills-development model
	Reflective models
	Project-based models
	Portfolios
	Action Research
	Use of teachers' narratives
	Generational or cascade model
	Coaching/mentoring

erable demand owing to the advent of technology in interactive simulations. Serious games differ from entertaining games in that they are designed primarily for an educational purpose. Boudreaux's (2018) literature review examined the usability of serious games for training and faculty development from the perspectives of viability of serious games as teaching tools, validity of serious games in professional training, motivation, faculty attitudes, and faculty professional development. Boudreaux (2018) referred to several research studies on the use of serious games for the professional development of teachers at the K-12 and K-16 levels on 21st century skills, delivering student learning materials (e.g., for developing psychomotor skills), increasing motivation, supplementing field-based training, and involving virtual worlds. Nevertheless, Boudreaux (2018) underlined a significant shortage of research when it comes to higher education faculty development, and encouraged future studies to be undertaken since the available research at the time (2015) did not show the value inherent in using serious games for training purposes. A more recent study by Yu (2019) has examined the factors influencing the effect of serious game-assisted learning, positive and negative findings in serious games in education, and the development of serious games in education. Based on a rigorous review of the literature, Yu suggested an interdisciplinary approach for further studies. Games are essentially a simplified version of reality (Schaffer, Squire, Halverson, & Gee, 2005) whereby players live through alternative "bodies" in simulated worlds. It would not be wrong to state that serious games are powerful mediums for creating immersive environments that make it possible to learn actively by doing (Stamets, 2016).

As previously indicated, advances in digital technologies for learning has made it possible to create more *personalized learning* environments using learner data for interventions or for determining strategies for learners to achieve their learning goals in a more effective manner through predictive modeling. Personalized learning environments, maybe more importantly, can help learners to become creators or curators. Personalized or connected learning offers astounding opportunities for professional development practices, moving them from a "closed setting of a course-redesign workshop to an open and networked community of peer-to-peer learners within and across institutions of higher education" (Fowler & Bond, 2016, p. 57).

e-Tutor: An Online Professional Development Program for Faculty Members to Teach Online

e-Tutor is a certificated online professional development program for faculty members to teach online designed and implemented by the authors for more than seven years in four languages, namely English, Russian, and Ukrainian[1], and also in Turkish[2,3]. *e-Tutor* was designed in order to provide faculty members with key pedagogical, technological and administrative skills for effective online teaching, based on concepts of Technological Pedagogical Content Knowledge (TPCK) (Mishra & Koehler, 2006), and adapted as an open educational resource under Creative Commons License within the scope of an international project. *e-Tutor* introduces the fundamental concepts, tools and processes of online learning for classroom management and the creation of digital content in 14 modules:

1. Basics of e-Learning (Basic Concepts, Types of e-Learning, Time vs. Place – Asynchronous vs. Synchronous, e-Facilitator [changing roles and responsibilities], Learning Environments and Interaction Types);
2. Application of Instructional Theories to Online Environments (Behaviorism, Cognitivism, Constructivism, Connectivism, Adult Learning and Self-Regulated Learning);

3. Learning and Content Management Systems (Online Learning Communities, e-Moderation, LMS/CMS Features, Moodle and MOOCS);
4. Virtual Classroom Applications and Webinars (Managing Virtual Learning Environments, Adobe Connect and BigBlueButton);
5. Instructional Design Issues (Knowledge Management, Learning Goals & Outcomes, Instructional Planning/Syllabus, Learning Opportunities/Activities and Course Structure);
6. Instructional Methods and Techniques (Presentation, Training, Concept Teaching, Collaborative Learning, Problem-based & Project-based Learning and Discussion);
7. Copyright and Ethical Issues, Plagiarism (Copyright, Digital Rights Management, Creative Commons and Plagiarism);
8. e-Assessment (Classical Assessment Approaches [tests, essays, matching, fill-in-the-blank etc.] and Alternative Assessment Approaches [webquest, e-portfolio etc.]);
9. Graphical Design (Graphical Design Principles, Graphical Organizers and Storyboarding);
10. Creating Effective Visuals (Posters, Mind Maps, Concept Maps, and Infographics);
11. Multimedia Content Development (Audio-visual Content, Narrated presentations and Educational Videos);
12. Creating Interactive Applications (Tools for Creating Interactive Application and Interactive Mobile Applications);
13. Social Media and Emerging Technologies (Social Networking, Document Sharing, Media Sharing, Collaboration Tools and Blogs & Microblogs);
14. Quality Assurance in e-Learning (Competencies, Usability, Course Evaluation and Satisfaction).

e-Tutor merges synchronous and asynchronous technologies through varied materials and features of the learning management system such as course handouts, narrated presentations, videos, audio files, interactive activities, tasks, e-portfolio objects, and weblinks. The program is conducted through one-hour virtual and practical face-to-face classes. *e-Tutor* is based on two aspects. In *e-Tutor*, participants principally experience being an online learner themselves in order to gain familiarity from "the other side of the screen" so as to help them "reflect on their online-learner experience and make inferences for their own instruction" (Adnan, 2018, p. 6). Secondly, following a hands-on approach, participants are expected to create an online course from scratch using sound instructional design practices including all components such as course syllabus, handouts, visuals, presentations, videos, interactive and assessment activities, and social platforms.

The overriding goal of *e-Tutor* is to prepare, equip and certify faculty members to start their own online classes after completing a course design that includes instructional materials (Rapp et al., 2016). Adnan et al. (2017) reported findings from the assessment of the initial international *e-Tutor* program that faculty member participants underlined the importance of well-organized programs balancing theoretical and practical dimensions, more time for hands-on activities, and collaborative projects to encourage interaction. Another assessment of the program conducted by Adnan (2018) with the participation of online language instructors, concluded that in addition to institution-based structured professional development programs, faculty members should also be supported by formal and informal peer support, mentoring, coaching, and ad hoc meetings.

These results link back to the mainstream models for professional development as listed by OECD's TALIS, the World Bank's InfoDev, the ASCD, and other academic research conducted in the areas of courses, workshops, seminars, certificate programs, communities of learning, mentoring, and peer coaching etc.

CONCLUSION

A shift can be seen from "which technologies and pedagogical approaches should be used for effective technology integration" to "what kind of integrated learning environments should be used to meet diverse needs of learners." This shift forces educators to think differently about the intersection of technology, pedagogy, teaching and learning without disregard for using online technologies for teaching and learning. Hence, studies and discussion will continue on media, technology and its role in creating effective and meaningful learning environments, yet in a more purposive and responsible manner by taking learning and learners, not technology or media, as the central point of inquiry. This is still a novel and unconventional universe for many teachers and instructors with which they may feel rather uncomfortable at times due to various reasons such as lack of knowledge and skills, feelings of insecurity or anxiousness about technology, fear of the unknown, moving out of their comfort zone, not believing in technology's usefulness, and so on. This resistance or reluctance has been studied by researchers for decades, since the introduction of instructional technologies, and on several occasions, it has been stated that people are claimed to be a major barrier to the acceptance of online education (Anderson, Brown, Murray, Simpson, & Mentis, 2006; Stein, Shephard, & Harris, 2011). Teachers and instructors play a key role in creating efficient online learning environments, and many of them in this unfamiliar universe require a level of support and guidance in order to find their way.

It is at this juncture that professional development comes to the stage in its various models, guises, and techniques. Research indicates that, amongst others, faculty development leads to higher levels of adoption and continued usage of online technologies (e.g., Stein et al., 2011). Professional development is not a one-time practice, but a lifelong experience starting from the initial stages a professional career until retirement. As a result of their 10-year longitudinal study, Englund, Olofsson, and Price (2017) concluded that professional development practices started in instructors' early careers would more likely lead to the anticipated lasting impact, and "supporting conceptual change should, therefore, be a central component of professional development activities if a more effective use of educational technology is to be achieved" (p. 73).

According to Bates (2000), the provision of all-inclusive structures and systemized professional support for faculty members contributes to overcoming certain issues in online teaching. As previously mentioned, teaching with online technologies places instructors within an unfamiliar context (Adnan, 2018) where they need to embrace different roles, responsibilities, and competencies. Professional development is of the utmost importance in helping instructors to learn and acclimatize to new roles through new pedagogies (Baran & Correia, 2014; Bates, 2000), and to enhance their awareness, knowledge and experience for online teaching. Hence, the talk should be of developing a well-structured professional development vision with a balance of digital literacy, content knowledge, and pedagogical knowledge that is accompanied with follow-up events like mentoring, peer support, workshops, online learning, and support communities or online instructor exchanges for technical or pedagogical issues.

REFERENCES

Adnan, M. (2018). Professional Development in the Transition to Online Teaching: Voice of Entrant Online Instructors. *ReCALL*, *30*(1), 88–111. doi:10.1017/S0958344017000106

Adnan, M., Kalelioğlu, F., & Gülbahar, Y. (2017). Assessment of a Multinational Online Faculty Development Program on Online Teaching: Reflections of Candidate e-Tutors. *The Turkish Online Journal of Distance Education-TOJDE*, *18*(1), 22–38. doi:10.17718/tojde.285708

Anderson, B., Brown, M., Murray, F., Simpson, M., & Mentis, M. (2006). *Global picture, local lessons: e-learning policy and accessibility*. Retrieved from http://www.educationcounts.govt.nz/__data/assets/pdf_file/0005/58289/AndersonFinalReport.pdf

Anderson, T., Rourke, L., Garrison, D., & Archer, W. (2001). Assessing teaching presence in a computer conferencing context. *Journal of Asynchronous Learning Networks*, *5*(2), 1–17.

Baran, E., & Correia, A. (2014). A professional development framework for online teaching. *TechTrends*, *58*(5), 96–102. doi:10.100711528-014-0791-0

Bates, A. W. (2000). *Managing technological change: Strategies for college and university leaders*. San Francisco, CA: Jossey-Bass.

Bates, A. W. (2015). *Teaching in a Digital Age: Guidelines for Designing Teaching and Learning*. Vancouver, BC: Tony Bates Associates.

Beaudoin, M. (2010). Experiences and Opinions of Online Learners - What Foster Successful Learning? In Y. Kats (Ed.), *Learning Management System Technologies and Software Solutions for Online Teaching: Tools and Applications* (pp. 372–393). Hershey, PA: IGI Global. doi:10.4018/978-1-61520-853-1.ch020

Berge, Z. L. (2001). *New roles for learners and teachers in online education*. Retrieved from http://its.fvtc.edu/langan/BB6/BergeZane2000.pdf

Boudreaux, K. (2018). Serious Games for Training and Faculty Development--A Review of the Current Literature. *Journal of Educators Online*, *15*(2). doi:10.9743/jeo.2018.15.2.5

Brinkley-Etzkorn, K. E. (2018). Learning to teach online: Measuring the influence of faculty development training on teaching effectiveness through a TPACK lens. *The Internet and Higher Education*, *38*, 28–35. doi:10.1016/j.iheduc.2018.04.004

British Council. (2017). New model to improve your professional development. *Vocational Education Exchange Magazine*. Retrieved from https://www.britishcouncil.org/education/skills-employability/what-we-do/vocational-education-exchange-online-magazine/april-2017/new-model-improve-your-professional-development

Carr, N. (2011). *The Shallows: What the Internet Is Doing to Our Brains*. New York: Norton.

Darling-Hammond, L., Hyler, M. E., & Gardner, M. (2017). *Effective Teacher Professional Development*. Palo Alto, CA: Learning Policy Institute; Retrieved from https://learningpolicyinstitute.org/product/teacher-prof-dev

Dede, C. (Ed.). (2004). *Online Professional Development for Teachers: Emerging Models and Methods.* Cambridge, MA: Harvard Education Press.

Dennis, B., Watland, P., Pirotte, S., & Verday, N. (2004). Role and competencies of the e-tutor. *Proceedings of the Networked Learning Conference 2004.* Retrieved from http://www.networkedlearningconference.org.uk/past/nlc2004/home.htm

Díaz-Maggioli, G. (2004). *Teacher-Centered Professional Development.* Alexandria, VA: ACSD.

Elliott, M., Rhoades, N., Jackson, C. M., & Mandernach, B. J. (2015). Professional Development: Designing Initiatives to Meet the Needs of Online Faculty. *Journal of Educators Online, 12*(1), 160–188. doi:10.9743/JEO.2015.1.2

Englund, C., Olofsson, A. D., & Price, L. (2017). Teaching with technology in higher education: Understanding conceptual change and development in practice. *Higher Education Research & Development, 36*(1), 73–87. doi:10.1080/07294360.2016.1171300

Fielding, M., Bragg, S., Craig, J., Cunnigham, I., Eraut, M., Gillinson, S., …Thorp, J. (2005). *Factors Influencing the Transfer of Good Practice.* London: Department for Education and Skills. Research Report 615. Retrieved from https://dera.ioe.ac.uk/21001/1/RR615.pdf

Fowler, S., & Bond, M. A. (2016). The Future of Faculty Development in a Networked World. *Educause Review, 51*(2), 56-57. Retrieved from https://er.educause.edu/articles/2016/3/the-future-of-faculty-development-in-a-networked-world

Gaible, E., & Burns, M. (2005). *Using Technology to Train Teachers: Appropriate Uses of ICT for Teacher Professional Development in Developing Countries.* Washington, DC: infoDev / World Bank. Retrieved from http://documents.worldbank.org/curated/en/900291468324835987/Using-technology-to-train-teachers-appropriate-uses-of-ICT-for-teacher-professional-development-in-developing-countires

Garrison, D. R., & Anderson, T. (2003). *E-learning in the 21st century: A framework for research and practice.* New York: Routledge Falmer. doi:10.4324/9780203166093

Goodyear, P., Salmon, G., Spector, J., Steeples, C., & Tickner, S. (2001). Competences for online teaching: A special report. *Educational Technology Research and Development, 49*(1), 65–72. doi:10.1007/BF02504508

Gregory, J., & Salmon, G. (2013). Professional development for online university teaching. *Distance Education, 34*(3), 256–270. doi:10.1080/01587919.2013.835771

Gregson, M., & Hillier, Y. (2015). *Reflective Teaching in Further, Adult and Vocational Education* (4th ed.). Bloomsbury Academic.

Gulbahar, Y., & Kalelioglu, F. (2015). Competencies for e-Instructors: How to Qualify and Guarantee Sustainability. *Contemporary Educational Technology, 6*(2), 140–154.

International Society for Technology in Education. (2018). *ISTE Standards for Educators.* Retrieved from https://www.iste.org/standards/for-educators

Kebritchi, M., Lipschuetz, A., & Santiague, L. (2017). Issues and Challenges for Teaching Successful Online Courses in Higher Education: A Literature Review. *Journal of Educational Technology Systems, 46*(1), 4–29. doi:10.1177/0047239516661713

Krathwohl, D. R. (2002). A Revision of Bloom's Taxonomy: An Overview. *Theory into Practice, 41*(4), 212–218. doi:10.120715430421tip4104_2

Laurillard, D. (2002). *Rethinking university teaching*. London: Routledge Falmer. doi:10.4324/9780203160329

Learning Forward. (2011). Standards for Professional Learning. *The Learning Professional, 32*(4), 41-44. Retrieved from https://learningforward.org/docs/august-2011/referenceguide324.pdf?sfvrsn=2

Macdonald, J., & Poniatowska, B. (2011). Designing the professional development of staff for teaching online: An OU (UK) case study. *Distance Education, 32*(1), 119–134. doi:10.1080/01587919.2011.565481

Mishra, P., & Koehler, M. (2006). Technological pedagogical content knowledge: A framework for teacher knowledge. *Teachers College Record, 108*(6), 1017–1054. doi:10.1111/j.1467-9620.2006.00684.x

Mohr, S. C., & Shelton, K. (2017). Best practices framework for online faculty professional development: A Delphi study. *Online Learning, 21*(4), 123–140. doi:10.24059/olj.v21i4.1273

Nelson, R., Spence-Thomas, K., & Taylor, C. (2015). *What makes great pedagogy and great professional development: final report. Teaching schools R&D network national themes project 2012-14*. National College for Teaching & Leadership. Retrieved from https://dera.ioe.ac.uk/22157/

OECD. (2005). *Creating Effective Teaching and Learning Environments - First Results from TALIS*. Paris: OECD Publishing.

Quality Matters. (2016). *Online Instructor Skills Set*. Retrieved from https://www.qualitymatters.org/qa-resources/rubric-standards/teaching-skills-set

Rapp, C., Gülbahar, Y., & Adnan, M. (2016). e-Tutor: A Multilingual Open Educational Resource for Faculty Development to Teach Online. *International Review of Research in Open and Distributed Learning, 17*(5), 284–289. doi:10.19173/irrodl.v17i5.2783

Roddy, C., Amiet, D. L., Chung, J., Holt, C., Shaw, L., McKenzie, S., ... Mundy, M. E. (2017). Applying Best Practice Online Learning, Teaching, and Support to intensive Online environments: An integrative Review. *Frontiers in Education, 2*(59), 1–10.

Schaffer, D. W., Squire, K. R., Halverson, R., & Gee, J. P. (2005). Video Games and the Future of Learning. *Phi Delta Kappan, 87*(2), 104–111.

Stamets, S. E. (2016). *Game on: redesign of a teacher professional development platform for use with the serious game alien rescue* (Master's thesis). University of Texas at Austin. Retrieved from https://repositories.lib.utexas.edu/handle/2152/43378

Starkey, L. (2011). Evaluating learning in the 21st Century: A digital age learning matrix. *Technology, Pedagogy and Education, 20*(1), 19–39. doi:10.1080/1475939X.2011.554021

Stein, S. J., Shephard, K., & Harris, I. (2011). Conceptions of e-learning and professional development for e-learning held by tertiary educators in New Zealand. *British Journal of Educational Technology, 42*(1), 145–165. doi:10.1111/j.1467-8535.2009.00997.x

UNESCO. (2011). *ICT Competency Framework for Teachers*. Retrieved from http://unesdoc.unesco.org/images/0021/002134/213475E.pdf

Villegas-Reimers, E. (2003). *Teacher Professional Development: An International Review of the Literature*. Paris: UNESCO International Institute for Educational Planning.

Wolf, M. (2018). *Reader, Come Home*. New York, NY: Harper Collins.

Yu, Z. (2019). A Meta-Analysis of Use of Serious Games in Education over a Decade. *International Journal of Computer Games Technology, 2019*, 4797032. doi:10.1155/2019/4797032

ENDNOTES

[1] http://e-tutor.sml.zhaw.ch/
[2] https://uzem.ankara.edu.tr/index.php/sertifika-programlari/135-e-egitmen-programi
[3] http://uzem.mu.edu.tr

Chapter 5
Flexible Higher Education Through Swayam

Varun Gupta
Universidade da Beira Interior, Portugal

Durg Singh Chauhan
GLA University, India

Thomas Hanne
University of Applied Sciences and Arts Northwestern Switzerland, Switzerland

ABSTRACT

Challenges in MOOC education for both practical and theoretical courses are identified by the researchers, both experimentally and through a case study. The insights brought by empirical studies helped researchers to propose a framework to make higher education in engineering and management truly online and tuition free. The objective of this chapter is to propose a flexible online degree framework through SWAYAM or any other online platform being approved by education regulator. The process involving course enrollment, learning, evaluation, and outcome is contained in the proposed flexible system that leads to tuition free online degrees. The proposed system not only gives students a freedom to choose their courses in accordance with their flexibility but also use earned credit towards online degrees of any university of their choice.

INTRODUCTION

The online degrees as offered by leading universities on online platform like Edx, Coursera etc offers masters degrees, credit courses and certificate courses online at tuition rates that are less compared to on campus courses. The degrees provide flexibility in time to complete and flexibility to learn due to online delivery. Candidates get benefit in terms of getting degree from foreign universities at their home country at less cost and at their own flexible time. Examinations also do not require proctored examinations in most of cases and could be given online without a need to visit their campus for examinations. The

DOI: 10.4018/978-1-7998-0115-3.ch005

courses offered require candidates to pay tuition fees which are in contrast to the credit courses offered by Indian Universities through SWAYAM platform under Study Webs of Active–Learning for Young Aspiring Minds (SWAYAM) program. Government of India, through University Grants Commission (UGC) had allowed Indian Universities to Offer online degrees through SWAYAM platform provided permission is taken before offering such degrees and no degree/courses being offered in areas that require laboratory work (**UGC** (**Online Courses**) **Regulations**, 2018). The Engineering degree which requires extensive laboratory work is thus difficult to be offered online through SWAYAM as compared to Management degrees. Both credit and non credit courses on SWAYAM platform are completely free and hence if a degree programme structure has all courses on this platform then the complete degree could be completed almost tuition free as offered in few European countries.

The objective of this paper is to propose a flexible online degree framework that offers complete flexibility to students and offers to them tuition free education. The challenges of laboratory and non laboratory courses considering engineering and management degrees will be bridged by the flexible framework.

PROPOSED FRAMEWORK

The framework for online Master's Degrees in Engineering and Management is discussed considering the typical stages in earning the degrees. These stages include the following:

- Application for Admission in University and selection.
- Selecting the credit based courses for a semester and all mandatory courses.
- Undergoing through the evaluations including assignments, tests, mid examinations, final examinations etc.
- Repeating the above process for all semesters followed by mandatory Project work (also called as Dissertation work or Project work).

In Masters Degrees involving Engineering, none of university offers through Distance mode, however large number of universities do offer Distance mode MBA's. The admission criteria are different for all universities with fewer of them ask for Entrance examinations while others offering on basis of marks in UG degree and satisfying of minimum criteria. The degrees are offered if candidate has earned the minimum credit points with CGPA above the minimum defined by individual universities. In engineering Masters Degrees, few courses have laboratory courses also while in MBA the courses are based on theory, numerical and case studies. Industrial case studies and interactions with Industry people thus are easier to be provided through online platform and enhance the effectiveness of learning. Laboratory courses are challenge to be offered through online learning and require continuous guidance of teachers.

Typical degrees have maximum duration within which candidates do have to complete their degrees and the final examinations are proctored examinations conducted as subjective examinations at established examination centres.

Online degrees must be fully online and must allow candidates to take examinations at locations convenient to them provided that such examinations do not involve any element of unfairness at the end of candidate. The proposed framework is divided into levels to correspond to the stages in earning degrees outlined above (Table 1 and Table 2). The levels differs for both Engineering and Management degrees due to involvement of laboratory work and finally these levels are mapped with each other to yield a common framework for Online Masters degrees in Engineering & Management (Table 3).

Case Study (Example of Master in Management Administration Degree)

The University requires a candidate to undertake 10 theory courses (total credits 40) and Project Work (40 credits) to earn MBA degree. Let's assume that SWAYAM had large number of online courses (which of course will be there as lots of universities are now offering such courses). Candidate is experienced one and had 10 Years experience at Manager Level. Since, the curriculum does not require any Laboratory sessions and Minor Projects, only core courses and Project work is required. Under proposed system, the candidate does not need to enroll for any degree. During his professional life, he may choose any SWAYAM courses that best match his interests.

Let's suppose that University requires following courses to complete course work:

Semester-I

- Research Methodology
- Managerial Economics.
- Organizational Structure
- Business Ethics
- Accounting.

Semester-II

- Human Resource Management
- Marketing Management
- Operation Management
- Strategic Management
- Financial Management.

Semester-III & IV

- Project work submitted at the end as a project thesis.

(Candidate must have 2 papers in leading conferences and Journals of repute, indexed by Scopus).
Now let's assume that candidate had undergone through, 4 credit courses as given below:

- Research Methodology.
- Accounts for Managers.
- Business Ethics & role.
- Human Resource Management.
- Strategic Management.
- Marketing Management.
- Operation Management.

Table 1. Framework for management degrees

S. No.	Level Number	Activities
1.	**Level 1: (Course Offerings)**	Indian Universities prepares the courses employing the best expertise they have into three levels – Basic (1 credit), Intermediate (2 Credit) and Advanced (4 Credits). Each course should have a Minor project condition which is offered as 1 credit course. The database will have large number of courses on same subject offered by large number of Indian universities.
2.	**Level 2: (Admission)**	Universities could admit students in two ways-preadmission before starting any course and Post admission. In pre admission, the students can select online courses that are there in their program structure. Under this scheme, the courses offered that makes up online degree, could be registered by candidate matching credits and undergoing through evaluations. Thus if a candidate enrolls for Pondicherry University, he may take Research Methodology course of same or any other university, provided the credits are at least same as required by home university say 4 credits. In post admission, once candidate has successfully passed large number of credit courses in their life time and could be awarded a degree, can select a particular university that best matches its interests and type of courses passed. On basis of micro projects undertaken, courses passed and parameters, universities will admit students with details of more courses/projects to be undertaken to fulfill the criteria of the degree. Under this system, candidate learns at his own pace and at any time could decide university and complete the courses to fulfill the degree criteria. Admission committee of university will compare the completed courses with the course requirements at their universities to transfer credits and suggests gaps to be bridged. Thus universities get approval for offering online courses and contributed by creating the online degree courses on SWAYAM. Candidates could however, choose all courses of the university of may create a basket of courses of various universities. This gives flexibility to candidate to learn, complete and enroll for degree award.
3.	**Level 3: (Evaluation of course)**	University courses will have frequent evaluations in form of MCQ tests, Assignments, MID examination and final examination. Challenging questions and assignments needs to be framed to check candidate knowledge. The university faculty will be available online to discuss and resolve candidate doubts but interacting with massive candidates would not be a feasible idea. Thus, the Indian universities could become as *Supporting Centres* even if they are not allowed to offer online degrees/courses. The candidates on basis of vicinity of the Supporting centres (Universities) from their work locations could interact with the faculty teaching the same course for the removal of their doubts. Supporting Centres They could also interact with the faculty of online course during online sessions announced by him, several times during the length of the course. Examinations could be proctored and conducted in all Supporting Centres. Candidate could appear in any Centre near to his work place.
4.	**Level 4: (Thesis/Final Project)**	For both pre admission and post admission based degree, the candidate will undertake project work as expected by master's degree requirement. Different universities may have expectations from project like publications etc. The candidate who had completed course work and also project work, could submit their research findings to the university in which they are enrolled (Pre Admission) or to university where candidate want to earn degree (post Admission). In post admission, once the admission committee has suggested fresh courses to be taken or have accepted all courses passed by candidate, the candidate can submit their thesis once he got admission to the university. The evaluation committee will review or get thesis reviewed and may conduct viva if required. Candidate can check for thesis requirements of the university and could select university accordingly.

Flexible Higher Education Through Swayam

Table 2. Framework for engineering degrees

S. No.	Level Number	Activities
1.	Level 1: (Course Offerings)	Indian Universities prepares the courses employing the best expertise they have into three levels – Basic (1 credit), Intermediate (2 Credit) and Advanced (4 Credits). Each course should have a Minor project condition which is offered as 1 credit course. Experience reports reporting the Live projects handling and results, published in leading journals may be awarded Minor project or Thesis grade for which candidate must have to enroll for particular project course. Also, Laboratory session is mandatory credit of 1 or 2 credits with core courses to be offered alone and together with entire course.
2.	Level 2: (Admission)	Universities could admit students in two ways-preadmission before starting any course and Post admission. If candidate is experienced and had good knowledge about the course and also undertaken credit course on SWAYAM then candidate could directly choose the University, apply for admission and admission committee will suggest few additional courses and/or laboratory exercises. They may directly approve admission if courses are well mapped to their degree requirements.
3.	Level 3: (Evaluation of course)	University courses will have frequent evaluations in form of MCQ tests, Assignments, MID examination and final examination. Challenging questions and assignments needs to be framed to check candidate knowledge. Active participation of *Supporting Centres* and Online course faculty live interaction is required. A part from this, *Supporting Centres* will run *Short Term Laboratory Course* either in Winter of Summer, where candidate must attend the Laboratory course to earn Laboratory credits. Such course could be in Winter, Summer of Weekends depending on the enrollments made by candidates. Small part of fees could be paid towards such courses. If candidate is already employed in some University then he may choose to enroll in the Laboratory course with full Time students and after passing through that course, his credits are mapped to SWAYAM credits. Examinations could be proctored and conducted in all Supporting Centres. Candidate could appear in any Centre near to his work place.
4.	Level 4: (Thesis/Final Project)	For both pre admission and post admission based degree, the candidate will undertake project work or submit his results and live projects case studies (which he did during his job after taking permission from his department) directly to the University after taking admission and completing course work.

The candidate will submit his application for MBA degree to any university. Admission committee will recommend the Three courses of 4 credits or higher each to candidate. Once done, candidate will submit his thesis and after evaluation, MBA will be awarded. That's how such proposal is flexible enough to support Indian population that want to add the higher degrees to their resumes.

Now let's suppose that University is offering Master in Software Engineering. It require candidate to complete 6 courses with research project. Course curriculum is s under:

Semester-I & II

- Research Methodology. (4 Credits Theory, 2 Credit Minor Project)
- Requirement Engineering. (4 Credits Theory, 2 Credit Laboratory)
- Software Testing & Evolution. (4 Credits Theory, 2 Credit Laboratory)
- Agile Methodology & Crowd Sourcing. (4 Credits Theory, 2 Credit Laboratory)
- Programming & Software Architecture (4 Credits Theory, 2 Credit Laboratory)

Table 3. Comparative framework for management degrees and engineering degrees

S. No.	Level Number	Activities in Engineering	Activities in Management
1.	Level 1: (Course Offerings)	Three levels – Basic (1 credit), Intermediate (2 Credit) and Advanced (4 Credits). Each course should have a Minor project condition which is offered as 1 credit course. Laboratory session is mandatory credit of 1 or 2 credits with core courses to be offered alone and together with entire course.	Same as Engineering Degree except that Laboratory sessions will not be offered.
2.	Level 2: (Admission)	Universities could admit students in two ways-pre admission before starting any course and Post admission.	Same as Engineering Degree.
3.	Level 3: (Evaluation of course)	University courses will have frequent evaluations in form of MCQ tests, Assignments, MID examination and final examination. Challenging questions and assignments needs to be framed to check candidate knowledge. *Supporting Centres* and Online course faculty live interaction. *Supporting Centres* will run *Short Term Laboratory Course* either in Winter of Summer, where candidate must attend the Laboratory course to earn Laboratory credits. Such course could be in Winter, Summer of Weekends depending on the enrollments made by candidates. Small part of fees could be paid towards such courses. If candidate is already employed in some University then he may choose to enroll in the Laboratory course with full Time students and after passing through that course, his credits are mapped to SWAYAM credits. Examinations could be proctored and conducted in all Supporting Centres. Candidate could appear in any Centre near to his work place.	Same as Engineering Degree except that *Supporting Centres* will not run Laboratory Sessions.
4.	Level 4: (Thesis/Final Project)	For both pre admission and post admission based degree, the candidate will undertake project work or submit his results and live projects case studies (which he did during his job after taking permission from his department) directly to the University after taking admission and completing course work.	Same as Engineering Degree.

Semester-III & IV

- Thesis. (40 Credits).

Suppose that the candidate is faculty and working in some University from past 10 years. He already has gone through SWAYAM courses as part of requirements for his Job or knowledge enhancement. But, candidate has completed last three courses along with Laboratory requirements, earning 18 credits. He also have undergone through theory courses on Research methodology and Requirement Engineering, earning 8 credits. Now he wants to enroll for Masters Degree. Admission committee will suggest him to enroll for two Laboratory courses of total at least 4 credits and then undertake Thesis component.

He will enroll for Laboratory component to earn 4 credits total and as he had already done lot of research published in leading Journals, which is submitted as Thesis. He can do Laboratory course in any Supporting Centres or even at his own University with Full Time students, if course if there. After evaluation of thesis, the degree is awarded to candidate.

CONFLICT OF INTERESTS

The work presented here is on basis of own personal views of researchers with the objective of improving education and making it accessible to masses, opportunity which is provided as a result of innovative schemes like SWAYAM.

REFERENCES

Al-Shabandar, R., Hussain, A. J., Liatsis, P., & Keight, R. (2018). Analyzing Learners Behavior in MOOCs: An Examination of Performance and Motivation Using a Data-Driven Approach. *IEEE Access: Practical Innovations, Open Solutions*, 6, 73669–73685. doi:10.1109/ACCESS.2018.2876755

Chen, G., Davis, D., Krause, M., Aivaloglou, E., Hauff, C., & Houben, G. (2018). From Learners to Earners: Enabling MOOC Learners to Apply Their Skills and Earn Money in an Online Market Place. IEEE Transactions on Learning Technologies, 11(2), 264-274. doi:10.1109/TLT.2016.2614302

Pickard, L., Shah, D., & De Simone, J. J. (2018). *Mapping Microcredentials Across MOOC Platforms. In 2018 Learning With MOOCS* (pp. 17–21). Madrid: LWMOOCS. doi:10.1109/LWMOOCS.2018.8534617

Psathas, G., Chalki, P., Demetriadis, S., & Tsiara, A. (2018). *Profiles and Motivations of Participants in Greek MOOC for Python Programming. In 2018 Learning With MOOCS* (pp. 70–73). Madrid: LWMOOCS.

Qiu, L., Liu, Y., & Liu, Y. (2018). An Integrated Framework With Feature Selection for Dropout Prediction in Massive Open Online Courses. *IEEE Access: Practical Innovations, Open Solutions*, 6, 71474–71484. doi:10.1109/ACCESS.2018.2881275

Reda, V., & Kerr, R. (2018). *The MOOC BA, a New Frontier for Internationalization. In 2018 Learning With MOOCS* (pp. 94–97). Madrid: LWMOOCS.

Section 2
Designing Online Courses for Meaningful Learning Experiences

Chapter 6
The Transition From Teaching F2F to Online

Steven Tolman
Georgia Southern University, USA

Matt Dunbar
Georgia Southern University, USA

K. Brooke Slone
Georgia Southern University, USA

Allie Grimes
Georgia Southern University, USA

Christopher A. Trautman
Fairleigh Dickinson University, USA

ABSTRACT

As online education continues to grow, more and more faculty find themselves transitioning from teaching face-to-face to online environments. Unsurprisingly, this can be challenging for many faculty as they go through this process. This book chapters examines the experience of a faculty member who transitioned from teaching exclusively face-to-face to online and lessons learned are shared. Additionally, four students share their experience learning online and provide recommendations to faculty members.

INTRODUCTION

The pathways to the professoriate within the academy can be as diverse as those who hold these positions. While some knew they wanted to be faculty early on in their academic and professional careers, not only was this not a desire for me, but in fact it never crossed my mind as a possibility. After completing my graduate degree in my respective discipline, I, like the majority of my classmates and colleagues, entered into my field as a practitioner. Over the next twelve years, my career progressed accordingly,

DOI: 10.4018/978-1-7998-0115-3.ch006

and I moved into senior university administrator positions. During the latter part of my administrative career, I recognized that moving from a senior to an executive leadership position would require a terminal degree. This epiphany led to my pursuit of a doctorate and (unknowingly) my ultimate career change into the professoriate.

While I worked toward my doctorate, it didn't cross my mind that faculty life would be the path for me or the fact that it was even a possibility. Out of happenstance, I was asked to teach a graduate level course as an adjunct, which as it turned out would change my career path. This opportunity helped me to find my true passion and calling in my professional life – teaching. I loved teaching in the face-to-face (F2F) environment and actively sought out opportunities to continue to do so both as an adjunct and ultimately as a full-time faculty member. With my love for being in the classroom firmly established, I never would have imagined that I would willingly accept a faculty position where I would teach almost exclusively online. Not only did this happen, but even more to my surprise, I have found that I enjoy teaching online even more than in a F2F environment.

This chapter is an autoethnography of my teaching and experience transitioning from teaching solely F2F to exclusively online. Beyond sharing my experience, I will compare and contrast my Student Ratings of Instruction (SRI) for these two formats. The inclusion of these teaching evaluations and student comments will help to illustrate the strategies, success, and challenges shared throughout the chapter. Furthermore, it would be remiss of me if this chapter only included my experience and not also the voices of my online students. To provide this student perspective, four of my former students have briefly written about their experiences learning online and provided a recommendation for future faculty teaching online.

BACKGROUND

Online education has continued to grow and play an increasingly important role in higher education. The enrollment of online learners has increased from 1.6 million students in 2002 to 6.7 million online students in 2012 (Allen & Seaman, 2013). These significant enrollment numbers have not gone unnoticed, as a recent study found almost two-thirds of college and university administrators perceived online education as critical to the institution's long-term strategy and success (Allen & Seaman, 2016). While it was previously found that students preferred traditional face-to-face courses over online courses with regard to course quality, counter to this they continued to enroll in online courses at increasing rates (Weldy, 2018). As online education programs increase in both size and scope, it is important that educators continue to establish online learning environments that not only foster learning, but also promote positive experiences for students.

It has been noted that online courses have some distinctive features that set them apart from the traditional face-to-face classroom experience, such as a reliance on technology, differences in learner participation and content delivery, college affordability, student flexibility, and accessibility (Ascough, 2002; Deming, Goldin, Katz & Yuchtman, 2015; Kauffman, 2015; Nguyen, 2015). Many factors impact the quality of online education and the learning experience, which has been a long-standing topic for consideration (Twigg, 2001; Yang & Cornelious, 2004). Twigg (2001) made the distinction that "any discussion about quality in a distributed learning environment must first ask: From whose perspective are we considering quality?" (p. 1). Students may perceive differences in the quality of their traditional face-to-face courses in comparison to the quality of their online courses; similarly, students may also perceive the quality of their online courses differently than faculty members guiding the online courses.

Positive Student Experiences in Online Courses

Much attention and effort has been given to enhancing the experience of online students. Students greatly value the accessibility and flexibility of online courses, especially in asynchronous formats (Boling, Hough, Krinsky, Saleem, & Stevens, 2012; Yang & Cornelious, 2004). Students have expressed that the online format works well for them if they work full-time or if they were unable to physically go to campus (Rodriguez, Ooms, and Montanez, 2008; Yang & Cornelious, 2004). Students generally believe that online education is more cost effective than attending face-to-face courses on campus, because they do not have any transportation or meal-related expenses associated with their education (Allen & Seamen, 2008; Deming et al., 2015; Kilburn, Kilburn, & Cates, 2014).

Beyond this, students appreciate the freedom of online discussion boards and find they enhance student learning (Cheng, Pare, Collimore & Jordens, 2011). Discussion boards allow greater opportunity for students to share their own experiences, especially for students who may not be confident enough to raise their hands in a traditional face-to-face classroom (Petrides, 2002; Sun, Tsai, Finger, Chen, & Yeh, 2008). Online students tend to have less self-consciousness about their contributions to class discussions when compared to their peers in face-to-face classrooms, who worry about how other students perceive them in class. Thus, online students feel more freedom to express themselves in online environments (Vonderwell, 2003) and through the nature of asynchronous learning have the opportunity to better reflect and formulate their thoughts before engaging in dialogue (Hill, Song, & West, 2009).

With regards to academic rigor, online students perceive these courses to have an added layer of complexity because of the emphasis on writing in online courses (Boling et al., 2012; Ni, 2013). In typical face-to-face classes, students interact with each other both physically and verbally; however, they typically only express their thoughts in writing to the instructor. In online courses, students have the opportunity to share their written reflections with their peers, which adds value to the student experience (Vonderwell, 2003). To this end, students value their opportunity to carefully craft written responses to more accurately reflect their ideas in the asynchronous online environment. Furthermore, students also believe this exercise allows them to better grasp the content of the online course.

Despite being in an online environment, pedagogical practices often involve students interacting with one another synchronously in live time (in-person, phone, or video conferencing). These social exchanges with other students, as well as assignments that involved real-world scenarios, are well-received by online students (Boling et al., 2012; Boss & Krauss, 2014; Jaggars & Xu, 2016). Furthermore, students favor activities that push them to interact with others in the community. This helps make up for the absence of a physical classroom community, which is one of the main motivations for students to engage in face-to-face learning (Boling et al., 2012).

Negative Student Experiences in Online Courses

While much literature illustrates the positive experiences of online students, there are other perspectives to the contrary. These negative perceptions can lead to online students being unsuccessful academically and in turn a decline in motivation and ultimate persistence (Kauffman, 2015). Students value and benefit from varied instructional methods in their online courses (Boling et al., 2012; Liu, Liu, Lee, & Magjuka, 2010). However, the experience described by online students does not always meet this expectation. Most online coursework described by students revolves around instructor distributed text-based content, often in the form of lectures or readings, with less interaction. Students share this style of teaching and learning leads to monotony (Boling et al., 2012; Sansone, Fraughton, Zachary, Butner & Heiner, 2011). Furthermore, students argued that this simplified structure tends to overload them with reading and stifle creative thinking while promoting academic regurgitation and less application (Boling et al., 2012).

Similarly, online students have shared that text-based content that promoted individualized learning (in place of interaction) was found to be less helpful than the varied pedagogical strategies professors often used in F2F classroom (Boling et al., 2012). Students also feel less of a connection to their instructors, course content, and classmates when online courses feature less interaction (Boling et al., 2012; Stuber-McEwen, Wisely, & Hoggatt, 2009). Students genuinely want to feel a connection: to each other, to the instructor, and to the university. This feeling is best described by one the participants in the study conducted by Boling et al. (2012) who stated, "I really wanted to feel a connection… like I was a part of the school… like I was a student and not just somebody sitting in her home somewhere" (p. 123).

As expected, online students note they generally do not experience the same social structure of a face-to-face classroom in an online format. Students do not feel the same "person to person interaction" online that they experience face-to-face; rather, they perceive it to be a "computer to computer interaction" (Vonderwell, 2003, p. 84). Students want to feel a one-on-one connection with their instructor. Yet, students have shared feelings of online instructor absence and the need to teach themselves (Jaggars, 2014). To this end, it is not surprising that students also express a desire for immediate, engaged, and individualized instructor feedback (Boling et al., 2012; Eom & Ashill, 2016). While students in a face-to-face classroom can generally obtain immediate feedback from an instructor or fellow student (by raising one's hand and receiving a response, for example), this method is generally not present in an asynchronous online classroom. Graham, Cagiltay, Lim, Craner, and Duffy (2001) and Vonderwell (2003) found that faculty response rates to students decreased over the duration of the semester. That is, students received prompt feedback in the beginning of the semester, but the frequency of feedback faded throughout the semester and students noticed this change. This is particularly disconcerting as more recently it has been shown that responding in a timely manner and providing timely feedback is very important to online students (Sheridan & Kelly, 2010).

While aspects of the discussion board activities are perceived positively by online students, they also express concerns and frustrations with these discussion activities (Boling et al., 2012; Vonderwell, 2003). Students have noted that many strategies to promote engagement felt inauthentic because they were teacher-driven (Boling et al., 2012). This included discussion board activities in which student grades were negatively impacted by non-participation (Boling et al., 2012). While some students find discussion board activities to be a worthwhile experience, others express that student answers were repetitive, lacked immediate discourse, and were not beneficial to the learning experience (Vonderwell, 2003). In other words, it was "busy work" for the sake of doing it. Students also doubt the content provided by other students, and they instead place more value on the expertise of the instructor (Petrides, 2002). Reinforcing these previous findings of Vonderwell (2003) and Petrides (2002), the recent study by Cho and Tobias (2016) found the inclusion of discussion boards had no influence on course satisfaction or student achievement. However, both Cho and Tobias (2016) and Akcaoglu and Lee (2016) found that discussion boards do positively influence feelings of social presence and group cohesion.

Perhaps the greatest concern for online education stems from the struggle's students can have with technical issues in online courses (Beaudoin, 2016; Wang, 2014; Wingo, Ivankova, & Moss, 2017). There are students who are less comfortable with computers or technology, and the technical support they need exceeds the scope of the instructor. While the instructor cannot control some of those technical issues, they are responsible for their organization of their online learning environment (Vai & Sosulski, 2015).

Acknowledging this, it is disconcerting that students have found poor course design and an inability to locate the necessary resources as struggles and barriers to their success in online courses (Eom & Ashill, 2016; Yang & Cornelious, 2004). Educators who develop these online courses should give attention to intentional design, creating an online community that fosters cohesion, and keeping familiar with emerging technology (Sun & Chen, 2016).

THE TRANSITION FROM TEACHING F2F TO ONLINE

While I would like to say the opportunities and experiences I was fortunate to have throughout my doctoral program were intentional, truthfully, they were anything but that. Haphazardly, I stumbled into elective courses that lead to developing faculty mentor relationships, opportunities to collaborate and be a part of scholarship, and learning from faculty who epitomize the notion of teacher-scholars. I stumbled into elective courses that lead me to develop faculty mentor relationships which provided me the opportunity to collaborate on scholarly works and learn from those who epitomize the notion of teacher-scholars. Though I did not recognize this at the time, the credentialing process of earning a terminal degree and engaging with these faculty mentors afforded me many privileges and opportunities those outside of the "one percent club" of terminal degree holders do not get to partake in.

As I completed my doctoral coursework and embraced (for better and/or worse) the three heavy letters of ABD, I was presented with several opportunities to teach undergraduate and graduate level courses as an adjunct. Little did I know that these experiences teaching would have such a great impact on me and help me find my true calling – to be a full-time faculty member. As I continued to teach courses each semester as an adjunct, it did not occur to me to become a full-time faculty member; rather, I viewed my continued career path to be as an administrator who would regularly adjunct. It was during this time that I was approached by a colleague who asked if I would consider applying for a newly created non-tenure track position to develop a graduate program for the discipline in which I served as an administrator for and taught adjunct courses within. As I moved into this position, I quickly realized my passion to be a faculty member and knew I wouldn't look back.

This non-tenure track position focused exclusively on program administration and teaching. There were no formal requirements for traditional faculty service nor scholarship expectations. My teaching load was a 2-2-2 (two courses in the fall, two in the spring, and two in the summer). The majority of the courses in the program were taught in a face-to-face environment over a 15-week semester, with classes being held in the evenings. This non-tenure track position reinforced my desire (and ability) to become a faculty member – which propelled me to move into a tenure track (TT) position at another institution. In this role as Assistant Professor, I have the typical faculty expectations to meet the "three legs" of the academy: teaching, scholarship, and service. While the program is almost identical in terms of content and curriculum to my previous non-tenure track position, the majority of the courses in the program are taught exclusively online. My teaching load is a 3-3-X, where I teach three courses online in the fall, three online in the spring, and have the option to teach courses in the summer.

When offered this TT Assistant Professor position, I was excited about every aspect of the offer (i.e. the reputation of the university, soon-to-be colleagues, types of students in the program, university commitment to teaching, etc.) except the one red flag I could not ignore – teaching online. I had serious reservations not only about whether I would I enjoy teaching online, but if I could actually do it and do it well. This concern was reinforced by the fact that it was my experience being IN the classroom teaching face-to-face that helped me realize my calling and passion to be a faculty member. Would this be the same in an online environment? How would I build relationships with students? How would I engage them? And most importantly, how would I ensure I have prepared them to be effective practitioners who will be working in face-to-face environments?

SOLUTIONS AND RECOMMENDATIONS

In answering these questions, my experience of transitioning from teaching F2F to online was that of trial and error. This was very much so a learning process for me – one that I embraced with an academic curiosity and persistence. I learned as much, if not more, from my failures as I did my initial successes in this transition. As I reflect on this transition, my experiences and insights revolve around four themes:

1. Good Teachers Transcend the Learning Format
2. Planned Intentionality
3. Paralleled Experience
4. Instructor Availability

Good Teachers Transcend the Learning Format

While I had apprehensions about transitioning from teaching F2F to a fully online environment, I have come to realize that good teachers transcend any learning environment. Teachers who care about students, are passionate to teach, responsive to student needs, have great interpersonal skills, are timely in communication, and view themselves as educators will likely be successful regardless of the medium. Palmer (2017) reinforces this assertion, stating "good teaching cannot be reduced to technique; good teaching comes from the identity and integrity of the teacher" (p.10). For myself, this can be seen in the comparison of the aggregated Student Ratings of Instruction (SRI) between the F2F and online courses I have taught. While the SRI's for these two institutions varied greatly in terms of the questions they posed to students, the four consistent questions were:

- How well were the course materials organized?
- How organized/prepared was the professor?
- How accessible was the professor (in and out of class)?
- The overall rating of the professor?

Supporting this assertion that good teachers transcend any medium are the findings from the SRI data between the nine courses I previously taught F2F compared to the nine courses I have taught as I transitioned to exclusively online (Figure 1). The nature of the comparison of this SRI data is "apples-to-apples", as these were all graduate level courses within the same academic discipline/curriculum. The only difference was F2F vs. online.

Figure 1. The student ratings of instruction comparing nine face-to-face courses with nine online courses. The ratings are a Likert-scale with five being the highest/best

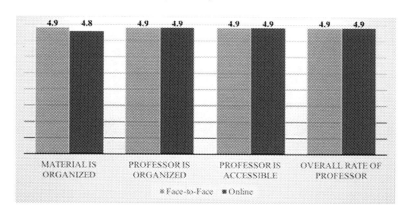

Planned Intentionality

I have always had a love for syllabus development. I ascribe to the belief it serves primary purposes; a contract for learning, a permanent record, and most importantly a tool for learning (Parkes & Harris, 2002). While other faculty groan at the idea of creating and updating their syllabi, I look forward to it each semester. This may come from my love of puzzles and solving riddles, but I feel the quest for developing the perfect syllabus is like the quest for the Holy Grail. We strive for it and make progress towards it, but ultimately, we'll never accomplish it. Nor should we. We are continually learning of new pedagogical practices, innovations in technology, changes within the curriculum and practices of our respective disciplines, and most importantly – the evolution of the needs and learning styles of our students.

With all that being said, I believe the nature of online courses warrants the need for more extensive planning prior to the semester beginning. Supporting this, it has been found that faculty believe it is time consuming and difficult to transfer a F2F course to the online medium (Ray, 2009). While this is obviously true for courses that open fully (having all content accessible at once) and allow students to progress at their own pace, it is also true for courses that open modules/sections at intervals over the course of the semester. From my experience, I have found my online students often seem to be more rigid and distressed with mid-semester changes compared to my F2F students. I think this is simply the product of the way online students have to structure their learning, along with a greater desire for autonomy and responsibility for self-directed learning.

One of the areas I put the most attention to when transitioning to teaching online was learning in-depth how to use every feature of the Learning Management Systems (LMS) that my new university used. While this happened to be Desire2Learn, there are a plethora of platforms out there including BlackBoard, Canvas, Sakai, etc. Thankfully, learning how to use an LMS was not part of my learning curve. As a F2F instructor, I integrated my courses through the LMS, so I had this experience in my favor as I transitioned to teaching online. However, despite being a self-proclaimed "techy", I did have the expected struggles of learning another LMS at my new institution. Despite my comfortability using several previous LMS', this is an aspect of teaching (especially online) that should not be underscored. It takes a significant amount of time and attention to learn to use the LMS, especially to the point to where it feels like a seamless experience from the student perspective. This success is reinforced throughout my SRI data. For example, one student commented:

I really appreciate how organized the course is. Each module has everything you need to know in one place, and there's no navigating between 10 different pages. I also think it's really nice that you do greeting videos to simply say hello and introduce the material for the week. You have been able to make an online course feel more personable than most in-person courses, so thank you!

As I developed my courses in the LMS, I was intentional in my planning and design. I recognized this would be the "face" of the class – not me as the instructor in a F2F that students saw each week in class. It was imperative to me to create an intuitive course layout that was engaging. As I structured my online courses for the 15-week semester, I broke each course down into 15 modules which corresponded with the respective week (i.e. Week 7 = Module 7). Each module contained the following components:

- Welcome video from me where I shared class updates and what was new with me professionally/personally
- Narrated PPT of the lecture I would give in class if it were F2F
- Task list of everything they must complete that week for the module
- Upcoming deadlines for assignments with hyperlinks to their descriptions
- Section for announcements/reminders
- Reminder that students can schedule a meeting with me at any point.

A video tutorial for the organization and navigation of my online courses can be found at tinyurl.com/Tolman-LMS. In the students' SRI feedback, one student shared, "He provided video's each week speaking to the class about the expectations of the week and he just spoke to the class like he would to a class in the classroom." Another student shared:

We were greeted each week with a short video that outlined what to expect the upcoming week. He prepared narrated PowerPoint presentations each week to accompany our lectures to give us the best "in class experience out of class". He was very engaged with the class and responded promptly to questions and comments.

Similarly, another student shared:

I think being an online class, it is easy to get caught up in just going through the motions and not getting excited about the material. There were several things that I liked about this course. The first was the introductory videos each week that are sometimes not even about the material but rather, what book he was reading or just something about his children. I thought that put a nice personal touch on the class.

Paralleled Experience

As I reflect on my experience teaching F2F, I think what greatly contributed to the student learning was the engaging discussions and activities that I orchestrated in the classroom. As is true in many graduate programs, while as the instructor I certainly have a wealth of knowledge, so does each individual in the class. It is the collectiveness of these experiences and inquiry that leads to engaged and effective teaching and learning. Recognizing this, when adapting my F2F teaching to online methods, I intrinsically believed that I needed to provide these same experiences to my online students. However, I quickly learned that trying to manipulate the online format to replicate what takes place in a physical classroom was like trying to place a square peg into a round hole.

It was at that point I realized that my F2F and online courses should not replicate one another, but rather the learning should parallel one another through the respective medium. This led me to focus on what I wanted the students to learn and from there using appropriate pedagogical practices for the online medium. Student feedback affirmed my focus on creating a paralleled experience, as they shared in the SRI feedback, "He does a wonderful job of morphing an online environment into a traditional environment and you can tell he puts great work into maintaining this environment throughout the term. He provides a model of online learning." and "I love the recorded lecture videos makes you feel like you are actually in a seminar course."

Instructor Availability

I have found that instructor availability, or perhaps more importantly, the perception of availability, is one of the fundamental components to successfully teaching online (Ladyshewsky, 2013; Richardson, Besser, Koehler, Lim, & Strait, 2016; Richardson, Koehler, Besser, Caskurlu, & Mueller, 2015; Sheridan & Kelly, 2010). In a F2F environment, students are afforded the opportunity to simply ask questions before/after class or to physically stop by the professor's office hours. For online students, this lack of a physical presence can be a barrier and create a sense of isolation for the student. To this end, it can cause them to feel they are in an "online abyss" and must sink or swim on their own. To proactively combat this feeling, I have incorporated two primary mechanisms into my online courses.

Firstly, I intentionally send out personalized emails to students at key periods of the semester. This includes an email prior to the class beginning, an email once the class begins, and follow up emails at weeks two, seven, and ten. Not only do these emails show students I care enough to reach out to them individually, but it also serves as a prompt for them to reply with challenges or questions they're having in the class or outside of it (i.e. questions about the academic program, troubles they're having academically, career advice, etc.). While students frequently reply to these emails with the concerns and questions, they may not have felt compelled to reach out on their own without seeing an email in their inbox from me.

Secondly, in an effort to provide students with a sense of connectedness to me as their professor and advisor, I have implemented the use of scheduling software that enables students to have direct access to my calendar and schedule appointments at their convenience. Whenever students would like to meet with me, they don't need to ask; instead, they can go directly to my youcanbook.me website to schedule an appointment (Figure 3). This expedites their meeting with me as it eliminates the back-and-forth of emails between professor and student to request and schedule the meeting. Students are able to select an in-person, phone, or Skype meeting. In recognition of their personal, academic, and professional work commitments, I provide generous availability including evening and weekend hours. The effort here was noticed and well received by students. In the students SRI feedback, students shared, "He provides amble [sic] opportunities for students to meet or speak with him and is highly engaging (which is hard in a mostly online format)." and "He made his self-available anytime for us to talk to him in any which way we liked! He is the best hands down!"

Figure 2. The YouCanBook.Me site which allows students to schedule in-person, phone, or Skype meetings at their convenience

ONLINE LEARNING: VOICES FROM STUDENTS AND WORDS OF WISDOM

While these have been my experiences as a tenure-track faculty member transitioning from teaching F2F to Online, I would be remiss to leave out the experience and voice of the most important individuals – the students. To this end, four students who have participated in a variety of online course with me (and other faculty) have shared their experiences below.

Student #1: Doctoral Student

My experience in online courses has featured both positive and negative experiences. I did not take any online courses throughout my undergraduate degree program nor my master's program. Consequently, I was a bit intimidated to join a doctoral cohort that featured some fully online coursework. Mostly, I was not sure what to expect and perhaps lacked confidence that my success in other educational formats would carry over. I always enjoyed traditional face-to-face classes, and I valued the dedicated time each week devoted to learning the subject material in a physical classroom with an instructor present. This method certainly increased my own personal accountability in my learning. Moving to an online format, I worried about how it might impact my learning experience. From possible miscommunications between students and/or instructors to a reduced sense of personal accountability via lack of physical presence in the learning environment, I feared that the online format may not be for me. Quickly, I learned that while the online learning environment did indeed possess a different feel, the adjustment was not overwhelming.

Several components of my online courses led to more positive experiences. The online courses that I have taken have all been asynchronous, meaning that I did not have any required course-related meeting times. This added a great deal of flexibility to my experience, allowing me to complete coursework on my own schedule (in accordance with course-mandated due dates). Online coursework also allowed me to interact with a more diverse group of students. By conducting coursework in a virtual environment, I was able to interact with students from many different backgrounds which really enriched my educational experience. Finally, I had instructors teach online courses who really took advantage of the online platform to shape their courses in a way that compared favorably to face-to-face courses. That is, instructors were able to implement technology and media in various ways, create and build student engagement, and deliver content effectively.

However, not every online course was a positive experience. Some online instructors did not possess the training or experience necessary to conduct an effective course in an online setting. These instructors were often unable to utilize media effectively to enhance the learning atmosphere and promote engagement. One unfortunate component of an online course is that the structure provides an opportunity for instructors and students to have lazy tendencies and be less accountable than they would otherwise be in a face-to-face course. This can leave students feeling disgruntled, as if they are not receiving the quality education they paid for. It is important that students and instructors come to an agreement on course expectations so as to maximize the greater learning experience.

Reflecting on both my positive and negative experiences in online courses, several recommendations come to mind. As a student, it is easy to look at the instructor and list off areas he or she could improve upon to enhance the learning experience. However, the instructor's tendencies are ultimately out of the student's control. As a result, I also think it is critical to look in the mirror and consider what I, the student, can do to positively impact my own learning experience. What can I do to promote my own engagement in the course content and positively influence my own learning in an online environment? How can I be accountable for my own learning experience? In an online environment that may not guarantee engagement or interaction, I think students need to sometimes be willing to go above and beyond to achieve the access and opportunities they desire. Yes, it is important for instructors to do what they can to create an engaging environment, but I think the student is an equal part of the puzzle to creating meaningful experiences in online courses.

Student #2: Graduate Student

As I reflect on the online classes that I have taken as part of my master's program, I can think of both positive and negative experiences I have had with this type of teaching platform. I was hesitant at first to complete an online master's, as I learn best by listening to discussions and interacting with others. However, the program I wanted to complete was only offered online so I had no other option but to go for it. After completing a few classes, I realized what was more important than the learning platform was the faculty member's engagement with the class and the sense of community that was built among the class participants. At the beginning of each term, I am eager for the class to start and dive right into the syllabus to see what the expectations are for the class but, more importantly, what assignments we will be completing and when they are due. I have to admit, there has been more than one semester I sighed after reading the syllabus, knowing that the class was going to be boring. The syllabus came across as uninspiring and uninteresting. Now, granted, it may have had something to do with the content of the class, but I believe that even the most boring of content can be tweaked to peak students' interest and engage them from the start. Unfortunately, this has not always been my experience.

In one class, we completed the same assignment every week. Read the chapter, take a quiz. We posted one discussion post at the beginning of the term to verify attendance, but no other discussion posts were required. I felt very disconnected from the class and gained little knowledge from the readings. There was no reason to actively engage with the text. Another negative experience was in a class where we read the week's reading from the textbook and then completed a 50-75 multiple-choice quiz that was created by the textbook company. We took two to three quizzes per week based on the amount of assigned reading. Any images or graphs that were associated with the quiz were not supported by our university's online platform, so we were forced to make a random guess since we were unable to see all of the question. The professor responded to a discussion post early on in the term but never again. This type of course setup was disheartening and left me ending the class with no real understanding of what I learned, or if I learned anything.

By far, the best classes I have taken are the ones where the faculty member is actively engaged in the class and is able to portray his/her love of the material to the students. When that happens, I find I am highly motivated to learn and readily accept more challenging projects because I know the faculty member cares about my learning and is not assigning a random project just to enter a grade in the gradebook. One professor consistently posted in our discussion posts and made comments that were thoughtful and pushed me to think further about my posts. This same professor provided timely and constructive feedback, which gave me a clear sense of how I was performing in the class and what I could do to improve. Feedback is crucial from faculty as well as fellow students. An environment which promotes interaction among the class is ideal, whether it is through discussion posts, video posts, or collaborating on projects (I prefer working with one or maybe two other students due to the nature of online master's programs where many of the students are working full-time or have families to work around. It can be tough to find a time that all parties are available when groups are larger).

The online communication tools that faculty incorporate into their virtual classrooms pave the way for greater engagement and better understanding of the content. Because of this, I recommend that instructors use up-to-date technological tools like Google Hangouts to encourage interactions between class participants, so all involved feel a sense of connection. This connection will promote learning and increase student participation. When students do not feel part of the classroom environment, they are less motivated and do not retain as much information. The functionality of an online learning platform is vital because when the mechanism for delivering course instruction is not functioning properly, students become frustrated and unfocused. In my opinion, professors should take the time to create quizzes, tests, and materials that work cohesively with the online platform and are tailored to the content being asked to learn versus generic content from a company. A factor that negatively impacts online learning is untimely responses from faculty as it can cause students to lose interest and feel uninspired to perform well in the course as well as learn the content.

Student #3: Graduate Student

I am an auditory learner, so I was nervous about the prospect of pursuing a degree fully-online. During my undergraduate career, I enjoyed the easy access to my professors before and after class, being able to discuss with classmates immediately upon learning new material and taking notes in class during face-to-face instruction. This transition from face-to-face learning to communicating via mostly computer screen was challenging but, in my opinion, well worth the cost.

The most beneficial part of completing my master's program online was the flexibility that it offered. I wanted to pursue a degree but could not afford to quit my job and go back to school full-time. At the time I began thinking about getting my masters, I was a college admissions recruiter; a job that took me miles out of town most weekdays, often for two to three weeks at a time. The online program offered me the flexibility to take classes that would have been impossible for me to attend if they were your typical Monday, Wednesday, Friday, in-person college course. My hotel room became my classroom and the coffee shop down the street became my library. I could even take a vacation and not worry about missing a quiz or getting behind on new material. My learning environment was versatile- something a face-to-face classroom could not ever offer me.

Additionally, an online learning environment helped improve both my writing and communication skills. Simply because of the nature of an online environment, I was challenged to write more often and to communicate my thoughts via written discussion posts on a weekly basis. I quickly learned the importance of proper, concise and clear language when communicating online. I was also asked often to produce scholarly writing that required the use of APA formatting, the expected standard in research. This helped me become a more organized writer and aided in communicating my thoughts more clearly. Because of the various means of communication the online environment allowed, I am more comfortable with my own writing and I'm no longer afraid to conduct and produce research.

While I enjoyed taking online courses, there were some unexpected challenges they posed. Online courses do offer flexibility, but they offer very little accountability if you don't know your classmates well. I missed the comradery of a cohort to experience face-to-face learning with me and then continue to push me outside the classroom. While I was able to meet some of my classmates through recruitment travel for my job, most of us were living in different cities, had varying work experiences and personal lives, and knew little about one another other than our initial introduction discussion post. Often, professors would assign a group project that was almost impossible to complete because of distance or difficulty finding time to communicate. I didn't realize how much I would miss the community of learners I was surrounded by in a normal classroom environment until it was no longer as easily accessible in an online environment.

Perhaps the most frustrating part of taking online courses was the repetitiveness of course content and assignments. It is important to add variety to course content, as it seems most online courses are simply reading then responding to discussion prompts, week after week. I'm ashamed to share that there were some courses where I grew so tired of our weekly discussion post that I would calculate how many I could skip and still get an "A" in the class! My favorite courses included not just reading and responding via typed out discussion posts, but opportunities to chat with my classmates via video or select my assignment from a list of options. When I could select an assignment, I felt like I could take ownership of it and cater the assignment toward my current job/role. Practical application was important to me as a student, but I feel as though only a few of my classes gave me the flexibility to make assignments relevant to my job. There is value in discussion posts, but offering varying assignments like video posts, lectures, small projects or interviews as an alternative will assist online students to stay engaged and find assignments to be more valuable.

Because of this, my recommendation to improve online courses would be for professors to consider their students' varying learning styles when creating assignments and offering the opportunity for students to select assignments that best fit their learning style. Because students typically know how they learn best, offering the chance for them to select assignments will boost confidence and aid in remaining engaged in their learning. Professors should consider the wide range of backgrounds likely present in an online setting and offer opportunities that support all learning types and demographics.

Student #4: Graduate Student

As both an undergraduate and graduate student, I've taken fully in-person, fully online, and blended courses, with those blended courses also featuring both synchronous and asynchronous elements. As an undergraduate student, I was initially skeptical of the prospect of taking online courses. In my mind, true learning could only occur in the classroom, engaging with a professor in person or discussing ideas with peers. My preconception of online courses was that they were "easy A's", a space where students could do minimal work with minimal accountability and where professors could do the same. This was based partially on anecdotes from friends, but more broadly from my bias that online spaces where illegitimate compared to physical classrooms.

After first needing to take an online course to fulfill a requirement during my junior year of college, I cannot say that I've become an apologist for them; however, I now believe that, when executed well by professors and taken seriously by students, online courses can produce meaningful learning.

Often during my online courses, professors would assign students a reading or pose a question and ask us to post a response and comment on our classmates' posts'. This was always asynchronous, wherein students would post at their own pace within a given timeframe (ex: requiring responses to be posted at any point in a week timeframe). At times, it felt as if I were posting into a void, developing a response that would never be read. I would also see classmates comment on posts by saying little more than "Great point! I hadn't thought of that before", followed by a bare minimum addition in order to receive credit for the week. My most positive experiences with online discussions have come when professors set clear expectations for the breadth and depth of posts/comments, and when they would also comment on a few posts with their own thoughts and follow-up questions. It was exciting to log onto our e-learning portal, see professors had read and responded to posts, and start sub-threads discussing ideas with them. The internet is often decried for its anonymizing influence, yet it also democratizes spaces. At least for me, it felt as if we were all on equal footing with our professors in these online forums, assuming identities as fellow scholars learning from and challenging each other.

Professors in online graduate classes I have taken have also required us to log on for live video lectures at a specific time and date (an example of synchronous online learning). In these instances, the central display on the screen would be of the professor's presentation for the week, and students could be seen via their webcams. One issue I saw with this format is that students often had technological challenges preventing them from being seen on a webcam or being heard, meaning they could only utilize an online chat feature to engage. This made for difficult class facilitation as the professor would need to monitor the chat room while teaching to see what questions students had, all while students who had webcams and microphones had a different type of dialogue that could drown out the chat. I also suspect that at least a few students misrepresented their technological challenges so that they could be less accountable in these spaces, which poses its own set of challenges. Looking back, I think the issue with this approach was that professors believed that the online space could be set up to mirror the physical classroom exactly, meaning that their teaching style would not need to adapt at all to an online environment. It seems to me that fully online courses are by definition and necessity different from classes held in rooms, and that professors could achieve more successful academic experiences by adapting their teaching and assessment methods to that.

My recommendation for professors of online courses is to set clear expectations for student performance and engagement. Furthermore, those expectations should be developed while keeping in mind the unique landscape of online learning, with all of the potential benefits and challenges it provides. Students should know that their work and ideas do not go into a void in an online class; that the professor is equally engaged as they would be in person. On a related note, professors should take steps to set up e-learning portals (like Canvas, Webcampus, etc.) that are comprehensive, offering class resources and technology tutorials that students can reference throughout the course. Online learning may not offer an identical experience to in-person learning, but it can offer one that is equally rich and edifying for students.

FUTURE RESEARCH DIRECTIONS

Online learning has (re)shaped the landscape of higher education and will continue to evolve as new innovative pedagogical practices are developed. To this end, continued research on all aspects of online education are warranted and will help to further strengthen the form of learning. Recognizing the growing number of online programs at all levels (undergraduate, graduate, and doctoral), there is a need to explore the support services that are afforded to online students. Furthermore, the work of student affairs professionals who are responsible for the experience of students outside the classroom should establish mechanisms to engage online students in the campus community just like they do students on the physical campus. This development of programs and resources will be strengthened through program evaluation and empirical research.

CONCLUSION

It is no longer a question of whether online education will "catch on", instead, the question is to what extent online education will continue to (re)shape the landscape of higher education. To be clear, it is not unrealistic to posit that not only will the numbers of online learners continue to grow, but in the future, they could become the majority of students taking courses in colleges and universities. Regardless of whether online education will ultimately dominate the academy, it is clear this medium for learning is here to stay (and will likely continue to grow). To this end, textbooks and chapters like this one serve as great primers to challenge current and future faculty to think about what it means to teach online and how to do it well. As on online faculty member who has a passion for teaching online, I am excited you are reading this chapter, as it gives me hope for the future of online educators, as you clearly care enough to further your knowledge in teaching online.

REFERENCES

Akcaoglu, M., & Lee, E. (2016). Increasing social presence in online learning through small group discussions. *The International Review of Research in Open and Distributed Learning, 17*(3), 1-17.

Allen, E., & Seaman, J. (2013). *Changing course: Ten years of tracking online education in the United States*. Newburyport, MA: Sloan Consortium.

Allen, E., & Seaman, J. (2016). *Online report card: Tracking online education in the United States.* Babson Survey Research Group Report. Retrieved from https://onlinelearningconsortium.org/read/online-report-card-tracking-online-education-united-states-2015

Ascough, R. S. (2002). Designing for online distance education: Putting pedagogy before technology. *Teaching Theology and Religion, 5*(1), 17–29. doi:10.1111/1467-9647.00114

Beaudoin, M. (2016). Issues in distance education: A primer for higher education decision makers. *New Directions for Higher Education, 2016*(173), 9–19. doi:10.1002/he.20175

Boling, E. C., Hough, M., Krinsky, H., Saleem, H., & Stevens, M. (2012). Cutting the distance in distance education: Perspectives on what promotes positive, online learning experiences. *Internet and Higher Education, 15*(2), 118–126. doi:10.1016/j.iheduc.2011.11.006

Boss, S., & Krauss, J. (2014). *Reinventing project-based learning: Your field guide to real-world projects in the digital age*. Eugene, OR: International Society for Technology in Education.

Cheng, C. K., Paré, D. E., Collimore, L. M., & Joordens, S. (2011). Assessing the effectiveness of a voluntary online discussion forum on improving students' course performance. *Computers & Education, 56*(1), 253–261. doi:10.1016/j.compedu.2010.07.024

Cho, M. H., & Tobias, S. (2016). Should instructors require discussion in online courses? Effects of online discussion on community of inquiry, learner time, satisfaction, and achievement. *The International Review of Research in Open and Distributed Learning, 17*(2), 123-139.

Deming, D. J., Goldin, C., Katz, L. F., & Yuchtman, N. (2015). Can online learning bend the higher education cost curve? *The American Economic Review, 105*(5), 496–501. doi:10.1257/aer.p20151024

Eom, S. B., & Ashill, N. (2016). The determinants of students' perceived learning outcomes and satisfaction in university online education: An update. *Decision Sciences Journal of Innovative Education, 14*(2), 185–215. doi:10.1111/dsji.12097

Graham, C., Cagiltay, K., Lim, B. R., Craner, J., & Duffy, T. M. (2001). Seven principles of effective teaching: A practical lens for evaluating online courses. *The Technology Source, 30*(5), 50–53.

Hill, J. R., Song, L., & West, R. E. (2009). Social learning theory and web-based learning environments: A review of research and discussion of implications. *American Journal of Distance Education, 23*(2), 88–103. doi:10.1080/08923640902857713

Jaggars, S. S. (2014). Choosing between online and face-to-face courses: Community college student voices. *American Journal of Distance Education, 28*(1), 27–38. doi:10.1080/08923647.2014.867697

Jaggars, S. S., & Xu, D. (2016). How do online course design features influence student performance? *Computers & Education, 95*, 270–284. doi:10.1016/j.compedu.2016.01.014

Kauffman, H. (2015). A review of predictive factors of student success in and satisfaction with online learning. *Research in Learning Technology, 23*, 1–13. doi:10.3402/rlt.v23.26507

Kilburn, A., Kilburn, B., & Cates, T. (2014). Drivers of student retention: System availability, privacy, value and loyalty in online higher education. *Academy of Educational Leadership Journal, 18*(4), 1–14.

Ladyshewsky, R. (2013). Instructor presence in online courses and student satisfaction. *International Journal for the Scholarship of Teaching and Learning, 7*(1), 1–23. doi:10.20429/ijsotl.2013.070113

Liu, X., Liu, S., Lee, S., & Magjuka, R. J. (2010). Cultural differences in online learning: International student perceptions. *Journal of Educational Technology & Society, 13*(3), 177–188.

Nguyen, T. (2015). The effectiveness of online learning: Beyond no significant difference and future horizons. *MERLOT Journal of Online Learning and Teaching, 11*(2), 309–319.

Ni, A. Y. (2013). Comparing the effectiveness of classroom and online learning: Teaching research methods. *Journal of Public Affairs Education, 19*(2), 199–215. doi:10.1080/15236803.2013.12001730

Palmer, P. J. (2017). *The courage to teach: Exploring the inner landscape of a teacher's life*. San Francisco, CA: Wiley.

Parkes, J., & Harris, M. B. (2002). The purposes of a syllabus. *College Teaching, 50*(2), 55–61. doi:10.1080/87567550209595875

Petrides, L. A. (2002). Web-based technologies for distributed (or distance) learning: Creating learning-centered educational experiences in the higher education classroom. *International Journal of Instructional Media, 29*(1), 69–77.

Ray, J. (2009). Faculty perspective: Training and course development for the online classroom. *Journal of Online Learning and Teaching / MERLOT, 5*(2), 263–276.

Richardson, J., Besser, E., Koehler, A., Lim, J., & Strait, M. (2016). Instructors' perceptions of instructor presence in online learning environments. *The International Review of Research in Open and Distributed Learning, 17*(4), 82–104. doi:10.19173/irrodl.v17i4.2330

Richardson, J. C., Koehler, A., Besser, E., Caskurlu, S., Lim, J., & Mueller, C. (2015). Conceptualizing and investigating instructor presence in online learning environments. *International Review of Research in Open and Distributed Learning, 16*(3), 256–297. doi:10.19173/irrodl.v16i3.2123

Rodriguez, M. C., Ooms, A., & Montañez, M. (2008). Students' perceptions of online-learning quality given comfort, motivation, satisfaction, and experience. *Journal of Interactive Online Learning, 7*(2), 105–125.

Sansone, C., Fraughton, T., Zachary, J. L., Butner, J., & Heiner, C. (2011). Self-regulation of motivation when learning online: The importance of who, why and how. *Educational Technology Research and Development, 59*(2), 199–212. doi:10.100711423-011-9193-6

Sheridan, K., & Kelly, M. A. (2010). The indicators of instructor presence that are important to students in online courses. *MERLOT Journal of Online Learning and Teaching, 6*(4), 767–779.

Stuber-McEwen, D., Wiseley, P., & Hoggatt, S. (2009). Point, click, and cheat: Frequency and type of academic dishonesty in the virtual classroom. *Online Journal of Distance Learning Administration, 12*(3), 1–10.

Sun, A., & Chen, X. (2016). Online education and its effective practice: A research review. *Journal of Information Technology Education, 15*, 157–190. doi:10.28945/3502

Sun, P.-C., Tsai, R. J., Finger, G., Chen, Y.-Y., & Yeh, D. (2008). What drives a successful e-learning? An empirical investigation of the critical factors influencing learner satisfaction. *Computers & Education, 50*(4), 1183–1202. doi:10.1016/j.compedu.2006.11.007

Twigg, C. A. (2001). *Quality for whom? Providers and consumers in today's distributed learning environment*. Troy, NY: The Pew Learning and Technology Program, Center for Academic Transformation.

Vai, M., & Sosulski, K. (2015). *Essentials of online course design: A standards-based guide*. New York, NY: Routledge. doi:10.4324/9781315770901

Vonderwell, S. (2003). An examination of asynchronous communication experiences and perspectives of students in an online course: A case study. *The Internet and Higher Education, 6*(1), 77–90. doi:10.1016/S1096-7516(02)00164-1

Wang, Y. D. (2014). Building student trust in online learning environments. *Distance Education, 35*(3), 345–359. doi:10.1080/01587919.2015.955267

Weldy, T. G. (2018). Traditional, blended, or online: Business student preferences and experience with different course formats. *E-Journal of Business Education & Scholarship of Teaching, 12*(2), 55–62.

Wingo, N. P., Ivankova, N. V., & Moss, J. A. (2017). Faculty perceptions about teaching online: Exploring the literature using the technology acceptance model as an organizing framework. *Online Learning, 21*(1), 15–35. doi:10.24059/olj.v21i1.761

Yang, Y., & Cornelious, L. F. (2004). Students' perceptions towards the quality of online education: A qualitative approach. *Association for Educational Communications and Technology, 27*, 19–23.

Chapter 7
Online Education Past, Current, and Future

Kieran Chidi Nduagbo
Independent Researcher, USA

ABSTRACT

This chapter addresses the paradigmatic shift in traditional education. It presents a historical overview of online education as a content and framework for understanding its current state and highlights how online education has become entrenched in business and in higher education worldwide. Beginning with distance education's contributions to the paradigmatic shift, this chapter provides a framework for understanding online education. It focuses on the connections and contributions of distance education to present day online education, the current trends in online education, and the projections of the future of online education. This chapter concludes that the nature and practice of online education across the globe will change in the next few years.

INTRODUCTION

Online education grew out of distance education, which has been in existence for the past 100 years. With the development of the Internet and the World Wide Web, online education can now reach students around the globe. Present day online education provides high quality educational resources in various forms of media to students. It supports both real-time and allochronous communication between students and instructors and between diverse students (Means, Toyama, Murphy & Jones, 2010). Institutions of higher learning now view online education as a means of boosting enrollment, aiding student who otherwise would not have been able to attend traditional college/university due to reasons that include distance, jobs, and family-related issues (Wilson, 2015). For students, however, online education is convenient, accessible, it has flexible scheduling, and it has accelerated courses. Additionally, online education provides opportunities for independent study at one's own pace, location, and time. Finally, compared to traditional education, online education allows for a faster degree acquisition, and promotes a high level of accountability for one's own learning (Sit, Chung, Meyric, & Chow, 2005).

DOI: 10.4018/978-1-7998-0115-3.ch007

Overall, online education is growing rapidly. For the past decade, it has grown significantly faster that overall college/university enrollment has grown (Allen & Seaman, 2009) and has remained steady for several years. According to Allen & Seaman (2009), over 4.6 million students were taking at least one online course during the fall of 2008, which represents a 17% increase over the number reported in 2007-fall term. By 2010, the number of college students taking at least one online courses rose to 6.1 million, which represents an increase of 560, or 1000 students more than the number reported in 2009.

WHAT IS ONLINE EDUCATION AND HOW DOES IT WORK?

Online education refers courses in which 80% or more of contents are delivered online via the Internet and without any face-to-face meetings or interactions (Allen & Seaman, 2009; Allen & Seaman, 2011; Wilson, 2015). Online education can be offered in several different ways:

- Synchronous: Students enrolled with this method of online education have the lectures and materials transmitted to them via the Internet at a specified time. Just as in physical classrooms, students in synchronous online education take part in a lecture, discussion, or class activity in real-time from different locations.
- Asynchronous: Here, students have access to pre-recorded lectures and materials given to or not given to a physical audience by an instructor in the form of a video at their own time with deadlines to keep the class on track. In asynchronous online education, students can also be provided with course objectives and a schedule. Additionally, they are allowed to work when they are able to and progress toward weekly or bi-weekly milestones.
- Distance students: Distance students do not have any need to come to campus, except at the end of their online education when they are ready for their final defense.
- Another method of online education is where students enroll as on-campus students, living close to the university or college, but chooses to attend and take courses offered by the university online.
- Free MOOCs: Students can also choose to taking non-credit hour courses offered free of charge through Massive Online Open Courses (MOOCs) by a university without being enrolled in the university. Recently, some higher institutions in the United Stated have started offering the MOOC courses for credit and with stipulations that include enrolling in the university, attending meetings with the instructor, and taking required additional coursework (Lewin, Allen & Seaman, 2015);.

The Early Years of Online Education

Online Education brings together many historical threads-distance learning, computers, and telecommunication. This means that the history of online education dates back much further than the birth of the internet. Online Education also merges educational theory, computer technology, and legislation. All of these play vital roles in the development of online education.

Correspondence Courses

Online education in the United States began with the first correspondence course offered by University of Chicago in the late 1800s. Correspondence courses are courses in which the instructor sends lessons and assignments to a student at a different location by mail and receives completed assignments by mail (McIsaac & Gunawardena, 2001). Prior to this time, education - especially in Europe - was available only to male children of rich elite families. The popular mode of instruction was bringing the male students together at a specified time and location to learn from one instructor. In 1890, notable educators, such as William Rainey Harper, attempted to establish an alternative form of education, but they were unsuccessful. Later, correspondence courses were developed to provide educational opportunities for people who were not from rich elite families and for those who could not afford to reside full-time at institutions of higher learning. At first, many people considered correspondence courses inferior to elite courses. Some educators viewed it as a form of business operations (Pittman, 1991; McIsaac & Gunawardena, 2001). Although many people did not accept correspondence courses at the beginning, it nevertheless later became a vital means of providing equal access to educational opportunities to all students, which is an integral part of our nation's democratic ideals (McIsaac & Gunwardena, 2001).

Industrial Age and Early Computers

The first computers were developed during the Industrial Age (1760-1820). A computer is any device that takes in information and deploys it for a certain outcome based on ordered instructions (History.com Editors, 2009). Historians regard the Industrial Age as the beginning of computers because it was during this period that the first semi-automated computing machines, radios, and motion pictures, which played significant roles in effectiveness of correspondence study, were developed. With the development of radios during World War I and television in the 1950s, people began to have more interest in instruction outside of traditional classrooms (Ferrer, 2013). Radios and television were used for the first time in schools to deliver instructions to students at distant locations. Wisconsin's School of the Air, for example, took the first initiative in the 1920s in engaging in distance learning. Today, audio and computer teleconferencing have influenced instructional delivery in many institutions of learning, universities, community colleges, elementary and secondary schools, military, industry, and business schools. Additionally, institutions of higher learning have established open universities based on a model that was developed in Britain in the 1970's. Universities worldwide are today using media to provide more effective distance education following Charles Wedemeyer's initial use of media in 1986 for instructional delivery to distance learning students (Ferrer, 2013).

In the early 1960's, University of Illinois created a computer system known as the Intranet for its students. The Intranet is a system that connected many computer terminals, making it possible for students to access course materials and to listen to recorded lecture without being physically present. The Intranet later evolved into PLATO (Programmed Logic for Automatic teaching Operations), the initial global computer-assisted instruction system (Woolley, 1994; Ferrer n.d.). University of Illinois used PLATO to offer coursework to its students in elementary school through university. PLATO included valuable pedagogical features, such as text, keywords, and feedbacks intended to respond to alternative answer (Stifle, 1971). Until the late 1970's, PLATO supported graphic terminals distributed worldwide and ran on varied networked mainframe computers (Dear, 2017; Ferrer, 2013). Today's modern idea of multi-user computing, such as forums, message boards, online testing, emails, chat rooms, picture languages, instant messaging, remote screen sharing, and multiplayer games, and MMORPGS was first created on PLATO (Ferrer, 2013, Dear, 2017).

Distance Education

Distance education is the education of students who are not or cannot be physically present at a traditional educational location, such as a classroom or a school (Moore, & Kearsley, 2005; Kang, 2009). During its early years, distance education involved Correspondence Studies and courses. It requires focused planning, organizational systems, teaching and learning systems, which address learning at varied locations. Today, distance education is synonymous to online education in its varied forms. More recent developments in online education include MOOS delivered through the Worldwide Web or other network technologies, e- learning, virtual classroom, and distributed learning, to mention a few.

According to Schlosser & Anderson (1994), distance education has been around for about 175 years. For example, in 1833, an ad in a Swedish newspaper announced the availability of studying "composition through the Post" (Holmberg, 1986; Schlosser & Anderson, 1994). In addition, in 1840, England's penny post granted Sir Isaac Pittman permission to deliver shorthand instruction through correspondence study. Later, in 1843, England legalized distance instruction with the establishment of Phonographic Correspondence Society, which existed before Sir Isaac Pittman's Correspondence Colleges (Holmberg, 1986; Scholsser & Anderson, 1994).

Furthermore, distance education developed in Germany in the form of correspondence study. Two university foreign language instructors, Charles Toussaint and Gustave Langenscheidt, began mailing out letters of correspondence in French to their students in 1856. Immediately after World War I, the percentage of students enrolled in distance education and the types of distance education grew significantly because many people who wanted to make up for lost time during the war enrolled in distance courses, hoping to enhance their scholastic and professional education (Steffen K, 1998).

In the United States in 1873, Anna Eliot Ticknor founded a society called Ticknor Society in Boston, Massachusetts, which was founded to encourage studies at home. The society consisted of a group of women instructing other women through the mail and offered courses in classical studies (Bergman, 2001). Within 24 years, it attracted more than 10,000 students (Schlosser & Anderson, 1994; Watkin, 1991) - mostly women - who enrolled in the classical studies curriculum. Through the mail, these women communicated with their instructors, who provided them with guided readings and recurrent tests on a monthly basis. New York State approved the academic degree of Ticknor students between 1883 and 1891 through Chautauqua College of Liberal Arts after their completion of summer institutes and correspondence courses. (Schlosser & Anderson, 1994). Following the example of the Ticknor Society, Thomas J. Foster, the editor of The Mining Herald, a daily newspaper based in eastern Pennsylvania, started proffering correspondence studies in mining and the prevention of mine accidents. In 20 years' time, Foster's business grew very fast and became an international school with student enrollment skyrocketing from 225,000 in 1900 to more than 2,000,000 in 1920 (Rose, 1991; Schlosser & Anderson, 1994). Meanwhile, correspondence education continued to grow in Europe with the establishment of Hermond's institute in 1898, the development of the Skerry's College in Edinburgh, England in 1978, and the Correspondence College in London in 1887.

Simultaneously, the university extension movement in the United States and in England encouraged correspondence study methods in Wesley, Illinois in 1877 and the University of Chicago in 1892 (Holmberg, 1986; Schlosser & Anderson, 1994). As part of Oxford, Cambridge's and London's models, Wesleyan Illinois provided courses that led to Bachelors, Masters, and doctoral degrees. About 750 students enrolled in Wesleyan from 1881-1890, among which 500 were in the degree programs. Unfortunately, in 1906, Wesleyan was forced to close due to concern regarding its program quality (Watkins, 1991). In the University of Chicago, Correspondence Study was successful in numbers and thus became an essential part of the university. Yearly, 3,000 students enrolled in the 350 correspondence courses offered and taught by 125 professors. Nonetheless, interest in the program gradually started to die out because of financial issues (Schlosser & Anderson, 1994; Watkins, 1991).

Across the globe, distance education began to impact high schools in the 1920s. For example, in the United States, teachers at high schools in Benton Harbor, Michigan provided students with vocation courses, while University of Nebraska experimented with correspondence courses in 1923. That same year, responding to the advent of the war, the French Ministry of Education created a government correspondence college called Centre National d' Eseignment par Correspondence to teach children (Holmberg, 1986; Schlosser & Anderson, 1994). In 1962, University of South Africa became a distance education University. This brought significant changes in the practice of distance education in many parts of the world. Additionally, in 1971, the United Kingdom established Open University, a degree-granting distance education university program providing varied programs, sophisticated courses, and innovative use of media (Holmberg, 1986; Schlosser & Anderson, 1994). Open University also enhanced the status of distance education, promoted the development of similar institutions in the developed world, such as Japan and Germany, and in the developing world, such as Pakistan and Sri Lanka (Schlosser & Anderson, 1994, Holmberg, 1986).

From the onset of distance education, its goal has always been to educate adults with occupational, social and family obligations. Today, this goal has not changed. Distance education still offers adults the chance to broaden their intellectual horizons, and to enhance and upgrade their professional knowledge while emphasizing individuality and flexibility of learning (Schlosser & Anderson, 1994).

The Current Trends in Online Education

Today, online education is entrenched in American higher education and is thriving. It is successfully providing more and more innovative possibilities for diverse students, faculty, and educational institutions across the globe. The majority of what practitioners learn today is already taught in blended courses (Mayadas, Bourne, & Bacsich, 2009). This approach is currently improving pedagogical and teaching methods, and it is decreasing the amount of time it takes to complete a college degree in traditional institutions. Online education today offers superior opportunities and access to education. Many students are already benefiting from it. These opportunities include diverse classes and graduate and postgraduate degrees in varied courses, such as Social Sciences, Arts and Humanities, pure sciences, applied sciences, Engineering and Technology, physical sciences, and Computer Science, to mention but a few (Keebler, 2014).

In an article published in 1995, Eli Noam of Columbia University declared that at the rate people are getting information from the Internet, the Internet would present significant challenges for traditional higher education institutions in the future. Noam also stated, "As one connects in new ways, one also disconnects the old ways" (Noam. 1995 p 247, Mayadas, Bourne & Bacsich 2009). About 28 years after internet was developed and 23 years after Noam's article, online education has become an essential component of education. Today, online learning is rapidly developing in K-12 education settings, and it is already widely used in the cooperate world and in higher institutions across the globe (Mayadas, Bourne, & Bacsich, 2009). In the cooperate world, Professionals us online learning to access short-term training modules, such as new product information, quality practices, orientation, and on-board training that employees can study on their own via their company's Internet. In doing so, businesses are replacing

CD-ROMS and printed materials, and they are simultaneously making distribution efficient and effective (Mayadas, Bourne, & Bacsich, 2009). Higher education institutions, however, uses online education to offer classes that are similar to traditional classes(for example, the cohort program) but are at the same different(hybrid/blended learning). In most institutions, online courses are taught by faculty members, who often require students to be actively involved in class discussion and in the exchange of ideas with other classmates online. For example, students can get help on a problem or request clarification of an assignment from classmates or from the faculty who are in another location via the Internet. This availability of student-to-student, student-to-faculty interactions immediate access to information and resources on the internet and the effective distributions of course materials differentiate current online education from its predecessor distance education (Mayadas, Bourne, & Bacsich, 2009; Bates, 2005). In today's online education, all that students in any part of the world need is a personal computer and an access to the Internet. Students connect to their classes at different times and in different locations. It is not necessary for the faculty to meet with students at a particular location or at a particular time as is with traditional classrooms. Students also use more recent innovative devices such as iPads, Second Life (SL) (online virtual world), mostly in cooperate environments for learning. However, institutions of higher learning are in the experimental stage with these devices (Downes, 2005, Brown & Diaz, 2010)

Presently, online education is changing the way students are taught. Students now learn in an environment that is constantly changing and is full of possibilities. These growing approaches to learning and pedagogy are part of innovative opportunities marked by "Web Mediation" (Ferrer, 2013).The following are some of the most current trends in online education across the globe:

Flipped Classroom

Salman Khan developed Flipped Classrooms, and teachers first used them Khan Academy. As the names indicate, Flipped Classroom turns things around, changing the time that students dedicate to lecture, class, and homework. In Flipped Classroom, students complete their assignments and projects in class. As a result, they always have access to a teacher when they have difficulty with a problem. However, faculty /teacher complete their lesson plans and classwork at home, using videos and on-screen tutorials. Most science and math classes today espouse Flipped Classroom as their model. Many math and science classrooms have adopted this model, made famous by the highly acclaimed founder of Khan Academy Salman Khan and chemistry teachers Jon Bergeman and Aaron Sams (Ferrer, 2013; Khan Academy, 2007; Bergman and Sams, 2012)

Project-Based Learning (PBL)

Project-Based Learning (PBL) is a new method of learning that teaches numerous skills essential for success in the twenty-first century. In PBL, instructors play the role of the facilitator, while students work collectively as a group, researching and constructing projects that mirror their knowledge (Bell, 2010). Learning in PBL occurs through inquiry. Students ask questions, research answers to their questions, and create projects based on knowledge gained from research. Online education today has broadened the use, interest, and benefits of PBL in education. It provides opportunities for students to use programs, such as blogs and Wikipedia, to create projects for public use and consumption. Using online education, students can also create Wiki classes to host their projects. Online PBLs also make gamification of learning easy, according to Kiang and Gee (2003). In gamification, students make some mistakes that have no long-lasting effects, while attempting to achieve their goal and use varied methods. They also go through many routes before achieving success or their goals. Project-based learning has similar characteristics as traditional learning. However, in PBL, the real world provides the many routes, the information, the mistakes or failures, and the success or goals that are needed as students work collaboratively to create their projects (Orlando, 2016).

Collaborative Online Learning

Currently, collaborative learning is progressively becoming very common in many online classrooms. Collaborative learning refers to the idea that students learn better while working together in groups (Ferrer, 2013). It also emphasizes that students learn from each other, through each other, and about each other as they collaborate to finish or complete projects. Realizing this, online educators are now incorporating collaborative learning into their online courses, and students are collaborating more in online education through social media technologies, such as videoconferencing, texting, email, teleconferencing, and workflow programs, including Trello, Slack, ClearSlide, Goggle Docs and Skype. These modern technologies make global collaboration simple and easy(Bowser, Davis, Singleton, & Small, 2017)

Blended Learning or Hybrid Learning

Blended learning has become an exciting instructional learning technique in higher education today. Many institutions now create or seek to create their own hybrid of learning courses as alternatives for students and instructors who wish to replace some part of traditional in-person class meeting time with online instruction (Olapiriyakul & Scher, 2006). Blended or hybrid learning is a combination of in-person class sessions or taking courses on-site with online learning (Kilmova & Kacetl, 2015). It entails delivering curricular materials, providing access to learning resources, and submitting tasks online. In blended learning, online discussion is either allochronic or synchronic in nature (Buzzetto-More & Sweat-Guy, 2006; Ferrer, 2013). At first, blended learning was not widely embraced by institutions of higher learning. However, today, according to Allen and Seaman (2003), the percentage of students registering in hybrid courses is significantly greater than the percentage of students in total online courses. Allen and Seaman (2003) also predicted that in the future, blended learning would continue to make considerable impacts on higher education globally. Other research (Hodges, 2004; Buzzetton-More & Sweat-Guy, 2006; Bhatti, Tubaisahat & El-Quawasmeh, 2005) found that blended learning has vital benefit for students. For example, Hodges, (2004) found that blended learning minimizes the feelings of isolation and frustration often experienced in full online learning. Bhatti, Tubaisahat and El-Quawasmeh (2005) showed that students' satisfaction increased with hybrid learning while their dependency on the instructors decreased. Research also reported that students consider hybrid learning viable, convenient, accessible, and favorable.

Mastery Learning

Many online colleges and schools today use mastery learning. Although the idea of Mastery learning has been around since 1968, when Benjamin Bloom first proposed it, it Khan Academy has made it very popular. Mastery learning is an instructional strategy that advocates the notion that students must master certain levels of performance before moving on to the next level (Slavin, 1987). For example, students must achieve 90% of the concept of knowledge tested before being allowed to move on to study and learn the next information. Thus, in mastery learning students who achieve a 60 or 70 percent must continue to learn a topic, concept, or set of information until they show that they have mastered it by answering at least 90% of the questions correctly before moving on. Many colleges and school that use mastery learning today rely greatly on online tutoring, to make it successful (Ferrer, 2013)

Virtual Learning Environments

Current virtual learning environments (e.g. Moodle, Blackboard, Canvas and Renweb) now extend both the classroom, the instructor's and the administrator's offices. Today educators use Moodle and Blackboard to complete their teaching responsibilities, such as gradebooks, attendance sheets and assessments, and administrative duties like enrollment, updating class lists, sending emails to absent students, tracking payroll and accounting information (Wilcox, Thall, & Griffin, 2017, Ferrer 2013)

Massive Open Online Courses

A more current development in online education that is rapidly gaining media attention is MOOCs. Massive Open Online Courses represent a growing practice of online education, and they were motivated by the philosophy of connectivism (i.e. the belief or idea that the ability to look for current information and the ability to filter secondary and unnecessary information must be present for learning to occur (Rodriguez, 2012). Both students and instructors need to conceptually change their perspective to implement and use it successfully. According to Rodriquez (2012), "massive" refers to the number of participants that can easily have quick access to one online course. For example, "Thousands of students simultaneously engaged in one courses; 'open' is related to several concepts: software as used is open-source, registration is open to anyone, and the curriculum is open or loosely structured and it can even change as the course evolves, the sources of information are open, the assessment processes (if they exit) are open, and the learners are open to range of difficult learning environment" (Rodriquez, 2012, p.3-4). MOOCs offer interactive opportunities for students and teachers. Characteristically, MOOCs do not provide credit or charge tuition. Institutions of higher learning, such as Stanford and MIT, and companies like Coursera and Udacity, provide and offer MOOCs that are currently reaching and educating many people worldwide (Rodriguez, 2012).

Unschooling

An area of innovation in online education originated from the homeschooling movement. Many homeschools use college-level online education, such as dual-enrollment classes, dual-credit classes, or college-level courseware for middle and high school students. Thus, online education has been beneficial in developments in the unschooling movement. Unschooling is a new trend in homeschooling in which students lead the way in directing their learning. Unschooled students learn at home and during fieldtrips. Unschooling is different from homeschool in that parents acts as teachers in homeschooling, directing their children's learning, whereas unschooling operates with the belief that children are naturally curious and will follow their interest in their own way. Thus, children direct their own learning (gary &Riley, 2013). Just like online education technology, which enables an expanded and almost infinite world of exploration, unschooling promotes a borderless world of learning. These current trends in online education are creating innovative avenues for learning and new models for success.

Redesigned Classrooms

Previously, online education entailed chatting with or sending emails back and forth with an instructor. Currently, our classrooms are "tech-savvy and act as smart rooms to facilitate better learning". (Lynch 2018, p.1). These classrooms allow students to interact with instructors in real time and to connect with guest speakers or business partners worldwide (Lynch, 2018)

ONLINE EDUCATION IN THE FUTURE

A country's economy is interlinked with the education system. Thus, for any country to complete successfully in the global market of the future or to be able to keep up with the fast-changing global market, the country needs to strengthen and reform its education system (Lynch 2018). Online education is the future of education at all levels, particularly in higher education. As distance education or learning evolved from cassette tapes and telephone learning to high-speed, interactive Internet learning, online education will provide access to education and learning for students who lack access to traditional education and for students for whom traditional education was not ineffective. The following are anticipated trends in online education in the next 5-10 years.

Course Management System (CMs)

According to Kyong-Jeep & Bonk (2006) Course management system (CMss) will increase substantially in the next few-ten years. Likewise, video streaming, online testing and exam tools and learning objectives libraries would be used greatly on campuses. Educational institutions will be using more videos for open education. These videos will be created so that students can pause and replay them anytime. Moreover, because these videos will be accessible through websites, such as YouTube, students can use them to review and study lesson or lectures that they did not understand in class the previous day. They can play the videos repeatedly until they have a good understanding of the lesson. Additionally, these videos will be very engaging, interactive and interesting so that students will not be bored, as they may be with textbooks. They will encourage students to ask questions that they may not feel comfortable asking in class...

More MOOCS

Ruth (2012) in her study titled Can MOOC's and Other E-Learning Paradigms Help Reduce College Costs. Can MOOC's and Existing E-Learning Efficiency Paradigms Help Reduce College Costs? Parad assert that MOOCS can help to solve the problem of rising costs and inaccessibility of higher education. MOOCS are free online courses, and, as such, they are accessible to everyone who has access to a computer and Internet. In the future, students worldwide will be able to view and join the courses and lectures that are taught in prestigious institutions by accessing MOOCS websites. Currently a not all students across the globe have access to these courses In the future Open Course Ware Courses will be available to all students. Then most students will not have to pay the high tuition that is currently required to attain a high-quality education.

More Adaptive Learning Platforms/Technologies

Adaptive Learning Platforms, such as, Khan Academy and Knewton, will help reshape the face of education in the near future. Currently, these websites already provide online materials for students based on their individual learning styles, thereby helping them to understand lessons or lectures immediately. Bill gates refer to this kind of education as "personalized education. Using adaptive learning platforms, such as Knewton and Khan Academy, students can create their own account, watch videos created by instructors view instructional materials, and answer virtual exams. The instructors, in turn, monitor and track students' progress as necessary. For example, the instructor can assist a student as soon as he or she notices that the student is stuck or is having significant difficulties with algebraic equations for a prolonged period of time (Linardopoulos, 2010). With current enrollment numbers in online higher education growing rapidly, the future of education lies in online education. As institutions of higher learning adapt to serve the increasing number of online learners, they will be making significant progress in educating students across the globe (Lynch 2018).

New Feedback System= Improved Teaching Approach

New Feedback System is a feedback channel that will enable teachers to assess whichever areas of their instructional approach need improvement to help them become more effective. In the future, with the use of this new feedback system, teachers or instructors will receive comprehensive feedback that will customize their methods to help their students learn more and excel in school.

Mobile Learning

In the past, access to online course materials were only possible with desktops or laptop computers. Now and in the future, all online course materials will be very easy to access on varied handheld devices, such as smartphones, iPads, tablets, and chrome books with special educational apps that facilitate instruction (Lynch, 2018), According to a Tehnavio study conducted in 2017, more and more students are enrolling in online education due to mobile access to courses andwith the high penetration of the Internet, students use these handheld devices to access course assignments, lesson plans, and complete coursework (Bogardus Cortez, 2017),

Free College Online: Driven Education

With student loan debts currently increasing to trillions of dollars, college education may change and become free, online-driven education in the future. Additionally, college may begin to align students' skills with in-demand jobs.

Blending the Traditional with the Technological

In the future, the Internet will play much more significant roles in higher education. While people are currently debating the need for traditional college degrees, progress is already being made in integrating traditional college education with online classes. The Internet is gradually becoming a vital learning tool for higher education, and its importance will continue to increase in the future. According to David L. Warren, president of National Association of Independent College and Universities, about 50% of all private colleges in the United States have some kind of online programs blending traditional classroom learning with online learning. This percentage is significantly higher in public institutions of higher learning Bhatti, A., Tubaisahat, A., & El-Qawasmeh, E. (2005 (www.goodcall.com).

Mobile-Friendly Course Content

Present-day online students have smartphones, iPads, or tablets, and the majority of them are already using these devices for their online studies. An International Staff study conducted in June of 2018 revealed that 87% of future or prospective online students use their handheld devices to search for potential programs online, and 67% of online students have completed their online coursework using their smart phones. Thus, higher institutions must adapt their websites and course content to function effectively with mobile platforms if they want to keep pace.

Open Online Courses

Open online courses are examples of what online education will look like in the future. According to Alemi and Maddox (2008), open online courses are courses that are offered and provided completely online. This means that the lectures, assignments, syllabi, class discussions, and projects, are all open for everyone to see online without disclosing students' personal information. Open Online Courses reduce the cost of marketing for higher institutions, and the customer relationship tools reduce the time that faculty spend on individual emails. Additionally, Open Online Courses enhance student-faculty interaction drastically because the provide students with quick and free access to online courses through varied search engines Furthermore, they allows for fast improvements of courses through ongoing feedback from the Internet.

Unlike other online education courses, where access to courses is limited to registered students with password and identifications, open online course provides lectures, assignments, student evaluations and students' comments online without a password or login information. Thus, students and non-students can read the course content without any limitations. Anyone from anywhere can see the video lectures and the software used to evaluate data, listen to instructions on difficult theories, write comments, see answers to questions posted by others, interrelate with other students, and, in some courses, they can even add their own lectures or projects. However, interaction with faculty is strictly limited to students who get grades for their assignments. Unregistered students are not permitted access to these parts of the courses. In open online courses, lectures are assigned as readings materials to students because the courses are not password protected. Faculty from different institutions can also access Open Online Courses, they and are free to use all or some parts of the course materials to teach their own courses. Open online courses have very rich content, are available in searches, and are often found on the first page of the search. Recently, open online courses have become a web destination.

Three –Dimensional Online Education

Three-Dimensional immersive spaces, such as Second Life (SL) are the new faces of online education. According to Staley and Hoffman (2010, p. 167), in the future, people will begin to navigate web spaces instead of webpages. Three-dimensional web spaces will then replace the current 2-dimensional webpages. Already, large corporations, such as Coca Cola, IBM, and Toyota, have purchased real estate inside of SL. Some businesses have tentatively begun to interview prospective candidates in a Second Life (SL) "virtual job fair". (Hoffman, 2010, p Similar to people who hide behind the mask of their avatars and play at different personas inside SL, businesses use the site as a way to play with different products and services or to test out and virtually marketing ideas that they might then launch in the real world (Hemp, 2006). Some institutions of higher learning intend to launch and use virtual spaces to attract prospective students and to permit them to "visit" their campuses without the cost of real trips to the real campus (Joly 2007). Others use virtual campuses to stay connected with their tech-savvy alumni, and some are already experimenting with virtual space as an educational space.

In the past, online education was criticized for not providing students with opportunities for "face-to-face" interaction, which is an important element of the educational experience. Three-dimensional virtual course in an SL-type environment would address this issue. For example, with three-dimensional web spaces, higher education institutions can construct a virtual classroom, seminar room, or theater, where a class of avatars might meet. This type of virtual classroom will replace the complex chat function presently used in most online education settings. In three-Dimensional virtual space students will meet and mingle freely, as in a real space. They can cluster together in groups to chat, work on group projects, or simply listen to a lecture together. As avatars become more communicative, body language, and other nonverbal cues will become possible (Hoffman, 2011, p. 157). Three-dimensional virtual immersive spaces will provide online students the "feeling of presence" that is now nonexistent in today's online education, which has only text and sometimes motionless photographs (New Media Consortium and EDUCAUSE Learning Initiative, 2007: Hoffman, 2011, p. 157).

Globalization of Online Education

Higher education is gradually experiencing the effects of globalization. For example, the demand for higher education is now a global phenomenon, and thus the demand for higher education services currently has no boundaries. Many U.S. institutions of higher learning are currently collaborating with other non-U.S. institutions of higher learning in different parts of the world. United States universities today have regional campuses in places including the Middle East, China, and India (Hoffman, 2010, p. 167). University of Maryland and Phoenix, for example, currently have online presences in Europe and Asia. Although the United States' higher education is currently considered to be the model of higher education worldwide, countries including China, India, and Brazil, which have a growing and steady rise in economic prominence, may in the near future present challenges to United States' prominent role as the leader in higher education. Chinese universities, for example already have their own version of online programs and online classes. With time, they will begin to attract students from around the world, including American students, and thus, they will become a significant competitor to United States due to their prominence in online education (Hoffman, 2011,).

Additionally, "online education from this non-Western world could represent an important new market for teachers; globalization reflects not only a global competition for students, but also a potential global supply of teachers. In an online world, where teaching and learning are asynchronous and not location-specific, it does not really matter if the teacher or the students are located in Illinois or in India". (Hoffman, 2010, p. 167)To readers in the Western world, it is possible that your next online teaching job will be working for a Chinese-based or Indian-based online college (Zhao, Zhang, & Li 2006; Hoffman, 2011, p. 157).

Online learning has roots in the tradition of distance education, which goes back at least 100 years to the early correspondence courses. With the advent of the Internet and the World Wide Web, the potential for reaching learners around the world has increased greatly., Online learning today offers rich educational resources in multiple media and the capability to support both real-time and asynchronous communication between instructors and learners as well as among different learners. Institutions of higher education and corporate training were quick to adopt online learning. The future of online is more than an upward trend line of boosting enrollments. The numerous trends identified here suggest that the nature and practice of online education will be changed in the next few years. Changes include how teaching and learning will happen, how online education will be managed and organized, and, most significantly, how people in the online environment will understand the meaning of education.

REFERENCES

Alemi, F. F., & Maddox, P. J. (2008). Open courses: One view of the future of education. *The Journal of Health Administration Education*, 25(4), 329–342. PMID:19655635

Amirault, R. J. (2012). Distance learning in the 21st century university: Key issues for leaders and faculty. *Quarterly Review of Distance Education*, 13(4), 253-265, 269.

Bates, A. W. (2005). *Technology, E-Learning and Distance Education* (2nd ed.). London: Routledge Taylor Francis Group. doi:10.4324/9780203463772

Bergmann, J., & Sams, A. (2012). Flip your classroom: Reach every student in every class every day. *International Society of Technology in Education*. Retrieved from https://www.liceopalmieri.edu.it/wp-content/uploads/2016/11/Flip-Your-Classroom.pdf

Bhatti, A., Tubaisahat, A., & El-Qawasmeh, E. (2005). Using technology-mediated learning environment to overcome social and cultural limitations in higher education. *Issues in Informing Science and Information Technology*, 2, 67–76. doi:10.28945/811

Bogardus-Cortez, M. (2017). *Emerging tech boost online education growth over next 4 years*. Retrieved from edtechmagazine.com

Bowser, A., Davis, K., Singleton, J., & Small, T. (2017). Professional learning: A collaborative model for online teaching and development. *SRATE Journal*, 26(1), 1–8.

Brown, M. B., & Diaz, V. (2010). Mobile learning: Context and prospects. *EDUCAUSE: Mobile Learning*. Retrieved from http://www.educause.edu/Resources/MobileLearningContextandProspe/204894

Buzzetto-More, N.A., & Sweat-Guy, R. (2006). Incorporating the hybrid learning model into minority education at a historically black university. *Journal of Information Technology Education*, 5(1), 153-164.

Dear, B. (2017). *The Friendly Orange Glow: The Untold story of the PLATO System and the Dawn of Cyberculture*. Audiobook.

Delisio, E. R. (2009). Merging online education with social networking: Welcome to present. *Podiatry Management, 28*(6), 73–76.

Downes, S. (2005). e-Learning 2.0. *ACM e-Learn Magazine*, (10). Retrieved from http://www.downes.ca/post/31741

Ferrer, D. (2013). *The One World Schoolhouse by Salman Khan—A Review*. New York: Twelve/Hachette Book Group.

Ferrer, D. (n.d.a). *The History of Online Education*. Retrieved from https://thebestschools.org/magazine/online-education-history/#pre1900

Ferrer, D. (n.d.b). *Current Trends in Online Education*. Retrieved from https://thebestschools.org/magazine/current-trends-online-education/

Gray, P., & Riley, G. (2013). The challenges and benefits of unschooling according to 232 families who have chosen that route. *Journal of Unschooling and Alternative Learning, 7*, 1–27.

Helm Coordinated Science Laboratory. (1960). *SL Quarterly Report*. Urbana, IL: Online Learning and Innovative Online Learning. Retrieved from http://www.innovativelearning.com/online_learning/timeline.html

Hodges, C. (2004). Designing to motivate: Motivational techniques to incorporate in e-learning experience. *Journal of Interactive Online Learning, 2*(3), 1–7.

Hoffman, D. D. (2016). Considering the Crossroads of Distance eEducation: The Experiences of Instructors as they Transitioned to Online or Blended Courses. *Education Database*. Retrieved from https://search-proquest-com.ezproxy.shu.edu/docview/1806944939?accountid=13793

Hoffman, S. J. (2011). *Teaching the Humanities Online: A Practical Guide to the Virtual Classroom: A Practical Guide to the Virtual Classroom*. Armonk: Routledge.

Holmberg, B. (1986). *Growth and Structure of Distance Education*. London: Croom.

Kang, H. (2009). *A comparative study of the distance education history in China and the United States: A socio-historical perspective* (Ph.D. Dissertation). The Pennsylvania State University.

Keebler, B. (2014). Online education: Past, present, and future. *Momentum, 45*, 35–37.

Klimova, B.F. & Kacet, J. (2014). Hybrid learning and its current role in the teaching of foreign languages. *Procedia-Social and Behavioral Sciences, 182*(2015), 477-481.

Kyong-Jee, K., & Bonk, C. J. (2006). The future of online teaching and learning in higher education: The survey says.... *EDUCAUSE Quarterly, 29*(4). Retrieved from http://faculty.weber.edu/eamsel/Research%20Groups/On-line%20Learning/Bonk%20(2006).pdf

Larreamendy-Joerns, J., & Leinhardt, G. (2006). Going the distance with online education. *Review of Educational Research, 76*(4), 567–605. doi:10.3102/00346543076004567

Linardopoulos, N. (2010). A cross-comparison of perceptions of online education: A case of an online MBA program. *Education Database*. Retrieved from https://search-proquest-com.ezproxy.shu.edu/docview/741224498?accountid=13793

Linda, L. (2015). The current conundrum of state authorization for online education programs and clinical placement. *Journal of Allied Health, 44*(3), 188–192. PMID:26342618

Lynch, M. (2008). *What is the Future of Online Learning in Higher Education*. Retrieved from https://www.thetechedvocate.org/future-online-learning-higher-education/

Mayadas, F., Bouren, J., & Bacsich, P. (2009). Online education today. Reprinted with permission from AAAS. *Journal of Asynchronous Learning Networks, 13*(2), 49. doi:10.1126cience.1168874

Moe, R. (2014). The evolution and impact of the massive open online course. *Education Database*. Retrieved from https: //search-proquest-com.ezproxy.shu.edu/docview/1554699058?accountid=1379

Moore, M., & Kearsley, G. (2005). *Distance education: A systems view* (2nd ed.). Belmont, CA: Wadsworth.

Nicoll, L. A. (2016). Bringing education online: Institutional logics in the legitimation of and resistance to online higher education. *Education Database*. Retrieved from https://search-proquest-com.ezproxy.shu.edu/docview/1785398290?accountid=13793

Noam, E. M. (1995). Electronics and the Dim Future of the University. *Science, 270*(5234), 247–249. doi:10.1126cience.270.5234.247

Olapiriyakul, K., & Scher, J. (2006). A guide to establishing hybrid learning courses: Employing information technology to create a new learning experience, and a case study. *The Internet and Higher Education, 9*(4), 287–301. doi:10.1016/j.iheduc.2006.08.001

Orlando, J. (2016). Understanding Project-Based Learning in Online Education. *Magna Publication*. Retrieved from https://www.facultyfocus.com

PLATO User's Guide. (1981). *CDC*. Retrieved from http://www.bitsavers.org/pdf/cdc/plato/97405900C_PLATO_Users_Guide_Apr81.pdf

Rodriguez, C. O. (2012). MOOCs and the AI_Stanford like courses: Two successful and distinct Courses Formats for Massive Open Online Course. *European Journal of Open, Distance and E- learning*. Retrieved from http://files.eric.ed.gov/fulltext/EJ9829.pdf

Rose, S. N. (1991). Collegiate-based noncredit courses. In B. B. Watkins & S. J. Wright (Eds.), *The foundations of American distance education* (pp. 67–92). Dubuque, IA: Kendall/Hunt.

Ruth, S. (2012, June 18). *Can MOOC's and Existing E-Learning Efficiency Paradigms Help Reduce College Costs?* Available at SSRN: doi:10.2139srn.2086689

Steffens, K. (1989). *Open and distance education in Germany*. Retrieved from https://scholar.google.com/scholar?cluster=18015051997387056388&hl

Stifle, J. (1972). *The Plato IV Architecture*. Retrieved from http://bitsavers.informatik.uni-stuttgart.de/pdf/univOfIllinoisUrbana/plato/X-20_The_Plato_IV_Architecture_May72.pdf

Watkins, B. L. (1991). A quite radical idea: The invention and elaboration of collegiate correspondence study. In B. L. Watkins & S. J. Wright (Eds.), *The foundations of American distance education* (pp. 1–35). Dubuque, IA: Kendall/Hunt.

Wilcox, D., Thall, J., & Griffin, O. (2017). One canvas, two audiences: How faculty and students use a newly adopted learning management system. In *Proceedings of the 2016 Society for Information Technology & teacher education international conference, USA* (pp. 1163–1168). Retrieved from http://er.dut.ac.za/bitstream/handle/123456789/193/LMS%20new%20adopted.pdf?sequence=1&isAllowed=y. Google Scholar

Wilkins, J. (2007). The future is now: Online education and the future of higher education. *Sheriff, 59*(3), 37.

Woolley, D. R. (1994). PLATO: The Emergence of Online Community. *Matrix News*. Retrieved from http://thinkofit.com/plato/dwplato.htm

Chapter 8
Quality Assurance:
Breaking Through the Online Learning Plateau

Jermaine S. McDougald
https://orcid.org/0000-0002-2558-5178
Universidad de La Sabana, Colombia

ABSTRACT

Online education has continued to increase at a rapid rate over the past decades, offering diverse learning programs at all levels of education. As a result, online programs continue to shift and change according to the demands of society. However, the demands for qualified online instructors (OI) are not increasing at the same rate and are not proportional to the number of instructors directly responsible for delivering quality online courses. Many OI do not know their learners; therefore, a gap is left in terms of their needs in an online environment. This chapter will provide insights into how the strategy "module hosts" for online discussion boards, and learner profiles are used in an online graduate program to promote effective communication, leadership, and collaboration. Moreover, the chapter discusses varied ways through which online instructors can incorporate a "bottom-up" approach in their instruction as part of being a change agent.

INTRODUCTION

Online learning or virtual learning continues to increase across the globe, in all academic areas for the past four decades (Zawacki-Richter & Latchem, 2018). As such there are still concerns surrounding the nature of online courses or programs as well as its validity (Agbebaku & Adavbiele, Justina, 2016; Markova, Glazkova, & Zaborova, 2017). It comes as no surprise as to the impact technology has had on education in the past few decades, in which distance education has grown rapidly into online, virtual education or even blended learning. Allen, Seaman, Poulin, and Straut (2016) claim that more than two-thirds of academic leaders believe online learning is a "critical" component to the long-term viability of the institution. This increase in online programs is partially attributed to its mobility, flexibility,

DOI: 10.4018/978-1-7998-0115-3.ch008

internationalization and increased job opportunities. The flexibility and mobility of online learning make studying attractive, in which potential students can access high-quality education, across borders, without having to completely interrupt their already active lives.

Although online programs help learners to overcome the hassle and constraints of time, other hurdles obstacles arise such as, real-time communication, which is a vital role in making online learning more authentic and natural. The later in hopes of connecting with shy, less confident students, providing them with practical and genuine opportunities to stay involved in their own learning. However, Jiang (2017, p. para. 1) suggest that "learner's online behavior and peer-interaction would be more regulated and stimulated by assigning roles to learners in discussion activities". There are an array of benefits to assigning roles with collaborative group assignments, such as allowing learners to stay on task, clear route for participation, encourage individual accountability while strengthening communication (Johnson, 2011; Villagonzalo, 2014). The diverse roles that could be assigned in online environments are mirrored from face-to-face interactions; however, they are still valid and extremely useful for online learners, such as being a *facilitator, recorder, presenter*, or even a *reflector*. In fact, additional roles such as *encourager, questioner* or even a *checker* (De Wever, Keer, Schellens, & Valcke, 2010) could also be used. Nevertheless, these roles can be assigned and distributed as needed in accordance with the topic or assignment at hand. Thus, this chapter will discuss how roles can be used managing online forum discussions, where learners become online instructors (OIs hereafter) for different periods during the online real-time sessions.

However, regardless of the increase and demand of online programs, many OIs still lack the essential knowledge of their learners as well as their online teaching context since OIs often carry over traditional face-to-face strategies into the online environment, making no significant adjustment, and simply changing the delivery modality. In fact, OIs are not truly aware of what or even who are their students, which in turn has a direct consequence on the teaching and learning process. Now, faculty members at higher education institutions (HEI, hereafter) across the globe are typically deemed "experts" in their field of study, but not in pedagogy, education or the like. Now, if a second or foreign language is involved, the recipe for teaching just got that much harder. Therefore, the combination of *[expertise (-) pedagogy] + foreign language equals challenges* in successfully acquiring the content at hand (Betts & Heaston, 2014; Tømte, Enochsson, Buskqvist, & Kårstein, 2015). Now, if this same formula is applied to an online course, the stakes just increased meaning that these professionals, now faculty at a HEI, often do not have competences to teach online, which in turn results in not so "positive" reactions from learners (i.e. high dropout rates, lack of field competences, limited cognition development, etc.).

HEIs try to off-set this lack of preparation/training by offering short courses, seminars and the like on various topics, unfortunately, teaching online is often not on "to-do list", because faculty believe that since they are "experts" in their field, they do not need an "upgrade" to teach online, because they claim that it is the same. Unfortunately, both HEIs and faculty alike perceive online education as such.

Nevertheless, online learners are unique in their own way; they all come from different walks of life, cultures or even across different time zones, where culture plays an even bigger role, an area still not addressed in online programs. The more OIs know about their learners, the more successful the teaching-learning process can evolve. Online instructors do not have the luxury of seeing their students in person, missing out on key body language (communication) and learners do not have their instructors there after class to consult, get tutored or just a simple greeting. However, regardless of the level of training that online instructors possess to deliver their courses online, there are several strategies (peer teaching and

Quality Assurance

creating learner profiles) that could be included into the instruction so that realistic communication, along with authentic tasks are incorporated/used.

The aforementioned aspects actually make a difference in determining the ultimate success and/or quality of an online program, as well as contribute to the quality of the teaching and learning process. Therefore, several pedagogical approaches that could be used in online learning will be discussed; indicating how these strategies along with increased professional development opportunities could make a difference to learners and the overall quality of the online program. Furthermore, specific examples employed in an online Master's Program in English Language Teaching for both faculty and students will be discussed, drawing from teaching experiences and research literature so that the intended audience can make a connection between the chapter and their own teaching practices.

BACKGROUND

Challenges to Online Learning

There are far too many online programs that are a mere replica of face-to-face classes, with an attempt to be delivered online, without considering that the context is different. In which different teaching strategies and tools should be used to fully support online learners (McDougald, 2018). Yet, this is not the only aspect that is carried over to online programs from the face-to-face scenarios, the overall mindset, and competences of instructors also start to become a problem, which is a direct reflection of their lack of online training/professional development. There are many practitioners that start teaching online, by accident, without preparation, which in turn lead to negative results in online learning. High dropout rates, lack of authentic communication in online courses, faulty evaluation/assessment practices with unrealistic tasks and assignments among others. These are only some of the issues surrounding the "negative press" that online programs receive.

Yet, there are actions that can be taken, without having to wait for 'top-down' decisions to make changes but using more of a 'bottom-up' approach for online instruction, in which the teacher/instructor is in control and who has a direct impact on how learners acquire new knowledge online and pretty much how they perceive their online education. If the online instructor is well trained, motivated and uses an array of strategies, techniques and/or approaches learners will achieve more in the online teaching and learning process, thereby providing positive insights about their process, if not then, they will report the unfortunate, which in turn leads to "negative press" about the online experience.

Some of the challenges that come with online programs can be categorized in several areas hardware (platforms, connectivity), software (applications, LMS), lack of qualified online instructors, lack of online teaching methods and strategies, communication and evaluation assessment procedures. (Markova et al., 2017; Okaz, 2015) Moreover, issues such as retention, (Betts & Heaston, 2014; Heyman, 2010; Shea & Bidjerano, 2018) qualified online instructors (Banegas & Manzur Busleimán, 2014; Okaz, 2015; Tømte et al., 2015), effective teaching practices and communication patterns also way heavy on how online courses are perceived. These elements actually make a difference in determining the ultimate success and or quality of an online program.

Professional Educational Development

Teacher Professional Development (TPD, hereafter) plays a vital role overall in education, where it still remains a constant learning process for teachers, regardless of their experience (Markova et al., 2017). In fact, professional development programs have also been considered as strategies to strengthen the overall teaching and learning process. These strategies come in all shapes and sizes, such as initial or short training programs, workshops or even formal educational programs (Graduate or Doctoral). Unfortunately, many of these programs have not considered including topics related to online learning environments, meaning that many online instructors, after receiving training in HEIs are not really prepared or qualified to teach online.

Many of these practitioners attempt to replicate what they do in traditional face-to-face classroom encounters. Nevertheless, close attention is not paid to the online context, the methods, approaches or even the learner themselves, making the online classes/instruction "teacher-centered". Yes, this lack of preparation often results in unsuccessful teaching and learning processes in an online environment, which in turn discredits online education overall. Unfortunately, because online instructors are not well versed in how to successfully deliver their courses the retention rates starts (Betts & Heaston, 2014; Heyman, 2010; Shea & Bidjerano, 2018) to become an even bigger issue.

Teacher Collaboration

According to Moutafidou and Sivropoulou (2010, p. 351) cooperation is defined as "the development of mutual relationships between individuals or groups with common goals" and Hargreaves (1994) notes that cooperation provides teachers with moral support, increases efficiency, improves effectiveness, reduces the burdens and pressures from work demands, promotes confidence, teacher learning and reflection and leads to continuous improvement. Thus, through cooperation, teachers plan together to evaluate the accomplishment of the established goals, where both in-service and pre-service teachers alike can find solutions to problematic situations that they would face in the classroom. Therefore, it is key that teachers' efficient cooperation is essential and can bring about positive changes in the teaching and learning process (Shachar & Shmuelevitz, 1997).

Teacher Collaboration (TC, hereafter) is often seen as a positive condition to develop teacher learning and usually the first step towards informal teacher training. This can be echoed by teachers who report the impact that collaboration has in order to build powerful learning environments in which teachers can exchange new ideas, reflect on their practice, develop and implement new materials, discuss certain issues, receive feedback and advice from other peers, and the moral support from each other (Meirink, Imants, Meijer, & Verloop, 2010). Furthermore, there are studies (Ellis, 2010; Vangrieken, Dochy, Raes, & Kyndt, 2015; Vinagre, 2017) that have reviewed the impact that teacher collaboration has on transforming students into proficient future collaborators in order to respond to the professional field. For example, teachers' collaboration can be reflected in cooperative learning for students to work together as a team (Shachar & Shmuelevitz, 1997; Vangrieken et al., 2015). Therefore, collaboration plays an important role in enhancing not only teaching practices but also addresses their professional growth, which in turn leads to personal benefits. Besides, teachers can also be a benefit to their context starting with their institution, then the educational community, their peers, and their students. A systematic review by Vangrieken et al. (2015) shows that collaboration is also mediated by internal organization in the institutions, based on the conditions and norms, different values are not appreciated and that is

Quality Assurance

when collaboration presents boundaries that need to be developed for teachers. These differences could be resolved, once all collaborators understand their role, in which their expertise is shared, along with a spirit of cooperation and mutual respect.

Quality Assurance in Online Education

Quality assurance (QA) in online programs help institutions ensure that the teaching and learning process is effective and efficient. However, easier said than done, this implies that several actors and stakeholders live up to their commitments so that the online class / programs are successful. As displayed in Figure 1 there are three key areas that should be attended to the 1) online learner, 2) online instructor and the 3) content development. Because of not connecting these three areas and not having them as the core of any online program, the overall quality of an online program is jeopardized. These three areas work together, simultaneously in which there is a continued sequence of phases, tasks or events that could occur in any given direction. For example, the more OIs know about learners, i.e. through a learner profile, the more realistic the tasks and assignments can become when developing content for the online course. In which this content can be adjusted making the learning process more meaningful to the online learner. Along the same lines, the online instructors are also well prepared and up to date in order to successful manage the changes that arise in a given online course, through initial training and continuous professional development. Therefore, regular or periodic assessment of online programs is essential to maintain and improve their quality (Marciniak, 2018). The assessment process should not be a long and tedious task, but a series of constant actions that take place regularly and as often as the online class meets. For example, OI could have learners self-assess themselves (3-5 close-ended questions) after each module, feedback from the tools and resources used throughout the platform, short questionnaires on engagement or interaction patterns or even online focus groups scheduled at different times throughout an online program that focuses on administrative, logistical and overall welfare and perceptions about the program. In any event, Marciniak (2018) proposes a model that could be used or adopted to assess online programs at higher education institutions (HEIs). However, if actions are seriously incorporated into a program as indicators for the quality of the online program, this in turn becomes a habit, which leads to best practices and could speak wonders about the quality of online education, where the OIs has a tremendous role and responsibility.

Issues, Controversies, Problems

Quality Assurance in Online Learning

Online education can be examined taking into account three main areas, *a) online learners b) online instructors, and c) content development,* areas that can help ensure success in online learning. These areas are crucial to how online programs can progress and eventually succeed (Markova et al., 2017). All three areas lead right back to the beginning, the lack of professional development in online learning (Baran & Correia, 2014). Faculty members/ instructors are essential in the success of an online learning program, and as such, it is paramount that professional development programs are put into place so that continuous training is made available. These online training programs are often omitted or seen as unnecessary, in which institutions overlook this aspect, thinking that the traditional training courses or

Figure 1. Factors for quality assurance in online programs (Created by the author)

Factors for Quality Assurance in Online Programs (Created by the author)

- Online Learner
  - Learner Profile
  - Experiences
  - Digital Literacies
  - Personal Development Plan (Organize time, Set Communication, Troubleshoot Channels)
  - Highly committed

- Online Instructor
  - Professional Development (Certified)
  - Social Competences
  - Pedagogical Competences
  - Technical Competences
  - Managerial Competences
  - Digital Literacies

- Content Development
  - Instructional Design
  - Blended Learning
  - Flipped Learning
  - Platforms
  - Hardware
  - Software

programs provided by face-to-face environments are sufficient. This traditional mindset not only hinders the entire success of online learning but also does not offer alternatives or real solutions.

Professional development should be incorporated into the institutional training plans and looked at as a requirement and not an option. Budgets should be set aside and in-house training plans should be established. Now, convincing faculty that they need to receive additional training and need to be in a constant process of improvement is not an easy task. Nevertheless, HEIs should set standards for the online instructors, where there are minimum standards that OIs should comply with. For example, as part of the faculty yearly performance evaluation, institutions should enforce a certain number of hours dedicated to the enforcement of digital competences, which include a combination of areas such as pedagogical, social, technical and managerial competences for online education. This is a way to train all members of an institution across the board and on a constant basis, ensuring that OIs are up to date with online technologies and pedagogy.

SOLUTIONS AND RECOMMENDATIONS

Considering that, there are diverse possibilities to engage online learners, knowing what tool or strategy to use can be challenging. These challenges constantly arise since instructors are not accustomed to the options that traditional face-to-face methodologies pose, they are not in tune with the online course objectives. On the other hand, OIs should be aware of the competences and/or skills of their learners that need to be developed in the online environment. For starters knowing about your learners should be a priority. Cipher, Urban, and Mancini (2019, p. 204) claim that "it is important to understand student characteristics that contribute to course and program-level success or persistence". Hence, knowing about

Quality Assurance

online learners is a vital step, as this provides more than basic information delivered to instructors before the online course starts, which is often not enough. Thereby, creating learner profiles could provide key aspects and insights as to what makes online learners operate effectively. Learner profiles are often used or seen in primary or secondary educational levels, however, they if used in higher educational online programs, the results would lead to better developed content, activities and tasks closer to the needs and realities of the online instructor's teaching context.

Creating Learner Profiles

What is a learner profile? A learner profile (LP, hereafter) comes in different shapes and sizes, such as a document, portfolio, or even a conversation with the learner that highlights key information about them that could be used to better help the learner successfully achieve their learning outcomes. Essentially an LP allows learners to:

- express who they are
- address assumptions people may have about them or their disability
- express their aspirations and passions
- have a say in what goes on for them at school/university and in their learning.

Learner profiles are often created by the student, with the support of those that know them best, their instructor. Now, by creating a LP, students develop a more profound understanding of who they are as learners – reflecting on what motivates and challenges them when learning (Trofimovich, Lightbown, & Halter, 2013). However, before developing the LP, a short discussion with the learner is needed, touching on a) the purpose of the LP, b) format to be used, and c) if the learner wants the LP to be connected to an e-portfolio or the institutional evaluation system. Developing a LP is especially important for online learners since they use their experience as a learner gained from years of being exposed to traditional face-to-face classes, then attempting to apply those same competencies in online environments; however, they are not always aware that additional competences and attitudes are needed in online learning environments. Cuesta Medina (2017, p. 43) claims that "interaction outcomes should favor satisfaction, participation, communication, exploration, and self-regulation processes". Accordingly, LPs also create an opportunity for self-advocacy: identifying the tools, learning materials and presentation options that will optimize their learning experiences.

Learner Profile Benefits for Online Instructors

A learner profile can assist online instructors in several different facets of the teaching and learning process. For starters, it could be used to *build a stronger, more connected relationship* with their students. This alone is a great advantage in that the learner becomes more confident and secure with the instructor, thereby lowering their effective filter (Du, 2014), which are an learner's emotional and physical state. When these two are blocked or increased, the learning process is directly affected and is impeded.

Another benefit for the instructor is being able to *recognize and/or remove potential barriers* to learning since the beginning of the learning process. This, in turn, provides more time for both the instructor and learner(s), where they can dedicate more time to actually acquiring new content with ease, while decreasing the learning curve. The LP can also be valuable to *design learning environments and opportunities* that build on student interests and experiences to maximize learner engagement. Providing learners with an ideal learning environment that has been contextualized to the actual learners, hence further motivating them towards the teaching and learning process online. On another note, *selecting curriculum materials and content* that learners will be able to access is also beneficial. Once again, knowledge of learners and the curriculum is quite important since the curriculum is not designed specifically for a specific learner in mind from the beginning and not as a consequence of other non-related actions.

Furthermore, online instructors can also *offer a range of options* for demonstrating thinking and learning that will work well for learners. This selection goes together with differentiated instruction to provide online instructors with key elements in helping students to become more successful in the classroom. Finally, LP can also *support positive transitions* to new environments. These positive transitions help to ensure that learners are prepared to take on more challenging tasks as they develop and the content evolves.

Alongside assessment data, a learner profile supports teachers in knowing about the learner, providing information from the student's perspective. It is not very common to use LP in Higher Education, however, is not unheard of either. The more information that can be collected collectively on or about learners leads to a positive outcome for all stakeholders. There is limited research into using LP for online educational environments, leaving the doors open for the future. Overall, helping students identify and understand how they learn best and how they can use this information can help students learn-to-learn throughout their lives.

Using Module Hosts

The usage of the "Module Hosts" strategy has proven to be a successful to both engage and boost learner´s motivation and performance in the online learning environment. At the start of each new cohort (online), students are assigned the role of "Module Hosts" (MH, hereafter), this role is often shared with 2 or 3 other students in the class and proportional to the number of students enrolled in the course.

Students have access to video and written guidelines on how to successfully play the role of "Module Hosts" (MH, hereafter) where they are encouraged to take charge of the module forum for the assigned course module (see Appendix). Each week, the appointed host(s) is/are responsible for promoting discussion and participation in the online discussion forum throughout the entire week. All students in the course must take part in these discussions. MH may pose a question, discussion topic or further reflection on the topic to be discussed. However, it is/are the responsibility of the module host(s) to encourage all students to actively participate and to begin new discussions when there is little activity. As a MH, the students take on several roles, which aid in their professional development as in-service language teachers. The roles that were chosen for MH correspond to the task at hand, which is to synthesize and analysis the information found in the online discussion forums. Furthermore, when assigning roles as shown in Table 1, they should always correspond to the assigned task(s).

Their participation as a "host" is considered for their online participation evaluation. At the start of the next module, the following week, hosts are allotted 10 minutes to present their synthesis and analysis of the online forum discussion to the rest of the class during the online real-time sessions (generally held in a 50-60 minute timeframe). They are granted moderator rights within the platform, in this case, Blackboard, where they teach the class. Often time additional time is requested and/or granted since hosts often produce a lot more information and material than required. They often have two or three tasks that they design to interact with their peers. Tasks range from 2-3 videos, to interactive mind maps,

Table 1. Role of module hosts

Role of Module Hosts

Role	Description
Coacher	Guides discussions to produce agreements, reach a consensus and get to final conclusions
Crusader	Prioritize topics discussed, stress issues that have the most important in the forum discussions
Controller	Call participants to focus on the topic and post on time
Provider	Provide additional information and sources related to the topic that is discussed in the Module.
Summarizer	Post an executive summary that highlights the most important points discussed in the Module at the end of the week before the next module begins. This summary can be in the form of a map (mind, conceptual, etc.), PowerPoint Presentation (Max 3 Slides), Infographic, or 1-page executive summary, videos, etc.

to interviews from their students or fellow colleagues from their educational institutions, all related to the assigned module topic. Thereby taking a simple task of forum discussion and converting that into reusable content for their peers in various formats, which also serves as a study guide or review.

Benefits of Module Hosts

There are multiple benefits as shown in Table 2 that take place within the online environment as a result of using the strategy of *Module Hosts* as a way to instill promote of the online environment. These benefits go a long way in providing students with life skills, increased ICT competences and of course a more authentic learning environment for students. This alone, does wonder for the online teaching and learning process. These benefits range from social competences and leadership skills to extended writing practice and cultural awareness.

These skills both soft and hard, are cultivated because of the combination of knowing learners more in-depth (Learner Profiles) and assigning their key roles within the online environment (Module Hosts). These two aspects are examples of what an OI can use in a course to ensure success in the teaching and learning process. Meaning that the online instructor is able to carefully select tasks and activities that correspond to their learners and the overall teaching objectives.

Thereby, making the online experience and learning much more enriching, practical and realistic. The extra added responsibility as "Module Hosts" empowers learners to not only participate but prepare themselves as leaders amongst their peers, making use of higher-order cognitive skills, among others. Furthermore, by assigning online learners roles, it encourages them to take a more active stance and responsibility for their own learning (Jiang, 2017). The "Module Host" strategy forces online learners to respond to discussion questions reply to peers, among others, all the while constructing knowledge, disputing and negotiating with their peers within the amount of time during the learning process. In

Table 2. Benefits of being a module host

Benefits of being a Module Host, (Created by the author)

Benefits of Module Hosts	Social Competences (Leadership Skills & Social Skills)	Communication	Extended Writing Practice	Metacognition	Cultural Awareness
Leadership skills (person who rules, guides or inspires others)	X	X			
Teamwork	X	X			
Increased communication oral and written	X	X	X		
More profound responses in the forum		X	X		
Quality responses in forum amongst peers			X	X	
Deeper engagement with course material content			X	X	
Leadership role amongst peers	X				
Problem Solving				X	
Critical thinking				X	
Analysis and synthesizing skills				X	
Creation of a community	X				
Closer, interpersonal relationships inside and outside the online environment	X				X
Creativity				X	

order to encourage and remind learners of their role within the online forum discussion, a checklist is used as seen in Table 3. Therefore, along with the roles that a learner takes during a module, they also have to be reminded of what criteria of quality posts.

Interaction in online environments

There are several other types of strategies that can increase interaction in online environments, thereby making the teaching-learning process that much more enriching. Moore (1989) organizes these interaction strategies into three categories *learner-content (LC), learner-instructor (LI) and learner-learner (LL) interaction.* Now, *online interaction* is a process that composes both learners' educational experience and an outcome resulting from their engagement with the [online] learning environment (Garrison & Cleveland-Innes, 2005). However, Ke (2013) highlights that there should be a combination of "asymmetrical (reading textbooks watching or even listening to OI´s lectures and/or videos) and symmetrical communication (learner is involved in two-way contact with classmates or the Online Instructor) (2013, p. 13). This combination adds to fostering real-world opportunities to communicate, stay in touch with content and relate with others, thereby strengthening the quality of the online program by catering to all types of learners, all the while emulating face-to-face occurrences.

Learner-Learner Interaction

For starters, *learner-learner interaction* happens with or without the online-instructor (OI). Often times online programs fail to include these very basic elements of communication, which in a face-to-face environment is common day practice. Social interaction, like this, is a key element to online programs

Quality Assurance

Table 3. Criteria for quality posts, sample taken from content and language integrated learning course, master's in english language teaching for self-directed learning

Criteria for quality posts, sample taken from Content and Language Integrated Learning Course, Master's in English Language Teaching for Self-Directed Learning.

CRITERIA*	Tick if met	Weight
* If the Forum is not the main activity of your course, a different assessment tool will be used (i.e. rubric for writing, rubric for learning objects, etc.).	Yes= ✓ No= X	0-5.0
INITIAL POST (Action 1) Generates and supports points of view showing a thorough knowledge of the topic and the input material/sources provided for the module.		1.5
RESPONSE POST (Action 2) Formulates critical questions and/or comments and builds on arguments posted in the conference based on reflection, peers and tutor´s feedback.		1.5
Uses bibliographical sources to support arguments and cites following APA style.		1.0
Is posted within time limits		0.5
Follows netiquette rules		0.5
SCORE		

as leaners get support from their classmates, where they are able to share the challenges of learning, interchange strategies, thereby increasing motivation and as such, more academic success. A simple way to include *learner-learner interaction* is by adding a "*Social Forum*", allowing learners to interact amongst each other, questioning, commenting or even sharing resources, all the while building community and fostering relationships within the online environment. Yet with *social forums*, online learners can also teach each other, experiment with the new concepts/ideas, clarify assumptions amongst their peers while reacting to course content.

Not to mention, adding social media applications such as Facebook (closed groups) which aid in bridging the gap between the online learner´s academic life and their personal lives. Several studies (Kirschner & Karpinski, 2010; Llorens Cerdà & Capdeferro Planas, 2011) have shown that using Facebook for academic purposes have proven to increase motivation, communication and have also increased success in acquiring new knowledge. Arbaugh and Benbunan-Fich (2007) for example remind us that this type of interaction has more success when small groups of learners get together to share and discuss information, which acts as a support mechanism in so it gives learners the motivation to excel, which models the behavior of collaborative learning models. Learner-learner communication can also include using basic emailing or online collaboration tools such as Dropbox, OneDrive, Evernote, OneNote or even Google Documents, Trello or even SKYPE.

Learner-Content Interaction

Learner-content interaction is what Moore (1989) defines as the moment in which the learners actually come into contact with the content/subject of study. He claims that without this type of interaction, "there can't be education since it is the process of intellectually interacting with content that results in changes in the learner's understanding, the learner's perspective, or the cognitive structures of the learner's mind (1989, p. 1). This type of interaction is by far the most important of the three because this is where learning takes place. This allows learners to actually use and manipulate the content in accordance with their needs or even learning styles. For example, providing online learners with case studies, scavenger hunts, simulations, problem-solving and the like allow them to interact more profoundly with the content in hopes of fully acquiring the topic at hand (Linton, 2017; Meillur, 2018). Therefore, the online course content should be designed for self-directed users, in that there are clear guidelines and instructions, where the learner can easily navigate through the content independently with ease and with minimal or no support from the online instructor. This is why all aspects of the content should be designed for learners so that they can successfully engage with that content (Linton, 2017). Now, the connection between the online learner and the content is mainly influenced by the characteristics of the subject and the design of the online environment (Arbaugh & Benbunan-Fich, 2007).

Learner-Instructor Interaction

The last of the three interactions by Moore (1989) is learner-instructor (LI) interaction, which is where the learner interacts with the subject expert or online instructor who prepared the subject materials. A few ingredients as seen in Table 4 are examples of how to ensure that this type of interaction is included in the online environment.

Table 4. Online Instructor behavior for Learner-instructor Interaction

Online Instructor Behavior	Description
Provide clearly formulated instructions for assignments	Online Instructors (OIs) need to be clear and precise what learning will be doing from one session to the next. Instructors could send weekly reminders via email, blog, forum entry, or o make it more interactive a video (Vlog) or VoiceThread. Assignments should be designed in accordance with Self-access materials (SAMS)
Promptly answer questions	Online Instructors (OIs) need to respond to learners within a 24-48 hour window. If not, online learners will start sending questions by e-mail. Thus removing the benefit of having the answers visible to all i.e. via a Q & A forum, general posts to forum or even the shared spaces in Social media. Online Instructors should encourage learners to use the Public Forums for questioning, not emails.
Provide precise and useful feedback	Feedback is a crucial part to learning, and often times not seen enough in online environments, therefore OIs must provide timely and accurate feedback, and this could be done via individually using the "review" option in MS Word, PowerPoint, etc., Short Videos, or even Screencast. However a good rule of thumb is to provide feedback to all learners during the real-time sessions, which emulates the face-to-face class sessions, where learners can also participate in that feedback.
Provide structured and "efficient" teaching sessions of views and to an extent some degree of freedom in interaction in the online environment.	Structured sessions online are a must in that learners do not have the benefit of the doubt, they only know what is going to happen or how it will the session will evolve, only if the OI plans accordingly. OI have to consider the diverse learning styles of their learners and should plan as such. For example provide a session outline, entitled "Week 2 E-tivity", which contains key elements for the learner to stay on target, such as Average Online Time, Average Offline Time, Total No. of Posts, Deadlines, lesson objectives and resources among others.
Use multiple communication channels	Communication is a key element to the teaching-learning process, however being flexible and providing diverse forms to communicate can go a long way, making the instructor accessible to learners in accordance to tools that they are comfortable with. As side from the online class, back channels can be incorporated such as SKYPE, SKYPE Business, Zoom, Google Hangouts, Facebook, traditional emails, Blogs, or other social media tools that are agreed upon.

CONCLUSION

This chapter provided strategies that could be used to promote soft skills such as leadership, increased communication and collaboration in online learning environments as well as have learners take charge of their own learning. As well as a more structured way to better know and understand the learning needs of online learners. However, there is still a need for more teacher training opportunities to certify online instructors so that they are prepared to successfully lead online courses and programs, which in turn lead to competences for online instruction. As more and more online programs appear, both formal and informal, the greater the need for more qualified instructors who possess proper training and derived certifications. Hence, quality assurance could be achievable, considering that the online instructor has a direct responsibility in delivering the online course content successfully, and in assembling wisely some of the essential components of a learning environment: the learners, the content and the instructors. For example, teachers need to realize that teaching online is very different from face-to-face teaching, and they need to know how to effectively use the tools for their course, so that they can help, aid and finally guide their learners in using the software, platform and basic troubleshooting issues. Learning to use and integrate technology with educational goals, more specifically content requires, time, planning and effort.

On the contrary, several questions arise about the quality of online programs and online instructors, which both go hand in hand. What do you know about technology and learning management systems? What type of instructional approach will be used? What type of instructional strategy/ies is appropriate for online learning? What is the best way to engage online learners? What core competencies are desired for online instructors? What face-to-face teaching methods or approaches could be adapted for online learning?

Now, for future research, this chapter leaves the door open to explore and document other successful approaches that would help online learners to develop more soft skills such as leading, making decisions, being a team player, being self-confident, possessing excellent communication skills (written and spoken), solving problems and being flexible. Additionally, researchers could explore other ways to promote authentic communication, in which all learners have an opportunity to participate.

Overall, online instructors (OI) should always strive to create opportunities for real-time communication that caters to all learners of a particular group/class. This communication does not only connect them to the online environment but makes the content that more appealing and attractive to the learners. Communication is at the forefront of any online program. Since the interaction patterns change from one-to-one, face-to-face to a more social interaction, many-to-many with an authentic audience. This type of interaction, finally leading to effective learning, assisting students in understanding information and constructing knowledge with help from OI and peers.

REFERENCES

Agbebaku, C. A., & Adavbiele, Justina, A. (2016). The reliability and oegality of online education. *Journal of Education and Practice*, *7*(5), 32–41.

Allen, I. E., Seaman, J., Poulin, R., & Straut, T. T. (2016). *Online report card: Tracking online education in the United States*. Retrieved from http://onlinelearningsurvey.com/reports/onlinereportcard.pdf

Banegas, D. L., & Manzur Busleimán, G. I. (2014). Motivating factors in online language teacher education in southern Argentina. *Computers & Education, 76*, 131–142. doi:10.1016/j.compedu.2014.03.014

Baran, E., & Correia, A. P. (2014). A professional development framework for online teaching. *TechTrends, 58*(5), 95–101. doi:10.100711528-014-0791-0

Betts, K., & Heaston, A. (2014). Build it but will they teach?: Strategies for increasing faculty participation & retention in online & blended Education. *Online Journal of Distance Learning Administration, 17*(2), 16–28.

Cipher, D. J., Urban, R. W., & Mancini, M. E. (2019). Factors associated with student success in online and face-to-face delivery of master of science in nursing programs. *Teaching and Learning in Nursing, 14*(3), 203–207. doi:10.1016/j.teln.2019.03.007

Cuesta Medina, L. (2017). Blended learning: Deficits and prospects in higher education. *Australasian Journal of Educational Technology, 34*(1), 42–56. doi:10.14742/ajet.3100

De Wever, B., & Van Keer, H., Schellens, T., & Valcke, M. (2010). Roles as a structuring tool in online discussion groups: The differential impact of different roles on social knowledge construction. *Computers in Human Behavior*. doi:10.1016/j.chb.2009.08.008

Du, X. (2014). The Affective Filter in Second Language Teaching. *Asian Social Science*. doi:10.5539/ass.v5n8p162

Ellis, R. (2010). Instructed second language acquisition a literature review. *Language Teaching, 43*. doi:10.1017/S0261444809990139

Hargreaves, D. H. (1994). The new professionalism: The synthesis of professional and institutional development. *Teaching and Teacher Education, 10*(4), 423–438. doi:10.1016/0742-051X(94)90023-X

Heyman, E. (2010). Overcoming student retention issues in higher education online programs. *Online Journal of Distance Learning Administration, 13*(4).

Jiang, W. (2017). Role assignment and sense of community in an online course. *Distance Education*. doi:10.1080/01587919.2017.1299564

Johnson, C. (2011). *Activities using Process-Oriented Guided Inquiry Learning (POGIL) in the foreign language classroom*. Die Unterrichtspraxis/Teaching German. doi:10.1111/j.1756-1221.2011.00090.x

Ke, F. (2013). Online interaction arrangements on quality of online interactions performed by diverse learners across disciplines. *Internet and Higher Education, 16*(1), 14–22. doi:10.1016/j.iheduc.2012.07.003

Markova, T., Glazkova, I., & Zaborova, E. (2017). Quality Issues of Online Distance Learning. *Procedia - Social and Behavioral Sciences, 237*, 685–691. doi:10.1016/j.sbspro.2017.02.043

McDougald, J. (2018). Innovating with ICTs in content and language environments. *Latin American Journal of Content & Language Integrated Learning, 10*(2), 181–188. doi:10.5294/laclil.2017.10.2.1

Meillur, C. (2018). Online learning: 6 types of interactions at play. Knowledge One. Retrieved August 27, 2019, from https://knowledgeone.ca/online-learning-6-types-of-interactions-at-play/

Meirink, J. A., Imants, J., Meijer, P. C., & Verloop, N. (2010). Teacher learning and collaboration in innovative teams. *Cambridge Journal of Education, 40*(2), 161–181. doi:10.1080/0305764X.2010.481256

Moore, M. G. (1989). Editorial: Three Types of Interaction. *American Journal of Distance Education*. doi:10.1080/08923648909526659

Moutafidou, A., & Sivropoulou, I. (2010). Cooperation in all-day kindergartens: Kindergarten teachers' beliefs. *Procedia: Social and Behavioral Sciences, 5*, 350–355. doi:10.1016/j.sbspro.2010.07.103

Okaz, A. A. (2015). Integrating Blended Learning in Higher Education. *Procedia: Social and Behavioral Sciences, 186*, 600–603. doi:10.1016/j.sbspro.2015.04.086

Shachar, H., & Shmuelevitz, H. (1997). Implementing cooperative learning, teacher collaboration and teachers' sense of efficacy in heterogeneous junior high schools. *Contemporary Educational Psychology, 22*(1), 53–72. doi:10.1006/ceps.1997.0924

Shea, P., & Bidjerano, T. (2018). Online course enrollment in community college and degree completion: The tipping point. *The International Review of Research in Open and Distributed Learning, 19*(2), 282–293. doi:10.19173/irrodl.v19i2.3460

Tømte, C., Enochsson, A. B., Buskqvist, U., & Kårstein, A. (2015). Educating online student teachers to master professional digital competence: The TPACK-framework goes online. *Computers & Education, 84*, 26–35. doi:10.1016/j.compedu.2015.01.005

Trofimovich, P., Lightbown, P. M., & Halter, R. (2013). Are certain types of instruction better for certain learners? *System, 41*(4), 914–922. doi:10.1016/j.system.2013.09.004

Vangrieken, K., Dochy, F., Raes, E., & Kyndt, E. (2015). Teacher collaboration: A systematic review. *Educational Research Review, 15*, 17–40. doi:10.1016/j.edurev.2015.04.002

Villagonzalo, E. C. (2014). Process oriented guided inquiry learning: An effective approach in enhancing students' academic performance. *The DLSU Research Congress*.

Vinagre, M. (2017). Developing teachers' telecollaborative competences in online experiential learning. *System, 64*, 34–45. doi:10.1016/j.system.2016.12.002

Zawacki-Richter, O., & Latchem, C. (2018). Exploring four decades of research in Computers & Education. *Computers and Education, 122*, 136–152. doi:10.1016/j.compedu.2018.04.001

KEY TERMS AND DEFINITIONS

Collaboration Roles: Collaboration roles are diverse roles that team members, colleagues, etc. take on in order to present ideas and lead discussions with other members of a team or group. These roles can change where the expertise is shared and requires members to have a cooperative spirit and mutual respect.

Learner Profile (LP): A learner profile comes in different shapes and sizes, such as a document, portfolio, or even a conversation with the learner that highlights key information about them, which could be used to better help the learner successfully achieve their learning outcomes.

Module Hosts (MH): A module host is responsible for promoting discussion and participation in an online discussion forum throughout a specific period of time, encouraging participants in the forum to actively participate and to begin new discussions when there is little activity, while playing different roles.

Online Instructor (OI)/Online Teacher (OT)/Online Tutor (OT): An online instructor/teacher/tutor teaches courses online using the internet and teaching methods that cater to online learning environments, possessing at a minimum pedagogical, social, technical and managerial competences.

Professional Development (PD): Professional development is formal and informal training sessions designed to improve, increase and/or update faculty in order to remain effective and efficient in their job performance. PD is also an essential part of quality assurance.

Quality Assurance: Quality assurance in online education is a way to maintain a target level of quality in online programs, by carefully paying attention to details of online learners, online instructors, and content development, in order to maintain retention rates.

Teacher Collaboration (TC): Teacher collaboration takes places when colleagues within a given learning community work towards a common goal to make the teaching and learning process more efficient, thereby increasing student learning.

Quality Assurance

APPENDIX

Table 5. Elements for a learner profile, sample taken from the learner autonomy and self-access materials (lasam) course, master's in english language teaching for self-directed learning

Background of Learners - age, gender, location, ethnicity, language, disability, level of education, etc.	
Prior Experience - Prior knowledge, skills, experience relevant for learners? - How will past experience influence their cognition and development? – How can this experience be drawn out and integrated into the learning?	
Learners' Objectives - What do you think the learners' objectives will be for completing the program/course/class?	
Learners' Motivation - What will make the program most relevant to the learners? - What will prove meaningful, and provide motivation to learn?	
Success Factors - What factors might affect learner success or failure in the program/course/class?	
Technology - Do the learners have access to learning technologies? -Are learners predisposed to using these technologies? - How would you rate learner's computer literacy?	
Learning Strategies - How will they best learn – participation, self-reflection, activities, practice? - How can different learning styles (e.g. visual, auditory, kinesthetic) be accommodated? - Are learners self-directed? (Access responsibility, views problems as challenges, is capable of self-discipline, able to use basic study skills, etc.)	
Support - What kinds of support will be needed (academic, peer, supervisor, technical, etc.) to help ensure learner success?	
Desired Competencies - List the learner competencies that need to be achieved. - State these as things that the learner will be able to do after participating in the program/course/class.	

Section 3
Fostering Faculty–Student and Student–Student Interactions

Chapter 9
The Effect of Membership in an Online Cohort Major on Baccalaureate Degree Completion

Mary Dobransky
Bellevue University, USA

ABSTRACT

Attaining an undergraduate college degree contributes to increased employment opportunities and greater compensation, yet many students who enroll fail to graduate within six years, including a growing number of online students. One promising model for increasing retention is cohort education, in which students take multiple courses together as a group. This chapter uses a quantitative data analysis to examine the relationship between membership in an online cohort major and degree completion of baccalaureate students. The study population includes students at a Midwestern university that offers online programs in cohort and non-cohort formats. Study results show a significant positive relationship between membership in an online cohort major and baccalaureate degree completion. The results suggest that higher education leaders seeking to improve baccalaureate degree completion rates may benefit from offering online courses in a cohort format.

INTRODUCTION

Attaining a college degree contributes to increased employment opportunities and greater compensation (Bureau of Labor Statistics, 2016), yet a third of U.S. students who enroll in an undergraduate certificate program, associate's degree, or bachelor's degree do not finish within six years (Johnson, 2012). This failure of students to complete their degrees has a negative impact on the students who drop out, the postsecondary institutions that recruit and teach those students, and the national workforce. Students who spend resources on a degree they fail to complete can face financial burdens and diminished future earning potential (Schneider & Yin, 2011). Postsecondary institutions similarly experience a loss of re-

DOI: 10.4018/978-1-7998-0115-3.ch009

sources when funds are used to recruit and teach students who drop out (Johnson, 2012). Finally, given that an estimated 35% of U.S. job openings through 2020 will require at least a bachelor's degree, the nation faces an estimated shortage of five million baccalaureate degree-qualified workers (Carnevale, Smith, & Strohl, 2013).

The problem extends beyond the United States—failure of students to complete their degrees is a worldwide concern. According to a 2016 report from the Organisation for Economic Co-operation and Development (OECD), only 41% of students across OECD member countries completed their bachelor's degrees in the typical time allotted for the program, and 69% completed within three more years (OECD, 2016). Across OECD countries, the average unemployment for college graduates was 4.9% compared to 12.4% for those with less than upper secondary education (OECD, 2016). In addition, compensation for workers with bachelor's degrees was an average of 48% greater than for employees with only upper secondary education (OECD, 2016).

Efforts to retain students may have greater impact from examining factors that influence them to stay in college. Kuh (2001, 2009) found that students stay in college thanks to their engagement in activities such as working with a faculty member on a project or participating in an internship. These and other activities are the basis of the National Survey of Student Engagement (NSSE), a widely-used survey tool that measures baccalaureate student engagement in academic activities empirical research has deemed purposeful (Kuh, 2001). Included in the activities assessed by the NSSE are high-impact practices of a transformational nature. These activities are characterized by factors like substantial time and effort, meaningful faculty-student interactions, peer-to-peer collaboration, learning that extends beyond the classroom, and substantive feedback (National Survey of Student Engagement, 2015). The NSSE examines participation in numerous high-impact practices, such as internships, study abroad programs, and interactions with classmates and faculty (National Survey of Student Engagement, 2015). A particularly successful practice is engaging students through learning communities (National Survey of Student Engagement, 2015).

An example of a learning community is the cohort education model, a structure in which students complete a set of courses together over a period of time (Barnett & Caffarella, 1992). Studies have shown the cohort education model can positively influence student retention (Barnett, Basom, Yerkes, & Norris, 2000; Bentley, Zhao, Reames, & Reed, 2004; Bista & Cox, 2014; Burnett, 1999; Pemberton & Akkary, 2010). Two aspects are frequently linked to the cohort education model's positive influence on retention. First, studies have shown taking a set of courses together as a group positively influences student engagement (Kuh, 2003; K. A. Martin, Goldwasser, & Galentino, 2016; Zhao & Kuh, 2004). Second, researchers have reported a positive correlation between student engagement and retention (Astin, 1984; Chickering & Gamson, 1987; Pace, 1984; Pascarella, 1985; Tinto & Cullen, 1973). Inherent in the connection between the cohort model and retention is social connectedness, a factor shown to predict retention (Roberts & Styron, 2010; Tinto, 1997; Zhao & Kuh, 2004).

The cohort education model has been studied at the doctoral (Barnett et al., 2000), baccalaureate (Beachboard, Beachboard, Li, & Adkison, 2011), and associate's (Linderman & Kolenovic, 2013) degree levels. However, there are few studies specific to online cohorts. This study seeks to contribute to that literature by examining the relationship between online cohort membership and baccalaureate degree completion. The study focuses on cohort majors, for example a business major or a computer science major taken by a group of students as a cohort. In addition, the study concentrates on online majors.

Online education is an increasingly popular format. There was a 7% increase in online enrollments at U.S. postsecondary institutions between 2012 and 2014, with 5.8 million students (28% of the total enrollment) taking one or more courses online in fall 2014 (I. E. Allen & Seaman, 2016). By fall of 2016, 6.3 million students (31.5% of the total enrollment) were enrolled in at least one online course (Seaman, Allen, & Seaman, 2018). Worldwide, reports indicate increased online enrollments in Australia, China, India, New Zealand, and South Africa (Palvia et al., 2018). Online education is predicted to grow as countries advance technologically and build related legal infrastructure (Palvia et al., 2018).

Some aspects attracting students to online courses are accessible course materials, time saved with no commute or class session, and flexibility to manage course work with other obligations (Dziuban, Moskal, & Hartman, 2005). Results of a study of online students attending Australian universities supported the importance of accessible course materials, and found that course quality and design, regular communication, teacher interaction, and technical assistance influenced student success (O'Shea, Stone, & Delahunty, 2015). In addition, studies have shown online students value building a learning community and collaborating with peers (Northrup, 2002).

Researchers have examined the effect of online education on student retention, though so far, the results are inconclusive. Some studies show students drop out of online courses at a higher rate than residential courses (Lee & Choi, 2011; Stone & O'Shea, 2019; Stone, O'Shea, & May, 2016; Xu & Jaggars, 2011), whereas a study of 656,258 records of students enrolled between 2009 and 2014 at multiple colleges reported little difference in retention of residential students and those who took both residential and online courses (James, Swan, & Daston, 2016). In other research, a study of students (n=45,557) at 30 community colleges in the State University of New York system found students who took 40% or less of their courses online were not more likely to drop out compared to students who took 100% of their courses residentially (Shea & Bidjerano, 2018).

This study focuses on fully online courses, contributing to online education research, as well as the literature on baccalaureate cohort education.

BACKGROUND

With many baccalaureate students failing to complete their degrees, and more students taking online courses, postsecondary leaders seek strategies to retain online baccalaureate students. One strategy is to engage students via learning communities like cohorts. This section provides a review of literature related to the topic. It will examine research in the primary themes of the study: baccalaureate student attrition, baccalaureate student retention, and the cohort education model.

Baccalaureate Student Attrition

Attaining a college degree contributes to increased employment opportunities and greater compensation (Bureau of Labor Statistics, 2016), yet a third of the students who enroll in U.S. postsecondary undergraduate education—associate's degree, baccalaureate degree, or certificate—fail to finish at any institution within six years (Johnson, 2012). Only half of those who enrolled as first-time, first-year students at a four-year institution in fall 2010 earned their baccalaureate degree at that institution within six years (Shapiro et al., 2016). After six years, about a fourth of the non-completers were no longer enrolled at any institution (Shapiro et al., 2016). Worldwide, 41% of students across OECD member countries completed their bachelor's degrees in the typical time allotted for the program, and 69% of students completed within three more years (OECD, 2016).

At a time when many students are failing to complete their degrees, more students are taking courses online. U.S. postsecondary institutions reported a 7% increase in online enrollments between 2012 and 2014, with 5.8 million students (28% of the total enrollment) taking one or more courses online in fall 2014 (I. E. Allen & Seaman, 2016). Since students may take a mix of online and residential courses, studies of online student attrition frequently discuss dropout rates of courses, rather than attrition rates of degrees. These studies suggest online students face higher course attrition rates than non-online students. Reports indicate dropout rates of online courses can be as much as 20% higher than residential rates (Carr, 2000; Greenland & Moore, 2014). Analysis by the Australian Government Department of Education and Training indicated 75.4% of residential domestic students who began a university program of study in 2005 completed by 2012, compared to 44.4% of online domestic students (Australian Government Department of Education, 2014). In another study, James, Swan, and Daston (2016) examined 656,258 undergraduate student records and found that students who enrolled only in online courses had higher course attrition rates than students who enrolled in only residential or a mix of online and residential courses.

Online courses are popular, yet these findings show online education may contribute to higher dropout rates. Given the growing demand of online education, strategies to mitigate the attrition of online students can contribute to the overall reduction of baccalaureate attrition, thus decreasing any associated costs which arise not only for students, but for nations.

A high baccalaureate dropout rate brings substantial costs for students. College is expensive, and resources spent on education, as well as loans taken out without successfully attaining a degree, can impose a heavy financial burden on students who drop out (Wine, Janson, & Wheeless, 2011). Students who do not complete their degrees may also diminish their future earning potential. A baccalaureate degree is not a guarantee of success, but it gives those who earn one a significant advantage in lifetime earnings compared to those who do not earn one (Schneider & Yin, 2011). As noted by Schneider and Yin (2011), U.S. Census Bureau data shows earnings are about 40% higher for college-degreed full-time workers aged 25-35, compared to full-time workers of the same age who dropped out of college. Compared to similar workers with only a high school diploma, the college-degreed U.S. population earns about 66% more. Across OECD countries, compensation for workers with bachelor's degrees was reported an average of 48% higher than for workers with only upper secondary education (OECD, 2016).

Along with costs to students, dropping out of college results in considerable costs to nations. Employers incur the costs of unfilled jobs, with a U.S. shortage of five million baccalaureate degree-qualified workers predicted through 2020 (Carnevale et al., 2013). For taxpayers, funding allocated to students who dropout is costly. In 2010, U.S. taxpayers spent over $9 billion through state appropriations and federal grants to educate first-year students who did not return the next year (Schneider, 2010). For the federal government, lower wages of college dropouts compared to those who complete their degrees represents a loss of taxable income. Using degree completion data from the U.S. Department of Education and median earnings estimates at national and state levels, Schneider and Yin (2011) calculated a national loss of $3.8 billion in wages for a single year alone, as well as a $730 million loss in federal and state income taxes (Schneider & Yin, 2011). The OECD noted that public benefits of higher education include greater tax revenues and social contributions from a larger proportion of adults holding degrees (OECD, 2016).

The substantial costs of baccalaureate student attrition have focused the attention of higher education administrators on the reasons students leave college before they finish their degrees. Johnson (2012) reported students drop out of their undergraduate programs for reasons such as academic problems, scheduling, dissatisfaction with their programs, family responsibilities, financial reasons, and personal matters. Another study analyzed approximately 10,000 National Survey of Student Engagement (NSSE) responses gathered between 2000 and 2003 (Kuh, Kinzie, Cruce, Shoup, & Gonyea, 2007). Results of the analysis showed lack of financial resources and poor academic performance were significant indicators for dropping out, although the number of dropouts among academically successful and financially stable students was also significant (Kuh et al., 2007).

Other research shows online students drop out for many of the same reasons as residential students. In interviews with students who dropped out of their online master's program at the University of Illinois, respondents reported personal, job-related, and program issues, with no one reason overriding the others (Willging & Johnson, 2009). Job-related issues, which were not noted in Johnson's (2012) study of residential students, included lack of employer support, changes in student/employee responsibilities, and difficulty attending college while working full time (Willging & Johnson, 2009). In another study, Hart (2012) confirmed that personal and job-related problems can influence an online student's decision to leave college. Hart's study highlighted factors prior research had shown to increase online student attrition. These included auditory learning style (Harrell & Bower, 2011), lack of academic engagement (Bunn, 2004; Ivankova & Stick, 2007; Morris, Finnegan, & Wu, 2005), lack of online resources (Bunn, 2004), and poor communication (Aragon & Johnson, 2008; Bunn, 2004). Hart's (2012) study shows online education may not be desirable for all students. Students without the technology they need to attend online courses, as well as those who prefer in-person interaction with their instructor and classmates, may find residential courses more appealing. Additional evidence of the reasons students drop out of online courses is found in a literature review by Bawa (2016), which noted factors such as student misperception of online course workload, ineffective course design, lack of instructor understanding of online learners, student and faculty limitations of using technology, and lack of faculty training.

These studies highlight the many reasons students drop out of college. While motives vary from one student to the next, the literature shows online students drop out for similar reasons as students who attend courses on a physical campus. However, understanding why students fail to complete their degrees is only one aspect of analyzing degree completion. Also important is knowing the reasons why students stay in college.

Baccalaureate Student Retention

Tinto (2010) noted that the reasons students stay in college are not necessarily the opposite of the reasons they drop out. To retain students, institutions should examine the reasons students leave college, as well as the factors that influence them to stay. As the review of baccalaureate student attrition literature pointed out, students drop out of college for a variety of reasons. Some reasons are external to the postsecondary institutions students choose to attend. For example, personal and job-related issues are critical from a student's standpoint. Other reasons, such as academic or scheduling problems, fall under the purview of the institution. Understanding the reasons students leave college, and the reasons they stay, can inform institutional actions for improving graduation rates.

The reasons students stay in college are reflected in student retention models. These models frequently link to factors like student effort, social interaction, institutional structure, student background, and student perceptions of the learning environment (Kuh et al., 2007). Early work by Pace (1984) found student effort influenced academic outcomes and retention. In separate studies, both Astin (1984) and Pascarella (1985) found that student involvement significantly affects retention. Tinto's (1987) student integration model emphasizes the importance of social and academic integration in retaining students. Research on institutional structure found that students who began their college education at two-year institutions were more likely to attain a bachelor's degree if they were successfully socially and academically integrated at the two-year institution they attended (Pascarella, Smart, & Ethington, 1986). Linkages between retention and student background have been established in studies of diverse student populations (W. Allen, 1992; Bennett & Okinaka, 1990; Hurtado & Carter, 1997). The importance of the learning environment was reinforced by a study of 6,700 undergraduate students that found a significant relationship between retention and students' perceptions of institutional support (Reason, Terenzini, & Domingo, 2006).

These student retention models illustrate that retention requires an integration of student and institutional perspectives. With many possible viewpoints, student retention models can serve as frameworks to guide a variety of retention efforts. For example, evaluating evidence from student retention models in conjunction with results from studies of online retention may help postsecondary leaders formulate strategies for retaining both residential and online students.

Given the growth of online education, there have been some studies specific to retaining online students. A study by Park and Choi (2009) compared factors like age, gender, family support, and academic experience satisfaction of online students who persisted with those of students who dropped out. An analysis of 147 students taking online courses at a U.S. university showed family support, organizational support, and satisfaction and relevance of the academic experience positively influenced online student retention (Park & Choi, 2009). Meanwhile, age, gender, and education level did not significantly influence retention.

In another study of online retention, Harrell and Bower (2011) examined characteristics of online students at five community colleges in Florida. Using an online survey, the researchers gathered information about learning styles, computer experience, online experience, and academic success. Results of the study indicated grade point average, computer skills, and auditory learning style had a significant positive influence on retention in online courses.

In addition to quantitative approaches, some studies of online retention have used qualitative methods. A qualitative case study by Boton and Gregory (2015) tested four aspects of online retention: cultural diversity, motivation, learning management system, and online pedagogy. The researchers investigated the methods of instructors who were considered successful in their delivery of online education. Study findings indicated sensitivity to cultural diversity was an important factor, as online students may be from all over the world. The findings also showed that increasing motivation through faculty presence and challenging activities positively influenced retention and student engagement.

These studies show student engagement has been the focus of retention research for online and residential students. For both populations, retention is an institutional effort. Student retention models integrate student and institutional views, and they offer empirical evidence to guide a variety of retention strategies. The next section focuses on a factor prominent in student retention models—student engagement.

Cohort Education Model

Several studies have shown the cohort education model can positively influence retention (Barnett et al., 2000; Bentley et al., 2004; Bista & Cox, 2014; Burnett, 1999; Pemberton & Akkary, 2010). A longitudinal study by Harris (2006) discovered peer support and encouragement were often cited as primary reasons for the completion of degrees by cohort students. In other research, Rausch and Crawford (2012) reported that attempts to increase bonding in a cohort contributed to a 90% retention rate. They found group interactions and a blend of online and residential course activities promoted student-student and student-faculty bonding.

Further research has indicated positive effects of the cohort education model on student engagement as well as other aspects of student life overall. Studies have reported cohort students have closer bonds than non-cohort students (Barnett et al., 2000; K. A. Martin et al., 2016). In a study of students enrolled in a graduate education program, students expressed a positive attitude towards the cohort education model, and the cohesiveness of the cohort group increased over time (Maher, 2005). A study of undergraduate students at a school of education found a positive correlation between cohort membership and nine factors: professional background, personal attributes, instructional skills, classroom management, application of knowledge, holistic understanding, student interactions, faculty interactions, and professional opportunities (Connor & Killmer, 2001). In summary, research shows the cohort education model can positively influence student retention by promoting peer support and growing student-to-student bonds.

Not all cohort education model research shows positive results. Barnett, Basom, Yerkes, and Norris (2000) found peer pressure can add stress for cohort students, and noted those who need to leave their cohort group may feel a sense of abandonment. Groupthink is another potential issue with the cohort education model. A case study by Mandzuk, Hasinoff, and Seifert (2003) reported cohort members tended to think and act alike. This was supported by Watts' (2013) finding that dominance by an individual student or clique can lead to groupthink among cohort members. Watts investigated the influence of cohorts on hyberbonding, a term denoting negative student behaviors that manifest from empowerment of a group. Watts recommended instructors engage frequently with their cohort students to prevent hyperbonding.

A study by Jaffee (2001) showed freshman cohorts sometimes reestablish negative behaviors common in high schools, such as excessive socializing, misbehavior, disruptive conduct, and cliques. Research by Barnett and Muse (1993) indicated personal issues can have a stronger negative effect on the group morale of cohort students compared to non-cohort students, and jealously among cohort groups is a potential issue.

These studies illustrate that institutions will not be able to rely on the cohort education model alone to improve student engagement and retention. In practice, the cohort education model would have to be supplemented by institutional measures to support student engagement, mitigate disengagement from the negative social factors described above, and improve the resulting quality of their education. These supplemental measures are beyond the scope of this study; however, they should be considered by institutions that desire to implement the cohort education model.

RESEARCH METHODOLOGY

Research Question and Hypothesis

The purpose of this quantitative study was to test whether a significant positive relationship exists between membership in an online cohort major and degree completion of baccalaureate students. Specifically, this study examined the following research question: What is the unique influence of membership in an online cohort major on degree completion of baccalaureate students, controlling for gender, age, race/ethnicity, Pell status, and academic discipline. To address this question, the following hypothesis was tested:

Hypothesis: There is a significant positive relationship between membership in an online cohort major and degree completion for baccalaureate students.

Research Design

The study was conducted at a private, not-for-profit, mostly online university in the Midwest region of the United States. The independent variable was defined as membership in an online cohort major, compared to membership in an online non-cohort major. The dependent variable was defined as baccalaureate degree completion. The study used a six-year period to define baccalaureate degree completion. Only degrees completed at the research site were included in the study.

The study population was students who enrolled in online majors at the research site between January 1, 2005 and January 1, 2012. The research site (University) had collected the data previously, allowing for a secondary data analysis. Student record data for the study included cohort membership, degree completion, online status, academic discipline, number of credits completed, Pell-eligibility, and demographic information. Cohort membership, degree completion, and online status facilitated comparison of degree completion of online cohort students and online non-cohort students. Information about academic discipline enabled analysis across different fields of study. The analysis examined demographic information including student gender, age, race/ethnicity, and Pell status. Age was the age of the student when he or she enrolled. The mean value replaced missing values for age. Financial aid data provided Pell status of eligible or not-eligible. Gender and race/ethnicity were self-reported. Missing values for gender were categorized as Unknown or Preferred not to Report.

The study uses statistical methods to determine whether there is a significant relationship between the dependent variable of degree completion and the independent variable of participation in an online cohort major. The study conducts three types of analysis to examine the relationship. First, the study conducts analysis of the correlations between degree completion rates and participation in an online cohort major. Second, the study fits a logistic regression model to the degree completion rate to examine the interactions between predictor variables. The third analysis is to perform a hypothesis test to determine if the degree completion rate for students participating in online cohort majors is greater than the degree completion rate for students in online non-cohort majors.

The study conducts correlation analysis with the Spearman's rho test. Hypothesis testing is conducted using the Pearson's chi-squared test. It is hypothesized that degree completion rates for students participating in online cohort majors are greater than degree completion rates for online non-cohort students. The Pearson's chi-squared test is used to test this against the null hypothesis. Because the dependent variable is binary, rather than a continuous value, the study employs a logistic regression model to analyze the second research question. Generally speaking, the coefficients of the logistic regression model help determine whether the variable of interest (participation in an online cohort major) affects degree completion while considering other predictor variables. In exploring the influence of online cohort membership on the dependent variable of degree completion, the current study controls for the potentially confounding variables of gender, age, ethnicity/race, Pell-eligibility, and academic discipline.

FINDINGS

Study Population

The study performed descriptive analysis to summarize demographics of the study populations, as shown in Table 1 (see Appendix 1). Study participants were students seeking baccalaureate degrees at the University and enrolled in an online major. There were 3,274 students who enrolled in online programs between 2005 and 2012. Of these, 2,773 (85%) took their major courses in a cohort format. The predominant age range was 25-34 years. Females accounted for 1,598 (49%) of students. The number of Pell-Eligible students was 30% of the population. The Unknown or Prefer not to Report category was the largest diversity percentage (46%), followed by White (40%). Overall, 1,882 (57%) of the students graduated from the University within six years.

Statistical Analyses

The statistical analysis examines the influence of membership in an online cohort major on baccalaureate degree completion, controlling for gender, age, race/ethnicity, Pell status, and academic discipline. The analysis includes correlation analysis, logistic regression analysis, and hypothesis testing through chi-squared tests. These methods determine whether there is a significant relationship between the dependent variable of baccalaureate degree completion and the independent variable of participation in an online cohort major.

Statistical testing began with correlation analysis. Spearman's rho (ρ) correlation was used to test for a monotonic relationship between cohort membership and degree completion for the 2005-2012 online baccalaureate students. The analysis found a positive correlation between degree completion and participation in a cohort program. For the population tested, the correlation coefficient of $\rho = 0.15$ indicated a significant (p = 0.000) positive correlation between participation in an online cohort and degree completion rates for a confidence interval at the 95% level.

After completing the correlation analysis, a logistic regression model examined the relationship between membership in an online cohort major and the dichotomous outcome of degree completion. Logistic regression, which conveys a non-linear relationship in a linear way, can be used to predict the probability of a variable given known values of other variables (Field, 2013; D. Martin, 1977). For this study, there is one predictor variable (online cohort membership) of a single outcome (baccalaureate degree completion). The analysis included only students who completed their courses online. Input variables included Age, Academic Discipline, Diversity, Course format, Pell-eligibility, and Gender. In fitting a logistic regression model, the study modeled the outcome variable of degree completion (y) using the following probability function, where b_0 is the constant intercept value, x_i is the value of the ith input variable, and b_i is the model coefficient for that variable.

$$P(y) = \frac{1}{1 + exp\left(-\left(b_0 + \sum_{i=1}^{N} b_i x_i\right)\right)}$$

Given the dichotomous outcome variable of degree completion, the logistic regression model was fit with the binomial family using the R programming language's Generalized Linear Models (GLM) function ("GLM: Fitting generalized linear models," n.d.). The algorithm chooses the best model by minimizing the Akaike information criterion (AIC). AIC is a function of the log-likelihood (LL) of the number of parameters, k, in the model. Log-likelihood and AIC are defined using the following equations:

$$LL = \sum_{i=1}^{N} Y_i ln(P(Y_i)) + (1-Y_i) ln(1-P(Y_i))$$

$$AIC = 2k - ln(\hat{LL})$$

The study assessed goodness of fit using the Receiver Operating Characteristics (ROC) Area under the Curve (AUC), and Accuracy. Accuracy is the percent of predictions the model correctly predicts. ROC is mainly used as a binary classifier (Fawcett, 2006). The ROC AUC is a value from 0.0 to 1.0 that assesses the goodness of fit for models with dichotomous output variables (Fawcett, 2006). The AUC is the probability the model will rank a randomly chosen positive instance (that the student completed their degree) higher than a negative instance (the student did not complete their degree). An AUC less than or equal to 0.5 indicates the model is worse than a model that picks one of the two classes at random.

The 2005-2012 online student logistic model contained N = 3326 records. Fifty-two students completed two majors within six years of their enrollment, resulting in a population larger than the overall 2005-2012 online population of N = 3274. Of the students in the logistic regression model, 56.79% completed their degrees within six years. Table 2 shows the results with the model coefficients. The model fit with AIC = 4207.35, Accuracy = 0.65, and AUC = 0.69. When using mean values for the other variables, the model predicts a 59.88% degree completion rate for online baccalaureate students in cohort programs compared to a 39.84% degree completion rate for those in non-cohort programs.

As shown in Table 2 (See Appendix 2), nine variables (in addition to the intercept) are statistically significant at the $p < 0.001$ level: Academic Discipline Computer, Academic Discipline Education, Academic Discipline Social Science Combined, Age, Diversity Unknown, Diversity White, Gender Male, and In Cohort. One variable, Academic Discipline Public Administration, is significant at the $p < 0.01$ level. Notable for this study, being in an online cohort has a statistically significant positive association with degree completion, controlling for other variables in the model.

An examination of the odds ratio Exp.(B) provides insights to interpret the strength of logistic regression results by quantifying the effect of the variables (Field, 2013). The odds ratio provides the effect on the odds of degree completion if the predictor variable is increased by one unit. The odds ratio is calculated with the following equation:

$$odds-ratio = \frac{p(x+1)}{p(x)}$$

If a variable has an odds ratio, Exp.(B), greater than one, increasing this variable increases the odds of the student graduating. If Exp.(B) is less than one, increasing this variable decreases the odds of the student graduating. As shown in Table 2, the Exp.(B) for the continuous variable Age is statistically significant. The effect is positive, and the odds ratio for Age (1.02) means increasing age by one year increases the odds of graduating by 1.02. Compared to the other variables that are statistically significant, the effect is weaker. Besides Age, all the other variables in the logistic regression model are categorical. For categorical variables, the odds ratio represents the effect of belonging to the category. For example, Table 2 shows that In Cohort has a statistically significant positive coefficient, with an odds ratio of

2.05. This means that membership in a cohort increases the odds of graduating 2.05 times, compared to not being in a cohort. All the statistically significant variables in the model have a positive effect.

To summarize the logistic regression analysis, the logistic regression model predicted a 59.88% degree completion rate for baccalaureate students in online cohort programs and a 39.84% degree completion rate for those in online non-cohort programs, with membership in an online cohort significant at the p < 0.001 level. This analysis suggests a significant relationship exists between the dependent variable of baccalaureate degree completion and the independent variable of participation in an online cohort major, controlling for the confounding factors in the model.

Multicollinearity was tested using the generalized variance-inflation factor (GVIF) for each categorical variable (Fox & Monette, 1992). The computed $GVIF^{\frac{1}{2df}}$ values were near one, suggesting little collinearity among the predictors. The next step in the analysis was to test the hypothesis.

The hypothesis proposes there is a significant positive relationship between membership in an online cohort major and degree completion for baccalaureate students. Statistical analyses provided a comparison between degree completion rates of students enrolled in online cohort programs and degree completion rates of students enrolled in online non-cohort programs. Given that the comparison in the hypothesis is of proportions (the rate of degree completion), the study used Pearson's chi-squared test χ^2 to test this hypothesis. Below are the equations for computing chi-squared.

$$\chi^2 = \sum_{i=1}^{n} \frac{(O_i - E_i)^2}{E_i}$$

$$\chi^2 = N \sum_{i=1}^{n} \frac{(O_i / N - p_i)^2}{p_i}$$

The null hypothesis is that the degree completion rates are the same, whereas the alternative hypothesis is that the degree completion rate for online cohort students is greater than the degree completion rate for online non-cohort students. The χ^2 statistics were used to calculate the p value from the chi-squared distribution. The effect size was calculated using Cohen's h (Cohen, 1995).

Calculations from the 2005-2012 online student dataset resulted in a mean degree completion rate of 59.88% for students enrolled in an online cohort major and a mean degree completion rate of 39.84% for those in an online non-cohort major. The results of the hypothesis test indicted p = 0.000. This indicates students enrolled in online cohort majors complete their degrees at higher rates than those enrolled in online non-cohort majors for this sample. Based on these results, the hypothesis that there is a significant positive relationship between membership in an online cohort major and degree completion for baccalaureate students is accepted.

SOLUTIONS AND RECOMMENDATIONS

The study used a logistic regression model to examine the relationship between membership in an online cohort major and degree completion. The results showed a statistically significant difference in degree completion rates between online cohort and online non-cohort students. This is consistent with prior studies indicating the cohort education model can positively influence student retention (Barnett et al., 2000; Bentley et al., 2004; Bista & Cox, 2014; Burnett, 1999; Pemberton & Akkary, 2010). The current study builds on the results of these prior studies and finds the cohort model's positive influence on retention applies to the online baccalaureate population at the research site. Based on the statistically significant difference in degree completion rates between online cohort (59.88%) and online non-cohort students (39.84%) for the 2005-2012 dataset, higher education institutions may benefit from offering array of online baccalaureate majors in the cohort format.

FUTURE RESEARCH DIRECTIONS

The findings of the study provide insights for areas of future research. Notably, the study found a statistically significant difference in degree completion rates between online cohort and online non-cohort students for the 2005-2012 dataset. While this supports the viability of the cohort education model for improving degree completion rates of online baccalaureate students at the research site, it also poses questions about the structure of the cohort model. For example, what portion of a baccalaureate degree should be delivered in a cohort to maximize retention? At what point in a degree does cohort education most influence retention? Does the cohort model have a similar influence on degree completion rates of residential students compared to online students? In terms of future research, the study results invite examination of the structure, timing, and underpinnings of the cohort education model, as well the influence of credit hours attained on degree completion. An additional area of future study is the application of pedagogy to the cohort model. For example, studies have reported that well-designed courses and student and faculty training positively influence online student retention (Bawa, 2016; Russell, Kleiman, Carey, & Douglas, 2009). What affect does the cohort model have on these pedagogical implications?

CONCLUSION

The goal of this study was to generate empirical findings to inform strategies for improving degree completion rates of online baccalaureate students. The study examined the relationship between membership in an online cohort major and degree completion of baccalaureate students. A quantitative secondary data analysis tested the relationships. Results of the study showed a statistically significant difference in degree completion rates between online cohort and online non-cohort students. Given the higher degree completion rates of online cohort students compared to online non-cohort students, offering cohort options to students may increase degree completion rates, which would benefit the students, the institution, and employers who are seeking workers who have earned baccalaureate degrees.

REFERENCES

Allen, I. E., & Seaman, J. (2016). *Online report card: Tracking online education in the United States.* Needham, MA: Babson Survey Research Group. Retrieved from http://onlinelearningsurvey.com/reports/onlinereportcard.pdf

Allen, W. (1992). The color of success: African-American college student outcomes at predominantly white and historically black public colleges and universities. *Harvard Educational Review*, *62*(1), 26–45. doi:10.17763/haer.62.1.wv5627665007v701

Aragon, S. R., & Johnson, E. S. (2008). Factors influencing completion and noncompletion of community college online courses. *American Journal of Distance Education*, *22*(3), 146–158. doi:10.1080/08923640802239962

Astin, A. W. (1984). Student involvement: A developmental theory for higher education. *Journal of College Student Development*, *25*(4), 297–308. Retrieved from https://eric.ed.gov/?id=EJ614278

Austrailan Government Department of Education. (2014). *Completion rates of domestic bachelor students: A cohort analysis*. Retrieved from https://docs.education.gov.au/system/files/doc/other/completion_rates_of_domestic_bachelor_students_-_a_cohort_analysis_-_updated_27032015.pdf

Barnett, B. G., Basom, M. R., Yerkes, D. M., & Norris, C. J. (2000). Cohorts in educational leadership programs: Benefits, difficulties, and the potential for developing school leaders. *Educational Administration Quarterly*, *36*(2), 255–282. doi:10.1177/0013161X00362005

Barnett, B. G., & Caffarella, R. S. (1992). *The use of cohorts: A powerful way for addressing issues of diversity in preparation programs*. Presented at the Annual Meeting of the University Council for Educational Administration, Minneapolis, MN. Retrieved from http://www.eric.ed.gov/ERICWebPortal/recordDetail?accno=ED354627

Barnett, B. G., & Muse, I. D. (1993). Cohort groups in educational administration: Promises and challenges. *Journal of School Leadership*, *3*(4), 400–415. doi:10.1177/105268469300300405

Bawa, P. (2016, January). Retention in online courses: Exploring issues and solutions — a literature review. *SAGE Open*, 1–11. doi:10.1177/2158244015621777

Beachboard, M. R., Beachboard, J. C., Li, W., & Adkison, S. R. (2011). Cohorts and relatedness: Self-Determination Theory as an explanation of how learning communities affect educational outcomes. *Research in Higher Education*, *52*(8), 853–874. doi:10.100711162-011-9221-8

Bennett, C., & Okinaka, A. M. (1990). Factors related to persistence among Asian, Black, Hispanic, and White undergraduates at a predominantly White university: Comparison between first and fourth year cohorts. *The Urban Review*, *22*(1), 33–60. doi:10.1007/BF01110631

Bentley, T., Zhao, F., Reames, E. H., & Reed, C. (2004). Frames we live by: Metaphors for the cohort. *Professional Educator*, *26*(2), 39–44. Retrieved from http://files.eric.ed.gov/fulltext/EJ728474.pdf

Bista, K., & Cox, D. W. (2014). Cohort-based doctoral programs: What we have learned over the last 18 years. *International Journal of Doctoral Studies*, *9*, 1–20. doi:10.28945/1941

Boton, E. C., & Gregory, S. (2015). Minimizing attrition in online degree courses. *Journal of Educators Online*, *12*(1), 62–90. doi:10.9743/jeo.2015.1.6

Bunn, J. (2004). Student persistence in a LIS distance education program. *Australian Academic and Research Libraries*, *35*(3), 253–269. doi:10.1080/00048623.2004.10755275

Bureau of Labor Statistics. (2016). *Unemployment rates and earnings by educational attainment, 2016*. Bureau of Labor Statistics, U.S. Department of Labor. Retrieved from https://www.bls.gov/emp/ep_chart_001.htm

Burnett, P. C. (1999). The supervision of doctoral dissertations using a collaborative cohort model. *Counselor Education and Supervision, 39*(9), 46–52. doi:10.1002/j.1556-6978.1999.tb01789.x

Carnevale, A. P., Smith, N., & Strohl, J. (2013). *Recovery: Job growth and education requirements through 2020*. Washington, DC: Georgetown Public Policy Institute, Center on Education and the Workforce. Retrieved from https://cew.georgetown.edu/wp-content/uploads/2014/11/Recovery2020.FR_.Web_.pdf

Carr, S. (2000). As distance education comes of age, the challenge is keeping the students. *The Chronicle of Higher Education, 46*(23), A39. Retrieved from https://eric.ed.gov/?id=EJ601725

Chickering, A. W., & Gamson, Z. F. (1987). Seven principles for good practice in undergraduate education. *AAHE Bulletin, 39*(7), 3–7. Retrieved from http://files.eric.ed.gov/fulltext/ED282491.pdf

Cohen, J. (1995). *Statistical power analysis for the behavioral sciences* (2nd ed.). Hillsdale, NJ: Erlbaum.

Connor, K. R., & Killmer, N. (2001). Cohorts, collaboration, and community: Does contextual teacher education really work? *Action in Teacher Education, 23*(3), 46–53. doi:10.1080/01626620.2001.10463074

Dziuban, C., Moskal, P., & Hartman, J. (2005). Higher education, blended learning and the generations: Knowledge is power-no more. In *Elements of quality online education: Engaging communities*. Retrieved from http://www.oswego.edu/~celt/Dziuban_Knowledge_is_Power_Oct_2004.doc

Fawcett, T. (2006). An introduction to ROC analysis. *Pattern Recognition Letters, 27*(8), 861–874. doi:10.1016/j.patrec.2005.10.010

Field, A. (2013). *Discovering statistics using IBM SPSS statistics* (4th ed.). Los Angeles, CA: SAGE Publications.

Fox, J., & Monette, G. (1992). Generalized collinearity diagnostics. *Journal of the American Statistical Association, 87*(417), 178–183. doi:10.1080/01621459.1992.10475190

GLM. (n.d.). *Fitting generalized linear models*. Retrieved from https://www.rdocumentation.org/packages/stats/versions/3.5.1/topics/glm

Greenland, S. J., & Moore, C. (2014). Patterns of student enrolment and attrition in Australian open access online education: A preliminary case study. *Open Praxis, 6*(1), 45–54. doi:10.5944/openpraxis.6.1.95

Harrell, I. L. II, & Bower, B. L. (2011). Student characteristics that predict persistence in community college online courses. *American Journal of Distance Education, 25*(3), 178–191. doi:10.1080/08923647.2011.590107

Hart, C. (2012). Factors associated with student persistence in an online program of study: A review of the literature. *Journal of Interactive Online Learning, 11*(1), 19–42. Retrieved from http://www.ncolr.org/jiol/issues/pdf/11.1.2.pdf

Hurtado, S., & Carter, D. F. (1997). Effects of college transition and perceptions of the campus racial climate on Latino college students' sense of belonging. *Sociology of Education, 70*(4), 324–345. doi:10.2307/2673270

Ivankova, N. V., & Stick, S. L. (2007). Students' persistence in a distributed doctoral program in educational leadership in higher education: A mixed methods study. *Research in Higher Education, 48*(1), 93–135. doi:10.100711162-006-9025-4

Jaffee, D. (2001). Peer cohorts and the unintended consequences of freshman learning communities. *College Teaching, 55*(2), 65–71. doi:10.3200/CTCH.55.2.65-71

James, S., Swan, K., & Daston, C. (2016). Retention, progression and the taking of online courses. *Journal of Asynchronous Learning Networks, 20*(2). doi:10.24059/olj.v20i2.780

Johnson, N. (2012). *The institutional costs of student attrition*. Washington, DC: Delta Cost Project at American Institutes for Research. Retrieved from http://eric.ed.gov/?id=ED536126

Kuh, G. D. (2001). Assessing what really matters to student learning: Inside the National Survey of Student Engagement. *Change: The Magazine of Higher Learning, 33*(3), 10–17. doi:10.1080/00091380109601795

Kuh, G. D. (2003). What we're learning about student engagement from NSSE: Benchmarks for effective educational practices. *Change: The Magazine of Higher Learning, 35*(2), 24–32. doi:10.1080/00091380309604090

Kuh, G. D. (2009). The National Survey of Student Engagement: Conceptual and empirical foundations. *New Directions for Institutional Research, 141*, 5–20. doi:10.1002/ir.283

Kuh, G. D., Kinzie, J., Cruce, T., Shoup, R., & Gonyea, R. M. (2007). *Connecting the dots: Multi-faceted analyses of the relationships between student engagement results from the NSSE, and the institutional practices and conditions that foster student success*. Bloomington, IN: Center for Postsecondary Research, Indiana University Bloomington. Retrieved from https://webmail.csuchico.edu/vpaa/wasc/docs/EERDocs/NSSE/NSSE_Connecting_the_Dots_Report.pdf

Lee, Y., & Choi, J. (2011). A review of online course dropout research: Implications for practice and future research. *Educational Technology Research and Development, 59*(5), 593–618. doi:10.100711423-010-9177-y

Linderman, D., & Kolenovic, Z. (2013). Moving the completion needle at community colleges: CUNY's accelerated study in associate programs (ASAP). *Change: The Magazine of Higher Learning, 45*(5), 43–50. doi:10.1080/00091383.2013.824350

Maher, M. A. (2005). The evolving meaning and influence of cohort membership. *Innovative Higher Education, 30*(3), 195–211. doi:10.100710755-005-6304-5

Mandzuk, D., Hasinoff, S., & Seifert, K. (2003). Inside a student cohort: Teacher education from a social capital perspective. *Canadian Journal of Education, 2*, 168–184. Retrieved from http://www.jstor.org/stable/10.2307/1602159

Martin, D. (1977). Early warning of bank failure. A logit regression approach. *Journal of Banking & Finance, 1*(3), 249–276. doi:10.1016/0378-4266(77)90022-X

Martin, K. A., Goldwasser, M. M., & Galentino, R. (2016). Impact of cohort bonds on student satisfaction and engagement. *Current Issues in Education, 19*(3), 1–14. Retrieved from http://cie.asu.edu/ojs/index.php/cieatasu/article/view/1550

Morris, L. V., Finnegan, C., & Wu, S.-S. (2005). Tracking student behavior, persistence, and achievement in online courses. *The Internet and Higher Education, 8*(3), 221–231. doi:10.1016/j.iheduc.2005.06.009

National Center for Education Statistics. (2000). *Classification of Instructional Programs (CIP 2000)*. Retrieved from https://nces.ed.gov/pubs2002/cip2000/

National Survey of Student Engagement. (2015). *Engagement indicators & high-impact practices*. Bloomington, IN: Indiana University Center for Postsecondary Research. Retrieved from http://nsse.indiana.edu/html/high_impact_practices.cfm

Northrup, P. (2002). Online learners' preferences for interaction. *Quarterly Review of Distance Education*. Retrieved from http://www.eric.ed.gov/ERICWebPortal/custom/portlets/recordDetails/detailmini.jshttps://eric.ed.gov/?id=EJ654234

O'Shea, S. E., Stone, C., & Delahunty, J. (2015). I 'feel' like I am at university even though I am online." Exploring how students narrate their engagement with higher education institutions in an online learning environment. *Distance Education, 36*(1), 41–58. doi:10.1080/01587919.2015.1019970

OECD (Ed.). (2016). How many students complete tertiary education? In *Education at a glance 2016: OECD indicators*. Paris, France: Organisation for Economic Cooperation and Development. Retrieved from https://www.oecd-ilibrary.org/education/data/education-at-a-glance/education-at-a-glance-graduation-and-entry-rates-edition-2016_a7768c94-en

Pace, C. R. (1984). Measuring the quality of student effort. *Current Issues in Higher Education, 2*, 10–16. Retrieved from http://files.eric.ed.gov/fulltext/ED255099.pdf

Palvia, S., Aeron, P., Gupta, P., Mahapatra, D., Rosner, R., & Sindhi, S. (2018). Online education: Worldwide status, challenges, trends, and implications. *Journal of Global Information Technology Management, 21*(4), 233–241. doi:10.1080/1097198X.2018.1542262

Park, J., & Choi, H. J. (2009). Factors influencing adult learners' decision to drop out or persist in online learning. *Journal of Educational Technology & Society, 12*(4), 202–217. Retrieved from https://www.researchgate.net/profile/Ji-Hye_Park/publication/220374458_Factors_Influencing_Adult_Learners'_Decision_to_Drop_Out_or_Persist_in_Online_Learning/links/00b495243f10b72a43000000.pdf

Pascarella, E. T. (1985). College environmental influences on learning and cognitive development: A critical review and synthesis. In J. C. Smart (Ed.), *Higher education handbook of theory and research* (pp. 1–61). New York, NY: Agatha Press.

Pascarella, E. T., Smart, J. C., & Ethington, C. A. (1986). Long-term persistence of two-year college students. *Research in Higher Education, 24*(1), 47–71. doi:10.1007/BF00973742

Pemberton, C. L. A., & Akkary, R. K. (2010). A cohort, is a cohort, is a cohort…or is it? *Journal of Research on Leadership Education, 5*(5), 179–208. doi:10.1177/194277511000500501

Rausch, D. W., & Crawford, E. (2012). Building the future with cohorts: Communities of inquiry. *Metropolitan Universities, 23*(1), 79–89. Retrieved from https://journals.iupui.edu/index.php/muj/article/view/20505/20103

Reason, R. D., Terenzini, P. T., & Domingo, R. J. (2006). First things first: Developing academic competence in the first year of college. *Research in Higher Education, 47*(2), 149–175. doi: 10.1007/sl1162-005-8884-4

Roberts, J., & Styron, R. (2010). Student satisfaction and persistence: Factors vital to student retention. *Research in Higher Education, 6*(3), 1–18. Retrieved from http://www.aabri.com/manuscripts/09321.pdf

Russell, M., Kleiman, G., Carey, R., & Douglas, J. (2009). Comparing self-paced and cohort-based online courses for teachers. *Journal of Research on Technology in Education, 41*(4), 443–466. doi:10.1080/15391523.2009.10782538

Schneider, M. (2010). *Finishing the first lap: The cost of first year student attrition in America's four year colleges and universities*. Washington, DC: American Institutes for Research. Retrieved from http://www.air.org/files/AIR_Schneider_Finishing_the_First_Lap_Oct101.pdf

Schneider, M., & Yin, L. (2011). *The high cost of low graduation rates: How much does dropping out of college really cost?* Washington, DC: American Institutes for Research. Retrieved from http://www.air.org/resource/high-cost-low-graduation-rates

Seaman, J. E., Allen, I. E., & Seaman, J. (2018). *Grade increase: Tracking distance education in the United States*. Needham, MA: Babson Survey Research Group. Retrieved from http://onlinelearningsurvey.com/reports/gradeincrease.pdf

Shapiro, D., Dundar, A., Wakhungu, P. K., Yuan, X., Nathan, A., & Hwang, Y. (2016). *Completing college: A national view of student attainment rates – Fall 2010 cohort (Signature Report No. 12)*. Herndon, VA: National Student Clearinghouse Research Center.

Shea, P., & Bidjerano, T. (2018). Online course enrollment in community college and degree completion: The tipping point. *International Review of Research in Open and Distributed Learning, 19*(2), 282–293. doi:10.19173/irrodl.v19i2.3460

Stone, C., & O'Shea, S. (2019). Older, online and first: Recommendations for retention and success. *Australasian Journal of Educational Technology, 35*(1), 57–69. doi:10.14742/ajet.3913

Stone, C., OShea, S. O., & May, J. (2016). Opportunity through online learning: Experiences of first-in-family students in online open-entry higher education. *Australian Journal of Adult Learning, 56*(2), 146–169. doi:10.1080/01587919.2015.1019970

Tinto, V. (1987). *Leaving college: Rethinking the causes and cures of student attrition*. Chicago, IL: University of Chicago Press.

Tinto, V. (1997). Classrooms as communities: Exploring the educational character of student persistence. *The Journal of Higher Education, 68*(6), 599–623. doi:10.2307/2959965

Tinto, V. (2010). From theory to action: Exploring the institutional conditions for student retention. In J. Smart (Ed.), *Higher Education: Handbook of Theory and Research* (Vol. 25, pp. 51–89). New York, NY: Springer. doi:10.1007/978-90-481-8598-6_2

Tinto, V., & Cullen, J. (1973). *Dropout in higher education: A review and theoretical synthesis of recent research.* Washington, DC: Office of Planning, Budgeting, and Evaluation. Retrieved from http://files.eric.ed.gov/fulltext/ED078802.pdf

U.S. Department of Education. (n.d.a). *IPEDS: About IPEDS.* Retrieved from https://nces.ed.gov/ipeds/about-ipeds

U.S. Department of Education. (n.d.b). *IPEDS: Definitions for new race and ethnicity categories.* Retrieved from https://nces.ed.gov/ipeds/report-your-data/race-ethnicity-definitions

Watts, J. (2013). Why hyperbonding occurs in the learning community classroom and what to do about it. *Learning Communities Research and Practice, 1*(3). Retrieved from http://washingtoncenter.evergreen.edu/lcrpjournal/vol1/iss3/4

Willging, P. A., & Johnson, S. D. (2009). Factors that influence students' decision to dropout of online courses. *Journal of Asynchronous Learning Networks, 13*(3), 115–127. Retrieved from http://files.eric.ed.gov/fulltext/EJ862360.pdf

Wine, J., Janson, N., & Wheeless, S. (2011). *2004/09 Beginning Postsecondary Students Longitudinal Study (BPS:04/09).* Washington, DC: National Center for Education Statistics, Institute of Education Sciences, U.S. Department of Education. Retrieved from http://nces.ed.gov/pubsearch

Xu, D., & Jaggars, S. S. (2011). *Online and hybrid course enrollment and performance in Washington State Community and Technical Colleges.* Retrieved from https://files.eric.ed.gov/fulltext/ED517746.pdf

Zhao, C.-M., & Kuh, G. D. (2004). Adding value: Learning communities and student engagement. *Research in Higher Education, 45*(2), 115–138. doi:10.1023/B:RIHE.0000015692.88534.de

KEY TERMS AND DEFINITIONS

Age: Age is the age of the student when he or she enrolled at the University, as calculated from the birthdate indicated in their student record.

Course Format: Course format reflects the independent variables cohort and non-cohort. The course format is cohort if the major includes all cohort courses, or non-cohort if the major includes all non-cohort courses.

Degree Completion: Degree completion reflects the dependent variable of degree completion. Student record data was used to determine if a student completed their baccalaureate degree at the research site within six years of their first enrollment. Data was not available for students who transferred out and completed their degree at another institution within six years.

Gender: As indicated in student record data, gender includes the categories male, female, and other/unknown.

Pell-Eligible: Students were categorized as Pell-eligible if they were eligible for Pell grants during any point in their baccalaureate enrollment at the research site, as indicated by student record data. An estimated 80% of baccalaureate students at the research site apply for federal financial aid.

APPENDIX 1

Table 1. Demographic information

Characteristic		2005-2012 Online Students (N)	2005-2012 Online Students (%)
Age	18 to 24	604	18.45
	25 to 34	1455	44.44
	35 to 44	798	24.37
	45 to 54	359	10.97
	55 to 64	57	1.74
	Unknown	1	0.03
Gender	Female	1598	48.81
	Male	1672	51.07
	Other	4	0.12
Pell-Eligibility	Eligible	979	29.90
	Ineligible	2295	70.10
Diversity	Am. Indian or Alaska Native	17	0.52
	Asian	38	1.16
	Black or African American	290	8.86
	Hispanic or Latino	115	3.51
	Native Hawaiian or Other Pacific Is.	8	0.24
	White	1299	39.68
	Unknown or Prefer Not to Report	1507	46.03
Course Format	Cohort	2773	84.70
	Non-Cohort	501	15.30
Graduated	Yes	1882	57.48
	No	1392	42.52
Total		3274	100.00

APPENDIX 2

Table 2. Logistic regression model for 2005-2012 online students

Variable	B	SE	Exp.(B)	Sig.	
(Intercept)	-2.30	0.23	0.10	0.000	***
AD Computer	0.74	0.11	2.09	0.000	***
AD Education	1.33	0.20	3.80	0.000	***
AD Health	-0.17	0.37	0.84	0.648	
AD Homeland Security	-0.16	0.36	0.85	0.666	
AD Misc.	-0.17	0.24	0.84	0.485	
AD Psychology	-13.85	282.79	0.00	0.961	
AD Public Administration	1.13	0.41	3.08	0.006	**
AD Social Science Combined	1.34	0.11	3.82	0.000	***
Age	0.02	0.00	1.02	0.000	***
Diversity Hispanic	0.31	0.23	1.36	0.177	
Diversity Other	0.53	0.29	1.70	0.067	
Diversity Unknown	0.84	0.14	2.33	0.000	***
Diversity White	0.64	0.14	1.90	0.000	***
Gender Male	0.27	0.08	1.31	0.001	***
In Cohort	0.72	0.12	2.05	0.000	***
Is Pell-Eligible	0.03	0.09	1.03	0.713	

Note. Significance Codes: 0 '***' 0.001 '**' 0.01 '*' 0.05 '.' 0.1 ' ' 1. AD=Academic Discipline; *B*=logistic coefficient; *SE*=Standard Error; Exp.(*B*)=odds ratio.

Chapter 10
Relationships in Online Learning Experiences:
Identifying and Creating Positive Relationships in Online Learning

Robyn J. Emde
The University of the Cumberlands, USA

Erin Kathleen Doherty
The University of the Cumberlands, USA

Bradley 'Scott' Ellis
The University of the Cumberlands, USA

Dina Flynt
The University of the Cumberlands, USA

ABSTRACT

A relationship is documented as a personal investment in another's life. Relationships add to learning environments as substantial to the growth of students. In an online learning environment, a relationship is defined by the mutual agreement between an educator and a learner in which expectations of increased knowledge gained through the education experience provided by the educator. It is evident that in an online environment it is vital to consistently evaluate in order to have the enrichment of relationships between student to professors and student to student. Research has shown that the creation of such environments results in a feeling of community and social presence for the students. Student satisfaction extends to the relationship students feel toward their professors. The strength of the student to professor relationship results in a key component in student retention. The method in which the relationships are established and built in an online environment are vital for student satisfaction and retention of students within a program of study.

DOI: 10.4018/978-1-7998-0115-3.ch010

INTRODUCTION: LEARNING IS RELATIONAL

Online education at its core is simply a contemporary extension of the concept of distance learning, which can be traced back to the 1700's (Harting & Erthal, 2005). Could we also consider a public library as a type of distance education? The famous libraries of antiquity attest to the mission of our ancestors to pass down knowledge they considered fundamental and critical to their descendant's success. This model of learning also assumes that there would be curious and self-motivated learners willing to invest their time to gain from other's experiences, and to then expand that knowledge and passes it down to successive generations. Now, as it was then, there is an implied contract, or relationship, between the educator and the learner: the learner seeks knowledge that the educator commits to provide. As consumers when we want a hamburger, we pay a set price and expect to receive a particular product. If we are fortunate, we may be able to engage with the product and increase enjoyment through the addition of some vegetation, dairy, grains and additional protein (i.e. a bacon cheeseburger with lettuce, tomato and mustard). Now we are getting somewhere! While this relationship on its face seems purely transactional, there should be no stigma associated with that implication. A relationship does not have to be exclusively intimate, familial or bound by proximity or time. We can take solace in a much-anticipated book, completing a household task, receiving good news, or just taking some personal time to meditate. Likewise, we can thoroughly enjoy that cheeseburger and/or the service of the individual who provided it and/or the environment in which it was provided and/or the price that we paid. There is a personal investment in all of our life transactions, big or small. These transactions can carry such weight in our lives that our trajectory can radically change through just one positive or negative transaction. Each of these transactions carry the fundamentals of a relationship, and our engagement in these transactions can influence our perceptions of that relationship.

Early human learning is necessarily relational. While small humans have basic impulses and inherent instincts, their true potential for learning is maximized based upon the knowledge, skills and goodwill of their caretakers. That caregiver-child relationship acts as a conduit through which the individual grows and develops. Over time, and with varying degrees of success, the young human grows, and their learning is expanded and aided by extended family relationships, social relationships, and cultural-social institutions. While each of these relationships is unique, individuals are still learning in relationship with each other. Primary education is based in large part on a series of relationships (with teachers, peers, school and community). This model has persisted for quite some time, and is more or less a collaborative process among the participants; although admittedly the young person's willingness and intrinsic motivation to learn can fluctuate due to a variety of factors.

How Can Educational Relationships Be Measured Reliably?

For the sake of online education, let us utilize the following parameters to define a relationship: a mutual agreement between an educator and a learner in which the learner has expectations of increased knowledge gained through the education experience provided by the educator. But measuring the quality and depth of online education relationships is difficult. The research regarding online educational relationships is scarce; although there is certainly no shortage of student survey data. Student surveys are a primary means to help educational institutions gauge their student's perceptions of the programs (Lowenthal, Bower, & Chen, 2015). These surveys, however, focus more on teacher feedback, content feedback and overall student experiences, not on the student's relationships to others or the content. It is difficult to benchmark overall relationships in context with online education unless it is compared to an alternative, such as residentially-based coursework. In some instances, students rate their online course experiences lower than those of face-to-face courses (Lowenthal et al., 2015). Interestingly, depending on the course content, students actually prefer a combination of face-to-face *and* online sessions, as opposed to purely online or face-to-face delivered content (Salter & Gardner, 2016). But the option of online education continues to motivate adults to pursue higher education with increased enrollments seen consistently year after year (Friedman, 2018). From this perspective, the implied relationship and perceived benefits can be seen as positive. As collaboration among peers increases in online learning, student positive perceptions of online learning also increase. In MBA programs, students who are able to engage with their peers report increased positive perceptions of the educational experience (Kyong-Lee et al, 2005). This research indirectly indicates that the quality of relationships within the program is important to the students even as far back as 2005.

Point, Counterpoint, Pivot

As technology evolves and changes the way a learner accesses educational content, the learning relationship and learner behaviors will also change. In years past, written correspondence, itinerant lecturers and textbooks morphed into radio broadcasts, telephone conferences, audio cassettes and televised lectures. Those methods continued to evolve and distance learning included VHS taped lectures and emails. A technology progressed, DVD lectures, online discussion boards and interactive content through learning management systems became popular in the online learning environment. Even now, online access and student engagement continues to increase. Interestingly, as engagement of students through various learning dimensions increases, online student commitment is somewhat opposite to their positive enrollment numbers. We now see that online students tend to drop out at higher rates than their traditional, on-campus counterparts (Park & Choi, 2009). Does this mean that the online educational relationship is disposable in the mind of the learner and that deeper relationships are required to help keep the student engaged? Does increased access to knowledge have the unintended consequence of devaluing that knowledge, and by extension then devalue the learning relationship? Or does this mean that there are a variety of external factors that affect the educational relationship of an online student in the home that are not as present or influential on campus? In the future, as educational content moves onto no-cost or low-cost platforms such as podcasts, YouTube and massive online courses (MOOCs) platforms, will the wave of free online content overtake the traditional fee-based educational model as it did with music? And if so, how will that influence the educational relationship? Exploring peer relationships and professor-student relationships within the Community of Inquiry Model first introduced by Garrison, Anderson and Archer (2000) will help to define the often-obscure element of relationships in online learning.

Community of Inquiry Model

Theorists have long addressed the importance of social interaction in learning. Bandura (2001) emphasized in his social cognitive theory that learning requires active engagement with others. Not only do high levels of engagement with course content influence academic achievement but so do high levels of engagement with peers and faculty (Kuh, 2003). In an online class, students may feel disconnected from their peers and instructor if there is little interaction among them. This lack of interaction can cause feelings of isolation and lack of support (by peers, faculty, and the school itself). When students do not feel supported, there is the risk they may not continue with their education. Getting students to engage in an online environment actively requires extra effort from the professor to initiate active and meaningful interaction between the students. Social presence is an important factor related to online learning. Short, Williams, and Christie (1976) developed social presence theory that which is defined as "the degree of salience of the other person in the mediated interaction and the consequent salience of the interpersonal relationships." Social presence theory postulates that the amount of social presence individuals have while using other mediums to communicate outside of face-to-face interactions have a direct impact on satisfaction. When discussing social presence as it relates to the online learning environment, social learning theory refers to how connected a student feels to the class, peers, and instructor. Adding to social presence theory, the Community Of Inquiry (COI) model formulates that deeper learning in an online setting occurs when a community of learners participates in reflective thinking and discussion (Garrison, Cleveland-Innes, & Fung, 2009). Cognitive presence, social presence, and teaching presence are the fundamental elements within the COI model. Cognitive presence refers to the extent that learners within the community can construct meaning through its communication (Garrison et.al., 2000). Teaching presence involves how the course content is designed and facilitated (Garrison et al., 2000). The element of social presence most directly addresses peer relationships and professor-student relationships and will be the emphasis of this chapter. In this instance, the definition for social presence is as "the ability of participants to identify with the community, communicate purposefully in a trusting environment and develop an inter-personal relationship by way of projecting the individual differences" (Garrison, 2009). As one can imagine, social presence and relationships are not a natural nor an automatic occurrence in the online environment. Social presence must be cultivated by the school, the professor, and the students for it to occur. Students with a sense of social presence are more likely to be comfortable interacting with their classmates, asking for help, assisting others, and sharing information with their classmates. Developing social presence leads to a feeling of a sense of community among students and is beneficial to overall learning and perception of satisfaction.

Peer Relationships in Online Learning

When students look for online educational programs, the quality of relationships they may have with other students is not usually at the forefront of their minds. Often potential students are looking for flexibility, they want to know how they can fit their education into their busy schedules. Building relationships or even having communication with their fellow students may not be a top priority. In contrast to what online learners' initial priorities may be, educators and researchers are growing more aware of just how important relationships among peers within the online learning community are. Social interaction and the quality of that interaction directly correlates with both course satisfaction (Croxton, 2014; Cheng & Chau, 2016; Drouin, 2008) and perceived learning outcomes (Eom & Ashill, 2016). Therefore, even though students may not be motivated for social connection in their online education, it is vital for their learning and overall satisfaction. Online education does not have to suffer in areas of social interaction and community. Despite the lack of in-person, face-to-face contact; social interaction, and the development of a sense of community within the online format are not only possible but also an important aspect of learning.

Creating a Social Presence and a Sense of Community

Online learning takes place in synchronous and/or asynchronous formats. Both synchronous and asynchronous online learning formats can foster a sense of isolation if there is not a mindful effort to build a sense of community among the students. Isolation can lead to the lack of socialization within the classroom (Lambert & Fisher, 2013). The online format is not the only cause of student community isolation. Student's busy lives and time constraints that include family and work obligations may make students resistant to the idea of interacting one another. The research shows, however, that student interactions are vital to learning and overall student satisfaction. Student satisfaction is an important indicator of whether a student decides to drop out of an online course (Levy, 2007). To achieve student satisfaction, a sense of community within the learning environment must be established. When students feel a sense of community and social presence, satisfaction with the course increases (Drouin, 2008).

Collaboration and Interaction Using Technology

Social presence and a sense of community occur as a result of intentional planning. The use of current technology can encourage student-to-student interaction, collaboration, and interactivity (Bickle & Rucker, 2018; Croxton, 2014; Stephens & Roberts, 2017). School leaders, faculty, and students can utilize technology to enhance student interactions, and help build community. As technology continues to get more sophisticated, so may the ways it is used within the learning environment.

At the school level, schools make a significant impact on community building utilizing social media platforms, such as Facebook, Twitter, Pinterest, and Instagram (Witzig, Spencer, & Myers, 2017). The use of social media fosters a sense of community as members can interact with each other outside the classroom environment. Tailored social media content engages students by sharing knowledge, promoting events, and encouraging conversation among students. Interestingly, online programs are not taking advantage of this community building opportunity as much as their traditional brick and mortar program counterparts (Witzig et al., 2017). Utilizing social media on the school and program level is an effective way to build both social presence and a sense of community.

Many schools also require mandatory in-person orientations or yearly residencies. Students are required to attend sessions/meetings on-campus or at a designated meeting place to acquire necessary information about the school/program. Course topics and instruction may also be introduced. The opportunities to learn the processes and procedures of the school also allows students to network and nurture relationships among one another in a bonding experience. When connecting with peers at an orientation type meeting, some online students find they want to continue the relationships they developed with their peers (Berry, 2019). This initial connection can be a starting point for students themselves to take the initiative to engage and develop relationships with their cohorts.

Students are not the only ones responsible for developing peer relationships within the community. It is essential for the professor of the class to also help facilitate social presence and community. As the steward of the class learning, the professor can utilize numerous tools that foster social presence and therefore lead to a sense of community. Discussion boards are the most common online tool used to help facilitate communication between students. "Threads" are created on different topics, and students can respond to questions. Students can also respond to each other's posts, mimicking a conversation on various subject content. When engaging in online discussion boards, students tend to participate more in this format than in face-to-face class conversation (Zhou, 2015). As students become comfortable with one other increased interaction and participation continue to grow. The discussions on the boards also tend to be more collaborative and constructive- possibly due to having time to process and develop a well thought out responses.

Discussion boards are one type of technology that can be used to help facilitate student interaction and create a social presence (Drange & Kargaard, 2017). Instant messaging (i.e. WhatsApp), audio/visual conferencing, virtual reality, vlogs, and blogs are all platforms that can be utilized in group projects and collaboration (Dailey-Hebert, 2018). Using these various applications allows students to "present" themselves to others and also see, hear, and interact with not just a computer but with real people. Personalities can shine through, and students can develop a stronger sense of who each person is and the attributes they bring to the class. The class can also be divided into small groups (just like in a traditional classroom), facilitating even deeper discourse. These interactions provide opportunities for stronger bonds to form, creating a sense of community and support for one another. Applications such as the ones mentioned above are ideal for the online learner. Students can collaborate and participate in-group work, yet they do not have to all be together in the same place or at the same time, a benefit unique to online classrooms.

As schools and faculty promote peer relationships, students in an online environment also forge relationships with their peers independent of specific class work assignments. Most students are already familiar with the technology used to connect people, and they use it independently to forge personal relationships. Students may text or call one another, bond through social media apps (public and private closed group forums), and may even meet face-to-face (Berry, 2019). These interactions may be more private as institutional authority does not oversee them. Private communications may also turn more personal in context, developing into genuine friendships, students supporting each other not only about their educational endeavors but in various other areas of their lives (Berry, 2019).

Not just one person or one entity is responsible for developing peer relationships in an online learning environment. Relationships between students can be fostered on a school level, by the course instructor or by the students themselves. The important factor is that these relationships do develop as the feeling of connectedness to peers can lead to overall course satisfaction and success.

Professor to Student Relationships in the Online Learning Environment

Online learning is growing at a rapid pace at universities and colleges across the United States. Students gravitate toward online schooling in order to meet personal needs and obligations such as work and family commitments. However, replacing the traditional brick-and-mortar educational setting with an online learning environment comes with its own unique challenges. One of those challenges is how the student will develop a relationship with their instructor in order to foster the academic development necessary to be successful in the educational setting. The importance of the professor-student relationship cannot be overlooked, as student engagement with the professor has been noted to be a factor in retention and graduation rates (Berry, 2018). One of the most frequently reported challenges to the online learning environment is of the quality of the professor-student interaction. A strong relationship between the professor and student is a key component in the academic success of the student (Underdown & Martin, 2016).

Perspectives on the Professor to Student Relationship

A qualitative study of 229 students in 16 graduate level business courses was done to determine how they perceived their relationship with their instructor. Most of these students had previous experience in a traditional classroom setting. Seven open-ended questions were posed to the students and over 6,400 individual comments were received. Over 80% of the students who were involved in the study had experience in a traditional higher education classroom setting (Berry, 2018). Responses to the survey indicated that students were aware of the differences in the professor's role in the online classroom compared to a traditional classroom setting. This was mentioned by more than 70% of respondents. Students felt that they were in a position to have to work more autonomously in the online classroom. Although this was a positive for some, they noted it is important that they demonstrate more self-discipline, have better time management skills, and be more committed. Some students reported that it was more difficult to develop relationships in the online learning environment. It was reported that electronic communication only provided necessary information and did not capture everything that face-to-face meetings could. Others, however, felt that the electronic communication allowed for increased opportunity for communication and responses. It was also noted by those surveyed felt that in the traditional classroom setting there are typically a few students who dominate classroom time and those that are shy may be less likely to talk. In contrast, the online classroom allows all students to participate more fully as there are various avenues within the online environment to communicate (Berry, 2018).

Willigeng and Johnson (2009) conducted a study to determine why students drop out of online courses. Participants of the study were previous students who dropped out of graduate programs at the University of Illinois at Urbana-Champaign. One of the reasons provided for leaving the program related to the lack of individual attention from professors in the program (Willigeng & Johnson, 2009).

Over the past decade, there has been an increase in the amount of students with diverse backgrounds entering online education (Willigeng & Johnson, 2009). With the growing number of students with different cultural backgrounds engaging in online higher education, it is critical for the professor to be aware of how to connect with those from varying backgrounds. Green, Hoffman, Donovan, and Phuntosog (2017) researched the level of connectedness that graduate students taking online courses felt they had with their professors. Their research utilized a mixed methods approach by using an online survey with follow-up interviews consisting of open-ended questions. The questions revolved around their feelings of connectedness to the program, their peers, and their professors. There were 50 who completed the study. The most prevalent theme in the responses was the concern of communication. Students reported that being able to communicate with professors electronically through "instant messaging and Voxer" helped them feel more connected (Green, Hoffman, Donovan, Phuntsog, 2017).

Students also reported that there was an increased level of connection with the professor when multimedia methods were employed in the online learning environment. Professors who utilized video within the classroom received higher feedback from students and they were perceived as being more engaged. When the professor was perceived as being more engaged, the students were also more engaged. Videos can be used for welcoming students, reviewing the syllabus, going over each week's assignments, and announcements (Undertown & Martin, 2016).

Social Presence

The student's level of satisfaction with a course increases as the instructor's social presence increases. Increasing student interaction was not found to be significant enough alone; it was crucial that the professor also maintain a positive social presence as well (Bickle, 2019). It is the task of the instructor to create an environment in which the professor-student relationship is positive and promotes student success. Students feel more connected and engaged when an online social presence has been established by the professor (Dickinson, 2017). The professor's personality, self-confidence, and attitude are also contributing factors to student engagement. (Gray, 2016).

In 2003, Richard and Swan examined the issue of social presence in the online classroom and concluded that social presence influenced student outcomes and satisfaction. Their research concluded that personal emails and specific feedback on assignments were more significant than the actual technology involved in the online course itself (Huss, 2013). Instructor presence is a critical piece to the student engagement process in online education. Whether it is through the development of the course, activities, or interaction with students, the instructor presence can enhance the learning process and strengthen the professor/student relationship. As technology has evolved, online learning classes have offered ways to improve social presence, such as the use of video to gauge facial expressions (Bickle, 2019). Utilizing personal video and audio, sharing personal stories, and participating in online discussions are all methods that can increase the instructor presence. This translates to the student feeling more connected to the professor and class (Gray, 2016).

Characteristics of Successful Online Instructors

Research continues to be conducted to determine what characteristics online instructors possess that best facilitates a strong professor-student relationship. Many studies show students rate instructor displays of understanding, caring and availability as important factors toward developing that relationship (Ratliff, 2018; Murphy& Rodriguez, 2012; Joyner, 2014). Instructors must make an effort to get to know their students, understand their unique needs and be flexible.

Online instructors must be understanding of the challenges online students may face (Ratliff, 2018). Assumptions cannot be made about a student's level of knowledge of the technology or the Learning Management System (LMS). Students appreciate the instructors that take the time to help the students navigate the virtual classroom. It is also important that online instructors also take in account students' individual circumstances such as work schedules, families, and living environment. When instructors show understanding as it relates to these various circumstances, they are in a better position to support the students' needs.

Rapport between faculty and students is also increased when professors communicate a sense of caring (Ratliff, 2018). Ways instructors can communicate caring is by being available to the students, being responsive, and providing sensitive feedback. Intentional caring by online professors can improve educational outcomes. In a study by Sitzman & Leners (2006), students identified specific behaviors they equated with professor caring. These behaviors included timely and frequent feedback, providing multiple ways for contact, clarity in communication and teacher's commitment to learning. Joyner (2014) found that students appreciated outside classroom communication such as consistent emailing, phone calls and the ability to video chat.

Strategies to Develop Relationships

There are various strategies that professors can employ to promote a positive professor-student relationship. Since most of the communication in the online educational environment is done electronically, the professor can improve the electronic communication by using a variety of methods to increase student engagement and connectedness. Students perform when they feel they have a positive relationship with the instructor and the instructor must work with the student to develop the positive relationship. The basis of an effective online class is the professor-student relationship.

Instructors struggle with making courses personal and interactive. Students desire a personal relationship with professors; however, the online learning format can be a hurdle (Martin, 2019). To combat the hurdle, instructors can make the effort to gather personal information of the students in the class (Murphy & Rodriguez, 2012). This can be done by having student's complete introduction posts where they discuss themselves. The professor can respond to student posts and even point out commonalities between the students or between the students and the professor (Ratliff, 2018).

In terms of corresponding with students via electronic communication, the tone can affect how students perceive the professor. Incorporating a more personal, positive, and friendly tone to the electronic communication works toward establishing better relationships with students. In order to develop effective online communication skills, the professor must be encouraging and supportive, which may be more difficult to convey in electronic communication. (Berry, 2018). It is the task of the professor to ensure that the student feels supported via electronic communication. The professor also has the difficult challenge of ensuring that discussion boards, emails, and other electronic communication are not impersonal or detached. Professors of online courses who have an online presence, give detailed course information, and provide prompt feedback are perceived with higher satisfaction from the students (Dickinson, 2017).

Another strategy to increase the professor-student relationship is to utilize a personalized video to enhance engagement between the professor and student. As previously mentioned, one of the primary methods of instruction and evaluation is the discussion forums. When professors insert personalized video into the discussion forum, there was an increase in student satisfaction and academic growth (Underdown & Martin, 2016).

Using videoconferencing is another way in which instructors can make connections with students. Professors can also create a video biography that shares information about their teaching experiences or personal information such as hobbies or interests. This activity can also be used for students to introduce themselves to classmates. A "coffee chat" can be used by the professor to meet with individual and/or small groups of students. This can be done via videoconferencing. YouTube or Vimeo make it simple for the instructor to create videos to share. Another tactic to improve upon relationships with students is to show a personal interest in the lives of the students and allow them the opportunity to share aspects of their lives in class or on discussion boards. FlipGrid is a web-based video message board that allows for recorded messages. Technology will forever evolve, so it is incumbent on the professor to remain current on new technology that can enhance the classroom experience for students., It is also vital that the professor uses a variety of methods to increase their social presence and improve the professor/student relationship (Martin, 2019).

There are many ways online instructors can facilitate the professor-student relationship. Many strategies that are utilized in the traditional classroom environment can also be used in the online classroom, with some adaptations. Student's value the professors that show commitment and caring toward their students, and online professors can communicate these with a little creativity. Creativity and knowledge of the resources available is essential in developing the positive professor-student relationship.

CONCLUSION

According to the Community of Inquiry (COI) model, deep and meaningful learning requires students to experience cognitive presence, teacher presence, and social presence (Garrison, 2009). A sense of social presence relates to students having the opportunity to communicate a sense of themselves to others and interact with others who are doing the same. A student experiencing a sense of presence creates a feeling of community amongst the learners and teacher. A sense of community leads to class satisfaction and perceived learning. Class satisfaction and perceived learning may lead to program retention. Following this evidence, it is easy to understand why creating opportunities for students to engage not only with course work, but relationships inevitably leads to the student feeling connected with peers.

Relationships in education continue to be vital for the growth of the student. As the evolution of education has arrived at online education the effort put forth into developing and nurturing relationships becomes more purposeful and meaningful. The relationship within a classroom is created on the foundation that the teacher establishes. As the foundation continues to strengthen, the learning environment is enriched and blossoms to each student's full potential.

REFERENCES

Bandura, A. (2001). Social cognitive theory: An agentic perspective. *Annual Review of Psychology*, *52*(1), 1–26. doi:10.1146/annurev.psych.52.1.1 PMID:11148297

Berry, G. (2018). Learning from the learners: Student perception of the online classroom. *Quarterly Review of Distance Education, 19*(3), 39-56.

Berry, S. (2019, April). The offline nature of online community: Exploring distance learners' extra-curricular interactions. *International Review of Research in Open and Distributed Learning, 20*(2). doi:10.19173/irrodl.v20i2.3896

Bickle, M. C. (2019). Online learning Examination of attributes that promote student satisfaction. *Online Journal of Distance Learning Administration, 22*(1).

Bickle, M. C., & Rucker, R. (2018). Student-to-student interaction: Humanizing the online classroom using technology and group assignments. *The Quarterly Review of Distance Education, 19*(1), 1–11. Retrieved from https://www.infoagepub.com/quarterly-review-of-distance-education.html

Cheng, G., & Chau, J. (2016). Exploring the relationships between learning styles, online participation, learning achievement, and course satisfaction: An empirical study of a blended classroom. *British Journal of Educational Technology, 47*(2), 257–278. doi:10.1111/bjet.12243

Croxton, R. A. (2014, June). The role of interactivity in student satisfaction and persistence in online learning. *MERLOT Journal of Online Learning and Teaching, 10*(2), 314-324. Retrieved from: http://jolt.merlot.org

Dailey-Hebert, A. (2018, December). Maximizing interactivity in online learning: Moving beyond discussion boards. *Journal of Educators Online*, *15*(3). doi:10.9743/jeo.2018.15.3.8

Dickinson, A. (2017). Communicating with the online student: The impact of e-mail tone on student performance and teacher evaluations. *Journal of Educators Online, 142*(2), 36-45.

Drange, T., & Kargaard, J. (2017, April 27-28). Increasing student/student and student/lecturer communication through available tools to create a virtual classroom feeling in online education. *The 13th International Scientific Conference e-learning and software for education.* 10.12753/2066-026x-17/058

Drouin, M. A. (2008). The relationship between students' perceived sense of community and satisfaction, achievement, and retention in an online course. *The Quarterly Review of Distance Education*, *93*(3), 267–284. Retrieved from https://www.infoagepub.com/quarterly-review-of-distance-education.html

Eom, S. B., & Ashill, N. (2016, April). The determinants of students' perceived learning outcomes and satisfaction in university online education: An Update. *Decision Sciences Journal of Innovative Education*, *14*(2), 185–215. doi:10.1111/dsji.12097

Friedman, J. (2018). 4 expectations for online education in 2018. *U.S. News & World Report.* Retrieved from https://www.usnews.com/higher-education/online-education/articles/2018-01-18/4-expectations-for-online-education-in-2018

Garrison, D., Cleveland-Innes, M., & Fung, T. S. (2009). Exploring Causal relationships among teaching, cognitive, and social presence: Student perceptions of the community of inquiry framework. *Internet and Higher Education.* doi:10.1016/j.iheduc.2009.10.002

Garrison, D. R. (2009). Communities of inquiry in online learning. In P. L. Rogers & ... (Eds.), *Encyclopedia of distance learning* (2nd ed.; pp. 352–355). Hershey, PA: IGI Global. doi:10.4018/978-1-60566-198-8.ch052

Garrison, D. R., Anderson, T., & Archer, W. (2000). Critical inquiry in a text-based environment: Computer conferencing in higher education. *The Internet and Higher Education*, *2*(2-3), 87–105. doi:10.1016/S1096-7516(00)00016-6

Gray, J. A., & Diloreto, M. (2016). The effects of student engagements, student's satisfaction, And perceived learning in online learning environments. *The International Journal of Educational Leadership Preparation*, *11*(1).

Green, T., Hoffman, M., Donovan, L., & Phuntsog, N., (2017). Cultural communication Characteristics and student connectedness in an online environment: perceptions of online graduate students. *International Journal of E-Learning & Distance Education, 32*(2).

Harting, K., & Erthal, M. J. (2005). History Of Distance Learning. *Information Technology, Learning, and Performance Journal*, *23*(1), 35-44. Retrieved from http:// ezproxy.liberty.edu/login?url=https://search-proquest-com.ezproxy.liberty.edu/docview/219815808?accountid=12085

Huss, J.A., & Estep, S. (2013). The perceptions of students toward online learning at a Midwestern University: What are students telling us and what are we doing about it? *I.E.: Inquiry in Education, 4*(2).

Joyner, S. A. (2014). The importance of student-instructor connections in graduate level online courses. *Journal of Online Learning and Teaching / MERLOT, 10*(3), 436–445.

Kuh, G. D. (2003). What we're learning about student engagement from NSSW: Benchmarks for effective educational practices. *Change, 35*(2), 24–32. doi:10.1080/00091380309604090

Kyong-Lee, K., Kiu, S., & Bonk, C. (2005). Online MBA students' perceptions of online learning: benefits, challenges, and suggestions. *The Internet and Higher Education, 8*(4), 335-344. Retrieved from https://www-sciencedirect.com.ezproxy.liberty.edu/science/article/pii/S1096751605000618

Lambert, J. L., & Fisher, J. L. (2013, Spring). Community of Inquiry Framework: Establishing community in an online class. *Journal of Interactive Online Learning, 13*(1), 1–16. Retrieved from www.ncolr.org/jiol

Levy, Y. (2007). Comparing dropouts and persistence in e-learning courses. *Computers & Education, 48*(2), 185–204. doi:10.1016/j.compedu.2004.12.004

Lowenthal, P., Bauer, C., & Chen, K. (2015). Student perceptions of online learning: An analysis of Online Course Evaluations. *American Journal of Distance Education, 29*(2), 85–97. doi:10.1080/08923647.2015.1023621

Martin, J. (2019). Building relationships and increasing engagement in the virtual classroom: Practical tools for the online instructor. *Journal of Educators Online, 16*(1), 1-8.

McClannon, T. W., Cheney, A. W., Bolt, L. L., & Terry, K. P. (2018, December). Predicting sense of presence and sense of community in immersive online learning environments. *Online Learning, 22*(4), 141-159. Retrieved from: https://olj.onlinelearningconsortium.org/index.php/olj

Murphy, E., & Rodriguez-Manzanares, M. A. (2012). Rapport in distance education. *The International Review of Research in Open and Distributed Learning, 13*(1), 167. doi:10.19173/irrodl.v13i1.1057

Park, J., & Choi, H. J. (2009). Factors influencing adult learners? Decision to drop out or persist in online learning. *Journal of Educational Technology & Society, 12*(4), 207–217. Retrieved from http://ezproxy.liberty.edu/login?url=https://search-proquest- com.ezproxy.liberty.edu/docview/2139084226?accountid=12085

Ratliff, K. (2018). Building rapport and creating a sense of community: Are relationships Important in the online classroom? *Internet Learning Journal,* 31-48. doi:10.18278/il.7.1.4

Salter, S., & Gardner, C. (2016). Online or face-to-face microbiology laboratory sessions? First year higher education student perspectives and preferences. *Creative Education, 7,* 1869-1880. Retrieved from https://www.scirp.org/journal/PaperInformation.aspx?PaperID=70022

Short, J., Williams, E., & Christie, V. (1976). *The social psychology of telecommunications.* London: John Wiley and Sons.

Stephens, G. E., & Roberts, K. L. (2017). Facilitating collaboration in online groups. *Journal of Educators Online, 14*(1). Retrieved from https://www.thejeo.com/

Underdown, K., & Martin, J. (2016). Engaging the online student: Instructor-created video Content for the online classroom. *Journal of Institutional Research*, *5*(1), 8–12. doi:10.9743/JIR.2016.2

Willging, P., & Johnson, S. (2009). Factors that influence students' decision to dropout of online Course. *Journal of Asynchronous Learning Networks*, *13*(3), 115–127.

Witzig, L., Spencer, J., & Myers, K. (2017). Social media: Online versus traditional universities and developing communities. *Journal of Higher Education Theory and Practice*, *17*(6), 39–52. Retrieved from http://www.na-businesspress.com/jhetpopen.html

Zhou, H. (2015). A systematic review of empirical studies on participants' interactions in internet-mediated discussion boards as a course component in formal higher education settings. *Online Learning Journal*, *19*(3). Retrieved from: www.onlinelearningconsortium.org

Chapter 11
A Framework for Student Engagement:
Strategies for Faculty Teaching Online

Desiree' Caldwell
Gwynedd Mercy University, USA

Tiffany Cresswell-Yeager
Gwynedd Mercy University, USA

Jennifer Aucoin
Gwynedd Mercy University, USA

Danielle Budenz
Gwynedd Mercy University, USA

ABSTRACT

When teaching online, many instructors are provided with a master course that contains the learning materials, discussion forums, assignments, and assessments. With more higher education institutions opting to offer master course shells, it can be difficult for instructors to know how to incorporate their personality, experiences, and insights into a pre-designed course. Faculty who teach online may be searching for ideas on how to personalize their master course and increase student engagement. Many faculty express concerns about students who are disconnected. Personalization of master courses increases student engagement while allowing students and instructors to feel more connected during the course. The authors will explore best practices to increase student engagement and provide a framework to implement these strategies that assist online instructors in demonstrating their personalities and expertise in master courses.

DOI: 10.4018/978-1-7998-0115-3.ch011

INTRODUCTION

Student engagement strategies and technology are a necessity for personalizing master courses and engaging students. When teaching online, many instructors are provided with a master course which contains the learning materials, discussion forums, assignments, and assessments. With more higher education institutions opting to offer master course shells, it can be difficult for instructors to know how to incorporate their personality, experiences, and insights into a pre-designed course. Faculty who teach online may be searching for ideas on how to personalize their master course and increase student engagement. Many faculty express concerns about students who are disconnected. Personalization of master courses increases student engagement while allowing students and instructors to feel more connected during the course. From personalized weekly announcements, individualized feedback and check-ins, to dialogue creation in discussion forums, and audio feedback, there are a variety of ways an instructor can incorporate strategies that increase engagement and add personality to the course.

In this chapter, the authors explore strategies to increase student engagement and provide a framework to implement these strategies that assist online instructors in demonstrating their personalities and expertise in master courses. Strategies can be separated into three components, engaging with the instructor, with peers and with course content.

Chapter Objectives

- Explore the student engagement framework for online teaching.
- Examine evidence-based strategies to build engagement.
- Share ideas to implement strategies in practice.

REVIEW OF LITERATURE

Engagement

In an online environment, engagement is a necessary component for learning to take place (Revere & Kovach, 2011). Students who actively participate learn more than those that do not (Zappala, 2012). Faculty who teach online must intentionally develop and implement strategies that increase students' engagement with the course content, with the instructor, and with peers (Nandi, Hamilton, & Harland, 2012; Briggs, 2015). Dail (2012) asserts that in the online environment technology enables this interaction. In this section, the authors explore the three types of engagement explaining the evidence-based strategies related to each.

Engaging with the Content

To engage with the content, assignments should be designed to connect texts, articles and other reading material to previous work or professional experience (Dail, 2012). Technology has allowed for students to engage with course content in the online classroom (Dyer, Aroz, & Larson, 2018). Many innovative tools and delivery methods provide ways for students to engage with the content. They add that "the use of technology helped students become invested and engaged in the classroom, making the material

A Framework for Student Engagement

more fun and appealing" (Dyer et al., 2018, p.113). Briggs (2015) finds that the use of multimedia and a variety of modalities keeps students with different learning styles engaged in the course content. Zappala (2012) adds that content must be relevant to the students' professional work and skills. He adds that the use of real-world examples and problem-based learning are valuable components to engage the student with the course content. This chapter will explore two strategies that enhance engagement with course content including using real-world examples and critical thinking with self-reflection and self-assessment.

Engaging with Peers

Instructors in online courses have many options to support students engaging with peers. This section will examine learning communities and the concept of socialization related to student engagement. Faculty must create learning communities within the online classroom to build relationships amongst students. Dyer et al. (2018) assert that improving the collaboration among peers will establish a "community of inquiry'. Learning communities have been found to increase social presence among and between the instructor and students and among and between the students and their peers. Dyer et al. (2018) explain that socialization is integral to the educational environment. Despite the distance within an online environment, they assert that active and collaborative learning occurs. In addition, learners must feel comfortable and confident with their peers to share information and become involved in discussion (Dyer et al., 2018). Socialization allows the student to build meaningful relationships and connect in the online environment. They add that socialization is a necessary component for open communication which will help develop group cohesion leading to active learning. This chapter will address two strategies related to engaging with peers such as building a community of learners through resource sharing and increasing student-to-student interaction.

Engaging with the Instructor

A great deal of research discusses the importance of students engaging with the instructor. Dyer et al., (2018) state the instructor's involvement is paramount to enhancing the academic outcomes, learning, and student satisfaction in an online classroom. They add that the "relationship between the instructor and the student is boosted through social presence" (p.111). Social presence can be established by instructors building and developing purposeful relationships with students online. Instructors who do this by investing time and energy to establish communication with students enhance learning and confidence (Briggs, 2015; Dyer et al., 2018). One of the most important roles of the instructor is to provide feedback (Dyer et al., 2018). To be effective, feedback should be holistic and include enough detail that students can understand its usefulness (Briggs, 2015; Dyer et al., 2018). This chapter will examine strategies that focus on engaging with the instructor such as increasing instructor presence online and personalizing feedback.

Being able to develop a connection to their instructor is critically important for students (Jaggars, Edgecombe, & Stacey, 2013). "One of the fundamental criticisms about online education is the lack of a teacher's presence and the ability to interact with him/her" (Das, 2012, p. 9). Traditional students and educators think that students miss out on the benefits of a teacher's presence in the classroom (Das, 2012). Students want to know instructors care about them as students and as people. Students feel an instructor cares about them based on the timeliness of communication, emotional responses such as affirmations, empathy, expressions of confidence in students' ability to be successful, frequent and caring feedback, availability, clear expectations and multiple methods of communication (Post, Mastel-Smith, & Lake, 2017).

An instructor is perceived as "present" in the online classroom when he/she is visible to the students. Teaching presence has been linked to increased affect and motivation in the students as well as being an important factor for creating a sense of community (Rapp & Anyikwa, 2016). Gray and DiLoreto (2016) found that the level of interpersonal interaction was the most important factor in predicting student grades in online courses. Students enrolled in low-interaction courses earned almost one letter grade lower than students in high-interaction courses. In an online environment, asserting teaching presence requires intentional preparation and action in terms of design, facilitation and direction of learning. Specific communication strategies such as addressing students by name, initiating discussions, asking probing questions, using humor, using self-disclosure, responding quickly, and conveying attentiveness should be utilized in order to model appropriate etiquette and effective use of the tools in the learning environment (Baker & Taylor, 2012).

In many instances, online instructors are teaching courses that were designed by an instructional designer. This can pose a challenge for instructors when it comes to creating a presence because the pre-designed activities may not have been constructed in such a way for instructors to easily engage with the students (Richardson, Besser, Koehler, Lim, & Strait, 2016). Online instructors should provide leadership in creating a caring environment that provides respect, authenticity, thoughtfulness, and emotional integrity (Lear, Isernhagen, LaCost, & King, 2009).

Online communication that is expressive, stimulating, and substantial is an important aspect of creating a sense of presence. There has to be a mutual awareness that the exchange occurring in the online classroom is between humans. A study conducted by Shea, Li, and Pickett in 2006 (as cited in Miller & Redman, 2010) of over 1000 students taking online courses at 32 colleges confirmed that teaching presence is crucial in creating a community of learners within an online course. Humans are social by nature thus they require human social interactions. Because these types of social interactions are difficult in an online environment, the online classroom can be social isolating and make students uncomfortable (Kennette & Redd, 2015). Instructor presence in the online classroom can be created in ways other than physical presence and ways that increase students' independence (Rapp & Anyikwa, 2016). The theory behind social connections is Constructivism. This theory asserts that students construct their own understanding through the connections they establish by attaching new information to past happenings. Students are active participants in an online classroom because they collect and reflect on information in a variety of ways (Lear et al., 2009).

Creating a sense of presence should begin prior to the commencement of the course (Kennette & Redd, 2015). Online instructors can engage students before the course commences through the use of pictures or avatars, the inclusion of a welcome or introduction video, and the building in of personalized graphics (Baker & Taylor, 2012). Aucoin and Budenz (2018) recommend sending a personalized email using the students' names. Kelly (2009) suggests sending students an introductory letter explaining what they need to do to prepare for the online course; a short video clip containing no course information is supplemented strictly to make students feel connected and welcome.

Research by Richardson et al., (2016) shows that students want available instructors who are willing to provide timely feedback, listen to concerns, and guide them through learning activities. Instructor presence is also visible through responding to all or almost all student discussion postings. This presence allows the instructor to push discussions forward and keep them on track (Sull, 2012). Students felt a sense of caring when the instructor frequently posted in discussion forums, invited students to ask questions and provided a quick response to those questions, provided detailed feedback on assignments, and asked for feedback about the course (Jaggars et al., 2013).

To be successful in the eyes of the students, an online course needs to be lively. One way to enliven a course is to integrate multimedia material such as interactive exercises and audio-visual materials (Das, 2012). Research conducted by Michael Scheuermann (2012) indicates that online students and instructors find considerable value in asynchronous course elements. When asked if the asynchronous chat sessions should be eliminated from a synchronous course, between 70 and 100% of students have said, "NO!" (pg. 4). Students said things like, "It makes me feel like I am in a more interactive environment, rather than 100% online."; "They bring a personal feel to the virtual class."; and "I look forward to these sessions" (p. 4). Miller and Redman (2010) concluded that video demonstrations are an effective means of creating instructor presence in an online course.

It is important for instructors to establish effective patterns of interactions from the very beginning of the course (Baker & Taylor, 2012). Be sure to respond to all student inquiries within 24 hours. The quick response tells them you are interested in what they are asking, want to help, and can be depended upon; qualities that keep students engaged. One participant in Richardson et al.'s (2016) study stated,

I respond a lot in opening discussions and the reason is because it sets the tone. The students take over after that. If you sit back in those first two discussions, that also sets the tone, and you are struggling from then on. You are wondering why they aren't responding, and they are just following what you did (p. 88-89).

Another participant in Richardson et al.'s (2016) study uses "small talk" to help learners feel connected; this includes campus trivia, facts or comments about sports or current events (p. 90). Another participant in Richardson et al.'s (2016) study stated the use of self-disclosure. The participant shares professional as well as personal experiences through storytelling.

Studies researched by Jaggars et al. (2013) found that students reported a higher level of engagement when instructors incorporated live audio and video chats using web conferencing software such as Adobe Connect. There are also a variety of free technological tools that can help increase instructor presence. Audacity software uses a computer's built-in microphone to allow an instructor to record an audio or video file, while Jing allows an instructor to create a five-minute voice over or screencast presentation. Using a Flip cam allows an instructor to make a video on the spot and upload it to the course through YouTube/TeacherTube. Ideas for the use of these technological tools include demonstrating how to solve difficult math problems, answering quick questions, walking students through the layout of the course, reminders for assignments, weekly updates, or provide students with necessary information (Baker & Taylor, 2012). Technological tools such as the ones mentioned are suitable for both visual and auditory learners. These tools not only add instructor visibility, but also pedagogical benefits. They also provide a chance for students to be able to go back and view or listen again if needed; a face to face environment does not allow for this opportunity (Das, 2012). Technology is deemed useful when it supports interpersonal interaction, allowing students to see, hear, and get to know their instructors despite the physical distance between them. When optimized, technological tools can help instructors establish a knowledgeable and approachable presence (Jaggars et al., 2013).

The idea of presence is a multi-dimensional construct, including social, cognitive, and teaching, as seen in the Community of Inquiry framework set forth by Garrison, Anderson, and Archer (as cited in Gurley, 2018). Social presence refers to an individual's ability to present him/herself online as unique and real while cognitive presence refers to the construction of meaning through communication. Teaching presence refers to the design of a student's educational experience, including content and learning activities (Richardson et al., 2016). Garrison et al. (as cited in Gray & DiLoreto, 2016) later expand on this framework by including three indicators of instructor presence: instructional management, building understanding, and direct instruction. Instructional management is referred to as course structure and organization. Through active intervention, the instructor can draw in less active participants, acknowledge individual contributions, reinforce appropriate contributions, focus the discussion, and facilitate an educational transaction in order to build understanding. Direct instruction includes any teaching such as lectures, videos, feedback, and readings that is provided directly or indirectly by the instructor (Gray & DiLoreto, 2016).

A participant in Kennette and Redd's (2015) study shared the various things that were done each week in the online course to increase social, cognitive, and teaching presence. In the first week of the course, the students completed an introduction activity where they posted a page about themselves and included a picture. The instructor created a conversation with the students by asking specific questions about their biographies. The next week, the instructor created a labeled class collage with the pictures used in the introduction activity. Each week after that, discussion questions were posted; some were icebreaker-type questions, and some were academic questions, but not related to the course. The instructor also personalized the feedback given to the students on the weekly assignments rather than using general language (Kennette & Redd, 2015). The different types of instructor presence are sometimes seen independent from each other as opposed to being interconnected. Some instructors do not associate grading and giving feedback on assignments as being "present;" social activities tend to be seen as more of creating a presence. This is not accurate as all three types of instructor presence work together to create a sense of community for the students (Richardson et al., 2015). Feedback from the instructor is an important piece of the puzzle because it lets students know when their thinking is on track and when it needs to be revised or redirected (Lear et al., 2009).

Barriers to Engagement

Briggs (2015) adds that faculty that teach online may find challenges engaging students. These barriers must be overcome to enhance and increase student learning. She explains that there are three types of barriers—social, administrative and motivational. In understanding social barriers, students may become isolated or disconnected in online courses. Administrative barriers are evident when students don't know how to contact the instructor or the instructor doesn't respond in a timely manner. Motivational barriers impact students because of workload, multiple responsibilities, and procrastination.

In addition, research has identified other barriers to engagement in the online environment. Dyer et al. (2018) explain that the potential lack of spontaneity and vitality is often cited as negative when comparing to traditional classrooms. Despite the importance of student to student interaction, many students preferred to work alone on assignments (Moore, Warner & Jones, 2016). In the qualitative portion of their study, some respondents indicated student to student interaction made learning more fun and enjoyable, but many of the statements questioned the effectiveness of student to student interaction. Students were more concerned with course content rather than student to student interaction. A suggestion was made to allow for student to student interaction with those who wanted to engage, but not to require it of everyone (Moore et al., 2016).

Balance within the framework is needed as excessive teaching presence can reduce student satisfaction due to the extra reading work it creates within a course, particularly at a post-graduate level where it can fuel a litany of responsive postings. This presents a challenge for online instructors. Excessive instructor posting can reduce student involvement in discussion forums; however, students often perceive instructors who post often as enthusiastic and possessing greater expertise (Ladyshewsky, 2013). Wehler (2018) recommends bringing the outside in; keep students abreast about campus happenings whether online or not. Some students might be interested in an event and make every effort to attend despite the distance. Baran, Correia, and Thompson (2013) suggest having interactive online guest lectures. Create social presence by creating a "café" discussion board since students are unable to actually gather outside of the "café" before or after class; be sure to partake in the discussions that would occur in this type of environment (Wehler, 2018).

EVALUATION OF PRACTICES LEADING TO NEW INITIATIVES

The results of the Ruffalo Noel Levitz Priorities Survey for Online Learners (PSOL), administered in 2016, were assessed to examine student engagement and student satisfaction. The authors found a great need to improve satisfaction of students in the online environment. Through a review of these results, the authors have focused on implementing the evidence-based strategies discussed in the next section. The authors are working with the Office of Institutional Research to conduct the study in 2019-2020 so the data can be compared. Table 1 provides the demographic information from the survey. Table 2 provides a summary of findings from the survey and Table 3 provides the responses from the data that were lower than the national average.

Strengths of the Survey Results

The Office of Institutional Research found several strengths of the online programs. Students felt the institution responded quickly to information requested by students. They also felt the coursework was applicable to their career.

Challenges of the Survey Results

The Office of Institutional Research found several challenges of the online learning programs. These challenges are being addressed in the section called evidence-based strategies. Students reported lower satisfaction on faculty providing timely feedback and that the feedback they receive supports their un-

Table 1. Demographic information

Item	N	%
Total respondents	274	100
Goal is to complete online degree	216	80.60
Some Previous experience online	100	39.06
Majority of classes are taken online	224	81.75

Table 2. Institutional summary

Item	Importance	Satisfaction	Gap	Strategy
Faculty provide timely feedback about student progress.	6.63	5.55	1.08	Personalizing Feedback
Faculty are responsive to student needs.	6.63	5.75	.88	Instructor Presence
The feedback supports further understanding.	6.62	5.54	1.08	Personalizing Feedback
The frequency of student instructor interactions is adequate	6.38	5.72	.66	Instructor Presence
My faculty are actively involved in discussion boards.	6.20	5.42	.78	Instructor Presence
Classwork relates to my professional goals.	6.61	5.81	.80	Using real-world examples
My coursework is applicable to my career.	6.61	5.90	.71	Using real-world examples
Online assignments are meaningful learning opportunities	6.50	5.59	.91	Critical thinking using self-reflection or self-awareness

derstanding. There were several instances where the student satisfaction was lower than the national average, providing an important challenge to be improved.

In addition, the students selected 5.43 (somewhat satisfied) with the quality of online instruction is excellent. Because of the challenges, the authors and other faculty have implemented strategies to increase student engagement and student satisfaction. These challenges provided an awareness of areas to improve and offered the faculty an opportunity to look at new ways to engage students in their online learning environments.

PRACTICAL APPLICATION OF EVIDENCE-BASED STRATEGIES

The authors have selected several strategies to provide in-depth explanation and practical applications in online courses. This section will provide an explanation of the strategy and tips for implementing it in the online course environment. The strategies discussed include increasing instructor presence, personalizing feedback, engaging with course content, and building a community of learners.

Table 3. Lower satisfaction than national online learners

Item	Campus Score	National Average	Gap
Faculty are responsive to student needs.	5.75	5.96	-.21
Faculty provide timely feedback about student progress.	5.55	5.86	-.31
The quality of online instruction is excellent.	5.43	5.88	-.45

Strategies for Increasing Instructor Presence

Instructor presence can be challenging to establish in an online environment. However, there are a variety of ways to let students know the instructor is there and cares. The typical ways online instructors can emit presence is through announcements, emails, discussion boards, and feedback provided on assignments. One of the authors does use all of these methods, but she is always looking to try something different each time a new course begins. However, engaging students before the course actually begins can be difficult. Students might not visit the course until the start date, new students might not have the necessary connections from the university, or instructors might not know how to engage the students. One of the authors incorporates a few things into her courses to try to engage students before it actually begins. She likes to do this because it gives the students time to be in the course without having to deal with the content yet. The first thing the author does is post a welcome image; she tries to choose one that will make the students laugh or at least smile. Instead of sending a welcome email, the author sends a welcome video. She titles it, "Introducing, Dr. Caldwell." The video includes an introduction about who she is both professionally and personally. She wants the students to see her and know who she is, just as if they were in a face to face environment. This helps when the students are reading something from the author because they truly know who it is coming from.

The author also created a separate video giving a brief overview of the course. Feedback from past students indicated this was helpful because even though students could read the information in the syllabus and in the course, hearing it from the instructor provided a different level of understanding. The author also sends a written announcement highlighting the first week of the course; weekly objectives are posted as well as a reminder about using rubrics to check assignments before submitting.

Another way the author lets her presence be known is by giving "shout outs" to highlight the work of those students who really shined that particular week. There are two purposes of the "shout outs": to provide recognition and to help other students see good examples in order to self-reflect on their own work. The author also makes it a point to respond to students' questions and concerns as soon as she is aware of them; even if the answer is yet to be known, she will respond with a statement like, "I received your question/concern. I will get back to you as soon as I can provide a specific answer." This lets the students know they have been heard immediately.

Strategies for Personalizing Feedback

Research shows that personalizing feedback is an important strategy for teaching online. One of the authors uses the sandwich feedback method to reduce the stress and anxiety associated with feedback not only from the students, but also the perspective of the author. The author takes an approach of giving positive feedback, followed by critical feedback if applicable, and ends with suggestions for improvement. When providing the constructive criticism it is suggested that only one or at most two should be provided at one time (Daniels, 2009). Table 4 can be provided to students along with a picture diagram of a hamburger to see how they will receive feedback and give them a visualization of what the feedback will look like. Since the author began using the sandwich feedback method students have been more appreciative and receptive to constructive feedback.

Table 5 is an example of feedback provided in the Announcement of an online course, demonstrating the instructor's explanation and integration of course content. The author creates this personalized group feedback for students as she creates personalized individual feedback. The information synthesized in

Table 4. Sandwich method for feedback

Positive Feedback	Thank you for the progress update. Your lesson planning seems to be coming along. I like your idea of targeting the two grade levels that will be making transitions.
Critical Feedback	While you have indicated that your lesson plan development has been informed by the results of your needs assessment, there is no review of the most relevant findings (even if it is made up for this assignment).
Suggestions for Improvement	A great way to do this is to pick the top 2-3 findings that pointed you in the direction that you are headed with your lesson development and explain them. Whenever possible, adding specific data (percentages) can help to support your rationale. You have a good basis for your lessons and the proposal. I'm looking forward to seeing the end result.

the table is created through several different methods. First, when grading assignments, the instructor is looking for questions students are asking regarding course content that would apply to everyone in the class. As the author provides personalized individual feedback to the student she is including the individual feedback in a word document to then be provided to all of the class as group feedback. Next, the author is continually looking for resources shared by other students in the class. She gathers these resources and shares them with the class in her group feedback as well as sharing her own resources as personalized individual feedback. Many students make relevant points through assignments that other students might not be able to see. The instructor takes those points and synthesizes them into the group feedback document to allow all students to be able to see a broader perspective of the course content through other students' perspectives. Finally, the author incorporates her own personal experiences as well as content knowledge to enhance the group feedback.

Strategies For Engaging Students With Content

From the results of the PSOL discussed previously, the authors knew that relevant course content was not only important, but integral to student satisfaction and student engagement. Dahl (2015) explains that hands-on learning connects students to the field of study. Assignments can create these connections by interviewing professionals, analyzing data and solving problems of practice (Dahl, 2015).

Real-World Examples

There are several important strategies for encouraging students to engage with content. Research has shown that the relevance to students' career aspirations and experiences is an important component in engaging students in the content (Dixson, 2010). Faculty can engage students with the content by encouraging interviews with professionals in the field or with case studies and problem-solving assignments. In one course, students are assigned to create a presentation as if they were presenting to the school board about a new initiative to be implemented at the school. This assignment requires the student to practically apply the theoretical knowledge or textbook concepts to best accomplish the learning outcomes. Dixson (2010) adds that creating an active learning environment is integral to student engagement. Table 6 shows an example of using real-world examples in assignments.

A Framework for Student Engagement

Table 5. Weekly announcement personalized feedback

Announcement
GUIDANCE/COUNSELING/PSYCHOTHERAPY Everyone did a great job differentiating between guidance, counseling, and psychotherapy. In the school counseling field, guidance is a term ASCA has tried to move away from. School counselors are trained to be in the middle of the diagram that was in your book which is counseling. For those of you who are training in the mental health track you will also be prepared to be in the counseling track. When you get into psychotherapy you are looking at additional training in very specific areas of counseling. If you begin working as an LPC, it is likely that the facility where you work will give you specific training to move into the psychotherapy range. Here is a good example posted in the discussion board: I also associate guidance with leading someone to a solution of a quick problem. In high school, I would go to my guidance counselor to inquire about how to apply for FAFSA or how to register for SATs and ACTs. Solutions to these issues were provided within a very short time period. Below is a question from the discussion board that I would like to address. How does this differ in schools across the state? Are most schools strictly guidance driven in the school counselor position? My Answer: This is why ASCA is trying to get away from the word guidance. There are plenty of therapeutic techniques that are appropriate for a school counselor to use and should use. However, you have to follow the guidelines of your district. It does vary widely from school to school. We should be using a more universal counseling approach in the schools. This is something that should be advocated for if you are at a school that only uses counselors for guidance. **PROFESSIONAL ORGANIZATIONS** As counselors one of the most important aspects of your job is joining a professional organization. Most professional organizations provide you with liability insurance. For this program you will need liability insurance, so you do need to join one of the organizations listed this week and sign up for the student insurance coverage. Besides getting insurance, being a member of a professional organization provides excellent professional development. You also need to attend conferences in order to grow professionally. The nice thing about technology now is you can attend most of the conferences virtually. There are also virtual webinars you can attend and most of the organizations send out a monthly or quarterly magazine. I know joining organizations can be expensive, but they are worth it. Licensure/Certification I am going to specifically talk about LPC licensure here because all of you are on an LPC track or school counseling track. School counselors, you can also go on to get your LPC. I recommend doing it if you have any inclination that you might want to be an LPC. It is something I did not do immediately after my school certification 15 years ago and I wish I had. Here are the Pennsylvania LPC Requirements: • Meet the educational requirement of a Master's in Counseling from an accredited program. (60 hours of coursework) • Complete a practicum as well as an internship during your graduate studies. • Pass a criminal background check. • Complete the supervised experience element. • Apply to take your National Counselor Examination (NCE) as administered by the National Board of Certified Counselors (NBCC). • Apply for your Licensed Professional Counselor (LPC) title.

Table 6. Real-world assignment example

Addressing the Needs of an Underserved Population
Propose a new program or charter school that supports the need or needs of an underserved population. **Identify** a specific educational goal for your program. Examples of goals may include, but are not limited to the following: • Access to preschool education • Community outreach • Giving students of diversity a voice • Reduction of suspension rates • High school graduation • College graduation **Research** current statistics on your identified goal for your selected underserved population. **Create** a plan to address the goals. **Prepare** a 5- to 8-minute presentation that you could present to a board of directors describing the goals and plans for your program or charter school. Your presentation may be a narrated Prezi, Microsoft® PowerPoint® presentation, or video. **Post** your presentation in the Addressing the Needs of an Underserved Population discussion forum by Friday. **Provide** feedback to one of your classmates' presentations by Sunday.

Table 7. Self-reflection example

Cultural Self-Assessment Paper
In this paper, you will conduct an analysis of the cultural influences on your own life. The National Center for Cultural Competence at Georgetown University explains that self-assessment helps individuals do the following: • Gauge the degree to which they are effectively addressing the needs of culturally and linguistically diverse groups • Determine their strengths and areas for growth • Strategically plan for the systematic incorporation of culturally and linguistically competent policy, structures, and practices **Complete** an online self-assessment inventory about your cultural intelligence, awareness or competence. There are several suggested options or you may choose another one. Some of the inventories have a fee associated with them; others are free for your use. **Write** a 500-word paper that analyzes your cultural intelligence. Analyze each dimension within Hofstede's theory of national culture and Livermore's framework for cultural intelligence. Provide personal experience and theoretical or empirical evidence to support your understanding. Your paper must: • Cite 3 to 5 outside sources to strengthen your analysis, especially when explaining the culture(s) selected. • Apply the results from the inventory to demonstrate your understanding.

Self-Reflection

Research shows the importance of self-reflection as a tool to connect with the course content (Briggs, 2015; Dai, 2012; Dahl, 2015). Students can participate in reflection through challenging discussion posts, surveys or inventories where there is opportunity to reflect within the assignment. Table 7 is an example of an assignment that uses self-reflection to build student's connection to the course.

Strategies for Building a Community of Learners

Briggs (2015) encourages instructors who teach online to establish a community of learners. One of the ways to build a community of learners is to increase student-to-student interaction. There are several evidence-based strategies to consider when building student-to-student interaction. First, asynchronous online discussion boards had a positive impact on student-to-student interaction (Osborne, Byrne, Massey, & Johnson, 2018) and have been a discussion in recent literature (Hampton et al., 2017; Hudson, 2014; & McGarry, Theobald, Lewis, & Coyer, 2015) An emerging theme was to build community, which allowed students to interact through introductions and ice breakers that would normally be seen in a face to face setting (Osborne, Byrne, Massey, & Johnson, 2018). Quantitative and qualitative research by Osborne et al., (2018) concluded that asynchronous online discussion boards created a collaborative environment which facilitated student to student interaction.

According to Drange and Kargaard, (2017), using an interactive site to chat such as Discord or Skype allowed students to interact with students quickly and answer questions at a faster rate. In addition, this not only assisted the students, but also the instructor. Students often work outside of traditional hours and the instructor is not always available for immediate assistance, but many times multiple students are available immediately. This type of interactive communication creates a similar feeling to a live class (Drange & Kargaard, 2017). Assigning roles had a positive impact on student to student interaction, while group reflections led to higher level of thought during student-to-student interactions throughout the semester (Truhlar, Walter & Williams, 2018). The findings of this longitudinal quasi-experimental study suggested that Facebook provides a platform for better student-to-student interaction through an asynchronous learning environment allowing for better student engagement similar to a face-to-face environment (Northey, Bucic, Chylinski, & Govind, 2015).

Resource Sharing

Building opportunities for students to exchange knowledge, share resources, and provide support within an online course or program is another way to facilitate a community of learning, inquiry and practice. A few strategies that instructors can implement as a means to accomplish this are by incorporating a virtual student lounge, providing professional resources and experiential stories, adding a resource sharing component to course assignments, and implementing peer review as part of the feedback loop.

Virtual Student Lounge

As each new course begins, one of the author adds a *virtual student lounge* discussion forum, which contains threads aimed at acquainting students with each other and setting up a culture of sharing; sharing about one's self, knowledge and support. An introductory discussion thread allows students to introduce themselves. Students are directed to provide information related to their current profession, their academic and career goals, what they hope to learn in the course, hobbies, family, etc., basically, any information that provides insight into who they are. Students typically accomplish this introduction through a written post; however, giving students other options like creating a virtual poster or recording a video allows for more creative means of sharing. The University of Massachusetts' (n.d.) Teaching and Learning Online faculty handbook notes that online instructors should,

incorporate opportunities for students to tell you something about themselves in a 'student lounge' or meeting place. A 'student lounge' can also be a place where students can share with each other, meet each other virtually, and learn more about each other without your presence (p. 30).

The addition of a space for informal discussion is a way to establish social capital and build community. A water cooler discussion board provides a place for students to engage in the before- and after-class chatter that frequently occurs in real time. Students conduct non-course related discussions that help to build camaraderie and a sense of community (Gallagher-Lepak, Reilly & Killion, 2009; Liu, Magjuka, Bonk & Lee, 2007). One online instructor introduced the concept of a "coffee shop" as a way for students to interact with each other; students were able to "learn about one another, support each other through life stresses, and celebrate personal accomplishments" (Donovan, 2015). A water cooler discussion thread provides an open discussion for students to post non-course related commentary. Students can come to this place to share news about themselves, vent about life's goings-on, and provide support and encouragement to those in need. Additionally, instructors could also use this water cooler discussion as a way to share resources from professional organizations related to the program of study or they could opt to create a Shared Resources discussion thread for this purpose.

Gallagher-Lepak, et al. (2009) interviewed students enrolled in an online RN to BSN program about their perceptions of community in online learning. Results indicated that an open discussion forum used for informal, non-content related discussion was used as a means to build community. Participant comments about the "water cooler" discussion included that it allowed students to "talk with other members in an offline sort of way", "it really…humanized the experience of an online program." Dwyer (as cited in Kelly, 2009) includes a pet gallery as an ice breaker in the introductory discussion board and finds that it is another way to build social presence. Students are asked to post a picture of their pet(s) and then to introduce themselves.

Experiential Stories and Professional Resources

Bigatel (2016) states that to keep students engaged, it is important for instructors to ensure that course content is applicable to real-world experiences. Working professionals who serve as instructors for pre-professional students have a great deal of real-life experience that is beneficial to relay to students looking to enter the workforce. Courses led by these professionals often include impromptu stories about the instructor's daily responsibilities, their perspective on the application of theory to practice, and issues that may arise from day-to-day. In face-to-face class sessions, instructors often sprinkle stories of what happened in their professional life throughout the class as a way to provide students with examples of practice or real-life scenarios that mimic what is being taught. Instructors of pre-designed online courses sometimes wonder how they can impart this valuable knowledge. In a virtual classroom, where instructor and students may not be engaging in the class at the same point in time, these real-life examples, or teachable moments, can be integrated into discussion forum responses. Engaging in discussion forums allows an instructor to share more deeply his/her area of professional expertise and on-the-job experiences thus enhancing student mastery of learning objectives (Shaw, 2016).

Instructors can add supplemental outcomes-specific resources to pre-designed courses as a way to help meet the learning objectives and to exercise academic freedom in determining how to best meet students' needs and engage the community of learners (Shaw, 2016).

In preparation for the start of a course, one of the authors first reviews a faculty instructional guide, which is basically a paper-version of the courses content, assignments, and assessments displayed in weekly modules. This review allows her to preview the content being covered each week so that she can locate supplemental materials available from professional organizations and pre-determine in which topic areas she has specific real-world examples that would be beneficial to share. Given that students are required to maintain membership in the professional organization throughout the duration of their program, the author likes to add available resources that will further support the students in their studies. Professional organizations frequently provide webinar-style professional development trainings that are free to members. Knowing that many of the students deal with the typical barriers that adult learners face, the author adds supplemental content and notifications in the course weekly announcements to students about upcoming professional development webinars and provides links to web-based resources related to the course content.

Additionally, because many of the adult students are already working in careers related to their course of study, the author also encourages students to share their real-world experiences as a way to make theoretical concepts more understandable.

Peer Review

Another strategy that the one of the authors employs is the use of small group peer review. In courses where students are working on a research-supported projects, the project components are chunked in such a way that students are completing draft versions of project sections. While the author would typically review and provide feedback on these drafts, she finds that having students share their work with a small group of peers allows for the writer to receive praise, critical review, suggestions for improvement, and support from a variety of perspectives. The peer review process also allows students to provide supplemental subject-matter and writing support resources.

FUTURE DIRECTIONS

Future Research

There are many opportunities for future research. First, the authors would like to review student engagement through reflection and learning in their assignments. For example, a course can remain as is for one section, but have revised assignments based on the type of presentation and delivery in another section. A comparison can then be made as to how the students engaged in the different ways they transacted with the material. In addition, the authors would like to assess the course evaluations for feedback related to the strategies presented and student engagement practices. Another possible future research project would be to survey the faculty about their practices.

Additional Assessment

Foremost, the authors would like to administer the Ruffalo Noel Levitz Online Learner Survey to compare current satisfaction with the data from the previous survey. This would allow for evidence-based evaluation of the initiatives implemented since 2017.

The university is now using IDEA, an instrument built on more than 45 years of research, for course evaluations (IDEA, 2019). Through IDEA, the students give feedback on teaching and learning based on their direct course experience, providing faculty with relevant information that can ultimately guide and strengthen teaching (IDEA, 2019). There will be opportunity to assess these practices in a more formal way evaluating student satisfaction and student engagement in which they report their experiences.

CONCLUSION

More research is needed to determine which actions, behaviors, and tools are most influential on the success of students in online courses. However, research shows that instructors who are actively present in the online classroom, whether it is in the role of a coach, advocate, facilitator, or mentor, create an environment more focused on the learner (Richardson et al., 2015). When instructors increase their social presence, students increase their social presence, which results in a stronger cognitive presence (Ladyshewsky, 2013). Participants in Thompson, Ballenger, and Templeton's (2018) case study on quality elements of online learning in doctoral programs appreciated instructor presence. One participant said, "I learned best when the instructor was present in the course such as chats and discussion boards. One instructor even held Google Hangouts and Adobe Connect sessions" (Thompson et al., 2018, p. 59). Another participant remarked, "I thought the discussion board was very helpful. Some instructors provided great feedback on the discussion board and the assignments" (Thompson et al., 2018, p. 59). Another participant added, "Online learning was just as effective as face to face for me because of teacher presence in the classroom" (Thompson et al., 2018, p. 59). Garrison, Anderson, and Archer (as cited in Ekmekci, 2013) said it best: "teaching presence is essential in balancing cognitive and social issues consistent with intended educational outcomes' whereby practical inquiry based upon experience becomes the framework for transforming practice" (p. 31).

Student engagement is imperative to enhancing learning online. Instructors must utilize a multi-level approach to engaging students. It is important to consider how to engage the student with the course content, with the instructor, and with the student's peers. This chapter explored several strategies in each category and provided a framework for implementing them in the online classroom.

REFERENCES

Aucoin, J., & Budenz, D. (2018, November). *Personalize your master course using student engage strategies*. PowerPoint presentation at the meeting of OLC Accelerate, Orlando, FL.

Baker, C., & Taylor, S. L. (2012). The importance of teaching presence in an online course. In *Online Student Engagement Tools and Strategies* (section 3). Retrieved from https://www.facultyfocus.com/wp-content/uploads/2019/02/FF-Online-Student-Engagement-Report.pdf

Baran, E., Correia, A., & Thompson, A. D. (2013). Tracing successful online teaching in higher education: Voices of exemplary online teachers. *Teachers College Record, 115*, 1–41.

Bigatel, P. M. (2016, March 14). Student engagement strategies for the online learning environment [Blog]. Retrieved from https://www.facultyfocus.com/articles/online-education/studentengagement-how-to-help-students-succeed-in-the-online-environment/

Briggs, A. (2015, February 11). Ten Ways to Overcome Barriers to Student Engagement Online. *Academic Technology at the College of William and Mary*. Retrieved from http://at.blogs.wm.edu/ten-ways-to-overcome-barriers-to-student-engagement-online/

Dahl, B. (2015). 7 Tips for increasing student engagement in online courses. Student Engagement [Blog]. Retrieved from http://www.d2l.com/blog/author/bdahl

Dail, T. (2012). Enabling: A strategy for improving learning. In *Online Student Engagement Tools and Strategies*, 6-7. Retrieved from https://www.facultyfocus.com/wp-content/uploads/2019/02/FF-Online-Student-Engagement-Report.pdf

Daniels, A. (2009). *Oops! 13 management practices that waste time and money (and what to do instead)*. Atlanta, GA: Performance Management Publications.

Das, S. (2012). Increasing instructor visibility in online courses through mini-videos and screencasting. In *Online Student Engagement Tools and Strategies* (section 4). Retrieved from https://www.facultyfocus.com/wp-content/uploads/2019/02/FF-Online-Student-Engagement-Report.pdf

Dixson, M. (2010). Creating effective student engagement in online courses: What do students find engaging? *The Journal of Scholarship of Teaching and Learning, 10*(2), 1–13.

Donovan, J. (2015). The importance of building online learning communities [Blog]. Retrieved from http://blog.online.colostate.edu/blog/online-education/the-importance-of-building-online-learning-communities/

Drange, T., & Kargaard, J. (2017, April). *Increasing student/student and student/lecturer communication through available tools to create a virtual classroom feeling in online education*. Paper presented at the meeting of The 13th International Scientific Conference eLearning and Software for Education, Bucharest, Romania.

Dyer, T., Aroz, J., & Larson, E. (2018). Proximity in the online classroom: Engagement, relationships, and personalization. *Journal of Institutional Research, 7*, 108–118.

Ekmekei, O. (2013). Being there: Establishing instructor presence in an online learning environment. *Higher Education Studies, 3*(1), 29–38.

Gallagher-Lepak, S., Reilly, J., & Killion, C. (2009). Nursing student perceptions of community in online learning. *Contemporary Nurse, 32*(1-2), 133–146. doi:10.5172/conu.32.1-2.133 PMID:19697984

Gray, J. A., & DiLoreto, M. (2016). The effects of student engagement, student satisfaction, and perceived learning in online learning environments. *The International Journal of Educational Leadership Preparation, 11*(1).

Gurley, L. E. (2018). Educators' preparation to teach, perceived teaching presence, and perceived teaching presence behaviors in blended and online learning environments. *Online Learning, 22*(2), 197–220.

Hampton, D., Pearce, P. F., & Moser, D. K. (2017). Preferred methods of learning for nursing students in an on-line degree program. *Journal of Professional Nursing, 33*(1), 27–37. doi:10.1016/j.profnurs.2016.08.004 PMID:28131145

Hudson, K. A. (2014). Teaching nursing concepts through an online discussion board. *The Journal of Nursing Education, 53*(9), 531–536. doi:10.3928/01484834-20140820-01 PMID:25138567

IDEA. (2019). *Services*. Retrieved from https://www.ideaedu.org/Services

Jaggars, S., Edgecombe, N., & Stacey, G. (2013). *Creating an effective online instructor presence*. Community College Research Center Teachers College, Columbia University. Retrieved from https://ccrc.tc.columbia.edu/media/k2/attachments/effective-online-instructor-presence.pdf

Kelly, R. (2009). Seven easy ways to personalize your online course [Blog]. Retrieved from https://www.facultyfocus.com/articles/online-education/seven-easy-ways-to-personalize-your-online-course/

Kennette, L. N., & Redd, B. R. (2015). Instructor presence helps bridge the gap between online and on-campus learning. *The College Quarterly, 18*(4).

Ladyshewsky, R. K. (2013). Instructor presence in online courses and student satisfaction. *International Journal for the Scholarship of Teaching and Learning, 7*(1), 1–23. doi:10.20429/ijsotl.2013.070113

Lear, J. L., Isernhagen, J. C., LaCost, B. A., & King, J. W. (2009). Instructor presence for web-based classes. *Delta Pi Epsilon Journal, 51*(2), 86–98.

Liu, X., Magjuka, R. J., Bonk, C. J., & Lee, S.-h. (2007). Does sense of community matter? *The Quarterly Review of Distance Education, 8*(1), 9–24.

McGarry, B. J., Theobald, K., Lewis, P. A., & Coyer, F. (2015). Flexible learning design in curriculum delivery promotes student engagement and develops metacognitive learners: An integrated review. *Nurse Education Today, 35*(9), 966–973. doi:10.1016/j.nedt.2015.06.009 PMID:26169287

Miller, S. T., & Redman, S. L. (2010). Improving instructor presence in an online introductory astronomy course through video demonstrations. *Astronomy Education Review, 9*(1).

Moore, G. E., Warner, W. J., & Jones, D. W. (2016). Student-to-student interaction in distance education classes: What do graduate students want. *Journal of Agricultural Education, 57*(2), 1–13. doi:10.5032/jae.2016.02001

Nandi, D., Hamilton, M., & Harland, J. (2012). Evaluating the quality of interaction in asynchronous discussion forums in fully online courses. *Distance Education, 33*(1), 5–30. doi:10.1080/01587919.2012.667957

Northey, G., Bucic, T., Chylinski, M., & Govin, R. (2015). Increasing student engagement using asynchronous learning. *Journal of Marketing Education, 37*(3), 171–180. doi:10.1177/0273475315589814

Osborne, D. M., Byrne, J. H., Massey, D. L., & Johnston, A. N. (2018). Use of online asynchronous discussion boards to engage students, enhance critical thinking, and foster staff-student/student-student collaboration: A mixed method study. *Nurse Education Today, 70*, 40–46. doi:10.1016/j.nedt.2018.08.014 PMID:30145533

Post, J., Mastel-Smith, B., & Lake, P. (2017). Online teaching: How students perceive faculty caring. *International Journal for Human Caring, 21*(2), 54–58. doi:10.20467/HumanCaring-D-16-00022.1

Rapp, L., & Anyikwa, V. (2016). Active learning strategies and instructor presence in an online research methods course: Can ourdecrease anxiety and increase perceived knowledge. *Advances in Social Work, 17*(1), 1–14. doi:10.18060/20871

Revere, L., & Kovach, J. (2011). Online technologies for engaged learners: A meaningful synthesis for educators. *The Quarterly Review of Distance Education, 12*(2), 113–124.

Richardson, J. C., Koehler, A. A., Besser, E. D., Caskurlu, S., Lim, J., & Mueller, C. M. (2015). Conceptualizing and investigating instructor presence in online learning environments. *International Review of Research in Open and Distributed Learning, 16*(3), 256–297. doi:10.19173/irrodl.v16i3.2123

Richardson, J. C., Koehler, A. A., Besser, E. D., Caskurlu, S., Lim, J., & Mueller, C. M. (2016). Instructors' perceptions of instructor presence in online learning environments. *International Review of Research in Open and Distributed Learning, 17*(4), 82–103. doi:10.19173/irrodl.v17i4.2330

Ruffalo Noel Levitz. (2015). *Priorities Survey for Online Learners*. Cedar Rapids: Ruffalo Noel Levitz.

Scheuermann, M. (2012). Engaging students with synchronous methods in online courses. In *Online Student Engagement Tools and Strategies* (section 1). Retrieved from https://www.facultyfocus.com/wp-content/uploads/2019/02/FF-Online-Student-Engagement-Report.pdf

Shaw, A. (2016). 4 Ways to personalize instruction in pre-designed online courses [Blog]. Retrieved from https://elearningindustry.com/4-ways-personalize-instruction-pre-designed-online-courses

Sull, E. C. (2012). Teaching online with Errol: A tried and true mini-guide to engaging online students. In *Online Student Engagement Tools and Strategies* (section 7). Retrieved from https://www.facultyfocus.com/wp-content/uploads/2019/02/FF-Online-Student-Engagement-Report.pdf

The University of Massachusetts. (n.d.). *Teaching and learning online - communication, community, and assessment: A handbook for UMass faculty*. Retrieved from https://www.umass.edu/oapa/sites/default/files/pdf/handbooks/teaching_and_learning_online_handbook.pdf

Thompson, J. R., Ballenger, J. N., & Templeton, N. R. (2018). Examining quality elements in a higher education fully online doctoral program: Doctoral students' perceptions. *The International Journal of Educational Leadership Preparation, 13*(1), 51–63.

Truhlar, A. M., Walter, T., & Williams, K. M. (2018). Student engagement with course content and peers in synchronous online discussions. *Online Learning, 22*(4), 289–312. doi:10.24059/olj.v22i4.1389

Wehler, M. (2018). Five ways to build community in online classrooms [Blog]. Retrieved from https://www.facultyfocus.com/articles/online-education/five-ways-to-build-community-in-online-classrooms/

Zappala, J. (2012). Promoting student participation and involvement in online instruction: Suggestions from the front. In *Online Student Engagement Tools and Strategies*, 18-20. Retrieved from https://www.facultyfocus.com/wp-content/uploads/2019/02/FF-Online-Student-Engagement-Report.pdf

Section 4
Considering Power, Privilege, and Inclusion in Online Courses

Chapter 12
Intentionally Creating an Inclusive and Welcoming Climate in the Online Learning Classroom

Jon P. Humiston
Central Michigan University, USA

Sarah M. Marshall
Central Michigan University, USA

Nicole L. Hacker
Central Michigan University, USA

Luis M. Cantu
Central Michigan University, USA

ABSTRACT

The online classroom environment may feel safer for students in marginalized groups because the sense of anonymity the environment can provide. While faculty purposely strive to ensure all students are treated equitably in traditional, in-person classrooms, faculty should not assume power and privilege are not impacting the online classroom environment for students, particularly students from underrepresented identities. Research indicates that marginalized students face different challenges in online classrooms than in traditional, in-person classrooms. Further, power and privilege manifests in the online classroom in different ways than in traditional classrooms. This chapter positions a critical lens on the ways that power and privilege impact the online environment, why marginalized students are drawn to the online classroom, the challenges they face, and how faculty contribute to the creation or resolution of these problems. Finally, the chapter concludes with strategies for intentionally promoting inclusion in online classrooms.

DOI: 10.4018/978-1-7998-0115-3.ch012

INTRODUCTION

The online classroom environment may feel safer for students from marginalized groups because the sense of anonymity the environment provides (Erichsen & Bolliger, 2011; Sullivan, 2002). While faculty purposely strive to ensure students are treated equitably in traditional, in-person classrooms, they should not assume power and privilege do not impact the online classroom environment for students, particularly students from marginalized identities (e.g., gender, gender identity, race/ethnicity, sexual orientation, different abilities, and other identities where power and privilege marginalize a student's identity/identities). These identities can affect motivation, retention, and classroom success. Being sensitive to difference and ensuring all students feel valued and respected can mean the difference between a student who successfully graduates and one who does not. Integrating the principles of diversity, inclusion, and equity into teaching are essential to ensuring student learning. An individual's ability to effectively learn is often influenced by their sense of belonging, and, without an intentional focus on inclusive teaching practices, instructors can unknowingly alienate certain learners, thus causing them to withdraw mentally, emotionally, or physically from the course.

Delivering a course via an online platform presents similar, yet often overlooked, challenges pertaining to the development of an inclusive learning environment. Perhaps most importantly, the ways in which power and privilege impact the online classroom cannot be overlooked. Rovai and Wightin (2005) acknowledged that the online environment provides a greater likelihood for marginalized students to feel alienated or disconnected from the social and learning community. Also, Sujo de Montes, Oran, and Willis (2002) cautioned faculty to not assume issues are not present in the online environment and that they should be proactive in addressing issues of bias and assumptions. Added challenges typically faced by marginalized students in traditional classroom settings may include imposter syndrome, implicit bias, and microaggressions (Sujo et. al, 2002). These same barriers to learning can easily present themselves in an online class.

This chapter positions a critical lens on the ways that power and privilege can impact the online environment for marginalized students and outlines the need for inclusive teaching. Also, the chapter details why marginalized students are drawn to the online classroom, the challenges they face and how faculty contribute to the creation or resolution of these problems. Finally, the chapter concludes with strategies for promoting inclusion in online classrooms.

Marginalization and Power in Theory and Pedagogy

Power and privilege play a key role in how faculty and students navigate the online classroom. The ways in which power and privilege impact the classroom is described later in this chapter. However, in order to understand how power and privilege can manifest in the online environment and reinforce marginalization, an understanding of the foundational theory of power and privilege, and how it is evident in pedagogy, is critical.

Bourdieu and Passeron (1977) state that cultural disparities among the social classes does not automatically suggest cultural poverty for the working class and cultural supremacy for the upper- and middle- class cultures. The overarching idea in Bourdieu's theory is the disparate control of cultural capital, which decides educational achievement or failure (Camilleri-Cassar, 2014). Bourdieu places blame on the educational system for the failure of the working class; stating that the system favors the higher social classes (Camilleri-Cassar, 2014). Furlong (2009) further explained:

Those who lack cultural capital run the risk of marginalization while those who possess cultural capital have a valuable asset that can be used to secure favourable outcomes, and which will offer a degree of protection in educational and labour market careers. (p. 7)

This clash between the social classes in school may cause working-class youth to resist authority and reject school-based values in terms of academic achievement (Willis, 1977). This resistance may be central to the population's marginalization; however, this explanation may be oversimplified (Camilleri-Cassar, 2014). While social class is only one aspect of marginalization, this sets the stage for how power disparities begin in the educational system. If we focus more on higher education, we look to Michel Foucault.

Michel Foucault, a French social theorist, was outspoken in his critique of popular methods of democratic adult education classroom discussions (Brookfield, 2005). While many educators felt that open conversations developed self-confidence and control in students manifested from liberatory power as opposed to repressive power, Foucault maintained that these activities resulted in oppression in addition to liberation (Brookfield, 2005). Foucault stated, "it would not be possible for power relations to exist without points of subordination which, by definition, are means of escape" (Foucault, 1982, p. 225). Overall, Foucault believed that power was too intricate to be separated into oppressive or liberatory (Brookfield, 2005). Foucault's writings suggested that modern society has transitioned from sovereign power, "power exercised from above by a clearly discernible authority such as a monarch or the president" (Brookfield, 2005, p. 120), to disciplinary power, "power that is exercised by people on themselves in the specific day-to-day practices of their lives" (Brookfield, 2005, p. 120). For adult educators, this means that they can no longer focus on sovereign power as the adversary and must confront that they may be complicit in disciplinary power and surveillance (Brookfield, 2017). In the end, Foucault was self-critical of his work and displayed an interminable pursuit of the part power plays in our lives; however, Foucault was not considered strictly a critical theorist (Brookfield, 2005). One person who was undoubtedly a critical theorist was Paulo Freire (Díaz, n.d.).

The first person credited with applying critical theory to education and pedagogy was Paulo Freire, a prominent educational philosopher in the twentieth century (Díaz, n.d.). Freire was known for several important contributions to philosophy and critical theory, most notably the banking concept of education, internalization, freedom, and critical consciousness (i.e., conscientização) (Díaz, n.d.). These ideas were discussed in Freire's seminal novel *Pedagogy of the Oppressed* (Díaz, n.d.).

Freire (2005/1970) highlighted oppression in terms of the oppressed finding freedom. The resultant emergence of a new human undertaking liberation may result in rectification of the oppressor-oppressed paradox (Freire, 2005/1970). In addition, Freire (2005/1970) stated that education is a machine-like process of narration, where students are "containers" waiting to be "filled" by the teacher (p. 72). As a result, education is basically a series of "deposits," where the teacher makes the communication deposit and the students obediently "receive, memorize, and repeat" (Freire, 2005/1970, p. 72). This "banking" idea of education does not allow for knowledge through inquiry, creativity, or innovation and creates an environment of oppression (Freire, 2005/1970, p. 73). The banking concept of education "between the teacher and the students is characterized by insecurity, suspicion of one another, the teacher's need to maintain control, and power dynamics within a hierarchy that are oppressive" (Díaz, n.d., para. 35). In contrast to the banking concept of education, Freire proposes a critical pedagogy (i.e., "problem-posing" education) where the teacher and students learn from each other, there is mutual respect, and each person realizes the value in the diverse experiences of others (Díaz, n.d.; Freire, 2005/1970, p. 79).

Freire (2005/1970) chooses critical pedagogy as his chosen pedagogy "because critical pedagogy utilizes dialogue among human beings who are equals rather than oppressive imposition" (Díaz, n.d., para. 37).

More recently, Morris and Stommel (2018) introduced the topic of Critical Digital Pedagogy, which focuses on dialogue and equity in the classroom rather than standardized content and tools. When defining Critical Digital Pedagogy, Morris and Stommel (2018) said it:

centers its practice on community and collaboration; must remain open to diverse, international voices, and thus requires invention to reimagine the ways that communication and collaboration happen across cultural and political boundaries; will not, cannot, be defined by a single voice but must gather together a cacophony of voices; must have use and application outside traditional institutions of education. (Chapter 1, Section 1, para. 23)

While this pedagogy aims to decenter the instructor, the presence of everyone in the classroom is important to move forward in the educational process (Morris & Stommel, 2018).

In the classroom, mutual sharing by both the teacher and students is vital to creating a sense of community (Morris & Stommel, 2018). Exclusively asking students to share their narrative and discussing diversity and marginalization creates a one-sided emphasis on the student (Morris & Stommel, 2018). The instructor's narrative should be included in the conversation as well, because "If we do not speak up about our own power — if we don't do more than simply concede the podium or the center of the room — we have done too little to undo that power" (Morris & Stommel, 2018, Chapter 2, Section 9, para. 7). However, as classrooms are moving increasingly to online settings, this dynamic changes.

There is a dearth of literature on power and privilege in online classrooms. Academic institutions have all the physical spaces needed on-campus to support students' curricular and co-curricular activities; however, few of these institutions mirror these spaces online (Morris & Stommel, 2018). Online programs need to make use of the Internet that supports current online courses to provide these spaces, because most ongoing courses are provided via a structured Learning Management System (LMS) (Morris & Stommel, 2018). Morris and Stommel (2018) discussed the contradiction of a LMS, which is linked to behaviorism, and critical pedagogy, stating that the LMS, and technology in general, "provides a data-driven means of controlling student behavior — modifying it through methods of reward and punishment — critical pedagogy's primary aim is the liberation of students from systems that oppress them" (Chapter 2, Section 6, para. 18). To accomplish critical pedagogy's goals, the focal point is similar to LMS but includes analysis and inquiry as well (Morris & Stommel, 2018). As a result, instructors should invite inspection of the LMS and the web as one way to create dialogue and a more equitable online experience (Morris & Stommel, 2018).

This foundational understanding of theory and pedagogy related to marginalization and power informs instructors of their position within the power structure of the classroom. The theory around power also informs instructors on the various ways that power manifests throughout the classroom. If instructors want to create an environment that is inclusive of all students, a foundational understanding of power is critical to have, as well as an understanding of why inclusive pedagogy and teaching is so important.

Importance of Inclusive Teaching

A dynamic aspect of American education is the diversity represented in student learners. Celebrating the diversity of our students and learning from their varying perspectives must be a top priority of our educators. As online learning involves a greater number and diversity of learners, instructors need to be concerned about how differences are managed. One-size-fits-all education is no longer an effective approach. Focusing on the language we use, covering material our learners can relate to, and removing obstacles to learning enhances the experience for our students. Within our classes we need to communicate respect, belonging, and caring. When learners do not experience these three, they may choose to not participate thus withdrawing their engagement (Sullivan, 2001). Withdrawal can manifest via their absence from class, failure to ask questions, lack of peer engagement, or lack of preparedness. They also may drop the class or leave the university all together. To promote inclusive educational opportunities, instructors must be aware of how learners are affected by the social interactions in a course and take steps to ensure a positive class culture (Xu & Jaggars, 2014).

Online learning presents new, accessible educational opportunities. Online classes can reach learners outside of the traditional-aged, in-person student. While online learning provides access for diverse learners, studies suggest that certain populations of students such as those with lower grade point averages, lower socioeconomic status, and minority learners struggle in an online setting (Jaggars, 2011). Knowing these groups struggle more in an online environment suggests more work needs to be done to encourage and support these populations.

Inclusion here relates to creating a learning environment where all learners feel respected and included. Most learners, including those from marginalized groups, may experience three barriers that hinder their learning. First, imposter syndrome relates to those students who are often accomplished but feel inferior to their peers (Sakulku & Alexander, 2011). Concerned that others will realize they are not as capable as they seem, they fear being perceived as less than competent. Cokley, McClain, Enciso, & Martinez (2013) claim that when it comes to imposter feelings for racial/ethnic minority students, gender does not have a significant impact; yet, Asian American students are more likely to be impacted by imposter syndrome than others due to cultural expectations of high performance.

The best way to offset imposter syndrome is via affirmations. Students need to know that they are smart, capable, and with hard work and persistence, they can succeed in the course. Some tangible ways to boost student confidence without compromising rigor include: 1) communicating clear learning objectives; 2) acknowledging when material is especially challenging and providing supplemental material or making yourself available for extra tutoring; and 3) breaking the material into manageable chunks and providing students feedback at each step. By building students' confidence, they will start to see themselves as competent and able to succeed.

Next, implicit bias may also threaten a student's ability to learn. Implicit bias refers to the "attitudes or stereotypes that affect our understanding, actions, and decisions in an unconscious manner. These biases, which encompass both favorable and unfavorable assessments, are activated involuntarily and without an individual's awareness or intentional control" (Kirwan Institute for the Study of Race & Ethnicity, 2015, para 1). Classroom bias can be defined as the subtle and blatant ways that prejudice, discrimination, and stereotypes emerge in teaching situations (Boyson, 2012). Implicit bias may come from instructors of students and may lead to negative stereotypes about a person's group and being concerned about being judged or treated negatively on the basis of this stereotype. This may lead to the perception that students are intellectually less capable than other groups and may perform worse academically as a result of this perception. Knowingly or unknowingly, bias can present a real barrier for marginalized students. Due to the stereotype about their group, marginalized students may face more pressure than a White student, a straight student, a male student, a cisgender student, a student without a disability, or a student with inherent privilege because of their demographic background. Studies have shown that extra pressure can undermine the targeted groups' performance, making it more difficult for them to succeed than for a non-stereotyped person (Spencer, Logel, & Davies, 2016). To help overcome the consequences of implicit bias, instructors must first start with examining their own implicit bias. Since implicit bias is often unconscious, instructors may not be aware of the assumptions they hold about students' learning behavior. Some examples may include: 1) expecting students whose first language is not English to be poor writers; 2) expecting students with substandard writing abilities to be stereotyped as lacking intellectual ability; or 3) expecting students who are affiliated with a particular identity group to be experts on issues related to that group. The first step to overcoming implicit bias within the classroom is for instructors to increase their personal awareness of their biases. This may be done formally by taking a self-assessment such as those offered by Project Implicit (2011) (see additional readings) or by soliciting feedback from students or an outside evaluator. Next, instructors can help reduce the threat by intervening with affirmations and creating identity-safe environments. This may be done by assuring students that their stigmatized social identities are not barriers to their success or by providing peer mentors or successful role models from the targeted group.

A third barrier faced by students from underrepresented, and often marginalized, groups is the receipt of regular microaggressions that frequently emerge from implicit bias. Microaggressions are often microinsults and microinvalidations by faculty and other students in the course based on someone's race, ethnicity, religion, nationality, sexual orientation, gender expression, gender identity, disability, age, socioeconomic status, and other diverse dimensions (Sue et al., 2007). The prejudice that students encounter is more likely to be subtle rather than blatant. Racial and ethnic minority students report that they frequently face subtle slights and insults that are offensive but largely unintentional (Boyson, 2012). In the context of teaching, microaggressions may be comments or questions directed at a student that communicate messages of exclusion based on their identity, inappropriate jokes, malicious comments, singling-out students, or stereotyping (Sue et al., 2007). Examples may include: 1) failing to learn to pronounce or continuing to mispronounce the names of students, especially after they corrected you; 2) scheduling tests or projects due dates on cultural or religious holidays; 3) assuming the gender of any student; or 4) singling out students because of their backgrounds. These actions may seem harmless, and often the person who is speaking has no ill intent; however, intent does not mean there is no impact. In other words, there may not be an intent of harm, but the impact of the comment may impart unintentional (or intentional) harm. Microaggressions are often committed by well-intentioned, good people not meaning to hurt anyone. Nevertheless, the outcome for the person impacted by microaggressive acts is anger, frustration, and withdrawal. Overall, microaggressions may contribute to an unwelcoming classroom environment. Some suggestions for addressing microaggressions in the classroom include: not expecting students to speak on behalf of their entire group; not assuming all groups are not represented in the classroom; establishing ground rules and expectations regarding discussions around diversity; being cognizant of microaggressions between students, and being prepared to interrupt and address those incidents. An instructor's silence, whether intentional or not, will equal acceptance of the act.

Instructors in traditional classrooms have a greater chance of monitoring and observing whether their marginalized students are struggling in the classroom with imposter syndrome and acts from others in the class based on implicit bias or microaggressions. For marginalized students, the impact of these acts may push them to seek education through alternative means, such as the online environment. As a result, online instructors need to be even more vigilant to see where marginalized students are experiencing barriers to their success.

Intentionally Creating an Inclusive and Welcoming Climate in the Online Learning Classroom

Why Marginalized Students Take Online Courses

There are varied reasons why a student may choose an online course. These reasons range from convenience in schedule, preference in learning style, or the ability to be invisible and not treated differently based on looks or mannerisms. To establish a foundation for understanding the experiences of marginalized students in the online classroom, this section discusses the reasons why marginalized students may intentionally choose to take online courses.

Marginalized students cite classrooms as the most common place on campus where they experience prejudicial behavior (i.e., being treated differently due to an aspect of their identity) from their instructor or other students. To avoid experiencing this, marginalized students may opt to take their classes online. However, just because the online classroom offers a different environment to students than traditional classrooms, students may still experience mistreatment, albeit in different forms than a traditional classroom.

One of the main reasons marginalized students may seek out online education is an opportunity to become anonymous or invisible (Sullivan, 2002), so that their physical characteristics are not factored into interactions. In other words, the differences that may be apparent in a traditional classroom become less visible within the virtual classroom (Rovai & Ponton, 2005).

Enger (2006) noted that in traditional college classrooms, the dominant culture provides a barrier for marginalized students. As mentioned earlier, these barriers may include bias or the prevalence of microaggressions. Caspi, Chajut, and Saporta (2008) share similar ideas about the dominant culture prohibiting success in a traditional classroom. They found that the online environment may lessen the impact of the dominant culture and discriminating behaviors, because there is less of an opportunity for implicit bias and prejudicial behavior to occur based on a student's identity. According to Caspi et al. (2008), the online classroom provides opportunities to lessen the impact of intimidation for marginalized students, because the environment levels the playing field for students. There is less opportunity to physically interact with each other, which means less of an opportunity to treat people differently.

Sullivan (2002) pointed out that somehow the online environment allows students to be more open and honest. Without the face-to-face interaction of a traditional classroom, students are freer to share their thoughts and ideas. In addition, the lack of physical appearance provides a decrease of stereotyping or bias by other students and the instructor. Sullivan (2002) pointed out that even the subtle classroom nuances of judgement, such as eye rolling or body language, disappear in the online classroom, which allows for the sharing of ideas without fear of being judged.

Next, Enger (2006) shared that the very structure of learning shifts in an online environment, which allows students to center their own learning. In a traditional classroom, professors act as a conduit for the learning process. In the online environment, the instructor guides and nurtures the students, and the students own the responsibility for their learning. Sullivan (2002) noted that the online environment allows for self-reflection and an opportunity to critically think about questions, as opposed to the traditional classroom which may put students on the spot for an instant answer. This structure of the online learning environment, combined with the ability to allow marginalized students a more welcoming learning environment, has significant potential to erase barriers that traditional classrooms still face. The online environment has the ability to intentionally create an environment that is free from traditional classroom culture and inequities. However, this does not mean that marginalized students in the online environment are free from barriers. Ashong and Commander (2012) argued that race/ethnicity and/or gender do impact students' perceptions of online learning, particularly for marginalized students.

Problems Faced by Marginalized Students in the Online Classroom

Luyt (2013) validated that the culture of academe is infused with power relations formed by the dominant or majority viewpoint, which excludes or marginalizes voices of those who are not part of the dominant or majority. Further Luyt (2013) pointed out that language, communication style, writing requirements, and textbook readings are all often slanted with the expectations of Western culture, which perpetuate the power role of the dominant culture. This power dynamic created by the dominant culture places marginalized students at an academic disadvantage in the online classroom, especially if they do not identify with the dominant or majority culture. Those who do identify with the dominant or majority culture have the privilege of participating in a class where they are set to succeed in the reading and writing assignments and expectations. Due to their identity with the majority culture, they will have a higher success rate. According to Luyt (2013), those students will understand the need to connect with the material because there is an expectation for the number of logins, the number of responses to discussion questions, and also identifying with and seeing themselves reflected in the reading material. Instructors must pay critical attention to how the dominant culture impacts their classroom and understand how learners construct their knowledge.

Erichsen and Bolliger (2011) noted that "Learners construct their knowledge when they are placed in active roles and in social learning environments that are safe" (p. 312). As such, the gathering of learners together (i.e., learning communities) is integral to learning the art of scholarship (Erichsen & Bolliger, 2011). In this setting, small breakout groups can be utilized to encourage knowledge-sharing to merge previous and new knowledge (Erichsen & Bolliger, 2011). However, Erichsen and Bolliger (2011) stated that this method of learning may be uniquely difficult in the online setting, which can lead to increased isolation.

Isolation of online students is concerning (Erichsen & Bolliger, 2011; Shaw & Polovina, 1999; Smith & Shwalb, 2007; Terry 2001). The risk of isolation increases with online students due to sometimes limited to no in-person interaction in a course or even an entire program (Erichsen & Bolliger, 2011). However, the online environment does have advantages such as allowing students extra time to reflect on material and developing responses to online question prompts and the ability to disguise gender, age, country of origin, English as a second language challenges, disabilities, and more (Erichsen & Bolliger, 2011). Cross (1998) and McClure (2007) discussed the importance of peer support and the ability to engage in learning communities, which online students do not experience as effectively and undergo increased levels of isolation as a result.

Similarly, Delahunty (2012) suggested that the use of technology and the online platform may increase frustration around communication, as it is difficult to discern another user's tone of voice, interpret their values and ethics, or discern whether one fits within a group or not. These factors lead to further communication barriers, which can lead to avoiding communication. If a student is unwilling to engage or communicate, there is no opportunity to help them feel included because they have isolated themselves.

While the online environment may shield students from bias and stereotypes faced in the face-to-face classroom, students may still face bias and stereotyping in the online environment (Delahunty, 2012). Phirangee and Malec (2017) stated that online instructors are encouraged to create a more social virtual learning environment that spurs student interaction and discourse. While it is thought that this more interactive pedagogy will lead to decreased isolation and increased retention, this discourse is not necessarily void of bias (Phirangee & Malec, 2017). Bias can emerge when students read comments, knowingly or unknowingly stereotyping their response, which results in treating students differently.

Phirangee and Malec (2017) agreed that when bias or microaggressions emerge, marginalized students feel less confident participating and are less likely to share, particularly about their background. Delahunty (2012) claimed that this dynamic causes students to treat each other differently, positively and negatively. In other words, they either align with each other or this unconscious bias begins to create a divide between them that they cannot overcome.

Regardless of the reason, marginalized students take online classes. While participation in these classes may allow for more anonymity or a more comfortable learning environment, there are still many barriers that negatively impact student learning. By promoting inclusive teaching environments and implementing culturally responsive pedagogies, students may find a more welcoming and encouraging environment where they can excel.

Strategies to Create and Maintain an Inclusive Online Learning Environment

This chapter concludes with intentional ways that instructors of online classes can create an inclusive learning environment. In addition to adhering to the optimal delivery and design practices put forth via Quality Matters through their National Standards for Quality Online Courses (2018) (https://www.qualitymatters.org), we recommend implementing culturally responsive pedagogies, eliminating inappropriate or uninformed comments, understanding student motivations, and removing alienating language or imagery. While our suggestions are not exhaustive, they are the beginning steps to create a more inclusive, virtual classroom climate.

Culturally Responsive Pedagogy

Culturally responsive pedagogy (CRP) is a "student-centered approach to teaching where a student's unique cultural strengths are identified and nurtured to promote student achievement and sense of well-being about the student's cultural place in the world" (Lynch, 2012, p. 1). Rooted in differentiated instruction, culturally responsive pedagogy strives to connect course content, teaching practices, and assessment to each individual. This may be realized through: 1) encouraging students to share their stories, perspectives, and thoughts; 2) integrating diverse and culturally-significant teaching strategies; and 3) understanding student backgrounds and learning styles.

To create an optimal learning environment for all students, instructors must be intentional in creating a virtual environment that is inclusive of all students. This can be difficult to accomplish when students from varying backgrounds bring different perceptions and expectations to the classroom. Understanding that each student and instructor has a vast background of intersecting identities is an initial step. The intersecting identities of the instructor impacts the classroom experience for students (Dixon-Saxon, 2009). Educators must lead by example in terms of bringing their authentic selves to the environment thus allowing others to do the same. Further, instructors should spend time deconstructing their identities, areas of privilege and oppression, and understanding their implicit biases. The best way for an instructor to do this is to understand their identities, educate themselves on ways people who hold identities that are different from their own experience the world, and to attend training sessions particularly geared toward identities that they do not hold. Committing to a culturally competent environment with a focus on equity, more so than equality, will have a drastic, positive impact in the online classroom.

Inappropriate or Uninformed Comments

As described earlier, microaggressions and stereotypes may appear, even in an online platform. As a result, these comments can lead to learners disengaging from the social community you aim to foster. As an instructor, employing various strategies can model a welcoming and inclusive online environment.

Classroom suggestions:

- Educate yourself in different kinds of microaggressions and be conscious of your language.
- Closely review all of your written or recorded materials for microaggressions.
- Monitor the interactions on forums or other online platforms.
- Establish ground rules prohibiting inappropriate comments and demonstrate a commitment to intergroup dialogue.
- Directly address and do not ignore inappropriate comments.

Lack of Motivation and Expectations

Online courses often demand high levels of learner motivation and self-regulation. You can support learners in your online course by empowering them and clearly reinforcing your support of all learners.

Classroom suggestions:

- Add a welcoming and encouraging message to your course.
- Promote growth and learning among your students to encourage them to persevere through difficult course material. Emphasize that all learners can succeed with practice and effort and intervene when you hear learners say otherwise. Affirming students' potential is critical.
- Reduce anxiety and associated imposter syndrome challenges by affirming that students can succeed in your course. Give students regular messages that, with sustained effort, they can incrementally advance toward mastery of course content. Regular assessments And ongoing feedback, with the possibility of resubmission, may help build student confidence.
- One aspect of online learning that is missing, according to Sullivan (2002), is the storytelling that happens in traditional classrooms. Online courses should make a point to allow students to share their experiences with each other, their history, experiences at work, and their travel. Stories help students understand each other and their differences and similarities. Delahunty (2012) urged instructors to look for the opportunities to encourage identity expression among students. Students are looking for the opportunity to share passion and align identities by social or cultural factors. This spurs success, particularly for marginalized students.

Alienating Language or Imagery

How you address learners and how they address one another can have a strong effect on feelings of belonging and inclusion, which impacts the learning community. The language and images used throughout your course (e.g., syllabus, PowerPoints, discussion boards, email) can affect whether learners feel as though they are welcome in your course.

For example, in terms of inclusive language, learners who identify as transgender or gender nonbinary may feel less engaged in a course where other individuals have misgendered them in the past or where only male or female pronouns are used. If your course material refers exclusively to experiences that resonate with the majority learner population, the remaining students will feel excluded. Additionally, if words like *crazy, nuts, or psychotic* are used, they have the power to marginalize students with a mental illness. Phrases such as *foreign students* used instead of *international students* or *illegal students* versus *undocumented students* will have an impact on the students taking your course in terms of perceptions of inclusivity.

In terms of imagery, if all of the images an instructor uses in the classroom depict White people, those of different racial or ethnic identities will feel excluded. Instructors should pay attention to whether their imagery depicts those with different marginalized identities when using imagery in the classroom in an effort to create a world view that is inclusive of everyone.

Classroom suggestions:

- Be mindful of the images and references you use throughout the course. Notice if you tend to depict only people with certain identities in the images you incorporate. Rewrite your materials, as needed, if you are focusing on cultural aspects that may not speak to learners of other cultures.
- In an online format, be extremely careful about the language that you choose to use and pay attention to the language that your students are using in discussion boards. If there is something that is written that would marginalize another student, be sure to address it.

Knowing who is in the classroom can improve the chances of creating a positive environment. By knowing our students, we are more likely to implement teaching practices that best meet their needs. Most importantly, instructors must remember that behind every face there is a story and that story impacts how a student learns. Knowing our students and genuinely demonstrating care for them and their well-being are essential to their academic success.

CONCLUSION

Sujo de Montes et al. (2002) provided guidelines for instructors of online classes, who wish to intentionally create safe spaces. The first step is helping students understand power and privilege and how it plays out in society and to provide judgement-free opportunities for students to examine their own behaviors. Instructors must also have the ability and knowledge to call out implicit bias in their words and actions, not only from their students, but from themselves and of the material they are using in the classroom. According to Sujo de Montes et al. (2002), the best way to intentionally create a climate in the classroom that is welcoming is to begin examining, as an instructor, your own power and privilege. We must examine our own thoughts, language, and actions in teaching. If we, as educators, are unable to do this, we should not expect to be successful in creating an online classroom that is conducive for marginalized students to learn.

REFERENCES

Ashong, C. Y., & Commander, N. E. (2012). Ethnicity, gender, and perceptions of online learning in higher education. *Journal of Online Learning and Teaching / MERLOT*, *8*(2), 98–110.

Bourdieu, P., & Passeron, J. (1977). *Reproduction in education, society, and culture*. London: Sage Publications.

Boysen, G. A. (2012). Teacher and student perceptions of microaggression in college classrooms. *Journal of College Teaching*, *60*(3), 122–129. doi:10.1080/87567555.2012.654831

Brookfield, S. (2005). *The power of critical theory: Liberating adult learning and teaching*. New York, NY: Open University.

Brookfield, S. D. (2017). *Becoming a critically reflective teacher*. New York, NY: John Wiley & Sons, Incorporated.

Camilleri-Cassar, F. (2014). Education strategies for social inclusion or marginalising the marginalised? *Journal of Youth Studies*, *17*(2), 252–268. doi:10.1080/13676261.2013.834312

Caspi, A., Chajut, E., & Saporta, K. (2008). Participation in class and gender in online discussions: Gender differences. *Computers & Education*, *50*(3), 718–724. doi:10.1016/j.compedu.2006.08.003

Cokley, K., McClain, S., Enciso, A., & Martinez, M. (2013). An examination of the impact of minority status stress and imposter feelings on the mental health of diverse ethnic minority college students. *Journal of Multicultural Counseling and Development*, *41*(2), 82–95. doi:10.1002/j.2161-1912.2013.00029.x

Cross, K. P. (1998). Why learning communities? Why now? *About Campus: Enriching the Student Learning Experience*, *3*(3), 4–11. doi:10.1177/108648229800300303

Delahunty, J. (2012). 'Who am I?': Exploring identity in online discussion forums. *International Journal of Educational Research*, *53*, 407–420. doi:10.1016/j.ijer.2012.05.005

Díaz, K. (n.d.). Paulo Freire. *Internet encyclopedia of philosophy*. Retrieved from https://www.iep.utm.edu/freire/#H11

Dixon-Saxon, S. V. (2009). Diversity and distance education: Cultural competence for online instructors. In R. A. R. Gurung & L. R. Prieto (Eds.), *Got diversity? Best practices for incorporating culture into the curriculum*. Sterling, VA: Stylus Publications.

Enger, K. B. (2006). Minorities and online higher education. *EDUCAUSE Quarterly*, *29*(4), 7–8.

Erichsen, E. A., & Bolliger, D. U. (2011). Towards understanding international graduate student isolation in traditional and online environments. *Educational Technology Research and Development*, *59*(3), 309–326. doi:10.100711423-010-9161-6

Foucault, M. (1982). The subject and power. In H. L. Dreyfus & P. Rabinow (Eds.), *Michel Foucault: Beyond Structuralism and Hermeneutics*. Chicago, IL: University of Chicago Press.

Freire, P. (2005). *Pedagogy of the oppressed* (M. Bergman Ramos, Trans.). New York, NY: Continuum. (Original work published 1970)

Furlong, A. (2013). Marginalized youth in education: Social and cultural dimensions of exclusion in Canada and the UK. In K. Tilleczek & H. B. Ferguson (Eds.), *Youth, Education, and Marginality: Local and Global Expressions*. Waterloo, UK: Wilfrid Laurier University Press.

Jaggars, S. S. (2011). *Online learning: Does it help low-income and underprepared students?* CCRC Working Paper No. 26. Assessment of Evidence Series. Columbia University: Community College Research Center. Retrieved from: https://ccrc.tc.columbia.edu/publications/online-learning-low-income-underprepared.html

Kirwan Institute for the Study of Race and Ethnicity. (2015). *Understanding implicit bias*. Retrieved from: http://kirwaninstitute.osu.edu/research/understanding-implicit-bias/

Luyt, I. (2013). Bridging spaces: Cross-cultural perspectives on promoting positive online learning experiences. *Journal of Educational Technology Systems, 42*(1), 3–20. doi:10.2190/ET.42.1.b

Lynch, M. (2012, February 13). What is culturally responsive pedagogy? *HuffPost*. Retrieved from: https://www.huffpost.com/entry/culturally-responsive-pedagogy_b_1147364

McClure, J. W. (2007). International graduates' cross-cultural adjustment: Experiences, coping strategies, and suggested programmatic responses. *Teaching in Higher Education, 12*(2), 199–217. doi:10.1080/13562510701191976

Morris, S. M., & Stommel, J. (2018). *An urgency of teachers: The work of critical digital pedagogy* [Kindle for Mac version]. Retrieved from Amazon.com

Phirangee, K., & Malec, A. (2017). Othering in online learning: An examination of social presence, identity, and sense of community. *Distance Education, 38*(2), 160–172. doi:10.1080/01587919.2017.1322457

Project Implicit. (2011). *Take a test*. Retrieved from https://implicit.harvard.edu/implicit/takeatest.html

Quality Matters. (2018). *National standards for quality online courses*. Retrieved from https://www.qualitymatters.org

Rovai, A. P., & Ponton, M. (2005). An examination of sense of classroom community and learning among African American and Caucasian graduate students. *Journal of Asynchronous Learning Networks, 9*, 77–92.

Rovai, A. P., & Wightin, M. J. (2005). Feelings of alienation and community among higher education students in a virtual classroom. *The Internet and Higher Education, 8*(2), 97–110. doi:10.1016/j.iheduc.2005.03.001

Sakulku, J., & Alexander, J. (2011). The impostor phenomenon. *International Journal of Behavioral Science, 6*(1), 75–97.

Shaw, S., & Polovina, S. (1999). Practical experiences of, and lessons learnt from, Internet technologies in higher education. *Journal of Educational Technology & Society, 2*(3), 16–24. Retrieved from http://www.ifets.info/journals/2_3/stephen_shaw.pdf

Smith, T. B., & Shwalb, D. A. (2007). Preliminary examination of international students' adjustment and loneliness related to electronic communications. *Psychological Reports, 100*(1), 167–170. doi:10.2466/pr0.100.1.167-170 PMID:17451020

Spencer, S. J., Logel, C., & Davies, P. G. (2016). Stereotype threat. *Annual Review of Psychology, 67*(1), 415–437. doi:10.1146/annurev-psych-073115-103235 PMID:26361054

Sue, D. W., Capodilupo, C. M., Torino, G. C., Bucceri, J. M., Holder, A. M. B., Nadal, K. L., & Esquilin, M. (2007). Racial microaggressions in everyday life: Implications for clinical practice. *The American Psychologist, 62*(4), 271–286. doi:10.1037/0003-066X.62.4.271 PMID:17516773

Sujo de Montes, L. E., Oran, S. M., & Willis, E. M. (2002). Power, language, and identity: Voices from an online course. *Computers and Composition, 19*(3), 251–271. doi:10.1016/S8755-4615(02)00127-5

Sullivan, P. (2001). Gender differences and the online classroom: Male and female college students evaluate their experiences. *Community College Journal of Research and Practice, 25*(10), 805–818. doi:10.1080/106689201753235930

Sullivan, P. (2002). "It's easier to be yourself when you are invisible": Female college students discuss their online classroom experiences. *Innovative Higher Education, 27*(2), 129–144. doi:10.1023/A:1021109410893

Terry, N. (2001). Assessing enrollment and attrition rates for the online MBA. *Technology Horizons in Education Journal, 28*. Retrieved from http://www.thejournal.com/articles/15251

VPTL. (n.d.). *Blended and Online Learning Design (BOLD) from Stanford*. Retrieved from https://lagunita.stanford.edu/courses/course-v1:VPTL+BOLD+ongoing/about

Willis, P. (1977). *Learning to labour*. Farnborough, UK: Saxon House.

Xu, D., & Jaggars, S. S. (2014). Adaptability to online learning: Differences across types of students and academic subject areas. *The Journal of Higher Education, 85*(5), 633–659. doi:10.1353/jhe.2014.0028

Chapter 13
Strategies for Efficient, Meaningful, and Inclusive Online Learning Environments:
It's About Time

Naomi Jeffery Petersen
Central Washington University, USA

ABSTRACT

Students and faculty rely on clear and unambiguous time targets to exchange information and pace their intersecting lives. Most students juggle work, family, and commuting demands, and increasing numbers also struggle with language needs and disabilities, requiring additional and flexible time to grasp the scope of assignments, read and gather information, process concepts into written products, and finally make sense of the experience. It all takes time. In this chapter, practical strategies for structuring time expectations are introduced in the context of a commitment to empower self-regulation and lifelong learning with particular attention to accessibility. The time dimension of each component of the syllabus, assignments, and gradebook are described with examples from a successful online course, with reference to theory and research on student engagement and satisfaction.

INTRODUCTION

A search through most professors' e-mail for words such as *sorry* or *late* will yield an impressive collection of student pathos. There is no end to the reasons why their work is delayed: personal tragedies, technological glitches, and admitted shortcomings of managing busy lives. Instructors, too, fall victim to inefficiency and distraction. This tendency is even more common in online learning environments. An online course is particularly challenging to a student with weak time-management skills, yet provides a rich opportunity to cultivate that very competence. In this chapter, we consider the time-sensitive aspects of postsecondary education in an online environment, based on a review of pertinent literature and informed by successful online undergraduate courses at a regional comprehensive university in the

DOI: 10.4018/978-1-7998-0115-3.ch013

United States. Beginning with a framework for understanding students' patterns and perspectives, ways to infuse growth-oriented perspectives and self-monitoring techniques are demonstrated with practical strategies for cultivating students' engagement and time management, with specific attention to troubleshooting vulnerability in an online context

In short, it's about time because it takes time to learn and it takes time to teach. It's about teachers and students both making the most of the time they have, but more importantly, making it worth their time.

BACKGROUND

Student-Centered Instruction

This article is written from a student-centered, or constructivist, perspective, with a concern for multiple dimensions of student success (conceptual understanding, personal proficiency, and practical application) in the context of postsecondary education. Decades of research (e.g. Beichner, 2008; Hake, 2008; Hattie, 2012; Hsiao, Mikolaj, & Shih, 2017; Oliver-Hoyo, 2011; Schreiber, 2017) confirm the effectiveness of strategic interaction between instructor and students, as well as among students, combined with metacognition and real world application, which are key components of student-centered pedagogy.

Universities are no longer – if they ever were – simple 'knowledge boxes' with students hungry for knowledge, sitting at the feet of gurus. Instead, campuses are complex self-supporting institutions with a keen interest in student retention and satisfaction, both resulting in tuition-based income for sustaining the institution. Whether a faculty member is motivated more by a sense of the university's business or by social justice, student success will be a primary goal.

Time management is widely recognized as a factor in student success in terms of both user experience and achievement. In France, Fernex, Lima, and de Vries (2015) explored time allocation for academic activities, noting, "At the heart of this exercise is the question of the time students dedicate to academic activities in competition with a whole range of other activities" (p. 399). They concluded that students' choices were influenced more by their past and current experiences than by their goals for the future. This confirms the current psychosocial constructivist model (Phillips et al., 2000) of facilitating student metacognition of experience and reflection on its meaning. Internal constraints and tendencies toward counterproductive behaviors are recognized in this chapter as vulnerabilities, with troubleshooting strategies offered to strengthen both students and instructors' capacities to manage the demands of learning and teaching.

The first vulnerability, then, is one of identity and purpose: both instructor and student are weaker if the instructor is in a traditional role of being the 'sage on the stage' focused only on transmitting knowledge and the student is in a passive role of absorbing information. The more progressive relationship of an instructor who is a 'guide on the side' facilitating the students' active engagement leads to a better use of time because the learning process and the student experience is realistically anticipated and monitored. It is therefore helpful for instructors to consider the reality of current students' lives. There are several individual vulnerability factors in the amount of time students have which in turn affects how they use it.

How Much Time Do Students Have?

Student characteristics have been studied as factors in time-related aspects of student success. Douglas, Bore, and Munro (2016) looked for influences on time management, finding a significant correlation between some personality traits and academic-work engagement. They used the 29-item time-management behavior scale (Macan, Shahani, Dipboye, & Phillips, 1990) of setting goals and priorities, mechanics of time management, and preference for organization. Douglas et al. found time-management behavior was positively predicted by the conscientiousness aspects of industriousness and orderliness. Their work focuses on identifying antecedent demographic characteristics of students: this approach assumes students have stable personality traits that help predict time management and work engagement rather than the reverse.

Similarly, Thill, Rosenzweig, & Wallis (2016) studied students' engagement in an online-library module and found that younger male students were more likely to avoid engagement. However, the module itself was not representative of most instruction, because it was a stand-alone exercise with no assessment or accountability. Their study also did not identify contextual factors such as whether the participants were dependent or independent, a status correlated with age and family role.

Finally, there is little consensus about the construct of personality beyond a collection of behaviors, with research casting doubt that such constructs are stable traits that allow valid interpretation (e.g. Dickson & Kelly, 1985; Lynne-Landsman, Graber, Nichols, & Botvin, 2011). Although it would be convenient to categorize students according to 'learning style', awareness of different modalities of learning simply informs the instructor of the need to use more than the traditional in order to increase engagement with all students.

Others view time management as a skill set to learn rather than an indication of personal disposition. In Canada, Wintre et al. (2011) found that, according to self-report, successful students rated their time-management skills higher than did students whose grades had declined since high school. An earlier study by Slaven and Totterdell (1993) questioned the value of time-management training, but Ebrahimi, Kohlahi, and Nabipour (2017) found that students at University of Tehran who were taught time-management strategies experienced less anxiety and procrastination. In Britain, Trueman and Hartley (1996) found differences in time-management capacity between different ages and genders, but only modest predictions of academic success, while Britton and Tesser (1991) concluded that better time-management practices were associated with higher GPAs. Motivation and competence, though, are tempered by circumstances. It is useful to see patterns in the students' life contexts that may suggest risk regarding their success and a need for support.

Student Parents

The Institute for Women's Policy Research (Reichlin Cruse, Gault, Suh, & DeMario, 2018) noted that as many as one-fifth of all students are also parents and that these students are particularly constrained, needing to satisfy many demands on their time. The choice of online classes provides greater flexibility for students needing to meet family demands, which suggests such students are not lacking in time-management skills but simply have less time available. Reichlin Cruse et al (2018) reported that students who were themselves still financially dependent spent far more time sleeping, studying, and socializing than did their counterparts who were responsible for their own finances. Student parents spent less time on sleep, study, and socializing – and more time on working, a logical consequence of supporting more people.

Student Employment

While age and parental status may explain different time management performance, employment is also a factor. The most recent U.S. Census Bureau (2015) data indicated that approximately half of all full-time students are employed, and 80% of part-time students are working full time. Online courses are a seductive means to economize time by eliminating travel to campus and increase flexibility, but (as discussed above) the simple demand for adequate time necessary to engage in the learning process is often underestimated by both instructors and students.

Divide and Conquer

The image of the dependent student serves as a traditional characterization of undergraduates, but universities are increasingly charged with recognizing that such a "traditional student" may not exist, or be representative of their student population. Although students' poor time management might be due to immaturity in prioritizing tasks and to being more vulnerable to distraction, it is also likely to be due to unrealistic overcommitment to competing tasks and responsibilities. Given that so many students are restricted in the time they have available, instructors must be mindful of their effort to be efficient. Therefore, instructions should include reasonable time estimates for completing each component of an assignment, including the reading in preparation, and organize the information to help students prioritize their tasks meaningfully. Also, instructors can be candid in acknowledging that they share the challenge.

Listen to the voice of a senior faculty sharing lessons learned from teaching online courses to non-traditional students:

Having mature students pursuing [this program] instead of [typical] undergrads has prompted me to carefully consider why I require ANYthing because they have even less time to squander on busywork but ironically I find them even more appreciative of specific instructions and sometimes more nervous about believing they have understood things—especially if it has been a while since they were in school. I am certainly learning to caution them against taking more than one course if they are working full time!

Students with Disabilities

University classrooms must serve people with a great range of abilities affecting cognitive, social and physical functioning, who nonetheless have a right to the opportunity to learn. The concept of universal design assumes that all environments can be designed for maximum full inclusion of people with a range of abilities (Null, 2013). Designing for all will result in fewer needs for individual accommodations such as those necessary to comply with risk management mandates like the Americans with Disabilities Act (ADA, 1990/2010). This approach is consistent with the social model of disability, which attributes most problems of engagement to an incompatibility with an environment that could be altered without compromising the nature of the activity (Smart, 2013). While universal design focuses primarily on the physical environment, whereas, in an educational environment, a universal design for learning, or UDL, means traditional pedagogical methods may unnecessarily disadvantage people who might otherwise be successful (CAST, 2011). More commonly used in K-12 than postsecondary education (Schreffler et al., 2019), UDL has focused on including children with learning difficulties in the regular classroom; in this postsecondary context, UDL has a broader interpretation of identifying barriers preventing the general student population's participation in class activity or in demonstrating their learning.

These barriers can be neutralized by providing flexible means of representation, expression, and engagement to achieve each of the predictable stages of learning. Especially important is flexibility in time (Seok, DaCosta, & Hodges, 2018). Therefore it is much easier for faculty if they simply assume that *all* students need some flexibility and adopt policies that accommodate such routine requests. Regarding such leniency, many faculty believe that setting strict deadlines is a beneficial motivation to complete tasks They may assume that students do not want to learn or to submit evidence of their learning, yet the student's reluctance to submit work may not be a matter of malingering. This begs the question of whether the faculty believe that a student does indeed have a disabling condition that warrants some flexibility. Most disabilities are invisible and suffer from stigma so it is a pity time is sometimes wasted trying to persuade cynical faculty to accept the word of Disability Services.

Another dimension of time concerns its role in defining course procedures. Such parameters include due dates and the degree of flexibility the instructor tolerates for individuals with varied degrees of access or ability. There is lively debate about different accommodation decisions for people who qualify (e.g., Lerner, 2004; Ranseen & Parks 2005), but in this chapter the validity of the need--and that every instructor can expect at least one person to require accommodation --is accepted as a given. Institutions' disability services frequently recommend additional time as an accommodation. Many students benefit from extra time, including those with atypical neurological conditions, such as attention deficit disorder and dyslexia; mental-health issues, such as anxiety over test situations; and autoimmune disorders, such as Crohn's disease. Students with visual impairment who require screen-reader translation of text or students whose first language is not English who rely on translation software to confirm their comprehension of text, are also disadvantaged when tests are timed and assignments must be completed within a limited turnaround. For all these groups, the commonality is that predicted functioning is inhibited.

Reasonable Accommodation

Why, indeed, are time limits imposed for any reason? The legal definitions for *reasonable accommodation* enlightens us, for according to Section 504 of the Rehabilitation Act of 1973 there are only three reasons an accommodation may be refused: (1) if there is a physical danger to someone other than the person requesting the accommodation (e.g., fear for the safety of the person with disability is not reason to deny the accommodation of the person chooses to engage in the activity necessary for the learning experience), (2) the instructional experience is varied to the point that the curriculum value is compromised, or (3) the accommodation causes undue administrative cost to the institution (Katsiyannis, Zhang, Landmark, & Reber, 2009).

It is important to distinguish K-12 from post-secondary education regarding accommodations. The Individuals with Disabilities Education Act (IDEA, 2004) funds special education that is focused particular learning outcomes or degrees of success in K12 school settings. By comparison, the Americans with Disabilities Act (1990) ensures "persons with disabilities are granted reasonable accommodations in order to ensure access and opportunity equal to others (Gotlieb, 2019, p. 43)". A significant difference is that the learning outcomes are actually modified in the K-12 Individual Education Plan (IEP), but not so in higher education. The methods may be modified but not the standard of performance.

Legal Aspects of Time Limits

Supporting students with inhibited functioning is of particular interest to instructors of online courses, because people with disabilities are disproportionately represented among their registrants. Students seeking to minimize the great challenges inevitable when navigating the physical environment may be well served by online instruction, thus increasing the probability of their presence in online courses. However, these students may also be disadvantaged by online instruction. As pointed out by instructional-technology specialist Kevin Andrews "time limits could be viewed as ableist and actually violate WCAG guidelines (2017)." Here he refers to the Web Content Accessibility Guidelines, prompted by the United Nations' Convention on the Rights of Persons with Disabilities (2006), which has been signed but not yet ratified by the United States.

The "ableism" Andrews mentions refers to the expectations by people with no limitations in their perception, mobility, or executive-function capacities that all other people to function at the same level. As Jones (2018) points out, "When students don't seem to live up to the smart, energetic, social, independent self-starters we were expecting online, that's ableism." Ableism is akin to racism in its assumptions, biases, and consequent behaviors that assert power. It behooves an instructor to be aware that students with diverse levels of ability may be quite sensitive to insensitivity: Any instructor ignorant of these students' additional struggles may be considered unprofessional. Such keen criticism of their instructional competence will be warranted and may explain low student evaluations of instructions at the end of term.

But what of accommodations made for students who do not qualify for disability-services interventions? "What about athletes, students with alternative religious holidays, students who participate in clubs that necessitate additional absences from class—[for example], student government" asks Gilivray. "If an institution provides institutional excuses for these situations (and most do), then it is inaccurate to assert that all other students are expected to meet the same attendance standards and students with disabilities are the only ones receiving an exception" (Kathleen Gilivray in private e-mail correspondence with the author, January 9, 2019). This alert raises the question of whether time limits are reasonable for *any* students, even those who do not have disabilities according to categories used to qualify people for accommodations.

Administrative Costs of Time Flexibility

Time limits tend to be an issue of administrative cost not to the institution but to the instructor, whose personal time is exhausted by repeated demands to reengage in the framework of an assignment in order to assess it meaningfully: Reading all the submitted assignments at once when one's frame of mind is oriented to the assessment rubric is far more efficient than having to refresh perspective repeatedly.

There is also a potential cost to the students, because the instructor may have a slightly different mindset when returning to the assignment for grading late papers, and thus students risk biased assessment (Chappuis & Stiggins, 2017). Here there is a considerable value in articulating rubrics to guarantee more reliable interpretations of evidence. Of course, well-articulated rubrics serve not just to reduce bias in grading but to improve students' understanding of quality work. Articulating rubrics does takes time but it is well-spent in order to increase student performance and provide instant feedback.

Strategies for Efficient, Meaningful, and Inclusive Online Learning Environments

Course Completion

There is a broader time limit than the individual assignments within a course: a student struggling with each deadline is likely to struggle with the whole course, and may request an extension of the term in order to complete the course. Each university has its own policies regarding *incompletes*, but it is commonly discouraged, with efforts to protect instructors from undue pressure from students by stipulating that most work must already be done, or there must be extenuating circumstances. There is considerable cost to the instructor to allow such an extension: The work is completed out of sequence and is less efficient to read and score.

However, there may be compelling reasons to allow an incomplete, especially if it is a course required for a degree program and may not be offered again soon. As pointed out in the words of this experienced online instructor, the incomplete avoids the cost to the student of another registration with duplicate tuition:

You know I've been pretty liberal with incompletes, erring on the side of people finishing, in part serving the mission of getting this knowledge base in place before the next courses in the sequence, but also to let people finish after their lives have fallen apart, but without having to spend the tuition again. I have developed a few routines to keep my sanity through this—admitting that it occurs often enough that I need to develop habits: I make it clear they must piggyback on when I am teaching the course again and that I cannot tutor them individually.

When the next course comes around, I reach out a month before to see if they are ready to resume. I require them to copy and paste everything they have already done into the new course shell. In some cases, if they started submitting substandard work before they realized they simply couldn't finish, I let them resubmit work for a higher grade. As I said, the goal is to get them through the whole program without too much interruption because the other courses require this knowledge base.

How Much Time Do Students and Instructors Need?

The 3:1 Rule

Management of time begs the question of how much time must be managed. The first vulnerability is underestimating how much time is needed. The time demands of both undergraduate students and their instructors can be estimated with the 3:1 Rule. Incoming freshmen are often advised to allow at least two hours outside of class, sometimes even three (for a course a student would perceive as "difficult"), for every hour spent in class (United States Department of Education, 2019; Utah State University Academic Success Center, n.d.). These estimates assume the class meets face-to-face. Thus a 3-credit course would require a 9-12 hour weekly budget; a 5-credit course would require at least 15 hours. The two to three outside hours are for reading assigned texts and completing assignments that serve two purposes: to develop mastery of course learning objectives and to demonstrate it. Students are cautioned that their reading pace might affect their time, as will their writing proficiency. If they are weak in either, they must factor in more time. In online courses, the reading requirement is even greater, and students usually do not have the benefit of an interactive conversation that can clarify concepts and instructions more efficiently than a series of online discussion board posts or e-mails.

A full-time course load is typically 15 credits, with 12 considered minimum according to financial aid requirements. Often, universities will allow up to 18 credits for a base tuition (Central Washington University, n.d.; Michigan State University, n.d.; University of Oklahoma, n.d.). Using the formula above, a 15-credit schedule would require that at least 45 hours be devoted to school work each week.

This Isn't High School

The 3:1 Rule helps students develop a different set of management skills than high school, where compulsory attendance occupies about 6 hours a day, or 30 hours a week. The proportion is thus reversed when young adults matriculate to the university campus, compared to their prior experience when they spent about twice as much time in school as on homework. Complicating this unfamiliar distribution of effort is the tendency for students to only schedule attendance in class, leaving outside work less structured. Worse, students might not monitor how much time they do spend on different assignments, and may allow some activities to consume more of their time resource than they can afford.

This means that each assignment should generate its own time estimate in order for students to budget their time accordingly, which in turn means that instructors should have a realistic idea of how much time is really needed for the typical student to accomplish the assigned reading and writing. Barre (2016) noted that "the research [regarding how much time effective reading and writing takes] is more limited" than we would hope, and that faculty may well be asking students for more than we realize we are. Her finding held true even for faculty who made reasonable assumptions regarding students as content novices, for instance, who would necessarily take longer on an academic task when compared to themselves. Online environments are particularly sensitive because the instructor does not observe all the students as they engage in class activities, demonstrating their pace of academic functioning and voicing their concerns.

This Isn't a 24-Hour Convenience Store or a Factory. It's a Garden.

The instructor's time is also limited, and it can also be easily misdirected. Barre's (2016) research alerts us that, when it comes to approximating our own and our students' time, "our estimates can be wildly mistaken" (2016), resulting in our underestimating, often, the actual time spent. Again, the number of credits is an indicator for total time demands, with each credit assuming twice that number of hours each week in preparation and assessment responsibilities. Although instructors publish due dates for students to submit work, they may not schedule a specific time for reading and scoring that work. However, doing so has several advantages for both instructor and student. With a firm target for grades to be posted, students can anticipate when they will receive feedback.

A common complaint on end-of-term student surveys is that papers are not returned in a timely fashion, or that students did not receive meaningful feedback in time to improve the quality of their work on subsequent assignments. Importantly, according to Salisbury (as cited in Gooblar, 2014), early feedback may be associated with an increase in positive, learning-oriented student behaviors. Thus, the instructor benefits in multiple ways from committing to a specific time for grading and commenting on work: by knowing sooner whether students are making progress toward the learning target or whether instruction must be modified, by being able to anticipate that student effort and focus may improve, and by increasing the likelihood that students will report greater satisfaction. This is the garden metaphor: the plant thrives with strategic watering and pruning. Given the importance of instructor input regarding student work, when an assignment is designed, the instructor should have a realistic idea of how much time will be required to read it thoughtfully and respond with meaningful feedback.

Finally, there is also the problem of additional (and perhaps avoidable) demands on both instructor and student time due to confusion about course content or assignments. This issue may be due to poorly communicated information in text or lecture, or failure on the part of the student to engage, but it always results in duplication of effort to clarify meaning. Ways to improve the structure of assignments for greater student engagement and comprehension are suggested below in connection with the predictable stages of learning, as well as ways to respond to student requests in order to redirect their energies to more self-regulated habits. However, the additional time required to read late submissions is a separate issue, also discussed below in the context of establishing policies for time-sensitive communication.

Clearly both instructors and students struggle with having too much to do and not enough time to do it. With attention to instructional decisions and communication, though, both can become more efficient and less frustrated. However, the vulnerability of underestimating time needed is complicated with the vulnerability of overestimating how much time will be available.

Technology Resources

The online-learning environment requires access to an online learning platform, such as Blackboard or Canvas, and the use of an Internet-based communication system. Faculty can assume that some students will require assistive technology, such as text-to-voice software. Any special editions for the visually impaired in the form of braille will be initiated by the university's disability services which will need to know the required texts far in advance. However, these are very expensive and cumbersome, and preparing text for screen readers is more common. People who do not have visual impairment may nonetheless benefit from text-to-voice software—especially those with reading-comprehension problems who may better perceive the concepts aurally. The software is also advantageous for people challenged not by perception problems but by socioeconomic and physical challenges—for example, they have no time to sit and read but do have time to listen to a lesson when they must commute considerable distances.

There are several innovative programs available for engaging students online, such as Flipgrid, which provides templates to use in a social media platform. It is commendable for prompting students to pose questions using videos, a practice that can be implemented within platforms of university courses. Having to access a different platform is an additional obstacle likely to dissuade students. Many features in standard platforms can be used to engage students but each new task and new platform increases the time burden. Thus there must be compelling pedagogical value in each task so it is not perceived as busy work.

Engagement and Self-Regulation

Student engagement is a broad term encompassing "the extent to which students devote time and energy to educationally purposeful activities" (Carini, Kuh, & Klein, 2006, p. 4). This is the subject of the National Survey of Student Engagement used by many universities to monitor quality of instruction. Class attendance (Durden & Ellis, 2003) is a simple way to monitor student engagement, and most instructors place a premium on it with penalties for skipping class and for late submission of assignments.

Regularly scheduled face-to-face sessions between student and teacher establish a routine of sustained attention, but the online environment lacks these monitors of student engagement (Beaudoin, 2002) unless the course includes synchronous meetings, in which case it would be considered a "distance-learning" environment. The need to monitor student engagement has prompted the growing field of learning analytics (Morten, 2014) to identify variables in data collected within learning-management systems, such as Canvas and Blackboard Learn. These data may be interpreted as measures of student engagement by considering logging in as the equivalent of attending class.

Log-in Behavior

The concept of self-regulation explains patterns of student engagement. Using Schunk and Zimmerman's (1998) triarchic model of self-regulation—that is, forethought, performance/volitional control, and self-reflection—Terry and Doolittle (2008) investigate the influence of instructor feedback at two different intervals (daily/weekly) in the form of an online time-management tool, finding increases in self-reported time-management behaviors. In Korea, Jo, Kim, and Yoon (2015) studied not the demographic characteristics of students but their behavior. Their interest is in finding a variable that predicts success, assessed at the end of the course by selected response examination. After analyzing the online log-in behavior of 200 professionals in a five-week lecture-based online course, Jo et al. found that irregularity of the learning interval had a significant negative correlation with the final test score. The duration and the frequency of visits were not as significant, leading them to conclude that long-term planning and sustained effort were key components of self-regulation. This could mean that frequency of instructor feedback about online behavior is as important as frequency of feedback about learning progress.

A promising application of such findings is the development of monitoring features within the learning-management system that would alert faculty and students to trends in log-in behavior. An immediate application of learning analytics is to raise awareness among students that their habits make a difference in their learning, a nod to the power of self-efficacy (Bandura, 1997) and control theory (Glasser, 1997). Instructors can help by informing students that logging in frequently for short periods of time is more effective than waiting until a single long stretch of time comes available. Instructors can prompt students to plan how frequently they will engage online, and instructors can include metacognitive questions in routine assignments and quizzes that ask students to reflect on their log-in behavior. In addition, instructor feedback can help students attribute their success to time management.

Although not all universities have such a reminder feature available, all faculty can focus on log-in frequency to cultivate student engagement. Given that this chapter focuses on actions faculty can take that will make a difference in student success while still managing their own time, it may be enough to raise student awareness of the correlation between their log on behavior and their performance, and to provide metacognitive moments for them to acknowledge the evidence of their own engagement. Thus the instructor would not be tasked with monitoring log-in data but with coaching students in their development of frequent log-in behavior, that is, in promoting self-regulation.

It Takes Time to Learn

There is widespread interest in ways time factors in student success, which means the process of learning must be understood along with the time each stage needs to master the course objectives. Instructors can benefit from Hattie's (2012) research in K–12 teaching that finds classroom discussion, feedback, and metacognitive strategies significantly effect learning, all of which require student engagement. Each of these strategies can occur in an online environment, and each is sensitive to timing. However, they can best be framed in the context of the sequence of learning itself, which includes a sequence of predictable stages of memory as well as self-regulation (Moos & Miller, 2015; Rutherford, Buschkuehl, Jaeggi, & Farkas, 2018). In the context of this chapter, stages of learning are posited as discrete steps on the continuum of memory acquisition and attrition as well as self-regulation which in turn relate to specific activities of engagement that contribute to student success.

The term *stages of learning* has been used to summarize various theoretical models, ranging from differences in cognition, (e.g., unconscious v. conscious) regarding one's own degree of competence () to motor skill acquisition (Luft & Buitrago, 2005) to the narrow focus on categorical learning in neurocomputational theory (Cantwell, Crossley & Ashby (2015). Piaget (1969) pioneered a theory of development describing predictable stages of thinking (e.g. concrete v. abstract) which explain students' capacities to learn Anderson et al. (2001) equated cognitive processes (e.g. remembering, understanding, applying, analyzing, evaluating, and creating) of different types of knowledge (e.g., facts, concepts, procedures, metacognition) with performance of learning outcomes while the stages of self-regulation (i.e., planning, monitoring, control, and reflection) to focus on behaviors of task completion Pintrich, 2000; Schunk 2008).

Each stage of memory requires instructional interaction, although instructors may focus only on the first and last stages—sensory input and sensory output. The first two—*sensory input* and *sensory register*—last only seconds, while *short-term memory* lasts less than a minute. It takes multiple and sustained engagements to store information meaningfully enough to retrieve it from storage. Advancing from sensory register and short-term memory through *working memory* to *long term* memory are prerequisite to the fluid abstract reasoning that most university courses expect of students. The last stage is attrition, or *memory loss*, which is important to recognize for people forget what they do not use or value, and then must re-learn the concept.

The problem is that the time spent in the early stages is necessary to achieve the fluent higher levels of thinking that can only be achieved in long term memory. Incomplete instructions perpetuate a false economy because the student may not believe that the intervening steps are valuable except for grading points generated when the instructor views the evidence. It contributes to arrogance because the student presumes that superficial exposure to facts will be sufficient to enable their application to a sophisticated problem. It therefore behooves the instructor to direct the students' attention to the specific steps necessary to achieving success.

Online students are vulnerable to underestimating the steps of memory function because they can easily scroll to the instructions and the software is likely to highlight the final due date (Moos 2013). Many instructors will assign readings and give instructions for a task, requiring sensory input and short-term memory, but may not mention the intervening steps before scoring it after the due date because they assume university students have learned to learn independently. The steps include thoughtful digestion of the information using working memory and thoughtful construction of the assigned task which requires long-term memory. The grading of the memory output does indeed measure learning, but it may also be a measure of students' lack of study skills or misplaced efficiency.

It is also helpful to recognize that we have a natural tendency to be distracted. As a species, this serves us well when we are in danger. Ideally, students are studying in a safe environment that does not require such constant vigilance, although, as noted above, some students are parents and therefore ever vigilant. Kahneman (2011) explained the difference between thinking fast and slow, which highlights the difference between the earlier and later stages of memory. The tendency to think fast, such as playing games or checking social networks, is instinctive and emotional, while deliberative and logical slow thinking is not so immediately satisfying. Procrastination is often an avoidance of the tedium of slow thinking, which means that coping with the experience of controlling distraction is more helpful than emphasizing the consequences failure.

Setting concrete short term goals is helpful, such as the Pomodoro technique (Burkeman, 2011) that uses timers to help people focus on sub-tasks of larger tasks. It is also helpful to give concrete examples of setting goals and prioritizing small task completion such as these pep talks:

There is no such thing as multi-tasking: you are just oscillating quickly between things, which means you are doing everything superficially. Give yourself time.

Give yourself twenty minutes without distraction and see how much you get done. Set a timer and wait to check email or texts until it goes off.

You paid a lot of money for the textbook. Get your money's worth. Don't let other things steal the value you can get.

You've seen that episode of Big Bang Theory. See how much you can read before the next commercial.

Finally, the software of the online environment may unintentionally encourage a narrow focus on task completion by alerting students to due dates without the context of a series of interactive steps designed to engage students in a richer instructional method. Thus the organization of the assignments must specify the steps and their connection to each other as part of the learning process. In the example below, more than one due date is routine for some types of activities in order to reinforce the stage sequence.

Strategies for Efficient, Meaningful and Inclusive Online Learning Environments

The strategies offered here are organized first according to stages of learning and then in association with the two main types of instructional documents (syllabus and instructions). Concerns for student engagement, memory, and inclusion are integrated in the decisions and priorities of the examples.

Sensory Register and the Physical Capacity to Read the Required Text

Instructors must consider the students' simple capacity to perceive. Students with visual impairments are the most vulnerable to exclusion from perceiving the information provided by an instructor. The online environment complicates this because students with technical limitations may struggle to engage just as students with medical limitations do. To be truly perceivable and operable, the online environment should be navigable without a mouse and without requiring students to download large files.

Screen readers and text-to-voice features are now common, but the instructors providing the materials to be read must be aware of unintentionally obstructing students' access—for example, by failing to provide alternate text for images and tables or by misusing tables to format pages rather than to organize information. Instructors may not realize that using the *style* feature in Word condenses the formatting code, (e.g. font and size and indentation), to an efficient indicator of the importance of the information. The raw code must otherwise read, which is distracting to the flow of content, creating additional, time-consuming work for students who are well aware of the simple capacity to remove the distraction.

Tables can be problematic if cells are merged. This is explained below in rubrics (Tables 1-3 and 6) and calendars (Tables 4 & 5).

It therefore appears rude and insensitive to continue manual formatting instead of using styles and students may resent it, which in turn can reduce their respect for the instructor's professionalism and civility. All these failures in formatting add time to the student's effort to perceive the information, and contribute to frustration.

Example: Guidelines for Accessible Documents

- *Use Styles to signal the hierarchy of thought for efficient use of screen readers.*
- *Format tables with alternate text and the option to repeat header rows across pages. Format tables this way in Word before copying and pasting into online documents. The table should be navigable with the Tab button.*
- *Do not use tables to format page content, only for organizing categorical information.*
- *Format images with alternate text. Use images only for meaning, not decoration. The information should be perceivable without the image.*
- *Save documents as PDFs by using the 'print' function to increase navigability.*
- *Any online page should be navigable without a mouse. Any responses should be logically placed in proximity with their prompts.*

Instructors also have no direct control over the way students navigating online text. An instructor may thoughtfully design a series of pages, organized in modules, but students may interrupt their own flow of understanding by jumping around as they scan a page for quick extraction of 'one right answer' instead of digesting the whole stream of logic to better digest the food for thought. Thus it is appropriate for instructors to caution students about the tendency to skim and to point out that their tuition dollar has purchased a full meal deal requiring ample time to process. In this way the students may realize that learning is a process of several steps, beginning with perception but proceeding through predictable stages of short and long term memory before they are able to produce higher levels of thinking.

That said, simply organizing information with a hierarchy of headings will help all students more efficiently perceive text. An undifferentiated mass of text will bury the key information and is likely to discourage students from reading closely. Instructions should be numbered, and the information most necessary to understanding should be easy to locate using key-word searches. This generates a checklist and facilitates the student's advancement from instant perception to meaningful incorporation. Finally, in the online environment of interactive discussion threads, students may need an instructor to point out that organizing texts with numbers, bullets, and headings help focus attention while off-topic comments and grammatical errors distract and take more time for people to read, illustrated in the example of assignment instructions in the syllabus and assignment examples below.

Early Stages of Learning: Reading is Neither Simple Nor Assumed

Reading is a way of nourishing the mind with food for thought. It requires time to ingest and digest the information received. The digestion of food for thought is a useful metaphor, made credible with such studies in sports medicine as Kerksick et al. (2017), who find that exercising individuals benefited from taking adequate amounts of protein but also from the pace of intake. This echoes the work of Jo et al.

(2015), mentioned here previously, who find students' pace and interval of logging on was a significant predictor of their academic success. This is the equivalent of simply showing up for a meal, which increases the probability that the meal will be eaten.

Before the nutrients are absorbed, however, there are confounding problems of distractions, whether caused by the student or suffered by the student. In the face-to-face classroom, instructors exert varying degrees of influence over the learning environment, with interventions occurring frequently to shift activities and redirect attention. By contrast, in an online environment, the instructor is not in immediate proximity and cannot intervene when a student is subject to distractions.

The instructor can merely acknowledge that distractions are likely to occur and express an interest in the students' autonomous efforts to control them. The acknowledgment begins with an estimate of the amount of time that each student can expect to spend engaging with the instructional text and required assigned texts. In addition, the instructor can mention that the type of reading required is not the absorption of simple factual information but is likely to be more demanding in order for students to successfully make learning connections, and thus progress will be undermined if the student is subject to many distractions.

Example: Prompts for Engaging Student Learning

The following questions prompt students' self-awareness and trigger their goals:

- *How long did it take you to read pages 150 to 210?*
- *In what specific circumstances were you able to read it, and how distracted were you?*
- *What helps you focus your attention long enough to complete the reading and writing?*

Purposeful Reading

There is a dimension other than the concrete experience of being exposed to print that can improve the student's use of time: it is the value of spending the time in the first place. It is important that the instructor explicitly state why the text is assigned in terms of achieving the learning outcomes of the course. Those learning outcomes should already be stated in the syllabus, defining the contract between the student and the school: tuition was paid in order to achieve those outcomes. The student has invested tuition dollars and now is being asked to invest time, both of which are commodities in short supply.

One might assume that having signed up for the course and committed to the payment due for its credits that the student will have been persuaded of its value, but there is a significant temporal disconnect between the money spent (or borrowed or granted) and the experience of the course itself. The student may need help connecting the value of the reading to the value of the course or, more immediately, the value of the reading to the completion of an assigned task. Therefore, the instructions can mention that the particular text passage is related to the particular course outcome and that the information gained from the passage will be useful in completing the particular assignment. It is even more helpful for instructors to point out how the passage relates to previous and future resources.

Trusting that the information is useful and organized will facilitate its storage. In a face-to-face course, the instructor can orient students to the context and purpose of the assignment in the process of explaining the task. However, in an online environment, students are free to skip all the background and framing in order to focus on the concrete activity. This is a false economy, because without the context, students might not engage in the full meaning of the assignment to develop their full understanding instead of merely memorizing isolated facts or practicing isolated skills. This is especially true in courses that try to influence disposition, belief, or value as well as the knowledge base.

All coursework, though, is more successfully learned and later applied if its intrinsic value in students' overall development is a conscious priority. The reverse is true: if students only focus on completion of task and accumulation of attendant grade points, they are less likely to persevere in difficult tasks and to extend their understanding to new situations. Thus faculty can cultivate self-regulation in their students in both directions: increasing the focus on intrinsic value and decreasing the emphasis on coercive grading tactics, or extrinsic motivation. Dweck (2012) popularized the educational implications of intrinsic motivation as a growth mind-set.

Example: Prompts for Engaging Student Learning

- *Most of the scenarios in this chapter will be familiar, but the terms used to describe them are likely to be new. As you read, please note the terms you don't typically use.*
- *This chapter will introduce many well-known theorists. In the next assignment you will be comparing several of them.*
- *The bibliography will probably be useful when you look for peer-reviewed articles to support your essay.*
- *Buying a gym membership doesn't guarantee fitness and paying tuition doesn't guarantee learning. In both cases, you must work out no matter who is watching.*

Processing Information Meaningfully

Having perceived the environment, the next stage in student learning is the processing of the information absorbed. *Was it understood? Was the material asking students to make specific conclusions? Was it connected to what was already known and to a real-world context?*

This stage is typically cultivated with reading-response logs. In traditional lectures, the professor would assign a text, and the students may or may not have read it but would attend class with the expectation that the text would be digested for them: it would be summarized and perhaps a tour of it provided. Certain textbooks provide accompanying slide decks, dense with text, that uninspired instructors read aloud. Online students are at least spared that misery but may not .

Critical to getting students to process their learning, though, is to get them to interact with the text—that is, actually read it. Far more effective than the traditional classroom lecture is a "flipped" classroom (Alvarez, 2011), requiring students to pose questions based on the text, to be submitted before the lecture. Again, time is a problem, in part because students may not have strategies for reading efficiently. The prompts in a reading-response log can help cultivate effective strategies, such as predicting and monitoring one's own comprehension. Thus it may benefit the students for the instructor to include certain prompts in the instructions, which both consider the time element and provoke an immediate awareness of personal experience.

Unfortunately, some instructors use reading logs for coercion, that is, to hold students accountable for reading, but not necessarily for getting anything out of the reading. In these examples notice the reference to assignments that will use the information as well as the students' existing knowledge base.

Example: Student-friendly prompts for guiding more meaningful reading.

- *Before you read the chapter, comment on how well you already know the objectives of this chapter listed on page x.*
- *Read the summary of the chapter on page x, and comment on how much sense it makes before you read the whole chapter.*
- *List six terms you are likely to include in the essay assignment due next Sunday.*

Time-Sensitivity in the Syllabus

Having established the importance of engaging students in each stage of memory development (sensory register and input; short-term, working, and long-term memory; and memory loss) as well as the steps of self-regulation (planning, cognition, action, and metacognition) in addition to the importance of a student-centered approach with adequate guidance and feedback, specific instructional strategies may be considered to promote more timely student success. This necessitates a learner-focused syllabus, which Palmer, Wheeler, and Aneece (2016) found results in students having "more positive perceptions of the document itself, the course described by the syllabus, and the instructor associated with the course" (p. 36). Such a syllabus includes course resources, policies, assessment framework, and time frames with the expressed purpose of maximizing time for meaningful effort without assuming prior mastery.

Elements of a quality syllabus are easier to communicate online that in a face to face class where the syllabus is distributed in paper form the first day of class and may not be consulted again. In the online platform, it is perpetually available and its components can be positioned for timely access. The face-to-face instructor may include all pertinent course documents in a coursepack while the online instructor can provide hot links to each component.

The syllabus is not only a legal contract for services in which instructor promises to deliver specific content and facilitate specific learning activities, and sets policies and procedures for student engagement in those activities, but it engages student perspective and self-efficacy in the way it is presented.

Predictable Course Purpose

An important function of the syllabus is to define the purpose and priorities of the course, but many syllabi focus first on the tasks intended to achieve the outcomes instead of the outcomes themselves. It is therefore a higher quality syllabus which first defines the course and then explains the means to that end. The learning outcomes are, after all, what the student is paying tuition to accrue. It is also valuable to identify the personal and/or professional context of the course in the larger scope of why the student is attending university at all, e.g. to prepare for a particular career or complete a certificate.

Example Course Overview

ASP 305 is the introductory course for the undergraduate Accessibilities Studies Program (ASP), an interdisciplinary opportunity to learn about the challenges facing people with disabilities and limitations and to become competent in recognizing where, when, and how to accommodate such needs. Competence includes facilitating accessible transitions and employment for people with disabilities and limitations, approached from different perspectives of employers, social service agencies, commercial enterprises, and the people requiring access themselves.

The Accessibility Studies Certificate and Minor document a familiarity with the scope of laws and conditions most commonly encountered in public venues of employment, learning, recreation, commerce, and independent living. Difficulties are reported in six categories by the American Community Census: hearing, vision, cognitive, ambulatory, self-care, and independent living. Each of these topics is an academic field which in turn intersect with many others, such as business, law, communication, construction, and education. ASP 305 synthesizes the interdisciplinary aspects and begins the process of adding practical depth to all careers, given the increasing prevalence and need for awareness of disability in the general population.

Example: Learning Outcomes

By the end of this course, you should have produced evidence of the following abilities:

1. Identify assumptions of mobility, perception, cognition, and engagement regarding common life activities (i.e. ableism).
2. Define disability etiquette.
3. Distinguish between theoretical models of disability, e.g. medical, social, economic, functional, identity, moral, charity, and destiny, and examine the implications of beliefs and attitudes about disability on public and personal perceptions of disability.
4. Differentiate categories and levels of disability and common barriers associated with them (i.e., eligibility and entitlement).
5. Define assistive technologies and their uses.
6. List prominent legal documents and landmark events related to disability and human rights.
7. Survey current careers requiring competence in troubleshooting accessibility.
8. Read, write and communicate in a professional manner.

Predictable Learning Environment

The tools used to accomplish the learning outcomes define the actual experience of the course. The syllabus alerts the student to the need to assemble them before class begins and to prepare to use them. Here are excerpts from a syllabus demonstrating student-friendly language.

Example: Required Resources

Required Readings. Each of the two main textbooks has more than 300 pages, resulting in approximately 60-80 pages of reading a week. You will also be reading or viewing links to articles, news items, and recordings such as TedTalks each week. Finally, you will be locating such resources yourself to investigate topics that interest you and producing the items that demonstrate your learning.

Required Technology. This is an online class, so you will obviously need Internet connection of adequate strength to open sizable files. You must have access to a computer with current levels of functionality, for instance you will need to hear recordings and be able to embed your voice recording in Canvas discussion boards.

Computer Competence. Your competence to use standard online and word processing and spreadsheet features is assumed for a 300-level course. If you need help with the required technology and skills, CWU provides computer labs and support services. Please allow extra time if you are new to any of these skills. If you need help, please seek it earlier, rather than later.

Canvas. All information will be disseminated via CWU e-mail and Canvas, our Learning Management System (LMS).
- You are expected to remain current with announcements and content added to Canvas. You are certainly expected to respond in a timely manner to any requests.
- Make sure your Canvas settings have announcements sent to your CWU email. *Beware of forwarding to your home email as it doesn't always recognize Canvas.

Professionalism. The short version: Be nice. Be on time. Be prepared. Be honest. Be alert. Be reliable.

Predictable Course Activities

Students without effective time-management orientations tend to have a binary sense of time: *now* or *never*. They have not developed a sense of pacing their time over a reasonable period. College courses tend to be two months (in a quarter system of 10 weeks) or four months (in a semester system of 16 weeks). The tendency is to focus only on the due date for submitting specific evidence, not on the sequential development of the thinking necessary to demonstrate adequate mastery. Thus the instructor can provide considerable support by subdividing the task into separate steps, each of which has a concrete target for completion.

However, it is even more important to help students reduce a long list of assignments into meaningful categories of similar activity, such as the following example of description of course activity categories and weekly time estimates followed by a gesture of personal interest in the students' individual experience.

Example: Student-Friendly Overview of Time Estimates for Predictable Course Activities

This 3-credit course is expected to require 9-10 hours each week. Required readings are likely to take at least 3 hours, but more if you read slowly. Seminar posts and responses, Open Forum participation, and feedback to Projects should take no more than 3 hours. Quizzes and Projects should take no more than 3-4 hours.

Please contact (the instructor) if you are taking significantly longer to complete the different categories of task.

It is especially important to help students predict a routine, thereby making it possible to organize their very busy lives. It is helpful to prompt them to assemble a combined calendar for all their courses, and if your course is one of a program and they are likely to take others related to your course, it is prudent to ask them what the other demands are and whether they are seeing conceptual links between the courses.

The following example summary of course activities is organized into types of experiences with weekly routines and target dates helping students plan a weekly schedule and overall to grasp the pace of the class. Each description outlines value in terms of learning and in terms of grading weights.

Strategies for Efficient, Meaningful, and Inclusive Online Learning Environments

Example: Student-Friendly Instructional and Assessment Framework

Several instructional methods are used to develop course outcomes. The products and performances are not checklists of labor completed but used as *measures of learning*.

8 Checkpoints

- The *Preview Survey* is a pre-assessment which is not graded but earns an automatic **10 points** for completion. It will help me know your baseline and whether I should adjust the instructional plans.
  - Two *Mandatory Individual Meetings* occur at the beginning and then toward the end of the quarter. Sign up for 15 minute sessions to be held via Blackboard Ultra. In these meeting we will touch base regarding your experience and progress in the course, your interest accessibility, and any other topics you would like to discuss. This serves as an advising opportunity to help you with courses to reach your personal goals. Each meeting produces 40 points for signing up in a timely manner and participating. **80 points** total.
- Four *Quizzes* demonstrate knowledge and skills of accessibility competence. They are based on readings and lecture information provided within the modules and they include reflections on your progress toward learning the course goals. They each generate 50 points for a total of **200 points**.
- A Final Reflection is an opportunity to recognize how well you have developed each of the learner outcomes and how you plan to apply them in other circumstances. It generates 50 pts, too.

10 Seminars

These discussion boards are opportunities to process the current topics (readings): to articulate your understanding of the reading and its connection to current events and life as you have experienced it; and to produce something that explains its significance related to the outcomes of the course. (The products themselves are assignments assessed separately for their demonstration of the seven course outcomes.) Each seminar includes two activities: your post and your responses to your colleagues' posts. Each seminar is graded for being punctual, complete, and collegial. 50 pts @ x 10 = **500 points**.

5 Products

Each assignment is an opportunity to apply knowledge to a real-world problems. Here are brief descriptions. Consult the Canvas assignment pages for more detailed instructions and take advantage of Open Forums to troubleshoot your ideas. 100 pts @ x 5 = **500 points** for products.

Products are posted on Canvas discussion boards and include reading and responding to colleagues' products. All scoring rubrics measure learner outcomes related to the specifications of the assignment. Typically, 20% is based on timely submission and professional writing.

1. *Construct an informational poster* showing the correspondence between different models of disability with different functions of models. Include examples from each of the major categories of disability.

2. ***Review a drama featuring a Person with Disability (PWD).*** You don't have to give us all the details of the whole movie, book, or television series. Use the story to connect several ideas: A person with disability (PWD); The category and prevalence of the disability; The PWD's interactions with other people and issues of disability etiquette; Interactions with routine environments and issues of access.
3. ***Spotlight an Everyday Environment.*** Post an image with a caption. Identify the context and discuss user experience of its functionality. Discuss career, legal, and social justice aspects.
4. *Write an Accessible Career Guide entry.* Investigate accessibility in a career from several perspectives: Employer, employee, consumer/client, and a morally just society.
5. ***Create a Public Service Announcement*** or write a letter to the editor or some other form of outreach that includes a real world issue, the significance for individuals and society, and recommended action. Record an explanation of the logic behind the product.

Predictable Grading

The culminating assignment or exam will not be the first opportunity for the instructor to find out whether or not the student is "getting it." In fact, students should be able to predict their degree of success in demonstrating the course outcomes. However, measures of task completion—or labor—are not measures of learning. A student's demonstration of learning may be compromised by the distractions of task-completion criteria, such as timely submission. Procedural skills, such as timely submission and university-level writing, must be explicitly articulated as course outcomes or policies, or they should not be considered criteria for success.

Chappuis and Stiggins (2017) recommend separating the two outcomes of (1) learning the objectives and (2) complying with procedural requirements. The rubric should be organized accordingly, with references to the assignment instructions listed as indicators of the course outcomes.

Example: Time as a Grading Criterion

Here is a routine discussion board description and rubric based on the course objective to **read, write and communicate** in a professional manner. It also emphasizes the purpose of timely submission and response in terms of effective engagement in the learning community:

This is an online class, and Canvas is our platform for developing our community of learners. I apologize in advance if you do not need the technology tutorials included here, but this will be my opportunity to provide support if you are new to online platforms.

Although we may be some distance from each other, we do share an interest in our topic: Accessibility and user experience. We will be reading the same texts and thinking through the same topics, and we are richer for having an opportunity to express our thoughts and hear others thoughts.

This is one of the most valuable aspects of taking a class as opposed to simply reading on your own: Finding our own voices for expressing what is important and finding out what others think is meaningful. In this way we can develop our skills of advocacy while adding depth to our understanding.

Strategies for Efficient, Meaningful, and Inclusive Online Learning Environments

Table 1. Scoring guide for punctuality

Weight	10.0 pts	3.0 pts	2.0 pts	0.0 pts
Punctuality indicator	Posted by 9PM due date	Posted within 24 hrs after due.	Posted more than 24 hrs after due	Not posted when grading occurred.

There is a 'seminar' for you to respond to every week that is based on the Module introduction page--the equivalent of a lecture/discussion if we were meeting face to face. It is technically a discussion board. You simply click 'reply' after these instructions, and add your responses to the textbox as indicated.

A few general guidelines:

- Organize your responses with the same numbers and letters as the prompts. That helps us know what you are answering!
- Please use complete sentences and conventional English in both your original post and in your responses to colleagues' posts.
- By the way, you will not be able to see anyone else's posts until you post your own.

Criteria for Success for Weekly Seminars (50 possible points)

Grading occurs on Mondays, according to the following criteria:

Punctual post of responses to prompts (10 pts)
Complete, thoughtful, and accurate responses (25 pts)
Prompt, professional responses to colleagues' posts (15 pts)

Example: Screen Reader-Friendly Rubric

To articulate the criteria in a a rubric, different levels of quality must be described. Because the different criteria have different weights, there are different numbers of levels. This means they cannot be combined into one table for screen readers because the columns. This means each criterion should be a separate table

Time as a Grading Criterion

At issue is the value placed on task completion versus the value placed on learning demonstrated. Most instructors believe that firm due dates are a motivation for students and that it helps students prepare for professional success, but unless they are teaching students how to submit things, they are not measuring the learning of course objectives when they . This is seen in penalties attached to late submissions, which can skew a grade to measure not how much was learned but how promptly evidence was submitted. Thus, instructors commonly weigh the timely submission of assignments often as much as they weigh the evidence of learning.

Table 2. Scoring guide for complete response to seminar prompts

Weight	30.0 pts	27.0 pts	24.0 pts	21.0 pts	18.0 pts	15.0 pts	0.0 pts
Completeness indicators	Responses to all prompts are complete, thoughtful, and in the spirit of the assignment.	Responses are complete but may not include citations.	Responses include all required topics but may lack logical cohesion.	All prompts responded to but answers may be cursory.	Responses contain errors of fact or reasoning.	Not all prompts responded to.	Incomplete or off topic.

One important strategy is specifying time in the rubric, making it a significant but graduated weight such that it is still possible to get a passing grade with a late submission but impossible to get an A. Here is one instructor's approach:

I have a general category of completing the assignment according to standards and instructions that is worth up to 30% of the whole grade. I announce when the gradebook closes and will give up to 5% submitting before finals week, meaning a possible 75% if all else is perfect. A common weakness is to fail to respond in the discussion board to colleagues' posts. For the first two weeks I add a reminder and offer to regrade it, but the third week I announce that the scores will stand from then on.

Example: Late Policy

Here is a student-friendly explanation emphasizing the logic of a late policy and the support provides instead of mentioning only the negative consequences.

The pace of assignments is intended to allow you to develop the concepts in the most efficient way by scaffolding your learning. The target dates coincide with the time I have reserved in a very busy schedule to read your work and give you meaningful feedback in time to help you improve your skills.

If you have circumstances that you believe require special consideration the earlier you contact me and discuss it the better. It is very difficult to make accommodations AFTER a due date has passed. Late and missing assignments are a cause of concern because they can quickly escalate into a failure.

Therefore I monitor your performance closely. Please respond to the feedback regarding your work.

If more than one assignment is missing and/or there is a pattern of late submissions or omissions of important parts, such as responding to your colleagues, I will file an **Early Alert** which notifies your major advisor that you are struggling. This typically prompts an inquiry regarding your well-being and an offer of support for your academic success.

Table 3. Scoring guide for collegial responses to colleagues

Weight	10.0 pts	9.0 pts	8.0 pts	5.0 pts	5.0 pts
Collegiality indicators	Responses to colleagues are on topic and professional with personal connection.	Responses to colleagues are on topic and professional.	Names might not be used to greet and close.	Responses to colleagues might not include observations on topic. Might have merely attaboys; or fewer than 2 responses.	5.0 pts No responses to colleagues.

Timely and Meaningful Feedback

The importance of strategic assessment is undeniable. Moos (2013), reports "extrinsic motivation significantly predicted the extent to which participants monitored their learning task goals" (p. 128) in a study of undergraduates using media to learn independently, suggesting that the frequency and quality of instructor feedback in the grading process can direct students to more intrinsically rewarding behaviors.

Feedback is a cybernetic concept better understood when considered alongside Newton's first law of motion: an object in motion will continue in motion unless it meets resistance. The cybernetic loop asserts that understanding will be improved with additional information from a different perspective, and it has become a principle of basic professionalism to value feedback. Thus instructors are expected to provide feedback so students can improve before a consequential assignment, and students are asked to give instructors feedback at the end of courses so instructors can improve as each iteration of the course emerges. Feedback is considered formative assessment; that is, it helps improve learning and guides further instruction to that end.

Instructors will have had opportunities to give feedback at all three stages of the students' short-term, working, and long-term memory functioning. The point is for the instructor to plan time enough to get something inviting meaningful feedback. Simply monitoring whether students have logged on and perceived the information is helpful, but it is more important to focus on whether they have learned the concepts. To be honest, this approach may seem time-intensive for both the instructor and the student, but it certainly pays off in student performance—if the focus is on the concepts to be learned not the labor of completing tasks.

Here is a strategy to give effective feedback efficiently.

Example: The Boilerplate Feedback Strategy

The strategy of collecting common feedback comments into one text selection, ready to copy and paste into the comment section of the students' online assignment submissions, is a great economy for instructors who can then simply

1. Personalize the message with the student's name
2. Delete the comments that do not apply, and, if necessary
3. Add further comments

Example: Explaining the Value of Feedback

Unfortunately a culture of continuous assessment that regards the final grade as a calculation of cumulative effort rather than a measure of cumulative learning has resulted in a precarious pedagogy where developmental tasks originally formulated to produce feedback have become overly consequential to the final grade. In such a classroom, thus, students may see only the points and not the point, as it were. One strategy to help students focus on the qualitative feedback instead of the quantitative data is for the instructor to weight the developmental tasks very lightly. However, this might result in students foregoing them because they are not a significant influence on their final grade. It is therefore helpful to make this explicit, such as the following:

This assignment is part of your preparation for the culminating assignment. Feedback on this assignment and the next, weighted at only 25 points each, will help you develop a high quality performance on the paper due at midterm, weighted at 100 points.

Example: Explaining the Value of Timely Submission in Order to Get Feedback

Another strategy is to deduct points if the development tasks are not completed. All those strategies, however, highlight the previous discussion of time limits that have unknown purpose. For this reason, it is a good idea for the instructor to simply identify the purpose of the developmental tasks. For example,

This task will help you rehearse the skills necessary to be successful on the final assignment. By turning it in by the date specified, you have the opportunity to receive feedback. Thus you can consider it a draft version of the final assignment. Although you can receive some credit for turning it in late, you will not receive the feedback.

For an example of this type of feedback focused not on academic performance but on academic behavior, a voice of experience from a long-time university instructor who had previously taught middle school shares a general feedback approach below. Notice that timely response is regarded with the same gravity as scholarly writing quality and the personalization is intended to foster a positive working relationship and therefore greater engagement:

I notice many struggling students are often in completely online programs and appear to be struggling in all their classes. An early indicator is if they fail to respond to emails or appear to answer prompts superficially or without reference to reading. I call them on this: "I am noticing a pattern of missing fine points of instruction" or "I am noticing a pattern of answering the questions based on experience but not citing page numbers" or "I am concerned about your use of unconventional English" or "I have written to you on this date and this date and received no response" or "Did you notice the feedback written in the commentary banner of the Canvas assignment?".

Predictable Time Targets

Instructors may think calendars are self-explanatory, but they do need interpretation for most students. For example, a list of assignments such as the example above can become a key to the calendar if each category of activity is color-coded or given a distinctive icon. Students also benefit from general information in practical terms such the following:

This is the calendar to consult for timely information about required readings and links to module resources, assignments, and discussions. Some events and due dates may be adjusted, but always with advance notice. You can trust the calendar on the home page of the (course) Canvas site to have the most current information. The calendar printed in the syllabus is current as of the date note in the footer.

Note that this introduction acknowledges the possibility of adjusting due dates in response to compelling circumstances, thus signaling a realistic degree of flexibility for both the instructor and the students.

Calendars generated by online platforms simply list assignments by due dates. It is important for instructors to realize that many students rely on the online alerts without fully engaging in the calendars that reveal routine habits or a sequence of related actions. Below are two ways to organize information for the same course: a traditional calendar with weeks and days identifying each separate action, and a list of weekly modules showing topical relation of the routine activities within it. Once constructed, the calendar is useful for continuous reference by inserting the current week in announcements and informational pages.

Examples of Modular and Weekly Calendars

Here are examples of two calendars included in a syllabus for a 4- credit undergraduate course in Accessibility Studies taught online in a 10-week summer term. While they both contain the same time-sensitive information, the first, Table 4, is organized according to module topics with explicit readings and assignments plus the due dates listed; the second, Table 5, transposes the information to a traditional weekly calendar with abbreviated categorical activities so students can perceive the pattern of weekly activities and responses. Both require explanations of the activity structure, (e.g. that projects and seminars each require responses to colleagues by a second due date). Table 5 also demonstrates use of text cues, (e.g. asterisks *; plus +) for activity categories.

Examples of Checking for Understanding of the Syllabus

Traditionally, professors use much of the first face-to-face class period marching students through the syllabus, but in an online environment, students are more likely to retrieve the components in more digestible separate pages according to the category of information. It is well worth allotting a few points for an activity that measures their reading and understanding the syllabus with questions such as the following. This activity could be structured as a selected response quiz, giving students immediate feedback. The following examples include time-related components.

Questions can address procedural understanding such as the following:

- *On what day of the week are discussion posts due?*
- *How many days are allowed after discussion posts to respond to colleagues' posts?*
- *What information is expected in the subject line of any email you send the instructor?*
- *During which week will you have read chapter 8?*
- *In the discussion board rubric, what weight is given to citing pages from the text?*

Questions should also highlight the academic context of the course, for example a course in a sequence with specific prerequisites might ask the following:

- *When did you complete (prerequisite course) and do you feel a need for any review?*

Metacognitive understanding can also be questioned, alerting students to the instructor's awareness of personal experience, such as these items:

Table 4. Example of 10-week calendar organized according to weekly topics

Week	Module Topics & Readings	Assignments	Due
I	1: Getting Started • Smart ch 1 *Introductions* • Shapiro ch 1 *Encounters* • Mullens' *My 12 Pair of Legs*	*Individual Meetings	Jun 17-20
		Preview Survey Quiz A	Jun 18
		+ Seminar 1 Join the Community	Jun 19/21
II	2: Conceptual Frameworks • Smart ch 2 *Models* • Shapiro ch 2 *Independence* • Hansen's *Embrace the Shake* • (Norman ch 1 *Psychopathology*)	+ Seminar 2: The Accessibility Landscape	Jun 26/28
		*Open Forum	Jun 27
		Project A: Models of Disability Poster	Jun 30/ Jul 2
III	3: Attitudes & Responses • Smart ch 3 *Prejudice* • Shapiro ch 3 *Celebration* • Young's *I'm not your inspiration* • (Norman ch 2 *Psychology*)	+ Seminar 3: Good news/Bad news	Jul 3/5
		Quiz B Ch 1-3	Jul 7
IV	4: Laws of the Land • Smart ch 4 *Media Depictions* • Shapiro ch 4 *ADA* • Grandin's *The world needs all* • (Norman ch 3 *Knowledge*)	+ Seminar 4: Formal and Informal Depictions	Jul 9/11
		Open Forum	Jul 10
		Project B: Stories of User Experience	Jul 14/16
V	5: Integrated Environments • Smart ch 5 *User Experience* • Shapiro ch 5 *Integration* • Solomon's *Depression* • (Norman ch 4 *Constraints*)	+ Seminar 5: Integration & Reaction	Jul 16/18
		Open Forum	Jul 17
		Midterm Quiz C Ch 4-5	July 21
VI	6: People First • Smart ch 6 *Stage Theory* • Shapiro ch 6 *People First* • Saks' *A tale of mental illness* • (Norman ch 5 *Errors*)	+ Seminar 6: People or Diagnosis First	Jul 23/25
		Open Forum	Jul 24
		Quiz D: Ch 6-7	Jul 27
VII	7: Assistive Technology • Smart ch 7 *Onset* • Shapiro ch 7 *Assisstive Tech* • McCallum's *Technology* • (Norman ch 6 *Design Thinking*)	+ Seminar 7: Assistance	Jul 29/31
		Open Forum	Jul 30
		Project C: Environment Spotlight	Aug 4
VIII	8: Invisible Citizens • Smart ch 8 *Diagnosis* • Shapiro ch 8 *Nursing Homes* • Shapiro ch 9 *Severely disabled* • Zayid's *I've got 99 problems*	+ Seminar 8: Diagnostic Complications	Aug 7/9
		Open Forum:	Aug 8
		Project D: Career Guide	Aug 11
IX	9: Stigma • Smart ch 9 *Stigma* • Shapiro ch 10 *Retardation* • Casey's *Looking past limits* • (Norman ch 7 *Business*)	+ Seminar 9: Stigma	Aug 14/16
		Open Forum	Aug 15
		Project E: Public Service Announcement	Aug 18/23
X	10: Reflections and Predictions • Smart ch 10 *Epilogue* • Shapiro ch 11 *Postscript* • All Colleagues' *Project E PSAs*	* Individual meetings	Aug 13-20
		+ Seminar 10: Looking beyond	Aug 21
Finals		Quiz E Ch 1-1	Aug 25
		Final Reflection	Aug 28

Strategies for Efficient, Meaningful, and Inclusive Online Learning Environments

Table 5. Example of Table 4 calendar organized with daily targets

Week	Sun	Mon	Tues	Wed	Thur	Friday
I.	**16 Jun**	**17** FIRST DAY Read Ch 1/1 Sign up to meet 1:1	**18** Quiz A Pretest	**19** Seminar 1 due	**20** Last day to meet 1:1	**21** Seminar 1 responses
II.	**23**	**24** Read Ch 2/2	**25**	**26** Seminar 2 due	**27** Open Forum: Project A	**28** Seminar 2 responses
III.	**30** Project A due	**1 Jul** Read Ch 3/3	**2** Project A responses	**3** Seminar 3 due	**4** HOLIDAY (No Open Forum)	**5** Seminar 3 responses
IV.	**7** Quiz B Ch 1-3	**8** Read Ch 4/4	**9**	**10** Seminar 4 due	**11** Open Forum: Project B	**12** Seminar 4 responses
V.	**14** Project B due	**15** Read Ch 5/5	**16** Project B responses	**17** Seminar 5 due	**18** Open Forum: Ch 4-5	**19** Seminar 5 responses
VI.	**21** Quiz C Ch 4-5	**22** Read Ch 6/6	**23**	**24** Seminar 6 due	**25** Open Forum: Project C	**26** Seminar 6 responses
VII.	**28** Project C due	**29** Read Ch 7/7	**30** Project C responses	**31** Seminar 7 due	**1 Aug** Open Forum: Ch 6-7	**2** Seminar 7 responses
VIII.	**4** Quiz D Ch 6-7	**5** Read Ch 8/8-9	**6** Sign up to meet 1:1	**7** Seminar 8 due	**8** Open Forum: Project D	**9** Seminar 8 responses
IX.	**11** Project D due	**12** Read Ch 9/10	**13** Project D responses	**14** Seminar 9 due	**15** Open Forum: Project E	**16** Seminar 9 responses
X.	**18** Project E due	**19** Read Ch 10/11 View all Project E	**20** Last day to meet 1:1	**21** Seminar 10 due	**21** LAST DAY (No Open Forum)	**23** (No Seminar 10 response) Project E responses
Finals	**25** Quiz E Ch 1-10	**26**	**27**	**28** Final Exam	**29**	**30**

- *The syllabus estimates you will need 12 hours a week to adequately engage in the reading and writing tasks of this 4-credit course. Comment on your expectation of keeping up with the pace. Mention any challenging circumstances that might affect your capacity to do so.*
- *Out of 12 hours a week, estimate how much time you expect to spend on each of the following: reading assigned texts, figuring out assignments, completing written work, responding to colleagues.*

Time Sensitivity in Assignment Directions

Framing the entire module around a compelling problem is an inquiry model of teaching found to be quite effective with adult learners (Alkahe & Dolan, 2011). The example of an assignment found here uses questions to organize the instructions. This assignment is from the same undergraduate Accessibility Studies course featured in the syllabus above. Note that the student-friendly instructions acknowledge the developmental stage of reading background material as well as time estimates for each step of completing the assignment. The assignment itself may be considered a strategy to process concepts at a higher level than the earlier digestion of information, leading to a culminating exam of recalling and applying concepts with an advanced degree of fluency. The stages of learning are addressed and the learning outcomes are identified.

Time dimensions are explicit in the instructions in the form of a checklist. Chappuis and Stiggins (2017) report that "students who received checklists turned in their work two to five times earlier that those who did not" (p. 42). However, there is a difference between a checklist of labor to be completed and a rubric which analyzes quality of the evidence to demonstrate mastery of the learning targets. The example of a complete assignment found in the example below which includes the rubric that articulates all the checklist steps as indicators of the criteria of success. Instructors can find economy by using generalized checklists to assist the student with the completion of all course elements, not just a single part to enhance student self-monitoring in their online courses.

Example of Student-Friendly Instructions: Models of Disability Poster Instructions

What will you produce?

A project explaining how each model of disability corresponds to different uses of the models, with examples from the range of disabilities.

You have several options for demonstrating what you've learned about the Models of Disability, including a scholarly poster, a short video, or a paper. Do you have another idea? Let me know in an e-mail and we'll decide if it is appropriate.

Whatever format you choose must be easily understood by others who want to know how the different models of disability function to explain the experiences of people with disabilities.

- It must be able to be **posted online and accessible using a screen reader**. This means that any images must have alternative text embedded. If you have questions about document accessibility, see this link to a very thorough resource page.
- It should be brief. **A one-or two page document**. We do NOT want a lengthy article explaining everything like the textbook. We DO want a simple reference tool for matching different models to different functions.

How long will it take?

1. Reading Ch 1-2 may have taken you 4 hours or so.
2. Reading the instructions and attending an open forum to discuss them should take about half an hour.
3. Planning your comparison and constructing your design might take 3 more.
4. Saving it in a file with a helpful label and posting it will take only a few minutes.
5. Viewing some colleagues' work and writing thoughtful feedback might require a half hour.

Strategies for Efficient, Meaningful, and Inclusive Online Learning Environments

Your total commitment to this project is estimated at about 8 hours.

What resources will help you?

Chapter 1-2 in Smart's *Disability, Society, and the Individual (3rd ed)*. In particular,

- Models are described pp. 52-78.

You don't have to explain what each model is other than a summary statement explaining how it is different from the other models. This is actually the point of the exercise: telling the different models apart in practical terms of using them. Five models are described here; there are also other models you are welcome to research, but these five are enough.

- Functions are described pp.50-52.

These 6 functions could be reduced to three. How well does each model work to accomplish each function? Describe how each model is likely to be focused on 1) causes of disability, 2) responsibility, and 3) problem-solving. You are welcome to focus in more depth on more specific functions, but those three are enough.

- 3-4 Categories of disability are described pp. 21-29.

Note that there are different ways to categorize disabilities, but for this assignment, 3 categories are enough: 1) **physical**, 2) **sensori-motor,** and 3) **cognitive.** Note that 4) **psychiatric** problems are sometimes grouped separately or as the same category as cognitive disabilities. Please use examples of different disabilities in your explanations of how the different models view disabilities and the functions related to them.

Please contact me directly if you have any doubts about how to tackle this! I will help!

How will you get feedback?

Bring up your questions at the Open Forum June 27.

After you post yours June 30, give at least two people feedback on their work, mentioning specifically some aspect of the assignment. You will get at least two responses with feedback.

What learning outcomes will this product develop and demonstrate?

1. Distinguish between theoretical models of disability, e.g. medical, social, economic, functional, identity, moral, charity, and destiny, and examine the implications of beliefs and attitudes about disability on public and personal perceptions of disability.
2. Differentiate categories and levels of disability and common barriers associated with them (i.e., eligibility and entitlement).

Table 6. Rubric for scoring models of disability comparison poster

Criteria	Exemplary	Reasonable	Disappointing	Pts
Models of Disability	5 models identified and described; may include models in addition to Smart's Ch. 2.	5 models identified and described but in cursory terms AND/OR with some inaccuracy or ambiguity.	Fewer than 5 models identified and described AND/OR descriptions are inaccurate.	20
Functions of Disability	3+ functions identified and explained thoughtfully; may include functions in addition to Smart's Ch. 2.	6 functions identified and described but in cursory terms AND/OR with some inaccuracy or ambiguity.	Fewer than 3 functions identified and described AND/OR descriptions are inaccurate.	20
Examples of disability	3+ categories of disability are depicted accurately in context of models and functions; insightful connections are made with corresponding models and functions of disability.	4 categories of disability are depicted accurately in context of models and functions.	Fewer than 3 categories of disability are depicted AND/OR depictions are inaccurate regarding context.	20
Correspondence between models and functions of disability	Every model thoughtfully analyzed according to every function.	Every model and function are connected but connections may not be thoughtfully analyzed or explained.	Not all models and functions are connected or explained.	20
Conventional English usage	No distracting patterns of speech or syntax. Objective voice. Sources are cited.	No distracting patterns of speech or syntax but voice may be colloquial (informal); Sources might not be cited.	Distracting patterns of speech or syntax AND/OR no sources are cited.	5
Logical Organization	Readers can easily navigate the correlation of information thanks to helpful labels and text cues.	Models, functions, and categories of disability are correlated, but readers may require instructions to navigate information.	Information is not organized, e.g. may be a series of list, may not have titles.	5
Accessible with Screen Reader	Content is organized in adequately linear fashion for Screen Reader to interpret; AND any images have adequate alternative text to be meaningful via Screen Reader.	Content may require interpretation to be understood via Screen Reader, AND/OR images may not have adequate alternative text.	Content is completely image-based, e.g. PDF, AND/OR is organized in nonlinear form, making it difficult to read via screen reader.	5
Prompt Submission	Final project is submitted via Models of Disability Comparison by due date. Colleague feedback is posted by second due date.	Final project is submitted via Models of Disability Comparison by due date.	Permission is requested to post after due date.	5
			TOTAL Points	**100**

What are the criteria for success?

Look at the rubric below. You can trust it. If what you design satisfies it, you're gold!

What are some examples?

Here are some examples students have produced in quarters past. Some are better than others according to the rubric. A few have problems with several criteria. Can you tell which ones are less accessible?

Strategies for Efficient, Meaningful, and Inclusive Online Learning Environments

SOLUTIONS AND RECOMMENDATIONS

This chapter focuses on practical strategies to cultivate students' success by infusing the course with time-management awareness and cultivating students' proficiency in planning and monitoring their own time. It further includes ways to raise students' awareness of the function of time and empower their efficacy to set time-sensitive goals and achieve them. Thus, two concrete time-management strategies are promoted here: term-long progressions of all assignments, and steps within each assignment that concretely identify decision points.

This approached is based on a compassionate acknowledgement of the limited time students have, their need for flexibility, and the importance of meaningful engagement. The focus points counteract common vulnerabilities with strategies of effective teaching.

Focus on **Active Engagement**

- Mention the importance of frequent, meaningful action in the syllabus.
- Set a reasonable target for frequency of logging in, including an estimate of time required.
- Monitor log-in frequency routinely—for example, whenever an assignment will be graded or weekly.
- Report significant lapses in logging in to the early-alert system used by the university to support student success.
- Give feedback on it—for example, a comment in connection to a missed assignment.
- Refer to it whenever a student asks for clarification.

Focus on **Intrinsic Value**

- In every assignment, mention the development of specific course goals by the end of the term.
- Mention real world applications to real life, especially those in the future.
- Prompt students to connect concepts and activities to course goals and real world applications.
- Prompt students to describe changes in their mastery of course goals.

Focus on **Civility**

- Specifically identify timely response as a component of developing working relationships.
- Use students' names in feedback.

Focus on **Time as a Limited Resource**

- "Do the math" of how many hours are going to be needed each week.
- Mention the limited instructional time to be managed, and how it is spent preparing, delivering, and monitoring student instruction.
- Point out the efficiency that results from using standard submission procedures.

Focus on **Predicting Time Needed for Each Subtask**

- Provide a checklist for completing all parts of the assignment successfully, including reading and submission procedures.
- Provide an estimate of minutes likely to be required for each of the checklist items.
- Set concrete short term goals.

Focus on **Personal Growth**

- Frame supports and engagement opportunities in ways students will value.
- Students will come to a workshop on test anxiety and learning styles, but not time management or subject area test prep.

FUTURE RESEARCH DIRECTIONS

Strategies known to have high impact on undergraduate learning must be studied in online contexts. The emerging trend of learning analytics allows collection of data in online environments that may better define the most effective interventions by instructors to focus attention and direct energy. Adequate quantity of time available for learning as well as the qualities of the individuals' learning environments should also be studied in order to help students recognize risk factors. There is considerable knowledge accumulated through research on student engagement, and items in most end-of-term student surveys include such concerns as clear instructions, prompt and meaningful feedback, and instructor interest, but research is needed to confirm whether there is indeed a trend of more student-centered syllabi and interactive lecture. The structuring of assignments and communication routines combined with online behaviors should be studied for their interactive effects.

Another trend is worth noting: As Davidson (2017) pointed out, the world is changing and higher education is often criticized for failing to prepare its students for emerging technologies and world problems. This chapter highlights an enduring problem that new technologies can perhaps help address while also anticipating new versions of it: There will always be complex organizations requiring people to interact in a timely manner, and there will always be constraints on one's capacity to do so.

CONCLUSION

Ultimately, the function of time management is to help students engage more fully with classroom expectations so that they can effectively receive information and produce evidence of learning. Both students and instructors are vulnerable to limits in time available as well as inefficient or misdirected use of what little time they have. All of the possible time-related factors explaining students' varying demonstrations of successful learning must be understood in the context of learning itself, which includes a sequence of predictable stages of memory as well as self-regulation. The online environment provides the opportunity for students' autonomy in their sequence of interacting with text and therefore requires more explicit outlines of the steps needed as well as realistic predictions of the time required.

It is important for instructors to recognize that students who do not spend an expected amount of time interacting with online text or who do not submit assignments by the due date might not be exhibiting behaviors of immaturity or disinterest but rather be revealing the challenges of circumstances that are not traditional—be those circumstances medical, socioeconomic, or geographical. Thus, instructors are better served by reconsidering the reasons for any time constraints they impose than by making assumptions about the motives of students who cannot satisfy those impositions.

ACKNOWLEDGMENT

This research received no specific grant from any funding agency in the public, commercial, or not-for-profit sectors. Wendy Holden, Deborah Justice, Michelle Osborn, and Rebecca L. Pearson contributed significantly to the conception, organization and framing of this chapter.

REFERENCES

Alkaher, I., & Dolan, E. (2011). Instructors' decisions that inquiry teaching into undergraduate courses: How do I make this fit? *International Journal for the Scholarship of Teaching and Learning*, *5*(2), 26. doi:10.20429/ijsotl.2011.050209

Alvarez, B. (2011). Flipping the classroom: Homework in class, lessons at home. *Education Digest*, *77*(8), 18–21.

Americans with Disabilities Act of 1990, (1990). Pub. L. No. 101–336, 104 Stat. 328

Americans With Disabilities Act of 1990, 42 U.S.C. § 12101 et seq. (1994)

Anderson, L., & Krathwohl, D. R. (2001). *A taxonomy for learning, teaching, and assessing: A revision of Bloom's taxonomy of educational objectives* (Complete ed.). New York: Longman.

Bälter, O., & Zimmaro, D. (2018). Keystroke-level analysis to estimate time to process pages in online learning environments. *Interactive Learning Environments*, *26*(4), 476–485. doi:10.1080/10494820.2017.1341941

Bandura, A. (1997). *Self-efficacy: The exercise of control*. New York: W.H. Freeman and Company.

Barre, E. (2016, July 11). *How much should we assign? Estimating out of class workload*. Retrieved from https://cte.rice.edu/blogarchive/2016/07/11/workload

Beaudoin, M. F. (2002). Learning or lurking? Tracking the "invisible" online student. *The Internet and Higher Education*, *5*(2), 147–155.

Beichner, R. (2008). *The Scale-UP Project: A student-centered, active learning environment for undergraduate programs*. National Academy of Sciences. Available from http://www7.nationalacademies.org/bose/Beichner_CommissionedPaper.pdf

Britton, B. K., & Tesser, A. (1991). Effects of time-management practices on college grades. *Journal of Educational Psychology*, *83*(3), 405–410. doi:10.1037/0022-0663.83.3.405

Cantwell, G., Crossley, M., & Ashby, J. (2015). Multiple stages of learning in perceptual categorization: Evidence and neurocomputational theory. *Psychonomic Bulletin & Review*, *22*(6), 1598–1613. doi:10.375813423-015-0827-2 PMID:25917141

Carini, R. M., Kuh, G. D., & Klein, S. P. (2006). Student engagement and student learning: Testing the linkages. *Research in Higher Education*, *47*(1), 1–32. doi:10.100711162-005-8150-9

Cavanaugh, T., Lamkin, M. L., & Hu, H. (2012). Using a generalized checklist to improve student assignment submission times in an online course. *Journal of Asynchronous Learning Networks*, *16*(4), 39–44.

Center for Applied Special Technology. (2011). *CAST timeline*. Retrieved January 5, 2019, from http://www.cast.org/about/timeline.html

Central Washington University. (n.d.). Retrieved July, 2019 from https://www.cwu.edu/registrar/sites/cts.cwu.edu.registrar/files/documents/Tuition_18-19_UG_Res_Ellensburg.pdf

Chappuis, J., & Stiggins, R. (2017). *An introduction to student-involved assessment FOR learning, 7*. Pearson.

Davidson, C. (2017). *The new education: How to revolutionize the university to prepare students for a world in flux*. New York: Basic Books.

De Chastelaine, M., Mattson, J., Wang, T., & Rugg, M. (2013). Stability across age and associative memory performance in the engagement of a core networking supporting recollection. *Journal of Cognitive Neuroscience*, *1*(1), 167.

Dickson, D. H., & Kelly, I. (1985). 'The Barnum Effect' in personality assessment: A review of the literature. *Psychological Reports*, *2*(57), 367–382. doi:10.2466/pr0.1985.57.2.367

Douglas, H. E., Bore, M., & Munro, D. (2016). Coping with university education: The relationships of time management behaviour and work engagement with the five factor model aspects. *Learning and Individual Differences*, *45*, 268–274. doi:10.1016/j.lindif.2015.12.004

Durden, G., & Ellis, L. (2003). Is class attendance a proxy variable for student motivation in economics classes? An empirical analysis. *International Social Science Review*, *78*(1–2), 42–46.

Dweck, C. S. (2012). *Mindset: The new psychology of success*. New York: Constable & Robinson.

Ebrahimi, E., Kolahi, P., & Nabipour, E. (2017). Time management education influence on decreasing exam anxiety and conditioned university students' negligence of Tehran universities. *European Psychiatry*, *41*(Suppl.), S606. doi:10.1016/j.eurpsy.2017.01.952

Ellis, A. (2001). *Teaching, learning, and assessment together: The reflective classroom*. Larchmont, NY: Eye on Education.

Fernex, A., Lima, L., & de Vries, E. (2015). Exploring time allocation for academic activities by university students in France. *Higher Education*, *69*(3), 399–420. doi:10.100710734-014-9782-5

Gibson, L. (2011). Student-directed learning: An exercise in student engagement. *College Teaching*, *59*(3), 95–101. doi:10.1080/87567555.2010.550957

Glasser, W. (1999). *Choice theory: A new psychology of personal freedom* (First HarperPerennial ed.). New York: HarperPerennial.

Gooblar, D. (2014, March 19). *Student feedback matters – and it goes beyond grading*. Retrieved from https://chroniclevitae.com/news/392-student-feedback-matters-and-it-goes-beyond-grading

Gotlib, D., Saragoza, P., Segal, S., Goodman, L., & Schwartz, V. (2019). Evaluation and management of mental health disability in post-secondary students. *Current Psychiatry Reports*, *21*(6), 1–7. doi:10.100711920-019-1024-1 PMID:31037483

Hake, R. (2008). Interactive-engagement versus traditional methods: A six-thousand-student survey of mechanics test data for introductory physics courses. *American Journal of Physics*, *66*(1), 64–74. doi:10.1119/1.18809

Hattie, J. (2012). *Visible learning for teachers: Maximising impact on learning*. Oxford, UK: Routledge. doi:10.4324/9780203181522

Hofer, B. K., Yu, S. L., & Pintrich, P. R. (1998). Teaching college students to be self-regulated learners. In D. H. Schunk & B. J. Zimmerman (Eds.), *Self-regulated learning: From teaching to self-reflective practice* (pp. 57–85). New York: Guilford Press.

Hsiao, E., Mikolaj, P., & Shih, Y. (2017). A design case of scaffolding hybrid/online student-centered learning with multimedia. *Journal of Educators Online*, *14*(1), 1–9.

Individuals With Disabilities Education Act, 20 U.S.C. § 1400 (2004).

Jo, I.-H., Kim, D., & Yoon, M. (2015). Constructing proxy variables to measure adult learners' time management strategies in LMS. *Journal of Educational Technology & Society*, *18*(3), 214–225.

Jones, C. (2018, August 21). *Accessibility must be more than an add-on to online pedagogy*. Retrieved from https://www.universityaffairs.ca/opinion/in-my-opinion/accessibility-must-be-more-than-an-add-on-to-online-pedagogy/

Kahneman, D. (2011). *Thinking, fast and slow*. Macmillan.

Katsiyannis, A., Zhang, D., Landmark, L., & Reber, A. (2009). Postsecondary education for individuals with disabilities: Legal and practice considerations. *Journal of Disability Policy Studies*, *20*(1), 35–45. doi:10.1177/1044207308324896

Kerksick, C. M., Arnet, S., Schoenfled, B. J., Stout, J. R., Campbell, B., Wilborn, C. D., ... Antonio, J. (2017). International society of sports nutrition position stand: Nutrient timing. *Journal of the International Society of Sports Nutrition*, *14*(33). doi:10.118612970-017-0189-4 PMID:28919842

Kupczynski, L., Gibson, A. M., Ice, P., Richardson, J., & Challoo, L. (2011). The impact of frequency on achievement in online courses: A study from a south Texas university. *Journal of Interactive Online Learning*, *10*(3), 141–149.

Kwon, S. (2009). The analysis of differences of learners' participation, procrastination, learning time and achievement by adult learners' adherence of learning time schedule in e-learning environments. *Journal of Learner-Centered Curriculum and Instruction*, *9*(3), 61–86.

Lerner, C. S. (2004). Accommodations for the learning disabled: A level playing field or affirmative action for elites. *Vanderbilt Law Review*, *57*, 1043.

Lightweis, S. (2013). College success: A fresh look at differentiated instruction and other student-centered strategies. *The College Quarterly*, *16*(3), 1–9.

List, A., & Nadasen, D. (2017). Motivation and self-regulation in community college transfer students at a four-year online university. *Community College Journal of Research and Practice*, *41*(12), 842–866. doi:10.1080/10668926.2016.1242096

Lonn, S., & Teasley, S. D. (2009). Saving time or innovating practice: Investigating perceptions and uses of learning management systems. *Computers & Education*, *53*(3), 686–694. doi:10.1016/j.compedu.2009.04.008

Luft, A., & Buitrago, M. (2005). Stages of motor skill learning. *Molecular Neurobiology*, *32*(3), 205–216. doi:10.1385/MN:32:3:205 PMID:16385137

Lynne-Landsman, S., Graber, D., Nichols, J., & Botvin, A. (2011). Is sensation seeking a stable trait or does it change over time? *Journal of Youth and Adolescence*, *40*(1), 48–58. doi:10.100710964-010-9529-2 PMID:20354775

Macan, T. H., Shahani, C., Dipboye, R. L., & Phillips, A. P. (1990). College students' time management: Correlations with academic performance and stress. *Journal of Educational Psychology*, *82*(4), 760–768. doi:10.1037/0022-0663.82.4.760

McClenney, K., & Oriano, A. (2012). From promising to high-impact. *Community College Journal*, *82*(5), 38–45.

Michigan State University. (2018). *Flat rate tuition: Frequently asked questions*. Retrieved July, 2019 from https://undergrad.msu.edu/uploads/files/FlatRateTuition-FAQ-2018-12-06b.pdf?fbclid=IwAR36SC59rvvS0-Je29kMMRrGBxlzbj_3ktsZbLlkcc4YBJkIFGsz24pqfnI

Mizrachi, D., & Bates, M. J. (2013). Undergraduates' personal academic information management and the consideration of time and task-urgency. *Journal of the American Society for Information Science and Technology*, *64*(8), 1590–1607. doi:10.1002/asi.22849

Moos, D., & Amanda, M. (2015). The Cyclical Nature of Self-Regulated Learning Phases: Stable Between Learning Tasks? *Journal of Cognitive Education and Psychology*, *14*(2), 199–218. doi:10.1891/1945-8959.14.2.199

Null, R. (2014). *Universal design: Principles and models* (2nd ed.). Boca Raton, FL: CRC Press.

Oliver-Hoyo, M. (2011). Lessons Learned from the Implementation and Assessment of Student-Centered Methodologies. *Journal of Technology and Science Education*, *1*(1), 2–11. doi:10.3926/jotse.2011.6

Palmer, M. S., Wheeler, L. B., & Aneece, I. (2016). Does the document matter? The evolving role of syllabi in higher education. *Change: The Magazine of Higher Learning*, *48*(4), 36–47. doi:10.1080/00091383.2016.1198186

Park, C. B., Jarrow, J. E., & Association on Handicapped Student Service Programs in Postsecondary Education. (1991). *Americans with Disabilities Act response kit*. Columbus, OH: AHSSPPE.

Phillips, D., & National Society for the Study of Education. (2000). *Constructivism in education: Opinions and second opinions on controversial issues* (Yearbook of the National Society for the Study of Education; 99th, pt. 1). Chicago, IL: National Society for the Study of Education.

Piaget, J. (1969). *The Child's Conception of Time*. London: Routledge and Kegan Paul.

Pintrich, P. (2000). The role of goal orientation in self-regulated learning. In M. Boekaerts, M. P. Pintrich, & M. Zeidner (Eds.), Handbook of self-regulation (pp. 452-502). Academic Press. doi:10.1016/B978-012109890-2/50043-3

Ranseen, J. D., & Parks, G. S. (2005). Test accommodations for postsecondary students: The quandary resulting from the ADA's disability definition. *Psychology, Public Policy, and Law*, *11*(1), 83–108. doi:10.1037/1076-8971.11.1.83

Rehabilitation Act of 1973 [as amended by through P.L. 114–95, enacted December 10, 2015]. (n.d.). Accessed January, 2019 at https://www2.ed.gov/policy/speced/leg/rehab/rehabilitation-act-of-1973-amended-by-wioa.pdf

Reichlin Cruse, L., Gault, B., Suh, J., & DeMario, M. A. (2018, May 10). *Time demands of single mother college students and the role of child care in their postsecondary success*. Briefing paper, IWPR #C468. Washington, DC: Institute for Women's Policy Research. Retrieved from https://iwpr.org/publications/single-mothers-college-time-use/

Rutherford, T., Buschkuehl, M., Jaeggi, S., & Farkas, G. (2018). Links between achievement, executive functions, and self-regulated learning. *Applied Cognitive Psychology*, *32*(6), 763–774. doi:10.1002/acp.3462

Schreiber, J. (2017). Universal design for learning: A student-centered curriculum Perspective. *Curriculum and Teaching*, *32*(2), 89–98. doi:10.7459/ct/32.2.06

Schunk, D. (2008). Metacognition, self-regulation, and self-regulated learning: Research recommendations. *Educational Psychology Review*, *20*(4), 463–467. doi:10.100710648-008-9086-3

Schunk, D. H., & Zimmerman, B. J. (1998). Conclusions and future directions for academic interventions. In D. H. Schunk & B. J. Zimmerman (Eds.), *Self-regulated learning: From teaching to self-reflective practice* (pp. 225–235). New York: Guilford Press.

Sclater, N. (2016). Developing a code of practice for learning analytics. *Journal of Learning Analytics*, *3*(1), 16–42. doi:10.18608/jla.2016.31.3

Seifert, K., & Sutton, R. (2009). *Educational psychology*. Center for Open Education. Available at https://open.umn.edu/opentextbooks/textbooks/educational-psychology

Seok, S., DaCosta, B., & Hodges, R. (2018). A systematic review of empirically based Universal Design for Learning: Implementation and effectiveness of Universal Design in education for students with and without disabilities at the postsecondary level. *Open Journal of Social Sciences*, *06*(05), 171–189. doi:10.4236/jss.2018.65014

Slaven, G., & Totterdell, P. (1993). Time management training: Does it transfer to the workplace? *Journal of Managerial Psychology*, *8*(1), 20–28. doi:10.1108/02683949310024432

Small, M. L., Waterman, E. A., & Lender, T. (2017). Time use during first year of college predicts participation in high-impact activities during later years. *Journal of College Student Development*, *58*(6), 954–960. doi:10.1353/csd.2017.0075 PMID:29200615

Smart, J. (2015). *Disability, society, and the individual* (3rd ed.). Austin, TX: Pro-ed.

Smith, H. J., McConnell, D., & Ryker, K. (2013). Starting to flip the class: Quality of student's pre-class work improves with the use of online just-in time teaching methods. *Abstracts with Programs— Geological Society of America*, *45*(7), 69.

Søby, M. (2014). Learning Analytics. *Nordic Journal of Digital Literacy*, *9*, 89–91.

Su, J., & Waugh, M. L. (2018). Online student persistence or attrition: Observations related to expectations, preferences, and outcomes. *Journal of Interactive Online Learning*, *16*(1), 63–79.

Sun, J. C.-Y., & Rueda, R. (2012). Situational interest, computer self-efficacy and self-regulation: Their impact on student engagement in distance education. *British Journal of Educational Technology*, *43*(2), 191–204. doi:10.1111/j.1467-8535.2010.01157.x

Terry, K. P., & Doolittle, P. E. (2008). Fostering self-efficacy through time management in an online learning environment. *Journal of Interactive Online Learning*, *7*(3), 195–207.

Thill, M., Rosenzweig, J. W., & Wallis, L. C. (2016). The relationship between student demographics and student engagement with online library instruction modules. *Evidence Based Library and Information Practice*, *11*(3), 4–15. doi:10.18438/B8992D

Trueman, M., & Hartley, J. (1996). A comparison between the time-management skills and academic performance of mature and traditional-entry university students. *Higher Education*, *32*(2), 199–215. doi:10.1007/BF00138396

United Nations General Assembly. (2006, December 13). *Convention on the rights of persons with disabilities: Resolution [A/RES/61/106]*. Retrieved from https://www.un.org/development/desa/disabilities/resources/general-assembly/convention-on-the-rights-of-persons-with-disabilities-ares61106.html

University of Oklahoma. (n.d.). *Flat-rate tuition*. Retrieved July, 2019 from http://www.ou.edu/bursar/flat-rate-tuition

U.S. Department of Commerce, Census Bureau, Current Population Survey (CPS). (2017). See Digest of Education Statistics 2018, table 503.40.

U.S. Department of Education Credit Hour Definition. (n.d.). Retrieved from https://www.ecfr.gov/cgi-bin/text-idx?rgn=div8&node=34:3.1.3.1.1.1.23.2

Utah State University Academic Success Center. (n.d.). *Estimate Study Hours*. Retrieved July, 2019 from https://www.usu.edu/asc/assistance/pdf/estimate_study_hours.pdf

Wajcman, J. (2019). The digital architecture of time management. *Science, Technology & Human Values*, *44*(2), 315–337. doi:10.1177/0162243918795041

Wintre, M. G., Dilouya, B., Pancer, S. M., Pratt, M. W., Birnie-Lefcovitch, S., Polivy, J., & Adams, G. (2011). Academic achievement in first-year university: Who maintains their high school average? *Higher Education*, *62*(4), 467–481. doi:10.100710734-010-9399-2

Xu, J., Du, J., & Fan, X. (2013). "Finding our time": Predicting students' time management in online collaborative groupwork. *Computers & Education*, *69*, 139–147. doi:10.1016/j.compedu.2013.07.012

Zimmerman, B. J. (2002). Becoming a self-regulated learner: An overview. *Theory into Practice*, *41*(2), 64–70. doi:10.120715430421tip4102_2

ADDITIONAL READING

Dweck, C. S. (2012). *Mindset: The new psychology of success*. New York: Constable & Robinson.

Hattie, J. (2012). *Visible learning for teachers: Maximising impact on learning*. Oxford: Routledge. doi:10.4324/9780203181522

Lightweis, S. (2013). College success: A fresh look at differentiated instruction and other student-centered strategies. *The College Quarterly*, *16*(3), 1–9.

Rutherford, T., Buschkuehl, M., Jaeggi, S., & Farkas, G. (2018). Links between achievement, executive functions, and self-regulated learning. *Applied Cognitive Psychology*, *32*(6), 763–774. doi:10.1002/acp.3462

Seok, S., DaCosta, B., & Hodges, R. (2018). A systematic review of empirically based Universal Design for Learning: Implementation and effectiveness of Universal Design in education for students with and without disabilities at the postsecondary level. *Open Journal of Social Sciences*, *06*(05), 171–189. doi:10.4236/jss.2018.65014

Smart, J. (2015). *Disability, society, and the individual* (3rd ed.). Austin, TX: Pro-ed.

Zimmerman, B. J. (2002). Becoming a self-regulated learner: An overview. *Theory into Practice*, *41*(2), 64–70. doi:10.120715430421tip4102_2

KEY TERMS AND DEFINITIONS

Accessibility: Proactive approach applying principles of universal design in order to reduce barriers for people with disabilities so they may participate more fully in everyday functions to which they have a right.

Accommodations: Typically, the decisions by individual instructors to allow variation in policy for individual students entitled to disability services recommendations in compliance with equity mandates.

Checklist: Differentiated tasks within an assignment, provided to help guide student accomplishment of a multi-faceted assignment that may involve an extended time period. Distinguished from a rubric which analyzes quality of evidence according to learner outcome-based criteria.

Due Dates: Calendar dates set by instructors by which evidence of completing assigned tasks must be submitted according to course-based procedures.

Engagement: Broad term referring to all student behaviors related to course-based prompts to develop knowledge, skill, and disposition of the content.

Feedback: Communication between students or between student and professor focused on evidence of demonstrating learner outcomes. Typically regarded as significant for motivating student engagement and informing development of student knowledge and skills before summative performance.

Late Policies: Instructor-based criteria for determining procedures for students to submit evidence of accomplishing learner outcomes. Typically associated with penalties unrelated to learner outcomes.

Metacognition: Student engagement in awareness of own thoughts and feelings, typically in the context of learner outcomes developed during assigned tasks. An essential component of learner-centered pedagogy.

Online Learning Environments: Instructional delivery model using web-based content and platform for course activities for perceiving, processing and producing evidence of mastering course objectives, typically asynchronous.

Self-Regulation: Theoretical model for explaining individual capacity to engage in tasks without close supervision or coercion. Typically including functions of planning, monitoring, and reflecting.

Student-Centered Instruction: Psychosocial constructivism as an instructional ideology, assuming the importance of associating new information with existing mindsets and making meaningful and purposeful connections across contexts.

Time Management: General term for initiating control of limited temporal resources, e.g. budgeting a limited amount of time and prioritizing its use. Often regarded as a skill university students are expected to have but also often compromised by circumstances beyond student control.

Vulnerable Populations: Groups of people with personal and context characteristics that constrain their capacity to function as is typically expected. Vulnerability is specific to context but may be conflated to limit individuals' perceived identities to their particular disability.

Chapter 14
Universal Design for Learning Enables Significant Learning in Digital Courses

Kimberly Coy
California State University, Fresno, USA

ABSTRACT

Universities serve a more diverse group of students than ever before, including students who are first generation, students from poverty, and students with learning disabilities. These institutions are also increasing the amount and types of digital learning environments students use. Meeting the needs of such a diverse student group with changing resources is a dynamic problem. The universal design for learning (UDL) framework has the potential to support professors, lecturers, and course designers as they create academic events for this wide group of learners in every field of study. This chapter examines the core concepts of UDL and presents specific examples in digital university teaching constructs. Students with diverse learning needs can be served in the same environments as more traditional students when this design framework is employed. UDL can be leveraged as an instructional superpower to the benefit of all learners in universities and post-secondary courses.

INTRODUCTION

It is critical for universities to shift to meet the need of a variety of students This includes race, social class, ethnicity, cognitive differences, gender, families, and many more. At the university level we should embrace these changes and take steps toward believing that diversity makes us stronger. If we believe that working to make changes, to create pathways for all students to be successful, and to provide rigorous content is important then we must take that step. Harnessing the power of UDL in digital courses is a platform for building that step; for raising people up, expanding opportunity, and creating an environment for divergent thinking. And at its core, this is what a university should be providing its students.

This chapter is created to take the reader through examples of how the UDL framework and checkpoints influence specific practices in digital post-secondary digital and online settings.

DOI: 10.4018/978-1-7998-0115-3.ch014

On a personal experiential note the first involvement I had designing online courses took place with very young students, ages five through twelve. Some of these students had learning disabilities, some experienced trauma in the form of bullying at their regular face to face schools, and most were just average learners whose parents had chosen to have them school online while in their home environment. I had not met any of these students face to face and had little to no experience with the technology I would use to deliver content, develop curriculum, or understand if these students were learning or not. As I took stock of what I did know a list formed that became the foundation of the next chapter in my educational career:

- *the students were all human, with human brains;*
- *the content was familiar, as I had already been teaching for over ten years;*
- *I could learn the technology with some help from my friends;*
- *and I was creative and hard working.*

As I reflect on those first experiences with online learning I can see now how that list still informs my teaching and design practices, and my research ten years later. My teaching now involves learners who are in post-secondary institutions, and they are still human, I still understand my content deeply, I am always learning new technology (and still with the help of my friends), and I am creative and hard working. Perhaps this list is all we need? Probably not, but it is a start.

There are more students accesing post-secondary education now, that is a fact. Along with this is the realization that all students are more varied in their approach to learning then previously conceptualized. Learning and neuroscience continues to demonstrate the complex and infinitely unique ways human brains understand content, connect to new learning ideas, and demonstrate their new learning. This combination of diversities is a great opportunity to examine how teaching occurs within post-secondary classrooms. Add onto this opportunity the vast growth of online learning spaces and an explosion in teaching innovation is on the horizon.

This chapter examines the use of the Universal Design for Learning framework to answer the need for innovation. First by looking at the UDL framework in the context of learner variability, then by looking at engagement by educational setting variability, in particular in the digital and online learning environments. Then we look closely at how students can show what learning they understand and what questions they still have through examining the UDL principle of action and expression in the online course development by asking questions around how students navigate the online learning environment, and how do they demonstrate knowledge acquisition. And lastly asking, how can change be supported by other aspects of the college or university structure. UDL is presented in this final section as an area that administration and staff can participate in: how information is represented.

FROM ARCHITECTURE TO PEDAGOGY

Ron Mace, an architect, coined the term Universal Design in the early 1980's (Bremer, Clapper, Hitchcock, Hall, & Kachgal, 2002). He saw a new focus in designed spaces that could be used by all of the people who might want be in the space.

Universal Design for Learning Enables Significant Learning in Digital Courses

Universal design is the design of products and environments to be usable by all people, to the greatest extent possible, without the need for adaptation or specialized design.

–Ron Mace

Spaces designed for people who are wheel chair mobile, have vision or hearing impairments, are impacted by cognitive challenges, and many of the other variations within the human experience. While initially this may sound like a tremendous lift, instead this encourages using creativity and skilled design practices and thinking. Some examples that are often expected currently include crosswalks with words, images, and auditory signals, bumps on sidewalks to denote when the street begins, and curb cuts. While these design features may initially have been for people with disabilities they also allow strollers, carts, baggage and bicycles to access areas with more safety and efficiency. Another example is closed captioning, initially developed for those with hearing impairments, now help all people in public spaces. And if we look at the common features on smart phones, or digital home assistants, the idea of designing without options becomes somewhat unthinkable: Just ask Siri, Alexa, or Google.

Universal Design for Learning (UDL) asks educational designers to shift this idea from architecture to education. Specifically, to ask the question: How do all educational environments, including online and digital spaces, become available to every human learner? It can be helpful to conceptualize this shift by looking at the goals, variability, and context. For example, the goals of the educational event, course, lesson, etc. should be defined and revisited to make sure educators are looking at the student's mastery of a complex issue such as cultural competence and not only grading on the conventions of an essay.

Variability refers to the variations in how humans learn and process information. Neuroscience is continuing to demonstrate that the human brain learns differently from one person to another, more than previously conceptualized. One example can be illustrated by the differences in humans who have attentional challenges. Currently one in fifteen children, and one in 40 adults are diagnosed with Attention Deficit Hyperactivity Disorder (ADHD) (Intramural Research Program, 2016).

That is a considerable about of variability within any group of learners. A study of variability in cognition and the human brain is currently occurring in the Human Connectome Project. A study with the NIH using neuroimaging is demonstrating this variation (Glasser et al, 2016). When working on online or digital courses this is an important consideration. Such a variety of students takes online courses. The digital space, access to internet speeds, and the physical technology involved in online courses can compound the variations that learners will have in background knowledge.

Context in an educational frame indicates the content or curricula, the delivery of the content, and the assessment process. Or, the educational event as presented in an online course where students learn and educators teach. Within the digital world this context can be quite varied. A learning management system like Canvas or Blackboard is the context as is a social media platform like Facebook, Twitter, or Pinterest. YouTube can be a context or place where learning takes place as well as digital games. Context also includes subject matter and the content of curricula. Co-occurring with all of these systems is the preferences of students to learn and perform better in one context verses another. For example, learners may learn best about the effects of laws in post-colonial countries by playing a digital game in groups, while they may understand the history of the country by reading first person accounts and discussing this in a closed Facebook group. Context is rich, varied, and unique to the specific goals of learning (Burgstahler & Cory, 2013; Coy, Marino, & Serianni, 2014).

The study of UDL as a lens through which to organize and deliver content, create curricula, and assess student learning needs to consider goals, variability, and context promotes learning experiences in online courses. Courses and learning experiences can be designed with the learner in mind to foster more dynamic practices.

UDL IN POST-SECONDARY SETTINGS

It can be said that UDL is a relatively new educational focus (Meyer, 2005). There is still ongoing debate on how to conceptualize what UDL should look like in practice (King-Sears, 2009). While definitions for UDL exist within the literature (Rose, Meyer, & Hitchcock, 2005; Meyer & Rose, 2005) and United States federal educational guidelines, including the Higher Education Act of 2008 (U.S. Department of Education, 2008), and Every Student Succeeds Act (ESSA) (U.S. Department of Education, 2012), the focus continues by researchers to illustrate what educational actions constitute UDL with teachers and students (Hitchcock, Meyer, Rose & Jackson, 2002). UDL in action, and the data needed to confirm positive educational benefits for a variety of students is promising (Katz and Sokal, 2016), and yet to define the framework in action is an ongoing quest.

An early study of UDL in Higher Education conducted in a course at Harvard taught by David Rose is a self-study titled *Universal Design for learning in postsecondary education: Reflections on principles and their application* (Rose, Harbour, Johnston, Daley, & Arbanell, 2006). The word "reflections" in the title points toward the prime focus of designing learning within the newer context of online courses and programs. Rose et al. made several small changes at first to increase student engagement while keeping the course goals the same. One was to have students share class notes taken during lectures with the entire class. This one change let to some substantial barrier breakers. One, students who needed special note takers did not need this accommodation anymore since note distribution became part of everyone's experiences. Another barrier that was removed was to reduce anxiety for students to understand their own thinking. With everyone eventually sharing their notes, students could see the variety of ways each learner decided what was significant.

Success in Online

It's interesting and worthwhile to think about what exposure to online learning takes place before students enter post-secondary settings. While online opportunities are increasing for younger students the reasons for high school students accessing online courses are interesting. Picciano, Seaman, Shea, & Swan (2011) founds the results of a survey with high school and school district administrators choosing options for the importance of online options in the following areas:

1. Provide courses that otherwise were not available (79%).
2. Permit students who failed a course to take it again – credit recovery (73%).
3. Provide additional Advanced Placement Courses (61%).
4. Provide for the needs of specific students (60%).

None of these areas allow for the view that online learning is an integral part of all student's high school experiences. Online experiences are seen as additional, or special for some, not all, students.

A systematic review of online learning in higher education by Broadbent and Poon (2015) looked at self-regulated learning strategies (SLR) used by students. Online students are perceived to need more self-directed learning strategies to achieve more independence (Serdyukov & Hill, 2013). The regulatory process that encompass those skills is referred to as self-regulated learning (Zimmerman, 2008). This meta-analysis by Broadbent and Poon found that SLR strategies of "time management, metacognition, critical thinking, and effort regulation were found to have significant positive correlations with academic success in online settings" (p. 13).

Rao (2019) identified some common barriers to learning for many students in higher education learning environments: Excessive reliance on text and ambiguity around expectations. While these common barriers were focused on face to face learning experiences, the toll of these barriers in online environments is compounded. Many course designers, faculty and instructors, use a heavy reliance on text to deliver content to students. Another consideration around text, is that students are expected to read and make meaning out of text using digital content. These instructions and content often not have supports for students. While they may have been taught to gain content knowledge in the past by physically writing notes and meaning making on texts, or using a process of sticky notes to support learning, most students have not been taught how to do that with a digital document. In addition, students may be expected to lean heavily into their own abilities with written text by the requirements of turning in assignments in essay form, or contributing to discussion boards with text.

Engagement in online learning is as important as engagement in face to face learning, and UDL can help point the way. Within the framework of UDL there are principles, guidelines, and checkpoints. (Image 1) While there are not meant to be a checklist, or a prescriptive way of teaching, there is much to be learned while conceptualizing online environments where students need to be engaged and self-directed. One of the three primary principles of UDL is to provide multiple options for engagement when designing the learning environment (CAST, 2019) University faculty can be intensely motivated to create experiences for there students where these learners really learn the content. Faculty want their students to be engaged, or involved in the content they are presenting. This is especially evident in higher education faculty who have worked for years to master content, and in most cases are intensely passionate about their subject matter.

How can this passion translate into a deeper learning experience for students in online courses? Let's look briefly again at UDL at the guidelines under engagement for a clearer vision of what needs to be provided for students. The guidelines read: recruiting interest, or sparking excitement and curiosity for learning. Just add in the subject matter being offered and faculty have a better idea of where to go. For example, an instructor may think: "I want to engage my students to be interested in social justice by providing a way for them to be excited and curious about the civil rights movement in South Africa after apartheid.

The next part of this chapter will focus on engagement using UDL as a framework for course designers to ask questions and be guided into creating an online experience that has the potential to enable significant learning in digital courses.

Barriers: Recognize and Act

Depending on where a person is on the digital spectrum the barriers on online learning will be identified differently. If an educational designer, in this case a university faculty, is a digital native then the barriers may seem lower. If a faculty course designer is confused between the differences in Facebook and

Snapchat, the barriers are going to be very related to the digital environment and the technology itself. This of course also applies to the students. This chapter proposes using the UDL frame as a guide to your barrier identification, and the actions to solve for those barriers. So, we will begin with faculty and student engagement by looking at recruiting interest, sustaining effort and persistence, and self-regulation from the student point of view. These guidelines are under the UDL principle of engagement. Focusing on engagement in online post-secondary course design narrows the scope of UDL to a chapter size level.

Recruiting Interest

To spark excitement and curiosity for learning (CAST, 2019) can be seen as a responsibility for both the learner (student) and the designer (instructor). A lot of barriers can develop around this concept on online environments. Below are some examples instructors can ask to help guide their course development:

- Are my learners already familiar with some of the core concepts in this course?
- Is the subject matter traditionally seen as anxiety producing for students? (Cue mathematics)
- When designing the course am I allowing for students to form their own questions?
- Am I providing narratives to help students see themselves as participants in this course?
- Have I asked students to generate their own questions around core concepts?
- Can I use specific student experiences to encourage excitement in course goals and content?
- Have I communicated the larger course goals to students in a way that may allow for individual excitement?
- During the course am I providing a clear picture for students to see the usefulness of content in their future academic life?

In creating a digital space for learners to be curious and excited about the content instructors can find ways to minimize threats and distractions (CAST, 2019). In using discussion boards students can be assigned responsibilities that can rotate. Belin (2019) proposes these ideas: One student facilitates the discussion, another student summarizes the main points, and another student poses counter arguments.

A technique I have used and had good results with is to have a routine of Keepers and Queries. As I assign readings, videos, podcasts, etc. for students to experience I ask them to post in the discussion area two ideas that they want to keep or remember and two questions that they have from the assigned content. This way there is no "correct" answer, and student responses are sure to vary. However, I have achieved the main goal of having students experience the content and react to in with a thoughtful exchange that demonstrates their thinking. To extend the Keepers and Queries routine another question can be posed. I ask students to share who in their organization they would like to read, watch, or listen to the assignment. This extends student thinking about the content again.

Attending to what is often termed Social Emotional Learning within educational events fosters academic learning (Zins, Bloodworth, Weissberg, & Walberg, 2004). Attending to the learners need for to have their excitement and curiosity gain a place at the table during content acquisition reduces barriers to learning in online courses.

Universal Design for Learning Enables Significant Learning in Digital Courses

Sustaining Effort and Persistence

Tackles challenges with focus and determination (CAST, 2019). Providing a design frame that encourages students to be successful in an online course often means designing entry points in the course that are varied. Below are some questions instructors can ask themselves to see if they are addressing the barriers of effort and persistence in both the asynchronous, and synchronous aspects of the course experience.

- Is the entire design of the course clear from the beginning?
- Does the student understand how much time is required each week to be successful in the course?
- Is there a predictable and easy way to ask for and receive help?
- Are complex concepts offered as building blocks?
- Are tasks learners might define as boring eliminated or reduced?
- Are there built in rewards for creative thinking and sustained involvement?

Students need to understand how a course works. From the basics of where to begin, to how and when instructors will give individualized feedback, learners take their cues from the design of the course, so the clearer the better. Having the overall scope and sequence displayed in more than one way can help achieve this goal. For example, using a calendar so students can plan their time can help students stay persistent over the semester. In addition, creating a graphic organizer of how the goals of the course, the content of the course, and the assessments of the course support each other will allow students to see the connections and encourage them to focus on what is important.

In addition to making the path of the course consistent and transparent from the beginning I have two specific techniques I use to encourage student persistence. The first is how I condition students in asynchronous discussions. At the beginning of the semester I make sure to plan my time so that I can respond to each person individually during discussions and make sure that I respond in a very timely manner. I also always ask the student posting a question about what they have contributed. First off, this communicates that I both read and value what they have to say, and second, I am modeling the type of back and forth discussion I expect to happen over the rest of the course time. I ease off of my contributions as the course continues as I see other students responding to each other. I then assign myself a group of students weekly to respond to so I am still involved, just not as much.

Another way to keep students in a framework of effort some professors have instituted is the Quest. Using game theory by Jane McGonnigal, have students go on a quest each week of the course. These quest tasks are high in creative load, and lower in cognitive load. For example, ask questions around motivation and production. Have students share who in their family or friend group supports their hard work at school. Or, have students identify the biggest time killers they encounter while doing assignments. This encourages students to be metacognitive about their own thinking and study habits, and gives them the support of seeing that other students also experience barriers, and overcome these barriers. The students get all of the points if they complete the quest during the week it is assigned, and none of the points if they are late. This rewards students for consistently getting into their online course every week. A fun task, that has a purpose of supporting their study habits, does double duty.

Self-Regulation

Harness the power of emotions and motivation in learning (CAST, 2019). As can likely be seen, these guidelines in the UDL framework can have some overlap. For example, emotions and motivation are certainly involved in the domains of student persisting in difficult or dull tasks. The idea behind this checkpoint is to explicitly address self-regulation within the course goals and tasks. Below are some questions instructors can ask themselves as they review and continue to build their online course.

- Have I provided an example of what a successful student looks like in this course?
- Have I connected the new learning with previous learning or knowledge students possess?
- Are there different modalities for students to learn new information, such as text, video, or speech?
- Is there more than one way for students to demonstrate their knowledge?
- Has the concept that failure toward a goal is a normal and encouraged part of building new knowledge been introduced?
- Have I provided examples of my own journey of failures toward successes?

Failure is a very powerful concept that all courses can benefit from. If instructors do not build in opportunities for failure, and eventual success, students are less likely to take chances with learning and thinking. One system I have often used is the encouragement to fail forward. There is even a website dedicated to this for business innovation and success: (See additional readings)

When is an assignment done? If the assignment meets all of the goals, then the assignment is complete. If the assignment is lacking, then it is not complete and needs more work or revision. Structuring revision time into an assignment, in addition to clear rubrics, supports the overall goal of mastering content, and takes the focus off of failing during the first or second attempt. This may be a radically different way of approaching assignments then some instructors may be used to. However, if the goal of the professor and the course is to have students master content, concepts, and complex ideas it may be worth rethinking outside the usual paradigms of time and only one swing at the apple.

These are the three guidelines of UDL under the principle of engagement: recruiting interest, sustaining effort and persistence, and self-regulation. Barriers to learning common to online courses were examined and possible solutions were proposed through both questions' instructors can ask, and specific examples of strategies in online courses. Another look at barriers through specific UDL framework checkpoints is represented in Table 1. Checkpoints are another step in the UDL framework.

The first column points out a potential barrier, the second column describes the specific UDL checkpoint, and the third column explains how the barrier was reduced in practice.

The continued popularity and wide acceptance of online courses and teaching environments in post-secondary educational settings brings with it many opportunities, and many challenges. When course designers and instructors view the process through potential barriers to learning for students, specific progress can be made for learning and achievement. Using the UDL framework to view the solutions to these barriers gives instructors a place to begin making changes. It is also important to note that not every barrier can be overcome at once. Small adjustments and additions to online courses can create large opportunities for student success.

Universal Design for Learning Enables Significant Learning in Digital Courses

Table 1. Potential barriers in online courses, and UDL focused solutions

Barrier	UDL checkpoint used as a guide to address the barrier (www.udlguidelines.org)	What does this look like in practice while building and running an online course
Supporting students or learners in accessing content — The guideline of recruiting interest		
Complicated or complex concepts can be a barrier to learning in themselves. Especially if students do not have a rich amount of background knowledge, or access to supporting information	Optimize individual choice and autonomy could include varying the levels of perceived challenge	Introduction of a complex topic, for example Feminism, can be illustrated in a variety of formats; video, scholarly article, popular article, graphic organizer, or podcast. Students can choose which ones to experience first.
Learners do not seem to understand why instructor is making certain course choices	Optimize relevance, value, and authenticity. This idea can be met by designing activities so that learning outcomes are authentic, communicate to real audiences, a reflect a purpose that is clear to the participants.	The instructor continually uses metacognition to explain how the course is composed. In an online course there are even more options for this. For example, at the beginning of each module the instructor writes, or better yet records with video the explanation of how the content coming up supports the course goals, and then talks specifically about how they made the decisions for the content and activities in the module.
Students lose track of resources	Minimize threats and distractions and create a supportive and accepting classroom climate	Accept that this is a normal part of the course experience. Provide an alternative to the storage of resources. An example is to create a Padlet at (see additional readings) and store course resources there as well
Supporting students or learners in building knowledge and skills — The guideline of sustaining effort and persistence		
Students are confused as to how to get help, or lose track of tasks	Heighten salience of goals and objectives can be done by prompting or requiring learners to explicitly formulate or restate goals	Asking students to state course goals at the beginning of each module, or week can help the instructor understand if there is a gap between what the instructor knows is important in the course, and what the student thinks is important. Weekly email detailing upcoming tasks, and where to get help sent by the instructor is also encouraged
Instructor becomes bored reading the same assignments	Vary demands and resources to optimize challenge and provide alternatives in the permissible tools and scaffolds for students to demonstrate knowledge	Invite students to demonstrate knowledge in unusual way. Include creativity in the grading considerations. One idea is to look up "dance your PhD" in Science Magazine's online platform. In this contest PhD students are allowed to create a dance of their PhD and compete for money.
Students demonstrate lack of effort or persistence in course	Foster collaboration and community by creating communities of learners engaged in common interests or activities	Use gamification techniques. For example, provide a public quest with high creative and low cognitive load to keep students connected to each other and course goals
Assignments students turn in do not demonstrate deep understanding of concept	Increase mastery-oriented feedback by providing feedback that emphasizes effort, improvement, and achieving a standard rather than on relative performance	Create and use a rubric to reflect progress and improvement. Have a schedule for the instructor to give feedback in recorded audio
Supporting students internalizing knowledge, and applying it — The guideline of self regulation		
Students appear to lack motivation	Promote expectations and beliefs that optimize motivation. Support activities that encourage self-reflection and identification of personal goals	Use weekly quests as a place for students and instructor to identify goals that are within small time units like weekly and larger goals, like progress toward degree
Learner does not read with deep comprehension using digital documents	Facilitate personal coping skills and strategies, managing frustrations	Teach specific digital strategies. Many students using online content may not have strategies to work with digital documents. One source: (see additional readings)
Students do not understand how to gage their own progress, get overwhelmed and stop engaging in the course	Develop self-assessment and reflection capacity by monitoring emotions to support progress	Provide more than one way for students to see progress in course. Charts, templates, feedback displays

All the Voices in the Room

I was working with a Professor at a large and very diverse University recently. This professor had been out of the classroom for almost fifteen years while serving as a Dean in a school of education. He was a very accomplished academic and had presided over significant creative changes at his institution. The course he taught when I was working with him was offered as hybrid. The technology itself was new, and he struggled as well with both the diversity of student experiences in his students, as well as the newer reality that students held full time jobs, and were often full of anxiety before ever entering class. By the end of the course he had decided his teaching years were over. He explained to me that the students were too stressed out so he had to "dumb down" the course too much. This caused him to give too many A's. This is a cautionary tale.

In a UDL framework inspired course many more students would receive higher grades, because many more students would reach the goals of the course. There is no lowering of expectations, or rigor. There is the increased potential to reach all of the voices in the room, face-to-face or digital.

Part of UDL address the responsibility of the educational environment to build expert learners. It is an ongoing puzzle to look at how much responsibility colleges and universities need to undertake of the particular work. Many people teaching in post-secondary institutions believe that students get to college in part because they are expert learners. The reality is, this is not true. The proliferation of programs aimed to shore up student's skills is a testament to this.

Another way to conceptualize this is to understand that the self-regulation skills that got students to college may not be the skills that allow for success once arrived. Especially if universities are hoping to create independent thinkers that can work through complex subject matter. "Doing the reading" is a very small part of success in the post-secondary setting. Understanding when, where, and how to do the reading, and how to apply this reading, and how to read when students don't know how to talk to professors during office hours because they are first generation to college, is not a skill many students have without support.

Building in these key skills and strategies to post-secondary courses, especially online courses, is a way to build success. This success will give the student more of a chance to earn that A in every course, it will also give the student a better base for success in college and university life. We want our students to earn that A, because we want every voice in the room to be heard.

Nothing Works for Everyone

Now we look closely at how students can show what they understand and ask questions they still have while working through an online course. The UDL principle of action and expression will be used as a lens to examine online course development by asking questions around how students navigate the online learning environment, and how do they demonstrate knowledge acquisition.

Physical Action

It is important to provide materials in an online course which all students can use (CAST, 2019). This means instructors should provide well designed materials that can be used with common accessibility tools for all of their students. It helps during this process for instructors to imagine that some of their students are different. Some will have physical disabilities, low vision or hearing, dyslexia, or need organizational or cognitive support. With the ease of access to adaptive materials, especially in digital and online spaces, this is not as heavy a lift as one may at first envision. Below are some examples instructors can ask to help guide their course development:

- How can I make sure a person with low vision can access my content?
- Have I checked to see what accessibility resources or experts are available at my institution to help me?
- Can I have another resource support me in important tasks like making sure my content is text to speech available?
- How will I allow students to turn in work to me that is created by video, speech-to-text, or another alternative method?

Table 2 gives specific tools examples for online courses that course designers, instructors and professors can access.

Expression and Communication

There is no one type of expression that is suited for all learners. Therefore, it is important to provide alternative modalities for learners (CAST, 2019). This can have more than one benefit. Providing options for students to show what they know can help professors reach their learning goals. It can also level the playing field for students that may have not have had as much experience with essay writing, or students with dyslexia, but these students may have an excellent grasp of the course content.

Below are some examples instructors can ask to help guide their course development:

- What is an assignment I can assign that is not an essay?
- Can I give students optional assignments?
- What would a rubric look like that was only based on content knowledge?
- Could I have a curiosity mindset by asking "what if" on student assignments?
- Is there a benefit to students by offering non traditional assignments?

The following Table 3 gives specific tools examples for online courses that course designers, instructors and professors can access.

Table 2. Tools and materials support options for physical action

Tool	UDL Checkpoint Frame	Example
\multicolumn{3}{c}{Interact with accessible tools and materials The guideline of physical action}		
Speech to text	Vary the methods of response and navigation. Interact with tools and environments that make learning physically accessible to all.	Use text to speech as the instructor. Let students know you are going to do this, and better yet video yourself to show the process.
Text to speech	Optimize access to tools and assistive technologies. Open doors to learning with accessible tools and devices.	Require one assignment be completed using text to speech toward the beginning of the course so students understand this option.

Table 3. Tools for digital courses that support options for expression and communication

Tool	UDL checkpoint frame	Example
Compose and share ideas using tools that help attain learning goals The guideline of expression and communication		
Viemo	Use multiple media for communication to express learning in flexible ways	Have students create a short video on how they solved a question generated by the content. An example might be solving a mathematical problem
Students!	Use multiple tools for construction and composition. Share thoughts and ideas using tools that complement the learning goal.	Have students generate ideas and teach the class how to use different digital tools. They may be able to make short videos and an example of a tool that meets the rubric of the assessment
Voice thread	Build fluencies with graduated levels of support for practice and performance. Apply and gradually release support for independent learning.	This is a digital tool where students can share their answers to questions posed by the professor with each other. This opens up other students metacognition and may help those who are confused or unsure (or have processing issues)

Executive Functions

Associated with the networks that include the prefrontal cortex, these capabilities allow humans to overcome impulsive, short term reactions to their environment and to instead set long term goals (CAST, 2019). While many believe it is not the job of higher education to work with students to reduce impulsivity, the best practice in educating learners is to accept that these difficulties apply to all learners, just in different contexts. For example, when college students are taking their first few years of courses, before selecting a major, they may have more difficulty in navigating classes with subject matter they find difficult or even dull. In addition, stressful events occur to all university students at some time or another during their academic career. For example, many students experience clinical depression or anxiety. This certainly affects executive functions, although the instructor may never be aware of these challenges.

Below are some examples instructors can ask to help guide their course development:

- Assuming at some point all of my students will have a time during the course where their executive function is compromised, how can I make sure assignment expectations are in more than one place and modality?
- Is it possible to dedicate a small portion of the course to self-care?
- Can I demonstrate a successful strategy for working through problems connected to this content?
- Can I highlight someone in the field who has overcome adversity?

Table 4 gives specific tools examples for online courses that course designers, instructors and professors can access.

As colleges and universities create more online and digital learning spaces, professors should be encouraged to examine their instructional practices and to be more creative. This can take institutional support, or even peer support. This process can be unsettling to instructors, after all this is very likely not how they learned their subject matter expertise.

Universal Design for Learning Enables Significant Learning in Digital Courses

Table 4. Tools and materials to support executive functions

Tool	UDL checkpoint frame	Example
\multicolumn{3}{c}{Interact with accessible tools and materials. The guideline of executive functions}		
Graphic organizers	Guide appropriate goal-setting and practice setting challenging and authentic goals.	Create a graphic organizer that shows how the objectives and goals of the course relate to specific assessments.
Mail Chimp	Support planning and strategy development and formulate reasonable plans for reaching goals.	Use this email generator tool to create guides for breaking down long-term assignments into short-term checkpoints. Schedule the emails to go out once a week after you created them. Better yet, eventually have students create the emails for future classes for you to send out.
Padlet	Facilitate managing information and resources to support organization and memory using flexible tools and processes.	This is an easy digital resource to store information in categories. All of the assignments, readings, and other resources can be placed in categories for students to access in an additionally categorized way at anytime.
Closed Facebook Groups	Enhance capacity for monitoring progress and analyze growth over time and demonstrate how to build from it.	Better then discussion boards, a closed Facebook group allows students and instructors to post videos, graphic organizers, and gifs. This can also be a place for students to post in progress work and ask for feedback from peers before turning in a project or assignment.

The Professor is In Charge

And lastly asking, how can change be supported by other aspects of the college or university structure? UDL is presented in this final section as an area that administration and staff can participate in: how information is represented. The UDL principle of representation will be highlighted here as a frame for the professor to lean into providing content in ways that will be optional for all learners. To support this process the UDL frame will give examples of actions professors can take to allow their content to be perceived in a variety of modalities and level up the comprehension of content by a larger variety of students taking their courses.

Perception

Learning is impossible if information is imperceptible to the learner, and difficult when information is presented in formats that require extraordinary effort or assistance (CAST, 2019). When professors teach content, they have had many years, and countless opportunities to make meaning of their subject matter. They are experts. Students in college courses are not experts. Whether students are undergraduates, masters students, or doctoral candidates, their expertise in the material is far below the level of the professor. However, professors of seldom taught the pedagogy of education, or the how of teaching before beginning courses. This is a bridge that can lead to frustration with the students, and ultimately to the professor.

Below are some examples instructors can ask to help guide their course development:

- How would I represent this material to a student I expect would someday become an expert in it?
- How would I represent this material to a student I would expect would someday become an expert in something else?
- How can I show how important this material is to these student's futures?
- How would I represent this material to a student from another country, culture, or planet?

The following Table 5 gives specific actions for professors in online courses that professors can creatively use to open up content to a variety of students.

Language and Symbols

Culture and family experiences can differ greatly among students. At institutions that serve Hispanic populations are one example, there are others of course. As a result, inequalities can arise when information is presented to all learners through a single form of representation (CAST, 2019). Deciding how to present information for a variety of students to use can be a challenge.

Below are some examples instructors can ask to help guide their course development:

- How can I consider the vast differences in student background knowledge when presenting information?
- How can I try to account for student's biases?
- Do I need to understand my own biases?

Table 6 gives specific actions for professors in online courses that professors can creatively use to open up content to a variety of students.

Table 5. Professor Actions to Support Student Perception of Content

Professor action	UDL checkpoint frame (www.udlguidelines.org)
Interact with flexible content that doesn't depend on a single sense like sight, hearing, movement, or touch The guideline of perception	
Ask yourself: how do you best learn something new in an area you are not familiar with? You tube can be an amazing and robust resource. For example, look at ideas for using digital assistants like Google and Alexa.	Offer ways of customizing the display of information and use flexible materials with settings that can be adjusted based on needs and preferences.
Harness the power of the digital world and save your own voice. Providing videos professors giving lectures is competing with professionally composed materials students have access to. Look for alternative ways to communicate: podcasts, videos, and graphic organizers.	Offer alternatives for auditory information and share information in more ways than sound and voice alone.
Use the student background knowledge and talents. For an assignment, have students work in groups to present findings using physical objects, like legos, clay, or dioramas.	Offer alternatives for visual information and share information in more ways than images and text alone.

Universal Design for Learning Enables Significant Learning in Digital Courses

Table 6. Options professors can choose to support understanding

Professor action	UDL checkpoint frame (www.udlguidelines.org)
Communicate though languages that create a shared understanding The guideline of language and symbols	
Digital environments have a multitude of ways to support symbols. Students can use google translate for language, the professor can imbed hyperlinks to challenging or new vocabulary words, and graphic symbols or organizers can be found in almost every subject.	Clarify vocabulary and symbols and construct meaning from words, symbols, and numbers using different representations.
While some students will understand more complex meaning right way, others will need more support. Provide additional information or background as a choice for students who may need this.	Clarify syntax and structure and make the patterns and properties of systems like grammar, musical notation, taxonomies, and equations explicit.
Allow and encourage the use of text to speech or speech to text.	Support decoding of text, mathematical notation, and symbols and make sure text and symbols don't get in the way of the learning goal
Make sure all text sources are screen reader accessible. Most institutions have a resources that will support professors in this area.	Promote understanding across languages and use translations, descriptions, movement, and images to support learning in unfamiliar or complex languages.
Present key concepts and important content in more then one way. Use a traditional form, maybe text or a mathematical equation. Then let yourself get creative with an alternative for. Some examples being: illustrations, video, comic strip or storyboard, and animations	Illustrate through multiple media and make learning come alive with simulations, graphics, activities, and videos

Comprehension

The purpose of a course is not to make information just accessible to learners, but to teach learners how to transform accessible information into usable knowledge (CAST, 2019). This is a powerful statement, and often at the core of all knowledge. Student should not be expected to just memorize and repeat, but rather to become themselves transformed into using this knowledge to create a more knowledgeable world.

Below are some examples instructors can ask to help guide their course development:

- What is the most important concept students need to walk away with from this course?
- What are the top ten concepts students need to walk away with from this course?
- How can the content knowledge in this course support other courses students may take?
- In five years, what concepts should students still use?
- If student want more information, where will they get it?

The following table 7 gives specific actions for professors in online courses that professors can creatively use to open up content to a variety of students.

Get creative, and get students to help not only with the course that is currently offered, but for future groups of students. The digital resources professors take the time to make last for semester after semester.

FUTURE RESEARCH: JUST USE ONE

Small changes lead to big results. As university and college instructors engaging in making changes with a UDL lens, both small and systemic, researchers need to be watching and reporting out what happens.

Table 7. Professor Actions to Support Comprehension

Professor action	UDL checkpoint frame (www.udlguidelines.org)
Construct meaning and generate new understandings The guideline of comprehension	
The digital classroom is the perfect place to make background information available to students without taking up face to face course time. Professors can provide background information to important concepts and students can use this option if they feel they need it.	Activate or supply background knowledge and build connections to prior understandings and experiences.
Take the opportunity to highlight patterns that students might not find on their own. Video yourself creating a graphic organizer, or timeline of important concepts.	Highlight patters, critical features, big ideas, and relationships and accentuate important information and how it relates to the learning goal.
Video yourself having a one on one conversation with a student who may be confused. This is a great opportunity for students to see your thinking and student thinking they might be able to relate to.	Guide information processing and visualization and support the process of meaning-making through models, scaffolds, and feedback.
Creating a really clear calendar of the course is a great way to help keep students on task and on track	Maximize transfer and generalization and apply learning to new contexts.

Encouraging self-study opportunities for faculty as they engage in this work is an excellent opportunity to see which changes are significant. This is especially important in online and digital environments where the educational playing field is a little more equal. New technologies in online course offerings can be new to both students and instructors. While these developments do not alter the expertise of the professor, it does position both the professor and the students as learners. During this time student voice is vitally important.

The second opportunity for research then is with the students and their perceptions of success. How have they changed during the span of an online course. Did they gain content knowledge, did they feel they had opportunities for success in the online platform, and did they grow as expert learners? All questions researchers should follow.

CONCLUSION

David Rose, one of the academics instrumental in developing the UDL framework, has said that change can be measured by the extent to which it is a disruption. Online post-secondary courses and learning environments are certainly a disruption in the landscape of university and colleges.

At its core UDL is a social justice movement. Universal design is intended for every learner. The potential for success for every learner is the north star of this design intent. This is a change from education where it was expected that professors would only give out a certain number of A's, B's, and C's. Where university courses were designed to weed out a certain number of learners. Where success was limited to a few. This is a disruptive concept.

What barrier did you lower today? How did you address learner variability?

I have enjoyed my journey in online learning from teaching Kindergarten math to students with special education needs, through creating and teaching courses on educational technology to doctoral candidates. There have been some radical differences. For example, the kindergarten students were mindful to introduce every class to their family pets, including chickens, during synchronous class sessions.

While doctoral students meeting during synchronous office hours rarely produced farm animals. The similarities however did include deep mentoring relationships.

REFERENCES

Allen, I. E., & Seaman, J. (2016). *Online Report Card: Tracking Online Education in the United States.* Babson Survey Research Group.

Altinay, Z., Altinay, F., Ossianilsson, E., & Aydin, C. H. (2018). Open Education Practices for Learners with Disabilities. *BRAIN. Broad Research in Artificial Intelligence and Neuroscience*, *9*(4), 171–176.

Belin, A. (2019). 5 Ways to Improve online discussion boards. *Emerging Ed Tech.* Retrieved from: https://www.emergingedtech.com/2019/05/5-ways-to-improve-online-discussion-boards/

Bracken, S., & Novak, K. (Eds.). (2019). *Transforming Higher Education Through Universal Design for Learning: An International Perspective.* Routledge. doi:10.4324/9781351132077

Bremer, C. D., Clapper, A. T., Hitchcock, C., Hall, T., & Kachgal, M. (2002). *Universal Design: A Strategy To Support Students' Access to the General Education Curriculum.* Information Brief.

Broadbent, J., & Poon, W. L. (2015). Self-regulated learning strategies & academic achievement in online higher education learning environments: A systematic review. *The Internet and Higher Education*, *27*, 1–13. doi:10.1016/j.iheduc.2015.04.007

Burgstahler, S. E., & Cory, R. C. (Eds.). (2013). *Universal Design in Higher Education.* Harvard Education Press.

CAST. (2019). *Universal Design for Learning guidelines.* Retrieved from http://udlguidelines.cast.org/

Center for Applied Special Technology. (2011). *Universal Design for Learning Guidelines version 2.0.* Wakefield, MA: Author.

Coy, K., Marino, M. T., & Serianni, B. (2014). Using Universal Design for Learning in Synchronous Online Instruction. *Journal of Special Education Technology*, *29*(1), 63–74. doi:10.1177/016264341402900105

Dell, C. A., Dell, T. F., & Blackwell, T. L. (2015). Applying universal design for learning in online courses: Pedagogical and practical considerations. *Journal of Educators Online*, *12*(2), 166–192. doi:10.9743/JEO.2015.2.1

Edyburn, D. L. (2010). Would you recognize universal design for learning if you saw it? Ten propositions for new directions for the second decade of UDL. *Learning Disability Quarterly*, *33*(1), 33–41. doi:10.1177/073194871003300103

Glasser, M. F., Smith, S. M., Marcus, D. S., Andersson, J. L., Auerbach, E. J., Behrens, T. E., ... Robinson, E. C. (2016). The human connectome project's neuroimaging approach. *Nature Neuroscience*, *19*(9), 1175–1187. doi:10.1038/nn.4361 PMID:27571196

He, Y. (2014). Universal Design for Learning in an Online Teacher Education Course: Enhancing Learners' Confidence to Teach Online. *MERLOT Journal of Online Learning and Teaching 10*(2), 283-297.

Hitchcock, C., Meyer, A., Rose, D., & Jackson, R. (2002). Providing new access to the general curriculum: Universal Design for Learning. *Teaching Exceptional Children*, *35*(2), 8–17. doi:10.1177/004005990203500201

Intramural Research Program. (2016). *NIH researchers identify heritable brain connections linked to ADHD*. Retrieved from https://irp.nih.gov/blog/post/2016/11/nih-researchers-identify-heritable-brain-connections-linked-to-adhd

Katz, J., & Sokal, L. (2016). Universal Design for Learning as a Bridge to Inclusion: A Qualitative Report of Student Voices. *International Journal of Whole Schooling*, *12*(2), 37–63.

King-Sears, M. (2009). Universal design for learning: Technology and pedagogy. *Learning Disability Quarterly*, *32*(4), 199–201. doi:10.2307/27740372

Kumar, K. L., & Wideman, M. (2014). Accessible by Design: Applying UDL Principles in a First Year Undergraduate Course. *Canadian Journal of Higher Education*, *44*(1), 125–147.

Larreamendy-Joerns, J., & Leinhardt, G. (2006). Going the Distance With Online Education. *Review of Educational Research*, *76*(4), 567–605. doi:10.3102/00346543076004567

MaceR. (n.d.). Retrieved from: https://projects.ncsu.edu/ncsu/design/cud/about_ud/about_ud.htm

Marino, M. T. (2010). Defining a technology research agenda for elementary and secondary students with learning and other high incidence disabilities in inclusive science classrooms. *Journal of Special Education Technology*, *25*(1), 1–28. doi:10.1177/016264341002500101

Meo, G. (2008). Curriculum planning for all learners: Applying universal design for learning (UDL) to a high school reading comprehension program. *Preventing School Failure*, *52*(2), 21–30. doi:10.3200/PSFL.52.2.21-30

Meyer, A., & Rose, D. H. (2005). The future is in the margins: The role of technology and disability in educational reform. In D. H. Rose, A. Meyer, & C. Hitchcock (Eds.), *The universally designed classroom: Accessible curriculum and digital technologies* (pp. 13–35). Cambridge, MA: Harvard Education Press.

Picciano, A. G., Seaman, J., Shea, P., & Swan, K. (2012). Examining the extent and nature of online learning in American K-12 education: The research initiatives of the Alfred P. Sloan Foundation. *The internet and higher education*, *15*(2), 127–135. doi:10.1016/j.iheduc.2011.07.004

Rose, D., Meyer, A., & Gordon, D. (2014). Reflections: Universal design for learning and the common core. *The Special Edge*, *2*(27), 3–5.

Rose, D. H., Harbour, W. S., Johnston, C. S., Daley, S. G., & Abarbanell, L. (2006). Universal design for learning in postsecondary education: Reflections on principles and their application. *Journal of postsecondary education and disability*, *19*(2), 135–151.

Rose, D. H., Meyer, A., & Hitchcock, C. (Eds.). (2005). *The universally designed classroom: Accessible curriculum and digital technologies*. Cambridge, MA: Harvard Educational Press.

Spooner, F., Baker, J. N., Harris, A. A., Ahlgrim-Delzell, L., & Browder, D. M. (2007). Effects of Training in Universal Design for Learning on Lesson Plan Development. *Remedial and Special Education, 28*(2), 108–116. doi:10.1177/07419325070280020101

Thompson, T. L. (2018). Disability resources in higher education, part 2: Mission and role of disability resources and services. *Dean and Provost, 19*(7), 7–7. doi:10.1002/dap.30431

U.S. Department of Education. (2008). *Higher Education Opportunity Act – 2008*. Retrieved from http://www2.ed.gov/policy/highered/leg/hea08/index.html

Zins, J. E., Bloodworth, M. R., Weissberg, R. P., & Walberg, H. J. (2004). The scientific base linking social and emotional learning to school success. In J. E. Zins, R. P. Weissberg, M. C. Wang, & H. J. Walberg (Eds.), *Building Academic Success on Social and Emotional Learning: What Does the Research Say?* (pp. 3–22). New York: Teachers College Press.

ADDITIONAL READING

Bracken, S., & Novak, K. (Eds.). (2019). *Transforming Higher Education Through Universal Design for Learning: An International Perspective*. Routledge. doi:10.4324/9781351132077

Burgstahler, S. E., & Cory, R. C. (Eds.). (2013). *Universal Design in Higher Education*. Massachusetts: Harvard Education Press.

CAST. (2019). *Universal Design for Learning guidelines*. Retrieved from http://udlguidelines.cast.org/

Coy, K. (2016). Post Secondary educators can increase educational reach with Universal Design for Learning. *Educational Renaissance, 5*(1), 27–36. doi:10.33499/edren.v5i1.94

Novak, K., & Thibodeau, T. (2016). *UDL in the cloud: How to design and deliver online education using Universal Design for Learning*. CAST Professional Publishing.

Rose, D. H., Harbour, W. S., Johnston, C. S., Daley, S. G., & Abarbanell, L. (2006). Universal design for learning in postsecondary education: Reflections on principles and their application. *Journal of postsecondary education and disability, 19*(2), 135–151.

KEY TERMS AND DEFINITIONS

Digital Learning: Learning that takes place through accessing an environment requiring a computer, tablet, or mobile device.

Emergent Bilingual: The continual growth of more than one language over the course of a person's lifetime.

First Generation Student: Students attending colleges or universities who are the first of the current generation in their families to do so.

Online Learning Environments: Courses that take place in an online space that is not tied to a physical space, to include college and university courses, as well as high school and elementary.

Pedagogy: The scientific study of educational theory.

Post-Secondary: Educational environments that occur after secondary education to include Universities, Colleges, and Community Colleges.

Universal Design for Learning: An educational framework based on research that opens up content and curricula for a wide variety of learners.

Section 5
Student Outcomes and Experiences

Chapter 15
Expectations, Experiences, and Preferences of Students in a Dual Mode Program:
A Thematic Analysis

Linh Cuong Nguyen
Charles Sturt University, Australia

Kate Davis
https://orcid.org/0000-0002-5135-0890
University of Southern Queensland, Australia

Elham Sayyad Abdi
https://orcid.org/0000-0003-2964-6078
University of Southern Queensland, Australia

Clare Thorpe
https://orcid.org/0000-0002-0974-4087
University of Southern Queensland, Australia

Katya Henry
https://orcid.org/0000-0003-0789-6308
Queensland University of Technology, Australia

Helen Partridge
University of Southern Queensland, Australia

ABSTRACT

While online-only programs are increasingly common, many universities today offer dual mode programs with both online and on campus cohorts undertaking the same program at the same time. This results in students having a range of experiences along a continuum from fully online study to a mix of online

DOI: 10.4018/978-1-7998-0115-3.ch015

and face-to-face study. This research aimed to develop an understanding of preferences, expectations, and experiences of students enrolled in a dual mode postgraduate coursework program in Australia. Outcomes are presented in themes along with rich description and explanation that capture different facets of recurring singular ideas delineating the experiences of students in relation to their learning in a flexible dual mode. The research findings provide insight into the student experience of online study as well as the broader experience of study in a dual mode cohort.

INTRODUCTION

Many tertiary education institutions today offer programs on campus, online, at a distance, or in a blend of different modes. Dual mode programs are programs that have both an on campus and an online cohort undertaking the same program at the same time. This results in students having a range of experiences along a continuum from fully online study, to a mix of online and face-to-face study. This type of delivery provides students with greater online engagement while they still take advantage of direct interaction and communication with instructors and peers (Anderson, Sutton, & Gergen, 2014). Other benefits of such a learning mode have been acknowledged, including travel cost savings (Michael, 2012), reducing burdensome relocation (O'Shea, Stone, & Delahunty, 2015), and allowing combination of paid employment and family commitments (Stone, O'Shea, May, Delahunty, & Partington, 2016). As this mode makes the most of both online and on campus learning, it is anticipated that it will gradually replace single mode learning (Daniel, 2012). There is a body of research exploring the perceptions and experiences of students in distance learning, online learning, face-to-face learning, and the mix of these modes. For example, the literature touches on the issue of social interaction and independent learning among distance students (Andeson, Upton, Dron, Malone, & Poelhuber, 2015), student satisfaction and experiences in online programs (Blackmon & Major, 2012; Bolliger & Wasilik, 2012), and the variations in student experiences of online and face-to-face classes (Okech, Barner, Segoshi, & Carney, 2014). However, there is little empirical research regarding experiences of students in a dual mode program, where students are invited to move fluidly across modes of engagement, from week to week, without altering the enrolment.

This article reports on a study that sought to explore students' expectations of study in a dual mode cohort, both before enrolment, and after experiencing the approaches to teaching used across in the program. It also sought to audit the specific approaches to learning and teaching used across the program, and to explore students' experiences and preferences with regard to those approaches. The teaching team sought to understand whether they were under or over delivering compared to students' expectations, whether expectations shifted over time, and where they should put their energy in terms of making improvements.

The project involved three sub-studies: an audit of approaches used by educators across the program; an online questionnaire open to all students; and in-depth semi-structured interviews with current students. This article reports primarily on a thematic analysis of the interview data, with some supporting data from the questionnaire. The thematic analysis presented may be used by instructors working in dual mode, blended and online programs to inform their understanding of how students experience dual mode learning where extreme flexibility in mode of learning is a core characteristic of the learning environment.

About the Programs

This research was conducted as a case study of two coursework Masters programs in Library and Information Studies at a university in Australia. The research was initially shaped around a single program, however, a new version of the program was introduced before data collection was undertaken. As the program content and approach to teaching remained largely unchanged despite the program being reshaped for the new program, both cohorts were included in the study.

The program was first offered as a dual mode program – that is, simultaneously for both an on campus and online cohort – in 2008, providing students with what the teaching team refer to as 'extreme flexibility' in mode of study. A key feature of the overall approach to learning was that students could enrol in either an internal (on campus) or external (online) study mode and move fluidly from one mode to the other, on a week-to-week and course-by-course basis. They could come to a class face-to-face one week, and engage online the next. Over the next eight years, course delivery evolved from an approach centred on recording live classes and posting the file on the learning management system (LMS), to using a range of approaches and technologies to provide students with the opportunity to tailor their learning experience. One key change over time was a shift to providing the opportunity for online students to virtually attend a class as it was being presented on campus (simultaneous face-to-face and online classes). The practice of running simultaneous online and face-to-face classes began in response to a desire on the part of the teaching team to provide more interactive experiences for online students. This practice involved running a class on campus and simultaneously live streaming it for the online cohort. In most courses, there was a dedicated online facilitator who was responsible for managing the online classroom and engaging the students in discussion there so that the instructor could concentrate on managing the on campus classroom.

Over time, the teaching team saw a shift in student online study preferences, however, since moving to simultaneous face-to-face and online classes, no empirical work had been done to understand students' experience in the program. The team had relied largely on anecdotal evidence in conjunction with course evaluations to get a sense of what students expected, what they preferred, and what their experiences were like. This project was born out of a desire to take a closer look at students' experience in the dual mode program.

LITERATURE REVIEW

A review and analysis of literature found that students experiences of dual mode learning resulted in the development of five key themes: (1) a rich and supported technological learning environment, (2) flexible and convenient course delivery (3) quality course content, (4) knowledgeable, engaged and supportive teaching staff, and (5) opportunities for interaction and a sense of connectedness.

A Rich and Supported Technological Learning Environment

Students expect a rich technological environment, including a comprehensive virtual learning environment that is consistently structured across courses (Beetham & White, 2014). They also expect technological support from both technical services staff and the course instructor (Harris, Larrier, & Castano-Bishop, 2011), as their expectations of the access and skills they will need for success are highly course-specific. These skills do not emerge fully until students have had considerable experience and opportunity to compare their experience with that of other students (Beetham & White, 2014). Students require time to build their confidence and competence within the digital environment (Killen, 2015).

It is important to provide students with necessary support rather than heavily investing in ICT (Anderson et al., 2014; Beetham & White, 2014; Masoumi & Lindström, 2012). Academic software and specialist systems require a structured introduction in the context of meaningful tasks (Beetham & White, 2014). It is also vital that students' anxiety is reduced by all means possible by using only current, user-friendly and accessible technologies (Fish & Wickersham, 2009; Okech et al., 2014). Technology used in a course must align with and support other components like assessment and learning activities (Andeson et al., 2015), be driven by consideration of learners' needs, curriculum content and availability of support for all learners (Hope 2006), and have an ability to bring about student engagement and learning opportunities (Meyer, 2014).

Flexible and Convenient Course Delivery

Factors relating to the pace of learning, flexibility and convenience are cited as the main reasons students select an online course over face-to-face delivery (Fortune, Spielman, & Pangelinan, 2011; Kuzma, Kuzma, & Thiewes, 2015; Okech et al., 2014). O'Shea, Stone and Delahunty (2015) reported that the best part of studying online was the flexibility and the opportunity to work around various professional and family commitments. The challenge for universities is that while students are choosing online courses for their flexibility, students' persistence, or the ability to endure in an online degree program until completion, has been found to be consistently lower in online learning experiences than in comparable face-to-face learning experiences (Budash, 2015).

The experiences and successes that students have when studying flexibly online depend largely on the technologies chosen by their instructor for course learning activities. The difference in the use of synchronous environments such as videoconferencing and instructor-facilitated social media chats, as opposed to asynchronous ones such as email and pre-recorded videos (Farnes et al., 2000; Mgutshini, 2013) has a great impact on students' preferences related to the pace of learning, time management, and personal autonomy. Sullivan and Freishtat (2013) argue that asynchronous delivery allows information sharing and discussion outside the constraints of time and place, extending learning beyond 'classroom time' and throughout the week. However asynchronous activities lack the benefit of instant feedback and can potentially exacerbate learning isolation (Mgutshini, 2013). Using a mix of approaches for forging connections between learners, content, universities and staff, therefore, reduces limitations and takes advantage of each approach (Holzweiss, Joyner, Fuller, Henderson, & Young, 2014; Mgutshini, 2013; O'Shea et al., 2015).

Quality Course Content

High quality course content is a common students' expectation. Whether in online or face-to-face mode, students understandably expect that course content will be interesting, relevant, accurate and up-to-date (Andrews & Tynan, 2012; Bolliger & Wasilik, 2012; Masoumi & Lindström, 2012). Students tend to be more active and engaged when they find the content and assignments to be relevant or meaningful to their daily lives (Bolliger & Wasilik, 2012; Harris et al., 2011; Sankey & Hunt, 2014). Poor online course design can be a key reason for student attrition (Budash, 2015; Harris et al., 2011). Regardless of modality, students are most concerned with learning course fundamentals and they expect to be in a stimulating learning environment (Brocato, Bonanno, & Ulbig, 2015).

The quality of an online course is dependent on good course design and the provision of integrated learning support (Fyle, Moseley, & Hayes, 2012). This should ensure that all students, regardless of their location, have equitable access to educationally appropriate core learning experiences (Taylor & Newton, 2013). Simply transferring course material used in face-to-face classes into a learning management system is not sufficient and may contribute to both intellectual and personal disengagement from activities (O'Shea et al., 2015). Hope (2006) argues that the quality of the educational experience outcomes should be consistent between both online and face-to-face modes; with effective student support made a requirement of all courses and built in to the design of course materials.

Knowledgeable, Engaged and Supportive Teaching Staff

Instructors play a major role in student learning. In both online and face-to-face modes, students pointed to the need to 'connect' with the teaching staff (Okech et al., 2014). Students have the expectation that their instructor will be engaged with and enthusiastic about the course content (Andeson et al., 2015; Andrews & Tynan, 2012; Bolliger & Wasilik, 2012) and an instructor's lack of enthusiasm is a clear demotivator for students (Bolliger & Wasilik, 2012). In addition, frequent interaction and prompt replies to students' questions about the course and assessment are expected (Farnes et al., 2000; Harris et al., 2011; Masoumi & Lindström, 2012; Muyinda, 2012). Instructors are responsible for establishing student rapport by being available to students to gain their trust and their confidence (Brocato et al., 2015), and this is a great influencer on students' learning experiences.

Additionally, the provision of feedback, both summative and formative, is a key motivator for students (Anderson et al., 2014). Students prize timely feedback (Brocato et al., 2015; O'Shea et al., 2015). To increase student engagement, feedback should be given often and in a timely manner (Andrews & Tynan, 2012; Bolliger & Wasilik, 2012; Harris et al., 2011; Sankey & Hunt, 2014). Brocato et al. (2015) describe these challenges as a double-edged sword for instructors working in dual-mode courses due to the communicative constraints that exist in the two learning environments. It is therefore critical for teaching staff to receive adequate training in both the use of technology and how to interact with diverse others in a virtual environment (Budash, 2015).

Opportunities for Interaction and a Sense of Connectedness

Many authors in the field reveal that students identify interaction with staff and peers as one of the most important elements of online leaning. The group dynamics of online learning are an important factor in creating a safe and comfortable learning environment (Herbert, 2006; Killen, 2015). Students need opportunities to participate in discussions and interact with each other in order to feel involved and stay engaged in online courses (Bolliger & Wasilik, 2012), particularly if they do not have such support at home or at work (Harris et al., 2011).

Having high levels of interaction within an online course can increase student engagement, foster trust, cooperation and belonging and allow for shared decision-making (Anderson et al., 2014). Interaction provides a feeling of being connected and involved, and this ability should be available in both formal and informal channels (Andrews & Tynan, 2012; Herbert, 2006; Todhunter, 2013). Within the dual mode experience where students may move between face-to-face and online modes throughout their degree program, many undergraduate students who move to an online course may not expect high levels of interaction in their new online learning environment. Conversely postgraduate students may expect high levels of peer collaboration, regardless of mode, as emerging members of a community of professional practice (Holzweiss et al., 2014). Postgraduate students place more value on the opportunity to develop professional relationships and a sense of a community (Oguz, Chu, & Chow, 2015).

METHODOLOGY

The project reported in this article took a mixed methods approach, and was comprised of three sub-studies. The first sub-study was an audit of approaches used by educators across the degree (Sub-Study 1). The second sub-study used an online questionnaire to develop an understanding of students' preferences, expectations and experiences related to online study (Sub-Study 2). The questionnaire design was informed by the audit of teaching approaches and used a mix of open and closed response questions to gather both qualitative and quantitative data. The third sub-study used in-depth semi-structured interviews to gather qualitative data about students' preferences, expectations and experiences (Sub-Study 3). This article reports primarily on a thematic analysis of the interview data, with some supporting data from the questionnaire.

Research participants for the qualitative interview study were students in one of two Masters programs in Information Studies at a university in Australia. All students enrolled in the two programs were invited to participate in an interview. Fourteen students, including four males and ten females participated in the study. Of the 14 participants, ten were enrolled as part-time students and four were full-time. Four students were enrolled as external students and ten as internal students. It should be noted that the students enrolled as internal students did not necessarily behave as traditional internal students. All students were encouraged to move flexibly between modes throughout the program, and even within individual courses. They might attend class online one week, on campus the next, and the following week they might choose not to attend class at all. Students' study progress ranged from completion of one semester (at least two subjects for part-time students) to graduation (completed the program within six months of their interview).

Interviews were conducted face-to-face, online, or via telephone, dependent on participant preference. All interviews were audio recorded and transcribed verbatim. The length of each interview was between 40 and 65 minutes. The interviews were conducted in a conversational manner using a semi-structured set of questions. To mitigate ethical concerns and put students at ease, interviews were conducted by a research assistant who was not a member of the teaching team. The interviews were broken into three stages:

1. Scene setting: In this stage, participants were asked about their enrolled mode of study, their actual study mode (ie their usual way of engaging in the program, which often differs from the official enrolled mode), when they expected to graduate, and what they knew about the program before commencing.
2. Expectations: In this stage, participants were asked about the expectations they had of their actual mode of study, including why they chose that mode, what they thought the mode would be like (before commencing), and any expectations they developed through talking with others about this type of study.
3. Experience: In this stage, students were asked about their experience of study. Students were asked what they liked most and least about their mode of study, which aspects of the program assisted or impeded their learning, which approaches to teaching (drawn from the audit of teaching approaches) they liked most and least, what barriers they had experienced in their studies, and strategies they used to overcome these challenges.

Data was analysed using a thematic analysis approach. The analysis process was mainly guided by Braun and Clarke (2006) in combination with the use of a constant comparison technique, a data analysis technique commonly used in grounded theory (Strauss & Corbin, 1990; Strauss & Corbin, 1998). Three main types of comparisons were made: data was compared to data, data was compared to emerging concepts, and concepts were compared with concepts. Such comparisons generated a list of concepts (codes), which were repeatedly validated against the data and other concepts. The use of this comparison technique aims to 'stimulate thought that leads to both descriptive and explanatory' themes (Lincoln & Guba, 1985, p. 334). Specifically, the following steps were carried out:

1. Preparation: reading transcripts twice and noting down initial main ideas.
2. Coding: breaking down and examining transcripts; generating codes (concepts) and collating excerpts relevant to each code.
3. Theme identification: collating and sorting codes (similar codes were grouped to establish potential sub-themes and themes); gathering all excerpts relevant to each potential (sub) themes.
4. Reviewing and defining themes: checking if each (sub) theme represents ideas in the relevant coded excerpts; refining and naming (sub) themes; creating a thematic table.
5. Interpreting and reporting: interpreting themes, giving examples, and writing the report.

In addition to the paper-based analysis, MAXQDA 10 software was used to help organise, manage, extract, and present data.

FINDINGS

The findings are presented here in two parts. Firstly, a summary of teaching approaches used across the programs (Sub-Study 1) are presented as background for the thematic analysis of interview data presented in the second findings section.

Expectations, Experiences, and Preferences of Students in a Dual Mode Program

Teaching Approaches

The audit of teaching approaches (Sub-Study 1) resulted in the development of definitions of various approaches used across the programs. These are outlined here to provide context for the findings.

Across the programs, a variety of different class types were used (Table 1). Type of class was dependent on the content and learning objectives of each course. Classes were offered in a variety of modes (Table 2), again dependent on content and learning objectives, but also dependent on the make up of the cohort (particularly, student preferences for delivery modes).

All courses had a dedicated Blackboard site (the university's Learning Management System (LMS), however in some courses, teaching staff opted to run WordPress multisite installations instead of Blackboard in order to support assignments that included blogging components, and build a dedicated community space. In later years, a consistent architecture and design was created for Blackboard sites, along with generic content related to assessment, support, and other general information. This allowed for a

Table 1. Class types

Class type	Description
Lecture	Primarily traditional lecture, with an instructor delivering a presentation, perhaps with some limited opportunities for questions or interaction.
Workshop	Hands-on activities, generally involving group work and reporting back to the whole class (e.g. design thinking workshop).
Discussion	Whole class or group discussions comprising majority of the class (e.g. reading discussion).
Lab	Students work on computers to execute a series of tasks or work through a tutorial activity (e.g. HTML tutorial).
Seminar	Integrated lecture, discussion, lab and/or workshop, moving fluidly between these types without clear breaks in the class.
Guest lectures	Guest lecturers from industry are invited to present on an area of their expertise related to course content.
Guest panels	Guests from industry are invited to participate in a panel discussion on an area of their expertise related to course content.
Assignment clinics	Optional drop-in sessions, supported by instructor or tutor, providing the opportunity to work on and receive guidance on assignments.

Table 2. Variety of modes

Mode	Description
Face-to-face only classes	Classes held on campus only. Classes are recorded for students who cannot attend, including online students.
Online only classes	Classes held online only. Classes are recorded for students who cannot attend.
Simultaneous online and face-to-face classes with dedicated online facilitator	Classes held online simultaneously with face-to-face classes. Students log-on via Collaborate (or similar tools, such as Adobe Connect). The online session is facilitated by a dedicated online facilitator who may or may not be in the on campus classroom.
Simultaneous online and face-to-face classes without dedicated online facilitator	Classes held online simultaneously with face-to-face classes. Students log-on via Collaborate (or similar tools, such as Adobe Connect). Both the online and on campus classes are facilitated by the instructor.

consistent student experience across the courses of the program. Course sites – whether on Blackboard or WordPress – were the hub for the courses, and teaching staff actively used announcement functionality to communicate key information to students.

Four key types of learning experiences (Table 3) were used across the courses to engage students outside of classes, with the course Blackboard or WordPress site being the central hub for distribution of content and activity instructions.

Teaching staff used a variety of social media tools (Table 4) to engage with students outside of classes, and to encourage peer-to-peer engagement. For courses that ran on the university's LMS, social media was used for structured discussions, informal discussions, information sharing, and assignment support. Generally, one social media channel was selected per course. These were selected based on course learning objectives or sometimes by negotiation with students. Where WordPress was used for the course site, two different functionalities were used for discussion on the site itself:

- Forums: A plugin was used to enable structured, traditional forums on the site.
- Activity page: A feed of all activity, site-wide, including on students' own blogs. Students could also post a status update, which appeared on this feed too.

This was sometimes supplemented by use of social media.

Table 3. Learning outside of classes

Type of experience	Description
Readings	A variety of readings, required and additional, assigned prior to weekly classes that support understanding of subject content. Includes academic journal articles, industry and government reports, websites, blogs, etc.
Mini lectures	Short videos, varying in duration from approximately 5 to 15 minutes, designed to deliver themed lecture content prior to weekly classes, in lieu of traditional lectures delivered in class.
Weekly introduction videos	Short videos, varying in duration from approximately 5 to 10 minutes, designed to welcome students to the week and outline what is happening in the unit in that week. These do not contain course content, but are more focused on administration and introducing the week's topic.
Online activities	Activities assigned prior to weekly classes that scaffold the development of skills or knowledge related to course content or assessment. Activities are followed up with in-class dissection.

Table 4. Social media usage

Social media channel	Description of usage
Google+ communities	A private space for students and staff in a particular course.
Facebook groups	A private space for students and staff in a particular course.
Twitter, including unit hashtags	Students were encouraged to sign up for Twitter and engage with each other and staff there. They were asked to post to Twitter using the unit hashtag when they had questions or comments about the unit, and they used the hashtag to share content. The hashtag is generally the unit code.

Themes from the Interview Data

The analysis of the interview data resulted in the development of five main themes that capture different facets of recurring singular ideas delineating the experiences of students in relation to their learning in a flexible dual mode. Each theme has sub-themes underneath that share the essence of the theme but focus on a notable specific element of the theme. The five main themes and their sub-themes are presented in Table 5.

A detailed description and interpretation of each theme is provided in the sections below.

Theme 1: Flexibility

Flexibility relates to being able to participate in any learning mode and the ability to easily tailor the program to suit individual circumstances. The extremely flexible nature of enrolment, where students could move seamlessly from internal to online study, without changing their enrolment, from week-to-week was a feature of the program that students did not expect initially, but highly prized. It was also a feature that they came to expect as they progressed through the program. The essence of the 'flexibility' theme is described by two sub-themes, namely 'fluid learning mode' and 'adaptable learning needs'.

Fluid Learning Modes

Students valued the ability to seamlessly move between internal and external modes, without changing their enrolled mode of study, according to their needs at any point in time. This extreme flexibility in mode of study did not necessarily match up with expectations: *'My expectation was there'd be so much face-to-face; I probably most enjoyed the flexibility that on the weeks where I couldn't physically come in, that I could take advantage of the online'* (Participant 9). Once in the program, students' expectations for flexibility were met or exceeded by the ability to move fluidly from mode to mode. In fact, the mode of learning was so flexible that students who participated in interviews were sometimes not certain of which mode they were enrolled in (Participant 14). The fact that a student could be enrolled as an internal student but attend classes as an external student (and vice versa) 'blurred the lines' between study modes.

Table 5. Themes and associated details representing students' experiences of dual mode learning

Themes	Sub-themes
Flexibility	Fluid learning modes
	Customisability
Empowerment	Autonomy and independence
	Comfort
Community	Connection
	Collaboration and sharing
Sense of inclusion	Feeling of neglect
	Understanding and caring
Online learning spaces	Technological learning environments
	Information organisation

I don't think there's a difference really between internal and external for this [program]. I think those internal students, if they miss a class, they can just go online like I do and get a recording, and so I think there's a better mix I guess. And so yeah, so that sort of changed...you know, sort of blurred lines I guess (Participant 5).

Some students who had initially enrolled as internal students found themselves surprised at the level of interactivity and engagement possible in the online mode.

I was initially very hesitant to actually attend online because a lot of the people that I talked to mentioned to me that, "Oh, doing a course online is really difficult. It's going to be really hard to follow," and all that... But I think my idea of attending online and attending face-to-face has changed as the [program] has developed... [L]ast time that I studied at university in 2008 didn't have any of the technology or didn't have any of this type of mode of studying that I can actually access now. So it was a very different study context. So I had no idea – I didn't know what to expect from studying online; I didn't know how it was going to be like, and I was very hesitant about it (Participant 2).

The availability of simultaneous online and face-to-face live classes made studying in the online mode more appealing to many students, which supported them in making the most of the fluidity of learning modes because they felt they would not be missing out if they attended a class online instead of face-to-face.

Customisability

Students experienced the fluidity of learning modes as very convenient because it allowed them to customise their approaches to engaging with the program. They appreciated that they could change the way they engaged with content to suit their individual needs and demands of their other responsibilities, including parenting:

I do like to work through the materials in my own time. So generally speaking, lectures are at a time when it's bedtime for the children. So I generally can't attend in person and that's okay. So I like to be able to access it when I want to, so when they're in bed or it's at five o'clock in the morning, if I want to. I will work at those different times. So for me, that's been a really - a really good benefit that I can chose when I work and how I work (Participant 6).

As students in a Masters program, many of the participants had jobs, family caring responsibilities, or both. The extreme flexibility the program offered allowed them to balance these competing priorities. *'It really does make life a lot easier when you've got work and home life... Having the freedom and the flexibility of online study is awesome' (Participant 1).*

In addition to customising their engagement to around their other priorities, the flexibility offered in the program allowed students to adjust learning strategies to suit their personality and their own study preferences (Participants 3, 9 and 13). One student preferred to attend classes on campus to avoid distractions at home:

Personally I have trouble studying at home, so actually being able to physically go to class helps me concentrate better rather than me being in my study at home where I actually watch a lot of TV and that sort of thing (Participant 11).

While this student wanted to come to class, other students appreciated the ability to stay at home and participate live online, or engage with content asynchronously.

Students reported that they valued the opportunity to learn with their peers in various learning spaces, both on campus and online, according to their own preferences and needs. Many students acknowledged that their peers' input is invaluable for their learning. In online spaces, they can quickly get a response to a question from a peer instead of waiting for a response from their instructor, and they recognised that sharing ideas was valuable as they worked through the programs (Participants 4 and 13). Students learned through interaction with peers using a variety of communication channels that meet their needs at particular times:

When we are not on Facebook talking to each other about assignments or the things that we need to do together as in group work, we're on Twitter. We meet face-to-face on campus sometimes. So I think what's really helping me to learn is that interaction, whichever way I can get that interaction happening, being it online or social media or face-to-face. 'Cause just sitting with a book and the context sometimes doesn't happen (Participant 2).

Theme 2: Empowerment

Empowerment relates to the availability of the course materials, the accessibility of the learning spaces, and the ways the program was delivered, all of which gave students a sense of agency and helped them develop as independent learners. Students experienced and appreciated a sense of empowerment that the dual mode offered? to shape their studies. *Empowerment* relates to the theme *Flexibility,* in that the extreme flexibility offered by the approach to dual mode delivery gave them options they could choose between and empowered them to make decisions that suited them. In that sense, *empowerment* is derived from flexibility. The essence of the theme *Empowerment* is described in the sub-themes *Autonomy and independence* and *Comfort*.

Autonomy and Independence

The freedom or openness that the dual mode program offered allowed students to study in an independent way, providing them with autonomy as learners. Students were able to actively determine what to learn, where to learn, and when to learn without being constrained to a scheduled timetable and a specific place (Participants 7 and 2). They had the ability to make decisions about their learning and the power to take control of their learning process. Commenting on one specific course, a student said:

I think what was good about that was that there were parameters, you know, that we needed to kind of fill in, but there was also a sense of autonomy where we could go and fill in with whatever else we liked. So I liked that idea of there being rules, but you can also add your own little flair to it - which was what I think made it interesting and fun (Participant 12).

Offering students autonomy, openness, and the ability to direct their own studies supports them to become independent lifelong learners. Their learning is initiated and directed by themselves rather than by the instructor. The practice of self-paced learning was therefore found to be effective. It allowed students to learn as much as they needed. Referring to their experience in a course that used short mini lecture recordings on key concepts for use outside of class, in lieu of traditional lectures, one student commented: *'They were awesome because you could watch them in your own time and then you could go back and re-watch them and you know, it was short sort of snippets of useful information, which were particularly helpful when it came to assessment.' (Participant 1)*. Providing content in small packages supported students to be self-directed learners, as they were able to engage with the content when and where they wished, and revisit core concepts should they feel the need to do so.

Comfort

The sub-theme of *Comfort* relates to a range of positive feelings students reported experiencing as they undertook their studies. These positive feelings towards their studies supported students in having agency, making decisions, and hence feeling empowered, in their studies. They used words such as entertainment, pleasure, enjoyment, and having fun when talking about their learning. For instance, a student reported being physically comfortable when participating in an evening class online:

Being able to sit in my [pyjamas] and being able to, you know, have dinner and not be starving, yeah. I think the convenience of being at home is actually quite compelling once you've done it a bit and go, ah actually, I'm getting my food given to me as I sit here and I can get comfy (Participant 3).

Another student who generally preferred to be in the physical classroom on campus highlighted that they also appreciated the informality and cosiness of online classes:

I probably, to be honest, enjoy being in the classroom the most because that's the way that I worked as a practitioner myself and because I like the interaction with those students. But then I mean really, I don't know whose great idea it was but the idea you can sit there at home with your feet up and a cup of tea and even have your dinner and even interact with your kids while you're working, is amazing (Participant 14).

The feeling of comfort when engaging online was also brought about by the 'look and feel' of the online learning environment, which students found easy to navigate due to consistency across courses. The atmosphere of the online learning environment also impacted on students' comfort, with the approaches to learning supporting students to feel comfortable and confident in the online study environment. Learning by playing, learning while having fun, and the idea that learning happens best when it comes naturally and is not constrained were all ideas shared by participants (Participants 5, 8, and 10). Showing pleasure in learning in social media spaces, a student excitedly stated: *'It wasn't really like studying. It was more like it was fun, like using any sort of social media' (Participant 1).*

Theme 3: Community

Community refers to a cohort of students, instructors, and practitioners who are involved in the program or component courses in some way, who interact with each other and learn together. The community built around the program shaped the experience of students. They were connected through different channels, both physical and virtual, and had a shared purpose of contributing to the success of students in their dual mode learning. The theme of *Community* has two sub-themes known as *Connection* and *Collaborative learning*.

Connection

Connection was acknowledged as a key attribute of the learning community. In order to establish a community for learning, it was noted that it was necessary for people to feel a sense of connection, through networking, making friends, and building relationships. These were ways to commence a good learning journey, as a student commented:

I think I was probably trying to build as many relationships as I could as well, both with instructors as well as with other students. I think they were the things that really helped me to cope [with difficulties in learning] (Participant 1).

As a strategy to better connect with teaching staff and peers, some external students attended face-to-face classes to develop relationship in the physical environment. It was then easier to communicate online as they had already got to know each other (Participants 10 and 13). Other students who preferred to study online connected through student blogs, the chat channel in online classes, social media, and group assignments. Through these activities, students built up a *'kind of a core group of us…that were moving through the degree together' (Participant 12)*. A student satisfied with their networking for learning strategy, said: *'it's the connections and the relationships that you build that really enhanced your learning' (Participant 1)*. Students valued opportunities to engage with and connect to their classmates and the learning community, regardless of their mode of study.

The program as a whole placed an emphasis on establishing personal learning networks, both within their cohort and more generally within the profession. When asked about memorable experiences in their studies, questionnaire respondents referred to a specific course that was designed to foster the development of personal learning networks, saying: *'It got me out of my comfort zone and showed me the benefit of interacting and forming personal learning networks'* (survey respondent). Another said *'I've enjoyed a lot of parts of this [program]. [This course] probably had the most interaction and engagement, and I enjoyed it'* (survey respondent). In this specific course, community was built through and around students' blogs: *Having one of your blog posts commented on by a student – and letting you know that they approved of what you said – nice!* (survey respondent).

Connection was believed especially beneficial when students were able to connect with professionals in industry who could help students stay up-to-date with what was happening in practice. For this reason, students found having guest lecturers was beneficial because *'I think most of us are in this, not just to learn but also to get jobs. You know it's not like, um, some of the creative industries where you're kind of just there 'cause you're interested in the subject. You're actually… we're here to learn and to go "Okay well this is what they're doing out in the real world when we're getting jobs"' (Participant 3)*.

Students were able to meaningfully connect with the guest lecturers who spoke in classes and engaged with them online, finding them to be *'incredibly generous with what they offer to students - contact me, have my notes, here's my card, you know what I mean?' (Participant 14)*. Students valued the connection to industry professionals and felt the benefits of this in their personal learning networks expanding beyond their cohort.

Collaborative Learning

Another attribute of community is the idea of collaboration. Collaboration was enabled through forming close relationships and strong connections with peers, which supported students in having a positive experience of learning in the dual mode environment. A student talked about their experience of group work:

Everyone I connected with for group work were mature-age students as well, so I think we brought a level of workplace experience maybe or that might have helped with why we worked together. And I tried to make sure that we had clear roles, so we weren't stepping on each other and we always created a calendar – okay, we're going to try this by then, do this by then, who's doing that? We met really regularly, either face-to-face or Skype (Participant 9).

Group work can often be difficult territory, however very few participants reported experiencing difficulties with working with their peers. This is perhaps attributable to the focus on community building across the program and to students' own practices around building relationships, which allowed them to work more effectively in group work. Participants reported supporting each other and learning from one another in group work and beyond. A student expressed their positive experience when working in a team, saying that *'I really like to talk with other people and kind of bounce ideas off of them and kind of gauge where they're sitting, to know how I'm doing'*. Working together helped students work more efficiently and also helped them gain a deeper understanding of the content. A good connection between like-minded people enabled students to advance their success in learning. Online students benefitted from collaborative learning not only through group work, but also through engaging with their peers on social media: *'I typically used social media such as Facebook/Twitter or email to discuss things about my classes with my peers'* (survey respondent).

The contribution and support from peers were not always related to academic issues. It might be about broader challenges they face or feelings they experience in learning. For instance, within their community, students might talk about the *'anxieties or fears or things' (Participant 10)* that would ease their difficulties.

Theme 4: Sense of Inclusion

While students might enrol in different learning modes, they had a shared expectation of being a real part of the learning community. This expectation related to emotional aspects such as seeing, being, and feeling. The *Sense of inclusion* theme is described in two sub-themes, labelled as *Feeling of neglect* and *Understanding and caring*.

Feeling of Neglect

Students' experiences were not always positive. There was a 'fear of isolation' that students might face in certain learning situations. They used the words such as 'neglect', 'loneliness', and 'separation' to describe this feeling. Whilst the feeling did not always exist, it was a concern, especially of those who were learning online. One student described the experience of online learning generally:

When you're an online student, it can be a bit isolating, particularly when you're not even in the same state. So you can't meet people for coffee and talk about you know, what you're learning and - it's really hard to build connections (Participant 1).

The practice of running simultaneous online and face-to-face classes began in response to a desire on the part of the teaching team to provide more interactive experiences for online students. This practice, however, was imperfect, as reported by one participant:

Sometimes it does feel a little bit like you're not seen when you're in the online cohort, even if you're talking like you're typing... you can feel a bit like, you're just kind of sitting in a corner, just watching but you can't always hear what is going on when the other students are talking, so you're kind of missing out... (Participant 3).

In such a situation when both physical and online classes occurred at the same time, online students might have a negative feeling, as another student added:

I did struggle a little bit with some aspects of the online study... You couldn't see the lecturer and couldn't see the other students and sometimes you felt a little bit sort of neglected (Participant 11).

Having a dedicated online facilitator was seen as important in synchronous learning classes. This is because *'it's almost too much for the lecturer to do both the online and the lecture at the same time' (Participant 4)*. Without such a facilitator, online students occasionally did not know what was going on in the class because they could not always hear what the instructor said or what questions and answers were presented by other on campus students. For this reason, a student stated that *'I definitely preferred the one [instructor] with the facilitator. I found it worked a lot better' (Participant 5)*.

Understanding and Caring

One of the aspects of feeling included in dual mode learning was the extent to which students' needs were understood, taken care of and addressed. When students felt they were understood and their needs are taken care of, the pitfalls of online learning can be avoided. Interestingly, this helped with the downside of online learning being avoided. One student appreciated the opportunity to participate in live classes:

I find that when a lecturer is delivering an actual lecture, they do reference to online students to encourage participation... They don't just deliver the lecture to the on-campus students and then just say it's a recording, off you go, you can source it. There's always an opportunity for online students to participate as well. So I don't feel like we're just being left in the dark. So there is a level of inclusion... (Participant 6).

Students also valued that instructors provided support and advice outside class hours by quickly responding to questions or helping with technological issues. When asked about the best aspects of the program in the online questionnaire, students responded that the care and attention of the teaching team had a positive impact on their sense of inclusion and experience of study. Students were extremely appreciative of the dedication, enthusiasm, and encouragement of staff.

For me, the most memorable experience in the [program] is the passionate, up-to-date to the latest knowledge, understanding, caring, supportive and kind... teaching team. Many LIS schools offer blended learning, but only few of them have strong relationships with their students and alumni outside class. For me, [the program] is not just a place to learn, it's a safe place full with caring and lovely people. It's a family (survey respondent).

Theme 5: Online Learning Spaces

Students of this dual mode delivery program expected to learn in an online environment comprised of fit-for-purpose technologies, where learning was actively facilitated by teaching staff. Effective facilitation allows students participating in any mode to feel up-to-date with their courses. This theme is comprised of two sub-themes: *Technological learning environment* and *Information organisation*.

Technological Learning Environment

Students acknowledged that technological advancements provide huge support to teaching and learning practice. While many students felt excited by new and emerging technologies, some students were surprised, confused, or overwhelmed on commencing their studies. This may in part be related to incoming students' perceptions of the nature of the profession they were entering, with a high proportion of students not fully appreciating that library and information science is a technology discipline, as is encapsulated by a participant: '*the continual keeping up with technology is important and continually integrating technology into the [program] is something I think is important because I think that I had no idea how much the library [program] would involve technology when I started' (Participant 4)*. For those students returning to study after many years (even internal students, the technological changes were sometimes confronting. One part time student admitted that he did not settle until semester three of the program (Participant 14). For these reasons, technologies, tools, and virtual learning spaces were expected to be carefully adopted for student learning.

In reflecting on online learning environments, most students revealed they preferred to have their learning occur outside the university's LMS, Blackboard. This was particularly evident when discussing tools and approaches to facilitating discussion. One student said Blackboard provides '*a poor discussion forum' (Participant 3)*. This participant recounted a story where she had asked the instructor to try to activate discussion on the Blackboard forums, and this had failed, however once the discussion function was migrated to a Facebook group, there was much more discussion. Many students believed that social media spaces such as Twitter and Google+ are better for learning. They found these tools were superior to the commercial ones in terms of functionality, usability, and friendliness (Participants 4, 11, and 12). With social media, *you just go to the website and then you're there, whereas with Blackboard, you've got to log in, ... you've got to get in to the actual discussion forum, which I think a lot of people don't even know where it is... [I]t's like too many layers deep and so people just forget about it or they just can't be bothered (Participant 3).*

This sentiment was echoed by a questionnaire respondent, who said *'Blackboard doesn't integrate into my existing workflows quite like social media (FB, Twitter, WordPress) does'*. They allow communicating more effectively. *'You can get a response within 10 minutes at times, which I find very useful'* (Participant 5). *'I think that moving away from it [Blackboard] into something like Facebook, to me, was a better learning experience (Participant 4)*. Similarly, another student preferred WordPress as a course site over Blackboard, commenting that: *'it's a good teaching tool as well because the teaching staff are only putting things in one spot, generally, and then it triggers out to all the other modes of communication, which is handy'* (Participant 6). While students who participated in interviews might not have initially expected learning to occur in online spaces outside the LMS, once they experienced learning in these spaces, they tended to prefer the way these alternative spaces functioned.

It should be noted that the questionnaire data revealed that a small proportion of students were reticent to use social media for various reasons. Some students did not appreciate the blurring of boundaries between personal life and study that occurs when discussion spaces are on Facebook.

Information Organisation

Whilst the diversity of technologies provided instructors and students with more choices it also introduced certain challenges to students' experience in relation to the format of learning materials, quantity and quality of information used for learning.

Although students valued audio recorded lectures as good backups to use for the purpose of learning at their own pace, they preferred to have something visual in the lectures. Audio lectures could be a considerable issue if they are too long. Students admitted that they have *'trouble focusing when they're just listening to audio'* (Participant 9). Another added that *'I had to listen to things a couple of times because if I'm just sitting there with nothing in front of me'* (Participant 13). Students appreciated mini lecture videos and recordings of live classes that included the visuals from the class.

Teaching staff placed a strong emphasis on community and engagement, and were active participants in the learning community, communicating regularly with students through announcements on the course site (in Blackboard or WordPress) and engaging with students in social media. This invariably increased the amount of content that students were presented with across the teaching spaces. This sometimes led to students being concerned they would miss an important communication:

I'm a bit scared I'm going to miss out on something. So I'm furiously checking all the modes of communication whereas I probably just need to pick the ones that I like and just stick with those but yeah, I end up overwhelming myself (Participant 6).

Similarly, students sometimes felt overwhelmed by the pace of discussion on Facebook groups:

I found them frustrating because it was a lot of people asking a lot of questions that had been answered in lectures or in the study guide or - and it just really felt like it was a bit of a waste of my time (Participant 8).

DISCUSSION

There is limited literature exploring postgraduate students' expectations, experiences and preferences with regards to studying in a dual mode program, particularly a program offering the degree of flexibility offered by the programs discussed in this article. This research provides insight into what students value in terms of their studies in a dual mode program: flexibility, convenience, community, sense of inclusion, and technology-enhanced facilitation of learning.

The findings presented here align with existing published literature in many ways. Both existing research and this study found that students appreciate flexibility and convenience, and that relationships play an important role in effective learning. For example, in the literature it is argued that flexibility and convenience are main reasons for students to select an online or dual-mode program instead of a face-to-face one (Fortune et al., 2011; Kuzma et al., 2015; Okech et al., 2014). This study found that students appreciated the extreme flexibility and convenience of the fluid learning modes offered. Although they were perhaps surprised by the level of flexibility when first entering the course, it became a valued feature. In addition, the advantage of such a learning mode is that it provides students with the ability to retain professional work while they still undertake family responsibilities (O'Shea et al., 2015). Connection with peers and instructors (Blackmon & Major, 2012; Holzweiss et al., 2014) is another similarity between this research and the existing ones. These aspects are either a theme or sub-theme in the current study.

There are variations in the level of detail presented here, when setting the current research's findings against those in earlier studies. The most notable difference is that while the existing studies provide some interesting information about students' preferences, perceptions, and experiences and comment on these to a certain extent, they tend to focus on identification of 'what' rather than 'how' and 'why' aspects of student experiences. On the contrary, this research discovers not only the students' preferences, expectations, and experiences in terms of themes, but also identifies sub-themes and draws out implications for dual mode course design, set against a background discussion of the approaches to teaching and learning used in the program. Together, these elements present a rich picture of students' experience in the program.

The research findings presented here can be used as a theoretical guideline for instructors, course coordinators and curriculum designers, who seek to develop sustainable courses and programs. The implications for dual mode programs provide practical advice for practitioners. The research results can also serve as a benchmark so that tertiary educators can set their existing curriculums against this research to identify areas for possible changes that will help enhance students' learning experiences.

A limitation of this research is that it is not possible to generalise the findings, given the qualitative nature of the analysis presented here. The results are specific to a postgraduate level cohort in a dual mode program and are not generalisable at a university wide scale due to those characteristics, and to the modes number of participants.

FUTURE RESEARCH DIRECTIONS

The research findings may be an empirical base for future research that adopts a different approach such as case study. This approach allows the researcher to make use of other sources of data, such as archival records and observation that may bring about other aspects influencing student learning experiences. This may also be an opportunity for a study to quantitatively test the results of the current research.

CONCLUSION

Aiming to develop an understanding of students' experiences of teaching and learning, this research found that a flexible and convenient learning environment with a strong sense of community has a great influence on the experience of students when they learn in a dual mode program. A well facilitated online learning environment can generate a sense of inclusion. The research findings will be a useful guide for educators in dual modes who seek to improve student learning experiences and care about a sustainable higher education in this type of delivery mode. They may also be useful to educators working with online programs, as they provide significant insight into postgraduate students' experiences of the online component of dual mode learning.

REFERENCES

Anderson, J., Sutton, S. R., & Gergen, T. (2014). *Student engagement in a dual-mode teaching environment: A pilot study*. Paper presented at the Society for Information Technology & Teacher Education International Conference.

Andeson, T., Upton, L., Dron, J., Malone, J., & Poelhuber, B. (2015). Social interaction in self-paced distance education. *Open Paraxis*, *7*(1), 7–23. doi: 10.5944/openpraxis.7.1.164

Andrews, T., & Tynan, B. (2012). Distance learners: Connected, mobile and resourceful individuals. *Australasian Journal of Educational Technology*, *28*(4), 565–579. doi:10.14742/ajet.828

Beetham, H., & White, D. (2014). Students' expectations and experiences of the digital environment. Bristol, UK: Academic Press.

Blackmon, S. J., & Major, C. (2012). Student experiences in online courses: A qualitative research synthesis. *Quarterly Review of Distance Education*, *13*(2), 77–85.

Bolliger, D. U., & Wasilik, O. (2012). Student satisfaction in large undergraduate online courses. *Quarterly Review of Distance Education*, *13*(3), 153–165.

Braun, V., & Clarke, V. (2006). Using thematic analysis in psychology. *Qualitative Research in Psychology*, *3*(2), 77–101. doi:10.1191/1478088706qp063oa

Brocato, B. R., Bonanno, A., & Ulbig, S. (2015). Student perceptions and instructional evaluations: A multivariate analysis of online and face-to-face classroom settings. *Education and Information Technologies*, *20*(1), 37–55. doi:10.100710639-013-9268-6

Budash, D. E. (2015). *Understanding persistence in an online master's degree program: A single case study of learners and faculty* (Unpublished doctoral dissertation). North Central University.

Creswell, J. W. (2003). *Research design: Qualitative, quantitative, and mixed method approaches*. Thousand Oaks, CA: Sage Publications.

Daniel, J. (2012). Dual-mode universities in higher education: Way station or final destination? *Open Learning: The Journal of Open, Distance and e-Learning*, *27*(1), 89-95.

Farnes, N., Ganor, M., Gil'ad, R., Guri-Rosenblit, S., Ovsyannikov, V., Shelley, M., & Libin-Levav, V. (2000). *Distance education for the information society: Policies, pedagogy and professional development*. UNESCO Institute for Information Technologies In Education.

Fish, W. W., & Wickersham, L. E. (2009). Best practices for online instructors: Reminders. *The Quarterly Review of Distance Education, 10*(3), 279–284.

Fortune, M. F., Spielman, M., & Pangelinan, D. T. (2011). Students' perceptions of online or face-to-face learning and social media in hospitality. *Journal of Online Learning and Teaching / MERLOT, 7*(1), 1–16.

Fyle, C. O., Moseley, A., & Hayes, N. (2012). Troubled times: The role of instructional design in a modern dual-mode university? *Open Learning: The Journal of Open, Distance and e-Learning, 27*(1), 53-64.

Harris, S. M., Larrier, Y. I., & Castano-Bishop, M. (2011). Development of the student expectations of online learning survey (SEOLS): A pilot study. *Online Journal of Distance Learning Administration, 19*(5), 1–12.

Herbert, M. (2006). Staying the course: A study in online student satisfaction and retention. *Online Journal of Distance Learning Administration, 9*(4), 300–317.

Holzweiss, P. C., Joyner, S. A., Fuller, M. B., Henderson, S., & Young, R. (2014). Online graduate students' perceptions of best learning experiences. *Distance Education, 35*(3), 311–323. doi:10.1080/01587919.2015.955262

Killen, C. (2015). *Enhancing the student digital experience: A strategic approach*. Retrieved February 9, 2016, from https://www.jisc.ac.uk/guides/enhancing-the-digital-student-experience

Kuzma, A., Kuzma, J., & Thiewes, H. (2015). Business student attitudes, experience, and satisfaction with online courses. *American Journal of Business Education (Online), 8*(2), 121. doi:10.19030/ajbe.v8i2.9134

Masoumi, D., & Lindström, B. (2012). Quality in e-learning: A framework for promoting and assuring quality in virtual institutions. *Journal of Computer Assisted Learning, 28*(1), 27–41. doi:10.1111/j.1365-2729.2011.00440.x

Meyer, K. A. (2014). Student engagement in online learning: What works and why. *ASHE Higher Education Report, 40*(6), 1–114. doi:10.1002/aehe.20018

Mgutshini, T. (2013). Online or not? A comparison of students' experiences of an online and an on-campus class. *Curationis, 36*(1), 1–7. doi:10.4102/curationis.v36i1.73 PMID:23718147

Michael, K. (2012). Virtual classroom: Reflections of online learning. *Campus-Wide Information Systems, 29*(3), 156–165. doi:10.1108/10650741211243175

Muyinda, P. B. (2012). Open and distance learning in dual mode universities: a treasure unexploited. In E. J. L. M. A. D. Benson (Ed.), International Perspectives of Distance Learning in Higher Education (p. 33). Academic Press.

O'Shea, S., Stone, C., & Delahunty, J. (2015). "I 'feel' like I am at university even though I am online." Exploring how students narrate their engagement with higher education institutions in an online learning environment. *Distance Education*, *36*(1), 41–58. doi:10.1080/01587919.2015.1019970

Oguz, F., Chu, C. M., & Chow, A. S. (2015). Studying online: Student motivations and experiences in ALA-Accredited LIS programs. *Journal of Education for Library and Information Science*, *56*(3), 213–231. doi:10.3138/jelis.56.3.213

Okech, D., Barner, J., Segoshi, M., & Carney, M. (2014). MSW student experiences in online vs. face-to-face teaching formats? *Social Work Education*, *33*(1), 121–134. doi:10.1080/02615479.2012.738661

Sankey, M., & Hunt, L. (2014). Flipped university classrooms: Using technology to enable sound pedagogy. *Journal of Cases on Information Technology*, *16*(2), 26–38. doi:10.4018/jcit.2014040103

Stone, C., O'Shea, S., May, J., Delahunty, J., & Partington, Z. (2016). Opportunity through online learning: Experiences of first-in-family students in online open-entry higher education. *Australian Journal of Adult Learning*, *56*(2), 146–169.

Sullivan, T. M., & Freishtat, R. (2013). Extending learning beyond the classroom: Graduate student experiences of online discussions in a hybrid course. *The Journal of Continuing Higher Education*, *61*(1), 12–22. doi:10.1080/07377363.2013.758555

Taylor, J. A., & Newton, D. (2013). Beyond blended learning: A case study of institutional change at an Australian regional university. *The Internet and Higher Education*, *18*, 54–60. doi:10.1016/j.iheduc.2012.10.003

Todhunter, B. (2013). LOL - limitations of online learning - are we selling the open and distance education message short? *Distance Education*, *34*(2), 232–252. doi:10.1080/01587919.2013.802402

Chapter 16
Supporting the Spiritual Experience in Online Faith-Based Education

Amanda Lanae Jones Ziemendorf
https://orcid.org/0000-0001-7270-8735
Grand Canyon University, USA

Sarah Schroyer
Grand Canyon University, USA

ABSTRACT

Faith-based institutions offer educators a unique set of challenges and opportunities as they are tasked with the integration of faith in the classroom experience while delivering content necessary to meet subject matter objectives. Evaluation of audience, context, and protection of the learning environment are key elements for consideration when incorporating faith within the online classroom. The purpose of this chapter is to support knowledge and competency in implementing faith-based content, integration techniques, and usable instructional solutions that promote authentic connections. When applied strategically and mindfully, faith components can support mutual trust between the learner and the educator, establish a foundation for deep personal growth, and actively fulfill the online instructional objectives. This chapter will cover the background and history of faith in adult education, evaluation of audience and context, protection of the learning environment, utility of faith-based instruction, mindfulness, and techniques for integration.

INTRODUCTION

The heritage and modern growth of faith-based institutions warrants the attention of the academic community in the application of inclusive and effective strategies toward positively supporting the spiritual experience in online education. Unique challenges include serving a broadly dispersed student population of many backgrounds, instructing across various geographical locations, and establishing

DOI: 10.4018/978-1-7998-0115-3.ch016

Supporting the Spiritual Experience in Online Faith-Based Education

common ground for group experiences. An additional challenge faced by online educators is the lack of face-to-face interaction. While spiritual experiences are important in faith-based learning, the focus of the program of study must also be at the forefront of instructional efforts. Both considerations can be met with common strategies in curricular and interactive arenas.

At the core of supporting the spiritual experience is mindfully recognizing opportunities for spiritual interaction and establishing the mutual trust that leads to learners seeking an immersive learning experience from the instructor as a mentor rather than an assigned facilitator. Learners may be assigned to an instructor, but unless they choose to learn from them, they are only engaging in a task-based experience. Mentorship may be compared to discipleship in some cases. The concept of discipleship is in every faith. This is a concept that is sincerely parallel to healthy learning. Discipleship demonstrates the essence of human caring and true immersion in the material, which may be missed in many modern platforms. When learners choose to engage with their assigned instructor as a mentor, they progress to a deeper, immersive learning experience. Many of the challenges that present for the online platform can be solved and the platform advantages leveraged to optimize individual experiences and connection with the instructor. This chapter will discuss the background and history of faith in adult education, prepare educators to evaluate the audience and context, apply strategies for protection of the learning environment, utility of faith-based instruction, mindfulness, and techniques for integration.

BACKGROUND

Historically, religion and spirituality have played an important role in formalized education. From ancient Greece to the Renaissance, faith served as a practical and conceptual foundation for learning. After the destruction of a massive collection of human knowledge in the burning of the library of Alexandria, humanity relied on remaining texts that had been copied and disseminated over a great expanse of geography. In the early years of American education, institutions were founded by the Church. John Harvard, a minister, founded Harvard in 1636 (Thelin, 2004). Practical association can be largely attributed to the lack of established texts, thus religious books such as the Bible offered perspectives in poetry, history, prophesy, theology, and the written word. Faith has always been a learning enterprise, and throughout history, religious entities are the prime promoters of faith. Additionally, many scientists and innovators, were theologians. Isaac Newton was one such theologian scientist (Haycock, 2004). While this chapter is focused on faith-based education in general, it is noteworthy that faith-based education historically has limited precedence from a religious standpoint. Its delivery is approached via universal concepts believed to transcend many religious contexts and backgrounds.

Over time, the expansion of material and knowledge has led to a massive amount of human knowledge documented in books, journals, and now electronic format. Online platforms make information available at lightning speeds that have never before been seen in human history. Even with the introduction of more material, faith remains an integral part of education for many institutions. Some institutions continue to focus on an evangelical approach to support proliferation of the heritage of faith while others seek to establish an environment that fosters fellowship and growth in spirituality. Many seek both.

Modern faith-based institutions may be very inclusive and often do not restrict attendance or employment to those who profess the same theological ideals. With this inclusiveness, administrators and educators are faced with a new challenging dynamic to preserve heritage and a commitment to faith-based education while serving their mission to provide higher education to the masses.

THE SPIRITUAL EXPERIENCE

The spiritual experience is unique to each learner and educator. Due to the individuality of spiritual experiences, supporting the concept of the spiritual experience may be intimidating for the educator. However, this same uniqueness is what allows the presentation of spirituality in the classroom adaptable to each individual encounter. Educational encounters in the online environment primarily occur at-will for both the educator and the learner, further individualizing how information is processed and interpreted. Achievement of continuity for learners manifests differently in the online environment, but can be achieved through consistent approach that optimizes the sharing of distinctive perceptions and mindsets.

Religion vs. Spirituality

Due to the magnitude of the role of spirituality in religion, the two terms may often be used erroneously as synonyms. Though the relationship between the two concepts is undeniable and ever-present, they are not one in the same. Spirituality is an innate element of the human composition and may be described as the personal engagement with the inimitable nonphysical component of the individual human being. Religion is an organized set of beliefs often characterized by learned structure and rituals that support fellowship and defined faith.

Nearly all religions could be considered as having a spiritual foundation, but not all spiritual practices or experiences could be considered religious. It is essential to remember that spirituality is translatable to all humans and supports individual religious journeys and beliefs. Thus, spirituality is powerful in that it is a universal agent for connection even in the face of great philosophical differences. When spirituality and religion are mistakenly converged into one concept, barriers form and spiritual opportunities may be missed or neglected. Religion is an attempt to organize spirituality. Organizing spirituality is almost an oxymoron, as society often perceives spirituality as being a measure of total freedom and egocentric in nature. Religion is more of a collective idea.

Over the years, many have tried to describe the essence of the spirit and the characteristics of spirituality. Some religious documents outline spiritual gifts, or fruits of the spirit. Ultimately, there is no concrete, objective, or infallible definition of spirituality as it is an intangible personal experience that can be individually perceived and defined. Some may argue that it takes faith to even believe in the concept of the spirit at all, or to find oneself in agreement with a specific definition of the spirit and spirituality. Faith is not just intellectual ascent; it is the certainty in the belief itself. We act upon belief and it becomes faith. Demonstration of faith occurs through action, which is a concept that can be purposed in the act of instruction.

The connection between religion and spirituality can be investigated in many capacities. Hilton & Plummer (2013) conducted a study that sought to determine if the affiliation of course faculty with either the Department of Religion or an extraneous department would impact student scores on their Religious Education Survey, and found they were significantly higher in the group assigned to Department of Religion faculty. Those who are religious may have a more structured approach to spirituality and may be more likely to engage in activities that support spiritual growth due to the major role of spirituality in religion. This does not mean that non-spiritual staff cannot tremendously impact the learner population, but it may indicate that a purposeful approach with specific preparation furthers the likelihood learners will engage in a greater depth of spiritual experience.

Even though spiritualty is subjective and intangible, it is translatable and associated with certain pathways of human action, growth, and achievement. The relationship between spirituality, religion, and social justice orientation was recently researched in an investigation into spirituality and religion as factors in U.S. college student career goals and their social justice orientation (Chenot & Kim, 2018). Using the Spiritual Identification Scale, researchers were able to establish relationships between spirituality and social justice orientation attitudes (Chenot & Kim, 2018). Spirituality, beliefs and faith impact people at their core and drive most thoughts responses and behaviors one does. They will fall under natures rule and that is to get the most from the least energy expended. They will do the most at the least cost. Pain is one of the few bridlers. While each study and project has a specific focus, connections from research may lend themselves to a greater attention toward spirituality as an area of strategic focus.

Fellowship

Fellowship is present both in informal spiritual practices and formal religious settings. Many people do not consider fellowship to be a part of the online learning environment. The online classroom has traditionally been viewed as an asynchronous learning environment where learners have little opportunity to form connections with others. With the advancement of technology and integration of evidence in this new modality, educators are more aware of curricular requirements that promote connections as part of the course structure. Fellowship is fostered when people engage with one another and are inspired to connect on a personal level. Facilitation of this involves the promotion of opportunities in discussion and group work.

It could be argued that the online learner has a greater opportunity to silo themselves due to the lack of face-to-face interaction. However, in reality online learners are required to engage in discussion whereas traditional face-to-face instruction may allow learners to decline to participate in discussion without being noticed. Consider the learner who always submits work, but sits at the back of the classroom and refrains from engaging in discussion. This could be due to social fear or personal attitude toward discussion. The online format offers the same learner a haven for open thought and at-will participation. Mandatory contribution from all members of the classroom supports a greater representation of all perspectives. Ultimately, there may be greater disadvantage in the classroom as not all thoughts are represented in every discussion.

When learners are allowed to feel comfortable expressing their spiritual worldview, discussion is enriched. Finding common ground and discussion of diverse beliefs may drive the collective spiritual experiences of the group. While spirituality is very personally perceived, it is not just personal in experience as it is possible to have tremendous collective experiences. Humans are wired to be connected.

KEY ELEMENTS FOR INCORPORATING FAITH IN THE ONLINE CLASSROOM

Individually, audience, context and protection of the learning environment may not directly drive actions in the instructional environment, but these key elements are important for consideration when developing or customizing strategies for supporting faith in the online classroom. Collectively, they become a strategic force and foundation for constructing a safe environment for spiritual growth and personal development.

Audience

Understanding your audience is essential in optimizing the delivery of education that supports spiritual experience. Part of understanding the audience is knowing that your audience changes with each course. The audience in a classroom should be approached from both an individual and collective standpoint. The learners have individual and private educational experiences, though they also work together, collaborate, and dialog as a group. Furthermore, the learners have individual and group spiritual experience through one-on-one communication and group fellowship. Mindfulness of this concept is important in each point of strategic application. In approaching this general task, educators should ask themselves the following questions:

- What is the organization's mission statement? (What are people signing up for?)- When learners enroll in an institution they may consider the mission in determining fit. Even when learners do not consider the mission, they are still agreeing to embark on a journey guided by the overarching mission. Staying true to the organizational vision supports continuity of academic experience, and provides a framework for context. Even when the mission is specific, the approach can be welcoming and inclusive. Instructors may choose to integrate the mission into the classroom by posing questions for group discussion pertaining to how the course material relates to the learner view of the organizational mission.
- What is the purpose of the course I am teaching? (where they are at in their program)- Purpose is not only a practical element, but a spiritual one. Instructors should strive to make the purpose personal. Opening discussion for how the purpose relates to the learner and the group may foster deepening of discussion and help the learners' self-identify utility of the course content both for their individual purpose and the purpose of preparing for the degree they aim for.
- What are the common characteristics of those who seek a degree at my academic institution? - Identifying common characteristics can be difficult, though it is useful to identify the general characteristics of the population. Just as in research, the population may not be exactly identical as individuals, but they will have common characteristics.
- What level of professional achievement is typical of my audience? Are they obtaining an undergraduate degree? Are they seeking a doctoral education? Are they already professionals in the industry?
- General organizational data on the student body population is helpful, but it is also ideal to understand the specific nature of those seeking a degree. For example, in a master's of nursing education program all learners are nurses. They may be from varied background, but nurses have a great deal of common ground in their profession alone.
- What information is available to me about my individual learners? (profile, class wall, initial communication, geographical location) Class biographies are also a great tool for identifying individual class or cohort characteristics that can help the instructor hone in on what might be important for group discussion and points of feedback.
- What are the requirements for spiritual and religious integration (if any)? - Understanding the policy and requirements is likely one of the most important elements of supporting the spiritual experience of the online learner. Rules and guidelines set forth by the organization must always be followed, and personal application of strategy should be tailored and designed to fit the needs of the organization and vision fed by the mission. Following guidelines protects the faculty, the

learner, and the organization. Breeches of policy not only cause conflict and breakdown protections, but they also reduce the effectiveness of faith integration and attempts toward spiritual experience support.

Context

Theological context is very clear in the instance of defined religious groups such as Mormon, Christian, or Jewish. This may be furthered by specific denominational doctrines. For example, in Christianity there are many different denominations that have very detailed theological beliefs and practices. While some faith-based institutions do ascribe to specific denominational beliefs, others focus on faith but remain non-denominational. If a context is prescribed by the organization through affiliation or articles of faith, these connections and descriptions of belief can be really useful in the classroom

Even when affiliations or specific beliefs are clearly articulated, the instructor may also be able to incorporate inspiration from other religions in discussions of comparison or inclusiveness. Delving into the specific manuscripts, articles of faith, and belief systems of great priority for an educator teaching in an environment guided by a specific doctrine. This is true even when the instructor does not individually subscribe to the belief.

Protection of the Learning Environment

Threats to the online learning environment can include incivility, the spread of misinformation, academic dishonesty, and lax behavior. Accountability is the primary key to protecting the learning environment. At times, peers will hold one another accountable, but their reach is limited to scholarly rebuttals and reporting in extreme cases. The facilitator, instructor, or educator is obligated to monitor the classroom and associated activities while facilitating resolution or mitigation of threats per academic and organizational policy. Setting clear expectations both at the beginning of the course of study and each individual course is a powerful pre-emptive strategy toward fostering a progressive and constructive learning environment. Expectations are essential in shaping mindset and preparing the individual for reception of content.

In faith-based institutions, the spiritual freedom of the online learning environment must also be protected. An instructor who is unsure or uneasy about expressing their faith or spirituality in a written format, students who dismiss or mock faiths other than their own, or professors who simply forget to post in their prayer forums all threaten the expression of spirituality of the class as a whole.

UTILITY OF FAITH-BASED INSTRUCTION

Integrating faith in the online classroom has many benefits. One of the most notable benefits is that faith and discussions on faith have been known to create a pathway for connection, even when beliefs are not the same. This may be due to the relationship between spirituality and characteristics such as social justice orientation which has been established in literature (Chenot & Kim, 2017). In other words, when people are engaged in spirituality, regardless of religion or individual belief, they are more likely to have a common interest and affinity for human caring. Caring connections lead to mutual trust between the learner and the educator. Prayer is an example of a caring, faith-based action. When an instructor offers to pray for an individual learner, or prayer is delivered in a written capacity within the online forum, learners may be inclined to view their educator as someone who cares for them as a spiritual being. The instructor must regularly engage in activities such as grading that are commonly perceived as criticism or corrective. The addition of enrichment communication or caring communication supports the perception that the educator desires to grow their scholars.

Sincerity is the essential in any caring action. Being sincere is important because not only do the words convey authentic meaning, but it causes the educator to shape their own nurturing mindset. As educators are in a position of leadership and authority, their words both written and verbal should always be sincere and authentic. Various disciplines have begun to recognize the value of authenticity and caring for the human condition in organizational success and the success of service professionals. Healthcare is a prime example. Examples of notable models for healthcare include Jean Watson's theory of human caring, the nursing as caring theory, the theory of caring and healing, and the quality caring model (Duffy, 2018). Many of these caring models and theories rely on the underlying belief that humans are naturally inclined to care, and that caring relationships and communications empower and strengthen both the individual and the interpersonal relationship (Duffy, 2018).

Authority should never be weaponized in the classroom, and the educator has a responsibility to protect their authoritative power from any level of corruption or bias (Pace & Hemmings, 2007). Authority is a powerful tool in leadership, but it does not automatically lend itself to learning or engagement. For some, authority has a negative connotation. This is unfortunate because in reality authority is very protective and guiding. Faith-based interaction and strategies are useful in channeling authority and supporting its ethical application.

- Prayer
    - Praying with students can be done in text or, ideally, anytime a phone conference/webinar occurs. It is useful to ask the learner's permission to pray for them.
    - "Before we conclude the call today, may I pray for you?"
    - It is amazing just how many learners accept prayer, and it is a venue for complete change in perception and atmosphere.
    - Prayer shows support on a personal and spiritual level.
    - Learners know that prayer is optional, and they are likely to perceive that the instructor cares about them as a human and as an individual.
- Prayer forums
    - Forums allow for learners to engage with one another in collective, spiritual fellowship.
    - Learners do not have to share religious beliefs to support one another.
    - Prayer forums create a positive community venue for encouragement.
    - Unlike general forums, learners are less likely to cause disruption and complain in a prayer forum.
- Faith-based encouragement
    - Including scripture passages in weekly announcements.
    - Allowing and responding to prayer requests.
- Use of bible verses/religious text in personal communication
- References to the Bible or other Articles of Faith in the classroom discussion.
- Using of inspirational quotes when delivering tough news or having hard conversations (see Table 1).

Supporting the Spiritual Experience in Online Faith-Based Education

Table 1. Bible verse/ religious texts

Verses/excerpt	Source
• "O Lord, You are my God; I will exalt You and praise Your name, for in perfect faithfulness You have done marvelous things, things planned long ago." (Isaiah 25:1) • "Oh, the depth and riches of the wisdom and the knowledge of God! How unsearchable His judgments, and His paths beyond tracing out." (Romans 11:33) • "When I said, 'My foot is slipping,' Your love, O Lord, supported me. When anxiety was great within me, Your consolation brought joy to my soul." (Psalm 94:18-19) • "I have told you these things, so that in Me you may have peace. In this world you will have trouble. But take heart! I have overcome the world." (John 16:33) • "Fear not, for I am with you; be not dismayed for I am your God; I will strengthen you, I will help you, I will uphold you with my righteous hand." (Isaiah 41:10) • "Therefore, my dear brothers and sisters, stand firm. Let nothing move you. Always give yourselves fully to the work of the Lord, because you know that your labor in the Lord is not in vain." (1 Corinthians 15:58) • "God is our refuge and strength, an ever present help in trouble. Therefore we will not fear, though the earth give way and the mountains fall into the heart of the sea." (Psalm 46:1-2) • "Do not throw away your confidence; it will be richly rewarded. You need to persevere so that when you have done the will of God, you will receive what He has promised." (Hebrews 10:35-36) • "We are God's workmanship, created in Christ Jesus to do good works, which God prepared in advance for us to do." (Ephesians 2:10) • "The steps of a good man/women are ordered by the Lord: and he delighteth in his/her way." Psalm 37:23 (KJV) • "'For I know the plans I have for you,' declares the Lord. 'Plans to prosper you and not to harm you, plans to give you hope and a future." — Jeremiah 29:11 (NIV). • "May the Lord bless you and protect you. May the Lord smile on you and be gracious to you. May the Lord show you his favor, and give you his peace." Numbers 6:24-26 • "She who kneels before God can stand before anyone" Romans 8:31 • "Then you will call on me and come and pray to me, and I will listen to you. You will seek me and find me when you seek me with all your heart." — Jeremiah 29:12-13 (NIV) • "Therefore, since we are surrounded by so great a cloud of witnesses, let us also lay aside every weight, and sin which clings so closely, and let us run with endurance the race that is set before us," (Hebrews 12:1) • "Because you know that the testing of your faith produces perseverance. Let perseverance finish its work so that you may be mature and complete, not lacking anything." (James 1:3-4, NIV)	Bible
• "But the Lord knoweth all things from the beginning; wherefore, he prepareth a way to accomplish all his works among the children of men; for behold, he hath all power unto the fulfilling of all his words. And thus it is. Amen." (1 Nephi 9:6) • "Whosoever shall put their trust in God shall be supported in their trials, and their troubles, and their afflictions, and shall be lifted up at the last day." (Alma 36:3) • "And if men come unto me I will show unto them their weakness. I give unto men weakness that they may be humble; and my grace is sufficient for all men that humble themselves before me; for if they humble themselves before me, and have faith in me, then will I make weak things become strong unto them." (Ether 2:27) • "But behold, I, Nephi, will show unto you that the tender mercies of the Lord are over all those whom he hath chosen, because of their faith, to make them mighty even unto the power of deliverance." (1 Nephi 1:20)	Book of Mormon

Mindfulness

Mindfulness is a necessity for both the learner and the educator as they navigate the course in their distinctive roles. The educator must be mindful of their audience, the communication trends, and the opportunities that arise from organic and unpredictable discussion between learners. Mindfulness is more than awareness, it is an active and purposeful thought process in which one seeks to gain and use information from their environment to shape their responses.

The concept of mindfulness is easily bogged down by abstract examination and over thinking. Presented plainly, mindfulness can be described as compassionate, self-awareness. This concept of how an individual carries themselves with honor, charity and caring in their day-to-day activities ties easily into faith-based values.

While those in the secular realm may contend that in order to be "mindful" a meditative state is a necessary precursor, prayer can be an invaluable substitute for mere inward examination. Within mindfulness, the natural problem-driven, solution-focused "monkey mind" is often blamed for wandering thoughts, disconnectivity, and absentmindedness. However, when faith is incorporated into this equation we get further from this animalistic state and are instead building our closeness with our higher power (Knabb & Vazquez, 2018).

Since the early 1980's the recognized effectiveness of mindfulness as an intervention within many varying service populations has grown, thanks in part to the diligent work of researchers from many fields (Ivtzan et al, 2016). Today, mindfulness has a place as an intervention for many different disorders such as mental illness and substance abuse recovery. An example of this is research that has demonstrated feasibility that those with Autistic traits can utilize self-control to eliminate undesirable behaviors (Singh et al., 2019). Moreover, per Singh et al. (2019) mindfulness among those with Autism may even result in decreased dependency on psychotropic medication for behavior management.

Another appeal of mindfulness is that it can be applied with favorable results, efficiently and across a wide variety of professional settings (Bartlett et al., 2019). This is an excellent way to frame the value of mindfulness in the eyes of a student who will benefit from applying mindfulness techniques in their future professional roles. For current learners, implementation of mindfulness exercises boast benefits in the areas of self-reliance, hardiness and has been shown to reduce stress among practitioners (Vidic & Cherup, 2019).

Reflection is the act of engaging in examination of one's inner thoughts, feelings, and motivations. Humans constantly engage in reflection, though it is not always considered ritualistic. Since reflection is not always intentional, it may not be optimized toward the spiritual experience, whereas purposeful reflection can be a powerful catalyst for actualization.

Similarly, there is a common misconception that in order to practice mindfulness one must enter into a trance-like state for several minutes or even hours. Studies have shown a brief mindfulness exercise at the beginning of a class (5-10 minutes) is sufficient to garner rewards from the practice (Chase-Cantarini & Christiaens, 2019). This means that beginning a mindfulness practice in a classroom setting need not be an overwhelming task. A simple prayer exercise wherein students are verbally guided through wishing fellow students and others success and kindness, defuses tension in the environment and helps students overcome classroom anxiety.

It is imperative to note that while mindfulness has a wealth of benefits and can be utilized gracefully, research has shown that it is likely to cause manifestations of negative symptoms in those with past traumatic experiences, such as (but not limited to) post-traumatic stress disorder (Calvert, 2019). To ensure that these populations are not adversely effected, instructors may make the disclaimer that students can chose not to participate in the practice or engage in their own prayer or faith-based routine during that time.

Constructive Spiritual Dialogue

Regardless of the organizational religious affiliation or non-affiliation, constructive spiritual dialog can happen in any classroom. The innate aspect of spirituality makes it relevant in all settings where humans are growing and developing. Fear of crossing the line between religion and spirituality often prevents educators and learners from engaging in dialog they feel may be offensive or inappropriate. When fear is relinquished, constructive dialog can not only further the spiritual experience but can open the mind for readiness of learning non-spiritual concepts. Constructive dialog also conveys caring, respect, and trust that can be mutually established between peers and within the learner-educator relationship.

Characteristics of constructive spiritual dialog include respectful tone, expanding on experiences shared by others, finding common ground, and acknowledging differences. Even when presented beliefs are not shared, the information can be purposed to help those in the classroom environment understand the world around them and grow in their ability to serve others regardless of the industry.

Escalations related to tone are a common theme amongst disgruntled students. Students may make statements such as:

- "My instructor is disrespectful to me"
- "My instructor is rude and critical"
- "I think my instructor is mad at me"
- "He/she talks down to me"
- "My instructor wants me to fail"

When these complaints are investigated, often there is no breach in policy or inappropriate language used. When the language pertaining to what was actually said is broken down, there are no elements that would precipitate punitive action or correction. While these statements may certainly be substantiated in some cases, many complaints such as these stem from a lack of established mutual respect. Unfortunately, when this point is reached it is difficult to re-establish the foundation. Thus, it is extremely important that the instructor work to establish mutual respect and a foundation that will support a feeling of trust from the beginning.

Even when learners are not objectively correct in their claims, it is possible to empathize with their perception of the academic experience. These moments are valuable opportunities to determine what strategies could have been implemented to prevent the negative experience in the first place.

At first glance, it may appear that the following strategies will cause responses to take more time. However, implementing strategies such as these will streamline communication, cause greater efficiency, establish expectations for professional communication, ensure you have covered all points requested, serve to protect the instructor from unsubstantiated claims, and establish a tone that supports interpersonal receptiveness (see Table 2). Furthermore, establishing full and organized communication demonstrates to the learner that you are committed to their success. Once strategies are implemented as part of personal educational practice, it actually saves time in composition and in reducing negative responses.

- Greet your learners in every communication
    - Though the online platform is certainly different from live didactic interaction, it is worthwhile to consider the simulation of face-to-face interaction whenever possible.
    - When responding to learner communication, greetings are important as you would greet a learner in person.
    - A greeting is a neutral statement that serves to acknowledge the person as an individual and supports communication as a formal event.
    - The action also models what is expected of the learner when sending communication to any figure of authority or guidance.

- Infuse caring communication prior to engaging in the business of the communication
  - Caring communication is special because it costs nothing, takes away nothing, and only benefits both the learner and the instructor.
  - It is encouraging and speaks to the spirit rather than the learners' actions, inactions, or questions.
  - It conveys unconditional concern for the individual regardless of the challenges they are facing.
  - Some instructors may be resistant to add caring communication when learners are engaging in especially negative or disrespectful behavior.
  - It is important to note that this communication does not condone negative behavior, it simply communicates unconditional caring.
- Ensure that all questions are answered
  - When learners reach out to locate information or to find the answers to their questions, they are often already frustrated. That frustration may deepen if the response lacks clarity, dismisses their thoughts or questions, or reprimands the learner for not being able to locate the information.
  - Even if the learner should have been able to locate the material, that can be reinforced while also providing an answer to the question. Reprimanding students for not being able to locate items or not noticing information within announcements is assumptive in that the instructor is assuming the learners did not fulfill their responsibility for material.
  - Technical difficulties, personal barriers with technology, and lack of mastery of new material may be culprits for questions that seem unnecessary. Even when questions seem unnecessary or reflect lack of review of course materials, the educator should treat all questions as necessary and give the learner the benefit of the doubt when responding. Learner errors in overlooking material are opportunities to redirect and help the learner develop effective habits for ownership of their learning experience. Dismissing seemingly unnecessary questions can lead to wariness of inquisitive activity and can weaken mutual trust.
  - Instructors can also ask, "Did you see my announcement on this subject? I think you will find that information useful. I will share it again here, but make sure you take a look at the original announcement as I want to make sure you have access to all the course materials"
- Provide rationale for any authoritative decisions
  - Sometimes we have to communicate difficult information to learners such as the decision to not accept an excessively late assignment, or to deduct late points. When this occurs, it is important to provide rationale:
    - "Hi Jenny, Thank you for reaching out! I hear your concerns about getting the assignment in on time, and I will share your options with you. Per university policy, there will be a 10% per day deduction for late submissions. Even though I cannot grant you an extension at this time, I encourage you to consider whether it is worth it to you to complete the entire work and take the late deduction. If you have questions please let me know. I am happy to help! If you feel you need additional accommodations, please reach out to your counsellor. They may be able to offer you information pertaining to university-level accommodations. I hope this helps!"
    - Personalize the reference to rationale.
- Include resources

- ○ Inclusion of resources is a service action that serves the core of instructional intent. Even if the resources are already available, it is often necessary to reinforce ideas just as one would within a live classroom. Humans require repetition in many areas of growth and development. Consider how many times one must be corrected throughout their childhood and even adult life. Learners are responsible for more information and platforms than ever before due to the accessibility of information. This strategy offers the opportunity to extend grace. We may not always be able to extend grace in areas such as university policy, thus it is important to seek other ways to do so. Grace communicates with the spirit. It is a caring action, and one that serves to bolster mutual trust. It is important for learners to be able to disclose their weaknesses without being reprimanded. If they are reprimanded each time, they will hide their shortcomings and instructors lose the opportunity to develop the learner.
- Infuse encouraging statements into the dialogue
- Conclude the communication formally- Essentially, place your name at the end. Use your credentials. Some professionals use the first name only to seem more approachable, however, it fails to support the role-respect that is innate with the position of instructor. Also, rewarding feedback or encouragement may mean more when the learner is faced with recognizing credentials. Feedback from Amanda or Sarah may be less mentally valuable than feedback from Dr. Ziemendorf, or Professor Schroyer.
- Finally-proofread!-Research has shown that mechanical errors in writing leads to significant impact on the perception of the audience. One such study found that errors in email messages had a negative impact on the recipient's perception of the author's intelligence and conscientiousness (Vignovic, & Thompson, 2010). Intelligence and conscientiousness are important for the educator. If the audience perception is damaged related to those two characteristics, the educator may lose learner engagement and trust. Make an effort to deliver complex information verbally.
- Honesty is key in all strategies. Do not tell the learner something that is not true. If they are not doing great, do not say, "You are doing great!" Instead, say: "It is truly evident that you wish to succeed!" or say, "I encourage you to continue your commitment to improvement"

SOLUTIONS AND RECOMMENDATIONS

For organizations, it is recommended that a strategic plan is developed and implemented to outline resources, techniques, and approaches that are consistent with the organizational mission. Some organizations require establishment of faith-based forums within the classrooms. It is also recommended that individual educators develop a process and plan for how they will support faith in the classroom. Practicing strategies consistently and continuously cultivates innovation toward the establishment of even more dynamic approaches that evolve with each new group of learners.

Most importantly, it is recommended that educators and administrators in online higher learning recognize and invest in the value of human caring. Caring is at the very core of the spirit of education in all modalities. Caring for the spirit of another creates natural responses in human interaction that transcend all other strategy and approach. Without it, no measure of action is effective in truly reaching the spirit.

Table 2. Strategies for individual learner communication

Strategy	Examples	Rationale
Greeting	• Hi Jenny, • Good Afternoon James, • Greetings Jerome, • Thank you Alicia!	• Establishes respect • Begins the communication on positive or neutral ground • Recognizes the learner as an individual • Reinforces professional communication in modeling what is expected.
Caring Communication	• I hope this message finds you well! • Thank you for reaching out with your questions! • Great questions! • I am happy to help! • I am glad to hear you are making progress. • Sounds like you are working really hard.	• Demonstrates a caring for the person, regardless of the circumstance • Acknowledges any effort or positive accomplishments.
Business	• Clearly provide explanations • State the course of action or options • Provide dates and times as applicable • Set measurable goals	• Establishes the necessary core of the communication
Rationale for Decisions	• Clearly deliver rationale, even if it seems to be apparent • Provide evidence as needed • Refer to policies	• Rationale supports instruction and helps the learner understand why the course of action is being taken, and thus why alternate courses may not be appropriate • Serves to demonstrate respect
Resources	• Direct learners to resources • Refer to any attachments to the communication • Provide links as applicable	• Delivers pertinent information related to resource availability and location • The delivery of resources supports the learner's understanding of how they can become more autonomous
Encouragement	• Include statement of encouragement or inspirational quotes • Prayer may be used in this area	• Encouragement is the voice of caring
Conclusion	• May be a short phrase • "I hope this helps!" • "Let me know if you have questions!" • "Your commitment to success is truly evident"	• Ends communication on a positive note • Demonstrates respect • Reinforces the modeling of formality
Proofread	• Use the features of the email or learning management system individual communication to spellcheck • Read through the communication before sending • Especially make sure the Learner's name is spelled correctly • Double check for any missed attachments	• Modeling expected behavior • Protects the instructor from unnecessary concerns • Supports perceptions that the instructor is qualified to give feedback pertaining to mechanics of writing.

FUTURE RESEARCH DIRECTIONS

Due to the modern growth of faith-based institutions in online education, the opportunities for research are not only available, but also plentiful. The authors of this chapter recommend expansion and focus on four main areas for future research:

- The willingness of learners to allow their instructor to pray for them regardless of belief.

- Barriers for faith integration faced by the educator.
- Barriers for faith discussion encountered by the learner.
- Faith integration and perception on caring.

It may also be valuable to investigate the level of autonomy, acumen, and duty to innovation faculty have in incorporating faith in the classroom. Learning more about student perspectives and the ultimate impact of spirituality on the learner's success following completion of an academic program could better inform higher learning entities regarding return on spiritual investment.

CONCLUSION

Spirituality and the human quest to nurture spiritual experiences is a timeless concept. Modern technology and the ever-changing modalities people use to communicate and learn offer special circumstances for consideration. Challenges arise when learning to connect across distance and in asynchronous environments, though these modalities also offer powerful advantages for eliciting participation and engagement.

Learning to leverage the characteristics of the online environment supports effective teaching practices that seamlessly marry professional instruction of curriculum and promotion of spiritual grown in varying theological contexts.

ACKNOWLEDGMENT

The authors wish to offer sincere and heartfelt thanks to David Schroyer, BSW, CMP and Rev. Steven Mark Jones, MDiv, MEd for the sharing of their experiences and inspiration for content.

REFERENCES

Allen, P. (2014). Divinings: Religion at Harvard from its origins in New England ecclesiastical history to the 175th anniversary. *Journal of Education & Christian Belief*, *18*(2), 286–290. doi:10.1177/205699711401800240

Bartlett, L., Martin, A., Neil, A. L., Memish, K., Otahal, P., Kilpatrick, M., & Sanderson, K. (2019). A systematic review and meta-analysis of workplace mindfulness training randomized controlled trials. *Journal of Occupational Health Psychology*, *24*(1), 108–126. doi:10.1037/ocp0000146 PMID:30714811

Calvert, R. (2019). *Advanced Mindfulness Practitice. PESI Comprehensive Training*. Eau Claire, WI: PESI.

Chase-Cantarini, S., & Christiaens, G. (2019). Introducing mindfulness moments in the classroom. *Journal of Professional Nursing*.

Chenot, D., & Kim, H. (2017). Spirituality, religion, social justice orientation, and the career aspirations of young adults. *Journal of Social Work Education*, *53*(4), 699–713. doi:10.1080/10437797.2017.1283267

Haycock, D. (2004). The long-lost truth': Sir Isaac Newton and the Newtonian pursuit of ancient knowledge. *Studies in History and Philosophy of Science, 35*(3), 605–623. doi:10.1016/j.shpsa.2004.06.009

Hilton, J. III, & Plummer, K. (2013). Examining student spiritual outcomes as a result of a general education religion course. *Christian Higher Education, 12*(3), 331–348. doi:10.1080/15363759.2013.824352

Ivtzan, I., Young, T., Martman, J., Jeffrey, A., Lomas, T., Hart, R., & Eiroa-Orosa, F. J. (2016). Integrating mindfulness into positive psychology: A randomized controlled trial of an online positive mindfulness program. *Mindfulness, 7*(6), 1396–1407. doi:10.100712671-016-0581-1

Knabb, J. J., & Vazquez, V. E. (2018). A randomized controlled trial of a 2-week internet-based contemplative prayer program for Christians with daily stress. *Spirituality in Clinical Practice, 5*(1), 37–53. doi:10.1037cp0000154

Pace, J., & Hemmings, A. (2007). Understanding authority in classrooms: A review of theory, ideology, and research. *Review of Educational Research, 77*(1), 4–27. doi:10.3102/003465430298489

Singh, N. N., Lancioni, G. E., Karazsia, B. T., Myers, R. E., Kim, E., Chan, J., ... Janson, M. (2019). Surfing the Urge: An informal mindfulness practice for the self-management of aggression by adolescents with autism spectrum disorder. *Journal of Contextual Behavioral Science, 12*, 170–177. doi:10.1016/j.jcbs.2018.10.003

Thelin, J. R. (2004). *A history of American higher education.* Baltimore, MD: The John Hopkins University Press.

Vidic, Z., & Cherup, N. (2019). Mindfulness in classroom: Effect of a mindfulness-based relaxation class on college students' stress, resilience, self-efficacy and perfectionism. *College Student Journal, 53*(1), 130–142.

Vignovic, J. A., & Thompson, L. F. (2010). Computer-mediated cross-cultural collaboration: Attributing communication errors to the person versus the situation. *The Journal of Applied Psychology, 95*(2), 265–276. doi:10.1037/a0018628 PMID:20230068

ADDITIONAL READING

Adrian, W. (2007). Globalization and the Christian idea of a university (or, the Lexus and the olive tree, and higher education). *Christian Higher Education, 6*(4), 299–320. doi:10.1080/15363750701268137

Ahn, J., Hinson, D. W., & Teets, S. T. (2016). Teachers' views on integrating faith into their professional lives: A cross-cultural glimpse. *AILACTE Journal, 13*(1), 41–57.

Borst, M. J. (2017). Online discussions improve student perceptions of instructor efforts to relate faith to learning in graduate occupational therapy courses. *Christian Higher Education, 16*(4), 255–265. doi:10.1080/15363759.2017.1328319

Byrd, J. C. (2016). Understanding the online doctoral learning experience: Factors that contribute to students' sense of community. *Journal of Educators Online, 13*(2), 102–135.

Carnevale, D. (2002). Virtual faith. *The Chronicle of Higher Education, 49*(13), 51–52.

Cosgrove, M. (2006). *Foundations of Christian thought: Faith, learning, and the Christian worldview.* Grand Rapids, MI: Kregel Publications.

Daniels, J. R. & Gustafson, J. N. (2016). Faith-based institutions, institutional mission, and the public good. *Higher Learning Research Communications, 6*(2).

Frye, S. (2007). Religious education and faith challenges in the college classroom. *Adult Learning, 18*(1/2), 12–14. doi:10.1177/104515950701800104

Herron, F. (2008). Technology initiative promotes catholic faith through cyberfaith. *Momentum, 39*(4), 48–50.

Hulme, E. E., Groom, D. E. Jr, & Heltzel, J. M. (2016). Reimagining Christian higher education. *Christian Higher Education, 15*(1/2), 95–105. doi:10.1080/15363759.2016.1107348

Reeder, G., & Pacino, M. A. (2013). Faith integration in the classroom. *The International Journal of Religion and Spirituality in Society, 2*(2), 121–127. doi:10.18848/2154-8633/CGP/v02i02/51199

Smith, D. (2013). Differentiation and diversification in higher education: The case of private, faith-based higher education in Manitoba. *Canadian Journal of Higher Education, 43*(1), 23–43.

Smith, P. V., & Baratta, A. (2016). Religion and literacies in higher education: Scoping the possibilities for faith-based meaning making. *Critical Studies in Teaching and Learning, 4*(2), 68.

Swezey, J. A. (2009). Faculty sense of religious calling at a Christian university. *Journal of Research on Christian Education, 18*(3), 316–332. doi:10.1080/10656210903333400

Zenner, C., Herrnleben-Kurz, S., & Walach, H. (2014). Mindfulness-based interventions in schools – A systematic review and meta-analysis. *Frontiers in Psychology, 5*, 603. doi:10.3389/fpsyg.2014.00603 PMID:25071620

KEY TERMS AND DEFINITIONS

Discipleship: Period of time when one follows a teacher, mentor, or leader.
Faith-Based: Affiliated with or supported by a religion or religious theology.
Fellowship: A group of people meeting and working toward a shared goal in a friendly manner.
Integration: The process of combining or bringing together in application.
Mindfulness: An active and purposeful thought process in which one seeks to gain and use information from their environment to shape their responses.
Prayer: Communication to a perceived superior being, God, or cosmic power.
Reflection: The act of engaging in examination of one's inner thoughts, feelings, and motivations.
Religion: An organized set of beliefs often characterized by learned structure and rituals that support fellowship and defined faith.
Spirituality: The personal engagement with the inimitable nonphysical component of the individual human being.

Chapter 17
The Effectiveness of Gamification on Student Engagement, Learning Outcomes, and Learning Experiences

Kenneth C. C. Yang
https://orcid.org/0000-0002-4176-6219
The University of Texas at El Paso, USA

Yowei Kang
https://orcid.org/0000-0002-7060-194X
National Taiwan Ocean University, Taiwan

ABSTRACT

Gamification has been widely used in the higher education to enhance users' learning experiences through the integration of game-like elements into the course materials. This study explores whether and how different levels of gamification in the instructional methods will influence student engagement with the course, overall learning experiences with the course, and learning outcomes with the course materials. The findings suggest that, among four indices to measure the success of gamification, three out of four show the positive gamification effects with a highly gamified class leads to higher level of student engagement than no or lowly gamified classes. The same positive gamification effects can be found in students' overall learning experience. Highly gamified classes result in better student learning outcomes as measured by their grades at different data collection points. Limitations of this study include small class sizes and no statistically significant results and only two gamified elements used. Implications and discussions were presented.

DOI: 10.4018/978-1-7998-0115-3.ch017

INTRODUCTION

The Rise of Digital Game Industry

According to Entertainment Software Association (henceforth, ESA) (2019), 65% of American adults play video game and the average age of gamers is 33 years old. Fifty-four percent of American gamers is male, while forty-six percent is female (ESA, 2019). Sixty-two percent of Millennial gamers (aged between 18 and 34 years old) who are attending college believe video games can be educational, while 68% of them believe playing video game can stimulate mental capacity (ESA, 2019). The video game industry has accumulated $43.4 billion in 2018 from three major categories: contents ($35.8 billion), hardware ($5.1 billion), and accessories and VR ($2.4 billion) (ESA, 2019). Nine out of the top 20 best-selling video games are classified as Mature, such as *Call of Duty: Black Ops III*, *Red Dead Redemption II*, *Grand Theft Auto V*, *Far Cry 5*, *God of War 2018*, etc. challenging previous perceptions that digital games are played by teenagers (ESA, 2019). The growing importance that digital games have played in Generation M's life has lent support to the integration of digital games into the higher education pedagogy.

Rapid growth of the digital game industry have generated enthusiasm among scholars from different disciplines to explore this phenomenon and its impacts in a variety of application contexts (Kang, 2015; Raessens & Goldstein, 2005; Wolf & Perron, 2003). Some emerging areas of digital game research include media effects of digital gameplay, addiction to digital games (Chuang, 2006), adoption behaviors of new game technologies (Chang, Lee, & Kim, 2006), methodological implications in researching digital games (Boellstorff, Nardi, Pearce, & Taylor, 2012), and educational applications (Adukaite, Zyl, Er, & Cantoni, 2017; de-Marcos, Domínguez, & Saenz-de-Navarrete, 2014; Gee, 2004; Leaning, 2015; Prensky, 2005). This book chapter will particularly focus on the applications of digital games in the higher education context (Adukaite et al., 2017; de-Marcos et al., 2014; Leaning, 2015).

Gamification as an Educational Tool in the Higher Education Context

The popularity of digital games and widespread applications have led educators to integrate game elements into their instructional methods and materials, in order to make the best of users' own desire for achievement, competition, and self-expression (Hamari & Eranti, 2011; Hamari, Koivisto, & Sarsa, 2014; Kang, 2015; Reeve & Read, 2009; Swallow, 2012). To study many game-like applications in the educational context, a comprehensive term, gamification, has been developed to address how educators take advantage of users' desire for achievement, education, entertainment, and stimulation through the use of game design elements in non-game contexts (Deterding, Sicart, Nacke, O'Hara, & Dixon, 2011a; Kang, 2015; Morschheuser, Rivera-Pelayo, Mazarakis, & Zacharias, 2014).

Gamification is also defined as "the application of game design principles in non-gaming contexts" (Robson, Plangger, Kietzmann, McCarthy, & Pitt, 2015, p. 411). The term, gamification, mainly refers to "an approach to enhancing people's experience of a service or system through incorporating game-like experiences into the service or practice" (Leaning, 2015, p. 159). As conceptualized by Leaning (2015), the process of gamifying a course "involves adding a different form of experience to an activity, adding a new layer to an existing process that incorporates a new level of symbolic or ludic meaning above and beyond the merely instrumental activity of the task. The new layer of meaning provides a greater experience for the user and encourages participation with the transformed activity" (p. 159).

Because there is a growing focus of students' learning experiences in a classroom (such as the flipped classroom approach), from the user experience (UX) perspective, this term, gamification, is also considered to be "an informal umbrella term for the use of video game elements in non-gaming systems to improve user experience and user engagement" (Deterding et al., 2011a, p. 1). In the business setting, this concept is related to how a business organization attempts to understand and influence human behaviors among its workforce and customers by integrating the challenge, fun, and play elements to the business processes (Dale, 2014). Recent popularity of digital games has prompted researchers and practitioners from other fields to explore the potential of game elements in other applications (Deterding et al., 2011).

In terms of its applications in the higher education context, "gamification" includes "game-based mechanics, aesthetic, and game thinking to engage people, motivate action, promote learning, and solve problems" (Blair & Mesch, 2013, p. 134). These educational studies often focus on the following areas of gamification in the higher education context: 1) mechanisms of gamification; 2) effects of gamification; 3) instructors' adoption behaviors.

In terms of mechanisms of gamification, some examples of gaming a college class include offering students with virtual badges as rewards when they complete extra quizzes through a social media site (Landers & Callan, 2011). Other examples include league tables, leader boards, medal or virtual goods (Paisley, 2013). Competition that does not involve substantial penalty, if failed, is also a popular form of gamification (Kapp, 2012). Some scholars (Morschheuser, Hassan, Werder, & Hamari, 2018) have interviewed 25 leading gamification experts and concluded that gamification can be seen as "a situational and iterative development process with a high degree of user involvement and early testing of design ideas" (Morschheuser et al., 2018, n.p.).

In terms of the effects of gamifications on course delivery, Leaning (2015) reports a qualitative focus group study to assess the integration of gamification into a media theory class. His qualitative data found that students who enjoyed the gamified course more lead to their motivation to be more prepared and generate better learning outcomes. Past research on the applications of gamification mainly focus on three areas: 1) The motivational 'affordances' (exploring how actual gamified activities give the subject or the mechanics of the game); 2) Psychological outcomes (studying subsequent changes in feeling about an activity during and after the gamified activity); 3) Behavioral outcomes (researching the usage experience in behavior following the gamified activity). Although playing digital games has been viewed as for entertainment and leisure purposes, the task-oriented and strategy-guided nature of advanced digital game applications has transformed digital games into potentially gamification practices for serious purposes (Kang, 2015). Hamari and Eranti (2011) have argued that games can be considered as gamified systems to accomplish some common objectives for applications in non-game contexts, making this application appropriate for instructional purposes. Gee argues well-developed gamified systems are expected to generate positive outcomes (Gee, 2007a, 2007b).

In terms of instructors' adoption behaviors, Adukaite et al. (2017) study predictors affecting the adoption of gamification among tourism teachers in South Africa. Their study identified these six factors (e.g., challenge, computer anxiety, curriculum fit, learning opportunities, playfulness, and self-efficacy) predicted their advocacy to accept a gamified application. Particularly, perceived playfulness and curriculum fit have positive and direct impacts on the adoption intention of these teachers, while challenge, computer anxiety, learning opportunities, and self-efficacy have indirect impacts on the same adoption intention. The past studies have pointed to the complexity of successful implementation of gamified pedagogy in the college classroom. This book chapter therefore aims to add to the existing literature by investigation whether gamification will help enhance students' learning experiences and outcomes.

BACKGROUND

The TeachTech Program at the University of Texas at El Paso

This study was based on a grant awarded by *the TeachTech Program* at The University of Texas at El Paso. Similar to many college and universities around the world, The University of Texas at El Paso (henceforth, UTEP) has launched many initiatives to transform traditional higher education pedagogy. Among them are Extended University (EU), an 100% online university that offers an intensive 7-8 weeks program per semester, as well as the *TeachTech Program* sponsored by Information Resources and Planning (henceforth, IRP) (TeachTech Program, n.d. https://admin.utep.edu/Default.aspx?tabid=74699).

The TeachTech Program at UTEP has been designed to answer two questions related to the applications of new instructional technologies in the university classrooms:

Q1: What can emerging instructional technologies do to facilitate integrative and applied learning in the university classroom?
Q2: Which types of instructional technology tools can best support faculty teaching and student success in their learning process?

The TeachTech Program aims to recruit faculty members from all levels (tenured, tenure-track, and adjunct) to work collaboratively with its university technology experts to deploy, develop, evaluate, and implement ground-breaking strategies to incorporate new instructional technologies into their curriculum and pedagogy (TeachTech Program, n.d.). The program gives special consideration to applicants "with little or no experience applying technology to the improvement of teaching and learning" (TeachTech Program, n.d.). According to its selection rubrics, the program particularly selects applicants whose proposals can describe and identify how research will be innovative and how the technology integration can be applied to a flipped classroom across disciplines and institutionally (TeachTech Program, n.d.). Since its launch in 2018, the program has trained over 20 faculty members to incorporate instructional technologies into their classroom. Their projects include gamification in nursing courses, gamification in advertising and communication classes, and virtual reality technology in training interview, among other interesting faculty-developed projects.

The Growing Importance of Instructional Technologies in University Classroom

Universities across the U.S. and around the world have been eagerly embracing instructional technologies. For example, the Center for Teaching and Learning at University of Washington is set up to offer faculty members to develop creative and constructive approaches to integrate technologies into their pedagogy and instructional materials (Center for Teaching and Learning, n.d.). Various instruction technologies are available to teachers who are interested in using a technologized classroom; they include *White Noise*, *Cold Turkey*, *Kahoot*, *Venngage*, *Trello*, *Plickers*, *Nearpod*, *Prezi*, and *Class Dojo* (McQuire, 2016). Other technologies include *Google Apps*, *PowerPoint*, *Canvas*, *Clickers*, *Smartphone*, *Panopto*, etc. (Center for Teaching and Learning, n.d.). Among many instructional technologies, streaming and Internet technologies seem to generate the most impacts among college instructors (Davies, Dean, & Ball, 2013).

The increasing popularity of instructional technologies in the higher educational classroom is attributed to many benefits claimed by their advocates. Saxena (2013) points out the following benefits of incorporating instructional technologies into faculty's pedagogy: 1) allowing faculty members to share resources and ideas online; 2) enabling students to be exposed to technologies and research skills when they are young; 3) allowing both teachers and students to access to a variety of online resources; 4) creating an environment for a technology-enabled flipped classroom; 5) taking advantage of the growing online learning market.

The growing importance of instructional technologies is also related to the changing demographics as more Generation Z students (born between 1996 and 2005) enter the campus (Burroughs, 2016). Some scholars even extend the demographic impacts for Net Generation and Millennials (Lohnez & Kinzer, 2007). Net Generation students are characterized as "digitally literate, connected, multitasking individuals" (Oblinger & Oblingers, cited in Lohnez & Kinzer, 2007, n.p.) The Generation Z cohort is very keen to collaborative learning, particularly through digital platforms (Burroughs, 2016). Generation Z students also prefer course materials to be delivered via mobile, rather than desktop, platforms (Burroughs, 2016). Given the technological preference of many incoming Generation Z, higher education institutions need to reconfigure their infrastructure that supports WiFi, multi-directional casting, and cloud-based content delivery (Burroughs, 2016).

MAIN FOCUS OF THE CHAPTER

Gamifications in Higher Education

Gamification (in education) mainly refers to "an approach to enhancing people's experience of a service or system through incorporating game-like experiences into the service or practice" (Leaning, 2015, p. 159). Gamification is also defined as "the application of game design principles in non-gaming contexts" (Robson, Plangger, Kietzmann, McCarthy, & Pitt, 2015, p. 411). Existing literature has often linked gamification "to motivate students to engage more with the core subject matter that is 'wrapped up' in a gamified activity" (Leaning, 2015, p. 160). In terms of its educational applications, ''gamification'' includes "game-based mechanics, aesthetic, and game thinking to engage people, motivate action, promote learning, and solve problems" (Blair & Mesch, 2013, p. 134). In practice, gamification has been used in the classroom by means of redesigning the traditional grading system to experience points accumulated throughout the class, awarding students with badges, incorporating video games into the curriculum, including competition among students or groups in the grading, etc (Holloway, 2018). To transform a traditional course to its gamified version successfully, Kapp (2012) argues that all teaching activities need to be re-designed to become games, instead of merely including game mechanics in the activities, to be considered a fully gamified course. More specifically, classroom activities that include gamifications in a task or a process usually involve league tables, leader boards, medals, virtual goods, or valueless reward points (Paisley, 2013).

Çakıroglu, Basıbüyük, Güler, and Memis (2017) provide more detailed descriptions of different gamification elements and their actual applications (p. 102). These gamification elements include quest (goal/mission) leaderboard, points, reputation, and real gifts. In terms of incorporating quest (goal/mission) leaderboard into the classroom, Çakıroglu et al. (2017) state that students can be ranked according to their performance of the learning task and be placed accordingly in the leaderboard to be shared on a Facebook or a Blackboard site to encourage participation and enhance motivation. The points system allows students to receive bonus points at the end of each task (such as a Q&A session) when they respond to a question correctly. Their performance will affect their position in the leaderboard. The reputation element will allow the instructor to identify the top performers (or leaders) in the class to transform them to become "instructors" in the class to help other students. The leader(s) in the class will be offered real gift to reward their outstanding performance (Refer to Table 1 below).

Past research on the applications of gamification and gamified activities mainly focus on three areas: 1) The motivational 'affordances' that study how gamified activities provide the subject or the mechanics of the game; 2) Psychological outcomes that study variations in students' feeling about a gamified activity during and after learning from these activities; 3) Behavioral results as a result of using the gamified activity) (Hamari, Koivisto, & Sarsa, 2014). These research areas are closely related to the study of gamification in the educational context. For example, one of the most popular topic, in terms of gamification in education, is to study how gamified pedagogy and activities could enhance student engagement in the classroom to better motivate students (Leaning, 2015; Paisley, 2013). Scholars have also focused on how gamified elements in the curriculum could help increase students' participation in their educational experiences and faculty members' instruction (Kapp, 2012; Leaning, 2015). The above discussion touches on the motivational affordances gamified elements are able to provide to generate students engagement and learning experiences (i.e., psychological outcomes) and their active participation in the learning activities (i.e., behavioral results).

Because a strong emphasis on the utility concerns of integrating gamification into the higher education institute, a growing body of literature has begun to explore and empirically assess the effectiveness of gamification. For example, Fitz-Walter, Tjondronegoro, and Wyeth (2012) examines whether gami-

Table 1. Gamification elements and their applications

Gamification Elements	Use of the Elements
Quest (Goal/Mission)	Related activities after lecturing for retention.
Leaderboard	Students were ranked according to their performance in the activities. The top five were placed on the leader board, and the leader board was then shared on a Facebook group for participation and motivation.
	Another list in addition to the top give was also presented on the Facebook group. This list included in the performance of the rest of the top 5 students, whether their performance had increased or decreased from previous works.
Points	Two extra points were assigned to those students who gave the correct answers to the questions at the end of the activities or during the presentation period of the lessons. This may be a chance for students who could not take place in leader board.
Reputation	After each activity, the top three leaders of the week (according to the best performance recorded on the activity evaluation rubrics) were assigned as "instructors" (namely, assistants to the course instructor) for the following week. This may provide a professional experience and also peer learning.
Real Gifts	The leader for the week was awarded with small gifts.

Source: Adapted from Çakıroglu, Basıbüyük, Güler, & Memis (2017), p. 102

fication will engage students in non-curricular activities. Decker and Lawley (2013) study is designed to examine whether gamification ultimately promotes students' behavioral changes in terms of their participation in peer tutoring sessions. Their study examines whether gamification affects learning in large classroom environments, participation rates, and positive attitudes toward these instructional technologies (Decker & Lawley, 2013).

To understand the effects of gamifications, Robson et al. (2015) propose the gamification principles and particularly focus on three aspects of gamification: mechanics, dynamics, and emotions (MDE) adapted from Hunicke, LeBlanc, and Zubek (2004) in the game design literature. The mechanics component refers to the decision made by the designer to consider the setting, the rules, the context, and the types of interactions, while the dynamics dimension refers to different behaviors as a result of using gamified elements (Robson et al., 2015). The emotion aspect refers to the "mental affective states and reactions evoked" after interacting with gamified elements (Robson et al., 2015, p. 416). These three MDE is common among gamified learning applications which, according to recent literature, has been found to increase student activity and subsequently improve learning outcomes in the higher education setting (Barata, Gama, Jorge, & Gonçalves, 2017). Barata et al.'s (2017) longitudinal study of three-year data and cluster analyzed students' learning experiences. Their study confirms the effects of gamifications in a positive manner. Among many pertinent variables related to the assessment of gamification effects, student engagement is one of the most discussed variables. Past literature has confirmed that increased student engagement often leads to the improvement of academic performance (Fitzgerald, Bruns, Sonka, Furco, & Swanson, 2012).

On the basis of the previous literature, this study aims to answer the following three questions:

RQ1: Will the level of gamification affect students' engagement with the course?
RQ2: Will the level of gamification affect students' learning experiences with the course?
RQ3: Will the level of gamification affect students' learning outcomes with the course?

Research Methods

This study employed a quasi-experimental design that is made of naturally formed classes taught by one of the authors during Spring 2018. This is an appropriate research method when the researchers conduct their study using existing classes (Davies et al., 2013). All three classes are technology-based with one-hour online and 2-hour face-to-face class meeting, using a flipped classroom approach explained in Davies et al. (2013). Gamified elements integrated into the instructor's pedagogy include *Goal/Task Completion* and *Point Accumulation* as discussed in the previous literature. Students from three classes were recruited to take part in the study, including the NO gamified course as the contrast group [COMM. 3339 (N=19 students)], [the HIGH gamified course as the experimental group: COMM. 2330: (N=12 students)], and [LOW gamified course as the control group: COMM. 3338 (N=13 students)]. Data are later analyzed using the cross-class and cross-subject approach, similar to Davies et al. (2013).

Independent variable of the study is the level of gamification that was operationalized at three levels (high, low, and no) (following Robson et al.,'s gamifications design principles, 2015 and Kang, 2015, H.I.R.E. gamification metrics as manipulation check). Manipulation check were done by a group of expert panelists to ensure the manipulation and implementation of gamification is successful.

The dependent variables were 1) students' engagement (adapted from Eryılmaz, 2014); 2) students' learning experiences (Domínguez, Saenz-de-Navarrete, de-Marcos, Fernández-Sanz, Pagés, & Martínez-

Herráiz, 2013); 3) students' learning outcomes (measured by academic scores, Hanus & Fox, 2015). Intervening variables include 1) past experiences with Blackboard or online teaching platforms (5-item Domínguez et al., 2013); 2) attitudes toward game-based learning (3-item Likert statements, from Landers & Armstrong, 2017); 3) intrinsic motivation (22-item Likert statements, from Hanus & Fox, 2015; Ryan, Koestner, & Deci, 1991); and demographic questions such as gender.

Student engagement variable is measured by the following 5-point Likert statements: *I often spend a lot of my free time looking for more information on topics discussed in an online class; When I'm reading, I try to understand the meaning of what the author wants me transmit; I review my notes regularly, even if a test is not coming up; I have done well in my studies if the class is taught online; I know how to prepare myself for the exams; I can act in class the way my teacher wants me to; What I'm learning in my online classes will be important in my future; After finishing my schoolwork, I check it over to see if it's correct; When I do schoolwork I check to see whether I understand what I'm doing; When I do well in school it's because I work hard.*

Learning experience variable is measured by the following 5-point Likert statements: *Online course contents are often presented more effectively (than their offline counterparts); I learned more about the course topic (than their offline counterparts); I enjoyed learning online; Using an online technology was easy for me; Online practical activities are often useful; There is sufficient time to complete the online exercises (than their offline counterparts); My level of involvement with online courses is usually high; I usually learn more about the course contents online; Online learning experience is usually worthwhile.*

Attitudes toward the gamified learning system is measured by the following 5-point Likert statements: *If I had the choice, I would choose to complete my education in which games were used; If I had to vote, I would vote in favor of using games in college classrooms; I am enthusiastic about using games in college classrooms.*

Students' intrinsic motivation is measured by a list of 5-point Likert statements. Some examples include: *I enjoy learning online very much; While I am learning online, I am thinking about how much I enjoy it; After learning online for a while, I feel pretty competent; I put a lot of effort into online learning; It is important to me to learn well online; I learn well online, compared to other students, etc.*

For example, experiences with instructional technologies are measured by questions such as

Have you used any online learning technologies (i.e., Blackboard) before?: ___ Yes ___ No; *In general, how many hours per week do you use these online learning technologies?* ____ Hour(s) ___ Minutes; or *How many months have you used these online learning technologies?* ___ Months.

Data were collected in the following periods through the semester. Students are required to complete the survey before they can continue the class: 1) 1st week: Baseline data on the first day of the class; 2) 7th week: After Exam 1; 3) 13th week: After Exam 2; and 4) 16th week: After the final project presentation. Composite scores are calculated for later analyses.

Findings

The small sample size does not allow the researcher to conduct inferential statistical procedures.

The following analyzes rely on the comparison of group means to examine if the levels of gamification could affect students' engagement with the course (RQ1), learning experiences with the course (RQ2), and learning outcomes with the course (RQ3).

The following preliminary findings rely on the comparison of group means to examine if the levels of gamification could affect students' engagement with the course (RQ1), learning experiences with the course (RQ2), and learning outcomes with the course (RQ3). Among four indices to measure the success of gamification, 3 out of 4 show the positive gamification effects with a highly-gamified class leads to higher level of student engagement than no or lowly gamified classes (3.62> 3.54>3.32 as in Mean $_{COMM.2330}$> Mean $_{COMM.3338}$ >Mean $_{COMM.3339}$). The same positive gamification effect can be found in students' overall learning experience (3.63> 3.58>3.40 as in Mean $_{COMM.2330}$> Mean $_{COMM.3338}$ >Mean $_{COMM.3339}$). While attitudes toward gamified learning systems did not show differences, but motivation to use these technologies similarly shows positive gamification results (3.67> 3.58>3.37 as in Mean $_{COMM.2330}$> Mean $_{COMM.3338}$ >Mean $_{COMM.3339}$). Using students' GPA (total points accumulated as to assess their learning outcomes), highly-gamified class results in better students' learning outcomes as measured by their grades at different data collection points. Gamified instructions in an online context also lead to better learning outcomes (measured by post-Exam 1, -Exam 2, and end-of-the-semester). In conclusion, gamified instructions in an online context seem to help with students' engagement and overall learning experiences. Among four indices to measure the success of gamification, 3 out of 4 show the positive gamification effects below (Refer to Table 2 below).

To demonstrate the gamification effects on students' learning outcomes as measured by their GPA (total points accumulated as to assess their learning outcomes), we collected data at the 7th, 13th, and 16th week after Exam 1 (7th week), Exam 2 (13th week), and final project presentation (16th week). As shown in Table 3 below, highly-gamified class results in better students' learning outcomes as measured by their grades (Mean $_{COMM.2330}$> Mean $_{COMM.3338}$> Mean $_{COMM.3339}$).

Table 2. Results from quasi-experiment

		N	Mean	S.D.
Group A Index (Engagement With Online Learning Technologies) (Alpha=0.93)	COMM3338 (Low Gamified)	23	3.54	.42
	COMM2330 (High Gamified)	25	3.64	.56
	COMM3339 (No Gamified)	48	3.32	.80
Group B Index (Overall Learning Experience) (Alpha=0.94)	COMM3338 (Low Gamified)	23	3.58	.63
	COMM2330 (High Gamified)	25	3.63	.58
	COMM3339 (No Gamified)	48	3.40	.74
Group C Index (Attitudes Toward Gamified Learning Systems) (Alpha=0.81)	COMM3338 (Low Gamified)	23	3.28	.70
	COMM2330 (High Gamified)	25	3.21	.81
	COMM3339 (No Gamified)	48	3.30	.71
Group D Index (Motivation To Use Online Learning Technologies) (Alpha=0.94)	COMM3338 (Low Gamified)	23	3.58	.49
	COMM2330 (High Gamified)	25	3.67	.57
	COMM3339 (No Gamified)	48	3.37	.68

Source: The Authors

Table 3. Students' academic performance (measured by total points accumulated) at three different data collection points

		N	Mean	S.D.
7th Week Data Collection Point (After Exam 1)	COMM3338 (Low Gamified)	25	501.94	35.94
	COMM2330 (High Gamified)	25	540.00	.00
	COMM3339 (No Gamified)	50	449.63	.00
13th Week Data Collection Point (After Exam 2)	COMM3338 (Low Gamified)	26	785.12	71.64
	COMM2330 (High Gamified)	25	861.00	.00
	COMM3339 (No Gamified)	50	730.00	.00
16th Week Data Collection Point (After Final Project Presentation)	COMM3338 (Low Gamified)	26	961.18	18.51
	COMM2330 (High Gamified)	25	980.79	.00
	COMM3339 (No Gamified)	50	965.79	.00

Source: The Authors

RECOMMENDATIONS, LIMITATIONS, AND FUTURE DIRECTIONS

The overall positive effects of gamification on students' engagement with online learning technologies, overall learning experiences, attitudes toward gamified learning systems, motivation to use online technologies, and students' GPA's confirm the efficiency of integrating gamified elements into instructional materials in the higher education classroom. As Leaning (2015) points out, the process of gamifying teaching materials allows college instructors to add "a different form of experience to an activity….. The new layer of meaning provides a greater experience for the user and encourages participation with the transformed activity" (p. 159). In the age of information overload, particularly among Generation Z and Net Generation college students, wrapping course materials up with gamified activities contributes to the engagement of students in the course contents by increasing students' attention level, motivation, and participation (Leaning, 2015).

Empirical evidence abounds in establishing the relationship between gamification and students' learning outcomes (Domínguez et al., 2013; Landers & Armstrong, 2017). For example, Landers and Armstrong (2017) uses an experiment to assign students to read scenarios about gamified instruction or traditional PowerPoint method. Results find that students expect greater values in the gamified group. Their study also finds that previous video game experience and attitudes toward game-based learning moderate the above relationships as demonstrated by students with more game experience and favorable attitudes (toward game-based learning) generate better learning outcomes than students with few experience and less favorable attitudes (Landers & Armstrong, 2017). Landers and Armstrong's (2017) study confirms our speculations that, for a gamified learning system, to be effective in the university classroom, factors such as students' demographics, and previous exposure to technologies related to digital games or instructional technologies are crucial.

As expected, gamification has a positive effect on four measures used to assess its usefulness (such as students' engagement with online learning technologies, overall learning experiences, attitudes toward gamified learning systems, motivation to use online technologies). In the literature, gamified elements such as leaderboards or point system, function as a good motivator to encourage students to learn (Domínguez et al., 2013). Hanus and Fox (2015) reports that virtual badge for acknowledge students' accomplishment can enhance students' engagement and promote their academic performance. Furthermore, students' academic performance as measured by their total points accumulated in three data collection point also confirms the positive effects of gamification on their learning outcomes (Attali & Arieli-Attali, 2015). Observable impacts on students' attitudes, behaviors, and overall learning experiences also concur with what Leaning (2015) has reported.

FUTURE RESEARCH DIRECTIONS

A thorough study of user experience in gamified pedagogy will be an important component of gamification research and will have significant theoretical and methodological implications for both researchers and practitioners interested in better incorporating gamified elements in their pedagogy. First, the exploration of user experience will obtain new data that can be analyzed in either qualitative or quantitative gamification research. Despite the breadth of gamification research and application as an interdisciplinary endeavor, the extant foci of conventional approaches seem mostly on the process of the causes and outcomes of gamifications in a variety of application contexts (Hamari et al., 2014). Previous gamification research in the education context has been derived from theories and approaches from psychology to understand the process and outcome of gamification (See Hamari et al., 2014 for literature review). The chapter focuses on its application in the higher education context as an important part of gamification because a surge of interests in incorporating instructional technologies in the university classroom and an increase number of online courses and degree around the world. For example, Harvard University is in the process of phasing out its conventional M.B.A. programs as more business students are interested in the online curriculum. As such, findings from this study that confirm the benefit of a gamified class may help university administrators and teachers to assess what gamification can offer to create a more meaningful and effective learning environment. Therefore, this book chapter aims to generate more discussions to explore how gamification can be instrumental to emerging pedagogical approaches (such as flipped classroom) (Davies et al., 2013).

The emergence of many instructional and digital game technologies will open up new avenues of research for gamification researchers and scholars in designing their game-based pedagogies. For example, alternate reality games (ARG) create a new gaming space to allow students to learn collectively and to focus on new media literacy skills (Chess & Booth, 2014). Another example is that context-based learning (CBL) through digital-physical games amply integrates users' cultural elements with game-based pedagogies to generate better students' learning experiences (Kwon, Kim, & Woo, 2015).

Another potential area of the gamification study in the higher education context is to examine the collaborative process by which students can work together as a team to complete a task in the gamified learning curriculum. Effective gamified learning system are expected to accomplish the same outcome in terms of modifying students' attitude, knowledge, purchase intention, and behavior (Burke, 2013). Variables that may affect the collaborative process in a gamified platform should be carefully studied to better assess whether a sense of collaboration could generate more positive learning experiences.

Extant research on the gamification in the university classroom mainly focuses on its effects on students' learning experiences and outcomes. Gamification researchers and practitioners will benefit from the study of determinants that affect instructors' adoption of instructional technologies in their courses

(Adukaite et al., 2017; Baran, Correia, & Thompson, 2011; Gonzalez, 2008). How do college instructors feel about the implementation of these emerging pedagogical platforms will be essential to the success or failure of integrating gamification into their teaching to create a meaningful learning experience for their students. The importance of providing faculty members a support system within the university will complement the positive effects of increased faculty technology literacy (Baran et al., 2011). As discussed earlier, many universities have created centers and grants to assist faculty's adoption of these instructional technologies, which may offer good examples of feasible solutions to address faculty's resistance and lack of motivation, due to concerns about their own research productivity (Meyer, 2012).

CONCLUSION

In conclusion, Gamification as an emerging area of research and applications faces similar theoretical and methodological challenges as seen in digital game research (Kang, 2015). For example, Aarseth (2003) is concerned with this lack of theories and methods in game research. Similarly, both researchers and practitioners that are interested in integrating gamification into higher education classroom face the same questions that past digital game researchers have to address. Therefore, the objectives of this book chapter provide a preliminary attempt to assess quantitatively to evaluate the implementation gamification into the university classrooms to investigate better this important area of gamification research in education.

Practical Implications

Gamification will be instrumental to various types of pedagogical innovations currently emerging in the higher education context. One of the promising applications that has been mentioned in the literature is the integration of gamification into a flipped classroom (Davies et al., 2013). A gamified instruction in a flipped class can turn less engaging teaching materials into more vivid learning experiences for students, due to the stimulation and competition in a gamified learning context (Davies et al., 2013). Furthermore, a gamified flipped classroom pedagogy also has the advantage of personalize the learning processes and materials to differentiate the instructional method from conventional ones (Davies et al., 2013). The positive effects on students' learning experiences and outcomes in a hybrid flipped classroom as demonstrated in this study lent support to the use of gamifications in the university classroom.

Limitations

Given the small sample size in each class, this quantitative study is limited by statistically supported inferential evidence to demonstrate the efficacy of the gamified approach over conventional non-gamified pedagogy. As a result, caution should be taken in generalizing and interpreting the findings. Furthermore, data were collected at the 1st, 7th, and 13th week of a regular 16th week semester commonly found among most higher education institutes in North America. Students taken these three classes belong to freshmen, sophomores, juniors, or seniors. The findings reported in this chapter might not be applicable to graduate and professional courses. Students' demographics might influence the effectiveness of gamifications on their learning outcomes and experiences and might be analyzed as intervening variables in the future. Lastly, this study only have two gamified elements integrated into the courses and may limit the full potential of gamification in the university classroom. Furthermore, different types of gamified elements may have distinctive effects that ultimately interact with course contents that these elements are embedded. Future research may benefit both gamification researchers and practitioners if different gamified elements can be studied as an independent variable.

REFERENCES

Aarseth, E. J. (1997). *Cybertext: Perspectives on Ergodic Literature.* Baltimore, MD: Johns Hopkins UP.

Adukaite, A., & Zyl, I. (2017). Teacher perceptions on the use of digital gamified learning in tourism education: The case of South African secondary schools. *Computers & Education, 111*, 172–190. doi:10.1016/j.compedu.2017.04.008

Baran, E., Correia, A.-P., & Thompson, A. (2011, November). Transforming online teaching practice: Critical analysis of the literature on the roles and competencies of online teachers. *Distance Education, 32*(3), 421–439. doi:10.1080/01587919.2011.610293

Barata, G., Gama, S., Jorge, J., & Gonçalves, D. (2017, June). Studying student differentiation in gamified education: A long-term study. *Computers in Human Behavior, 71*, 550–585. doi:10.1016/j.chb.2016.08.049

Boellstorff, T., Nardi, B., Pearce, C., & Taylor, T. L. (2012). *Ethnography and virtual worlds: A handbook of method.* Princeton, NJ: Princeton University Press. doi:10.2307/j.cttq9s20

Burke, B. (2013, January 21). *The Gamification of Business.* Retrieved from http://www.forbes.com/sites/gartnergroup/2013/2001/2021/the-gamification-of-business/

Burroughs, A. (2019, June 11). UBTech 2019: Gen Z learners will push the limits of mobile-first, digital-first learning. *EdTech.* Retrieved on June 11, 2019 from https://edtechmagazine.com/higher/article/2019/2006/ubtech-2019-gen-z-learners-will-push-

Çakıroglu, Ü., Basıbüyük, B., Güler, M., Atabay, M., & Yılmaz Memiş, B. (2017). Gamifying an ICT course: Influences on engagement and academic performance. *Computers in Human Behavior, 69*, 98–107. doi:10.1016/j.chb.2016.12.018

Chang, B.-H., Lee, S.-E., & Kim, B.-S. (2006, April). Exploring factors affecting the adoption and continuance of online games among college students in South Korea: Integrating uses and gratification and diffusion of innovation approaches. *New Media & Society, 8*(2), 295–319. doi:10.1177/1461444806059888

Chess, S., & Booth, P. (2014). Lessons down a rabbit hole: Alternate reality gaming in the classroom. *New Media & Society, 16*(6), 1002–1017. doi:10.1177/1461444813497554

Chuang, Y.-C. (2006). Massively multiplayer online role-playing game-induced seizures: A neglected health problem in internet addiction. *Cyberpsychology & Behavior, 9*(4), 451–456. doi:10.1089/cpb.2006.9.451 PMID:16901249

Dale, S. (2014, June). Gamification: Making work fun, or making fun of work? *Business Information Review, 31*(2), 80–90. doi:10.1177/0266382114538350

Davies, R. S., Dean, D. L., & Ball, N. (2013, August). Flipping the classroom and instructional technology integration in a college-level information systems spreadsheet course. *Educational Technology Research and Development, 61*(4), 563–580. doi:10.100711423-013-9305-6

de-Marcos, L., Domínguez, A., Saenz-de-Navarrete, J., & Pagés, C. (2014). An empirical study comparing gamification and social networking on e-learning. *Computers & Education, 75*, 82–91. doi:10.1016/j.compedu.2014.01.012

Decker, A., & Lawley, E. L. (2013). Life's a game and the game of life: how making a game out of it can change student behavior. In *Proceeding of the 44th ACM Technical Symposium on Computer Science Education.* Denver, CO: ACM. 10.1145/2445196.2445269

Deterding, S., Dixon, D., Khaled, R., & Nacke, L. (2011b). *From game design elements to gamefulness: Defining "gamification."* Paper presented at the MindTrek '11, Tampere, Finland. Retrieved November 27, 2014 from https://www.cs.auckland.ac.nz/courses/compsci747s2c/lectures/paul/definition-deterding.pdf

Deterding, S., Sicart, M., Nacke, L., O'Hara, K., & Dixon, D. (2011a). *Gamification: Using game design elements in non-gaming contexts.* Paper presented at the CHI 2011, Vancouver, BC, Canada. Retrieved November 25, 2014 from http://gamification-research.org/wp-content/uploads/2011/04/01-Deterding-Sicart-Nacke-OHara-Dixon.pdf

Domínguez, A., Saenz-de-Navarrete, J., De-Marcos, L., Fernández-Sanz, L., Pagés, C., & Martínez-Herráiz, J. J. (2013). Gamifying learning experiences: Practical implications and outcomes. *Computers & Education, 63*, 380–392. doi:10.1016/j.compedu.2012.12.020

Entertainment Software Association. (2019). *2019 Essential Facts About the Computer and Video Game Industry.* Retrieved on June 11, 2019 from https://www.theesa.com/wp-content/uploads/2019/2005/2019-Essential-Facts-About-the-Computer-and-Video-Game-Industry.pdf

Ermi, L., & Mäyrä, F. (2005). *Fundamental components of the gameplay experience: Analyzing immersion.* Paper presented at the DiGRA 2005 Conference: Changing View-Worldds in Play, Vancouver, Canada.

Fitz-Walter, Z., Tjondronegoro, D., & Wyeth, P. (2012). A gamified mobile application for engaging new students at university orientation. In *Proceedings of the 24th Australian Computer Human Interaction Conference* (pp. 138-141). Melbourne, Australia: ACM. 10.1145/2414536.2414560

Fitzgerald, H. E., Bruns, K., Sonka, S. T., Furco, A., & Swanson, L. (2012). The centrality of engagement in higher education. *Journal of Higher Education Outreach & Engagement, 16*(2), 7–28.

Gee, J. P. (2004). *What video games have to teach us about learning and literacy.* New York, NY: Palgrave Macmillan.

Gee, J. P. (2007a). What video games have to teach us about learning and literacy (Rev. and updated ed.). New York: Palgrave Macmillan.

Gee, J. P. (2007b). *Good video games + good learning: Collected essays on video games, learning and literacy.* New York: Peter Lang. doi:10.3726/978-1-4539-1162-4

Goldstein, J. (2005). Violent video games. In J. Raessens & J. Goldstein (Eds.), Handbook of computer game studies (pp. 341-357). Cambridge, MA: The MIT Press.

Gonzalez, C. (2009). Conceptions of, and approaches to, teaching online: A study of lecturers teaching postgraduate distance courses. *Higher Education*, *57*(3), 299–314. doi:10.100710734-008-9145-1

Gunter, B. (2005). Psychological effects of video games. In J. Raessens & J. Goldstein (Eds.), Handbook of computer game studies (pp. 145-160). Cambridge, MA: The MIT Press.

Hamari, J., & Eranti, V. (2011). Framework for designing and evaluating game achievements. *Proceedings of DiGRA 2011 Conference: Think Design Play*. Retrieved November 27, 2014 from http://www.quilageo.com/wp-content/uploads/2013/07/Framework-for-Designing-Eval-11307.59151.pdf

Hamari, J., Koivisto, J., & Sarsa, H. (2014). *Does gamification work? A literature review of empirical studies on gamification*. Paper presented at The 47th Hawaii International Conference on System Sciences. 10.1109/HICSS.2014.377

Hanus, M. D., & Fox, J. (2015). Assessing the effects of gamification in the classroom: A longitudinal study on motivation, satisfaction, effort, and grades. *Computers & Education*, *80*, 152–161. doi:10.1016/j.compedu.2014.08.019

Holloway, S. (2018, May 2). Gamification in Education: 4 Ways To Bring Games To Your Classroom. *Top Hat Blog*. Retrieved on June 12, 2019 from https://tophat.com/blog/gamification-education-class/

Johnson, T. (2014, April). *Gamification and User Engagement in E-learning and Documentation*. Academic Press.

Kang, Y. W. (2015, August). Development of the "Hybrid Interactive Rhetorical Engagement" (H.I.R.E.) Scale: Implications for Digital Gamification Research. In H. Gangadharbatla & D. Z. Davis (Eds.), *Emerging Research and Trends in Gamification* (pp. 72–92). Hershey, PA: IGI Global.

Kapp, K. M. (2012). *The Gamification of Learning and Instruction: Game-based Methods and Strategies for Training and Education*. New York: Wiley.

Kerr, A. (2006). *The business and culture of digital games: Gamework/gameplay*. London, UK: Sage Publications.

Kiousis, S. (2002). Interactivity: A concept explication. *New Media & Society*, *4*(3), 355–383. doi:10.1177/146144480200400303

Korhonen, H., Montola, M., & Arrasvuori, J. (2009). *Understanding playful user experience through digital games*. Paper presented at the International Conference on Designing Pleasurable of Products and Interface, Compiegne University of Technology. Compiegne, France.

Kwon, C., Kim, Y., & Woo, T. (2015). Digital-physical reality game: Mapping of physical space with fantasy in context-based learning games. *Games and Culture*, 1–32.

Landers, R. N., & Armstrong, M. B. (2017). Enhancing instructional outcomes with gamification: An empirical test of the Technology-Enhanced Training Effectiveness Model. *Computers in Human Behavior*, *71*, 499–507. doi:10.1016/j.chb.2015.07.031

Landers, R. N., & Callan, R. C. (2012). Training evaluation in virtual worlds: Development of a model. *Journal of Virtual Worlds Research*, *5*(3), 1–20. doi:10.4101/jvwr.v5i3.6335

Leaning, M. (2015). A study of the use of games and gamification to enhance student engagement, experience and achievement on a theory-based course of an undergraduate media degree. *Journal of Media Practice*, *16*(2), 155–170. doi:10.1080/14682753.2015.1041807

Lohnes, S., & Kinzer, C. (2007). Questioning assumptions about students' expectations for technology in college classrooms. *Innovate (North Miami Beach, Fla.)*, *3*(5). Retrieved from http://www.innovateonline.info/index.php?view=article&id=2431

McGuire, S. (2016, August 5). 9 technology tools to engage students in the classroom. *TeachThrough: We Grow Teachers*. Retrieved on June 11, 2019 from https://www.teachthought.com/technology/2019-technology-tools-engage-students-classroom/

Meyer, K. A. (2012). The influence of online teaching on faculty productivity. *Innovative Higher Education*, *37*(1), 37–52. doi:10.100710755-011-9183-y

Morschheuser, B., Hassan, L., Werder, K., & Hamari, J. (2018, March). How to design gamification? A method for engineering gamified software. *Information and Software Technology*, *95*, 217–239. doi:10.1016/j.infsof.2017.10.015

Morschheuser, B. S., Rivera-Pelayo, V., Mazarakis, A., & Zacharias, V. (2014). Interaction and reflection with quantified self and gamification: An experimental study. *Journal of Literacy and Technology*, *15*(2), 136–156.

Nardi, B. (2010). *My life as a night elf priest: An anthropological account of World of Warcraft*. Ann Arbor, MI: University of Michigan Press.

O'Brien, H. L., & Toms, E. G. (2007). What is user engagement? A conceptual framework for defining user engagement with technology. *Journal of the American Society for Information Science and Technology*, *59*(6), 938–955. doi:10.1002/asi.20801

Paisley, V. (2013). *Gamification of tertiary courses: An exploratory study of learning and engagement*. Paper presented at the Electric Dreams 30th Asclite Conference, Sydney, Australia.

Prensky, M. (2005). Computer games and learning: Digital game-based learning. In J. Raessens & J. Goldstein (Eds.), Handbook of computer game studies (pp. 97-122). Cambridge, MA: The MIT Press.

Robson, K., Plangger, K., Kietzmann, J. H., McCarthy, I., & Pitt, L. (2015). Is it all a game? Understanding the principles of gamification. *Business Horizons*, *58*(4), 411–420. doi:10.1016/j.bushor.2015.03.006

Ryan, M.-L. (1999). Immersion vs. interactivity: Virtual reality and literary theory. *SubStance*, *28*(2), 110–137. doi:10.1353ub.1999.0015

Ryan, R. M., Koestner, R., & Deci, E. L. (1991). Varied forms of persistence: When free-choice behavior is not intrinsically motivated. *Motivation and Emotion*, *15*(3), 185–205. doi:10.1007/BF00995170

Saxena, S. (2013, October 8). How important is use of technology in education. *EdTech Review*. Retrieved on June 11, 2019 from http://edtechreview.in/news/2681-technology-in-education

Steinkuehler, C. (2006, July). The mangle of play. *Games and Culture*, *1*(3), 199–213. doi:10.1177/1555412006290440

Steinkuehler, C. A., & Williams, D. (2006). Where everybody knows your (screen) name: Online games as "third place". *Journal of Computer-Mediated Communication, 11*(4), 885–909. doi:10.1111/j.1083-6101.2006.00300.x

Swallow, E. (2012, September 18). Can gamification make customer support fun? *Forbes*. Retrieved from http://www.forbes.com/fdc/welcome_mjx.shtml

Zagal, J., Chan, S. S., & Zhang, J. (2011). Measuring flow experience of computer game players. *AMCIS 2010 Proceedings*. Retrieved from http://aisel.aisnet.org/amcis2010/137

ADDITIONAL READING

Bogost, I. (2007, July). *Persuasive games: The expressive power of videogames*. Cambridge, M.A.: MIT Press. Cai, X. (2005, February). An experimental examination of the computer's time displacement effects. *New Media & Society, 7*(1), 8–21.

Bolter, J. D., & Grusin, R. (2000). Remediation: Understanding new media. Cambridge, M.A.: The MIT Press.

Burke, B. (2013, January 21). The gamification of business. *Forbes.com*, Retrieved November 27, 2014 from http://www.forbes.com/sites/gartnergroup/2013/01/21/the-gamification-of-business/

Calvert, S. L. (2005). Cognitive effects of video games. In J. Raessens & J. Goldstein (Eds.), Handbook of computer game studies (pp. 125-131). Cambridge, M.A.: The MIT Press.

Calvillo-Gámez, E. H., Cairns, P., & Cox, A. L. (2009, September). Assessing the core elements of the gaming experience. Retrieved November 27, 2014 from http://www.eduardocalvillogamez.info/2009/09/assessing-core-elements-of-gaming.html

Calvillo-Gámez, E. H., Cairns, P., & Cox, A. L. (2011). Assessing the core elements of the gaming experience. In R. Bernhaupt (Ed.), *Evaluating user experience in games: Concepts and methods* (pp. 41–71). London: Springer.

Csikszentmihalyi, M. (1990). *Flow: The psychology of optimal experience*. New York, N.Y.: Harper.

Donath, J. (1999). Identity and deception in the virtual community. In M. Smith & P. Kollack (Eds.), *pp*. London: Routledge; http://smg.media.mit.edu/people/judith/Identity/IdentityDeception.html

Elverdam, C., & Aarseth, E. (2007, January). Game classification and game design: Construction through critical analysis. *Games and Culture, 2*(1), 3–22. doi:10.1177/1555412006286892

Friedman, T. (1995). Making sense of software: Computer games and interactive textuality. In S. Jones (Ed.), Cybersociety: Computer-mediated communication and community. Thousand Oaks, C.A.: Sage.

Fuller, M., & Jenkins, H. (1995). Nintendo and new world travel writing: A dialogue. In Jones, S. (Ed.), Cybersociety: Computer-mediated communication and community (pp. 73-89). Thousand Oaks, C.A.: Sage.

Helmes, R. M., & Pellegrini, A. D. (2005). Children's social behavior during video game play. In Raessens, J., & Goldstein, J. (Eds.), Handbook of Computer Game Studies (pp. 133-144). Cambridge, M.A.: The MIT Press.

Herz, J. C. (1997). Joystick nation: How video game ate our quarters, won our hearts, and rewired our minds. Boston, M.A.: Little, Brown.

Hussan, Z., & Griffiths, M. D. (2008). Gender swapping and socializing in cyberspace: An exploratory study. *Cyberpsychology & Behavior, 11*(1), 47–53. doi:10.1089/cpb.2007.0020 PMID:18275312

Jansz, J., & Martens, L. (2005, June). Gaming at a LAN event: The social context of playing video games. *New Media & Society, 7*(3), 333–355. doi:10.1177/1461444805052280

Kafai, Y. B. (1998). Video game designs by girls and boys: Variability and consistency of gender differences. In J. Cassell & H. Jenkins (Eds.), From Barbie to Mortal Combat: Gender and computer games. Cambridge, M.A.: MIT Press.

Klabbers, J. H. G. (2003, November 4-6). *The gaming landscape: A taxonomy for classifying games and simulations.* Paper presented at the LEVEL UP: Digital Games Research Conference, University of Utrecht, The Netherlands.

McBirney, K. (2004, December). Nested selves, networked communities: A case study of diablo ii: Lord of destruction as an agent of cultural change. *Journal of American Culture, 4*(4), 415–421. doi:10.1111/j.1542-734X.2004.00146.x

Miklaucic, S. (2001). Virtual real(i)ty: Simcity and the production of urban cyberspace, Association of Internet Researchers. Minneapolis, M.N.

Mikula, M. (2003, March). Gender and videogames: The political valency of Lara Croft. *Continuum (Perth), 17*(1), 79–87. doi:10.1080/1030431022000049038

Nielsen, R. P. (1996). *The politics of ethics: Methods for acting, learning, and sometimes fighting with others in addressing ethics problems in organizational life.* New York: Oxford University Press.

Okorafor, N., & Davenport, L. (2001, August). Virtual women: Replacing the real, *The Association for Education in Journalism and Mass Communication.* Washington, D.C.

Peña, J., & Hancock, J. T. (2006, February). An analysis of socio-emotional and task communication in online multimedia video games. *Communication Research, 33*(1), 92–109. doi:10.1177/0093650205283103

Reeves, B., & Read, J. L. (2009). Total engagement: Using games and virtual worlds to change the way people work and businesses compete. Cambridge, M.A.: Harvard Business Press.

Richard, B., & Zaremba, J. (2005). Gaming with grrls: Looking for sheroes in computer games. In J. Raessens & J. Goldstein (Eds.), Handbook of computer game studies (pp. 283-300). Cambridge, M.A.: The MIT Press.

Salen, K., & Zimmerman, E. (2005). Game design and meaningful play. In J. Raessens & J. Goldstein (Eds.), Handbook of computer game studies (pp. 59-79). Cambridge, M.A.: The MIT Press.

Stanley, R. (2014, March 24). Top 25 best examples of gamification in business, *ClickPedia: A ClickSoftware Blog*. Retrieved November 28, 2014 from http://blogs.clicksoftware.com/clickipedia/top-25-best-examples-of-gamification-in-business/

Steinkuehler, C. A., & Williams, D. (2006). Where everybody knows your (screen) name: Online games as "third place". *Journal of Computer-Mediated Communication, 11*(4), 885–909. doi:10.1111/j.1083-6101.2006.00300.x

Subrahmanyam, K., & Greenfield, P. M. (1998). Computer games for girls: What makes them play. In J. Cassell & H. Jenkins (Eds.), From barbie to mrotal kombat: Gender and computer games (pp.?-?). Cambridge, M.A.: The M.I.T. Press.

Turkle, S. (1984). *The second self: Computers and the human spirit*. New York, N.Y.: Simon and Schuster.

Vorderer, P., & Bryant, J. (2006). *Playing video games: Motives, responses, and consequences*. Mahwah, N.J.: Lawrence Erlbaum Associates.

Williams, D. (2005, December). Bridging the methodological divide in game research. *Simulation & Gaming, 36*(4), 1–17. doi:10.1177/1046878105282275

Williams, D., Caplan, S., & Xiong, L. (2005). Can you hear me now? The impact of voice in an online gaming community. *Human Communication Research, 33*(4), 427–449. doi:10.1111/j.1468-2958.2007.00306.x

Yates, S. J., & Littleton, K. (1999, December). Understanding computer game cultures: A situated approach. *Information Communication and Society, 2*(4), 566–583. doi:10.1080/136911899359556

Yee, N. (2006, January). The labor of fun: How video games blur the boundaries of work and play. *Games and Culture, 1*(1), 68–71. doi:10.1177/1555412005281819

KEY TERMS AND DEFINITIONS

EdTech: A term that is used to refer to different types of instructional technologies (such as the internet, streaming technologies, cloud storage, digital games, etc.).

Engagement: A popular term commonly found in the discussion of how users may experience with of information-communication technology (ICT). In the context of gamification in education, this term refers to a psychological state that gamers and user experience with digital game and other gamified systems and applications that explain the reason and the result that gamers and users want to interact with them to demonstrate a connection to deep and meaning learning. In the context of digital games, the level of engagement that gamers can experience in these environments cannot be understated because it constitutes an important part of their gamification.

Flipped Classroom: A term that recently gains prominence because of new innovations in instruction technologies to allow the instructor to offer online resources and to gamify a class to allow students to learn actively. Its application implies that learning will go beyond the traditional classroom and students can learn at their own pace, before each face-to-face lecture, and to personalize their own learning experiences.

Gamification: Gamification is defined as the application of game design principles and the inclusion of game elements in non-gaming contexts. From the user experience (UX) perspective, this term is also considered to be an informal umbrella term to describe the inclusion of game design elements in non-game applications such as business, education, health care, human resources, to name a few.

Generation Z: The terms Generation Z or Gen Z are used by demographers to refer to this generation cohort has been receiving increased Google search queries since 2014 with the highest weekly search volume, in comparison with that of Post-Millennials, iGeneration, or Homelanders.

Interactivity: A term that is often associated with an important part of the gameplay. This term refers to the process that users of gamified system can modify, based on the context and characters involved, the state and happening in a digital game by some action through an interface.

Motivation: A term to describe underlying reasons to explain human behaviors. Scholars have differentiated two types of motivation, such as intrinsic or extrinsic.

Online Learning: A term to describe an emerging approach to learn at students' premise through advanced information-communication technologies (such as Blackboard, Moodle, YouTube) either asynchronously or synchronously. Researchers have pointed out online learning can be informative/individual learning focused, or communicative/networked learning focused.

Pedagogy: This term refers to a systematic instruction method employed by an instructor to convey core subject matters to students.

Compilation of References

Aarseth, E. J. (1997). *Cybertext: Perspectives on Ergodic Literature.* Baltimore, MD: Johns Hopkins UP.

Adnan, M. (2018). Professional development in the transition to online teaching: The voice of entrant online instructors. *ReCALL, 30*(1), 88–111. doi:10.1017/S0958344017000106

Adnan, M., Kalelioğlu, F., & Gülbahar, Y. (2017). Assessment of a Multinational Online Faculty Development Program on Online Teaching: Reflections of Candidate e-Tutors. *The Turkish Online Journal of Distance Education-TOJDE, 18*(1), 22–38. doi:10.17718/tojde.285708

Adukaite, A., & Zyl, I. (2017). Teacher perceptions on the use of digital gamified learning in tourism education: The case of South African secondary schools. *Computers & Education, 111*, 172–190. doi:10.1016/j.compedu.2017.04.008

Agbebaku, C. A., & Adavbiele, Justina, A. (2016). The reliability and oegality of online education. *Journal of Education and Practice, 7*(5), 32–41.

Akcaoglu, M., & Lee, E. (2016). Increasing social presence in online learning through small group discussions. *The International Review of Research in Open and Distributed Learning, 17*(3), 1-17.

Alemi, F. F., & Maddox, P. J. (2008). Open courses: One view of the future of education. *The Journal of Health Administration Education, 25*(4), 329–342. PMID:19655635

Alexiou-Ray, J., & Bentley, C. C. (2015). Faculty professional development for quality online teaching. *Online Journal of Distance Learning Administration, 18*(4), 1–7.

Alexiou-Ray, J., & Bentley, C. C. (2016). Faculty professional development for quality online teaching. *Journal of Distance Learning Administration, 18*(4), 1–6.

Alkaher, I., & Dolan, E. (2011). Instructors' decisions that inquiry teaching into undergraduate courses: How do I make this fit? *International Journal for the Scholarship of Teaching and Learning, 5*(2), 26. doi:10.20429/ijsotl.2011.050209

Allen, E., & Seaman, J. (2016). *Online report card: Tracking online education in the United States.* Babson Survey Research Group Report. Retrieved from https://onlinelearningconsortium.org/read/online-report-card-tracking-online-education-united-states-2015

Allen, I. E., Seaman, J., Poulin, R., & Straut, T. T. (2016). *Online report card: Tracking online education in the United States.* Retrieved from http://onlinelearningsurvey.com/reports/onlinereportcard.pdf

Allen, E., & Seaman, J. (2013). *Changing course: Ten years of tracking online education in the United States.* Newburyport, MA: Sloan Consortium.

Allen, I. E., & Seaman, J. (2016). *Online Report Card: Tracking Online Education in the United States.* Babson Survey Research Group.

Compilation of References

Allen, I. E., & Seaman, J. (2016). *Online report card: Tracking online education in the United States.* Needham, MA: Babson Survey Research Group. Retrieved from http://onlinelearningsurvey.com/reports/onlinereportcard.pdf

Allen, P. (2014). Divinings: Religion at Harvard from its origins in New England ecclesiastical history to the 175th anniversary. *Journal of Education & Christian Belief, 18*(2), 286–290. doi:10.1177/205699711401800240

Allen, W. (1992). The color of success: African-American college student outcomes at predominantly white and historically black public colleges and universities. *Harvard Educational Review, 62*(1), 26–45. doi:10.17763/haer.62.1.wv5627665007v701

Al-Shabandar, R., Hussain, A. J., Liatsis, P., & Keight, R. (2018). Analyzing Learners Behavior in MOOCs: An Examination of Performance and Motivation Using a Data-Driven Approach. *IEEE Access: Practical Innovations, Open Solutions, 6*, 73669–73685. doi:10.1109/ACCESS.2018.2876755

Altinay, Z., Altinay, F., Ossianilsson, E., & Aydin, C. H. (2018). Open Education Practices for Learners with Disabilities. *BRAIN. Broad Research in Artificial Intelligence and Neuroscience, 9*(4), 171–176.

Alvarez, B. (2011). Flipping the classroom: Homework in class, lessons at home. *Education Digest, 77*(8), 18–21.

Americans with Disabilities Act of 1990, (1990). Pub. L. No. 101–336, 104 Stat. 328

Americans With Disabilities Act of 1990, 42 U.S.C. § 12101 et seq. (1994)

Amirault, R. J. (2012). Distance learning in the 21st century university: Key issues for leaders and faculty. *Quarterly Review of Distance Education, 13*(4), 253-265, 269.

Anderson, B., Brown, M., Murray, F., Simpson, M., & Mentis, M. (2006). *Global picture, local lessons: e-learning policy and accessibility.* Retrieved from http://www.educationcounts.govt.nz/__data/assets/pdf_file/0005/58289/AndersonFinalReport.pdf

Anderson, J., Sutton, S. R., & Gergen, T. (2014). *Student engagement in a dual-mode teaching environment: A pilot study.* Paper presented at the Society for Information Technology & Teacher Education International Conference.

Anderson, L., & Krathwohl, D. R. (2001). *A taxonomy for learning, teaching, and assessing: A revision of Bloom's taxonomy of educational objectives* (Complete ed.). New York: Longman.

Anderson, T., Rourke, L., Garrison, D., & Archer, W. (2001). Assessing teaching presence in a computer conferencing context. *Journal of Asynchronous Learning Networks, 5*(2), 1–17.

Andeson, T., Upton, L., Dron, J., Malone, J., & Poelhuber, B. (2015). Social interaction in self-paced distance education. *Open Paraxis, 7*(1), 7–23. doi: 10.5944/openpraxis.7.1.164

Andrews, T., & Tynan, B. (2012). Distance learners: Connected, mobile and resourceful individuals. *Australasian Journal of Educational Technology, 28*(4), 565–579. doi:10.14742/ajet.828

Aragon, S. R., & Johnson, E. S. (2008). Factors influencing completion and noncompletion of community college online courses. *American Journal of Distance Education, 22*(3), 146–158. doi:10.1080/08923640802239962

Ascough, R. S. (2002). Designing for online distance education: Putting pedagogy before technology. *Teaching Theology and Religion, 5*(1), 17–29. doi:10.1111/1467-9647.00114

Ashong, C. Y., & Commander, N. E. (2012). Ethnicity, gender, and perceptions of online learning in higher education. *Journal of Online Learning and Teaching / MERLOT, 8*(2), 98–110.

Astin, A. W. (1984). Student involvement: A developmental theory for higher education. *Journal of College Student Development*, *25*(4), 297–308. Retrieved from https://eric.ed.gov/?id=EJ614278

Aucoin, J., & Budenz, D. (2018, November). *Personalize your master course using student engage strategies*. PowerPoint presentation at the meeting of OLC Accelerate, Orlando, FL.

Austrailan Government Department of Education. (2014). *Completion rates of domestic bachelor students: A cohort analysis*. Retrieved from https://docs.education.gov.au/system/files/doc/other/completion_rates_of_domestic_bachelor_students_-_a_cohort_analysis_-_updated_27032015.pdf

Babson Survey Research Group. (2018). *Babson College, New Study: Distance Education up, Overall Enrollment Down*. Retrieved from http://www.babson.edu/about/news- events/babson-announcements/babson-survey-research-group-tracking-distance- education-report/

Baker, C., & Taylor, S. L. (2012). The importance of teaching presence in an online course. In *Online Student Engagement Tools and Strategies* (section 3). Retrieved from https://www.facultyfocus.com/wp-content/uploads/2019/02/FF-Online-Student-Engagement-Report.pdf

Baker, D. M., & Unni, R. (2018). USA and Asia hospitality & tourism students' perceptions and satisfaction with online learning versus traditional face-to-face instruction. *E-Journal of Business Education & Scholarship of Teaching*, *12*(2), 40–54. Retrieved from https://lopes.idm.oclc.org/login?url=https://search.ebscohost.com/login.aspx?direct=true&db=ehh&AN=132335757&site=eds-live&scope=site

Bälter, O., & Zimmaro, D. (2018). Keystroke-level analysis to estimate time to process pages in online learning environments. *Interactive Learning Environments*, *26*(4), 476–485. doi:10.1080/10494820.2017.1341941

Bandura, A. (1997). *Self-efficacy: The exercise of control*. New York: W.H. Freeman and Company.

Bandura, A. (2001). Social cognitive theory: An agentic perspective. *Annual Review of Psychology*, *52*(1), 1–26. doi:10.1146/annurev.psych.52.1.1 PMID:11148297

Banegas, D. L., & Manzur Busleimán, G. I. (2014). Motivating factors in online language teacher education in southern Argentina. *Computers & Education*, *76*, 131–142. doi:10.1016/j.compedu.2014.03.014

Baran, E., & Correia, A. (2014). A professional development framework for online teaching. *TechTrends*, *58*(5), 96–102. doi:10.100711528-014-0791-0

Baran, E., Correia, A.-P., & Thompson, A. (2011, November). Transforming online teaching practice: Critical analysis of the literature on the roles and competencies of online teachers. *Distance Education*, *32*(3), 421–439. doi:10.1080/01587919.2011.610293

Baran, E., Correia, A., & Thompson, A. D. (2013). Tracing successful online teaching in higher education: Voices of exemplary online teachers. *Teachers College Record*, *115*(3), 1–41.

Barata, G., Gama, S., Jorge, J., & Gonçalves, D. (2017, June). Studying student differentiation in gamified education: A long-term study. *Computers in Human Behavior*, *71*, 550–585. doi:10.1016/j.chb.2016.08.049

Barnett, B. G., & Caffarella, R. S. (1992). *The use of cohorts: A powerful way for addressing issues of diversity in preparation programs*. Presented at the Annual Meeting of the University Council for Educational Administration, Minneapolis, MN. Retrieved from http://www.eric.ed.gov/ERICWebPortal/recordDetail?accno=ED354627

Barnett, B. G., Basom, M. R., Yerkes, D. M., & Norris, C. J. (2000). Cohorts in educational leadership programs: Benefits, difficulties, and the potential for developing school leaders. *Educational Administration Quarterly*, *36*(2), 255–282. doi:10.1177/0013161X00362005

Compilation of References

Barnett, B. G., & Muse, I. D. (1993). Cohort groups in educational administration: Promises and challenges. *Journal of School Leadership*, *3*(4), 400–415. doi:10.1177/105268469300300405

Barre, E. (2016, July 11). *How much should we assign? Estimating out of class workload*. Retrieved from https://cte.rice.edu/blogarchive/2016/07/11/workload

Bartlett, M. (2018). Online Professional Development for Part-time Instructors: FaculTEA. In E. Langran & J. Borup (Eds.), *Proceedings of Society for Information Technology & Teacher Education International Conference* (pp. 514-519). Washington, DC: Association for the Advancement of Computing in Education (AACE). Retrieved from https://www.learntechlib.org/primary/p/182573/

Bartlett, L., Martin, A., Neil, A. L., Memish, K., Otahal, P., Kilpatrick, M., & Sanderson, K. (2019). A systematic review and meta-analysis of workplace mindfulness training randomized controlled trials. *Journal of Occupational Health Psychology*, *24*(1), 108–126. doi:10.1037/ocp0000146 PMID:30714811

Bates, A. W. (2000). *Managing technological change: Strategies for college and university leaders*. San Francisco, CA: Jossey-Bass.

Bates, A. W. (2005). *Technology, E-Learning and Distance Education* (2nd ed.). London: Routledge Taylor Francis Group. doi:10.4324/9780203463772

Bates, A. W. (2015). *Teaching in a Digital Age: Guidelines for Designing Teaching and Learning*. Vancouver, BC: Tony Bates Associates.

Bawa, P. (2016). *Retention in online courses: Exploring issues and solutions*. Purdue University. doi:10.1177/2158244015621777

Beachboard, M. R., Beachboard, J. C., Li, W., & Adkison, S. R. (2011). Cohorts and relatedness: Self-Determination Theory as an explanation of how learning communities affect educational outcomes. *Research in Higher Education*, *52*(8), 853–874. doi:10.100711162-011-9221-8

Beaudoin, M. (2010). Experiences and Opinions of Online Learners - What Foster Successful Learning? In Y. Kats (Ed.), *Learning Management System Technologies and Software Solutions for Online Teaching: Tools and Applications* (pp. 372–393). Hershey, PA: IGI Global. doi:10.4018/978-1-61520-853-1.ch020

Beaudoin, M. (2016). Issues in distance education: A primer for higher education decision makers. *New Directions for Higher Education*, *2016*(173), 9–19. doi:10.1002/he.20175

Beaudoin, M. F. (2002). Learning or lurking? Tracking the "invisible" online student. *The Internet and Higher Education*, *5*(2), 147–155.

Beetham, H., & White, D. (2014). Students' expectations and experiences of the digital environment. Bristol, UK: Academic Press.

Beichner, R. (2008). *The Scale-UP Project: A student-centered, active learning environment for undergraduate programs*. National Academy of Sciences. Available from http://www7.nationalacademies.org/bose/Beichner_CommissionedPaper.pdf

Belin, A. (2019). 5 Ways to Improve online discussion boards. *Emerging Ed Tech*. Retrieved from: https://www.emergingedtech.com/2019/05/5-ways-to-improve-online-discussion-boards/

Bennett, C., & Okinaka, A. M. (1990). Factors related to persistence among Asian, Black, Hispanic, and White undergraduates at a predominantly White university: Comparison between first and fourth year cohorts. *The Urban Review*, *22*(1), 33–60. doi:10.1007/BF01110631

Bentley, T., Zhao, F., Reames, E. H., & Reed, C. (2004). Frames we live by: Metaphors for the cohort. *Professional Educator, 26*(2), 39–44. Retrieved from http://files.eric.ed.gov/fulltext/EJ728474.pdf

Berge, Z. L. (2001). *New roles for learners and teachers in online education.* Retrieved from http://its.fvtc.edu/langan/BB6/BergeZane2000.pdf

Bergmann, J., & Sams, A. (2012). Flip your classroom: Reach every student in every class every day. *International Society of Technology in Education.* Retrieved from https://www.liceopalmieri.edu.it/wp-content/uploads/2016/11/Flip-Your-Classroom.pdf

Berry, G. (2018). Learning from the learners: Student perception of the online classroom. *Quarterly Review of Distance Education, 19*(3), 39-56.

Berry, S. (2019, April). The offline nature of online community: Exploring distance learners' extracurricular interactions. *International Review of Research in Open and Distributed Learning, 20*(2). doi:10.19173/irrodl.v20i2.3896

Betts, K., & Heaston, A. (2014). Build it but will they teach?: Strategies for increasing faculty participation & retention in online & blended Education. *Online Journal of Distance Learning Administration, 17*(2), 16–28.

Bhatti, A., Tubaisahat, A., & El-Qawasmeh, E. (2005). Using technology-mediated learning environment to overcome social and cultural limitations in higher education. *Issues in Informing Science and Information Technology, 2*, 67–76. doi:10.28945/811

Bickle, M. C. (2019). Online learning Examination of attributes that promote student satisfaction. *Online Journal of Distance Learning Administration, 22*(1).

Bickle, M. C., & Rucker, R. (2018). Student-to-student interaction: Humanizing the online classroom using technology and group assignments. *The Quarterly Review of Distance Education, 19*(1), 1–11. Retrieved from https://www.infoagepub.com/quarterly-review-of-distance-education.html

Bigatel, P. M. (2016, March 14). Student engagement strategies for the online learning environment [Blog]. Retrieved from https://www.facultyfocus.com/articles/online-education/studentengagement-how-to-help-students-succeed-in-the-online-environment/

Bista, K., & Cox, D. W. (2014). Cohort-based doctoral programs: What we have learned over the last 18 years. *International Journal of Doctoral Studies, 9*, 1–20. doi:10.28945/1941

Blackmon, S. J., & Major, C. (2012). Student experiences in online courses: A qualitative research synthesis. *Quarterly Review of Distance Education, 13*(2), 77–85.

Boellstorff, T., Nardi, B., Pearce, C., & Taylor, T. L. (2012). *Ethnography and virtual worlds: A handbook of method.* Princeton, NJ: Princeton University Press. doi:10.2307/j.cttq9s20

Boettcher, J. V. (2013). *Ten best practices for teaching online: Quick guide for new online faculty.* Retrieved from http://www.designingforlearning.info/services/writing/ecoach/tenbest.html

Bogardus-Cortez, M. (2017). *Emerging tech boost online education growth over next 4 years.* Retrieved from edtechmagazine.com

Boling, E. C., Hough, M., Krinsky, H., Saleem, H., & Stevens, M. (2012). Cutting the distance in distance education: Perspectives on what promotes positive, online learning experiences. *Internet and Higher Education, 15*(2), 118–126. doi:10.1016/j.iheduc.2011.11.006

Bolliger, D. U., & Wasilik, O. (2012). Student satisfaction in large undergraduate online courses. *Quarterly Review of Distance Education, 13*(3), 153–165.

Boss, S., & Krauss, J. (2014). *Reinventing project-based learning: Your field guide to real-world projects in the digital age*. Eugene, OR: International Society for Technology in Education.

Boton, E. C., & Gregory, S. (2015). Minimizing attrition in online degree courses. *Journal of Educators Online, 12*(1), 62–90. doi:10.9743/jeo.2015.1.6

Boudreaux, K. (2018). Serious Games for Training and Faculty Development--A Review of the Current Literature. *Journal of Educators Online, 15*(2). doi:10.9743/jeo.2018.15.2.5

Bourdieu, P., & Passeron, J. (1977). *Reproduction in education, society, and culture*. London: Sage Publications.

Bowser, A., Davis, K., Singleton, J., & Small, T. (2017). Professional learning: A collaborative model for online teaching and development. *SRATE Journal, 26*(1), 1–8.

Boysen, G. A. (2012). Teacher and student perceptions of microaggression in college classrooms. *Journal of College Teaching, 60*(3), 122–129. doi:10.1080/87567555.2012.654831

Bozkurt, A. (2019). From Distance Education to Open and Distance Learning: A Holistic Evaluation of History, Definitions, and Theories. In S. Sisman-Ugur, & G. Kurubacak (Eds.), Handbook of Research on Learning in the Age of Transhumanism (pp. 252-273). Hershey, PA: IGI Global. doi:10.4018/978-1-5225-8431-5.ch016

Bracken, S., & Novak, K. (Eds.). (2019). *Transforming Higher Education Through Universal Design for Learning: An International Perspective*. Routledge. doi:10.4324/9781351132077

Braun, V., & Clarke, V. (2006). Using thematic analysis in psychology. *Qualitative Research in Psychology, 3*(2), 77–101. doi:10.1191/1478088706qp063oa

Bremer, C. D., Clapper, A. T., Hitchcock, C., Hall, T., & Kachgal, M. (2002). *Universal Design: A Strategy To Support Students' Access to the General Education Curriculum*. Information Brief.

Briggs, A. (2015, February 11). Ten Ways to Overcome Barriers to Student Engagement Online. *Academic Technology at the College of William and Mary*. Retrieved from http://at.blogs.wm.edu/ten-ways-to-overcome-barriers-to-student-engagement-online/

Brinkley-Etzkorn, K. E. (2018). Learning to teach online: Measuring the influence of faculty development training on teaching effectiveness through a TPACK lens. *The Internet and Higher Education, 38*, 28–35. doi:10.1016/j.iheduc.2018.04.004

British Council. (2017). New model to improve your professional development. *Vocational Education Exchange Magazine*. Retrieved from https://www.britishcouncil.org/education/skills-employability/what-we-do/vocational-education-exchange-online-magazine/april-2017/new-model-improve-your-professional-development

Britton, B. K., & Tesser, A. (1991). Effects of time-management practices on college grades. *Journal of Educational Psychology, 83*(3), 405–410. doi:10.1037/0022-0663.83.3.405

Broadbent, J., & Poon, W. L. (2015). Self-regulated learning strategies & academic achievement in online higher education learning environments: A systematic review. *The Internet and Higher Education, 27*, 1–13. doi:10.1016/j.iheduc.2015.04.007

Brocato, B. R., Bonanno, A., & Ulbig, S. (2015). Student perceptions and instructional evaluations: A multivariate analysis of online and face-to-face classroom settings. *Education and Information Technologies*, *20*(1), 37–55. doi:10.100710639-013-9268-6

Brookfield, S. (2005). *The power of critical theory: Liberating adult learning and teaching*. New York, NY: Open University.

Brookfield, S. D. (2017). *Becoming a critically reflective teacher*. New York, NY: John Wiley & Sons, Incorporated.

Brown, M. B., & Diaz, V. (2010). Mobile learning: Context and prospects. *EDUCAUSE: Mobile Learning*. Retrieved from http://www.educause.edu/Resources/MobileLearningContextandProspe/204894

Budash, D. E. (2015). *Understanding persistence in an online master's degree program: A single case study of learners and faculty* (Unpublished doctoral dissertation). North Central University.

Bunn, J. (2004). Student persistence in a LIS distance education program. *Australian Academic and Research Libraries*, *35*(3), 253–269. doi:10.1080/00048623.2004.10755275

Bureau of Labor Statistics. (2016). *Unemployment rates and earnings by educational attainment, 2016*. Bureau of Labor Statistics, U.S. Department of Labor. Retrieved from https://www.bls.gov/emp/ep_chart_001.htm

Burgstahler, S. E., & Cory, R. C. (Eds.). (2013). *Universal Design in Higher Education*. Harvard Education Press.

Burke, B. (2013, January 21). *The Gamification of Business*. Retrieved from http://www.forbes.com/sites/gartner-group/2013/2001/2021/the-gamification-of-business/

Burnett, P. C. (1999). The supervision of doctoral dissertations using a collaborative cohort model. *Counselor Education and Supervision*, *39*(9), 46–52. doi:10.1002/j.1556-6978.1999.tb01789.x

Burroughs, A. (2019, June 11). UBTech 2019: Gen Z learners will push the limits of mobile-first, digital-first learning. *EdTech*. Retrieved on June 11, 2019 from https://edtechmagazine.com/higher/article/2019/2006/ubtech-2019-gen-z-learners-will-push-

Buzzetto-More, N.A., & Sweat-Guy, R. (2006). Incorporating the hybrid learning model into minority education at a historically black university. *Journal of Information Technology Education, 5*(1), 153-164.

Çakıroglu, Ü., Basıbüyük, B., Güler, M., Atabay, M., & Yılmaz Memiş, B. (2017). Gamifying an ICT course: Influences on engagement and academic performance. *Computers in Human Behavior*, *69*, 98–107. doi:10.1016/j.chb.2016.12.018

Calvert, R. (2019). *Advanced Mindfulness Practitice. PESI Comprehensive Training*. Eau Claire, WI: PESI.

Camilleri-Cassar, F. (2014). Education strategies for social inclusion or marginalising the marginalised? *Journal of Youth Studies*, *17*(2), 252–268. doi:10.1080/13676261.2013.834312

Campana, J. (2014). *Learning for work and professional development: The significance of Informal learning networks of digital media industry professionals*. Academic Press.

Cantwell, G., Crossley, M., & Ashby, J. (2015). Multiple stages of learning in perceptual categorization: Evidence and neurocomputational theory. *Psychonomic Bulletin & Review*, *22*(6), 1598–1613. doi:10.375813423-015-0827-2 PMID:25917141

Carini, R. M., Kuh, G. D., & Klein, S. P. (2006). Student engagement and student learning: Testing the linkages. *Research in Higher Education*, *47*(1), 1–32. doi:10.100711162-005-8150-9

Carnevale, A. P., Smith, N., & Strohl, J. (2013). *Recovery: Job growth and education requirements through 2020*. Washington, DC: Georgetown Public Policy Institute, Center on Education and the Workforce. Retrieved from https://cew.georgetown.edu/wp-content/uploads/2014/11/Recovery2020.FR_.Web_.pdf

Carr, N. (2011). *The Shallows: What the Internet Is Doing to Our Brains*. New York: Norton.

Carr, S. (2000). As distance education comes of age, the challenge is keeping the students. *The Chronicle of Higher Education, 46*(23), A39. Retrieved from https://eric.ed.gov/?id=EJ601725

Casey, G., & Evans, T. (2011). Designing for learning: Online social networks as a classroom environment. *International Review of Research in Open and Distance Learning, 12*(7), 1–26. doi:10.19173/irrodl.v12i7.1011

Caspi, A., Chajut, E., & Saporta, K. (2008). Participation in class and gender in online discussions: Gender differences. *Computers & Education, 50*(3), 718–724. doi:10.1016/j.compedu.2006.08.003

CAST. (2019). *Universal Design for Learning guidelines*. Retrieved from http://udlguidelines.cast.org/

Cavanaugh, T., Lamkin, M. L., & Hu, H. (2012). Using a generalized checklist to improve student assignment submission times in an online course. *Journal of Asynchronous Learning Networks, 16*(4), 39–44.

Center for Applied Special Technology. (2011). *CAST timeline*. Retrieved January 5, 2019, from http://www.cast.org/about/timeline.html

Center for Applied Special Technology. (2011). *Universal Design for Learning Guidelines version 2.0*. Wakefield, MA: Author.

Central Washington University. (n.d.). Retrieved July, 2019 from https://www.cwu.edu/registrar/sites/cts.cwu.edu.registrar/files/documents/Tuition_18-19_UG_Res_Ellensburg.pdf

Chang, B.-H., Lee, S.-E., & Kim, B.-S. (2006, April). Exploring factors affecting the adoption and continuance of online games among college students in South Korea: Integrating uses and gratification and diffusion of innovation approaches. *New Media & Society, 8*(2), 295–319. doi:10.1177/1461444806059888

Chappuis, J., & Stiggins, R. (2017). *An introduction to student-involved assessment FOR learning, 7*. Pearson.

Chase-Cantarini, S., & Christiaens, G. (2019). Introducing mindfulness moments in the classroom. *Journal of Professional Nursing*.

Chen, G., Davis, D., Krause, M., Aivaloglou, E., Hauff, C., & Houben, G. (2018). From Learners to Earners: Enabling MOOC Learners to Apply Their Skills and Earn Money in an Online Market Place. IEEE Transactions on Learning Technologies, 11(2), 264-274. doi:10.1109/TLT.2016.2614302

Cheng, C. K., Paré, D. E., Collimore, L. M., & Joordens, S. (2011). Assessing the effectiveness of a voluntary online discussion forum on improving students' course performance. *Computers & Education, 56*(1), 253–261. doi:10.1016/j.compedu.2010.07.024

Cheng, G., & Chau, J. (2016). Exploring the relationships between learning styles, online participation, learning achievement, and course satisfaction: An empirical study of a blended classroom. *British Journal of Educational Technology, 47*(2), 257–278. doi:10.1111/bjet.12243

Chen, K., Lowenthal, P. R., Bauer, C., Heaps, A., & Nielsen, C. (2017). Moving beyond smile sheets: A case study on the evaluation and iterative improvement of an online faculty development program. *Online Learning, 21*(1), 85–111. doi:10.24059/olj.v21i1.810

Chenot, D., & Kim, H. (2017). Spirituality, religion, social justice orientation, and the career aspirations of young adults. *Journal of Social Work Education, 53*(4), 699–713. doi:10.1080/10437797.2017.1283267

Chess, S., & Booth, P. (2014). Lessons down a rabbit hole: Alternate reality gaming in the classroom. *New Media & Society, 16*(6), 1002–1017. doi:10.1177/1461444813497554

Chickering, A. W., & Ehrmann, S. C. (1996). Implementing the seven principles: Technology as a lever. *AAHE Bulletin, 49*(2), 3–6. Retrieved from https://www.aahea.org/articles/sevenprinciples.htm

Chickering, A. W., & Gamson, Z. F. (1987). Seven principles for good practice in undergraduate education. *AAHE Bulletin, 39*(7), 3–7. Retrieved from http://files.eric.ed.gov/fulltext/ED282491.pdf

Ching, Y. H., Hsu, Y. C., & Baldwin, S. (2018). Becoming an Online Teacher: An Analysis of Prospective Online Instructors' Reflections. *Journal of Interactive Learning Research, 29*(2), 145-168. Retrieved from https://www.learntechlib.org/primary/p/181339/

Cho, M. H., & Tobias, S. (2016). Should instructors require discussion in online courses? Effects of online discussion on community of inquiry, learner time, satisfaction, and achievement. *The International Review of Research in Open and Distributed Learning, 17*(2), 123-139.

Chuang, Y.-C. (2006). Massively multiplayer online role-playing game-induced seizures: A neglected health problem in internet addiction. *Cyberpsychology & Behavior, 9*(4), 451–456. doi:10.1089/cpb.2006.9.451 PMID:16901249

Cipher, D. J., Urban, R. W., & Mancini, M. E. (2019). Factors associated with student success in online and face-to-face delivery of master of science in nursing programs. *Teaching and Learning in Nursing, 14*(3), 203–207. doi:10.1016/j.teln.2019.03.007

Cohen, J. (1995). *Statistical power analysis for the behavioral sciences* (2nd ed.). Hillsdale, NJ: Erlbaum.

Cokley, K., McClain, S., Enciso, A., & Martinez, M. (2013). An examination of the impact of minority status stress and imposter feelings on the mental health of diverse ethnic minority college students. *Journal of Multicultural Counseling and Development, 41*(2), 82–95. doi:10.1002/j.2161-1912.2013.00029.x

Connor, K. R., & Killmer, N. (2001). Cohorts, collaboration, and community: Does contextual teacher education really work? *Action in Teacher Education, 23*(3), 46–53. doi:10.1080/01626620.2001.10463074

Costley, J., & Lange, C. (2016). The effects of instructor control of online learning environments on satisfaction and perceived learning. *Electronic Journal of E-Learning, 14*(3), 169–180.

Cox, E. (2015). Coaching and adult learning: Theory and practice. *New Directions for Adult and Continuing Education, 2015*(148), 27–38. doi:10.1002/ace.20149

Coy, K., Marino, M. T., & Serianni, B. (2014). Using Universal Design for Learning in Synchronous Online Instruction. *Journal of Special Education Technology, 29*(1), 63–74. doi:10.1177/016264341402900105

Creswell, J. W. (2003). *Research design: Qualitative, quantitative, and mixed method approaches*. Thousand Oaks, CA: Sage Publications.

Cross, K. P. (1998). Why learning communities? Why now? *About Campus: Enriching the Student Learning Experience, 3*(3), 4–11. doi:10.1177/108648229800300303

Croxton, R. A. (2014, June). The role of interactivity in student satisfaction and persistence in online learning. *MERLOT Journal of Online Learning and Teaching, 10*(2), 314-324. Retrieved from: http://jolt.merlot.org

Compilation of References

Cuesta Medina, L. (2017). Blended learning: Deficits and prospects in higher education. *Australasian Journal of Educational Technology, 34*(1), 42–56. doi:10.14742/ajet.3100

Dahl, B. (2015). 7 Tips for increasing student engagement in online courses. Student Engagement [Blog]. Retrieved from http://www.d2l.com/blog/author/bdahl

Dail, T. (2012). Enabling: A strategy for improving learning. In *Online Student Engagement Tools and Strategies*, 6-7. Retrieved from https://www.facultyfocus.com/wp-content/uploads/2019/02/FF-Online-Student-Engagement-Report.pdf

Dailey-Hebert, A. (2018, December). Maximizing interactivity in online learning: Moving beyond discussion boards. *Journal of Educators Online, 15*(3). doi:10.9743/jeo.2018.15.3.8

Dale, S. (2014, June). Gamification: Making work fun, or making fun of work? *Business Information Review, 31*(2), 80–90. doi:10.1177/0266382114538350

Daniel, J. (2012). Dual-mode universities in higher education: Way station or final destination? *Open Learning: The Journal of Open, Distance and e-Learning, 27*(1), 89-95.

Daniels, A. (2009). *Oops! 13 management practices that waste time and money (and what to do instead)*. Atlanta, GA: Performance Management Publications.

Darling-Hammond, L., Hyler, M. E., & Gardner, M. (2017). *Effective teacher professional development*. Palo Alto, CA: Learning Policy Institute.

Darling-Hammond, L., Hyler, M. E., & Gardner, M. (2017). *Effective Teacher Professional Development*. Palo Alto, CA: Learning Policy Institute; Retrieved from https://learningpolicyinstitute.org/product/teacher-prof-dev

Das, S. (2012). Increasing instructor visibility in online courses through mini-videos and screencasting. In *Online Student Engagement Tools and Strategies* (section 4). Retrieved from https://www.facultyfocus.com/wp-content/uploads/2019/02/FF-Online-Student-Engagement-Report.pdf

Davidson, C. (2017). *The new education: How to revolutionize the university to prepare students for a world in flux*. New York: Basic Books.

Davies, R. S., Dean, D. L., & Ball, N. (2013, August). Flipping the classroom and instructional technology integration in a college-level information systems spreadsheet course. *Educational Technology Research and Development, 61*(4), 563–580. doi:10.100711423-013-9305-6

De Chastelaine, M., Mattson, J., Wang, T., & Rugg, M. (2013). Stability across age and associative memory performance in the engagement of a core networking supporting recollection. *Journal of Cognitive Neuroscience, 1*(1), 167.

De Wever, B., & Van Keer, H., Schellens, T., & Valcke, M. (2010). Roles as a structuring tool in online discussion groups: The differential impact of different roles on social knowledge construction. *Computers in Human Behavior*. doi:10.1016/j.chb.2009.08.008

Dear, B. (2017). *The Friendly Orange Glow: The Untold story of the PLATO System and the Dawn of Cyberculture*. Audiobook.

Decker, A., & Lawley, E. L. (2013). Life's a game and the game of life: how making a game out of it can change student behavior. In *Proceeding of the 44th ACM Technical Symposium on Computer Science Education*. Denver, CO: ACM. 10.1145/2445196.2445269

Dede, C. (Ed.). (2004). *Online Professional Development for Teachers: Emerging Models and Methods*. Cambridge, MA: Harvard Education Press.

Delahunty, J. (2012). 'Who am I?': Exploring identity in online discussion forums. *International Journal of Educational Research*, *53*, 407–420. doi:10.1016/j.ijer.2012.05.005

Delisio, E. R. (2009). Merging online education with social networking: Welcome to present. *Podiatry Management*, *28*(6), 73–76.

Dell, C. A., Dell, T. F., & Blackwell, T. L. (2015). Applying universal design for learning in online courses: Pedagogical and practical considerations. *Journal of Educators Online*, *12*(2), 166–192. doi:10.9743/JEO.2015.2.1

de-Marcos, L., Domínguez, A., Saenz-de-Navarrete, J., & Pagés, C. (2014). An empirical study comparing gamification and social networking on e-learning. *Computers & Education*, *75*, 82–91. doi:10.1016/j.compedu.2014.01.012

Deming, D. J., Goldin, C., Katz, L. F., & Yuchtman, N. (2015). Can online learning bend the higher education cost curve? *The American Economic Review*, *105*(5), 496–501. doi:10.1257/aer.p20151024

Dennis, B., Watland, P., Pirotte, S., & Verday, N. (2004). Role and competencies of the e-tutor. *Proceedings of the Networked Learning Conference 2004*. Retrieved from http://www.networkedlearningconference.org.uk/past/nlc2004/home.htm

Deterding, S., Dixon, D., Khaled, R., & Nacke, L. (2011b). *From game design elements to gamefulness: Defining "gamification."* Paper presented at the MindTrek '11, Tampere, Finland. Retrieved November 27, 2014 from https://www.cs.auckland.ac.nz/courses/compsci747s2c/lectures/paul/definition-deterding.pdf

Deterding, S., Sicart, M., Nacke, L., O'Hara, K., & Dixon, D. (2011a). *Gamification: Using game design elements in non-gaming contexts*. Paper presented at the CHI 2011, Vancouver, BC, Canada. Retrieved November 25, 2014 from http://gamification-research.org/wp-content/uploads/2011/04/01-Deterding-Sicart-Nacke-OHara-Dixon.pdf

Díaz, K. (n.d.). Paulo Freire. *Internet encyclopedia of philosophy*. Retrieved from https://www.iep.utm.edu/freire/#H11

Díaz-Maggioli, G. (2004). *Teacher-Centered Professional Development*. Alexandria, VA: ACSD.

Dickinson, A. (2017). Communicating with the online student: The impact of e-mail tone on student performance and teacher evaluations. *Journal of Educators Online*, *142*(2), 36-45.

Dickson, D. H., & Kelly, I. (1985). 'The Barnum Effect' in personality assessment: A review of the literature. *Psychological Reports*, *2*(57), 367–382. doi:10.2466/pr0.1985.57.2.367

Dixon-Saxon, S. V. (2009). Diversity and distance education: Cultural competence for online instructors. In R. A. R. Gurung & L. R. Prieto (Eds.), *Got diversity? Best practices for incorporating culture into the curriculum*. Sterling, VA: Stylus Publications.

Dixson, M. (2010). Creating effective student engagement in online courses: What do students find engaging? *The Journal of Scholarship of Teaching and Learning*, *10*(2), 1–13.

Dolan, V. (2011, Feb). The isolation of online adjunct faculty and its impact on their performance. *The International Review of Research in Open and Distributed Learning*, *12*(2).

Domínguez, A., Saenz-de-Navarrete, J., De-Marcos, L., Fernández-Sanz, L., Pagés, C., & Martínez-Herráiz, J. J. (2013). Gamifying learning experiences: Practical implications and outcomes. *Computers & Education*, *63*, 380–392. doi:10.1016/j.compedu.2012.12.020

Donovan, J. (2015). The importance of building online learning communities [Blog]. Retrieved from http://blog.online.colostate.edu/blog/online-education/the-importance-of-building-online-learning-communities/

Douglas, H. E., Bore, M., & Munro, D. (2016). Coping with university education: The relationships of time management behaviour and work engagement with the five factor model aspects. *Learning and Individual Differences*, *45*, 268–274. doi:10.1016/j.lindif.2015.12.004

Downes, S. (2005). e-Learning 2.0. *ACM e-Learn Magazine*, (10). Retrieved from http://www.downes.ca/post/31741

Drange, T., & Kargaard, J. (2017, April 27-28). Increasing student/student and student/lecturer communication through available tools to create a virtual classroom feeling in online education. *The 13th International Scientific Conference e-learning and software for education*. 10.12753/2066-026x-17/058

Drange, T., & Kargaard, J. (2017, April). *Increasing student/student and student/lecturer communication through available tools to create a virtual classroom feeling in online education.* Paper presented at the meeting of The 13th International Scientific Conference eLearning and Software for Education, Bucharest, Romania.

Drouin, M. A. (2008). The relationship between students' perceived sense of community and satisfaction, achievement, and retention in an online course. *The Quarterly Review of Distance Education*, *93*(3), 267–284. Retrieved from https://www.infoagepub.com/quarterly-review-of-distance-education.html

Durden, G., & Ellis, L. (2003). Is class attendance a proxy variable for student motivation in economics classes? An empirical analysis. *International Social Science Review*, *78*(1–2), 42–46.

Du, X. (2014). The Affective Filter in Second Language Teaching. *Asian Social Science*. doi:10.5539/ass.v5n8p162

Dweck, C. S. (2012). *Mindset: The new psychology of success*. New York: Constable & Robinson.

Dyer, T., Aroz, J., & Larson, E. (2018). Proximity in the online classroom: Engagement, relationships, and personalization. *Journal of Institutional Research*, *7*, 108–118.

Dziuban, C., Moskal, P., & Hartman, J. (2005). Higher education, blended learning and the generations: Knowledge is power-no more. In *Elements of quality online education: Engaging communities*. Retrieved from http://www.oswego.edu/~celt/Dziuban_Knowledge_is_Power_Oct_2004.doc

Ebrahimi, E., Kolahi, P., & Nabipour, E. (2017). Time management education influence on decreasing exam anxiety and conditioned university students' negligence of Tehran universities. *European Psychiatry*, *41*(Suppl.), S606. doi:10.1016/j.eurpsy.2017.01.952

Edyburn, D. L. (2010). Would you recognize universal design for learning if you saw it? Ten propositions for new directions for the second decade of UDL. *Learning Disability Quarterly*, *33*(1), 33–41. doi:10.1177/073194871003300103

Ekmekei, O. (2013). Being there: Establishing instructor presence in an online learning environment. *Higher Education Studies*, *3*(1), 29–38.

Elliott, M., Rhoades, N., Jackson, C. M., & Mandernach, B. J. (2015). Professional development: Designing initiatives to meet the needs of online faculty. *Journal of Educators Online*, *12*(1), 160–188. doi:10.9743/JEO.2015.1.2

Ellis, R. (2010). Instructed second language acquisition a literature review. *Language Teaching*, *43*. doi:10.1017/S0261444809990139

Ellis, A. (2001). *Teaching, learning, and assessment together: The reflective classroom*. Larchmont, NY: Eye on Education.

Enger, K. B. (2006). Minorities and online higher education. *EDUCAUSE Quarterly*, *29*(4), 7–8.

Englund, C., Olofsson, A. D., & Price, L. (2017). Teaching with technology in higher education: Understanding conceptual change and development in practice. *Higher Education Research & Development*, *36*(1), 73–87. doi:10.1080/07294360.2016.1171300

Entertainment Software Association. (2019). *2019 Essential Facts About the Computer and Video Game Industry.* Retrieved on June 11, 2019 from https://www.theesa.com/wp-content/uploads/2019/2005/2019-Essential-Facts-About-the-Computer-and-Video-Game-Industry.pdf

Eom, S. B., & Ashill, N. (2016). The determinants of students' perceived learning outcomes and satisfaction in university online education: An update. *Decision Sciences Journal of Innovative Education, 14*(2), 185–215. doi:10.1111/dsji.12097

Erichsen, E. A., & Bolliger, D. U. (2011). Towards understanding international graduate student isolation in traditional and online environments. *Educational Technology Research and Development, 59*(3), 309–326. doi:10.100711423-010-9161-6

Ermi, L., & Mäyrä, F. (2005). *Fundamental components of the gameplay experience: Analyzing immersion.* Paper presented at the DiGRA 2005 Conference: Changing View-Worldds in Play, Vancouver, Canada.

Farnes, N., Ganor, M., Gil'ad, R., Guri-Rosenblit, S., Ovsyannikov, V., Shelley, M., & Libin-Levav, V. (2000). *Distance education for the information society: Policies, pedagogy and professional development.* UNESCO Institute for Information Technologies In Education.

Fawcett, T. (2006). An introduction to ROC analysis. *Pattern Recognition Letters, 27*(8), 861–874. doi:10.1016/j.patrec.2005.10.010

Fernex, A., Lima, L., & de Vries, E. (2015). Exploring time allocation for academic activities by university students in France. *Higher Education, 69*(3), 399–420. doi:10.100710734-014-9782-5

Ferrer, D. (n.d.a). *The History of Online Education.* Retrieved from https://thebestschools.org/magazine/online-education-history/#pre1900

Ferrer, D. (n.d.b). *Current Trends in Online Education.* Retrieved from https://thebestschools.org/magazine/current-trends-online-education/

Ferrer, D. (2013). *The One World Schoolhouse by Salman Khan—A Review.* New York: Twelve/Hachette Book Group.

Field, A. (2013). *Discovering statistics using IBM SPSS statistics* (4th ed.). Los Angeles, CA: SAGE Publications.

Fielding, M., Bragg, S., Craig, J., Cunnigham, I., Eraut, M., Gillinson, S., …Thorp, J. (2005). *Factors Influencing the Transfer of Good Practice.* London: Department for Education and Skills. Research Report 615. Retrieved from https://dera.ioe.ac.uk/21001/1/RR615.pdf

Fink, L. D. (2003). *Creating Significant Learning Experiences: An Integrated Approach to Designing College Courses.* Hoboken, NJ: John Wiley & Sons.

Fischer, C., Fishman, C., Dede, C., Eisenkraft, A., Frumin, K., Foster, B., & McCoy A. (2018). *Investigating relationships between school context, teacher professional development, teaching practices, and student achievement in response to a nationwide science reform.* Academic Press.

Fish, W. W., & Wickersham, L. E. (2009). Best practices for online instructors: Reminders. *The Quarterly Review of Distance Education, 10*(3), 279–284.

Fitzgerald, H. E., Bruns, K., Sonka, S. T., Furco, A., & Swanson, L. (2012). The centrality of engagement in higher education. *Journal of Higher Education Outreach & Engagement, 16*(2), 7–28.

Fitz-Walter, Z., Tjondronegoro, D., & Wyeth, P. (2012). A gamified mobile application for engaging new students at university orientation. In *Proceedings of the 24th Australian Computer Human Interaction Conference* (pp. 138-141). Melbourne, Australia: ACM. 10.1145/2414536.2414560

Compilation of References

Fortune, M. F., Spielman, M., & Pangelinan, D. T. (2011). Students' perceptions of online or face-to-face learning and social media in hospitality. *Journal of Online Learning and Teaching / MERLOT, 7*(1), 1–16.

Foucault, M. (1982). The subject and power. In H. L. Dreyfus & P. Rabinow (Eds.), *Michel Foucault: Beyond Structuralism and Hermeneutics*. Chicago, IL: University of Chicago Press.

Fowler, S., & Bond, M. A. (2016). The Future of Faculty Development in a Networked World. *Educause Review, 51*(2), 56-57. Retrieved from https://er.educause.edu/articles/2016/3/the-future-of-faculty-development-in-a-networked-world

Fox, J., & Monette, G. (1992). Generalized collinearity diagnostics. *Journal of the American Statistical Association, 87*(417), 178–183. doi:10.1080/01621459.1992.10475190

Freire, P. (2005). *Pedagogy of the oppressed* (M. Bergman Ramos, Trans.). New York, NY: Continuum. (Original work published 1970)

Friedman, J. (2018). 4 expectations for online education in 2018. *U.S. News & World Report*. Retrieved from https://www.usnews.com/higher-education/online-education/articles/2018-01-18/4-expectations-for-online-education-in-2018

Furlong, A. (2013). Marginalized youth in education: Social and cultural dimensions of exclusion in Canada and the UK. In K. Tilleczek & H. B. Ferguson (Eds.), *Youth, Education, and Marginality: Local and Global Expressions*. Waterloo, UK: Wilfrid Laurier University Press.

Fyle, C. O., Moseley, A., & Hayes, N. (2012). Troubled times: The role of instructional design in a modern dual-mode university? *Open Learning: The Journal of Open, Distance and e-Learning, 27*(1), 53-64.

Gaible, E., & Burns, M. (2005). *Using Technology to Train Teachers: Appropriate Uses of ICT for Teacher Professional Development in Developing Countries*. Washington, DC: infoDev / World Bank. Retrieved from http://documents.worldbank.org/curated/en/900291468324835987/Using-technology-to-train-teachers-appropriate-uses-of-ICT-for-teacher-professional-development-in-developing-countires

Gallagher-Lepak, S., Reilly, J., & Killion, C. (2009). Nursing student perceptions of community in online learning. *Contemporary Nurse, 32*(1-2), 133–146. doi:10.5172/conu.32.1-2.133 PMID:19697984

Garrison, D. R. (2009). Communities of inquiry in online learning. In P. L. Rogers & ... (Eds.), *Encyclopedia of distance learning* (2nd ed.; pp. 352–355). Hershey, PA: IGI Global. doi:10.4018/978-1-60566-198-8.ch052

Garrison, D. R., & Anderson, T. (2003). *E-learning in the 21st century: A framework for research and practice*. New York: Routledge Falmer. doi:10.4324/9780203166093

Garrison, D. R., Anderson, T., & Archer, W. (2000). Critical inquiry in a text-based environment: Computer conferencing in higher education. *The Internet and Higher Education, 2*(2-3), 87–105. doi:10.1016/S1096-7516(00)00016-6

Garrison, D., Cleveland-Innes, M., & Fung, T. S. (2009). Exploring Causal relationships among teaching, cognitive, and social presence: Student perceptions of the community of inquiry framework. *Internet and Higher Education*. doi:10.1016/j.iheduc.2009.10.002

Gee, J. P. (2007a). What video games have to teach us about learning and literacy (Rev. and updated ed.). New York: Palgrave Macmillan.

Gee, J. P. (2004). *What video games have to teach us about learning and literacy*. New York, NY: Palgrave Macmillan.

Gee, J. P. (2007b). *Good video games + good learning: Collected essays on video games, learning and literacy*. New York: Peter Lang. doi:10.3726/978-1-4539-1162-4

Geldenhuys, J. L., & Oosthuizen, L. C. (2015). Challenges influencing teachers' involvement in continuous professional development: A South African perspective. *Teaching and Teacher Education*, *51*, 203–212. doi:10.1016/j.tate.2015.06.010

Gibson, L. (2011). Student-directed learning: An exercise in student engagement. *College Teaching*, *59*(3), 95–101. doi:10.1080/87567555.2010.550957

Gillett-Swan, J. (2017). The challenges of online learning: Supporting and engaging the isolated learner. *Journal of Learning Design*, *10*(1), 20–30. doi:10.5204/jld.v9i3.293

Ginda, M., Richey, M. C., Cousino, M., & Börner, K. (2019). Visualizing learner engagement, performance, and trajectories to evaluate and optimize online course design. *PLoS One*, *14*(5). doi:10.1371/journal.pone.0215964 PMID:31059546

Glasser, W. (1999). *Choice theory: A new psychology of personal freedom* (First HarperPerennial ed.). New York: HarperPerennial.

Glasser, M. F., Smith, S. M., Marcus, D. S., Andersson, J. L., Auerbach, E. J., Behrens, T. E., ... Robinson, E. C. (2016). The human connectome project's neuroimaging approach. *Nature Neuroscience*, *19*(9), 1175–1187. doi:10.1038/nn.4361 PMID:27571196

Glazier, R. A. (2016). Building rapport to improve retention and success in online classes. *Journal of Political Science Education*, *12*(4), 437–456. doi:10.1080/15512169.2016.1155994

GLM. (n.d.). *Fitting generalized linear models*. Retrieved from https://www.rdocumentation.org/packages/stats/versions/3.5.1/topics/glm

Goldstein, J. (2005). Violent video games. In J. Raessens & J. Goldstein (Eds.), Handbook of computer game studies (pp. 341-357). Cambridge, MA: The MIT Press.

Gonzalez, C. (2009). Conceptions of, and approaches to, teaching online: A study of lecturers teaching postgraduate distance courses. *Higher Education*, *57*(3), 299–314. doi:10.100710734-008-9145-1

Gooblar, D. (2014, March 19). *Student feedback matters – and it goes beyond grading*. Retrieved from https://chroniclevitae.com/news/392-student-feedback-matters-and-it-goes-beyond-grading

Goodman, J., Melkers, J., & Pallais, A. (2019). Can online delivery increase access to education? *Journal of Labor Economics*, *37*(1), 1–34. doi:10.1086/698895

Goodyear, P., Salmon, G., Spector, J., Steeples, C., & Tickner, S. (2001). Competences for online teaching: A special report. *Educational Technology Research and Development*, *49*(1), 65–72. doi:10.1007/BF02504508

Gotlib, D., Saragoza, P., Segal, S., Goodman, L., & Schwartz, V. (2019). Evaluation and management of mental health disability in post-secondary students. *Current Psychiatry Reports*, *21*(6), 1–7. doi:10.100711920-019-1024-1 PMID:31037483

Graham, C., Cagiltay, K., Lim, B. R., Craner, J., & Duffy, T. M. (2001). Seven principles of effective teaching: A practical lens for evaluating online courses. *The Technology Source*, *30*(5), 50–53.

Gray, J. A., & DiLoreto, M. (2016). The effects of student engagement, student satisfaction, and perceived learning in online learning environments. *The International Journal of Educational Leadership Preparation*, *11*(1).

Gray, J. A., & Diloreto, M. (2016). The effects of student engagements, student's satisfaction, And perceived learning in online learning environments. *The International Journal of Educational Leadership Preparation*, *11*(1).

Gray, P., & Riley, G. (2013). The challenges and benefits of unschooling according to 232 families who have chosen that route. *Journal of Unschooling and Alternative Learning*, *7*, 1–27.

Compilation of References

Green, T., Hoffman, M., Donovan, L., & Phuntsog, N., (2017). Cultural communication Characteristics and student connectedness in an online environment: perceptions of online graduate students. *International Journal of E-Learning & Distance Education, 32*(2).

Greenland, S. J., & Moore, C. (2014). Patterns of student enrolment and attrition in Australian open access online education: A preliminary case study. *Open Praxis, 6*(1), 45–54. doi:10.5944/openpraxis.6.1.95

Gregory, J., & Salmon, G. (2013). Professional development for online university teaching. *Distance Education, 34*(3), 256–270. doi:10.1080/01587919.2013.835771

Gregson, M., & Hillier, Y. (2015). *Reflective Teaching in Further, Adult and Vocational Education* (4th ed.). Bloomsbury Academic.

Gulbahar, Y., & Kalelioglu, F. (2015). Competencies for e-Instructors: How to Qualify and Guarantee Sustainability. *Contemporary Educational Technology, 6*(2), 140–154.

Gunter, B. (2005). Psychological effects of video games. In J. Raessens & J. Goldstein (Eds.), Handbook of computer game studies (pp. 145-160). Cambridge, MA: The MIT Press.

Gurley, L. E. (2018). Educators' preparation to teach, perceived teaching presence, and perceived teaching presence behaviors in blended and online learning environments. *Online Learning, 22*(2), 197–220.

Hake, R. (2008). Interactive-engagement versus traditional methods: A six-thousand-student survey of mechanics test data for introductory physics courses. *American Journal of Physics, 66*(1), 64–74. doi:10.1119/1.18809

Hamari, J., & Eranti, V. (2011). Framework for designing and evaluating game achievements. *Proceedings of DiGRA 2011 Conference: Think Design Play*. Retrieved November 27, 2014 from http://www.quilageo.com/wp-content/uploads/2013/07/Framework-for-Designing-Eval-11307.59151.pdf

Hamari, J., Koivisto, J., & Sarsa, H. (2014). *Does gamification work? A literature review of empirical studies on gamification.* Paper presented at The 47th Hawaii International Conference on System Sciences. 10.1109/HICSS.2014.377

Hampton, D., Pearce, P. F., & Moser, D. K. (2017). Preferred methods of learning for nursing students in an on-line degree program. *Journal of Professional Nursing, 33*(1), 27–37. doi:10.1016/j.profnurs.2016.08.004 PMID:28131145

Hanus, M. D., & Fox, J. (2015). Assessing the effects of gamification in the classroom: A longitudinal study on motivation, satisfaction, effort, and grades. *Computers & Education, 80*, 152–161. doi:10.1016/j.compedu.2014.08.019

Hargreaves, D. H. (1994). The new professionalism: The synthesis of professional and institutional development. *Teaching and Teacher Education, 10*(4), 423–438. doi:10.1016/0742-051X(94)90023-X

Harrell, I. L. II, & Bower, B. L. (2011). Student characteristics that predict persistence in community college online courses. *American Journal of Distance Education, 25*(3), 178–191. doi:10.1080/08923647.2011.590107

Harris, S. M., Larrier, Y. I., & Castano-Bishop, M. (2011). Development of the student expectations of online learning survey (SEOLS): A pilot study. *Online Journal of Distance Learning Administration, 19*(5), 1–12.

Hart, C. (2012). Factors associated with student persistence in an online program of study: A review of the literature. *Journal of Interactive Online Learning, 11*(1), 19–42. Retrieved from http://www.ncolr.org/jiol/issues/pdf/11.1.2.pdf

Harting, K., & Erthal, M. J. (2005). History Of Distance Learning. *Information Technology, Learning, and Performance Journal, 23*(1), 35-44. Retrieved from http:// ezproxy.liberty.edu/login?url=https://search-proquest-com.ezproxy.liberty.edu/docview/219815808?accountid=12085

Hassar, W., & Bailey, T. (2014). *Projections of education statistics to 2022*. National Center for Education Statistics, US Dept. of Education.

Hattie, J. (2012). *Visible learning for teachers: Maximising impact on learning*. Oxford, UK: Routledge. doi:10.4324/9780203181522

Haycock, D. (2004). The long-lost truth': Sir Isaac Newton and the Newtonian pursuit of ancient knowledge. *Studies in History and Philosophy of Science, 35*(3), 605–623. doi:10.1016/j.shpsa.2004.06.009

He, Y. (2014). Universal Design for Learning in an Online Teacher Education Course: Enhancing Learners' Confidence to Teach Online. *MERLOT Journal of Online Learning and Teaching 10*(2), 283-297.

Helm Coordinated Science Laboratory. (1960). *SL Quarterly Report*. Urbana, IL: Online Learning and Innovative Online Learning. Retrieved from http://www.innovativelearning.com/online_learning/timeline.html

Herbert, M. (2006). Staying the course: A study in online student satisfaction and retention. *Online Journal of Distance Learning Administration, 9*(4), 300–317.

Herman, J. H. (2012). Faculty development programs: The frequency and variety of professional development programs available to online instructors. *Journal of Asynchronous Learning Networks, 16*(5), 87–106. https://doi-org.proxy1.ncu.edu/10.24059/olj.v16i5.282

Hersman, B. L. (2014). Increasing student engagement in online classes. *Chronicle of Kinesiology & Physical Education in Higher Education, 25*(2), 23–25.

Hewett, B. L., & Bourelle, T. (2017). Online teaching and learning in technical communication: Continuing the conversation. *Technical Communication Quarterly, 26*(3), 217–222. doi:10.1080/10572252.2017.1339531

Heyman, E. (2010). Overcoming student retention issues in higher education online programs. *Online Journal of Distance Learning Administration, 13*(4).

Hill, J. R., Song, L., & West, R. E. (2009). Social learning theory and web-based learning environments: A review of research and discussion of implications. *American Journal of Distance Education, 23*(2), 88–103. doi:10.1080/08923640902857713

Hilton, J. III, & Plummer, K. (2013). Examining student spiritual outcomes as a result of a general education religion course. *Christian Higher Education, 12*(3), 331–348. doi:10.1080/15363759.2013.824352

Hitchcock, C., Meyer, A., Rose, D., & Jackson, R. (2002). Providing new access to the general curriculum: Universal Design for Learning. *Teaching Exceptional Children, 35*(2), 8–17. doi:10.1177/004005990203500201

Hodges, C. (2004). Designing to motivate: Motivational techniques to incorporate in e-learning experience. *Journal of Interactive Online Learning, 2*(3), 1–7.

Hofer, B. K., Yu, S. L., & Pintrich, P. R. (1998). Teaching college students to be self-regulated learners. In D. H. Schunk & B. J. Zimmerman (Eds.), *Self-regulated learning: From teaching to self-reflective practice* (pp. 57–85). New York: Guilford Press.

Hoffman, D. D. (2016). Considering the Crossroads of Distance eEducation: The Experiences of Instructors as they Transitioned to Online or Blended Courses. *Education Database*. Retrieved from https://search-proquest-com.ezproxy.shu.edu/docview/1806944939?accountid=13793

Hoffman, S. J. (2011). *Teaching the Humanities Online: A Practical Guide to the Virtual Classroom: A Practical Guide to the Virtual Classroom*. Armonk: Routledge.

Holbeck, R., & Hartman, J. (2018). Efficient strategies for maximizing online student satisfaction: Applying technologies to increase cognitive presence, social presence, and teaching presence. *Journal of Educators Online, 15*(3), 91–95. https://doi- org.lopes.idm.oclc.org/10.9743/jeo.2018.15.3.6

Holloway, S. (2018, May 2). Gamification in Education: 4 Ways To Bring Games To Your Classroom. *Top Hat Blog*. Retrieved on June 12, 2019 from https://tophat.com/blog/gamification-education-class/

Holmberg, B. (1986). *Growth and Structure of Distance Education*. London: Croom.

Holzweiss, P. C., Joyner, S. A., Fuller, M. B., Henderson, S., & Young, R. (2014). Online graduate students' perceptions of best learning experiences. *Distance Education, 35*(3), 311–323. doi:10.1080/01587919.2015.955262

Hsiao, E., Mikolaj, P., & Shih, Y. (2017). A design case of scaffolding hybrid/online student-centered learning with multimedia. *Journal of Educators Online, 14*(1), 1–9.

Hudson, K. A. (2014). Teaching nursing concepts through an online discussion board. *The Journal of Nursing Education, 53*(9), 531–536. doi:10.3928/01484834-20140820-01 PMID:25138567

Hurtado, S., & Carter, D. F. (1997). Effects of college transition and perceptions of the campus racial climate on Latino college students' sense of belonging. *Sociology of Education, 70*(4), 324–345. doi:10.2307/2673270

Huss, J.A., & Estep, S. (2013). The perceptions of students toward online learning at a Midwestern University: What are students telling us and what are we doing about it? *I.E.: Inquiry in Education, 4*(2).

IDEA. (2019). *Services*. Retrieved from https://www.ideaedu.org/Services

Individuals With Disabilities Education Act, 20 U.S.C. § 1400 (2004).

International Society for Technology in Education. (2018). *ISTE Standards for Educators*. Retrieved from https://www.iste.org/standards/for-educators

Intramural Research Program. (2016). *NIH researchers identify heritable brain connections linked to ADHD*. Retrieved from https://irp.nih.gov/blog/post/2016/11/nih-researchers-identify-heritable-brain-connections-linked-to-adhd

Ivankova, N. V., & Stick, S. L. (2007). Students' persistence in a distributed doctoral program in educational leadership in higher education: A mixed methods study. *Research in Higher Education, 48*(1), 93–135. doi:10.100711162-006-9025-4

Ivtzan, I., Young, T., Martman, J., Jeffrey, A., Lomas, T., Hart, R., & Eiroa-Orosa, F. J. (2016). Integrating mindfulness into positive psychology: A randomized controlled trial of an online positive mindfulness program. *Mindfulness, 7*(6), 1396–1407. doi:10.100712671-016-0581-1

Jaafar, R., & Schwartz, J. (2018). Applying holistic adult learning theory to the study of calculus. *Journal of University Teaching & Learning Practice, 15*(3), 6–16.

Jaffee, D. (2001). Peer cohorts and the unintended consequences of freshman learning communities. *College Teaching, 55*(2), 65–71. doi:10.3200/CTCH.55.2.65-71

Jaggars, S. S. (2011). *Online learning: Does it help low-income and underprepared students?* CCRC Working Paper No. 26. Assessment of Evidence Series. Columbia University: Community College Research Center. Retrieved from: https://ccrc.tc.columbia.edu/publications/online-learning-low-income-underprepared.html

Jaggars, S., Edgecombe, N., & Stacey, G. (2013). *Creating an effective online instructor presence*. Community College Research Center Teachers College, Columbia University. Retrieved from https://ccrc.tc.columbia.edu/media/k2/attachments/effective-online-instructor-presence.pdf

Jaggars, S. S. (2014). Choosing between online and face-to-face courses: Community college student voices. *American Journal of Distance Education, 28*(1), 27–38. doi:10.1080/08923647.2014.867697

Jaggars, S. S., & Xu, D. (2016). How do online course design features influence student performance? *Computers & Education, 95*, 270–284. doi:10.1016/j.compedu.2016.01.014

James, S., Swan, K., & Daston, C. (2016). Retention, progression and the taking of online courses. *Journal of Asynchronous Learning Networks, 20*(2). doi:10.24059/olj.v20i2.780

Jiang, W. (2017). Role assignment and sense of community in an online course. *Distance Education*. doi:10.1080/01587919.2017.1299564

Johnson, T. (2014, April). *Gamification and User Engagement in E-learning and Documentation*. Academic Press.

Johnson, C. (2011). Activities using Process-Oriented Guided Inquiry Learning (POGIL) in the foreign language classroom. *Die Unterrichtspraxis/Teaching German*. doi:10.1111/j.1756-1221.2011.00090.x

Johnson, N. (2012). *The institutional costs of student attrition*. Washington, DC: Delta Cost Project at American Institutes for Research. Retrieved from http://eric.ed.gov/?id=ED536126

Jo, I.-H., Kim, D., & Yoon, M. (2015). Constructing proxy variables to measure adult learners' time management strategies in LMS. *Journal of Educational Technology & Society, 18*(3), 214–225.

Jones, C. (2018, August 21). *Accessibility must be more than an add-on to online pedagogy*. Retrieved from https://www.universityaffairs.ca/opinion/in-my-opinion/accessibility-must-be-more-than-an-add-on-to-online-pedagogy/

Joyner, S. A. (2014). The importance of student-instructor connections in graduate level online courses. *Journal of Online Learning and Teaching / MERLOT, 10*(3), 436–445.

Kahneman, D. (2011). *Thinking, fast and slow*. Macmillan.

Kang, H. (2009). *A comparative study of the distance education history in China and the United States: A socio-historical perspective* (Ph.D. Dissertation). The Pennsylvania State University.

Kang, Y. W. (2015, August). Development of the "Hybrid Interactive Rhetorical Engagement" (H.I.R.E.) Scale: Implications for Digital Gamification Research. In H. Gangadharbatla & D. Z. Davis (Eds.), *Emerging Research and Trends in Gamification* (pp. 72–92). Hershey, PA: IGI Global.

Kapp, K. M. (2012). *The Gamification of Learning and Instruction: Game-based Methods and Strategies for Training and Education*. New York: Wiley.

Katsiyannis, A., Zhang, D., Landmark, L., & Reber, A. (2009). Postsecondary education for individuals with disabilities: Legal and practice considerations. *Journal of Disability Policy Studies, 20*(1), 35–45. doi:10.1177/1044207308324896

Katz, J., & Sokal, L. (2016). Universal Design for Learning as a Bridge to Inclusion: A Qualitative Report of Student Voices. *International Journal of Whole Schooling, 12*(2), 37–63.

Kauffman, H. (2015). A review of predictive factors of student success in and satisfaction with online learning. *Research in Learning Technology, 23*, 1–13. doi:10.3402/rlt.v23.26507

Kebritchi, M., Lipschuetz, A., & Santiague, L. (2017). Issues and Challenges for Teaching Successful Online Courses in Higher Education: A Literature Review. *Journal of Educational Technology Systems, 46*(1), 4–29. doi:10.1177/0047239516661713

Keebler, B. (2014). Online education: Past, present, and future. *Momentum, 45*, 35–37.

Ke, F. (2013). Online interaction arrangements on quality of online interactions performed by diverse learners across disciplines. *Internet and Higher Education*, *16*(1), 14–22. doi:10.1016/j.iheduc.2012.07.003

Kelly, R. (2009). Seven easy ways to personalize your online course [Blog]. Retrieved from https://www.facultyfocus.com/articles/online-education/seven-easy-ways-to-personalize- your-online-course/

Kelly, J. (2017). Professional learning and adult learning theory: A connection. *Northwest Journal of Teacher Education*, *12*(2), 4–18. doi:10.15760/nwjte.2017.12.4

Kennette, L. N., & Redd, B. R. (2015). Instructor presence helps bridge the gap between online and on-campus learning. *The College Quarterly*, *18*(4).

Kerksick, C. M., Arnet, S., Schoenfled, B. J., Stout, J. R., Campbell, B., Wilborn, C. D., ... Antonio, J. (2017). International society of sports nutrition position stand: Nutrient timing. *Journal of the International Society of Sports Nutrition*, *14*(33). doi:10.118612970-017-0189-4 PMID:28919842

Kerr, A. (2006). *The business and culture of digital games: Gamework/gameplay*. London, UK: Sage Publications.

Kilburn, A., Kilburn, B., & Cates, T. (2014). Drivers of student retention: System availability, privacy, value and loyalty in online higher education. *Academy of Educational Leadership Journal*, *18*(4), 1–14.

Killen, C. (2015). *Enhancing the student digital experience: A strategic approach*. Retrieved February 9, 2016, from https://www.jisc.ac.uk/guides/enhancing-the-digital-student-experience

Kincey, S., Farmer, E., Errick, D., Wiltsher, C., McKenzie, D., & Mibiza, S. (2019, January). From chalkboard to digital media: The evolution of technology and its relationship to minority students' learning experiences. *Journal of Faculty Development*, *33*(1), 65–76.

King-Sears, M. (2009). Universal design for learning: Technology and pedagogy. *Learning Disability Quarterly*, *32*(4), 199–201. doi:10.2307/27740372

Kiousis, S. (2002). Interactivity: A concept explication. *New Media & Society*, *4*(3), 355–383. doi:10.1177/146144480200400303

Kirwan Institute for the Study of Race and Ethnicity. (2015). *Understanding implicit bias*. Retrieved from: http://kirwaninstitute.osu.edu/research/understanding-implicit-bias/

Klimova, B.F. & Kacet, J. (2014). Hybrid learning and its current role in the teaching of foreign languages. *Procedia- Social and Behavioral Sciences, 182*(2015), 477-481.

Knabb, J. J., & Vazquez, V. E. (2018). A randomized controlled trial of a 2-week internet-based contemplative prayer program for Christians with daily stress. *Spirituality in Clinical Practice*, *5*(1), 37–53. doi:10.1037cp0000154

Korhonen, H., Montola, M., & Arrasvuori, J. (2009). *Understanding playful user experience through digital games*. Paper presented at the International Conference on Designing Pleasurable of Products and Interface, Compiegne University of Technology. Compiegne, France.

Kragler, S., Martin, L. E., & Sylvester, R. (2014). Lessons learned: What our history and research tell us about teachers' professional learning. In Handbook of professional development in education: Successful models and practices, preK-12. Guilford.

Krathwohl, D. R. (2002). A Revision of Bloom's Taxonomy: An Overview. *Theory into Practice*, *41*(4), 212–218. doi:10.120715430421tip4104_2

Kuh, G. D. (2001). Assessing what really matters to student learning: Inside the National Survey of Student Engagement. *Change: The Magazine of Higher Learning*, *33*(3), 10–17. doi:10.1080/00091380109601795

Kuh, G. D. (2003). What we're learning about student engagement from NSSE: Benchmarks for effective educational practices. *Change: The Magazine of Higher Learning, 35*(2), 24–32. doi:10.1080/00091380309604090

Kuh, G. D. (2009). The National Survey of Student Engagement: Conceptual and empirical foundations. *New Directions for Institutional Research, 141*, 5–20. doi:10.1002/ir.283

Kuh, G. D., Kinzie, J., Cruce, T., Shoup, R., & Gonyea, R. M. (2007). *Connecting the dots: Multi-faceted analyses of the relationships between student engagement results from the NSSE, and the institutional practices and conditions that foster student success.* Bloomington, IN: Center for Postsecondary Research, Indiana University Bloomington. Retrieved from https://webmail.csuchico.edu/vpaa/wasc/docs/EERDocs/NSSE/NSSE_Connecting_the_Dots_Report.pdf

Kumar, K. L., & Wideman, M. (2014). Accessible by Design: Applying UDL Principles in a First Year Undergraduate Course. *Canadian Journal of Higher Education, 44*(1), 125–147.

Kupczynski, L., Gibson, A. M., Ice, P., Richardson, J., & Challoo, L. (2011). The impact of frequency on achievement in online courses: A study from a south Texas university. *Journal of Interactive Online Learning, 10*(3), 141–149.

Kuzma, A., Kuzma, J., & Thiewes, H. (2015). Business student attitudes, experience, and satisfaction with online courses. *American Journal of Business Education (Online), 8*(2), 121. doi:10.19030/ajbe.v8i2.9134

Kwon, C., Kim, Y., & Woo, T. (2015). Digital-physical reality game: Mapping of physical space with fantasy in context-based learning games. *Games and Culture*, 1–32.

Kwon, S. (2009). The analysis of differences of learners' participation, procrastination, learning time and achievement by adult learners' adherence of learning time schedule in e-learning environments. *Journal of Learner-Centered Curriculum and Instruction, 9*(3), 61–86.

Kyong-Jee, K., & Bonk, C. J. (2006). The future of online teaching and learning in higher education: The survey says.... *EDUCAUSE Quarterly, 29*(4). Retrieved from http://faculty.weber.edu/eamsel/Research%20Groups/On-line%20Learning/Bonk%20(2006).pdf

Kyong-Lee, K., Kiu, S., & Bonk, C. (2005). Online MBA students' perceptions of online learning: benefits, challenges, and suggestions. *The Internet and Higher Education, 8*(4), 335-344. Retrieved from https://www-sciencedirect.com.ezproxy.liberty.edu/science/article/pii/S1096751605000618

Ladyshewsky, R. (2013). Instructor presence in online courses and student satisfaction. *International Journal for the Scholarship of Teaching and Learning, 7*(1), 1–23. doi:10.20429/ijsotl.2013.070113

Lambert, J. L., & Fisher, J. L. (2013, Spring). Community of Inquiry Framework: Establishing community in an online class. *Journal of Interactive Online Learning, 13*(1), 1–16. Retrieved from www.ncolr.org/jiol

Landers, R. N., & Armstrong, M. B. (2017). Enhancing instructional outcomes with gamification: An empirical test of the Technology-Enhanced Training Effectiveness Model. *Computers in Human Behavior, 71*, 499–507. doi:10.1016/j.chb.2015.07.031

Landers, R. N., & Callan, R. C. (2012). Training evaluation in virtual worlds: Development of a model. *Journal of Virtual Worlds Research, 5*(3), 1–20. doi:10.4101/jvwr.v5i3.6335

Larkin, K., & Jamieson-Proctor, R. (2015). Using transactional distance theory to redesign an online mathematics education course for pre-service primary teachers. *Mathematics Teacher Education and Development, 17*(1), 44–61.

Larreamendy-Joerns, J., & Leinhardt, G. (2006). Going the distance with online education. *Review of Educational Research, 76*(4), 567–605. doi:10.3102/00346543076004567

Compilation of References

Laurillard, D. (2002). *Rethinking university teaching*. London: Routledge Falmer. doi:10.4324/9780203160329

Leaning, M. (2015). A study of the use of games and gamification to enhance student engagement, experience and achievement on a theory-based course of an undergraduate media degree. *Journal of Media Practice, 16*(2), 155–170. doi:10.1080/14682753.2015.1041807

Lear, J. L., Isernhagen, J. C., LaCost, B. A., & King, J. W. (2009). Instructor presence for web- based classes. *Delta Pi Epsilon Journal, 51*(2), 86–98.

Learning Forward. (2011). Standards for Professional Learning. *The Learning Professional, 32*(4), 41-44. Retrieved from https://learningforward.org/docs/august-2011/referenceguide324.pdf?sfvrsn=2

Lee, Y., & Choi, J. (2011). A review of online course dropout research: Implications for practice and future research. *Educational Technology Research and Development, 59*(5), 593–618. doi:10.100711423-010-9177-y

Lerner, C. S. (2004). Accommodations for the learning disabled: A level playing field or affirmative action for elites. *Vanderbilt Law Review, 57*, 1043.

Levy, Y. (2007). Comparing dropouts and persistence in e-learning courses. *Computers & Education, 48*(2), 185–204. doi:10.1016/j.compedu.2004.12.004

Lightweis, S. (2013). College success: A fresh look at differentiated instruction and other student-centered strategies. *The College Quarterly, 16*(3), 1–9.

Linardopoulos, N. (2010). A cross-comparison of perceptions of online education: A case of an online MBA program. *Education Database*. Retrieved from https://search-proquest-com.ezproxy.shu.edu/docview/741224498?accountid=13793

Linda, L. (2015). The current conundrum of state authorization for online education programs and clinical placement. *Journal of Allied Health, 44*(3), 188–192. PMID:26342618

Linderman, D., & Kolenovic, Z. (2013). Moving the completion needle at community colleges: CUNY's accelerated study in associate programs (ASAP). *Change: The Magazine of Higher Learning, 45*(5), 43–50. doi:10.1080/00091383.2013.824350

List, A., & Nadasen, D. (2017). Motivation and self-regulation in community college transfer students at a four-year online university. *Community College Journal of Research and Practice, 41*(12), 842–866. doi:10.1080/10668926.2016.1242096

Liu, X., Liu, S., Lee, S., & Magjuka, R. J. (2010). Cultural differences in online learning: International student perceptions. *Journal of Educational Technology & Society, 13*(3), 177–188.

Liu, X., Magjuka, R. J., Bonk, C. J., & Lee, S.-h. (2007). Does sense of community matter? *The Quarterly Review of Distance Education, 8*(1), 9–24.

Lohnes, S., & Kinzer, C. (2007). Questioning assumptions about students' expectations for technology in college classrooms. *Innovate (North Miami Beach, Fla.), 3*(5). Retrieved from http://www.innovateonline.info/index.php?view=article&id=2431

Lonn, S., & Teasley, S. D. (2009). Saving time or innovating practice: Investigating perceptions and uses of learning management systems. *Computers & Education, 53*(3), 686–694. doi:10.1016/j.compedu.2009.04.008

Loudon, M., & Sharp, M. (2006). Online class review: Using streaming-media technology. *Journal of College Science Teaching, 36*(3), 39–43.

Lowenthal, P., Bauer, C., & Chen, K. (2015). Student perceptions of online learning: An analysis of Online Course Evaluations. *American Journal of Distance Education, 29*(2), 85–97. doi:10.1080/08923647.2015.1023621

Luft, A., & Buitrago, M. (2005). Stages of motor skill learning. *Molecular Neurobiology, 32*(3), 205–216. doi:10.1385/MN:32:3:205 PMID:16385137

Luyt, I. (2013). Bridging spaces: Cross-cultural perspectives on promoting positive online learning experiences. *Journal of Educational Technology Systems, 42*(1), 3–20. doi:10.2190/ET.42.1.b

Lynch, M. (2008). *What is the Future of Online Learning in Higher Education.* Retrieved from https://www.thetechedvocate.org/future-online-learning-higher-education/

Lynch, M. (2012, February 13). What is culturally responsive pedagogy? *HuffPost.* Retrieved from: https://www.huffpost.com/entry/culturally-responsive-pedagogy_b_1147364

Lynne-Landsman, S., Graber, D., Nichols, J., & Botvin, A. (2011). Is sensation seeking a stable trait or does it change over time? *Journal of Youth and Adolescence, 40*(1), 48–58. doi:10.100710964-010-9529-2 PMID:20354775

Macan, T. H., Shahani, C., Dipboye, R. L., & Phillips, A. P. (1990). College students' time management: Correlations with academic performance and stress. *Journal of Educational Psychology, 82*(4), 760–768. doi:10.1037/0022-0663.82.4.760

Macdonald, J., & Poniatowska, B. (2011). Designing the professional development of staff for teaching online: An OU (UK) case study. *Distance Education, 32*(1), 119–134. doi:10.1080/01587919.2011.565481

MaceR. (n.d.). Retrieved from: https://projects.ncsu.edu/ncsu/design/cud/about_ud/about_ud.htm

Maher, M. A. (2005). The evolving meaning and influence of cohort membership. *Innovative Higher Education, 30*(3), 195–211. doi:10.100710755-005-6304-5

Mahoney, P., Macfarlane, S., & Ajjawi, A. (2019). A qualitative synthesis of video feedback in higher education. *Teaching in Higher Education, 24*(2), 157–179. doi:10.1080/13562517.2018.1471457

Mandzuk, D., Hasinoff, S., & Seifert, K. (2003). Inside a student cohort: Teacher education from a social capital perspective. *Canadian Journal of Education, 2,* 168–184. Retrieved from http://www.jstor.org/stable/10.2307/1602159

Marino, M. T. (2010). Defining a technology research agenda for elementary and secondary students with learning and other high incidence disabilities in inclusive science classrooms. *Journal of Special Education Technology, 25*(1), 1–28. doi:10.1177/016264341002500101

Markova, T., Glazkova, I., & Zaborova, E. (2017). Quality Issues of Online Distance Learning. *Procedia - Social and Behavioral Sciences, 237,* 685–691. doi:10.1016/j.sbspro.2017.02.043

Martin, J. (2019). Building relationships and increasing engagement in the virtual classroom: Practical tools for the online instructor. *Journal of Educators Online, 16*(1), 1-8.

Martin, K. A., Goldwasser, M. M., & Galentino, R. (2016). Impact of cohort bonds on student satisfaction and engagement. *Current Issues in Education, 19*(3), 1–14. Retrieved from http://cie.asu.edu/ojs/index.php/cieatasu/article/view/1550

Martin, D. (1977). Early warning of bank failure. A logit regression approach. *Journal of Banking & Finance, 1*(3), 249–276. doi:10.1016/0378-4266(77)90022-X

Masoumi, D., & Lindström, B. (2012). Quality in e-learning: A framework for promoting and assuring quality in virtual institutions. *Journal of Computer Assisted Learning, 28*(1), 27–41. doi:10.1111/j.1365-2729.2011.00440.x

Mayadas, F., Bouren, J., & Bacsich, P. (2009). Online education today. Reprinted with permission from AAAS. *Journal of Asynchronous Learning Networks, 13*(2), 49. doi:10.1126cience.1168874

Compilation of References

McClannon, T. W., Cheney, A. W., Bolt, L. L., & Terry, K. P. (2018, December). Predicting sense of presence and sense of community in immersive online learning environments. *Online Learning, 22*(4), 141-159. Retrieved from: https://olj.onlinelearningconsortium.org/index.php/olj

McClenney, K., & Oriano, A. (2012). From promising to high-impact. *Community College Journal, 82*(5), 38–45.

McClure, J. W. (2007). International graduates' cross-cultural adjustment: Experiences, coping strategies, and suggested programmatic responses. *Teaching in Higher Education, 12*(2), 199–217. doi:10.1080/13562510701191976

McDougald, J. (2018). Innovating with ICTs in content and language environments. *Latin American Journal of Content & Language Integrated Learning, 10*(2), 181–188. doi:10.5294/laclil.2017.10.2.1

McGarry, B. J., Theobald, K., Lewis, P. A., & Coyer, F. (2015). Flexible learning design in curriculum delivery promotes student engagement and develops metacognitive learners: An integrated review. *Nurse Education Today, 35*(9), 966–973. doi:10.1016/j.nedt.2015.06.009 PMID:26169287

McGuire, S. (2016, August 5). 9 technology tools to engage students in the classroom. *TeachThrough: We Grow Teachers*. Retrieved on June 11, 2019 from https://www.teachthought.com/technology/2019-technology-tools-engage-students-classroom/

Meillur, C. (2018). Online learning: 6 types of interactions at play. Knowledge One. Retrieved August 27, 2019, from https://knowledgeone.ca/online-learning-6-types-of-interactions-at-play/

Meirink, J. A., Imants, J., Meijer, P. C., & Verloop, N. (2010). Teacher learning and collaboration in innovative teams. *Cambridge Journal of Education, 40*(2), 161–181. doi:10.1080/0305764X.2010.481256

Meo, G. (2008). Curriculum planning for all learners: Applying universal design for learning (UDL) to a high school reading comprehension program. *Preventing School Failure, 52*(2), 21–30. doi:10.3200/PSFL.52.2.21-30

Meyer, A., & Rose, D. H. (2005). The future is in the margins: The role of technology and disability in educational reform. In D. H. Rose, A. Meyer, & C. Hitchcock (Eds.), *The universally designed classroom: Accessible curriculum and digital technologies* (pp. 13–35). Cambridge, MA: Harvard Education Press.

Meyer, K. A. (2012). The influence of online teaching on faculty productivity. *Innovative Higher Education, 37*(1), 37–52. doi:10.100710755-011-9183-y

Meyer, K. A. (2014). An analysis of the research on faculty development for online teaching and identification of new directions. *Journal of Asynchronous Learning Networks, 17*(4), 93–112.

Meyer, K. A. (2014). Student engagement in online learning: What works and why. *ASHE Higher Education Report, 40*(6), 1–114. doi:10.1002/aehe.20018

Meyer, K. A., & Murrell, V. S. (2014). A national study of training content and activities for faculty development for online learning. *Journal of Asynchronous Learning Networks, 18*(1), 3–18.

Mezirow, J. (1997). Transformative Learning: Theory to Practice. In P. Cranton (Ed.), *New Directions for Adult and Continuing Education 74*. San Francisco, CA: Jossey-Bass. doi:10.1002/ace.7401

Mgutshini, T. (2013). Online or not? A comparison of students' experiences of an online and an on-campus class. *Curationis, 36*(1), 1–7. doi:10.4102/curationis.v36i1.73 PMID:23718147

Michael, K. (2012). Virtual classroom: Reflections of online learning. *Campus-Wide Information Systems, 29*(3), 156–165. doi:10.1108/10650741211243175

Michigan State University. (2018). *Flat rate tuition: Frequently asked questions*. Retrieved July, 2019 from https://undergrad.msu.edu/uploads/files/FlatRateTuition-FAQ-2018-12-06b.pdf?fbclid=IwAR36SC59rvvS0-Je29kMMRrGBxlzbj_3ktsZbLlkcc4YBJkIFGsz24pqfnI

Miller, S. T., & Redman, S. L. (2010). Improving instructor presence in an online introductory astronomy course through video demonstrations. *Astronomy Education Review*, *9*(1).

Mishra, P., & Koehler, M. (2006). Technological pedagogical content knowledge: A framework for teacher knowledge. *Teachers College Record*, *108*(6), 1017–1054. doi:10.1111/j.1467-9620.2006.00684.x

Mizrachi, D., & Bates, M. J. (2013). Undergraduates' personal academic information management and the consideration of time and task-urgency. *Journal of the American Society for Information Science and Technology*, *64*(8), 1590–1607. doi:10.1002/asi.22849

Moe, R. (2014). The evolution and impact of the massive open online course. *Education Database*. Retrieved from https://search-proquest-com.ezproxy.shu.edu/docview/1554699058?accountid=1379

Mohr, S., & Shelton, K. (2017). Best practices framework for online faculty professional development: A Delphi study. *Online Learning*, *21*(4), 123–143.

Money, W., & Dean, B. P. (2019). Incorporating student population differences for effective online education: A content-based review and integrative model. *Computers & Education*, *138*, 57–82. doi:10.1016/j.compedu.2019.03.013

Moore, M. (1997). Theory of transactional distance. In Theoretical Principles of Distance Education. Routledge.

Moore, G. E., Warner, W. J., & Jones, D. W. (2016). Student-to-student interaction in distance education classes: What do graduate students want. *Journal of Agricultural Education*, *57*(2), 1–13. doi:10.5032/jae.2016.02001

Moore, M. G. (1989). Editorial: Three Types of Interaction. *American Journal of Distance Education*. doi:10.1080/08923648909526659

Moore, M., & Kearsley, G. (2005). *Distance education: A systems view* (2nd ed.). Belmont, CA: Wadsworth.

Moore, R. L. (2016). Interacting at a distance: creating engagement in online learning environments. In L. Kyei-Blankson, J. Blankson, E. Ntulli, & C. Agyeman (Eds.), *Handbook of Research on Strategic Management of Interaction, Presence, and Participation in Online Courses* (pp. 401–425). Hershey, PA: IGI Global. doi:10.4018/978-1-4666-9582-5.ch016

Moore, R. L., & Fodrey, B. (2018). Distance education and technology infrastructure: Strategies and opportunities. In A. Pina, V. Walker, & B. Harris (Eds.), *Leading and Managing elearning: What the e-learning learner needs to know* (pp. 87–100). Cham: Springer. doi:10.1007/978-3-319-61780-0_7

Moos, D., & Amanda, M. (2015). The Cyclical Nature of Self-Regulated Learning Phases: Stable Between Learning Tasks? *Journal of Cognitive Education and Psychology*, *14*(2), 199–218. doi:10.1891/1945-8959.14.2.199

Morris, S. M., & Stommel, J. (2018). *An urgency of teachers: The work of critical digital pedagogy* [Kindle for Mac version]. Retrieved from Amazon.com

Morris, L. V., Finnegan, C., & Wu, S.-S. (2005). Tracking student behavior, persistence, and achievement in online courses. *The Internet and Higher Education*, *8*(3), 221–231. doi:10.1016/j.iheduc.2005.06.009

Morschheuser, B. S., Rivera-Pelayo, V., Mazarakis, A., & Zacharias, V. (2014). Interaction and reflection with quantified self and gamification: An experimental study. *Journal of Literacy and Technology*, *15*(2), 136–156.

Morschheuser, B., Hassan, L., Werder, K., & Hamari, J. (2018, March). How to design gamification? A method for engineering gamified software. *Information and Software Technology*, *95*, 217–239. doi:10.1016/j.infsof.2017.10.015

Moskal, P., Thompson, K., & Futch, L. (2015). Enrollment, engagement, and satisfaction in the BlendKit faculty development open, online course. *Online Learning, 19*(4), 1–12. doi:10.24059/olj.v19i4.555

Moutafidou, A., & Sivropoulou, I. (2010). Cooperation in all-day kindergartens: Kindergarten teachers' beliefs. *Procedia: Social and Behavioral Sciences, 5*, 350–355. doi:10.1016/j.sbspro.2010.07.103

Murphy, E., & Rodriguez-Manzanares, M. A. (2012). Rapport in distance education. *The International Review of Research in Open and Distributed Learning, 13*(1), 167. doi:10.19173/irrodl.v13i1.1057

Muyinda, P. B. (2012). Open and distance learning in dual mode universities: a treasure unexploited. In E. J. L. M. A. D. Benson (Ed.), International Perspectives of Distance Learning in Higher Education (p. 33). Academic Press.

Nandi, D., Hamilton, M., & Harland, J. (2012). Evaluating the quality of interaction in asynchronous discussion forums in fully online courses. *Distance Education, 33*(1), 5–30. doi:10.1080/01587919.2012.667957

Nardi, B. (2010). My life as a night elf priest: An anthropological account of World of Warcraft. Ann Arbor, MI: University of Michigan Press.

National Center for Education Statistics. (2000). *Classification of Instructional Programs (CIP 2000)*. Retrieved from https://nces.ed.gov/pubs2002/cip2000/

National Survey of Student Engagement. (2015). *Engagement indicators & high-impact practices*. Bloomington, IN: Indiana University Center for Postsecondary Research. Retrieved from http://nsse.indiana.edu/html/high_impact_practices.cfm

Nelson, R., Spence-Thomas, K., & Taylor, C. (2015). *What makes great pedagogy and great professional development: final report. Teaching schools R&D network national themes project 2012-14*. National College for Teaching & Leadership. Retrieved from https://dera.ioe.ac.uk/22157/

Nguyen, T. (2015). The effectiveness of online learning: Beyond no significant difference and future horizons. *MERLOT Journal of Online Learning and Teaching, 11*(2), 309–319.

Ni, A. Y. (2013). Comparing the effectiveness of classroom and online learning: Teaching research methods. *Journal of Public Affairs Education, 19*(2), 199–215. doi:10.1080/15236803.2013.12001730

Nicolaides, A., & Marsick, V. J. (2016). Understanding adult learning in the midst of complex social "Liquid Modernity.". *New Directions for Adult and Continuing Education, 2016*(149), 9–20. doi:10.1002/ace.20172

Nicoll, L. A. (2016). Bringing education online: Institutional logics in the legitimation of and resistance to online higher education. *Education Database*. Retrieved from https://search-proquest-com.ezproxy.shu.edu/docview/1785398290?accountid=13793

Noam, E. M. (1995). Electronics and the Dim Future of the University. *Science, 270*(5234), 247–249. doi:10.1126cience.270.5234.247

Northey, G., Bucic, T., Chylinski, M., & Govin, R. (2015). Increasing student engagement using asynchronous learning. *Journal of Marketing Education, 37*(3), 171–180. doi:10.1177/0273475315589814

Northrup, P. (2002). Online learners' preferences for interaction. *Quarterly Review of Distance Education*. Retrieved from http://www.eric.ed.gov/ERICWebPortal/custom/portlets/recordDetails/detailmini.jshttps://eric.ed.gov/?id=EJ654234

Null, R. (2014). *Universal design: Principles and models* (2nd ed.). Boca Raton, FL: CRC Press.

O'Brien, H. L., & Toms, E. G. (2007). What is user engagement? A conceptual framework for defining user engagement with technology. *Journal of the American Society for Information Science and Technology, 59*(6), 938–955. doi:10.1002/asi.20801

O'Hara, S., & Pritchard, R. (2012). "I'm teaching what?!": Preparing university faculty for online instruction. *Journal of Educational Research and Practice, 2*(1), 42–53.

O'Shea, S. E., Stone, C., & Delahunty, J. (2015). I 'feel' like I am at university even though I am online." Exploring how students narrate their engagement with higher education institutions in an online learning environment. *Distance Education, 36*(1), 41–58. doi:10.1080/01587919.2015.1019970

OECD (Ed.). (2016). How many students complete tertiary education? In *Education at a glance 2016: OECD indicators*. Paris, France: Organisation for Economic Cooperation and Development. Retrieved from https://www.oecd-ilibrary.org/education/data/education-at-a-glance/education-at-a-glance-graduation-and-entry-rates-edition-2016_a7768c94-en

OECD. (2005). *Creating Effective Teaching and Learning Environments - First Results from TALIS*. Paris: OECD Publishing.

Oguz, F., Chu, C. M., & Chow, A. S. (2015). Studying online: Student motivations and experiences in ALA-Accredited LIS programs. *Journal of Education for Library and Information Science, 56*(3), 213–231. doi:10.3138/jelis.56.3.213

Okaz, A. A. (2015). Integrating Blended Learning in Higher Education. *Procedia: Social and Behavioral Sciences, 186*, 600–603. doi:10.1016/j.sbspro.2015.04.086

Okech, D., Barner, J., Segoshi, M., & Carney, M. (2014). MSW student experiences in online vs. face-to-face teaching formats? *Social Work Education, 33*(1), 121–134. doi:10.1080/02615479.2012.738661

Olapiriyakul, K., & Scher, J. (2006). A guide to establishing hybrid learning courses: Employing information technology to create a new learning experience, and a case study. *The Internet and Higher Education, 9*(4), 287–301. doi:10.1016/j.iheduc.2006.08.001

Oliver-Hoyo, M. (2011). Lessons Learned from the Implementation and Assessment of Student-Centered Methodologies. *Journal of Technology and Science Education, 1*(1), 2–11. doi:10.3926/jotse.2011.6

Orlando, J. (2016). Understanding Project-Based Learning in Online Education. *Magna Publication*. Retrieved from https://www.facultyfocus.com

Ormrod, J. (2008). *Human learning*. Pearson Prentice-Hall.

Osborne, D. M., Byrne, J. H., Massey, D. L., & Johnston, A. N. (2018). Use of online asynchronous discussion boards to engage students, enhance critical thinking, and foster staff-student/student-student collaboration: A mixed method study. *Nurse Education Today, 70*, 40–46. doi:10.1016/j.nedt.2018.08.014 PMID:30145533

Pace, C. R. (1984). Measuring the quality of student effort. *Current Issues in Higher Education, 2*, 10–16. Retrieved from http://files.eric.ed.gov/fulltext/ED255099.pdf

Pace, J., & Hemmings, A. (2007). Understanding authority in classrooms: A review of theory, ideology, and research. *Review of Educational Research, 77*(1), 4–27. doi:10.3102/003465430298489

Paisley, V. (2013). *Gamification of tertiary courses: An exploratory study of learning and engagement*. Paper presented at the Electric Dreams 30th Asclite Conference, Sydney, Australia.

Palmer, M. S., Wheeler, L. B., & Aneece, I. (2016). Does the document matter? The evolving role of syllabi in higher education. *Change: The Magazine of Higher Learning, 48*(4), 36–47. doi:10.1080/00091383.2016.1198186

Palmer, P. J. (2017). *The courage to teach: Exploring the inner landscape of a teacher's life*. San Francisco, CA: Wiley.

Palvia, S., Aeron, P., Gupta, P., Mahapatra, D., Rosner, R., & Sindhi, S. (2018). Online education: Worldwide status, challenges, trends, and implications. *Journal of Global Information Technology Management, 21*(4), 233–241. doi:10.1080/1097198X.2018.1542262

Compilation of References

Park, C. B., Jarrow, J. E., & Association on Handicapped Student Service Programs in Postsecondary Education. (1991). *Americans with Disabilities Act response kit*. Columbus, OH: AHSSPPE.

Parkes, J., & Harris, M. B. (2002). The purposes of a syllabus. *College Teaching, 50*(2), 55–61. doi:10.1080/87567550209595875

Park, J., & Choi, H. J. (2009). Factors influencing adult learners? Decision to drop out or persist in online learning. *Journal of Educational Technology & Society, 12*(4), 207–217. Retrieved from http://ezproxy.liberty.edu/login?url=https://search-proquest- com.ezproxy.liberty.edu/docview/2139084226?accountid=12085

Park, J., & Choi, H. J. (2009). Factors influencing adult learners' decision to drop out or persist in online learning. *Journal of Educational Technology & Society, 12*(4), 202–217. Retrieved from https://www.researchgate.net/profile/Ji-Hye_Park/publication/220374458_Factors_Influencing_Adult_Learners'_Decision_to_Drop_Out_or_Persist_in_Online_Learning/links/00b495243f10b72a43000000.pdf

Pascarella, E. T. (1985). College environmental influences on learning and cognitive development: A critical review and synthesis. In J. C. Smart (Ed.), *Higher education handbook of theory and research* (pp. 1–61). New York, NY: Agatha Press.

Pascarella, E. T., Smart, J. C., & Ethington, C. A. (1986). Long-term persistence of two-year college students. *Research in Higher Education, 24*(1), 47–71. doi:10.1007/BF00973742

Patterson, D. (2019). The Power of the Human Face in Online Education. *International Journal of Adult Vocational Education and Technology, 10*(1), 13–26. doi:10.4018/IJAVET.2019010102

Pemberton, C. L. A., & Akkary, R. K. (2010). A cohort, is a cohort, is a cohort…or is it? *Journal of Research on Leadership Education, 5*(5), 179–208. doi:10.1177/194277511000500501

Petrides, L. A. (2002). Web-based technologies for distributed (or distance) learning: Creating learning-centered educational experiences in the higher education classroom. *International Journal of Instructional Media, 29*(1), 69–77.

Phillips, D., & National Society for the Study of Education. (2000). *Constructivism in education: Opinions and second opinions on controversial issues* (Yearbook of the National Society for the Study of Education; 99th, pt. 1). Chicago, IL: National Society for the Study of Education.

Phirangee, K., & Malec, A. (2017). Othering in online learning: An examination of social presence, identity, and sense of community. *Distance Education, 38*(2), 160–172. doi:10.1080/01587919.2017.1322457

Piaget, J. (1969). *The Child's Conception of Time*. London: Routledge and Kegan Paul.

Picciano, A. G., Seaman, J., Shea, P., & Swan, K. (2012). Examining the extent and nature of online learning in American K-12 education: The research initiatives of the Alfred P. Sloan Foundation. *The internet and higher education, 15*(2), 127–135. doi:10.1016/j.iheduc.2011.07.004

Pickard, L., Shah, D., & De Simone, J. J. (2018). *Mapping Microcredentials Across MOOC Platforms. In 2018 Learning With MOOCS* (pp. 17–21). Madrid: LWMOOCS. doi:10.1109/LWMOOCS.2018.8534617

Pintrich, P. (2000). The role of goal orientation in self-regulated learning. In M. Boekaerts, M. P. Pintrich, & M. Zeidner (Eds.), Handbook of self-regulation (pp. 452-502). Academic Press. doi:10.1016/B978-012109890-2/50043-3

PLATO User's Guide. (1981). *CDC*. Retrieved from http://www.bitsavers.org/pdf/cdc/plato/97405900C_PLATO_Users_Guide_Apr81.pdf

Post, J., Mastel-Smith, B., & Lake, P. (2017). Online teaching: How students perceive faculty caring. *International Journal for Human Caring, 21*(2), 54–58. doi:10.20467/HumanCaring-D-16-00022.1

Prensky, M. (2005). Computer games and learning: Digital game-based learning. In J. Raessens & J. Goldstein (Eds.), Handbook of computer game studies (pp. 97-122). Cambridge, MA: The MIT Press.

Project Implicit. (2011). *Take a test*. Retrieved from https://implicit.harvard.edu/implicit/takeatest.html

Psathas, G., Chalki, P., Demetriadis, S., & Tsiara, A. (2018). *Profiles and Motivations of Participants in Greek MOOC for Python Programming. In 2018 Learning With MOOCS* (pp. 70–73). Madrid: LWMOOCS.

Qiu, L., Liu, Y., & Liu, Y. (2018). An Integrated Framework With Feature Selection for Dropout Prediction in Massive Open Online Courses. *IEEE Access: Practical Innovations, Open Solutions*, 6, 71474–71484. doi:10.1109/ACCESS.2018.2881275

Quality Matters. (2016). *Online Instructor Skills Set*. Retrieved from https://www.qualitymatters.org/qa-resources/rubric-standards/teaching-skills-set

Quality Matters. (2018). *National standards for quality online courses*. Retrieved from https://www.qualitymatters.org

Ragan, L. C., Bigatel, P. M., Kennan, S. S., & Dillon, J. M. (2012). From research to practice: Towards the development of an integrated and comprehensive faculty development program. *Journal of Asynchronous Learning Networks*, 16(5), 71–86.

Ranseen, J. D., & Parks, G. S. (2005). Test accommodations for postsecondary students: The quandary resulting from the ADA's disability definition. *Psychology, Public Policy, and Law*, 11(1), 83–108. doi:10.1037/1076-8971.11.1.83

Rapp, C., Gülbahar, Y., & Adnan, M. (2016). e-Tutor: A Multilingual Open Educational Resource for Faculty Development to Teach Online. *International Review of Research in Open and Distributed Learning*, 17(5), 284–289. doi:10.19173/irrodl.v17i5.2783

Rapp, L., & Anyikwa, V. (2016). Active learning strategies and instructor presence in an online research methods course: Can ourdecrease anxiety and increase perceived knowledge. *Advances in Social Work*, 17(1), 1–14. doi:10.18060/20871

Ratliff, K. (2018). Building rapport and creating a sense of community: Are relationships Important in the online classroom? *Internet Learning Journal*, 31-48. doi:10.18278/il.7.1.4

Rausch, D. W., & Crawford, E. (2012). Building the future with cohorts: Communities of inquiry. *Metropolitan Universities*, 23(1), 79–89. Retrieved from https://journals.iupui.edu/index.php/muj/article/view/20505/20103

Ray, J. (2009). Faculty perspective: Training and course development for the online classroom. *Journal of Online Learning and Teaching / MERLOT*, 5(2), 263–276.

Reason, R. D., Terenzini, P. T., & Domingo, R. J. (2006). First things first: Developing academic competence in the first year of college. *Research in Higher Education, 47*(2), 149–175. doi: 10.1007/sl 1162-005-8884-4

Reda, V., & Kerr, R. (2018). *The MOOC BA, a New Frontier for Internationalization. In 2018 Learning With MOOCS* (pp. 94–97). Madrid: LWMOOCS.

Reed, P. (2015, July). Technology and the contemporary library. *Insights, 28*(2).

Rehabilitation Act of 1973 [as amended by through P.L. 114–95, enacted December 10, 2015]. (n.d.). Accessed January, 2019 at https://www2.ed.gov/policy/speced/leg/rehab/rehabilitation-act-of-1973-amended-by-wioa.pdf

Reichlin Cruse, L., Gault, B., Suh, J., & DeMario, M. A. (2018, May 10). *Time demands of single mother college students and the role of child care in their postsecondary success*. Briefing paper, IWPR #C468. Washington, DC: Institute for Women's Policy Research. Retrieved from https://iwpr.org/publications/single-mothers-college-time-use/

Revere, L., & Kovach, J. (2011). Online technologies for engaged learners: A meaningful synthesis for educators. *The Quarterly Review of Distance Education*, *12*(2), 113–124.

Richardson, J. C., Koehler, A., Besser, E., Caskurlu, S., Lim, J., & Mueller, C. (2015). Conceptualizing and investigating instructor presence in online learning environments. *International Review of Research in Open and Distributed Learning*, *16*(3), 256–297. doi:10.19173/irrodl.v16i3.2123

Richardson, J., Besser, E., Koehler, A., Lim, J., & Strait, M. (2016). Instructors' perceptions of instructor presence in online learning environments. *The International Review of Research in Open and Distributed Learning*, *17*(4), 82–104. doi:10.19173/irrodl.v17i4.2330

Rienties, B., Brouwer, N., & Lygo-Baker, S. (2013). The effects of online professional development on higher education teachers' beliefs and intentions towards learning facilitation and technology. *Teaching and Teacher Education*, *29*, 122–131. doi:10.1016/j.tate.2012.09.002

Rios, T. (2019, January). The relationship between students' personalities and their perception of online course experiences. *Journal of Educators Online.*, *16*(1). doi:10.9743/jeo.2019.16.1.11

Rios, T., Elliott, M., & Jean Mandernach, B. (2018). Efficient instructional strategies for maximizing online student satisfaction. *Journal of Educators Online*, *15*(3), 158–166. doi:10.9743/jeo.2018.15.3.7

Roberts, J. (2018). Future and changing roles of staff in distance education: A study to identify training and professional development needs. *Distance Education*, *39*(1), 37–53. doi:10.1080/01587919.2017.1419818

Roberts, J., & Styron, R. (2010). Student satisfaction and persistence: Factors vital to student retention. *Research in Higher Education*, *6*(3), 1–18. Retrieved from http://www.aabri.com/manuscripts/09321.pdf

Robson, K., Plangger, K., Kietzmann, J. H., McCarthy, I., & Pitt, L. (2015). Is it all a game? Understanding the principles of gamification. *Business Horizons*, *58*(4), 411–420. doi:10.1016/j.bushor.2015.03.006

Roddy, C., Amiet, D. L., Chung, J., Holt, C., Shaw, L., McKenzie, S., ... Mundy, M. E. (2017). Applying Best Practice Online Learning, Teaching, and Support to intensive Online environments: An integrative Review. *Frontiers in Education*, *2*(59), 1–10.

Rodriguez, C. O. (2012). MOOCs and the AI_Stanford like courses: Two successful and distinct Courses Formats for Massive Open Online Course. *European Journal of Open, Distance and E- learning*. Retrieved from http://files.eric.ed.gov/fulltext/EJ9829.pdf

Rodriguez, M. C., Ooms, A., & Montañez, M. (2008). Students' perceptions of online-learning quality given comfort, motivation, satisfaction, and experience. *Journal of Interactive Online Learning*, *7*(2), 105–125.

Rose, D. H., Harbour, W. S., Johnston, C. S., Daley, S. G., & Abarbanell, L. (2006). Universal design for learning in postsecondary education: Reflections on principles and their application. *Journal of postsecondary education and disability*, *19*(2), 135–151.

Rose, D. H., Meyer, A., & Hitchcock, C. (Eds.). (2005). *The universally designed classroom: Accessible curriculum and digital technologies*. Cambridge, MA: Harvard Educational Press.

Rose, D., Meyer, A., & Gordon, D. (2014). Reflections: Universal design for learning and the common core. *The Special Edge*, *2*(27), 3–5.

Rose, S. N. (1991). Collegiate-based noncredit courses. In B. B. Watkins & S. J. Wright (Eds.), *The foundations of American distance education* (pp. 67–92). Dubuque, IA: Kendall/Hunt.

Rovai, A. P., & Ponton, M. (2005). An examination of sense of classroom community and learning among African American and Caucasian graduate students. *Journal of Asynchronous Learning Networks*, *9*, 77–92.

Rovai, A. P., & Wightin, M. J. (2005). Feelings of alienation and community among higher education students in a virtual classroom. *The Internet and Higher Education*, *8*(2), 97–110. doi:10.1016/j.iheduc.2005.03.001

Ruffalo Noel Levitz. (2015). *Priorities Survey for Online Learners*. Cedar Rapids: Ruffalo Noel Levitz.

Russell, M., Kleiman, G., Carey, R., & Douglas, J. (2009). Comparing self-paced and cohort-based online courses for teachers. *Journal of Research on Technology in Education*, *41*(4), 443–466. doi:10.1080/15391523.2009.10782538

Ruth, S. (2012, June 18). *Can MOOC's and Existing E-Learning Efficiency Paradigms Help Reduce College Costs?* Available at SSRN: doi:10.2139srn.2086689

Rutherford, T., Buschkuehl, M., Jaeggi, S., & Farkas, G. (2018). Links between achievement, executive functions, and self-regulated learning. *Applied Cognitive Psychology*, *32*(6), 763–774. doi:10.1002/acp.3462

Ryan, M.-L. (1999). Immersion vs. interactivity: Virtual reality and literary theory. *SubStance*, *28*(2), 110–137. doi:10.1353ub.1999.0015

Ryan, R. M., Koestner, R., & Deci, E. L. (1991). Varied forms of persistence: When free-choice behavior is not intrinsically motivated. *Motivation and Emotion*, *15*(3), 185–205. doi:10.1007/BF00995170

Sakulku, J., & Alexander, J. (2011). The impostor phenomenon. *International Journal of Behavioral Science*, *6*(1), 75–97.

Salter, S., & Gardner, C. (2016). Online or face-to-face microbiology laboratory sessions? First year higher education student perspectives and preferences. *Creative Education*, *7*, 1869-1880. Retrieved from https://www.scirp.org/journal/PaperInformation.aspx?PaperID=70022

Sankey, M., & Hunt, L. (2014). Flipped university classrooms: Using technology to enable sound pedagogy. *Journal of Cases on Information Technology*, *16*(2), 26–38. doi:10.4018/jcit.2014040103

Sansone, C., Fraughton, T., Zachary, J. L., Butner, J., & Heiner, C. (2011). Self-regulation of motivation when learning online: The importance of who, why and how. *Educational Technology Research and Development*, *59*(2), 199–212. doi:10.100711423-011-9193-6

Saxena, S. (2013, October 8). How important is use of technology in education. *EdTech Review*. Retrieved on June 11, 2019 from http://edtechreview.in/news/2681-technology-in-education

Scarpena, K., Riley, M., & Keathley, M. (2018). Creating successful professional development activities for online faculty: A reorganized framework. *Journal of Distance Learning Administration*, *2*(1), 1–8.

Schaffer, D. W., Squire, K. R., Halverson, R., & Gee, J. P. (2005). Video Games and the Future of Learning. *Phi Delta Kappan*, *87*(2), 104–111.

Scheuermann, M. (2012). Engaging students with synchronous methods in online courses. In *Online Student Engagement Tools and Strategies* (section 1). Retrieved from https://www.facultyfocus.com/wp-content/uploads/2019/02/FF-Online-Student-Engagement-Report.pdf

Schlager, M. S., Farooq, U., Fusco, J., Schank, P., & Dwyer, N. (2009). Analyzing online teacher networks: Cyber networks require cyber research tools. *Journal of Teacher Education*, *60*(1), 86–100. doi:10.1177/0022487108328487

Schmidt, S. W., Tschida, C. M., & Hodge, E. M. (2016). How faculty learn to teach online: What administrators need to know. *Online Journal of Distance Learning Administration*, *19*(1), 1–8.

Compilation of References

Schneider, M. (2010). *Finishing the first lap: The cost of first year student attrition in America's four year colleges and universities*. Washington, DC: American Institutes for Research. Retrieved from http://www.air.org/files/AIR_Schneider_Finishing_the_First_Lap_Oct101.pdf

Schneider, M., & Yin, L. (2011). *The high cost of low graduation rates: How much does dropping out of college really cost?* Washington, DC: American Institutes for Research. Retrieved from http://www.air.org/resource/high-cost-low-graduation-rates

Schreiber, J. (2017). Universal design for learning: A student-centered curriculum Perspective. *Curriculum and Teaching*, *32*(2), 89–98. doi:10.7459/ct/32.2.06

Schunk, D. (2008). Metacognition, self-regulation, and self-regulated learning: Research recommendations. *Educational Psychology Review*, *20*(4), 463–467. doi:10.100710648-008-9086-3

Schunk, D. H., & Zimmerman, B. J. (1998). Conclusions and future directions for academic interventions. In D. H. Schunk & B. J. Zimmerman (Eds.), *Self-regulated learning: From teaching to self-reflective practice* (pp. 225–235). New York: Guilford Press.

Sclater, N. (2016). Developing a code of practice for learning analytics. *Journal of Learning Analytics*, *3*(1), 16–42. doi:10.18608/jla.2016.31.3

Seaman, J. E., Allen, I. E., & Seaman, J. (2018). *Grade increase: Tracking distance education in the United States*. Needham, MA: Babson Survey Research Group. Retrieved from http://onlinelearningsurvey.com/reports/gradeincrease.pdf

Seifert, K., & Sutton, R. (2009). *Educational psychology*. Center for Open Education. Available at https://open.umn.edu/opentextbooks/textbooks/educational-psychology

Seok, S., DaCosta, B., & Hodges, R. (2018). A systematic review of empirically based Universal Design for Learning: Implementation and effectiveness of Universal Design in education for students with and without disabilities at the postsecondary level. *Open Journal of Social Sciences*, *06*(05), 171–189. doi:10.4236/jss.2018.65014

Serrano, D., Dea-Avuela, M., Gonzalez-Burgos, E., Serrano-Gil, A., & Lalatsa, A. (2019, April 5). Technology-enhanced learning in higher education: How to enhance student engagement through blended learning. *European Journal of Education: Research. Development and Policy*, *54*(2), 273–286.

Shachar, H., & Shmuelevitz, H. (1997). Implementing cooperative learning, teacher collaboration and teachers' sense of efficacy in heterogeneous junior high schools. *Contemporary Educational Psychology*, *22*(1), 53–72. doi:10.1006/ceps.1997.0924

Shapiro, D., Dundar, A., Wakhungu, P. K., Yuan, X., Nathan, A., & Hwang, Y. (2016). *Completing college: A national view of student attainment rates – Fall 2010 cohort (Signature Report No. 12)*. Herndon, VA: National Student Clearinghouse Research Center.

Shaw, A. (2016). 4 Ways to personalize instruction in pre-designed online courses [Blog]. Retrieved from https://elearningindustry.com/4-ways-personalize-instruction-pre-designed-online-courses

Shaw, S., & Polovina, S. (1999). Practical experiences of, and lessons learnt from, Internet technologies in higher education. *Journal of Educational Technology & Society*, *2*(3), 16–24. Retrieved from http://www.ifets.info/journals/2_3/stephen_shaw.pdf

Shea, P., & Bidjerano, T. (2018). Online course enrollment in community college and degree completion: The tipping point. *The International Review of Research in Open and Distributed Learning*, *19*(2), 282–293. doi:10.19173/irrodl.v19i2.3460

Sheridan, K., & Kelly, M. A. (2010). The indicators of instructor presence that are important to students in online courses. *MERLOT Journal of Online Learning and Teaching, 6*(4), 767–779.

Short, J., Williams, E., & Christie, V. (1976). *The social psychology of telecommunications*. London: John Wiley and Sons.

Simplico, J. (2019). Strategies to improve online student academic success and increase university persistence rates. *Education, 139*(3), 173–177.

Singh, E. (2014). Learning theory and online technologies. *Open Learning: The Journal of Open, Distance and e-Learning, 29*(1), 89-92.

Singh, N. N., Lancioni, G. E., Karazsia, B. T., Myers, R. E., Kim, E., Chan, J., ... Janson, M. (2019). Surfing the Urge: An informal mindfulness practice for the self-management of aggression by adolescents with autism spectrum disorder. *Journal of Contextual Behavioral Science, 12*, 170–177. doi:10.1016/j.jcbs.2018.10.003

Slaven, G., & Totterdell, P. (1993). Time management training: Does it transfer to the workplace? *Journal of Managerial Psychology, 8*(1), 20–28. doi:10.1108/02683949310024432

Small, M. L., Waterman, E. A., & Lender, T. (2017). Time use during first year of college predicts participation in high-impact activities during later years. *Journal of College Student Development, 58*(6), 954–960. doi:10.1353/csd.2017.0075 PMID:29200615

Smart, J. (2015). *Disability, society, and the individual* (3rd ed.). Austin, TX: Pro-ed.

Smith, H. J., McConnell, D., & Ryker, K. (2013). Starting to flip the class: Quality of student's pre-class work improves with the use of online just-in time teaching methods. *Abstracts with Programs— Geological Society of America, 45*(7), 69.

Smith, T. B., & Shwalb, D. A. (2007). Preliminary examination of international students' adjustment and loneliness related to electronic communications. *Psychological Reports, 100*(1), 167–170. doi:10.2466/pr0.100.1.167-170 PMID:17451020

Søby, M. (2014). Learning Analytics. *Nordic Journal of Digital Literacy, 9*, 89–91.

Spencer, S. J., Logel, C., & Davies, P. G. (2016). Stereotype threat. *Annual Review of Psychology, 67*(1), 415–437. doi:10.1146/annurev-psych-073115-103235 PMID:26361054

Spooner, F., Baker, J. N., Harris, A. A., Ahlgrim-Delzell, L., & Browder, D. M. (2007). Effects of Training in Universal Design for Learning on Lesson Plan Development. *Remedial and Special Education, 28*(2), 108–116. doi:10.1177/07419325070280020101

Stamets, S. E. (2016). *Game on: redesign of a teacher professional development platform for use with the serious game alien rescue* (Master's thesis). University of Texas at Austin. Retrieved from https://repositories.lib.utexas.edu/handle/2152/43378

Starkey, L. (2011). Evaluating learning in the 21st Century: A digital age learning matrix. *Technology, Pedagogy and Education, 20*(1), 19–39. doi:10.1080/1475939X.2011.554021

Steffens, K. (1989). *Open and distance education in Germany*. Retrieved from https://scholar.google.com/scholar?cluster=18015051997387056388&hl

Steinkuehler, C. (2006, July). The mangle of play. *Games and Culture, 1*(3), 199–213. doi:10.1177/1555412006290440

Steinkuehler, C. A., & Williams, D. (2006). Where everybody knows your (screen) name: Online games as "third place". *Journal of Computer-Mediated Communication, 11*(4), 885–909. doi:10.1111/j.1083-6101.2006.00300.x

Stein, S. J., Shephard, K., & Harris, I. (2011). Conceptions of e-learning and professional development for e-learning held by tertiary educators in New Zealand. *British Journal of Educational Technology, 42*(1), 145–165. doi:10.1111/j.1467-8535.2009.00997.x

Stephens, G. E., & Roberts, K. L. (2017). Facilitating collaboration in online groups. *Journal of Educators Online, 14*(1). Retrieved from https://www.thejeo.com/

Stifle, J. (1972). *The Plato IV Architecture*. Retrieved from http://bitsavers.informatik.uni-stuttgart.de/pdf/univOfIllinoisUrbana/plato/X-20_The_Plato_IV_Architecture_May72.pdf

Stone, C., & O'Shea, S. (2019). Older, online and first: Recommendations for retention and success. *Australasian Journal of Educational Technology, 35*(1), 57–69. doi:10.14742/ajet.3913

Stone, C., O'Shea, S., May, J., Delahunty, J., & Partington, Z. (2016). Opportunity through online learning: Experiences of first-in-family students in online open-entry higher education. *Australian Journal of Adult Learning, 56*(2), 146–169.

Stuber-McEwen, D., Wiseley, P., & Hoggatt, S. (2009). Point, click, and cheat: Frequency and type of academic dishonesty in the virtual classroom. *Online Journal of Distance Learning Administration, 12*(3), 1–10.

Sue, D. W., Capodilupo, C. M., Torino, G. C., Bucceri, J. M., Holder, A. M. B., Nadal, K. L., & Esquilin, M. (2007). Racial microaggressions in everyday life: Implications for clinical practice. *The American Psychologist, 62*(4), 271–286. doi:10.1037/0003-066X.62.4.271 PMID:17516773

Su, J., & Waugh, M. L. (2018). Online student persistence or attrition: Observations related to expectations, preferences, and outcomes. *Journal of Interactive Online Learning, 16*(1), 63–79.

Sujo de Montes, L. E., Oran, S. M., & Willis, E. M. (2002). Power, language, and identity: Voices from an online course. *Computers and Composition, 19*(3), 251–271. doi:10.1016/S8755-4615(02)00127-5

Sull, E. C. (2012). Teaching online with Errol: A tried and true mini-guide to engaging online students. In *Online Student Engagement Tools and Strategies* (section 7). Retrieved from https://www.facultyfocus.com/wp-content/uploads/2019/02/FF-Online-Student-Engagement-Report.pdf

Sullivan, P. (2001). Gender differences and the online classroom: Male and female college students evaluate their experiences. *Community College Journal of Research and Practice, 25*(10), 805–818. doi:10.1080/106689201753235930

Sullivan, P. (2002). "It's easier to be yourself when you are invisible": Female college students discuss their online classroom experiences. *Innovative Higher Education, 27*(2), 129–144. doi:10.1023/A:1021109410893

Sullivan, T. M., & Freishtat, R. (2013). Extending learning beyond the classroom: Graduate student experiences of online discussions in a hybrid course. *The Journal of Continuing Higher Education, 61*(1), 12–22. doi:10.1080/07377363.2013.758555

Sun, A., & Chen, X. (2016). Online education and its effective practice: A research review. *Journal of Information Technology Education, 15*, 157–190. doi:10.28945/3502

Sun, J. C.-Y., & Rueda, R. (2012). Situational interest, computer self-efficacy and self-regulation: Their impact on student engagement in distance education. *British Journal of Educational Technology, 43*(2), 191–204. doi:10.1111/j.1467-8535.2010.01157.x

Sun, P.-C., Tsai, R. J., Finger, G., Chen, Y.-Y., & Yeh, D. (2008). What drives a successful e-learning? An empirical investigation of the critical factors influencing learner satisfaction. *Computers & Education, 50*(4), 1183–1202. doi:10.1016/j.compedu.2006.11.007

Swallow, E. (2012, September 18). Can gamification make customer support fun? *Forbes*. Retrieved from http://www.forbes.com/fdc/welcome_mjx.shtml

Taylor, J. A., & Newton, D. (2013). Beyond blended learning: A case study of institutional change at an Australian regional university. *The Internet and Higher Education*, *18*, 54–60. doi:10.1016/j.iheduc.2012.10.003

Templeton, L., & Linder, K. E. (2017). *Establishing an e-Learning Division. In Leading and managing e-learning: What the e-learning leader needs to know*. Springer.

Terry, N. (2001). Assessing enrollment and attrition rates for the online MBA. *Technology Horizons in Education Journal*, *28*. Retrieved from http://www.thejournal.com/articles/15251

Terry, K. P., & Doolittle, P. E. (2008). Fostering self-efficacy through time management in an online learning environment. *Journal of Interactive Online Learning*, *7*(3), 195–207.

The University of Massachusetts. (n.d.). *Teaching and learning online - communication, community, and assessment: A handbook for UMass faculty*. Retrieved from https://www.umass.edu/oapa/sites/default/files/pdf/handbooks/teaching_and_learning_online_handbook.pdf

Thelin, J. R. (2004). *A history of American higher education*. Baltimore, MD: The John Hopkins University Press.

Thill, M., Rosenzweig, J. W., & Wallis, L. C. (2016). The relationship between student demographics and student engagement with online library instruction modules. *Evidence Based Library and Information Practice*, *11*(3), 4–15. doi:10.18438/B8992D

Thompson, J. R., Ballenger, J. N., & Templeton, N. R. (2018). Examining quality elements in a higher education fully online doctoral program: Doctoral students' perceptions. *The International Journal of Educational Leadership Preparation*, *13*(1), 51–63.

Thompson, T. L. (2018). Disability resources in higher education, part 2: Mission and role of disability resources and services. *Dean and Provost*, *19*(7), 7–7. doi:10.1002/dap.30431

Tinto, V. (1993). *Leaving college: Rethinking the causes and cures of student attrition* (2nd ed.). Chicago: University of Chicago Press.

Tinto, V. (1997). Classrooms as communities: Exploring the educational character of student persistence. *The Journal of Higher Education*, *68*(6), 599–623. doi:10.2307/2959965

Tinto, V. (2010). From theory to action: Exploring the institutional conditions for student retention. In J. Smart (Ed.), *Higher Education: Handbook of Theory and Research* (Vol. 25, pp. 51–89). New York, NY: Springer. doi:10.1007/978-90-481-8598-6_2

Tinto, V., & Cullen, J. (1973). *Dropout in higher education: A review and theoretical synthesis of recent research*. Washington, DC: Office of Planning, Budgeting, and Evaluation. Retrieved from http://files.eric.ed.gov/fulltext/ED078802.pdf

Todhunter, B. (2013). LOL - limitations of online learning - are we selling the open and distance education message short? *Distance Education*, *34*(2), 232–252. doi:10.1080/01587919.2013.802402

Tømte, C., Enochsson, A. B., Buskqvist, U., & Kårstein, A. (2015). Educating online student teachers to master professional digital competence: The TPACK-framework goes online. *Computers & Education*, *84*, 26–35. doi:10.1016/j.compedu.2015.01.005

Trofimovich, P., Lightbown, P. M., & Halter, R. (2013). Are certain types of instruction better for certain learners? *System*, *41*(4), 914–922. doi:10.1016/j.system.2013.09.004

Compilation of References

Trueman, M., & Hartley, J. (1996). A comparison between the time-management skills and academic performance of mature and traditional-entry university students. *Higher Education, 32*(2), 199–215. doi:10.1007/BF00138396

Truhlar, A. M., Walter, T., & Williams, K. M. (2018). Student engagement with course content and peers in synchronous online discussions. *Online Learning, 22*(4), 289–312. doi:10.24059/olj.v22i4.1389

Trust, T. (2017). Motivation, empowerment, and innovation: Teachers' beliefs about how participating in the Edmodo Math Subject Community shapes teaching and learning. *Journal of Research on Technology in Education, 49*(1), 16–30. doi:10.1080/15391523.2017.1291317

Twigg, C. A. (2001). *Quality for whom? Providers and consumers in today's distributed learning environment*. Troy, NY: The Pew Learning and Technology Program, Center for Academic Transformation.

U.S. Department of Commerce, Census Bureau, Current Population Survey (CPS). (2017). See Digest of Education Statistics 2018, table 503.40.

U.S. Department of Education Credit Hour Definition. (n.d.). Retrieved from https://www.ecfr.gov/cgi-bin/text-idx?rgn=div8&node=34:3.1.3.1.1.1.23.2

U.S. Department of Education, National Center for Education Statistics, Integrated Postsecondary Education Data System (NCES). (2017). *Fall Enrollment component; IPEDS, Fall 2016, Completions component; and IPEDS, Winter 2016-17, Graduation Rates component*. Retrieved from https://nces.ed.gov/programs/digest/d17/tables/dt17_311.33.asp?current=yes

U.S. Department of Education. (2008). *Higher Education Opportunity Act – 2008*. Retrieved from http://www2.ed.gov/policy/highered/leg/hea08/index.html

U.S. Department of Education. (n.d.a). *IPEDS: About IPEDS*. Retrieved from https://nces.ed.gov/ipeds/about-ipeds

U.S. Department of Education. (n.d.b). *IPEDS: Definitions for new race and ethnicity categories*. Retrieved from https://nces.ed.gov/ipeds/report-your-data/race-ethnicity-definitions

Underdown, K., & Martin, J. (2016). Engaging the online student: Instructor-created video Content for the online classroom. *Journal of Institutional Research, 5*(1), 8–12. doi:10.9743/JIR.2016.2

UNESCO. (2011). *ICT Competency Framework for Teachers*. Retrieved from http://unesdoc.unesco.org/images/0021/002134/213475E.pdf

United Nations General Assembly. (2006, December 13). *Convention on the rights of persons with disabilities: Resolution [A/RES/61/106]*. Retrieved from https://www.un.org/development/desa/disabilities/resources/general-assembly/convention-on-the-rights-of-persons-with-disabilities-ares61106.html

University of Oklahoma. (n.d.). *Flat-rate tuition*. Retrieved July, 2019 from http://www.ou.edu/bursar/flat-rate-tuition

Uppal, M. A., Ali, S., & Gulliver, S. R. (2018). Factors determining e-learning service quality. *British Journal of Educational Technology, 49*(3), 412–426. doi:10.1111/bjet.12552

Utah State University Academic Success Center. (n.d.). *Estimate Study Hours*. Retrieved July, 2019 from https://www.usu.edu/asc/assistance/pdf/estimate_study_hours.pdf

Vaill, A. L., & Testori, P. A. (2012). Orientation, mentoring and ongoing support: A three-tiered approach to online faculty development. *Journal of Asynchronous Learning Networks, 16*(2), 111–119. doi:10.24059/olj.v16i2.256

Vai, M., & Sosulski, K. (2015). *Essentials of online course design: A standards-based guide*. New York, NY: Routledge. doi:10.4324/9781315770901

Vangrieken, K., Dochy, F., Raes, E., & Kyndt, E. (2015). Teacher collaboration: A systematic review. *Educational Research Review*, *15*, 17–40. doi:10.1016/j.edurev.2015.04.002

VanPortfliet, P., & Anderson, M. (2013). Moving from online to hybrid course delivery: Increasing positive student outcomes. *Journal of Research in Innovative Teaching*, *6*(1), 80–87. Retrieved from https://search-ebscohost-com.proxy1.ncu.edu/login.aspx?direct=true&db=ehh&AN=88176006&site=eds-live

Vedder, R. (2017, Aug 29). *Seven challenges facing higher education*. Center for College Affordability and Productivity. Retrieved from https://www.forbes.com/sites/ccap/2017/08/29/seven-challenges-facing-higher-education/#4e96eac43180

Vidic, Z., & Cherup, N. (2019). Mindfulness in classroom: Effect of a mindfulness-based relaxation class on college students' stress, resilience, self-efficacy and perfectionism. *College Student Journal*, *53*(1), 130–142.

Vignovic, J. A., & Thompson, L. F. (2010). Computer-mediated cross-cultural collaboration: Attributing communication errors to the person versus the situation. *The Journal of Applied Psychology*, *95*(2), 265–276. doi:10.1037/a0018628 PMID:20230068

Villagonzalo, E. C. (2014). Process oriented guided inquiry learning: An effective approach in enhancing students' academic performance. *The DLSU Research Congress*.

Villegas-Reimers, E. (2003). *Teacher Professional Development: An International Review of the Literature*. Paris: UNESCO International Institute for Educational Planning.

Vinagre, M. (2017). Developing teachers' telecollaborative competences in online experiential learning. *System*, *64*, 34–45. doi:10.1016/j.system.2016.12.002

Violino, B. (2014, Aug/Sep). The future is now. *Community College Journal, 85*(1), 18-23.

Vonderwell, S. (2003). An examination of asynchronous communication experiences and perspectives of students in an online course: A case study. *The Internet and Higher Education*, *6*(1), 77–90. doi:10.1016/S1096-7516(02)00164-1

VPTL. (n.d.). *Blended and Online Learning Design (BOLD) from Stanford*. Retrieved from https://lagunita.stanford.edu/courses/course-v1:VPTL+BOLD+ongoing/about

Wajcman, J. (2019). The digital architecture of time management. *Science, Technology & Human Values*, *44*(2), 315–337. doi:10.1177/0162243918795041

Waltemeyer, S. & Cranmore, J. (2018). Screencasting technology to increase student engagement in online higher education courses. *e-Learn, 2018*(12), 50-54.

Wang, Y. D. (2014). Building student trust in online learning environments. *Distance Education*, *35*(3), 345–359. doi: 10.1080/01587919.2015.955267

Watkins, B. L. (1991). A quite radical idea: The invention and elaboration of collegiate correspondence study. In B. L. Watkins & S. J. Wright (Eds.), *The foundations of American distance education* (pp. 1–35). Dubuque, IA: Kendall/Hunt.

Watts, J. (2013). Why hyperbonding occurs in the learning community classroom and what to do about it. *Learning Communities Research and Practice, 1*(3). Retrieved from http://washingtoncenter.evergreen.edu/lcrpjournal/vol1/iss3/4

Wehler, M. (2018). Five ways to build community in online classrooms [Blog]. Retrieved from https://www.facultyfocus.com/articles/online-education/five-ways-to-build-community-in-online-classrooms/

Weidlich, J., & Bastiaens, T. J. (2018). Technology matters--The impact of transactional distance on satisfaction in online distance learning. *International Review of Research in Open and Distributed Learning*, *19*(3), 222–242. doi:10.19173/irrodl.v19i3.3417

Weldy, T. G. (2018). Traditional, blended, or online: Business student preferences and experience with different course formats. *E-Journal of Business Education & Scholarship of Teaching*, *12*(2), 55–62.

Weller, M., Jordan, K., DeVries, I., & Rolfe, V. (2018). Mapping the open education landscape: Citation network analysis of historical open and distance education research. *Open Praxis*, *10*(2), 109–126. doi:10.5944/openpraxis.10.2.822

West, J., & Turner, W. (2016). Enhancing the assessment experience: Improving student perceptions, engagement and understanding using online video feedback. *Innovations in Education and Teaching International*, *53*(4), 400–410. doi:10.1080/14703297.2014.1003954

Wilcox, D., Thall, J., & Griffin, O. (2017). One canvas, two audiences: How faculty and students use a newly adopted learning management system. In *Proceedings of the 2016 Society for Information Technology & teacher education international conference, USA* (pp. 1163–1168). Retrieved from http://er.dut.ac.za/bitstream/handle/123456789/193/LMS%20new%20adopted.pdf?sequence=1&isAllowed=y.Google Scholar

Wilkins, J. (2007). The future is now: Online education and the future of higher education. *Sheriff*, *59*(3), 37.

Willging, P. A., & Johnson, S. D. (2009). Factors that influence students' decision to dropout of online courses. *Journal of Asynchronous Learning Networks*, *13*(3), 115–127. Retrieved from http://files.eric.ed.gov/fulltext/EJ862360.pdf

Willging, P., & Johnson, S. (2009). Factors that influence students' decision to dropout of online Course. *Journal of Asynchronous Learning Networks*, *13*(3), 115–127.

Willis, P. (1977). *Learning to labour*. Farnborough, UK: Saxon House.

Wine, J., Janson, N., & Wheeless, S. (2011). *2004/09 Beginning Postsecondary Students Longitudinal Study (BPS:04/09)*. Washington, DC: National Center for Education Statistics, Institute of Education Sciences, U.S. Department of Education. Retrieved from http://nces.ed.gov/pubsearch

Wingo, N. P., Ivankova, N. V., & Moss, J. A. (2017). Faculty perceptions about teaching online: Exploring the literature using the technology acceptance model as an organizing framework. *Online Learning*, *21*(1), 15–35. doi:10.24059/olj.v21i1.761

Wintre, M. G., Dilouya, B., Pancer, S. M., Pratt, M. W., Birnie-Lefcovitch, S., Polivy, J., & Adams, G. (2011). Academic achievement in first-year university: Who maintains their high school average? *Higher Education*, *62*(4), 467–481. doi:10.100710734-010-9399-2

Witzig, L., Spencer, J., & Myers, K. (2017). Social media: Online versus traditional universities and developing communities. *Journal of Higher Education Theory and Practice*, *17*(6), 39–52. Retrieved from http://www.na-businesspress.com/jhetpopen.html

Wolf, M. (2018). *Reader, Come Home*. New York, NY: Harper Collins.

Woolley, D. R. (1994). PLATO: The Emergence of Online Community. *Matrix News*. Retrieved from http://thinkofit.com/plato/dwplato.htm

Xiao, J. (2018, January 28). On the margins or at the center? Distance education in higher education. *Journal of Distance Education*, *29*(2), 22–36.

Xiaoxia, H., Chandra, A., DePaolo, C. A., & Simmons, L. L. (2016). Understanding transactional distance in web-based learning environments: An empirical study. *British Journal of Educational Technology*, *47*(4), 734–747. https://doi- org.lopes.idm.oclc.org/10.1111/bjet.12263

Xu, D., & Jaggars, S. S. (2011). *Online and hybrid course enrollment and performance in Washington State Community and Technical Colleges*. Retrieved from https://files.eric.ed.gov/fulltext/ED517746.pdf

Xu, D., & Jaggars, S. S. (2014). Adaptability to online learning: Differences across types of students and academic subject areas. *The Journal of Higher Education, 85*(5), 633–659. doi:10.1353/jhe.2014.0028

Xu, J., Du, J., & Fan, X. (2013). "Finding our time": Predicting students' time management in online collaborative groupwork. *Computers & Education, 69*, 139–147. doi:10.1016/j.compedu.2013.07.012

Yang, Y., & Cornelious, L. F. (2004). Students' perceptions towards the quality of online education: A qualitative approach. *Association for Educational Communications and Technology, 27*, 19–23.

Yu, Z. (2019). A Meta-Analysis of Use of Serious Games in Education over a Decade. *International Journal of Computer Games Technology, 2019*, 4797032. doi:10.1155/2019/4797032

Zagal, J., Chan, S. S., & Zhang, J. (2011). Measuring flow experience of computer game players. *AMCIS 2010 Proceedings*. Retrieved from http://aisel.aisnet.org/amcis2010/137

Zappala, J. (2012). Promoting student participation and involvement in online instruction: Suggestions from the front. In *Online Student Engagement Tools and Strategies*, 18-20. Retrieved from https://www.facultyfocus.com/wp-content/uploads/2019/02/FF-Online-Student-Engagement-Report.pdf

Zawacki-Richter, O., & Latchem, C. (2018). Exploring four decades of research in Computers & Education. *Computers and Education, 122*, 136–152. doi:10.1016/j.compedu.2018.04.001

Zawacki-Richter, O., & Latchem, C. (2017, June 14). Exploring four decades of research in computer & education. *Computers & Education, 122*(36), 136–152.

Zhao, C.-M., & Kuh, G. D. (2004). Adding value: Learning communities and student engagement. *Research in Higher Education, 45*(2), 115–138. doi:10.1023/B:RIHE.0000015692.88534.de

Zhou, H. (2015). A systematic review of empirical studies on participants' interactions in internet-mediated discussion boards as a course component in formal higher education settings. *Online Learning Journal, 19*(3). Retrieved from: www.onlinelearningconsortium.org

Zimmerman, B. J. (2002). Becoming a self-regulated learner: An overview. *Theory into Practice, 41*(2), 64–70. doi:10.120715430421tip4102_2

Zins, J. E., Bloodworth, M. R., Weissberg, R. P., & Walberg, H. J. (2004). The scientific base linking social and emotional learning to school success. In J. E. Zins, R. P. Weissberg, M. C. Wang, & H. J. Walberg (Eds.), *Building Academic Success on Social and Emotional Learning: What Does the Research Say?* (pp. 3–22). New York: Teachers College Press.

About the Contributors

Lydia Kyei-Blankson is an Associate Professor in the Educational Administration and Foundations (EAF) department at Illinois State University. Her expertise is in research methods, applied statistics, and psychometrics. Her teaching assignment includes graduate research methods and statistics courses. Dr. Kyei-Blankson's research agenda focuses on the scholarship of teaching and learning, online education, and the implications of effective technology integration in teaching and learning at the K-20 level.

Esther Ntuli is an Associate Professor in the Department of Teaching and Educational Studies at Idaho State University (ISU). Her expertise and training is in curriculum and instruction, early childhood education, and instructional technology. Her research interest focuses on technology use and practice in early childhood instruction, teacher education, assessment, and culturally responsive education.

Joseph Blankson, PhD, is the Educational Technology Manager at Ohio Northern University in Ada, Ohio. Joseph has extensive experience in supporting innovative curriculum development, including integration of technologies into higher education programs. He has designed and facilitated numerous professional development activities in the use of educational technologies, online/hybrid course design and provided instructional development services particularly with Learning Management Systems for faculty, staff and students. He has also taught educational technology courses at the undergraduate and graduate levels. Joseph has particular interest in using emerging technologies to promote excellence in teaching and learning, the design of web-based instruction and faculty development in the use of technology for teaching and learning.

* * *

Müge Adnan is currently a faculty member in the Department of Computer Education and Instructional Technology at Muğla Sıtkı Koçman University, Turkey. She also manages the Informatics Department, and serves as the Director of Distance Learning Centre in the same university. She has previously performed various key roles in national education and technology projects financed by the World Bank in Turkey. She graduated with a PhD in Computer Education and Instructional Technology from Middle East Technical University in 2005. She received her associate professorship in instructional technology in 2018. Her research interests include open and distance learning, technology training and integration, technology adoption, faculty development, and digital divide.

Danielle Budenz, EdD, currently works as a lecturer for Gwynedd Mercy University and as a instructional design contractor for Synergis Education. She has experience in higher education administration as an Associate Dean in Academic Affairs and as a Director and Assistant Professor for online graduate education programs. She has taught courses related to school counselor, teacher, and administrator preparation, both in the hybrid and online formats. Dr. Budenz earned a BA degree in English with a Psychology minor and Secondary Education certification from DeSales University, an MA degree in Counseling Psychology from Immaculata University, School Counseling certification from Gwynedd Mercy University, and K-12 Principal certification and an EDD in Educational Leadership from Widener University. Additionally, she is an alumna of Harvard University's Management Development Program ('15) and OLC's Institute for Emerging Leadership in Online Learning [IELOL] ('16).

Desiree' Caldwell is an assistant professor in the Master Teacher program at Gwynedd Mercy University. She teaches in both the Master Teacher program as well as the Doctoral in Educational Leadership program. She is also a dissertation advisor for doctoral students. With a background in elementary education, her classroom teaching experience spans 15 years and includes a variety of grade levels in both elementary and middle school settings. Her primary focus at the middle school level was English Language Arts. Desiree' also spent 5 years being an adjunct professor in the Master Teacher program at Gwynedd Mercy University before becoming a full-time faculty member. Desiree' earned her Ed.D. in General Education from Northcentral University. She earned her Masters Degree in Education from Cabrini University and is also a graduate of Gwynedd Mercy University with a Bachelor's Degree in Elementary Education. Her research interests include effective online teaching strategies, faculty development for online instructors, and tracking the progress of student teachers from the beginning of their journey throughout their first few years of teaching. Her professional memberships include Kappa Delta Pi, Kappa Gamma Pi, and PAC-TE. In addition to her professional experience, Desiree' has over 10 years of experience being a Disc Jockey, playing music for various private events such as weddings, parties, and showers. She also enjoys working out, reading books by Nicholas Sparks, and watching movies.

Kimberly Coy has done extensive work; research, writing, and speaking, on Universal Design for Learning (UDL) in a variety of educational environments. These include elementary, post secondary, and digital, environments. Kimberly is interested in UDL primarily because she believes it is not the learners that need to change to be better at school, but schools need to change to be better for students. Learners are not disabled, bored, or lazy. Instead the current educational structures and environments are disabling.

Jeff Cranmore has been a high school counselor for the past 13 years. He has presented numerous sessions on counseling issues at a wide variety of conferences, including the Texas Counselling Association (TCA), Texas School Counseling Association, and the International Association of Truancy and Dropout Prevention. He has been awarded the TCA awards for research and scholarly writing. His research appears in a number of state and national journals. Additionally, he works as a dissertation chair and teaches doctoral psychology classes at Grand Canyon University.

Tiffany J. Cresswell-Yeager is an assistant professor of Higher Education Leadership at Gwynedd Mercy University. She teaches in the doctoral program in educational leadership, specifically in the higher education concentration. Previously, she taught courses in public speaking, small group communication, multicultural and leadership communication, organizational development, and intercultural community

About the Contributors

building. With a background in higher education administration, her career experience includes leading and supervising student services, intercollegiate athletics, enrollment services, and alumni relations. She has varied experience in strategic planning, social media, student affairs, student conduct, crisis management, and threat assessment. Her research interests include leadership development, the scholarship of teaching and learning, first-generation college students' college choice, and the first-year experience. Tiffany earned her Ph.D. in administration and leadership studies from the Indiana University of Pennsylvania. She is a graduate of the Pennsylvania State University with a bachelor's degree in journalism and a master's degree in training and development. She was a 2015 fellow for the Educational Leadership Policy Center in Harrisburg, Pa. In addition to her professional experience, she is a member of the Walk In Arts Center board and Schuylkill County's VISION board of directors. She enjoys CrossFit, weightlifting, yoga, and cycling to stay healthy.

Kate Davis is a social scientist who researches information experience, particularly in the context of social media, using qualitative approaches designed to get to the heart of people's experience. She is at the forefront of this emerging area of scholarship. Her doctoral study exploring the information experience of new mothers in social media produced the first theoretical rendering of information experience as an object of study. In 2014, she co-edited the volume Information experience: approaches to theory and practice, a book designed to initiate dialogue on information experience as a research domain. In addition to her information experience research, Kate has a strong track record as an applied researcher in information studies, built on her experience as a practitioner-researcher and developed in more recent years through a range of projects exploring social technologies and their use in the library and information professions. Find Kate online at katedavis.info or follow her on Twitter @katiedavis.

Mary Dobransky is dean of the College of Science and Technology at Bellevue University. She has facilitated development of programs such as business analytics, cybersecurity, data science, game studies, information technology, mathematics, multidisciplinary studies, project management, sustainability management, and web development. Her teaching and research interests include technology, leadership, and innovation in teaching and learning. Mary holds a doctorate in interdisciplinary leadership from Creighton University, and a master's degree in systems science from SUNY Binghamton. She received Nebraska's College Technology Educator of the Year Award in 2010, and Bellevue University's Innovation Award in 2017.

Erin Kathleen Doherty has been practicing in the mental health field for 23 years, working primarily with the severe and chronically mentally ill population. She has worked in a variety of settings, but have spent most of my time doing inpatient work. She has experience with psychotic disorders, trauma, borderline personality disorder, and substance abuse. She also has 16 years experience working with children/adolescents and their families. Most of those children and adolescents have trauma in their background. Additionally, she works with various social justice organizations in her community and has a particular interest in multicultural and social justice issues.

Matt Dunbar is the Director of the Graduate Academic Services Center in the College of Education at Georgia Southern University. In this capacity, he oversees the Graduate Academic Services Center's support of graduate students and graduate programs in the College of Education, including roles with admissions, recruitment, advisement, enrollment management, and other student and program-related support services. His research interests include online education, self-efficacy, and program effectiveness in higher education.

Bradley 'Scott' Ellis is a married father of three, Scott is a School Counselor working with at-risk students, as well as a Nationally Certified Counselor with a background in In-Home Counseling (IHC) with at-risk children, teens, adults, couples and families. Like many individuals, early life circumstances provided barriers to college opportunities. As a result, Scott began earning his B.S in Psychology at the age of 39, followed by his M.Ed. in School Counseling summa cum laude. Currently, Scott is earning a Ph.D in Counselor Education and Supervision from the University of the Cumberlands with the goal of training future counselors in the areas of school counseling with at-risk students, ethics, IHC, and the integration of counselor identity and personality.

Robyn Emde, PhD, LPC, graduated with a PhD in Counselor Education Supervision with a specialty in Forensics. She currently serves University of the Cumberlands as an Assistant Professor. Her research focus is on strengthening relationships within schools. Her passion for strengthening relationships has been shared at both state, national and international conferences. In the summer of 2018 she presented at the International Marriage and Family Associations International Institute at Oxford University. Her service includes being appointed by the governor to the Michigan Board of Counseling where she currently serves as chair. In addition, she works with a team of school counselors from across America to yearly revise the American School Counselor Associations position statements. In her free time, Dr. Emde enjoys walking her dog, Bartley along the shore of Lake Michigan.

Dina Flynt is a Licensed Mental Health Counselor and Qualified Supervisor in Florida. She is also a Ph.D. student at the University of the Cumberlands in the Counselor Education and Supervision program. Dina is currently in private practice and has worked in a variety of settings in the past, including community mental health, juvenile justice, and the school system. Dina provides trainings for professionals and the community on various mental health topics.

Allie Grimes is the Coordinator of Scholarship Programs at Georgia Southern University. Master of Education (M.Ed.) in Higher Education Administration from Georgia Southern University. Proud wife and lover of cross-stitch, cooking, and exercise.

Yasemin Gulbahar has got received BS degree from the Department of Mathematics of Science Faculty at Middle East Technical University (METU) in 1992. The same year she started working as a programmer at METU Computer Center. Then, in 1998, she became a research assistant to the Department of Computer Education and Instructional Technologies (CEIT) in the Faculty of Education, METU while studying her MS degree at the same department. She earned his MS degree in the field of Science Education at METU Graduate School of Science in 1999 and she received her PhD in Department of Computer Education and Instructional Technologies (CEIT) from Graduate School of Sciences in 2002. After, she worked for Başkent University Faculty of Education Department of Computer Education and Instructional Technologies (CEIT) for about 9 years. Between years 2011-2017 she worked in Ankara University as the head of Department of Informatics and meanwhile served as the Chairman of Distance Education Center. Since 2018 she is a faculty member of Faculty of Educational Sciences in the Department of Computer Education and Instructional Technologies (CEIT). Dr. Gulbahar has got her Associate

About the Contributors

Professor degree in 2009 and full Professor Degree in 2014. Yasemin Gulbahar has lectured on many topics such as programming languages, problem solving and algorithms, instructional technologies, instructional design, material design and development, distance learning, web design, measurement and evaluation, research methods, teaching methods, software development, technology integration and planning both in undergraduate and graduate level. She has also many national and international publications as books, book chapters, journal articles, and proceeding papers.

Varun Gupta received his Ph.D & Master of Technology (By Research) in Computer Science & Engineering from Uttarakhand Technical University and Bachelor of Technology (Hon's) from Himachal Pradesh University respectively. He is pursuing Doctor of Science (Post-Doctoral Degree) from GLA University, Mathura under the supervision of Prof. Durg Singh Chauhan, Vice chancellor, GLA University. He had qualified State Eligibility Test (SET) conducted by Himachal Pradesh Public Service Commission (HPPSC) Shimla (Accredited by University Grants Commission as equivalent to UGC-NET). Presently he is working as Assistant Professor in the Department of Computer Science & Engineering at Amity University, Noida and had worked with National Institute of Technology, Hamirpur, PEC University of Technology, Chandigarh (Formerly Punjab Engineering College), Jawaharlal Nehru Govt. Engineering College (JNGEC), Sundernagar and Indian Institute of Technology- Mandi, M.G Institute of Engineering & Technology. He had also worked as Scientist-C in Chronicler Solutions, IT Park, Chandigarh. He was Coordinator of Remote Center for National Mission on Education through ICT (NMEICT) project of MHRD for IIT Bombay, Resource Center for Spoken Tutorial project and National Knowledge Network (NKN) coordinator at Jawaharlal Nehru Govt. Engineering College, Sundernagar. His area of interest is Software Engineering (Requirement Engineering, Requirement prioritization, Global Software Development, Software Testing). He had authored a book titled "Software Industry Compatible Projects: For The New Engineer" with "epubli GmbH" publisher, Berlin, Germany. (ISBN: 978-3-7375-2613-5). He has authored numerous research papers in peer reviewed, referred International Journals and various International and National Conferences that were held in India and Abroad. He is Associate Editor of IEEE Access (IEEE Journal, SCIE Indexed), Associate Editor of International Journal of Computer Aided Engineering & Technology (Inderscience Publishers, Scopus indexed), Editor, BJET (Wiley), Deputy Editor-In Chief of International Journal of Software Engineering And Computing (Serial Publishers, Scopus Indexed), Guest editor and review panel board member of many renowned international journals published by Inderscience, Springer, Wiley, IGI Global etc. He also holds lifetime memberships in various technical societies like IEEE, IEEE Industry Applications Society, IAENG etc. He is also on reviewer panel of Tata McGraw-Hill publisher and is subject matter expert of Software Engineering.

Nicole Hacker is a PhD student in Educational Leadership with an emphasis in Higher Education Administration at Central Michigan University (CMU). She is also a research graduate assistant in the Department of Educational Leadership at CMU. Prior to joining the PhD program at CMU, she was an Assistant Professor and Externship Coordinator in the School of Audiology at Pacific University in Oregon. She earned her Doctor of Audiology (AuD) from CMU and her BS in Hearing and Speech Sciences from Ohio University. Her research interests include emotional intelligence in higher education, peer mentorship, equity and inclusion in online learning, and global citizenship, specifically related to developing intercultural competence, conceptualizing equity pedagogy, and promoting social justice.

Jon Humiston is Executive Assistant to the Provost at Central Michigan University and adjunct professor in Educational Leadership. They are a leading expert on transgender and nonbinary students. They conduct campus climate research and recently completed their dissertation related to how transgender and nonbinary student experience campus climate.

Yowei Kang (Ph.D.) is Assistant Professor at Degree Program of Oceanic Cultural Creative Design Industry, National Taiwan Ocean University, TAIWAN. His research interests focus on new media design, digital game research, visual communication, and experiential rhetoric. Some of his works have been published in International Journal of Strategic Communication, and Journal of Intercultural Communication Studies.

Sarah Marshall is a Professor of Educational Leadership and Higher Education Administration at Central Michigan University. She conducts research related to gender studies and work/life management.

Jermaine McDougald is Director of Faculty and Research at the Department of Foreign Languages & Cultures, Universidad de La Sabana (Bogotá, Colombia). Currently the Editor of the Latin American Journal of Content & Language Integrated Learning. His research interest includes TELL, CLIL, YLs, teacher development, bilingual and international education on which topics he has published in a number of indexed journals and conference proceedings.

Kieran Nduagbo is a seasoned educator. She has taught kindergarten, elementary school, middle school, special education and secondary school. Dr. Nduagbo holds a B.S. Ed in Special Education, M.A. in education administration and a PhD in higher education. She currently resides in Brooklyn, New York Dr. Nduagbo enjoys reading, writing and conducting research on current issues in education. When she is not a computer, she is reclining on a couch listening to and enjoying some classical music.

Linh Nguyen is a sessional lecturer in library and information management at the School of Information Studies, Charles Sturt University (CSU), Wagga Wagga, Australia. His current research interests include online learning experiences, open educational practices, and the application of emerging technologies such as social media, artificial intelligence and social robots in library and information practice.

Naomi Petersen is Professor in the School of Education at Central Washington University since 2006. She teaches assessment and orientation courses in the Teacher Certification, STEM, and Elementary Education Programs. She originated, directs, and teaches the Accessibility Studies Program. Her research interests are interdisciplinary and collaborative.

Kathleen Pierce-Friedman received her M.S. in Education Leadership and Ph.D. in K-12 Future Studies from Capella University, Minneapolis, Minnesota. Her current appointments include serving an Associate Professor at Ashford University in San Diego, California and a Senior Doctoral Chair at Grand Canyon University, Arizona. Prior to this appointment she worked for a competency-based university, as a 2nd and 3rd grade teacher and assistant principal for one of the first online public schools in the United States and got her start in the teaching field teaching grades 1st-3rd at an intercity school in Sacramento, California. Her research interest include self-efficacy, isolation and online K-6th grade teaching.

About the Contributors

Sarah Schroyer, MSN, RN, CHPN, NE-BC, CNE, has spent her nursing career in various areas of community health. In nursing leadership positions in both hospice and homeless healthcare, Sarah has spent time educating her staff, patients, and the community on health initiatives while working to serve those around her. Currently at Grand Canyon University, Sarah serves as the Lead for both the MSN-Leadership and the Masters in Health Administration programs. She focuses serving her students in a faith-based online environment daily.

Brooke Slone earned her first bachelor's degree in Sociology from the College of Wooster and her second bachelor's degree in Education from Western Michigan University. After teaching 5th grade math for ten years, she began a career in higher education and is pursuing her Master of Arts in Higher Education Administration at Georgia Southern University. She has two sons, Andrew and Nicholas.

Clare Thorpe is the Associate Director (Library Experience) at University of Southern Queensland. She has worked in academic and state libraries since 2001, using evidence-based approaches to develop and apply best practices in collection management, user experience, staff development, and information literacy design. Clare was awarded the Australian Library and Information Association's Metcalfe Award in 2005 and the Queensland Library Achiever of the Year in 2016.

Steven Tolman, Ed.D., is an Assistant Professor of Higher Education Administration at Georgia Southern University. His previous roles included serving as a Higher Education Administration program director and 12 years as a student affairs administrator in Residence Life, Student Conduct, and Student Life. He holds a Doctorate from Rutgers University, Master's from Texas Tech University, and Bachelor's from Central Michigan University. His research is theoretically informed and guided by the tenets of student development theory. In particular, he explores the application of Maslow's Hierar-chy of Needs, Kolb's Experiential Learning, Sanford's Model of Challenge and Support, and Astin's Theory of Involvement. This theoretical framework is intertwined with the two streams of his scholarly agenda: 1) The profession of student affairs and 2) The residential and co-curricular experience of college students.

Christopher Trautman is a scholar and student affairs practitioner based at Fairleigh Dickinson University in Madison, New Jersey. His scholarly areas include financial expenditures in higher education and the efficacy of training programs for student affairs professionals and paraprofessionals.

Shaunna Waltemeyer is full-time faculty member in the Colangelo College of Business at Grand Canyon University. She teaches graduate and undergraduate classes in leadership, organizational behavior, management, marketing, and sports business.

Laurie Wellner, Ed.D., is the Vice President of Academic Affairs at Northcentral University in San Diego, California and has worked in education for the past 25 years. Dr. Wellner specializes in issues regarding autism, special education and organizational leadership, ADHD, Educationally Related Mental Health Services, faculty development, course design and program development and the successful communication and collaboration with stakeholders for the improvement of the educational process. Dr. Wellner has served as an adjunct professor at Claremont Graduate University, and Touro College (New York). She has served on many committees pertaining to systems change in education. Dr. Wellner is the author of several articles, a meta-analysis of the literature in the area of trust theory, a curriculum guide for Applied Behavior Analysis, as well as other writing, leadership, conferences and research projects. She regularly chairs and participates in committees for dissertation research at the doctoral level. She is a passionate advocate for the success of all.

Jill Winnington has been Assistant Dean and Business Program Director at Gwynedd Mercy University since June 2015. She previously served as Director of Academic Affairs at University of Phoenix. She earned her BA in Economics from the University of Delaware- Lerner College of Business and Economics, her MM in Management and MBA in Finance from Goldey-Beacom College, and her DBA from Wilmington University.

Kenneth C. C. Yang is a Professor at the Department of Communication. His research focuses on new media and advertising, consumer behavior in East Asia, impacts of new media in Asia.

Amanda Ziemendorf is a graduate of Oklahoma State University, Central Texas College, and Grand Canyon University. She has experience in executive hospital leadership, nursing education, adult critical care, and neonatal critical care. As an educator, Amanda has experience teaching in the clinical, didactic, ground, and online environments, with a presence at the LPN, ADN, RN to BSN, and Doctor of Nursing Practice levels. She has contributed as a subject matter expert, and has played a key role in refining program processes for doctoral education at her institution.

Index

A

accessibility 29, 68-69, 187, 192, 203, 206, 211, 213, 225, 236, 259
accommodations 190-192, 208, 225
adult learning theory 5
age 1, 38-39, 87, 122, 124-128, 137, 178, 180, 189-190, 287, 295
attrition 16, 121-123, 197, 252

B

bachelor's degree 119-120, 124
best practices 1-2, 4, 7-8, 14, 16, 18, 22, 28-30, 34, 48, 105, 153
blended learning 43-44, 90-91, 101, 264

C

checklist 110, 199, 214, 225, 231
classroom 2, 4-5, 7, 14, 16-17, 19-22, 26-28, 41-42, 45-46, 49, 51-52, 68-71, 74-76, 78-81, 88, 90, 92, 95-96, 104, 108, 120, 125, 144-149, 154-156, 166-168, 173-183, 191, 196, 200-201, 209, 218, 235, 250-251, 260, 270, 272-276, 278-279, 281, 283, 288-292, 295-297, 305
cohort education 119-121, 124-125, 130
Collaboration roles 115
college 5, 7, 15, 27, 68, 79-80, 85-86, 88-89, 93-95, 97, 119-124, 179, 204, 228, 236, 238-239, 241, 246, 273, 287-289, 293, 295, 297
community 2, 7, 17, 25, 27-28, 30, 34-36, 52, 69, 71, 77, 79, 81, 87, 104, 111, 116, 120-121, 124, 140-145, 149, 155-158, 160, 164-166, 174, 176, 182, 203, 206, 246, 253, 255, 261-262, 265-267, 270
Community of Inquiry Model 142
computer 6, 21, 39, 70, 79, 86-87, 89-90, 93, 120, 124, 128, 145, 157, 246, 288
correspondence 3, 86-89, 97, 142, 192
Course format 127, 137

D

degree completion 28, 119-120, 122-123, 125-130, 137
delivery of content 5
digital 14, 18, 37-41, 45-46, 49, 52, 54, 106, 176, 227-229, 231-232, 236, 238, 241-242, 246, 251, 287-288, 290, 295-297, 305
digital learning 39-40, 45, 227, 238, 246
Discipleship 271, 285
distance 3, 5, 14-16, 19, 22, 30, 34, 38, 60, 79, 85, 87-90, 93, 97, 101, 141-142, 155, 157, 159, 206, 249, 283
dual mode learning 250, 261, 263, 267
due dates 77, 178, 191, 194, 198, 207, 210-211, 226

E

EdTech 305
Emergent Bilingual 246
evidence-based strategies 25-26, 35-36, 154, 159-160, 164

F

face-to-face 1-2, 4, 7-8, 14-15, 20, 22, 28, 39, 41, 44, 53, 67-73, 76-79, 86, 96, 102-104, 106-107, 110, 113, 142-146, 164, 166, 179-180, 193, 195, 200, 202, 211, 236, 249-253, 257-259, 261-263, 266, 271, 273, 292, 305
faculty 1-2, 5, 7-9, 14, 25-39, 46-54, 64, 67-68, 70-73, 76-78, 81, 89-90, 95, 102-103, 105-106, 116, 120, 123-125, 130, 142, 144-145, 147, 153-155, 158-160, 162, 165-167, 173-174, 178, 187-188, 190-191, 194-196, 201, 231-232, 242, 272, 283, 289-291, 297

faculty development 25-31, 33-36, 39, 47, 50-52, 54
faculty professional development 1-2, 8, 27, 37, 49, 52
faith-based 270-271, 275-276, 278, 281-282, 285
feedback 6-7, 14, 16-19, 22, 27, 29-34, 41-44, 46-47, 70, 74-75, 78, 94-95, 104-105, 120, 141, 146-148, 154-162, 165-167, 177-178, 192, 194-196, 202, 204, 208-211, 215, 218, 226, 233, 251-252
fellowship 271-274, 285
First Generation Student 246
flipped classroom 90, 288-290, 292, 296-297, 305

G

gamification 18, 90, 286-298, 305
gender 124-128, 137, 174, 177-180, 183, 227, 293
Generation Z 290, 295, 305
graduation 123, 145, 253

H

higher education 3-6, 14-16, 25, 38, 44, 46, 48, 52, 59, 68, 81, 85, 89-91, 93-97, 102, 105, 108, 119, 122, 130, 142, 146, 153-154, 175, 191, 218, 230-231, 238, 267, 271, 286-292, 295-297

I

inclusive teaching 174, 176, 181
institution 6, 25-26, 35, 41, 44, 68, 71, 73, 101, 104, 106, 121, 123-124, 130, 137, 159, 188, 191-192, 235
instructional technology 38
instructor 1, 4-7, 9, 15-19, 21-22, 28, 31-32, 37, 41-44, 46-47, 54, 69-70, 73-77, 86-87, 92-94, 103, 105, 107, 109-110, 112-113, 116, 123, 142-143, 145-148, 154-162, 164-168, 176, 178-179, 181-183, 188-189, 191-202, 204, 206, 208-211, 218, 231-232, 238, 250-252, 259-260, 263-264, 271, 275-276, 279, 291-292, 305
Instructor characteristics 6
instructor feedback 70, 196, 209
instructor presence 147, 155-158, 160-161, 167
integration 29-30, 39, 49, 54, 123-124, 161, 270-271, 273, 285-289, 297
interactivity 144, 258, 305

L

Late Policies 226
Learner Profile(s) (LP) 44, 101, 103, 107, 109

learning 1-9, 14-22, 26-32, 34-54, 59-60, 67-81, 85-97, 101-113, 115-116, 120-121, 123-124, 140-149, 153-156, 158-160, 162, 164-167, 173-174, 176-182, 187-191, 193-209, 214-215, 218, 226-232, 234, 236-239, 242, 246, 249-253, 255-267, 270-271, 273, 275-276, 279, 281, 283, 286, 288-297, 305
learning experience 3, 37, 44, 68, 70, 76-77, 191, 231, 250, 265, 271, 286, 293-294, 297
Learning Management System(s) 5, 28, 31, 43, 53, 73, 113, 124, 142, 147, 176, 229, 250, 252, 255
learning outcomes 2, 6, 46, 107, 115, 143, 162, 191, 197, 200, 202-203, 214-215, 286, 288, 292-297
live conferencing 14

M

marginalized identities 174, 183
marginalized students 173-174, 177-181, 183
Masters degrees 59-61
metacognition 188, 197, 202, 226, 231
mindfulness 270-271, 274, 277-278, 285
Module Hosts (MH) 116
motivation 5-6, 9, 16, 44, 52, 69, 108, 111, 124, 141, 156, 174, 182, 189, 191, 201, 207, 209, 233-234, 288, 290, 293-295, 297, 305

O

online education 2-4, 15, 25-26, 46, 54, 67-70, 81, 85-86, 88-97, 101-106, 116, 120-124, 141-143, 146-147, 149, 155, 179, 270, 282
online engagement 36, 249
online instruction 3-5, 7, 9, 28-29, 31-32, 46, 91, 103, 113, 160, 192
online instructor 1, 21, 28, 32, 41-44, 46, 54, 70, 103, 105, 107, 109-110, 112-113, 116, 165, 193, 202
Online Instructor (OI)/Online Teacher (OT) 116
online learning 2-5, 7, 14-16, 20-22, 29, 36, 41, 45, 52, 54, 60, 68, 70, 75-76, 78-81, 89, 91, 95, 97, 101-108, 113, 116, 140, 142-148, 159-160, 165, 167, 173, 177, 179, 181, 187, 195, 198, 226, 228, 230-231, 236, 242, 246, 249, 251-253, 260, 263-264, 267, 273, 275, 290, 293, 295, 305
online learning environments 41, 54, 68, 104, 107, 113, 116, 160, 187, 198, 226, 228, 246, 264
Online Teacher 45, 116

P

pedagogy 2, 4-6, 9, 26, 28-30, 34, 48-49, 54, 90, 102, 106, 124, 130, 174-176, 180-181, 188, 209, 226, 228, 239, 246, 287-292, 296-297, 305
Pell-Eligible 127, 137
personal connections 14
post-secondary 191, 227-228, 230, 232, 234, 236, 242, 246
power and privilege 173-174, 176, 183
Prayer 275, 278, 285
present 4, 46, 70, 76, 80, 85, 87-89, 92, 96, 108, 115, 142, 145, 156-158, 167, 174, 177, 240, 254, 266, 271, 273
Professional Development (PD) 1-2, 7-9, 26-28, 33, 37, 39, 46-54, 103-106, 108, 116, 166
project 19, 45, 52, 61, 63, 78-79, 120, 166-167, 178, 214-215, 229, 249-250, 253, 273, 293-294

Q

Quality Assurance 101, 105-106, 113, 116
quantitative 34, 119, 124-125, 130, 164, 209, 253, 296-297

R

reflection 7, 34, 44, 103-104, 108, 164, 167, 188, 197, 278, 285
religion 178, 271-273, 275, 278, 285
retention 4, 6, 16, 22, 103-104, 116, 119-121, 123-125, 130, 140, 145, 149, 174, 180, 188

S

Screencasting 19, 21-22
self-regulation 107, 182, 187, 195-197, 201-202, 218, 226, 232, 234, 236

social interaction 19, 110, 113, 123, 142-143, 249
social media 38-39, 91, 111, 144-145, 195, 229, 251, 256, 259-262, 264-265, 288
spirituality 271-273, 275, 278, 283, 285
student engagement 21, 28, 42, 45, 77, 120, 123-125, 142, 145, 147-148, 153-155, 159-160, 162, 164, 167, 187, 195-196, 198, 202, 218, 226, 230, 232, 251-253, 286, 291-294
student experience 26, 69, 188, 249, 256
Student Ratings of Instruction 68, 72-73
Student-Centered Instruction 188, 226
support for online instructors 7, 46
SWAYAM 59-61, 64-65

T

Teacher Collaboration (TC) 104, 116
technology 3-5, 7-9, 14-15, 19-22, 26, 33, 37-40, 44-46, 49, 52, 54, 68, 70-71, 73, 77, 81, 86, 89, 92, 101, 113, 123, 142, 144-145, 147-148, 154, 157, 176, 180, 195, 206, 228-229, 232, 236, 242, 251-252, 258, 264, 273, 283, 289, 293, 297, 305
thematic analysis 248-249, 253-254
time management 4, 21, 45, 146, 188-190, 196, 218, 226, 231, 251
transactional distance 14-15, 22

U

Universal Design for Learning 70-71, 73, 78, 85-89, 96,

V

video feedback 19
virtual learning 92, 101, 180, 251, 264
Vulnerable Populations 226

Purchase Print, E-Book, or Print + E-Book

IGI Global's reference books are available in three unique pricing formats:
Print Only, E-Book Only, or Print + E-Book.
Shipping fees may apply.

www.igi-global.com

Recommended Reference Books

ISBN: 978-1-5225-9348-5
© 2019; 454 pp.
List Price: $255

ISBN: 978-1-5225-7763-8
© 2019; 253 pp.
List Price: $175

ISBN: 978-1-5225-7531-3
© 2019; 324 pp.
List Price: $185

ISBN: 978-1-5225-7802-4
© 2019; 423 pp.
List Price: $195

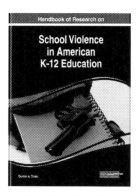

ISBN: 978-1-5225-6246-7
© 2019; 610 pp.
List Price: $275

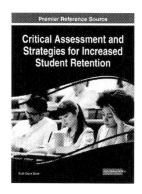

ISBN: 978-1-5225-2998-9
© 2018; 352 pp.
List Price: $195

Do you want to stay current on the latest research trends, product announcements, news and special offers?
Join IGI Global's mailing list today and start enjoying exclusive perks sent only to IGI Global members.
Add your name to the list at **www.igi-global.com/newsletters**.

Publisher of Peer-Reviewed, Timely, and Innovative Academic Research

www.igi-global.com Sign up at www.igi-global.com/newsletters facebook.com/igiglobal twitter.com/igiglobal linkedin.com/igiglobal

Ensure Quality Research is Introduced to the Academic Community

Become an IGI Global Reviewer for Authored Book Projects

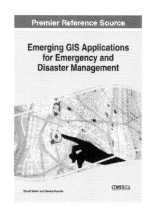 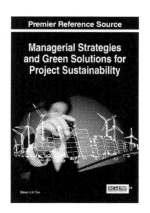  

The overall success of an authored book project is dependent on quality and timely reviews.

In this competitive age of scholarly publishing, constructive and timely feedback significantly expedites the turnaround time of manuscripts from submission to acceptance, allowing the publication and discovery of forward-thinking research at a much more expeditious rate. Several IGI Global authored book projects are currently seeking highly-qualified experts in the field to fill vacancies on their respective editorial review boards:

Applications and Inquiries may be sent to:
development@igi-global.com

Applicants must have a doctorate (or an equivalent degree) as well as publishing and reviewing experience. Reviewers are asked to complete the open-ended evaluation questions with as much detail as possible in a timely, collegial, and constructive manner. All reviewers' tenures run for one-year terms on the editorial review boards and are expected to complete at least three reviews per term. Upon successful completion of this term, reviewers can be considered for an additional term.

If you have a colleague that may be interested in this opportunity,
we encourage you to share this information with them.

IGI Global Proudly Partners With eContent Pro International

Receive a 25% Discount on all Editorial Services

Editorial Services

IGI Global expects all final manuscripts submitted for publication to be in their final form. This means they must be reviewed, revised, and professionally copy edited prior to their final submission. Not only does this support with accelerating the publication process, but it also ensures that the highest quality scholarly work can be disseminated.

English Language Copy Editing

Let eContent Pro International's expert copy editors perform edits on your manuscript to resolve spelling, punctuaion, grammar, syntax, flow, formatting issues and more.

Scientific and Scholarly Editing

Allow colleagues in your research area to examine the content of your manuscript and provide you with valuable feedback and suggestions before submission.

Figure, Table, Chart & Equation Conversions

Do you have poor quality figures? Do you need visual elements in your manuscript created or converted? A design expert can help!

Translation

Need your documjent translated into English? eContent Pro International's expert translators are fluent in English and more than 40 different languages.

Hear What Your Colleagues are Saying About Editorial Services Supported by IGI Global

"The service was very fast, very thorough, and very helpful in ensuring our chapter meets the criteria and requirements of the book's editors. I was quite impressed and happy with your service."

– Prof. Tom Brinthaupt,
Middle Tennessee State University, USA

"I found the work actually spectacular. The editing, formatting, and other checks were very thorough. The turnaround time was great as well. I will definitely use eContent Pro in the future."

– Nickanor Amwata, Lecturer,
University of Kurdistan Hawler, Iraq

"I was impressed that it was done timely, and wherever the content was not clear for the reader, the paper was improved with better readability for the audience."

– Prof. James Chilembwe,
Mzuzu University, Malawi

Email: customerservice@econtentpro.com   **www.igi-global.com/editorial-service-partners**

www.igi-global.com

Celebrating Over 30 Years of Scholarly Knowledge Creation & Dissemination

InfoSci®-Books

A Database of Over 5,300+ Reference Books Containing Over 100,000+ Chapters Focusing on Emerging Research

GAIN ACCESS TO **THOUSANDS** OF REFERENCE BOOKS AT **A FRACTION** OF THEIR INDIVIDUAL LIST **PRICE**.

InfoSci®-Books Database

The **InfoSci®-Books** database is a collection of over 5,300+ IGI Global single and multi-volume reference books, handbooks of research, and encyclopedias, encompassing groundbreaking research from prominent experts worldwide that span over 350+ topics in 11 core subject areas including business, computer science, education, science and engineering, social sciences and more.

Open Access Fee Waiver (Offset Model) Initiative

For any library that invests in IGI Global's InfoSci-Journals and/or InfoSci-Books databases, IGI Global will match the library's investment with a fund of equal value to go toward **subsidizing the OA article processing charges (APCs) for their students, faculty, and staff** at that institution when their work is submitted and accepted under OA into an IGI Global journal.*

INFOSCI PLATFORM FEATURES

- No DRM
- No Set-Up or Maintenance Fees
- A Guarantee of No More Than a 5% Annual Increase
- Full-Text HTML and PDF Viewing Options
- Downloadable MARC Records
- Unlimited Simultaneous Access
- COUNTER 5 Compliant Reports
- Formatted Citations With Ability to Export to RefWorks and EasyBib
- No Embargo of Content (Research is Available Months in Advance of the Print Release)

*The fund will be offered on an annual basis and expire at the end of the subscription period. The fund would renew as the subscription is renewed for each year thereafter. The open access fees will be waived after the student, faculty, or staff's paper has been vetted and accepted into an IGI Global journal and the fund can only be used toward publishing OA in an IGI Global journal. Libraries in developing countries will have the match on their investment doubled.

To Learn More or To Purchase This Database:
www.igi-global.com/infosci-books

eresources@igi-global.com • Toll Free: 1-866-342-6657 ext. 100 • Phone: 717-533-8845 x100

www.igi-global.com

Publisher of Peer-Reviewed, Timely, and Innovative Academic Research Since 1988

www.igi-global.com

IGI Global's Transformative Open Access (OA) Model:
How to Turn Your University Library's Database Acquisitions Into a Source of OA Funding

In response to the OA movement and well in advance of Plan S, IGI Global, early last year, unveiled their OA Fee Waiver (Offset Model) Initiative.

Under this initiative, librarians who invest in IGI Global's InfoSci-Books (5,300+ reference books) and/or InfoSci-Journals (185+ scholarly journals) databases will be able to subsidize their patron's OA article processing charges (APC) when their work is submitted and accepted (after the peer review process) into an IGI Global journal.*

How Does it Work?

1. When a library subscribes or perpetually purchases IGI Global's InfoSci-Databases including InfoSci-Books (5,300+ e-books), InfoSci-Journals (185+ e-journals), and/or their discipline/subject-focused subsets, IGI Global will match the library's investment with a fund of equal value to go toward subsidizing the OA article processing charges (APCs) for their patrons.

   Researchers: Be sure to recommend the InfoSci-Books and InfoSci-Journals to take advantage of this initiative.

2. When a student, faculty, or staff member submits a paper and it is accepted (following the peer review) into one of IGI Global's 185+ scholarly journals, the author will have the option to have their paper published under a traditional publishing model or as OA.

3. When the author chooses to have their paper published under OA, IGI Global will notify them of the OA Fee Waiver (Offset Model) Initiative. If the author decides they would like to take advantage of this initiative, IGI Global will deduct the US$ 1,500 APC from the created fund.

4. This fund will be offered on an annual basis and will renew as the subscription is renewed for each year thereafter. IGI Global will manage the fund and award the APC waivers unless the librarian has a preference as to how the funds should be managed.

Hear From the Experts on This Initiative:

"I'm very happy to have been able to make one of my recent research contributions, 'Visualizing the Social Media Conversations of a National Information Technology Professional Association' featured in the *International Journal of Human Capital and Information Technology Professionals*, freely available along with having access to the valuable resources found within IGI Global's InfoSci-Journals database."

– **Prof. Stuart Palmer**, Deakin University, Australia

For More Information, Visit: www.igi-global.com/publish/contributor-resources/open-access or contact IGI Global's Database Team at eresources@igi-global.com.

Are You Ready to Publish Your Research?

IGI Global offers book authorship and editorship opportunities across 11 subject areas, including business, computer science, education, science and engineering, social sciences, and more!

Benefits of Publishing with IGI Global:

- Free one-on-one editorial and promotional support.
- Expedited publishing timelines that can take your book from start to finish in less than one (1) year.
- Choose from a variety of formats including: Edited and Authored References, Handbooks of Research, Encyclopedias, and Research Insights.
- Utilize IGI Global's eEditorial Discovery® submission system in support of conducting the submission and blind review process.
- IGI Global maintains a strict adherence to ethical practices due in part to our full membership with the Committee on Publication Ethics (COPE).
- Indexing potential in prestigious indices such as Scopus®, Web of Science™, PsycINFO®, and ERIC – Education Resources Information Center.
- Ability to connect your ORCID iD to your IGI Global publications.
- Earn royalties on your publication as well as receive complimentary copies and exclusive discounts.

Get Started Today by Contacting the Acquisitions Department at:
acquisition@igi-global.com

Printed in the United States
By Bookmasters